NE SANS DROICT.

William Shakespeare

HENRY VI, PART ONE

HENRY VI, PART TWO

HENRY VI, PART THREE

With New Dramatic Criticism
and an Updated Bibliography

The Signet Classic Shakespeare
GENERAL EDITOR: SYLVAN BARNET

C

A SIGNET CLASSIC

SIGNET CLASSIC
Published by New American Library, a division of
Penguin Putnam Inc., 375 Hudson Street,
New York, New York 10014, U.S.A.
Penguin Books Ltd, 27 Wrights Lane,
London W8 5TZ, England
Penguin Books Australia Ltd, Ringwood,
Victoria, Australia
Penguin Books Canada Ltd, 10 Alcorn Avenue,
Toronto, Ontario, Canada M4V 3B2
Penguin Books (N.Z.) Ltd, 182–190 Wairau Road,
Auckland 10, New Zealand

Penguin Books Ltd, Registered Offices:
Harmondsworth, Middlesex, England

Published by Signet Classic, an imprint of New American Library,
a division of Penguin Putnam Inc.

First Signet Classic Printing, April 1986
14   13   12   11   10   9   8   7   6   5

Henry VI, Part One:
    Copyright © 1967, 1989 by Lawrence V. Ryan
    Copyright © 1963, 1989 by Sylvan Barnet

Henry VI, Part Two:
    Copyright © 1967, 1989 by Arthur Freeman
    Copyright © 1963, 1989 by Sylvan Barnet

Henry VI, Part Three:
    Copyright © 1968 by Milton Crane
    Copyright © 1963, 1989 by Sylvan Barnet
All rights reserved.

These books previously appeared as single volumes in Signet
Classic editions published by New American Library.

 REGISTERED TRADEMARK—MARCA REGISTRADA

Library of Congress Catalog Card Number: 85-63517

Printed in the United States of America

BOOKS ARE AVAILABLE AT QUANTITY DISCOUNTS WHEN USED TO PROMOTE PROD-
UCTS OR SERVICES. FOR INFORMATION PLEASE WRITE TO PREMIUM MARKETING DIVI-
SION, PENGUIN PUTNAM INC., 375 HUDSON STREET, NEW YORK, NEW YORK 10014.

If you purchased this book without a cover you should be aware that this book
is stolen property. It was reported as "unsold and destroyed" to the publisher
and neither the author nor the publisher has received any payment for this
"stripped book."

Shakespeare: Prefatory Remarks

Between the record of his baptism in Stratford on 26 April 1564 and the record of his burial in Stratford on 25 April 1616, some forty documents name Shakespeare, and many others name his parents, his children, and his grandchildren. More facts are known about William Shakespeare than about any other playwright of the period except Ben Jonson. The facts should, however, be distinguished from the legends. The latter inevitably more engaging and better known, tell us that the Stratford boy killed a calf in high style, poached deer and rabbits, and was forced to flee to London, where he held horses outside a playhouse. These traditions are only traditions; they may be true, but no evidence supports them, and it is well to stick to the facts.

Mary Arden, the dramatist's mother, was the daughter of a substantial landowner; about 1557 she married John Shakespeare, who was a glove-maker and trader in various farm commodities. In 1557 John Shakespeare was a member of the Council (the governing body of Stratford), in 1558 a constable of the borough, in 1561 one of the two town chamberlains, in 1565 an alderman (entitling him to the appellation "Mr."), in 1568 high bailiff—the town's highest political office, equivalent to mayor. After 1577, for an unknown reason he drops out of local politics. The birthday of William Shakespeare, the eldest son of this locally prominent man, is unrecorded; but the Stratford parish register records that the infant was baptized on 26 April 1564. (It is quite possible that he was

v

born on 23 April, but this date has probably been assigned by tradition because it is the date on which, fifty-two years later, he died.) The attendance records of the Stratford grammar school of the period are not extant, but it is reasonable to assume that the son of a local official attended the school and received substantial training in Latin. The masters of the school from Shakespeare's seventh to fifteenth years held Oxford degrees; the Elizabethan curriculum excluded mathematics and the natural sciences but taught a good deal of Latin rhetoric, logic, and literature. On 27 November 1582 a marriage license was issued to Shakespeare and Anne Hathaway, eight years his senior. The couple had a child in May, 1583. Perhaps the marriage was necessary, but perhaps the couple had earlier engaged in a formal "troth plight" which would render their children legitimate even if no further ceremony were performed. In 1585 Anne Hathaway bore Shakespeare twins.

That Shakespeare was born is excellent; that he married and had children is pleasant; but that we know nothing about his departure from Stratford to London, or about the beginning of his theatrical career, is lamentable and must be admitted. We would gladly sacrifice details about his children's baptism for details about his earliest days on the stage. Perhaps the poaching episode is true (but it is first reported almost a century after Shakespeare's death), or perhaps he first left Stratford to be a schoolteacher, as another tradition holds; perhaps he was moved by

> Such wind as scatters young men through the world,
> To seek their fortunes further than at home
> Where small experience grows.

In 1592, thanks to the cantankerousness of Robert Greene, a rival playright and a pamphleteer, we have our first reference, a snarling one, to Shakespeare as an actor and playwright. Greene warns those of his own educated friends who wrote for the theater against an actor who has presumed to turn playwright:

There is an upstart crow, beautified with our feathers, that with his *tiger's heart wrapped in a player's hide* supposes he is as well able to bombast out a blank verse as the best of you, and being an absolute Johannes-factotum is in his own conceit the only Shake-scene in a country.

The reference to the player, as well as the allusion to Aesop's crow (who strutted in borrowed plumage, as an actor struts in fine words not his own), makes it clear that by this date Shakespeare had both acted and written. That Shakespeare is meant is indicated not only by "Shake-scene" but by the parody of a line from one of Shakespeare's plays, *3 Henry VI:* "O, tiger's heart wrapped in a woman's hide." If Shakespeare in 1592 was prominent enough to be attacked by an envious dramatist, he probably had served an apprenticeship in the theater for at least a few years.

In any case, by 1592 Shakespeare had acted and written, and there are a number of subsequent references to him as an actor: documents indicate that in 1598 he is a "principal comedian," in 1603 a "principal tragedian," in 1608 he is one of the "men players." The profession of actor was not for a gentleman, and it occasionally drew the scorn of university men who resented writing speeches for persons less educated than themselves, but it was respectable enough: players, if prosperous, were in effect members of the bourgeoisie, and there is nothing to suggest that Stratford considered William Shakespeare less than a solid citizen. When, in 1596, the Shakespeares were granted a coat of arms, the grant was made to Shakespeare's father, but probably William Shakespeare (who the next year bought the second-largest house in town) had arranged the matter on his own behalf. In subsequent transactions he is occasionally styled a gentleman.

Although in 1593 and 1594 Shakespeare published two narrative poems dedicated to the Earl of Southampton, *Venus and Adonis* and *The Rape of Lucrece,* and may well have written most or all of his sonnets in the middle nineties, Shakespeare's literary activity seems to have been almost entirely devoted to the theater. (It may be sig-

nificant that the two narrative poems were written in
years when the plague closed the theaters for several
months.) In 1594 he was a charter member of a theatrical company called the Chamberlain's Men (which in
1603 changed its name to the King's Men); until he retired to Stratford (about 1611, apparently), he was with
this remarkably stable company. From 1599 the company acted primarily at the Globe Theatre, in which
Shakespeare held a one-tenth interest. Other Elizabethan
dramatists are known to have acted, but no other is known
also to have been entitled to a share in the profits of the
playhouse.

Shakespeare's first eight published plays did not have
his name on them, but this is not remarkable; the most
popular play of the sixteenth century, Thomas Kyd's *The
Spanish Tragedy*, went through many editions without
naming Kyd, and Kyd's authorship is known only because
a book on the profession of acting happens to quote (and
attribute to Kyd) some lines on the interest of Roman
emperors in the drama. What is remarkable is that after
1598 Shakespeare's name commonly appears on printed
plays—some of which are not his. Another indication of
his popularity comes from Francis Meres, author of
Palladis Tamia: Wit's Treasury (1598): in this anthology
of snippets accompanied by an essay on literature, many
playwrights are mentioned, but Shakespeare's name occurs
more often than any other, and Shakespeare is the only
playwright whose plays are listed.

From his acting, playwriting, and share in a theater,
Shakespeare seems to have made considerable money.
He put it to work, making substantial investments in
Stratford real estate. When he made his will (less than a
month before he died), he sought to leave his property
intact to his descendants. Of small bequests to relatives
and to friends (including three actors, Richard Burbage,
John Heminges, and Henry Condell), that to his wife of
the second-best bed has provoked the most comment;
perhaps it was the bed the couple had slept in, the best
being reserved for visitors. In any case, had Shakespeare

not excepted it, the bed would have gone (with the rest
of his household possessions) to his daughter and her
husband. On 25 April 1616 he was buried within the
chancel of the church at Stratford. An unattractive monument to his memory, placed on a wall near the grave, says
he died on 23 April. Over the grave itself are the lines,
perhaps by Shakespeare, that (more than his literary
fame) have kept his bones undisturbed in the crowded
burial ground where old bones were often dislodged to
make way for new:

> Good friend, for Jesus' sake forbear
> To dig the dust enclosed here.
> Blessed be the man that spares these stones
> And cursed be he that moves my bones.

Thirty-seven plays, as well as some nondramatic poems,
are held to constitute the Shakespeare canon. The dates
of composition of most of the works are highly uncertain,
but there is often evidence of a *terminus a quo* (starting
point) and/or a *terminus ad quem* (terminal point) that
provides a framework for intelligent guessing. For example, *Richard II* cannot be earlier than 1595, the publication date of some material to which it is indebted; *The
Merchant of Venice* cannot be later than 1598, the year
Francis Meres mentioned it. Sometimes arguments for a
date hang on an alleged topical allusion, such as the lines
about the unseasonable weather in *A Midsummer Night's
Dream,* II.i.81–117, but such an allusion (if indeed it is an
allusion) can be variously interpreted, and in any case
there is always the possibility that a topical allusion was
inserted during a revision, years after the composition of
a play. Dates are often attributed on the basis of style,
and although conjectures about style usually rest on other
conjectures, sooner or later one must rely on one's literary
sense. There is no real proof, for example, that *Othello*
is not as early as *Romeo and Juliet,* but one feels *Othello*
is later, and because the first record of its performance is
1604, one is glad enough to set its composition at that
date and not push it back into Shakespeare's early years.

The following chronology, then, is as much indebted to informed guesswork and sensitivity as it is to fact. The dates, necessarily imprecise, indicate something like a scholarly consensus.

PLAYS

1588–93	*The Comedy of Errors*
1588–94	*Love's Labor's Lost*
1590–91	*2 Henry VI*
1590–91	*3 Henry VI*
1591–92	*1 Henry VI*
1592–93	*Richard III*
1592–94	*Titus Andronicus*
1593–94	*The Taming of the Shrew*
1593–95	*The Two Gentlemen of Verona*
1594–96	*Romeo and Juliet*
1595	*Richard II*
1594–96	*A Midsummer Night's Dream*
1596–97	*King John*
1596–97	*The Merchant of Venice*
1597	*1 Henry IV*
1597–98	*2 Henry IV*
1598–1600	*Much Ado About Nothing*
1598–99	*Henry V*
1599	*Julius Caesar*
1599–1600	*As You Like It*
1599–1600	*Twelfth Night*
1601–02	*Troilus and Cressida*
1600–01	*Hamlet*
1597–1601	*The Merry Wives of Windsor*
1602–04	*All's Well That Ends Well*
1603–04	*Othello*
1604	*Measure for Measure*
1605–06	*King Lear*
1605–06	*Macbeth*
1606–07	*Antony and Cleopatra*
1605–08	*Timon of Athens*
1607–09	*Coriolanus*
1608–09	*Pericles*

1609–10	*Cymbeline*
1610–11	*The Winter's Tale*
1611	*The Tempest*
1612–13	*Henry VIII*

POEMS

1592	*Venus and Adonis*
1593–94	*The Rape of Lucrece*
1593–1600	*Sonnets*
1600–01	*The Phoenix and the Turtle*

Shakespeare's Theater

In Shakespeare's infancy, Elizabethan actors performed wherever they could—in great halls, at court, in the courtyards of inns. The innyards must have made rather unsatisfactory theaters: on some days they were unavailable because carters bringing goods to London used them as depots; when available, they had to be rented from the innkeeper; perhaps most important, London inns were subject to the Common Council of London, which was not well disposed toward theatricals. In 1574 the Common Council required that plays and playing places in London be licensed. It asserted that

> sundry great disorders and inconveniences have been found to ensue to this city by the inordinate haunting of great multitudes of people, specially youth, to plays, interludes, and shows, namely occasion of frays and quarrels, evil practices of incontinency in great inns having chambers and secret places adjoining to their open stages and galleries,

and ordered that innkeepers who wished licenses to hold performances put up a bond and make contributions to the poor.

The requirement that plays and innyard theaters be licensed, along with the other drawbacks of playing at inns, probably drove James Burbage (a carpenter-turned-

actor) to rent in 1576 a plot of land northeast of the
city walls and to build here—on property outside the
jurisdiction of the city—England's first permanent construction designed for plays. He called it simply the
Theatre. About all that is known of its construction is
that it was wood. It soon had imitators, the most famous
being the Globe (1599), built across the Thames (again
outside the city's jurisdiction), out of timbers of the
Theatre, which had been dismantled when Burbage's
lease ran out.

There are three important sources of information about
the structure of Elizabethan playhouses—drawings, a contract, and stage direction in plays. Of drawings, only the
so-called De Witt drawing (c. 1596) of the Swan—
really a friend's copy of De Witt's drawing—is of much
significance. It shows a building of three tiers, with a
stage jutting from a wall into the yard or center of the
building. The tiers are roofed, and part of the stage is
covered by a roof that projects from the rear and is supported at its front on two posts, but the groundlings, who
paid a penny to stand in front of the stage, were exposed
to the sky. (Performances in such a playhouse were held
only in the daytime; artificial illumination was not used.)
At the rear of the stage are two doors; above the stage
is a gallery. The second major source of information,
the contract for the Fortune, specifies that although the
Globe is to be the model, the Fortune is to be square,
eighty feet outside and fifty-five inside. The stage is to
be forty-three feet broad, and is to extend into the middle
of the yard (i.e., it is twenty-seven and a half feet deep).
For patrons willing to pay more than the general admission charged of the groundlings, there were to be three
galleries provided with seats. From the third chief source,
stage directions, one learns that entrance to the stage was
by doors, presumably spaced widely apart at the rear
("Enter one citizen at one door, and another at the
other"), and that in addition to the platform stage there
was occasionally some sort of curtained booth or alcove
allowing for "discovery" scenes, and some sort of playing
space "aloft" or "above" to represent (for example)

the top of a city's walls or a room above the street. Doubtless each theater had its own peculiarities, but perhaps we can talk about a "typical" Elizabethan theater if we realize that no theater need exactly have fit the description, just as no father is the typical father with 3.7 children. This hypothetical theater is wooden, round or polygonal (in *Henry V* Shakespeare calls it a "wooden *O*"), capable of holding some eight hundred spectators standing in the yard around the projecting elevated stage and some fifteen hundred additional spectators seated in the three roofed galleries. The stage, protected by a "shadow" or "heavens" or roof, is entered by two doors; behind the doors is the "tiring house" (attiring house, i.e., dressing room), and above the doors is some sort of gallery that may sometimes hold spectators but that can be used (for example) as the bedroom from which Romeo—according to a stage direction in one text—"goeth down." Some evidence suggests that a throne can be lowered onto the platform stage, perhaps from the "shadow"; certainly characters can descend from the stage through a trap or traps into the cellar or "hell." Sometimes this space beneath the platform accommodates a sound-effects man or musician (in *Antony and Cleopatra* "music of the hautboys is under the stage") or an actor (in *Hamlet* the "Ghost cries under the stage"). Most characters simply walk on and off, but because there is no curtain in front of the platform, corpses will have to be carried off (Hamlet must lug Polonius' guts into the neighbor room), or will have to fall at the rear, where the curtain on the alcove or booth can be drawn to conceal them.

Such may have been the so-called "public theater." Another kind of theater, called the "private theater" because its much greater admission charge limited its audience to the wealthy or the prodigal, must be briefly mentioned. The private theater was basically a large room, entirely roofed and therefore artificially illuminated, with a stage at one end. In 1576 one such theater was established in Blackfriars, a Dominican priory in London that had been suppressed in 1538 and confiscated by the Crown and thus was not under the city's jurisdiction. All the actors in the Blackfriars theater were boys about eight to thirteen years old (in the public theaters similar boys played female parts; a boy Lady Macbeth played to a man Macbeth). This private theater had a precarious existence, and ceased operations in 1584. In 1596 James Burbage, who had already made theatrical history by building the Theatre, began to construct a second Blackfriars theater. He died in 1597, and for several years this second Blackfriars theater was used by a troupe of boys, but in 1608 two of Burbage's sons and five other actors (including Shakespeare) became joint operators of the theater, using it in the winter when the open-air Globe was unsuitable. Perhaps such a smaller theater, roofed, artificially illuminated, and with a tradition of a courtly audience, exerted an influence on Shakespeare's late plays.

Performances in the private theaters may well have had intermissions during which music was played, but in the public theaters the action was probably uninterrupted, flowing from scene to scene almost without a break. Actors would enter, speak, exit, and others would immediately enter and establish (if necessary) the new locale by a few properties and by words and gestures. Here are some samples of Shakespeare's scene painting:

> This is Illyria, lady.

> Well, this is the Forest of Arden.

> This castle hath a pleasant seat; the air
> Nimbly and sweetly recommends itself
> Unto our gentle senses.

On the other hand, it is a mistake to conceive of the Elizabethan stage as bare. Although Shakespeare's Chorus in *Henry V* calls the stage an "unworthy scaffold" and urges the spectators to "eke out our performance with your mind," there was considerable spectacle. The last act of *Macbeth*, for example, has five stage directions calling for "drum and colors," and another sort of appeal to the eye is indicated by the stage direction "Enter Mac-

duff, with Macbeth's head." Some scenery and properties
may have been substantial; doubtless a throne was used,
and in one play of the period we encounter this direction:
"Hector takes up a great piece of rock and casts at Ajax,
who tears up a young tree by the roots and assails
Hector." The matter is of some importance, and will be
glanced at again in the next section.

The Texts of Shakespeare

Though eighteen of his plays were published during
his lifetime, Shakespeare seems never to have supervised
their publication. There is nothing unusual here; when a
playwright sold a play to a theatrical company he sur-
rendered his ownership of it. Normally a company would
not publish the play, because to publish it meant to allow
competitors to acquire the piece. Some plays, however,
did get published: apparently, treacherous actors sometimes pieced together a play for a publisher, sometimes
a company in need of money sold a play, and sometimes a
company allowed a play to be published that no longer
drew audiences. That Shakespeare did not concern himself with publication, then, is scarcely remarkable; of his
contemporaries only Ben Jonson carefully supervised the
publication of his own plays. In 1623, seven years after
Shakespeare's death, John Heminges and Henry Condell
(two senior members of Shakespeare's company, who had
performed with him for about twenty years) collected his
plays—published and unpublished—into a large volume,
commonly called the First Folio. (A folio is a volume
consisting of sheets that have been folded once, each sheet
thus making two leaves, or four pages. The eighteen plays
published during Shakespeare's lifetime had been issued
one play per volume in small books called quartos. Each
sheet in a quarto had been folded twice, making four
leaves, or eight pages.) The First Folio contains thirty-six
plays; a thirty-seventh, *Pericles,* though not in the Folio
is regarded as canonical. Heminges and Condell suggest
in an address "To the great variety of readers" that the

republished plays are presented in better form than in the quartos: "Before you were abused with diverse stolen and surreptitious copies, maimed and deformed by the frauds and stealths of injurious impostors that exposed them; even those, are now offered to your view cured and perfect of their limbs, and all the rest absolute in their numbers, as he [i.e., Shakespeare] conceived them."

Whoever was assigned to prepare the texts for publication in the First Folio seems to have taken his job seriously and yet not to have performed it with uniform care. The sources of the texts seem to have been, in general, good unpublished copies or the best published copies. The first play in the collection, *The Tempest*, is divided into acts and scenes, has unusually full stage directions and descriptions of spectacle, and concludes with a list of the characters, but the editor was not able (or willing) to present all of the succeeding texts so fully dressed. Later texts occasionally show signs of carelessness: in one scene of *Much Ado About Nothing* the names of actors, instead of characters, appear as speech prefixes, as they had in the quarto, which the Folio reprints; proofreading throughout the Folio is spotty and apparently was done without reference to the printer's copy; the pagination of *Hamlet* jumps from 156 to 257.

A modern editor of Shakespeare must first select his copy; no problem if the play exists only in the Folio, but a considerable problem if the relationship between a quarto and the Folio—or an early quarto and a later one—is unclear. When an editor has chosen what seems to him to be the most authoritative text or texts for his copy, he has not done with making decisions. First of all, he must reckon with Elizabethan spelling. If he is not producing a facsimile, he probably modernizes it, but ought he to preserve the old form of words that apparently were pronounced quite unlike their modern forms—"lanthorn," "alablaster"? If he preserves these forms, is he really preserving Shakespeare's forms or perhaps those of a compositor in the printing house? What is one to do when one finds "lanthorn" and "lantern" in adjacent lines? (The editors of this series in general, but not invariably, assume that words should be spelled in their modern form.) Elizabethan punctuation, too, presents problems. For example in the First Folio, the only text for the play, Macbeth rejects his wife's idea that he can wash the blood from his hand:

> no: this my Hand will rather
> The multitudinous Seas incarnardine,
> Making the Greene one, Red.

Obviously an editor will remove the superfluous capitals, and he will probably alter the spelling to "incarnadine," but will he leave the comma before "red," letting Macbeth speak of the sea as "the green one," or will he (like most modern editors) remove the comma and thus have Macbeth say that his hand will make the ocean *uniformly* red?

An editor will sometimes have to change more than spelling or punctuation. Macbeth says to his wife:

> I dare do all that may become a man,
> Who dares no more, is none.

For two centuries editors have agreed that the second line is unsatisfactory, and have emended "no" to "do": "Who dares do more is none." But when in the same play Ross says that fearful persons

> floate vpon a wilde and violent Sea
> Each way, and moue,

need "move" be emended to "none," as it often is, on the hunch that the compositor misread the manuscript? The editors of the Signet Classic Shakespeare have restrained themselves from making abundant emendations. In their minds they hear Dr. Johnson on the dangers of emending: "I have adopted the Roman sentiment, that it is more honorable to save a citizen than to kill an enemy." Some departures (in addition to spelling, punctuation, and lineation) from the copy text have of course been made, but the original readings are listed in a note following the play, so that the reader can evaluate them for himself.

The editors of the Signet Classic Shakespeare, following tradition, have added line numbers and in many cases act and scene divisions as well as indications of locale at the beginning of scenes. The Folio divided most of the plays into acts and some into scenes. Early eighteenth-century editors increased the divisions. These divisions, which provide a convenient way of referring to passages in the plays, have been retained, but when not in the text chosen as the basis for the Signet Classic text they are enclosed in square brackets [   ] to indicate that they are editorial additions. Similarly, although no play of Shakespeare's published during his lifetime was equipped with indications of locale at the heads of scene divisions, locales have here been added in square brackets for the convenience of the reader, who lacks the information afforded to spectators by costumes, properties, and gestures. The spectator can tell at a glance he is in the throne room, but without an editorial indication the reader may be puzzled for a while. It should be mentioned, incidentally, that there are a few authentic stage directions—perhaps Shakespeare's, perhaps a prompter's—that suggest locales: for example, "Enter Brutus in his orchard," and "They go up into the Senate house." It is hoped that the bracketed additions provide the reader with the sort of help provided in these two authentic directions, but it is equally hoped that the reader will remember that the stage was not loaded with scenery.

No editor during the course of his work can fail to recollect some words Heminges and Condell prefixed to the Folio:

It had been a thing, we confess, worthy to have been wished, that the author himself had lived to have set forth and overseen his own writings. But since it hath been ordained otherwise, and he by death departed from that right, we pray you do not envy his friends the office of their care and pain to have collected and published them.

Nor can an editor, after he has done his best, forget Heminges and Condell's final words: "And so we leave you to other of his friends, whom if you need can be your guides. If you need them not, you can lead yourselves, and others. And such readers we wish him."

SYLVAN BARNET
Tufts University

William Shakespeare

HENRY VI, PART ONE

Edited by Lawrence V. Ryan

Contents

Introduction

The First Part of Henry the Sixth is a play with many imperfections, so many, indeed, that editors and critics have often been reluctant to attribute the greater part of it to Shakespeare. "That Drum-and-trumpet Thing," the eighteenth-century critic Maurice Morgann called it in his essay on Sir John Falstaff, "written doubtless, or rather exhibited, long before *Shakespeare* was born, tho' afterwards repaired, I think, and furbished up by him with here and there a little sentiment and diction."

Such reluctance of ascription has led to the expenditure of much scholarly energy on attempts to isolate as undeniably Shakespearean a few scenes, in particular the finely managed quarrel of the Yorkists and Lancastrians in the Temple Garden (II.iv), and to assign the bulk of the work to various teams of collaborators, among them Christopher Marlowe, George Peele, Thomas Nashe, and Robert Greene. Another consequence has been an exceptional tentativeness in much of the critical speculation about *1 Henry VI,* though several fine studies have been made of its significance in Shakespeare's evolution from prentice playwright to master dramatist.

Arguments against Shakespeare's authorship, or primacy within a group of collaborators, have focused mainly upon resemblances in the text to patterns of diction and versification characteristic of other Elizabethan playwrights. The evidence amassed has been considerable, though sometimes contradictory; at times impressive, but never conclusive. For it is likely enough that a Shakespeare who was just setting out on his literary career would have tended to imitate the stylistic mannerisms of already established dramatists. Even Allison Gaw, among the champions of multiple authorship one of the most sensitive to the potential and actual virtues of the play, failed to associate the unusual effort to integrate historical theme and dramatic structure in a theatrically meaningful way with the designing hand of Shakespeare.

Against the collaborationist theory, however, have stood a number of commentators, among them Charles Knight and Hermann Ulrici in the nineteenth century and Peter Alexander, J. P. Brockbank, Leo Kirschbaum, Hereward Price, and E. M. W. Tillyard in our own time. These critics perceive the three dramas on the reign of Henry VI as of one piece, and regard the case for denying the Shakespearean authorship of any part as not proved. It would be rash to assert categorically that *1 Henry VI* as printed in the Folio of 1623 is entirely by Shakespeare, or that no version involving extensive collaboration with others ever did exist. But an approach to the play through the relationship between theme and dramatic design, rather than through its stylistic echoes of various contemporary writers, does considerably strengthen the argument that Shakespeare played the major, if not an exclusive, role in its composition.

Any reader or spectator coming to *1 Henry VI* after exposure to the chronicle plays of other Elizabethan authors is suddenly aware that here he is being asked not simply to observe the pageant of history, but to ponder the meaning of man's role in history. Most other works of the period in this dramatic kind are, even more evidently than the civic and national chronicles upon which they are based, mere strings of episodes in sequence of time, governed, if by any sense of theme at all, by the notion of the capriciousness of the goddess Fortune. Very few are concerned with seeking any other guiding principle in history or with the dramatic interaction of personalities within the pattern of historical events. Very few are concerned with the meaning of history at all, their authors often preferring instead, like a certain kind of modern historical novelist, to invent romantic situations involving historical personages within a bare framework of actual events.

The theme that runs throughout the tetralogy of plays composed by Shakespeare on the reigns of Henry VI and Richard III, and in fact throughout all of his dramatizations of English history, is the individual's, and a people's, response to the continuing alternations of order and disorder allowed by divine providence in the political life of a nation. A strong and heroic king whose regime brings glory and harmony to the commonwealth is succeeded by a monarch lacking, through extreme youth or defect of character, in the virtues necessary for unifying all the diverse constituents of society. The ineptitude or negligence of the sovereign looses the restraints on ambitious and unscrupulous subjects, whose schemes and counterschemes for self-aggrandizement promote faction, public disorder, and eventually civil war. As Tillyard points out in the selections printed later in this volume, in the struggle for domination degree, or acknowledgment of one's proper place in the hierarchically constituted political, and even cosmic, order, is forgotten. "Vaulting ambition" causes men to o'erleap themselves and drag the rest of society with them to the brink of chaos. Finally, when a ruler appears who is powerful and virtuous enough to triumph over the contending parties and restore degree and order, the hallmarks to the Elizabethan mind of good political economy, the wheel comes full circle.

Like the sixteenth-century chronicler Edward Hall, Shakespeare seems, officially at least, to have regarded the larger cycle of order emerging from disorder as having come round fully with the rise of the Tudor dynasty. Hall, whose book is entitled *The Union of the Two Noble and Illustre Families of Lancaster and York,* believed that the cause of the civil warfare which plagued England intermittently throughout the fifteenth century had been removed by the coronation of Henry VIII, whose father was connected with the Lancastrian, or Red-Rose, branch of the royal family, and whose mother was the daughter and heir of the Yorkist, or White-Rose, King Edward IV. For Shakespeare and his contemporaries, the full benefit of this restoration of harmony and degree after the near-anarchy of the Wars of the Roses was manifest in the long and prosperous reign of their virgin queen. "This royal infant," prophesies Archbishop Cranmer of the just-christened Elizabeth in the final scene of *Henry the Eighth,*

> Though in her cradle, yet now promises
> Upon this land a thousand thousand blessings
> Which time shall bring to ripeness. (V.v.18–21)

Nor will the maiden queen's death, continues Cranmer (how unprophetic the playwright here becomes of later Stuart history!) set the old cycle in motion again, because phoenix-like her "blessedness" will be reborn in her successor.

But Shakespeare was more concerned with presenting the ill effects of disrupted order than with depicting the glories of successful monarchs. Of all his plays on British historical or pseudohistorical subjects, only one, *Henry V,* concentrates on the personality of an all-prosperous ruler and an undeniably glorious moment in England's past. Despite the good fortune of the kingdom during most of Elizabeth's reign, he apparently brooded about the possibility that the cycle might recur, especially if men should ignore the lessons taught by history. Within the larger cycle described by Hall and accepted as complete by many writers of his age, Shakespeare saw smaller cycles or undulations of order and chaos that should have reminded men how precarious any state of equilibrium is in their moral and political lives.

This is not to suggest that in his earliest years as a playwright he had already blocked out in his mind a whole series of dramas to illustrate the pattern and point the historical lessons for his audiences. The order of composition of his various "chronicle histories" should dispel any such assumption. The later-written tetralogy on the troubled history of England toward the end of the Middle Ages—*Richard II, Henry IV: Parts I and II,* and *Henry V*—deals with events that antedate those of the three *Henry VI* plays and *Richard III.* There also exists some possibility that the second and third parts of *Henry VI* were composed before and provided suggestions for the first. Even the earlier tetralogy, therefore, hints at a gradually emerging and changing conception in Shakespeare's mind of what his subject signified and how that significance might be rendered in dramatic terms.

The breakdown of good order, manifest in the undermining of ancient chivalric ideals that had earlier held society together, has its origins for Shakespeare in the events leading to the deposition of King Richard II at the close of the fourteenth century. Richard, a minor at his accession and as an adult deficient in the private and public virtues requisite in a king, is forced to abdicate by his cousin Henry Bolingbroke, whom he has wronged. Bolingbroke, reigning as King Henry IV, is haunted by the rebellions consequent upon Richard's death; his own success in violating degree has ironically given rise to ambition in others. His son Henry V, however, brings to the throne a clearer conscience and the qualities needed for effective rule. His triumphant kingship marks the close of one of the smaller historical cycles, and is epitomized in his ability to control the anarchical forces in society and weld its different elements into the efficient little army that defeats the French at Agincourt (1415).

Yet this brief period of glory is only an interval in the larger pattern. The hero-king has scotched, not killed, "civil dissension," the "viperous worm / That gnaws the bowels of the commonwealth" (*1 Henry VI*, III.i.72–73). The opening scene of *1 Henry VI* is shrewdly designed to give warning of the impending disorder. At the funeral of Henry V the four speeches by the king's brothers and uncles convey an awesome sense of cosmic upheaval and heavy finality. Their foreboding is immediately justified, for within less than three dozen lines the lamentations dissolve into a quarrel between the Duke of Gloucester and the Bishop of Winchester. This altercation symbolizes the release of disruptive forces within a society deprived of its main source of unity. Bedford, the new king's uncle, in fact responds to the quarrel with a desperate invocation, asking Henry V's spirit, as his living presence had done, to

> Prosper this realm, keep it from civil broils,
> Combat with adverse planets in the heavens!

Nor does the playwright waste any further time before showing how disastrous has been the untimely death of this "king of so much worth." Bedford's prayer is interrupted by the entrance of a courier, who rushes in unceremoniously with news of English reversals in France. He is succeeded by two others, each arriving with worse tidings, worst of all being the account of Lord Talbot's capture. The remarkable economy of the scene is evident from the impact made by this trio of messengers. Their accounts project to the audience the importance for England's success in France of the efforts of such leaders as Salisbury, Talbot, and Bedford, who reacts to the news by preparing to go immediately to the aid of the others. Through this sequence of speeches the dramatist focuses attention on the three warriors, who stand for the ideals that have caused English arms until now to prosper. Yet all three worthy nobles are represented as advanced in years and fated to die later in the play. They carry with them to their graves not only the hopes of England's monarchs for possessing the crown of France, but also the chivalric ideals of a more innocent and masculine era. Their kind will be displaced, at least temporarily, by a self-seeking breed of new "risers," the Winchesters, the Suffolks, and the Yorks.

In spite of Bedford's resolve, there can be no doubt as the scene concludes that all coherence is already gone, that the downturn in England's fortunes has begun. With a real instinct for symmetrical design, the author concludes the scene by repeating the pattern of its opening. The royal brothers and uncles take their leave in precisely the order in which they have been introduced as speakers. As each goes his way to carry out his separate function in governing the realm, there is a momentary feeling that if they can work to one end, all may yet be well. Lest the audience presume, however, that shared grief and determination to act will lead to an effective coalition, the sense of division, of a pilotless ship of state, is emphasized by the words and pageantry of the departures. When all the rest are gone, there remains the unscrupulous politician Winchester, whose earlier altercation with Gloucester has already struck the note of discord, and who regards his nephew's death as an opportunity for him to seize control "And sit at chiefest stern of public weal."

The masterful construction of this introductory scene is more evident in theatrical performance than from silent reading. For it wants, as does the play on the whole, that poetic fire one is accustomed to look for in the work of Shakespeare. But as has often been remarked about his career, he seems to have developed a keen feeling for construction and for what is theatrically right before he evolved a poetic style that can thrill the auditor with its justness for the occasion or discriminate for the sensitive ear subtle differences of mood and character.

Symmetry and purposefulness of design, unlike the formlessness of most Elizabethan chronicle plays, are indeed the keynotes of this work, and of the Lancaster-York tetralogy as a whole. If later—beginning with *Richard II* and *Henry IV* and at length most impressively in *King Lear* and *Macbeth*—Shakespeare learned to portray characters helping to shape as well as enduring history or growing in perception and self-knowledge from their interaction with events, in *1 Henry VI* he is not yet ready for such an achievement. Here the problem of man's role in history is reduced to simpler terms: a dramatic personage responds in a particular way to events and to other persons involved in the action because he has a fixed character, rather than the possibility of an evolving one. This simple consistency is, in a way, true even of the heroicomical portrayal of Joan of Arc. Although she gives an impression at the outset of being admirably eloquent, efficient, and patriotic, and then of degenerating into wantonness and diabolism, the unsavory side of her character is hinted at in her very first scene. If we are

disturbed by the seemingly inconsistent and finally unchivalrous treatment of the Maid of Orleans, we should
remind ourselves that in Shakespeare's day she had not
yet been canonized or become the subject of more sympathetic characterizations by dramatists like Schiller, Shaw,
and Anouilh. Character in Shakespeare's play is conceived
broadly, flatly; the peculiar quality of every personage is
unequivocally represented.

The solution for him, consequently, was to develop
his dramatic theme mainly through formal structure;
that is, through symbolically parallel and contrasting
episodes, and through confrontations between characters representing sharply defined ethical and political
values.

The first clue to this intention is the extremely cavalier
handling of chronology, a disruption of time-sequence far
beyond that in any of Shakespeare's other plays based on
chronicles. Rather than demonstrating an ignorance of
history or indifference to order, the rearrangement of
events indicates a sense on the author's part that dramatic
logic and the historical lesson are better served by recre-
ating than by retelling what happened in the past. Thus,
while *1 Henry VI* is grounded upon chronicle materials,
it employs them so freely that one is not always certain
how much indebted to the sources a given scene may be,
or even, except in manifest instances, whether the principal inspiration is the work of Edward Hall or that of
Raphael Holinshed.

The play also includes totally fictional scenes, among
them the dispute in the Temple Garden and Talbot's encounter with the Countess of Auvergne. Unlike the arbi-
trarily invented episodes common in other history plays
of the age, those in *1 Henry VI* serve to clarify the meaning of actual events, far more effectively than anything
available to the author in his historical sources. The dis-
jointing of time, moreover, enables him to achieve striking dramatic and didactic effects. The episodes cover a
period of more than thirty years, from the beginning
of Henry VI's reign in 1422 to the death of the Talbots
near Bordeaux in 1453, but from the opening lines incidents are juxtaposed that were in actuality separated

by a number of years. Thus, the siege of Orleans (1428–29) is already taking place during the funeral of Henry V seven years earlier. The dramaturgical reason is evident: to introduce immediately the main conflict, between Joan of France and Talbot of England. In Act Five, the capture of Joan (1430) is succeeded directly and without even a scene division by Suffolk's fictitious capture and wooing of Margaret of Anjou, though the negotiations for the king's marriage did not actually take place until 1444. Finally, the death of the Talbots, chronologically the last in the long series of events here dramatized, precedes these other carefully paired episodes. Apparently this dislocation was made in order to maintain as long as possible the symbolical conflict between the mirror of English chivalry and the diabolically assisted Joan, and also to imply that Margaret is about to arise from Joan's ashes to carry on the scourging of England in the remainder of the trilogy.

Divine providence allows England to be plagued by infernal as well as political enemies because her people have sinned. How the nation might have remained true to itself is signified by the words and deeds of Talbot. What she is in danger of becoming is signified in the shortcomings of the French, failings that crop up increasingly among Englishmen as the action of the play proceeds. The dissension that breaks out at home in the opening lines begins immediately to sap the English strength abroad, for it is accompanied by the decay of feudal loyalties and forgetfulness of degree. Also manifest are an English decline toward French effeminacy and the beginnings of reliance on fraud and cunning rather than manly courage and straightforward knightly virtue.

In the second scene, which shifts to Orleans, the playwright quickly sketches in the defective moral character of Frenchmen, as epitomized in the behavior of the Dauphin. A braggart like his counterpart in Shakespeare's *Henry V,* he begins a sortie against the English with the cry to his followers,

> Him I forgive my death that killeth me
> When he sees me go back one foot or fly. (I.ii.20–21)

Some moments later, his forces are beaten back, and he excuses his retreat in words a Talbot or a Salisbury would have died rather than utter:

> I would ne'er have fled,
> But that they left me 'midst my enemies. (I.ii.23–24)

Nothing they can do as men, it is apparent from the ensuing conversation among the French leaders, can overcome these dogged Englishmen.

At this point Joan comes onstage, and the Dauphin's conversation with her brings out two grave defects of Frenchmen that also begin gradually to taint the characters of Englishmen in the play. After bowing to her in single combat, Charles woos Joan in the language not of her royal prince, but of the fashionable courtly lover, asking to be her "servant and not sovereign," and imploring her "mercy" (that is, the favor of her love) as her "prostrate thrall." Such domination by the female is obviously scorned by an audience of Tudor Englishmen; it confirms their prejudices against Gallic dandyism and effeminacy. For in spite of Joan's high-sounding claims and self-assertive dash, one's admiration of her must stop far short of the Dauphin's; she is, after all, no more than a shepherd's daughter from Lorraine. The comedy of the scene is also obvious. From the number of double entendres in the Ovidian tradition of lovemaking as armed combat, the audience can scarcely be expected to take seriously Joan's claims to divine inspiration and vow to maintain her virginity while Englishmen remain on her country's soil.

All doubt about the tenor of the scene is dispelled by Charles's final ecstatic response to her messianic claims:

> Was Mahomet inspirèd with a dove?
> Thou with an eagle art inspirèd then.
> Helen, the mother of great Constantine,
> Nor yet Saint Philip's daughters, were like thee.

Bright star of Venus, fall'n down on the earth,
How may I reverently worship thee enough?
(I.ii.140–45)

Not only are the allusions to other lofty examples of
divine inspiration too characteristic of the Dauphin's lack
of moderation to be taken seriously, but their very extravagance is a strong hint that Joan's pretensions are
false. When Charles climaxes his apostrophe with the
words "Bright star of Venus," the imagery of courtly
wooing and the bawdy overtones of the earlier part of
the scene intrude themselves again. Besides, "star of
Venus, fall'n down on the earth," calls to mind not only
the goddess of profane love, but also Lucifer, that brightest of angelic stars tumbled out of the heavens for his
aspiration to divinity. Feminine wiles are thus linked by
the epithet with diabolical fraud and deception. Charles
is blameworthy for allowing himself to be dominated by
a woman—a peasant girl at that!—and for resorting to
preternatural aid in his efforts to rid his country of the
English. "Coward of France!" exclaims Bedford,

how much he wrongs his fame,
Despairing of his own arm's fortitude,
To join with witches and the help of hell. (II.i.16–18)

The rest of the scenes in France are fashioned to contrast the reprehensible behavior of Joan and the Dauphin,
as well as of Englishmen whose characters become similarly stained as the moral fiber of their leaderless country
weakens, with that of the upright Talbot. These contrasts
are effectively brought out through patterns, as Ernest
Talbert calls them, of "intensified repetition." One such
pattern is the strategic paralleling of episodes either to
heighten the opposition between worthy and reprehensible
forms of behavior or to point up symbolical relationships
between apparently unconnected incidents. The playwright is also fond of grouping characters and episodes
in climactic triads to underscore several of the main
themes of the play.

Thus, since Talbot is the standard by which the measure of the other characters is taken, his first meeting with Henry VI is presented as an idealized interview between an unselfishly devoted vassal and his sovereign. For his loyal service and recovery in France of

> fifty fortresses,
> Twelve cities, and seven wallèd towns of strength,
> Beside five hundred prisoners of esteem,
>
> (III.iv.6–8)

Talbot is created Earl of Shrewsbury. But the episode distinctly recalls the first scene of the same act, where the already scheming Plantagenet is made Duke of York without having done anything to merit his elevation and pledges his fealty to the king with a hollow heart. Again, in the opening scene of Act Four Talbot tears the Garter from Falstaff's* leg for cowardice in battle and delivers a speech on what it means to bear "the sacred name of knight." His action is a clear example of how noblemen, in helping the monarch to maintain true order and degree, should deal with the presumptions of their subordinates.

As soon as Talbot departs, however, Vernon and Basset disrupt the coronation scene with their demands for trial by combat in behalf of their respective masters, York and Somerset. In order to further their own ambitions, Henry's nobles are obviously willing to let faction breed rather than suppress their contentious retainers. Toward the end of the scene York even appears to be on the point of exclaiming to Warwick (line 180) that he would prefer to have the king himself take sides against him since he might then turn it to his own advantage. This is but one of several scenes in which Talbot's conduct is sharply contrasted with that of other characters. The dramatist's intentions are unmistakable: Talbot is the ideal, the centripetal force of order that gradually gives

---

* Not the famous fat knight of *Henry IV*, whose death is described in *Henry V*, but rather a character based on the historical Sir John Fastolfe (c. 1378–1459), a prominent retainer of the Duke of Bedford and, according to the chronicles, one of the most valiant captains in the regent's armies.

way to the centrifugal forces of chaos represented by
York and others of the rising new breed.

Dramatic triads appear in many places in *1 Henry VI*
from the opening scene onward: the sense of climactic
urgency in the arrival of the three messengers hot on one
another's heels; the trio of ambitious nobles—Winchester,
York, Suffolk; the focusing on the three stout but aging
generals—Salisbury, Bedford, and Talbot—each of whose
deaths is a more discouraging blow, the last the final blow,
to English dynastic ambitions in France. Talbot opposes
the French and their sorceress champion on all three of
these occasions: at Orleans, where Salisbury is shot; at
Rouen, where Bedford dies; and finally near Bordeaux,
where he and his son meet their heroic end.

In each incident, fraud at first succeeds, not force of
arms, and the placing of blame in each indicates pro-
gressive deterioration on the English side. At Orleans,
Salisbury is killed by chance and Talbot is temporarily
set back, to his complete bewilderment, by Joan's "art
and baleful sorcery." His martial enterprise and trust in
God, however, in contrast with the Frenchmen's lax discipline and reliance on "the help of hell," win the day for
him when he returns to the attack. At Rouen (III.ii) Joan
gains entrance by means of a stratagem historically employed by the English on another occasion, according to
Holinshed, and transferred in the play to the French as
an instance of their treachery. Eventually, Talbot overcomes again, while Bedford watches the struggle from
"his litter sick." But now it is not only the French who
are cowardly, who, as Talbot complains,

> keep the walls
> And dare not take up arms like gentlemen. (III.ii.69–70)

Just before the victory is assured and Bedford dies content, Falstaff again shows the white feather, this time on
stage instead of in a messenger's report, and runs like a
Frenchman from the battle scene. It is this defection that
provides the occasion for Talbot later to tear the badge
of the Order of the Garter from his leg at Henry's coronation in Paris.

At Bordeaux, where the audience might expect a final confrontation between Talbot and Joan, none is provided, nor does Joan make use of any cunning device to gain advantage over the English. The dramatist's reasons are clear enough. They are placed in the mouth of Sir William Lucy as he vainly begs York and Somerset to come to Talbot's relief. It is "the vulture of sedition" and "Sleeping neglection" that are causing the loss of Henry V's conquests:

> The fraud of England, not the force of France,
> Hath now entrapped the noble-minded Talbot.
> (IV.iv.36–37)

Malice and cunning deceit are beginning to corrupt even the highest English nobility, and Talbot is the sacrifice to their dissension. Yet even against the forces of hell and the wily allurements of womankind, England might have stood fast, if only all her noblemen had been like her stoutest champion. But when men place their self-interest ahead of the common good, the old ideals are readily forgotten. Joan's cunning becomes no longer necessary; the English are now their own worst enemies, having succumbed to the vices of the French.

This eroding of English virtue is nowhere more skillfully depicted than in the triad of scenes involving the first appearances of each of the three evil-designing Frenchwomen (interestingly enough, the only feminine characters in the play!). The scenes in question are Joan's introduction to the Dauphin, Talbot's reception by the Countess of Auvergne (II.iii), and Suffolk's wooing of Margaret of Anjou (V.iii). All three women represent a threat to English fortunes; the manner in which the three men respond to them neatly dramatizes the lesson.

Earlier it was pointed out that not only the Dauphin's accepting the demoniacally inspired assistance of Joan but also his self-debasement to servant-lover of a peasant girl, is conduct inexcusable in a prince. And even if his behavior were not a burlesque of courtly traditions, it runs counter to the ruggedly heroic ideal represented by

Talbot. Not that Talbot is a boor: he does know how to treat a lady as becomes a worthy English chevalier. The Dauphin's involvement with Joan is a breaking of degree and serves, moreover, to unhinge her judgment of herself even beyond what traffic with fiends has done. When she is finally on her way to the stake, this peasant maiden who has been graced with sovereignty over her infatuated monarch pretends to "noble birth" and "gentler blood" than that of her shepherd father. Even the phrase with which she rejects the old man—"Decrepit miser!"— accentuates her disdain for her lowly origins; *miser* is the worst term of opprobrium in the vocabulary of the courtly tradition.

But the true measure of the Dauphin's folly is the scene between Talbot and the fictional Countess. This lady too plots evil to the English through her ruse for capturing "the terror of the French." There is even a suggestion that she, like Joan, may have resorted to witchcraft by practicing sympathetic magic on her guest's portrait:

> Long time thy shadow hath been thrall to me,
> For in my gallery thy picture hangs.
> But now the substance shall endure the like.
>
> (II.iii.36–38)

The resourceful Talbot, however, outwits her by a simple counterstratagem and, refusing like a true and valiant gentleman to avenge himself on so weak an adversary, asks only honest entertainment for himself and his men before they take their leave.

Obviously if all of Talbot's compatriots had been thus immune to the allure of scheming Frenchwomen, all might have remained well enough for England. But the third encounter of this kind, that between Suffolk and Reignier's daughter Margaret, shows that Englishmen no longer are men of true honor, who, in contrast with the French, place their country's interests above their own selfish desires. Suffolk is dazzled, almost bewitched, by Margaret's beauty when he first gazes on her. And while he is the active, she almost entirely the passive, agent in this scene, from the course taken by the remaining action there can be little doubt that this woman will supplant Joan as the punishment for the sins of faction and ambition among Englishmen. Having Joan's and Margaret's captures occur in the same scene, in another of those symbolically meaningful parallelings of seemingly unconnected episodes, is theatrically most effective. And even though Joan's final scenes are far different in tone from Margaret's entry into the action, they serve a twofold function in helping to knit up the events of *1 Henry VI* and to anticipate the subsequent development of the trilogy.

In defiance of historical fact, but with excellent dramatic sense, York is made to be Joan's captor and judge. But even as he is mercilessly taunting his prisoner about her past affairs with the Dauphin and his nobles, another game of man and woman is being played that will prove his undoing. The parting curses of Joan are not the impotent ragings of a "fell banning hag"; they are prophecies of ambitious York's own downfall and of the miserable years for England that are being engendered in the dalliance of Suffolk with Margaret of Anjou.

Suffolk would enjoy this lady's love and use her to further his own ends at the sacrifice of English interests in France. Worse still, his "wondrous rare description" of Margaret's beauty serves to corrupt King Henry's mind and causes him to break his pre-contract of marriage with the daughter of the Earl of Armagnac. That the choice is both impolitic and immoral is clear from the king's own inner turmoil in the last moments of the play: the "sharp dissension" that he feels within makes him "sick with working of my thoughts," and he finally departs in a state of "grief" rather than expectant elation at "This sudden execution of my will."

The threat latent in Henry's impending marriage to Margaret, with whose arrival in England the second part of the trilogy opens, is brilliantly suggested by a pair of images in the last scene of Part One. The king compares his infatuation to a tempest, driving his soul against its more settled inclinations like a ship against the tide:

So am I driven by breath of her renown
Either to suffer shipwreck or arrive
Where I may have fruition of her love. (V.v.7–9)

The sudden intrusion here of the conventional figure of,
the lover as a vessel in danger of shipwreck on the stormy
seas of passion calls to mind the dangers that Petrarch
(*"Passa la nave mia colma d'oblio"*) and his imitator Sir
Thomas Wyatt ("My galley chargèd with forgetfulness")
lamented as besetting the soul of the man tossed by sexual
desire. For a king to make such an admission, and then
to overrule good counsel and follow the inclination of his
will rather than reasons of state, is a most unregal kind
of behavior.

Most disturbing of all, however, are the verses with
which the drama concludes. If restoration of order were
to be implied at the end of the action, according to the
usual Shakespearean closing formula there would be a
speech explicitly saying so. But here the final words,
coming after the king's confused withdrawal, are left for
Suffolk, who exults in his success and departs for Anjou

As did the youthful Paris once to Greece,
With hope to find the like event in love,
But prosper better than the Trojan did. (V.v.104–106)

The image could hardly be lost on an Elizabethan audience, whose own mythmaking historians traced the an-
cestry of the British race to Troy. French Margaret will
bring disaster to England as certainly as Spartan Helen
brought ruin to "the topless towers of Ilium."

The remainder of the trilogy portrays Margaret, though
she is in neither play the solely dominating figure, as an
evil influence in England's domestic affairs. In Part Two
it is she and her lover Suffolk, along with the malevolent
Winchester, who engineer the downfall of the Duke of
Gloucester. In Part Three, her monstrous treatment of
her archrival York is the climax of her role as England's
scourge. Eventually, in *Richard III,* this figure of nemesis
who for long has borne a "tiger's heart wrapped in a
woman's hide," becomes inactive though not silent, an

unheeded Cassandra warning the now-dominant House of York of its own impending doom.

Though not a great poetic drama, *1 Henry VI* is by no means a failure as a play for theatrical performance. It exhibits a thoughtful design through which important themes are vigorously, if somewhat crudely, realized in the completed action. Nor is the affair of Margaret and Suffolk, as some critics would have it, only an after-thought. Strange as the final act and scene divisions in the Folio may be, the matter of these last episodes is not something inexpertly tacked onto what was originally con-ceived as an independent tragedy of Talbot simply be-cause the author, or reviser, needed a way to patch together a trilogy. All that previously transpires is too carefully articulated with the concluding scenes for that. Act Five is the logical conclusion to the events set in motion at the play's beginning, and at the same time an effective opening-out to the even greater disorder and calamities of Parts Two and Three. The close is nearly symmetrical with the opening, and far more ominous though more restrained and economical in its language. A nation that is leaderless because its king is an infant as the play begins, is still leaderless, or subject to dangerous misguidance, as the action ends because its now-grown king has succumbed to a destructive passion. And the unscrupulous new risers have now found an instrument for gaining the illicit power to which they aspire.

The bad news from Orleans that marked the downturn of England's fortunes in France is superseded by bad news from Angers that will lead to misery on England's soil itself. All this the maker of *1 Henry VI* was capable of rendering theatrically effective. By 1592 Shakespeare may not yet have been a supreme dramatic craftsman, but neither was he a mere botcher of other men's work, a snapper-up of other playwrights' unconsidered trifles.

LAWRENCE V. RYAN
Stanford University

The First Part of Henry the Sixth

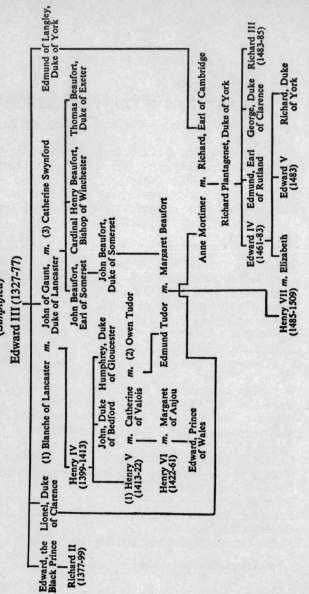

THE HOUSES OF LANCASTER AND YORK
(Simplified)

Edward III (1327-77)

[*Dramatis Personae*

King Henry the Sixth
Humphrey, Duke of Gloucester, uncle to the King, and
    Protector
John, Duke of Bedford, uncle to the King, and Regent
    of France
Thomas Beaufort, Duke of Exeter, great-uncle to the King
Henry Beaufort, Bishop of Winchester, and afterwards
    Cardinal, great-uncle to the King
John Beaufort, Earl, afterwards Duke, of Somerset
Richard Plantagenet, afterwards Duke of York, son of
    Richard, late Earl of Cambridge
Earl of Warwick
Earl of Salisbury
William de la Pole, Earl of Suffolk
Lord Talbot, afterwards Earl of Shrewsbury
John Talbot, Lord Lisle, his son
Edmund Mortimer, Earl of March
Sir John Falstaff*
Sir William Lucy
Sir William Glansdale
Sir Thomas Gargrave
Mayor of London
Woodville, Lieutenant of the Tower
Vernon, of the White-Rose or York faction
Basset, of the Red-Rose or Lancaster faction
A Lawyer. Mortimer's Jailers. A papal Legate

Charles, Dauphin, and afterwards King, of France
Reignier, Duke of Anjou, and titular King of Naples
Duke of Burgundy
Duke of Alençon
Bastard of Orleans
Governor of Paris
Master-Gunner of Orleans, and his Son

* See note, Introduction, p. xxxiv.

General of the French forces in Bordeaux
A French Sergeant. A Porter
An old Shepherd, father to Joan la Pucelle

Margaret, daughter to Reignier, afterwards married to
    King Henry
Countess of Auvergne
Joan la Pucelle, commonly called Joan of Arc

Lords, Ambassadors, Warders of the Tower, Heralds,
    Officers, Soldiers, Messengers, Attendants

Fiends appearing to La Pucelle

Scene: England; France]

The First Part of Henry the Sixth

ACT I

Scene I. [*Westminster Abbey.*]

Dead March.°¹ *Enter the Funeral of King Henry the Fifth, attended on by the Duke of Bedford, Regent of France; the Duke of Gloucester, Protector; the Duke of Exeter, Warwick, the Bishop of Winchester, and the Duke of Somerset, [with Attendants].*

Bedford. Hung be the heavens with black,° yield day
    to night!
  Comets, importing change of times and states,°
  Brandish your crystal° tresses in the sky,
  And with them scourge the bad revolting stars
  That have consented unto° Henry's death!   5
  King Henry the Fifth, too famous to live long!
  England ne'er lost a king of so much worth.

---

1 The degree sign (°) indicates a footnote, which is keyed to the text by line number. Text references are printed in **boldface** type; the annotation follows in roman type.
I.i.s.d. Dead March a solemn piece of music for a funeral procession   **1 black** i.e., as a stage was draped in black for a tragedy   **2 Comets . . . states** i.e., the appearance of comets portending some misfortune   **3 crystal** bright   **5 consented unto** conspired to bring about

Gloucester. England ne'er had a king until his time.
  Virtue he had, deserving to command;
  His brandished sword did blind men with his°
10 beams;
  His arms spread wider than a dragon's wings;
  His sparkling eyes, replete with wrathful fire,
  More dazzled and drove back his enemies
  Than midday sun fierce bent against their faces.
15 What should I say? His deeds exceed all speech:
  He ne'er lift° up his hand but conquerèd.

Exeter. We mourn in black; why mourn we not in blood?°
  Henry is dead and never shall revive.
  Upon a wooden° coffin we attend,
20 And death's dishonorable victory
  We with our stately presence glorify,
  Like captives bound to a triumphant car.°
  What! shall we curse the planets of mishap°
  That plotted thus our glory's overthrow?
25 Or shall we think the subtle-witted French
  Conjurers and sorcerers that, afraid of him,
  By magic verses have contrived his end?

Winchester. He was a king blessed of the King of Kings.
  Unto the French the dreadful judgment day
30 So dreadful will not be as was his sight.
  The battles of the Lord of Hosts he fought;
  The church's prayers made him so prosperous.

Gloucester. The church! Where is it? Had not churchmen prayed,
  His thread of life had not so soon decayed.
35 None do you like but an effeminate prince,
  Whom, like a schoolboy, you may overawe.

10 **his** its   16 **lift** lifted   17 **in blood** i.e., by shedding blood, probably of the French in order to avenge the king's death (see lines 25–27)   19 **wooden** unfeeling   22 **car** chariot   23 **of mishap** causing misfortune

Winchester. Gloucester, whate'er we like, thou art
    Protector°
    And lookest° to command the prince and realm.
    Thy wife is proud; she holdeth thee in awe
    More than God or religious churchmen may.   *40*

Gloucester. Name not religion, for thou lov'st the
    flesh,
    And ne'er throughout the year to church thou go'st
    Except it be to pray against thy foes.

Bedford. Cease, cease these jars° and rest your minds
    in peace;
    Let's to the altar. Heralds, wait on us.   *45*
    Instead of gold, we'll offer up our arms,°
    Since arms avail not now that Henry's dead.
    Posterity, await for wretched years,
    When at their mothers' moistened eyes babes shall
    suck,
    Our isle be made a nourish° of salt tears,   *50*
    And none but women left to wail the dead.
    Henry the Fifth, thy ghost I invocate:
    Prosper this realm, keep it from civil broils,°
    Combat with adverse planets in the heavens!
    A far more glorious star thy soul will make   *55*
    Than Julius Caesar° or bright—

Enter a Messenger.

Messenger. My honorable lords, health to you all!
    Sad tidings bring I to you out of France,
    Of loss, of slaughter, and discomfiture:
    Guienne, Champagne, Rheims, Orleans,   *60*
    Paris, Guysors, Poictiers, are all quite lost.

Bedford. What say'st thou, man, before dead Henry's
    corse?°

---

37 Protector governor of the realm during the king's minority   **38
lookest** expect   **44 jars** quarrels   **46 arms** weapons   **50 nourish**
nurse   **53 broils** disorders   **56 Julius Caesar** (whose soul, according to Ovid, *Metamorphoses*, xv. 843–51, became a star in the
heavens after his assassination)   **62 corse** corpse

Speak softly, or the loss of those great towns
Will make him burst his lead° and rise from death.

65 *Gloucester*. Is Paris lost? Is Rouen yielded up?
If Henry were recalled to life again,
These° news would cause him once more yield the
ghost.

Exeter. How were they lost? What treachery was
used?

Messenger. No treachery, but want of men and
money.
70 Amongst the soldiers this is mutterèd,
That here you maintain several factions,°
And whilst a field should be dispatched and fought,
You are disputing of your generals:
One would have ling'ring wars with little cost;
75 Another would fly swift, but wanteth wings;
A third thinks, without expense at all,
By guileful fair words peace may be obtained.
Awake, awake, English nobility!
Let not sloth dim your honors new begot;°
80 Cropped are the flower-de-luces° in your arms;
Of England's coat° one half is cut away.

Exeter. Were our tears wanting° to this funeral,
These tidings would call forth her° flowing tides.

Bedford. Me they concern; Regent° I am of France.
85 Give me my steelèd coat; I'll fight for France.
Away with these disgraceful wailing robes!
Wounds will I lend the French, instead of eyes,
To weep their intermissive° miseries.

---

64 **lead** lining of the coffin   67 **These** (since *news* was originally
plural)   71 **factions** (trisyllabic; the endings *-ion* and *-ions* are
often pronounced as two syllables in Shakespeare)   79 **new begot**
recently obtained   80 **flower-de-luces** fleur-de-lis, or lilies of France
(heraldic symbol of the French monarchs)   81 **coat** coat of arms
(the English royal family, as a sign of its pretensions to the throne
of France, included the fleur-de-lis in its coat of arms from the
fourteenth through the eighteenth centuries)   82 **wanting** lacking
83 **her** i.e., England's   84 **Regent** ruler in the king's absence   88
intermissive coming at intervals

Enter to them another Messenger.

Second Messenger. Lords, view these letters full of
　　bad mischance.
　France is revolted from the English quite,　　　　　　*90*
　Except some petty towns of no import.°
　The Dolphin° Charles is crownèd king in Rheims;
　The Bastard of Orleans with him is joined;
　Reignier, Duke of Anjou, doth take his part;
　The Duke of Alençon flieth to his side.　　　*Exit. 95*

Exeter. The Dolphin crownèd king? All fly to him?
　O, whither shall we fly from this reproach?°

Gloucester. We will not fly, but to our enemies'
　　throats.
　Bedford, if thou be slack, I'll fight it out.

Bedford. Gloucester, why doubt'st thou of my for-
　　wardness?　　　　　　　　　　　　　　*100*
　An army have I mustered in my thoughts,
　Wherewith already France is overrun.

Enter another Messenger.

Third Messenger. My gracious lords, to add to your
　　laments,
　Wherewith you now bedew° King Henry's hearse,
　I must inform you of a dismal fight　　　　　　*105*
　Betwixt the stout Lord Talbot and the French.

Winchester. What? Wherein Talbot overcame, is't so?

Third Messenger. O no, wherein Lord Talbot was
　　o'erthrown.
　The circumstance I'll tell you more at large.°
　The tenth of August last, this dreadful lord,　　　*110*
　Retiring from the siege of Orleans,
　Having full° scarce six thousand in his troop,

---

91 import importance　92 Dolphin Dauphin, title of the heir to
the French throne　97 reproach disgrace　104 bedew moisten
109 The circumstance . . . large I shall tell you the details at greater
length　112 full all told (?)

By three and twenty thousand of the French
Was round encompassèd and set upon.
115 No leisure had he to enrank° his men;
He wanted pikes° to set before his archers;
Instead whereof, sharp stakes plucked out of hedges
They pitchèd in the ground confusedly,
To keep the horsemen off° from breaking in.
120 More than three hours the fight continuèd;
Where valiant Talbot, above human thought,
Enacted wonders with his sword and lance.
Hundreds he sent to hell, and none durst stand him;
Here, there, and everywhere, enraged he slew.
125 The French exclaimed the devil was in arms;
All the whole army stood agazed° on him.
His soldiers, spying his undaunted spirit,
"A Talbot! a Talbot!" cried out amain,°
And rushed into the bowels of the battle.
130 Here had the conquest fully been sealed up,
If Sir John Falstaff had not played the coward.
He, being in the vanward,° placed behind
With purpose to relieve and follow them,
Cowardly fled, not having struck one stroke.
135 Hence grew the general wrack and massacre:
Enclosèd were they with their enemies.
A base Walloon,° to win the Dolphin's grace,
Thrust Talbot with a spear into the back,
Whom all France, with their chief assembled
        strength,
140 Durst not presume to look once in the face.

Bedford. Is Talbot slain then? I will slay myself
For living idly here in pomp and ease
Whilst such a worthy leader, wanting aid,
Unto his dastard foemen is betrayed.

---

115 **enrank** set in ranks   116 **pikes** stakes with sharpened iron
points, set in the ground to impale the enemy's horses if the
mounted troops charged the archers   119 **off** (apparently redun-
dant, and inserted for metrical purposes)   126 **agazed** astounded
(probably a variant of aghast)   128 **amain** with all their might
132 **vanward** vanguard   137 **Walloon** inhabitant of the region
between northeastern France and the Netherlands

Third Messenger. O no, he lives, but is took prisoner, 145
　　And Lord Scales with him and Lord Hungerford;
　　Most of the rest slaughtered or took likewise.

Bedford. His ransom there is none but I shall pay.
　　I'll hale the Dolphin headlong from his throne;
　　His crown shall be the ransom of my friend; 150
　　Four of their lords I'll change for one of ours.
　　Farewell, my masters, to my task will I;
　　Bonfires in France forthwith I am to make
　　To keep our great Saint George's feast° withal.°
　　Ten thousand soldiers with me I will take, 155
　　Whose bloody deeds shall make all Europe quake.

Third Messenger. So you had need, for Orleans is be-
　　　　sieged;
　　The English army is grown weak and faint;
　　The Earl of Salisbury craveth supply
　　And hardly keeps his men from mutiny 160
　　Since they, so few, watch such a multitude.

Exeter. Remember, lords, your oaths to Henry sworn:
　　Either to quell° the Dolphin utterly
　　Or bring him in obedience to your yoke.

Bedford. I do remember it and here take my leave 165
　　To go about my preparation.°　　*Exit Bedford.*

Gloucester. I'll to the Tower° with all the haste I can
　　To view th' artillery and munition,
　　And then I will proclaim young Henry king.
　　　　　　　　　　　　　　　　Exit Gloucester.

Exeter. To Eltham will I, where the young king is, 170
　　Being ordained his special governor,
　　And for his safety there I'll best devise.　　*Exit.*

Winchester. Each hath his place and function to at-
　　　　tend;
　　I am left out; for me nothing remains.

---

154 **Saint George's feast** April 23　　154 **withal** with　　163 **quell** destroy　166 **preparation** (five syllables)　167 **Tower** Tower of London

175 But long I will not be Jack out of office.°
The king from Eltham I intend to send
And sit at chiefest stern of public weal.°
                              Exit [with Attendants].

[Scene II. *France. Before Orleans.*]

*Sound a Flourish.° Enter Charles [the Dauphin],
Alençon, and Reignier, marching with Drum and
                              Soldiers.*

Dauphin. Mars his° true moving, even as in the
    heavens,
  So in the earth, to this day is not known.
  Late did he shine upon the English side;
  Now we are victors; upon us he smiles.
5 What towns of any moment° but we have?
  At pleasure here we lie near Orleans;
  Otherwhiles° the famished English, like pale ghosts,
  Faintly besiege us one hour in a month.

Alençon. They want their porridge and their fat bull-
    beeves:°
10 Either they must be dieted° like mules
  And have their provender° tied to their mouths,
  Or piteous they will look, like drownèd mice.

Reignier. Let's raise the siege; why live we idly here?
  Talbot is taken, whom we wont° to fear;
13 Remaineth none but mad-brained Salisbury,

175 **Jack out of office** a person deprived of official function   177
And . . . weal and maintain control of the government   I.ii.s.d.
Flourish fanfare of trumpets   1 **Mars his** Mars's   5 **moment** importance   7 **Otherwhiles** at times   9 **bull-beeves** (eating of bull-
beef was believed to give one courage)   10 **dieted** fed   11 **pro-
vender** food   14 **wont** were accustomed

And he may well in fretting spend his gall;°
Nor° men nor money hath he to make war.

Dauphin. Sound, sound alarum!° we will rush on
   them.
  Now for the honor of the forlorn French!
  Him I forgive my death that killeth me   20
  When he sees me go back one foot or fly.   *Exeunt.*

*Here alarum; they are beaten back by the English with
great loss. Enter Charles [the Dauphin], Alençon,
and Reignier.*

Dauphin. Who ever saw the like? What men have I?
  Dogs! cowards! dastards! I would ne'er have fled,
  But that they left me 'midst my enemies.

Reignier. Salisbury is a desperate homicide;   25
  He fighteth as one weary of his life.
  The other lords, like lions wanting food,
  Do rush upon us as their hungry prey.°

Alençon. Froissart,° a countryman of ours, records
  England all Olivers and Rowlands° bred   30
  During the time Edward the Third did reign.
  More truly now may this be verified,
  For none but Samsons and Goliases°
  It sendeth forth to skirmish. One to ten!
  Lean raw-boned rascals!° who would e'er suppose 35
  They had such courage and audacity?

Dauphin. Let's leave this town, for they are
   hare-brained slaves,
  And hunger will enforce° them to be more eager.°
  Of old I know them; rather with their teeth
  The walls they'll tear down than forsake the siege. 40

---

16 **gall** bitterness of spirit   17 **Nor** neither   18 **alarum** call to arms
28 **their hungry prey** prey for which they hunger   29 **Froissart** chronicler of fourteenth-century French, English, and Spanish affairs   30
Olivers and Rowlands heroes of the French medieval epic, *La Chan-
son de Roland*   33 **Goliases** Goliaths   35 **rascals** lean, inferior deer
38 **enforce** compel   38 **eager** (1) hungry (2) fierce

Reignier. I think, by some odd gimmors° or device
　　Their arms are set, like clocks, still to strike on;
　　Else ne'er could they hold out so as they do.
　　By my consent, we'll even let them alone.

45 *Alençon.* Be it so.

　　　　　Enter the Bastard of Orleans.

Bastard. Where's the Prince Dolphin? I have news
　　for him.

Dauphin. Bastard of Orleans, thrice welcome to us.

Bastard. Methinks your looks are sad, your cheer
　　appaled.°
　　Hath the late overthrow wrought this offense?
50　　Be not dismayed, for succor is at hand:
　　A holy maid hither with me I bring,
　　Which by a vision sent to her from heaven
　　Ordainèd is to raise this tedious siege
　　And drive the English forth° the bounds of France.
55　　The spirit of deep prophecy she hath,
　　Exceeding the nine sibyls° of old Rome:
　　What's past and what's to come she can descry.
　　Speak, shall I call her in? Believe my words,
　　For they are certain and unfallible.°

Dauphin. Go, call her in. [*Exit Bastard.*] But first, to
60　　try her skill,
　　Reignier, stand thou as Dolphin in my place;
　　Question her proudly; let thy looks be stern:
　　By this means shall we sound° what skill she hath.

　　Enter [*the Bastard of Orleans, with*] *Joan* [*la*]
　　　　　　　Pucelle.°

Reignier. Fair maid, is't thou wilt do these wondrous
　　feats?

---

41 **gimmors** (variant of *gimmals*) connecting parts for transmitting
motion   48 **cheer appaled** countenance pale with fear   54 **forth**
beyond   56 **nine sibyls** nine books of prophetic utterances offered
to King Tarquin of Rome by the sibyl at Cumae   59 **unfallible**
infallible   63 **sound** test   63s.d. **la Pucelle** the virgin

Pucelle. Reignier, is't thou that thinkest to beguile me?   65
   Where is the Dolphin? Come, come from behind;
   I know thee well, though never seen before.
   Be not amazed, there's nothing hid from me;
   In private will I talk with thee apart.
   Stand back, you lords, and give us leave awhile.   70

Reignier. She takes upon her bravely at first dash.°

Pucelle. Dolphin, I am by birth a shepherd's daughter,
   My wit° untrained in any kind of art.
   Heaven and our Lady° gracious hath it pleased
   To shine on my contemptible estate.   75
   Lo, whilst I waited on my tender lambs,
   And to sun's parching heat displayed my cheeks,
   God's mother deignèd to appear to me
   And in a vision full of majesty
   Willed me to leave my base vocation°   80
   And free my country from calamity.
   Her aid she promised and assured success;
   In complete glory she revealed herself;
   And, whereas I was black and swart° before,
   With those clear rays which she infused° on me   85
   That beauty am I blessed with which you may see.
   Ask me what question thou canst possible,
   And I will answer unpremeditated;
   My courage try by combat, if thou dar'st,
   And thou shalt find that I exceed my sex.   90
   Resolve on this,° thou shalt be fortunate
   If thou receive me for thy warlike mate.°

Dauphin. Thou hast astonished me with thy high
   terms;°
   Only this proof I'll of thy valor make,
   In single combat thou shalt buckle° with me,   95
   And if thou vanquishest, thy words are true;
   Otherwise I renounce all confidence.

71 **She . . . dash** she acts bravely at the first encounter   73 **wit** mind
74 **our Lady** the Virgin Mary   80 **vocation** occupation   84 **swart**
dark-complexioned   85 **infused** shed   91 **resolve on this** be assured of this   92 **mate** (1) comrade (2) sweetheart (?)   93 **high
terms** i.e., mastery of the grand rhetorical style   95 **buckle** (1)
grapple (2) embrace as lovers

Pucelle. I am prepared: here is my keen-edged sword,
     Decked with fine flower-de-luces on each side,
     The which at Touraine, in Saint Katherine's
100   churchyard,
     Out of a great deal of old iron I chose forth.

Dauphin. Then come, a° God's name, I fear no
     woman.

Pucelle. And while I live, I'll ne'er fly from a man.

Here they fight, and Joan la Pucelle overcomes.

Dauphin. Stay, stay thy hands! thou art an Amazon
105   And fightest with the sword of Deborah.°

Pucelle. Christ's mother helps me, else I were too
     weak.

Dauphin. Whoe'er helps thee, 'tis thou that must help
     me:
     Impatiently I burn with thy desire;
     My heart and hands thou hast at once subdued.
110   Excellent Pucelle, if thy name be so,°
     Let me thy servant° and not sovereign be;
     'Tis the French Dolphin sueth to° thee thus.

Pucelle. I must not yield to any rites of love,
     For my profession's sacred from above;
115   When I have chasèd all thy foes from hence,
     Then will I think upon a recompense.

Dauphin. Meantime look gracious on thy prostrate
     thrall.°

Reignier. My lord, methinks, is very long in talk.

Alençon. Doubtless he shrives this woman to her
     smock;°
120   Else ne'er could he so long protract his speech.

---

102 a in   105 Deborah prophetess who delivered Israel from oppression by the Canaanites (Judges 4–5)   110 if thy name be so
if you really are a virgin   111 servant lover   112 sueth to woos
117 thrall slave   119 shrives . . . smock (1) questions her closely
(2) hears her confession to the most minute detail

Reignier. Shall we disturb him, since he keeps no
　　mean?°

Alençon. He may mean more than we poor men do
　　know:
　　These women are shrewd tempters with their
　　tongues.

Reignier. My lord, where are you? What devise you
　　on?°
　　Shall we give o'er Orleans, or no?　　　　　*125*

Pucelle. Why, no, I say, distrustful recreants!°
　　Fight till the last gasp; I'll be your guard.

Dauphin. What she says I'll confirm: we'll fight it out.

Pucelle. Assigned am I to be the English scourge.
　　This night the siege assuredly I'll raise;　　　*130*
　　Expect Saint Martin's summer,° halcyon's days,°
　　Since I have enterèd into these wars.
　　Glory is like a circle in the water,
　　Which never ceaseth to enlarge itself
　　Till by broad spreading it disperse to nought.　　*135*
　　With Henry's death the English circle ends;
　　Dispersèd are the glories it included.
　　Now am I like that proud insulting° ship
　　Which Caesar and his fortune bare° at once.

Dauphin. Was Mahomet inspirèd with a dove?　　*140*
　　Thou with an eagle° art inspirèd then.
　　Helen,° the mother of great Constantine,
　　Nor yet Saint Philip's daughters,° were like thee.

---

121 **keeps no mean** does not control himself　124 **devise you on**
are you deliberating　126 **recreants** cowards　131 **Saint Martin's
summer** Indian summer (named after the feast of Saint Martin of
Tours, November 11)　131 **halcyon's days** peaceful times (the an-
cients believed that the bird called the halcyon nested on the sea
and that the waters remained calm during its breeding season)
138 **insulting** insolently triumphant　139 **bare** bore　141 **eagle** i.e.,
like Saint John the Evangelist, with the highest source of inspiration　142 **Helen** Saint Helena, inspired by a vision to find the cross
of Jesus　143 **Saint Philip's daughters** (who had the gift of prophecy; see Acts 21:9)

Bright star of Venus, fall'n down on the earth,
145   How may I reverently worship thee enough?

Alençon. Leave off delays, and let us raise the siege.

Reignier. Woman, do what thou canst to save our
      honors;
   Drive them from Orleans and be immortalized.

Dauphin. Presently° we'll try. Come, let's away about
      it;
150   No prophet will I trust, if she prove false.   *Exeunt.*

[Scene III. *London. Before the Tower.*]

Enter Gloucester, with his Servingmen [in blue coats°].

Gloucester. I am come to survey° the Tower this
      day:
   Since Henry's death, I fear, there is conveyance.°
   Where be these warders,° that they wait not here?
   Open the gates; 'tis Gloucester° that calls.

First Warder. [*Within*] Who's there that knocks so
5   imperiously?

Gloucester's First [Serving]man. It is the noble Duke
      of Gloucester.

Second Warder. [*Within*] Whoe'er he be, you may not
      be let in.

Gloucester's First [Serving]man. Villains, answer you
      so the Lord Protector?

---

149 **Presently** immediately I.iii.s.d. **blue coats** (blue clothing was
customary for servants) 1 **survey** inspect 2 **conveyance** under-
hand dealing 3 **warders** guards 4 **Gloucester** (trisyllabic here
and often, for metrical purposes, elsewhere in the play)

First Warder. [*Within*] The Lord protect him! so we
    answer him;
  We do no otherwise than we are willed.   10

Gloucester. Who willèd you? Or whose will stands
    but mine?
  There's none Protector of the realm but I.
  Break up the gates, I'll be your warrantize;°
  Shall I be flouted thus by dunghill grooms?°
      Gloucester's men rush at the Tower gates, and
           Woodville the Lieutenant speaks within.

Woodville. What noise is this? What traitors have
    we here?   15

Gloucester. Lieutenant, is it you whose voice I hear?
  Open the gates; here's Gloucester that would enter.

Woodville. Have patience, noble duke, I may not
    open;
  The Cardinal of Winchester forbids:
  From him I have express commandment°   20
  That thou nor none of thine shall be let in.

Gloucester. Faint-hearted Woodville, prizest him 'fore
    me?°
  Arrogant Winchester, that haughty prelate,
  Whom Henry, our late sovereign, ne'er could
    brook?°
  Thou art no friend to God or to the king;   25
  Open the gates, or I'll shut thee out shortly.

Servingmen. Open the gates unto the Lord Protector,
  Or we'll burst them open, if that° you come not
    quickly.

*Enter to the Protector at the Tower gates Winchester
    and his men in tawny coats.°*

<hr />

13 **warrantize** pledge of security   14 **dunghill grooms** vile servingmen   20 **commandment** (trisyllabic; spelled *commandement* in the
Folio)   22 **prizest him 'fore me** rank him above me   24 **brook**
endure   28 **if** that if   28s.d. **tawny coats** (servants of churchmen
traditionally wore tawny, or brownish-yellow, coats)

Winchester. How now, ambitious Humphrey, what
means this?

Gloucester. Peeled° priest, dost thou command me to
30   be shut out?

Winchester. I do, thou most usurping proditor,°
And not Protector, of the king or realm.

Gloucester. Stand back, thou manifest conspirator,
Thou that contriv'dst to murder our dead lord,
35   Thou that giv'st whores indulgences° to sin;
I'll canvas thee in thy broad cardinal's hat,°
If thou proceed in this thy insolence.

Winchester. Nay, stand thou back, I will not budge
a foot;
This be Damascus,° be thou cursèd Cain,
40   To slay thy brother° Abel, if thou wilt.

Gloucester. I will not slay thee, but I'll drive thee
back;
Thy scarlet robes as a child's bearing-cloth°
I'll use to carry thee out of this place.

Winchester. Do what thou dar'st, I beard° thee to
thy face.

Gloucester. What! am I dared and bearded to my
45   face?
Draw, men, for all this privilegèd place,°
Blue coats to tawny coats. Priest, beware your
beard;
I mean to tug it, and to cuff you soundly.
Under my feet I stamp thy cardinal's hat;

---

30 **Peeled** tonsured, bald   31 **proditor** traitor   35 **indulgences** (the
brothels near the theaters on the south bank of the Thames were
within the jurisdiction of the Bishops of Winchester)   36 **canvas
. . . hat** toss you in your wide-brimmed ecclesiastical hat as if it were
a blanket   39 **Damascus** (supposed to have been built in the place
where Cain killed Abel)   40 **brother** (Winchester was half-brother
to Gloucester's father, King Henry IV)   42 **bearing-cloth** christen-
ing robe   44 **beard** defy   46 **for . . . place** (even though drawing
of weapons is forbidden under pain of death in royal residences)

In spite of pope or dignities of church,°   50
Here by the cheeks I'll drag thee up and down.

Winchester. Gloucester, thou wilt answer this before
   the pope.

Gloucester. Winchester goose,° I cry, a rope!° a rope!
Now beat them hence; why do you let them stay?
Thee I'll chase hence, thou wolf in sheep's array.   55
Out, tawny coats! out, scarlet° hypocrite!

*Here Gloucester's men beat out the Cardinal's men,
and enter in the hurly-burly° the Mayor of London
and his Officers.*

Mayor. Fie, lords! that you, being supreme
   magistrates,°
Thus contumeliously° should break the peace!

Gloucester. Peace, mayor! thou know'st little of my
   wrongs:
Here's Beaufort, that regards nor God nor king,   60
Hath here distrained° the Tower to his use.

Winchester. Here's Gloucester, a foe to citizens,
One that still motions° war and never peace,
O'ercharging your free purses with large fines,°
That seeks to overthrow religion   65
Because he is Protector of the realm,
And would have armor here out of the Tower
To crown himself king and suppress° the prince.

Gloucester. I will not answer thee with words,
   but blows.   *Here they skirmish again.*

Mayor. Nought rests for me in this tumultuous strife   70
But to make open proclamation.

---

50 **dignities of church** your high ecclesiastical rank   53 **Winchester
goose** (1) venereal infection (2) prostitute (see note to line 35)   53
rope hangman's cord   56 **scarlet** (a derisive allusion to the red
robes of the cardinal)   56 s.d. **hurly-burly** tumult   57 **magistrates**
administrators of the kingdom   58 **contumeliously** insolently   61
distrained seized   63 **still motions** always proposes   64 **O'ercharging . . . fines** overburdening you with excessive special taxes
68 **suppress** depose

Come, officer, as loud as e'er thou canst,
Cry.

[*Officer.*] All manner of men assembled here in arms
75   this day against God's peace and the king's, we
charge and command you, in his highness' name,
to repair° to your several° dwelling-places; and not
to wear, handle, or use any sword, weapon, or
dagger henceforward, upon pain° of death.

80   *Gloucester.* Cardinal, I'll be no breaker of the law,
But we shall meet, and break our minds at large.°

Winchester. Gloucester, we'll meet to thy cost, be
sure:
Thy heart-blood I will have for this day's work.

Mayor. I'll call for clubs,° if you will not away.
85   This cardinal's more haughty than the devil.

Gloucester. Mayor, farewell; thou dost but what thou
mayst.

Winchester. Abominable Gloucester, guard thy head,
For I intend to have it ere long.   *Exeunt.*

Mayor. See the coast cleared, and then we will depart.
Good God, these nobles should such stomachs
90   bear!°
I myself fight not once in forty year.   *Exeunt.*

---

77 **repair** return   77 **several** own   79 **pain** penalty   81 **break . . .
large** reveal our thoughts fully   84 **call for clubs** i.e., summon the
apprentices of the city to come with clubs and assist the officers in
putting down the riot   90 **these . . . bear** that these noblemen
should have such quarrelsome tempers

[Scene IV. *Orleans.*]

Enter the Master Gunner of Orleans and his Boy.

Master Gunner. Sirrah,° thou know'st how Orleans is
    besieged,
  And how the English have the suburbs won.

Boy. Father, I know, and oft have shot at them,
  Howe'er, unfortunate, I missed my aim.

Master Gunner. But now thou shalt not. Be thou ruled
    by me: 5
  Chief master-gunner am I of this town;
  Something I must do to procure me grace.°
  The prince's espials° have informèd me
  How the English, in the suburbs close intrenched,
  Went through a secret grate of iron bars   10
  In yonder tower to overpeer° the city
  And thence discover how with most advantage
  They may vex us with shot or with assault.
  To intercept° this inconvenience,
  A piece of ordnance° 'gainst it I have placed,   15
  And even these three days have I watched
  If I could see them. Now do thou watch,
  For I can stay no longer.
  If thou spy'st any, run and bring me word,
  And thou shalt find me at the governor's.   *Exit.* 20

Boy. Father, I warrant you, take you no care;
  I'll never trouble you, if I may spy them.   *Exit.*

*Enter Salisbury and Talbot on the turrets, with [Sir
William Glansdale, Sir Thomas Gargrave, and] others.*

I.iv.1 **Sirrah** a term used in addressing children or inferiors 7
grace favor 8 **espials** spies 11 **overpeer** look down upon 14
intercept stop 15 **piece of ordnance** cannon

Salisbury. Talbot, my life, my joy, again returned!
　　How wert thou handled, being prisoner?
25　　Or by what means gots thou° to be released?
　　Discourse,° I prithee,° on this turret's top.

Talbot. The Earl of Bedford had a prisoner
　　Called the brave Lord Ponton de Santrailles;
　　For him was I exchanged and ransomèd.
30　　But with a baser° man of arms by far
　　Once in contempt they would have bartered me;
　　Which I disdaining scorned and cravèd death
　　Rather than I would be so pilled-esteemed.°
　　In fine,° redeemed I was as I desired.
35　　But O! the treacherous Falstaff wounds my heart,
　　Whom with my bare fists I would execute,
　　If I now had him brought into my power.

Salisbury. Yet tell'st thou not how thou wert enter-
　　　tained.

Talbot. With scoffs and scorns and contumelious
　　　taunts,
40　　In open marketplace produced they me,
　　To be a public spectacle to all:
　　Here, said they, is the terror of the French,
　　The scarecrow that affrights° our children so.
　　Then broke I from the officers that led me,
45　　And with my nails digged stones out of the ground
　　To hurl at the beholders of my shame.
　　My grisly° countenance made others fly;
　　None durst come near for fear of sudden death.
　　In iron walls they deemed me not secure;
50　　So great fear of my name 'mongst them were spread
　　That they supposed I could rend bars of steel
　　And spurn in pieces posts of adamant.°
　　Wherefore a guard of chosen shot° I had

25 **gots thou** did you manage　26 **Discourse** relate　26 **prithee**
pray thee　30 **baser** less well born　33 **pilled-esteemed** poorly
valued　34 **In fine** finally　43 **affrights** frightens　47 **grisly** grim
52 **adamant** indestructible material　53 **chosen shot** picked marks-
men

That walked about me every minute while,°
And if I did but stir out of my bed,   55
Ready they were to shoot me to the heart.

Enter the Boy with a linstock.°

Salisbury. I grieve to hear what torments you endured,
But we will be revenged sufficiently.
Now it is supper-time in Orleans;
Here, through this grate, I count each one   60
And view the Frenchmen how they fortify;
Let us look in; the sight will much delight thee.
Sir Thomas Gargrave, and Sir William Glansdale,
Let me have your express° opinions
Where is best place to make our batt'ry° next.   65

Gargrave. I think at the north gate, for there stands
lords.

Glansdale. And I, here, at the bulwark° of the bridge.

Talbot. For aught I see, this city must be famished,
Or with light skirmishes enfeeblèd.°   *Here they
shoot, and Salisbury [and Gargrave] fall down.*

Salisbury. O Lord, have mercy on us, wretched
sinners!   70

Gargrave. O Lord, have mercy on me, woeful man!

Talbot. What chance is this that suddenly hath
crossed° us?
Speak, Salisbury; at least, if thou canst speak,
How far'st thou, mirror of° all martial men?
One of thy eyes and thy cheek's side struck off!   75
Accursèd tower! accursèd fatal hand°
That hath contrived this woful tragedy!
In thirteen battles Salisbury o'ercame;
Henry the Fifth he first trained to the wars;

---

54 every minute while incessantly 56s.d. linstock staff to hold the
match for lighting a cannon 64 express precise 65 make our
batt'ry direct our fire 67 bulwark fortification 69 enfeeblèd
weakened 72 crossed thwarted 74 mirror of model for 76 fatal
hand hand of fate

80   Whilst any trump° did sound, or drum struck up,
      His sword did ne'er leave striking in the field.
      Yet liv'st thou, Salisbury? Though thy speech doth
          fail,
      One eye thou hast, to look to heaven for grace.
      The sun with one eye vieweth all the world.
85   Heaven, be thou gracious to none alive
      If Salisbury wants° mercy at thy hands!
      Bear hence his body; I will help to bury it.
      Sir Thomas Gargrave, hast thou any life?
      Speak unto Talbot; nay, look up to him.
90   Salisbury, cheer thy spirit with this comfort:
      Thou shalt not die whiles°—
      He beckons with his hand and smiles on me,
      As who° should say, "When I am dead and gone,
      Remember to avenge me on the French."
95   Plantagenet,° I will; and like thee, [Nero,]
      Play on the lute, beholding the towns burn.
      Wretched shall France be only in° my name.

Here an alarum, and it thunders and lightens.

      What stir° is this? What tumult's in the heavens?
      Whence cometh this alarum, and the noise?

Enter a Messenger.

Messenger. My lord, my lord, the French have gath-
100   ered head:°
      The Dolphin, with one Joan la Pucelle joined,
      A holy prophetess new risen up,
      Is come with a great power to raise the siege.

Here Salisbury lifteth himself up and groans.

Talbot. Hear, hear how dying Salisbury doth groan!
105   It irks his heart he cannot be revenged.

80 **trump** trumpet 86 **wants** lacks 91 **whiles** until 93 **As who**
as if he 95 **Plantagenet** (though Salisbury's name was Thomas
Montacute, he was related to the royal family, which adopted the
name Plantagenet in the fifteenth century) 97 **only in** merely at
the sound of (?) 98 **stir** commotion 100 **gathered head** raised
forces

Frenchmen, I'll be a Salisbury to you.
Pucelle or pussel,° Dolphin or dogfish,
Your hearts I'll stamp out with my horse's heels,
And make a quagmire of your mingled brains.
Convey me° Salisbury into his tent,   110
And then we'll try what these dastard Frenchmen
    dare.

                              Alarum. Exeunt.

               [Scene V. *Orleans.*]

*Here an alarum again, and Talbot pursueth the
Dauphin, and driveth him. Then enter Joan la Pucelle, driving Englishmen before her [and exit after
them]. Then [re-]enter Talbot.*

Talbot. Where is my strength, my valor, and my
    force?
  Our English troops retire, I cannot stay them;
  A woman clad in armor chaseth them.

               Enter [La] Pucelle.

  Here, here she comes. I'll have a bout with thee;
  Devil or devil's dam,° I'll conjure thee:°   5
  Blood will I draw on thee,° thou art a witch,
  And straightway give thy soul to him thou serv'st.

Pucelle. Come, come, 'tis only° I that must disgrace
    thee.   *Here they fight.*

Talbot. Heavens, can you suffer hell so to prevail?
  My breast I'll burst with straining of my courage   10

---

107 **pussel** lewd woman, strumpet   110 **convey me** carry   I.v.5 **dam**
(1) mistress (2) mother   5 **conjure thee** i.e., back to hell whence
you came   6 **Blood . . . thee** (whoever could draw blood from a
witch was free of her power)   8 **only** with no other assistance

And from my shoulders crack my arms asunder,
But I will chastise this high-minded° strumpet.
They fight again.

Pucelle. Talbot, farewell; thy hour is not yet come;
I must go victual° Orleans forthwith.°

A short alarum. Then enter the town with soldiers.

15 O'ertake me if thou canst; I scorn thy strength.
Go, go, cheer up thy hungry-starvèd men;
Help Salisbury to make his testament;
This day is ours, as many more shall be.   *Exit.*

Talbot. My thoughts are whirlèd like a potter's wheel;
20 I know not where I am, nor what I do.
A witch, by fear, not force, like Hannibal,°
Drives back our troops and conquers as she lists;°
So bees with smoke and doves with noisome stench
Are from their hives and houses driven away.
25 They called us for our fierceness English dogs;
Now, like to whelps,° we crying run away.
A short alarum.
Hark, countrymen! either renew the fight,
Or tear the lions° out of England's coat;
Renounce your soil,° give sheep in lions' stead:
30 Sheep run not half so treacherous° from the wolf,
Or horse or oxen from the leopard,
As you fly from your oft-subduèd slaves.
Alarum. Here another skirmish.
It will not be. Retire into your trenches.
You all consented unto Salisbury's death,
35 For none would strike a stroke in his revenge.
Pucelle is entered into Orleans
In spite of us or aught that we could do.

---

12 **high-minded** arrogant   14 **victual** bring provisions into   14 **forthwith** immediately   21 **Hannibal** (who terrified the Romans by driving among them oxen with lighted torches fixed to their horns)
22 **lists** pleases   26 **whelps** puppies   28 **lions** heraldic royal symbol of England   29 **soil** (possibly a misprint for *style*; the line appears to mean: replace the lions in your royal coat of arms with
sheep)   30 **treacherous** fearfully

O, would I were to die with Salisbury!
The shame hereof will make me hide my head.
Exit Talbot. Alarum. Retreat.°

[Scene VI. *Orleans.*]

*Flourish. Enter on the walls [La] Pucelle, Dauphin,
Reignier, Alençon, and Soldiers.*

Pucelle. Advance° our waving colors on the walls;
Rescued is Orleans from the English.
Thus Joan la Pucelle hath performed her word.

Dauphin. Divinest creature, Astraea's daughter,°
How shall I honor thee for this success?   5
Thy promises are like Adonis'° garden
That one day bloomed and fruitful were the next.
France, triumph in thy glorious prophetess!
Recovered is the town of Orleans;
More blessèd hap° did ne'er befall our state.   10

Reignier. Why ring not out the bells aloud throughout
     the town?
Dolphin, command the citizens make bonfires
And feast and banquet in the open streets
To celebrate the joy that God hath given us.

Alençon. All France will be replete with mirth and joy   15
When they shall hear how we have played the
     men.°

Dauphin. 'Tis Joan, not we, by whom the day is won;

39s.d. **Retreat** signal for withdrawal from battle **I.vi.1 Advance**
raise **4 Astraea's daughter** daughter of the goddess of justice
(compare *Deborah*, I.ii.105) **6 Adonis'** of the youth loved by
Venus (for a description of his garden, see Edmund Spenser,
Faerie Queene, III.vi.29–50) **10 hap** good fortune **16 played the
men** proved our courage

For which I will divide my crown with her,
And all the priests and friars in my realm
20   Shall in procession sing her endless praise.
A statelier pyramis° to her I'll rear
Than Rhodope's° or Memphis' ever was.
In memory of her when she is dead,
Her ashes, in an urn more precious
25   Than the rich-jeweled coffer of Darius,°
Transported shall be at high festivals
Before the kings and queens of France.
No longer on Saint Denis° will we cry,
But Joan la Pucelle shall be France's saint.
30   Come in, and let us banquet royally,
After this golden day of victory.   *Flourish. Exeunt.*

21 **pyramis** pyramid   22 **Rhodope's** (according to legend, the
famous Greek courtesan Rhodopis built the third pyramid)
25 **coffer of Darius** (the Persian monarch's jewel chest, said to
have been used by Alexander the Great to hold a copy of
Homer)   28 **Saint Denis** patron saint of France

ACT II

Scene I. [*Orleans.*]

Enter a [French] Sergeant of a band, with two Sentinels.

Sergeant. Sirs, take your places and be vigilant;
 If any noise or soldier you perceive
 Near to the walls, by some apparent sign
 Let us have knowledge at the court of guard.°

Sentinel. Sergeant, you shall. Thus are poor servitors,°   [*Exit Sergeant.*]   5
 When others sleep upon their quiet beds,
 Constrained to watch in darkness, rain, and cold.

Enter Talbot, Bedford, and Burgundy, [and forces,] with scaling-ladders, their drums beating a dead march.

Talbot. Lord Regent, and redoubted° Burgundy,
 By whose approach° the regions of Artois,
 Wallon, and Picardy° are friends to us,   10

II.i.4 **court of guard** headquarters of the guard   5 **servitors** soldiers 8 **redoubted** distinguished   9 **approach** presence   9–10 **Artois, Wallon, and Picardy** (provinces in northeastern France, parts of which are now in Belgium)

This happy night the Frenchmen are secure,°
Having all day caroused and banqueted;
Embrace we° then this opportunity
As fitting best to quittance° their deceit

13   Contrived by art° and baleful° sorcery.

Bedford. Coward of France! how much he wrongs his
      fame,
   Despairing of his own arm's fortitude,
   To join with witches and the help of hell.

Burgundy. Traitors have never other company.

20   But what's that Pucelle whom they term so pure?

Talbot. A maid, they say.

Bedford.   A maid? And be so martial?

Burgundy. Pray God she prove not masculine° ere
      long,
   If underneath the standard of the French
   She carry armor as she hath begun.

Talbot. Well, let them practice° and converse with
25   spirits.
   God is our fortress, in whose conquering name
   Let us resolve to scale their flinty° bulwarks.

Bedford. Ascend, brave Talbot; we will follow thee.

Talbot. Not all together: better far, I guess,
30   That we do make our entrance several° ways;
   That, if it chance the one of us do fail,
   The other yet may rise against their force.

Bedford. Agreed; I'll to yond° corner.

Burgundy.   And I to this.

Talbot. And here will Talbot mount, or make his
      grave.

---

11 **secure** careless   13 **Embrace we** let us seize   14 **quittance** repay   15 **art** (black) magic   15 **baleful** harmful   22 **prove not masculine** (1) does not turn out to be a man (?) (2) does not become
pregnant with a male child   24 **practice** conjure   27 **flinty** rugged
30 **several** by separate   33 **yond** yonder

Now, Salisbury, for thee, and for the right   33
Of English Henry, shall this night appear
How much in duty I am bound to both.

Sentinel. Arm! arm! the enemy doth make assault!
    [*The English, scaling the walls,*] *cry "St. George!*
                    a Talbot!" [*and enter the town*].

*The French leap o'er the walls in their shirts. Enter
several ways Bastard, Alençon, Reignier, half ready,°
and half unready.*

Alençon. How now, my lords! what, all unready so?

Bastard. Unready? Ay, and glad we 'scaped so well.   40

Reignier. 'Twas time, I trow,° to wake and leave our
    beds,
Hearing alarums at our chamber doors.

Alençon. Of all exploits since first I followed arms,
Ne'er heard I of a warlike enterprise
More venturous or desperate than this.   45

Bastard. I think this Talbot be a fiend of hell.

Reignier. If not of hell, the heavens, sure, favor him.

Alençon. Here cometh Charles; I marvel how he
    sped.°

            Enter Charles [*the Dauphin*] *and Joan.*

Bastard. Tut, holy Joan was his defensive guard.

Dauphin. Is this thy cunning,° thou deceitful dame?   50
Didst thou at first, to flatter us withal,°
Make us partakers of a little gain,
That now our loss might be ten times so much?

Pucelle. Wherefore is Charles impatient with his
    friend?
At all times will you have my power alike?   55
Sleeping or waking must I still° prevail,

38s.d. **ready** dressed   41 **trow** think   48 **marvel how he sped** wonder how he fared   50 **cunning** craftiness   51 **to flatter us withal**
in order to deceive us   56 **still** always

Or will you blame and lay the fault on me?
Improvident° soldiers! had your watch been good,
This sudden mischief never could have fall'n.

60 *Dauphin.* Duke of Alençon, this was your default,°
That, being captain of the watch tonight,
Did look no better to that weighty charge.°

Alençon. Had all your quarters been as safely kept
As that whereof I had the government,°
65 We had not been thus shamefully surprised.

Bastard. Mine was secure.

Reignier.   And so was mine, my lord.

Dauphin. And, for myself, most part of all this night,
Within her quarter° and mine own precinct°
I was employed in passing to and fro,
70 About relieving of the sentinels.
Then how or which way should they first break in?

Pucelle. Question, my lords, no further of the case,
How or which way; 'tis sure they found some place
But weakly guarded, where the breach was made.
75 And now there rests no other shift° but this,
To gather our soldiers, scattered and dispersed,
And lay new platforms to endamage them.°

*Alarum. Enter an [English] Soldier, crying, "A Tal-
bot! a Talbot!" They fly, leaving their clothes behind.*

Soldier. I'll be so bold to take what they have left.
The cry of Talbot serves me for a sword,
80 For I have loaden me° with many spoils,
Using no other weapon but his name.   *Exit.*

---

58 **Improvident** unwary   60 **default** fault   62 **weighty charge** important responsibility   64 **government** command   68 **quarter** (1)
assigned area for defense (2) chamber   68 **precinct** area of command   75 **shift** expedient, stratagem   77 **lay . . . them** make new
plans to harm the English   80 **loaden me** burdened myself

[Scene II. *Orleans. Within the town.*]

Enter Talbot, Bedford, Burgundy, [a Captain, and others].

Bedford. The day begins to break, and night is fled,
 Whose pitchy° mantle over-veiled the earth.
 Here sound retreat, and cease our hot pursuit.
           Retreat.

Talbot. Bring forth the body of old Salisbury,
 And here advance it° in the marketplace,   *5*
 The middle center of this cursèd town.
 Now have I paid my vow unto his soul;
 For every drop of blood was drawn from him
 There hath at least five Frenchmen died tonight.
 And that hereafter ages may behold   *10*
 What ruin happened in revenge of him,
 Within their chiefest temple° I'll erect
 A tomb, wherein his corpse shall be interred;
 Upon the which, that everyone may read,
 Shall be engraved the sack° of Orleans,   *15*
 The treacherous manner of his mournful death,
 And what a terror he had been to France.
 But, lords, in all our bloody massacre,
 I muse° we met not with the Dolphin's grace,°
 His new-come champion, virtuous Joan of Arc, *20*
 Nor any of his false confederates.°

Bedford. 'Tis thought, Lord Talbot, when the fight began,
 Roused on the sudden from their drowsy beds,

II.ii.2 pitchy dark **5 advance it** raise it up **12 chiefest temple**
cathedral **15 sack** plundering **19 muse** wonder why **19 the**
Dolphin's grace i.e., his grace, the Dauphin **21 confederates** companions

They did amongst the troops of armèd men
25 Leap o'er the walls for refuge in the field.

Burgundy. Myself, as far as I could well discern
For° smoke and dusky vapors of the night,
Am sure I scared the Dolphin and his trull,°
When arm in arm they both came swiftly running,
30 Like to a pair of loving turtle-doves
That could not live asunder day or night.
After that things are set in order here,
We'll follow them with all the power we have.

Enter a Messenger.

Messenger. All hail, my lords! Which of this princely
train°
35 Call ye the warlike Talbot, for his acts
So much applauded through the realm of France?

Talbot. Here is the° Talbot; who would speak with
him?

Messenger. The virtuous lady, Countess of Auvergne,
With modesty admiring thy renown,
40 By me entreats, great lord, thou wouldst vouchsafe°
To visit her poor castle where she lies,°
That she may boast she hath beheld the man
Whose glory fills the world with loud report.

Burgundy. Is it even so? Nay, then, I see our wars
45 Will turn unto a peaceful comic sport,
When ladies crave to be encountered° with.
You may not, my lord, despise her gentle suit.°

Talbot. Ne'er trust me then; for when a world of men
Could not prevail with all their oratory,
50 Yet hath a woman's kindness overruled;°

---

27 **For** because of   28 **trull** concubine, harlot   34 **princely train**
noble company   37 **the** (used with the surname to designate the
head of a family or clan)   40 **vouchsafe** condescend   41 **lies** re-
sides   46 **encountered** met (for an amatory interview)   47 **gentle
suit** mannerly request   50 **overruled** prevailed

And therefore tell her I return great thanks
And in submission° will attend on her.
Will not your honors bear me company?

Bedford. No, truly, 'tis more than manners will,°
And I have heard it said, unbidden°guests   55
Are often welcomest when they are gone.

Talbot. Well then, alone, since there's no remedy,
I mean to prove this lady's courtesy.°
Come hither, captain. (*Whispers*) You perceive my
mind?°

Captain. I do, my lord, and mean accordingly.   60
                                        Exeunt.

[Scene III. *Auvergne. The Countess' castle.*]

Enter Countess [and her Porter].

Countess. Porter, remember what I gave in charge,°
And when you have done so, bring the keys to me.

Porter. Madam, I will.   *Exit.*

Countess. The plot is laid; if all things fall out right,
I shall as famous be by this exploit   5
As Scythian Tomyris° by Cyrus' death.
Great is the rumor° of this dreadful knight,
And his achievements of no less account;
Fain° would mine eyes be witness with mine ears,
To give their censure° of these rare reports.   10

Enter Messenger and Talbot.

52 **in submission** deferentially   54 **will** require   55 **unbidden** un-
invited   58 **prove . . . courtesy** try out this lady's hospitality   59
perceive my mind understand my plan   II.iii.1 **gave in charge** instructed you to do   6 **Tomyris** queen of a fierce Central Asian people who slew Cyrus the Great in battle   7 **rumor** reputation   9
Fain gladly   10 **censure** judgment

Messenger. Madam,
    According as your ladyship desired,
    By message craved,° so is Lord Talbot come.

Countess. And he is welcome. What! is this the man?

Messenger. Madam, it is.

15 *Countess.*   Is this the scourge of France?
    Is this the Talbot, so much feared abroad
    That with his name the mothers still° their babes?
    I see report is fabulous° and false.
    I thought I should have seen some Hercules,
20   A second Hector, for his grim aspect°
    And large proportion of his strong-knit° limbs.
    Alas, this is a child, a silly° dwarf!
    It cannot be this weak and writhled° shrimp
    Should strike such terror to his enemies.

25 *Talbot.* Madam, I have been bold to trouble you,
    But since your ladyship is not at leisure,
    I'll sort° some other time to visit you.

Countess. What means he now? Go ask him whither
    he goes.

Messenger. Stay, my Lord Talbot, for my lady craves
30   To know the cause of your abrupt departure.

Talbot. Marry,° for that° she's in a wrong belief,
    I go to certify° her Talbot's here.

              Enter Porter with keys.

Countess. If thou be he, then art thou prisoner.

Talbot. Prisoner! to whom?

Countess.   To me, bloodthirsty lord;
35   And for that cause I trained° thee to my house.
    Long time thy shadow hath been thrall to me,

---

13 **craved** invited 17 **still** silence 18 **fabulous** merely fictional
20 **aspect** countenance 21 **strong-knit** well-muscled 22 **silly** feeble
23 **writhled** wrinkled 27 **sort** choose 31 **Marry** why 31 **for that**
because 32 **certify** inform 35 **trained** lured

For in my gallery thy picture° hangs.
But now the substance shall endure the like,
And I will chain these legs and arms of thine
That hast by tyranny these many years   40
Wasted our country, slain our citizens,
And sent our sons and husbands captivate.°

Talbot. Ha, ha, ha!

Countess. Laughest thou, wretch? Thy mirth shall turn
    to moan.

Talbot. I laugh to see your ladyship so fond°   45
    To think that you have aught but Talbot's shadow
    Whereon to practice your severity.°

Countess. Why, art not thou the man?

Talbot.   I am indeed.

Countess. Then have I substance too.

Talbot. No, no, I am but shadow of myself: 50
    You are deceived, my substance is not here,
    For what you see is but the smallest part
    And least proportion of humanity.
    I tell you, madam, were the whole frame° here,
    It is of such a spacious lofty pitch,°   55
    Your roof were not sufficient to contain 't.

Countess. This is a riddling merchant° for the
    nonce;°
    He will be here, and yet he is not here.
    How can these contrarieties° agree?

Talbot. That will I show you presently.   60
                    *Winds° his horn; drums strike up; a peal
                        of ordnance;° enter Soldiers.*
    How say you, madam? Are you now persuaded
    That Talbot is but shadow of himself?

37 **picture** (possibly implying that the Countess was trying to practice witchcraft on him)   42 **captivate** captive   45 **fond** foolish   47
severity cruelty   54 **frame** structure   55 **pitch** stature   57 **riddling
merchant** enigmatic fellow   57 **for the nonce** for the occasion
(merely a line-filler)   59 **contrarieties** contradictions   60s.d. **Winds**
blows   60s.d. **peal of ordnance** salute of guns

These are his substance, sinews, arms, and strength,
With which he yoketh° your rebellious necks,
65   Razeth your cities and subverts° your towns,
And in a moment makes them desolate.

Countess. Victorious Talbot, pardon my abuse;
I find thou art no less than fame hath bruited°
And more than may be gathered by thy shape.
70   Let my presumption not provoke thy wrath,
For I am sorry that with reverence°
I did not entertain thee as thou art.

Talbot. Be not dismayed, fair lady, nor misconster°
The mind of Talbot, as you did mistake
75   The outward composition° of his body.
What you have done hath not offended me,
Nor other satisfaction do I crave,
But only, with your patience, that we may
Taste of your wine and see what cates° you have,
80   For soldiers' stomachs always serve them well.

Countess. With all my heart, and think me honorèd
To feast so great a warrior in my house.   *Exeunt.*

[Scene IV. *London. The Temple Garden.°*]

Enter Richard Plantagenet, Warwick, Somerset, [William de la] Pole [Earl of Suffolk, Vernon, and another Lawyer].

Plantagenet. Great lords and gentlemen, what means
this silence?
Dare no man answer in a case of truth?

64 yoketh brings into subjection   65 subverts overthrows   68
bruited reported   71 reverence respect   73 misconster misunder-
stand   75 composition form   79 cates choice foods   II.iv.s.d.
Temple Garden (the Inner and Middle Temples were residences for
students of the common law)

Suffolk. Within the Temple Hall we were too loud;
  The garden here is more convenient.

Plantagenet. Then say at once if I maintained the
    truth;   *5*
  Or else was wrangling° Somerset in th' error?

Suffolk. Faith,° I have been a truant° in the law,
  And never yet could frame° my will to it,
  And therefore frame° the law unto my will.

Somerset. Judge you, my lord of Warwick, then,
  between us.   *10*

Warwick. Between two hawks, which flies the higher
    pitch;
  Between two dogs, which hath the deeper mouth;°
  Between two blades, which bears the better temper;
  Between two horses, which doth bear him° best;
  Between two girls, which hath the merriest eye— *15*
  I have perhaps some shallow spirit° of judgment;
  But in these nice sharp quillets° of the law,
  Good faith, I am no wiser than a daw.°

Plantagenet. Tut, tut, here is a mannerly forbearance.
  The truth appears so naked on my side   *20*
  That any purblind° eye may find it out.

Somerset. And on my side it is so well appareled,°
  So clear, so shining, and so evident,
  That it will glimmer through a blind man's eye.

Plantagenet. Since you are tongue-tied and so loath
  to speak,   *25*
  In dumb significants° proclaim your thoughts:
  Let him that is a true-born gentleman
  And stands upon° the honor of his birth,

---

6 **wrangling** quarrelsome 7 **Faith** in truth 7 **truant** lazy student
8 **frame** dispose 9 **frame** twist 12 **mouth** bark, bay 14 **bear him**
behave himself 16 **shallow spirit** small amount 17 **nice sharp
quillets** precise and subtle distinctions 18 **daw** simpleton 21
purblind nearly blind 22 **appareled** (1) dressed (2) ordered 26 **In
dumb significants** by mute signs 28 **stands upon** takes pride in

If he suppose that I have pleaded truth,
30   From off this brier pluck a white rose with me.

Somerset. Let him that is no coward nor no flatterer,
      But dare maintain the party of the truth,
      Pluck a red rose from off this thorn with me.

Warwick. I love no colors;° and without all color
35   Of base insinuating flattery
      I pluck this white rose with Plantagenet.

Suffolk. I pluck this red rose with young Somerset
      And say withal° I think he held the right.

Vernon. Stay, lords and gentlemen, and pluck no more
40   Till you conclude that he upon whose side
      The fewest roses are cropped° from the tree
      Shall yield the other in the right opinion.

Somerset. Good Master Vernon, it is well objected;°
      If I have fewest, I subscribe in silence.

45 *Plantagenet.* And I.

Vernon. Then for the truth and plainness of the case,
      I pluck this pale and maiden° blossom here,
      Giving my verdict on the white rose side.

Somerset. Prick not your finger as you pluck it off,
50   Lest bleeding you do paint the white rose red
      And fall on my side so against your will.

Vernon. If I, my lord, for my opinion bleed,
      Opinion shall be surgeon to my hurt
      And keep me on the side where still I am.

55 *Somerset.* Well, well, come on, who else?

Lawyer. Unless my study and my books be false,
      The argument you held was wrong in you;
      In sign whereof I pluck a white rose too.

Plantagenet. Now, Somerset, where is your argument?

---

34 colors (1) pretenses (2) adornments of speech   38 withal thereby
41 cropped plucked   43 objected proposed   47 maiden flawless

Somerset. Here in my scabbard, meditating° that　　60
　Shall dye your white rose in a bloody red.

Plantagenet. Meantime your cheeks do counterfeit°
　　our roses,
　For pale they look with fear, as witnessing
　The truth on our side.

Somerset.　　　　　　　No, Plantagenet,
　'Tis not for fear, but anger that thy cheeks　　65
　Blush for pure shame to counterfeit our roses,
　And yet thy tongue will not confess thy error.

Plantagenet. Hath not thy rose a canker,° Somerset?

Somerset. Hath not thy rose a thorn, Plantagenet?

Plantagenet. Ay, sharp and piercing, to maintain his
　　truth　　70
　Whiles thy consuming canker eats his falsehood.

Somerset. Well, I'll find friends to wear my bleeding
　　roses,
　That shall maintain what I have said is true
　Where false Plantagenet dare not be seen.

Plantagenet. Now, by this maiden blossom in my
　　hand,　　75
　I scorn thee and thy fashion,° peevish boy.

Suffolk. Turn not thy scorns this way, Plantagenet.

Plantagenet. Proud Pole, I will, and scorn both him
　　and thee.

Suffolk. I'll turn my part thereof into thy throat.

Somerset. Away, away, good William de la Pole!　　80
　We grace the yeoman° by conversing with him.

Warwick. Now, by God's will, thou wrong'st him,
　　Somerset;

60 **meditating** planning　62 **counterfeit** imitate　68 **canker** (1) disease (2) caterpillar larva　76 **fashion** (1) manner of behavior (2) faction (?)　81 **grace the yeoman** dignify this commoner

His grandfather° was Lionel Duke of Clarence,
Third son to the third Edward King of England:
85   Spring crestless° yeomen from so deep a root?

Plantagenet. He bears him on the place's privilege,°
Or durst not, for his craven heart, say thus.

Somerset. By him that made me, I'll maintain my
words
On any plot of ground in Christendom.
90   Was not thy father, Richard Earl of Cambridge,
For treason executed in our late king's days?
And, by his treason, stand'st not thou attainted,
Corrupted, and exempt from ancient gentry?°
His trespass° yet lives guilty in thy blood,
95   And, till thou be restored, thou art a yeoman.°

Plantagenet. My father was attachèd,° not attainted,
Condemned to die for treason, but no traitor;
And that I'll prove° on better men than Somerset,
Were growing time once ripened to my will.°
100 For your partaker° Pole and you yourself,
I'll note you in my book of memory
To scourge you for this apprehension.°
Look to it well and say you are well warned.

Somerset. Ah, thou shalt find us ready for thee still,
105 And know us by these colors for thy foes,
For these my friends in spite of thee shall wear.

Plantagenet. And, by my soul, this pale and angry
rose,
As cognizance° of my blood-drinking° hate,

---

83 **grandfather** i.e., great-great-grandfather   85 **crestless** not having the right to a coat of arms   86 **privilege** i.e., of sanctuary (since
the Temple was founded as a religious house)   92–93 **attainted . . .
gentry** (legal penalties by which the heirs of a person convicted of
treason were prevented from inheriting his property and titles)   94
trespass crime   95 **And . . . yeoman** (therefore, you shall remain a
commoner until your titles are legally restored)   96 **attachèd** arrested   98 **prove** establish through trial by combat   99 **Were . . .
will** i.e., if I should ever be restored to the nobility   100 **partaker**
partisan   102 **apprehension** notion, display of wit   108 **cognizance**
a badge   108 **blood-drinking** bloodthirsty

Will I forever and my faction wear
Until it wither with me to my grave   *110*
Or flourish to the height of my degree.°

Suffolk. Go forward and be choked with thy ambition!
  And so farewell until I meet thee next.   *Exit.*

Somerset. Have with thee,° Pole. Farewell, ambitious Richard.   *Exit.*

Plantagenet. How I am braved° and must perforce°
  endure it!   *115*

Warwick. This blot that they object against your house
  Shall be whipped° out in the next parliament
  Called for the truce of Winchester and Gloucester,
  And if thou be not then created York,°
  I will not live to be accounted° Warwick.   *120*
  Meantime, in signal of my love to thee,
  Against proud Somerset and William Pole,
  Will I upon thy party° wear this rose.
  And here I prophesy: this brawl° today,
  Grown to this faction in the Temple garden,   *125*
  Shall send, between the red rose and the white,
  A thousand souls to death and deadly night.

Plantagenet. Good Master Vernon, I am bound to
  you
  That you on my behalf would pluck a flower.

Vernon. In your behalf still will I wear the same.   *130*

Lawyer. And so will I.

Plantagenet. Thanks, gentle [sir].
  Come, let us four to dinner: I dare say
  This quarrel will drink blood° another day. *Exeunt.*

---

111 **to . . . degree** until I regain my high rank   114 **Have with thee**
I'll go with you   115 **braved** defied   115 **perforce** necessarily
117 **whipped** quickly stricken   119 **York** i.e., Duke of York   120
accounted considered   123 **upon thy party** in support of you   124
brawl quarrel   134 **drink blood** result in bloodshed

[Scene V. *The Tower of London.*]

Enter Mortimer, brought in a chair, and Jailers.

Mortimer. Kind keepers of my weak decaying age,
　　Let dying Mortimer here rest himself.
　　Even like a man new halèd from the rack,°
　　So fare my limbs with long imprisonment,
5　　And these gray locks, the pursuivants° of death,
　　Nestor-like° agèd in an age of care,
　　Argue° the end of Edmund Mortimer.
　　These eyes, like lamps whose wasting° oil is spent,
　　Wax° dim, as drawing to their exigent;°
10　　Weak shoulders, overborne with burthening° grief,
　　And pithless° arms, like to a withered vine
　　That droops his sapless branches to the ground.
　　Yet are these feet, whose strengthless stay° is numb,
　　Unable to support this lump of clay,
15　　Swift-wingèd with desire to get a grave,
　　As witting I no other comfort have.
　　But tell me, keeper, will my nephew come?

First Jailer. Richard Plantagenet, my lord, will come:
　　We sent unto the Temple, unto his chamber,
20　　And answer was returned that he will come.

Mortimer. Enough; my soul shall then be satisfied.
　　Poor gentleman! his wrong doth equal mine.
　　Since Henry Monmouth° first began to reign,
　　Before whose glory I was great in arms,

II.v.3 **new . . . rack** just released from the torturer's rack   5 **pur-
suivants** heralds   6 **Nestor-like** (the Greek king Nestor, in Homer's
Iliad, is a type of old age)   7 **Argue** foretell   8 **wasting** consuming   9 **Wax** grow   9 **exigent** end   10 **burthening** (dissyllabic)
burdensome   11 **pithless** strengthless   13 **stay** support   23 **Henry
Monmouth** King Henry V

This loathsome sequestration° have I had;   25
And even since then hath Richard been obscured,°
Deprived of honor and inheritance.
But now the arbitrator of despairs,
Just Death, kind umpire° of men's miseries,
With sweet enlargement° doth dismiss me hence.   30
I would his° troubles likewise were expired,
That so he might recover what was lost.

Enter Richard [Plantagenet].

First Jailer. My lord, your loving nephew now is
    come.

Mortimer. Richard Plantagenet, my friend, is he
    come?

Plantagenet. Ay, noble uncle, thus ignobly used,   35
    Your nephew, late despisèd° Richard, comes.

Mortimer. Direct mine arms I may° embrace his neck
    And in his bosom spend my latter gasp.°
    O, tell me when my lips do touch his cheeks,
    That I may kindly give one fainting kiss.   40
    And now declare, sweet stem from York's great
        stock,°
    Why didst thou say, of late thou wert despised?

Plantagenet. First, lean thine agèd back against mine
        arm,
    And, in that ease, I'll tell thee my disease.°
    This day, in argument upon a case,   45
    Some words there grew 'twixt Somerset and me;
    Among which terms he used his lavish° tongue
    And did upbraid° me with my father's death:
    Which obloquy° set bars before my tongue,
    Elsè with the like I had requited° him.   50

---

25 **sequestration** imprisonment 26 **obscured** degraded 29 **umpire** arbitrator 30 **enlargement** release 31 **his** i.e., Plantagenet's 36 **late despisèd** just insulted 37 **I may** (so that) I may 38 **spend my latter gasp** draw my last breath 41 **stock** trunk (i.e., lineage) 44 **disease** source of my discomfort 47 **lavish** licentious, unrestrained 48 **upbraid** insult 49 **obloquy** reproach 50 **requited** repaid

Therefore, good uncle, for my father's sake,
In honor of a true Plantagenet,
And for alliance' sake, declare the cause°
My father, Earl of Cambridge, lost his head.

Mortimer. That cause, fair nephew, that imprisoned
55   me
And hath detained me all my flow'ring° youth
Within a loathsome dungeon, there to pine,
Was cursèd instrument of his decease.

Plantagenet. Discover° more at large what cause that
was,
60   For I am ignorant and cannot guess.

Mortimer. I will, if that my fading breath permit
And death approach not ere my tale be done.
Henry the Fourth, grandfather to this king,
Deposed his nephew° Richard, Edward's son,
65   The first-begotten and the lawful heir
Of Edward king, the third of that descent:°
During whose reign the Percies° of the north,
Finding his usurpation most unjust,
Endeavored my advancement to the throne.
70   The reason moved° these warlike lords to this
Was, for that—young° Richard thus removed,
Leaving no heir begotten of his body—
I was the next by birth and parentage:
For by my mother° I derivèd° am
75   From Lionel Duke of Clarence, third son
To King Edward the Third; whereas he
From John of Gaunt doth bring his pedigree,
Being but fourth of that heroic line.
But mark:° as in this haughty° great attempt

---

53 **the cause** for what reason   56 **flow'ring** vigorous, flourishing
59 **Discover** explain   64 **nephew** (cousin)   64–66 **Edward's . . .
descent** i.e., Richard II, son of Edward the Black Prince and grand-
son of King Edward III   67 **Percies** noble family of Northumberland   70 **moved** that provoked   71 **young** (Richard was actually
over thirty at the time of his deposition)   74 **mother** (actually,
grandmother)   74 **derivèd** descended   79 **mark** listen attentively
79 **haughty** lofty

They labored to plant the rightful heir,   80
I lost my liberty and they their lives.
Long after this, when Henry the Fifth,
Succeeding his father Bolingbroke, did reign,
Thy father, Earl of Cambridge, then derived
From famous Edmund Langley, Duke of York,   85
Marrying my sister that thy mother was,
Again, in pity of my hard distress,
Levied an army, weening to redeem
And have installed me in the diadem;°
But, as the rest, so fell that noble earl   90
And was beheaded. Thus the Mortimers,
In whom the title rested, were suppressed.

Plantagenet. Of which, my lord, your honor is the
        last.

Mortimer. True; and thou seest that I no issue have
        And that my fainting words do warrant° death.   95
        Thou art my heir; the rest I wish thee gather,°
        But yet be wary in thy studious care.°

Plantagenet. Thy grave admonishments prevail with
        me,
        But yet, methinks, my father's execution
        Was nothing less than bloody tyranny.   100

Mortimer. With silence, nephew, be thou politic:
        Strong-fixèd is the house of Lancaster,
        And like a mountain, not to be removed.
        But now thy uncle is removing hence,
        As princes do their courts, when they are cloyed° 105
        With long continuance in a settled place.

Plantagenet. O, uncle, would some part of my young
        years

88–89 **Levied . . . diadem** raised an army, with the intention of
rescuing me and having me crowned king   95 **warrant** give assurance of   96 **the rest . . . gather** (1) I want you to conclude for yourself (2) I hope that you may gain all that is rightfully yours   97
But . . . care i.e., but always be careful even as you take pains in
this enterprise   105 **cloyed** satiated

Might but redeem the passage° of your age!

Mortimer. Thou dost then wrong me, as that
    slaughterer doth
110 Which giveth many wounds when one will kill.
Mourn not, except thou sorrow for my good;
Only give order° for my funeral.
And so farewell, and fair be all thy hopes,
And prosperous be thy life in peace and war! *Dies.*

Plantagenet. And peace, no war, befall thy parting
115   soul!
In prison hast thou spent a pilgrimage°
And like a hermit overpassed° thy days.
Well, I will lock his counsel in my breast,
And what I do imagine, let that rest.
120 Keepers, convey him hence, and I myself
Will see his burial better than his life.°

      [*Exeunt Jailers with the body of Mortimer.*]

Here dies the dusky° torch of Mortimer,
Choked with ambition of the meaner sort.°
And for those wrongs, those bitter injuries
125 Which Somerset hath offered to my house,
I doubt not but with honor to redress.°
And therefore haste I to the parliament,
Either to be restorèd to my blood,
Or make my will th'advantage of my good.°
                    Exit.

108 **redeem the passage** buy back the passing   112 **give order** make
arrangements   116 **pilgrimage** full life's journey   117 **overpassed**
lived out   121 **Will . . . life** will see that he receives the honor in
his funeral that was denied him during his lifetime   122 **dusky**
gloomy   123 **Choked . . . sort** stifled by the ambition of men of
inferior birth (i.e., the House of Lancaster)   126 **redress** remedy
129 **will . . . good** determination of purpose the means of achieving
my ambition (see Textual Note)

ACT III

Scene I. [*London. The Parliament-house.*]

Flourish. Enter King, Exeter, Gloucester, Winchester, Warwick, Somerset, Suffolk, Richard Plantagenet. Gloucester offers to put up a bill;° Winchester snatches it, tears it.

Winchester. Com'st thou with deep premeditated
    lines,°
With written pamphlets studiously devised?
Humphrey of Gloucester, if thou canst accuse
Or aught intend'st to lay unto my charge,
Do it without invention,° suddenly,   *5*
As I with sudden and extemporal° speech
Purpose to answer what thou canst object.

Gloucester. Presumptuous priest! this place commands
    my patience,
Or thou shouldst find thou hast dishonored me.
Think not, although in writing I preferred°   *10*
The manner of thy vile outrageous crimes,

III.i.s.d. **offers . . . bill** attempts to post a statement of accusations
1 **deep premeditated lines** statements carefully thought out in advance   5 **invention** (seeking out the grounds for argument in the manner of a rhetorician or a lawyer trained in oratory)   6 **extemporal** extemporaneous   10 **preferred** set forth

That therefore I have forged,° or am not able
Verbatim to rehearse the method of my pen.°
No, prelate, such is thy audacious wickedness,
15 Thy lewd, pestiferous, and dissentious pranks,°
As very° infants prattle of thy pride.
Thou art a most pernicious usurer,°
Froward° by nature, enemy to peace,
Lascivious, wanton, more than well beseems°
20 A man of thy profession and degree.
And for thy treachery, what's more manifest?
In that thou laid'st a trap to take my life,
As well at London Bridge as at the Tower.
Beside, I fear me, if thy thoughts were sifted,°
25 The king, thy sovereign, is not quite exempt
From envious malice of thy swelling° heart.

Winchester. Gloucester, I do defy thee. Lords,
      vouchsafe
To give me hearing what I shall reply.
If I were covetous, ambitious, or perverse,
30 As he will have me,° how am I so poor?
Or how haps it° I seek not to advance
Or raise myself, but keep my wonted calling?°
And for dissension, who preferreth peace
More than I do?—except I be provoked.
35 No, my good lords, it is not that offends;
It is not that that hath incensed° the duke:
It is, because no one should sway° but he,
No one but he should be about the king,
And that engenders thunder in his breast
40 And makes him roar these accusations forth.
But he shall know I am as good—

---

12 **forged** fabricated lies   13 **rehearse . . . pen** repeat the contents
of what I have written   15 **lewd . . . pranks** wicked, mischievous,
and quarrelsome offenses   16 **As very** that even   17 **pernicious
usurer** (alluding to Winchester's reputation for gaining riches
through extortions and loans made at exorbitant rates of interest)
18 **Froward** inclined to evil   19 **beseems** is fitting to   24 **sifted**
closely examined   26 **swelling** proud   30 **have me make me out to
be   31 **haps it** does it happen   32 **calling** religious vocation   36
incensed enraged   37 **sway** rule

Gloucester.   As good?
  Thou bastard° of my grandfather!

Winchester. Ay, lordly° sir; for what are you, I pray,
  But one imperious° in another's throne?

Gloucester. Am I not Protector, saucy priest?   45

Winchester. And am not I a prelate of the church?

Gloucester. Yes, as an outlaw in a castle keeps
  And useth it to patronage° his theft.

Winchester. Unreverent Gloucester!

Gloucester.   Thou art reverent
  Touching thy spiritual function,° not thy life.   50

Winchester. Rome shall remedy this.

Warwick.   Roam thither, then.
  My lord, it were your duty to forbear.

Somerset. Ay, see the bishop be not overborne.°
  Methinks my lord° should be religious
  And know the office° that belongs to such.   55

Warwick. Methinks his lordship° should be humbler;
  It fitteth not a prelate so to plead.

Somerset. Yes, when his holy state is touched so
  near.°

Warwick. State holy or unhallowed,° what of that?
  Is not his grace° Protector to the king?   60

Plantagenet. [*Aside*] Plantagenet, I see, must hold
  his tongue,
  Lest it be said, "Speak, sirrah, when you should;

---

42 **bastard** (Winchester was an illegitimate son of John of Gaunt,
Duke of Lancaster) 43 **lordly** haughty 44 **imperious** ruling 48
patronage defend 50 **Touching . . . function** only in respect of
your high ecclesiastical office 53 **overborne** prevailed over 54
lord i.e., Gloucester 55 **office** respect 56 **lordship** Winchester
58 **holy . . . near** ecclesiastical office is so directly involved 59
holy or unhallowed ecclesiastical or secular 60 **grace** i.e.,
Gloucester

Must your bold verdict° enter talk with lords?"
Else would I have a fling at° Winchester.

65 *King.* Uncles of Gloucester and of Winchester,
    The special watchmen° of our Engish weal,°
    I would prevail, if prayers might prevail,
    To join your hearts in love and amity.
    O, what a scandal is it to our crown,
70 That two such noble peers as ye should jar!
    Believe me, lords, my tender years can tell
    Civil dissension is a viperous worm°
    That gnaws the bowels of the commonwealth.

       A noise within, "Down with the tawny-coats!"

    What tumult's this?

Warwick   An uproar, I dare warrant,°
75 Begun through malice of the bishop's men.

           A noise again, "Stones! stones!"

                Enter Mayor.

Mayor. O my good lords, and virtuous Henry,
    Pity the city of London, pity us!
    The bishop° and the Duke of Gloucester's men,
    Forbidden late° to carry any weapon,
80 Have filled their pockets full of pebble stones
    And banding themselves in contrary parts°
    Do pelt so fast at one another's pate°
    That many have their giddy° brains knocked out.
    Our windows are broke down in every street,
85 And we for fear compelled to shut our shops.

*Enter [Servingmen of Gloucester and Winchester]
    in skirmish, with bloody pates.*

King. We charge you, on allegiance to ourself,
    To hold your slaught'ring hands and keep the
       peace.

---

63 **bold verdict** presumptuous opinion   64 **have a fling at** reprove
66 **watchmen** guardians   66 **weal** state   72 **worm** serpent   74 **warrant** swear   78 **bishop** bishop's   79 **late** recently   81 **parts** parties
82 **pate** head   83 **giddy** foolish

Pray, uncle Gloucester, mitigate° this strife.

First Servingman. Nay, if we be forbidden stones,
we'll fall to it with our teeth.   90

Second Servingman. Do what ye dare, we are as
resolute.   *Skirmish again.*

Gloucester. You of my household, leave this peevish
broil
And set this unaccustomed° fight aside.

Third Servingman. My lord, we know your grace to be
a man   95
Just and upright; and, for your royal birth,
Inferior to none but to his majesty,
And ere that we will suffer° such a prince,
So kind a father of the commonweal,
To be disgracèd by an inkhorn mate,°   100
We and our wives and children all will fight
And have our bodies slaughtered by thy foes.

First Servingman. Ay, and the very parings of our
nails
Shall pitch a field° when we are dead. *Begin again.*

Gloucester.   Stay, stay, I say!
And if you love me, as you say you do,   105
Let me persuade you to forbear awhile.

King. O, how this discord doth afflict my soul!
Can you, my Lord of Winchester, behold
My sighs and tears and will not once relent?
Who should be pitiful, if you be not?   110
Or who should study° to prefer a peace,
If holy churchmen take delight in broils?

Warwick. Yield, my Lord Protector; yield, Winchester,

---

88 **mitigate** appease   94 **unaccustomed** indecorous   98 **suffer** permit   100 **inkhorn mate** scribbling fellow (an unlettered person's
disparaging allusion to the literacy of clergymen)   104 **pitch a
field** i.e., serve as stakes in a pitched battlefield   111 **study** make
it his aim

Except° you mean with obstinate repulse°
115 To slay your sovereign and destroy the realm.
You see what mischief and what murder too
Hath been enacted through your enmity;
Then be at peace, except ye thirst for blood.

Winchester. He shall submit, or I will never yield.

Gloucester. Compassion on the king commands me
120   stoop;
Or I would see his heart out ere the priest
Should ever get that privilege° of me.

Warwick. Behold, my Lord of Winchester, the duke
Hath banished moody discontented fury,
125 As by his smoothèd brows it doth appear:
Why look you still so stern and tragical?°

Gloucester. Here, Winchester, I offer thee my hand.

King. Fie, uncle Beaufort! I have heard you preach
That malice was a great and grievous sin,
130 And will not you maintain the thing you teach,
But prove a chief offender in the same?

Warwick. Sweet king! the bishop hath a kindly gird.°
For shame, my Lord of Winchester, relent!
What, shall a child instruct you what to do?

Winchester. Well, Duke of Gloucester, I will yield
135   to thee
Love for thy love, and hand for hand I give.

Gloucester. [*Aside*] Ay, but, I fear me, with a hollow°
heart.
[*Aloud*] See here, my friends and loving countrymen;
This token° serveth for a flag of truce
140 Betwixt ourselves and all our followers.
So help me God, as I dissemble not!

---

114 **Except** unless 114 **repulse** refusal 122 **privilege** advantage
yielded   126 **tragical** gloomy   132 **kindly gird** fitting gibe   137
hollow insincere   139 **token** i.e., handclasp

Winchester. [*Aside*] So help me God, as I intend it
    not!

King. O loving uncle, kind Duke of Gloucester,
    How joyful am I made by this contract!°
    Away, my masters! trouble us no more,   *145*
    But join in friendship, as your lords have done.

First Servingman. Content; I'll to the surgeon's.

Second Servingman.   And so will I.

Third Servingman. And I will see what physic° the
    tavern affords.°   *Exeunt*.

Warwick. Accept this scroll,° most gracious sovereign,   *150*
    Which in the right of Richard Plantagenet
    We do exhibit to your majesty.

Gloucester. Well urged, my Lord of Warwick: for,
        sweet prince,
    And if° your grace mark° every circumstance,
    You have great reason to do Richard right,   *155*
    Especially for those occasions°
    At Eltham Place I told your majesty.

King. And those occasions, uncle, were of force.
    Therefore, my loving lords, our pleasure is
    That Richard be restorèd to his blood.°   *160*

Warwick. Let Richard be restorèd to his blood;
    So shall his father's wrongs be recompensed.

Winchester. As will the rest, so willeth Winchester.

King. If Richard will be true, not that all alone
    But all the whole inheritance I give   *165*
    That doth belong unto the house of York,
    From whence you spring by lineal descent.

Plantagenet. Thy humble servant vows obedience
    And humble service till the point of death.

---

144 **contract** agreement   148 **physic** remedy   149 **affords** provides
150 **scroll** document   154 **And if** if   154 **mark** take notice of   156
occasions reasons   160 **blood** i.e., title and rights of nobility

170 *King.* Stoop then and set your knee against my foot,
    And in reguerdon° of that duty done,
    I girt° thee with the valiant sword of York.
    Rise, Richard, like a true Plantagenet,
    And rise created princely Duke of York.

Plantagenet. And so thrive Richard as thy foes may
175   fall!
    And as my duty springs, so perish they
    That grudge one thought° against your majesty!

All. Welcome, high prince, the mighty Duke of York!

Somerset. [*Aside*] Perish, base prince, ignoble Duke
    of York!

180 *Gloucester.* Now will it best avail your majesty
    To cross the seas and to be crowned in France:
    The presence of a king engenders love
    Amongst his subjects and his loyal friends,
    As it disanimates° his enemies.

King. When Gloucester says the word, King Henry
185   goes,
    For friendly counsel cuts off many foes.

Gloucester. Your ships already are in readiness.

             Sennet.° Flourish. Exeunt. Manet° Exeter.

Exeter. Ay, we may march in England or in France,
    Not seeing what is likely to ensue.
190   This late dissension grown betwixt the peers
    Burns under feignèd ashes of forged° love
    And will at last break out into a flame;
    As festered members° rot but by degree°
    Till bones and flesh and sinews fall away,
195   So will this base and envious discord breed.
    And now I fear that fatal prophecy

171 **reguerdon** ample reward   172 **girt** gird   177 **grudge one
thought** entertain one grudging thought   184 **disanimates** disheart-
ens   187s.d. **Sennet** trumpet signal for the exit of an important
personage   187s.d. **Manet** remains (Latin)   191 **forged** pretended
193 **members** parts of the body   193 **by degree** little by little,
gradually

Which in the time of Henry named the Fifth
Was in the mouth of every sucking° babe,
That Henry born at Monmouth should win all
And Henry born at Windsor lose all: 200
Which is so plain that Exeter doth wish
His days may finish ere that hapless time.   *Exit.*

[Scene II. *France. Before Rouen.*]

Enter [La] Pucelle disguised, with four Soldiers
    with sacks upon their backs.

Pucelle. These are the city gates, the gates of Rouen,
    Through which our policy° must make a breach.
    Take heed, be wary how you place your words;
    Talk like the vulgar° sort of market men°
    That come to gather money for their corn.°   5
    If we have entrance, as I hope we shall,
    And that we find the slothful watch but weak,
    I'll by a sign give notice to our friends
    That Charles the Dolphin may encounter° them.

Soldier. Our sacks shall be a mean° to sack the city, 10
    And we be lords and rulers over Rouen;
    Therefore we'll knock.   *Knock.*

Watchman. [*Within*] *Qui est là?*°

Pucelle. Paysans là, pauvres gens de France:°
    Poor market folks that come to sell their corn.   15

Watchman. Enter, go in, the market bell is rung.

Pucelle. Now, Rouen, I'll shake thy bulwarks to the
        ground.   *Exeunt.*

---

198 **sucking** nursing III.ii.2 **policy** stratagem 4 **vulgar** common
4 **market men** people going to market 5 **corn** grain 9 **encounter**
assail 10 **mean** means 13 **Qui est là** who is there? 14 **Paysans**
... **France** peasants here, poor folk of France

*Enter Charles [the Dauphin], Bastard, Alençon,
[Reignier, and forces].*

Dauphin. Saint Denis bless this happy stratagem,
  And once again we'll sleep secure in Rouen!

20 *Bastard.* Here entered Pucelle and her practisants.°
  Now she is there, how will she specify:
  Here is the best and safest passage in?

Reignier. By thrusting out a torch from yonder tower,
  Which, once discerned, shows that her meaning is:
25 No way to° that, for weakness, which she entered.

*Enter [La] Pucelle on the top, thrusting out a
torch burning.*

Pucelle. Behold, this is the happy wedding torch
  That joineth Rouen unto her countrymen,
  But burning fatal to the Talbonites!°   [*Exit.*]

Bastard. See, noble Charles, the beacon of our friend,
30 The burning torch, in yonder turret stands.

Dauphin. Now shine it° like a comet of revenge,
  A prophet to the fall of all our foes!

Reignier. Defer° no time, delays have dangerous
    ends;
  Enter and cry, "The Dolphin!" presently,
33 And then do execution on the watch.

               Alarum. [*Exeunt.*]

An alarum. Talbot in an excursion.°

Talbot. France, thou shalt rue this treason with thy
    tears,
  If Talbot but survive thy treachery.
  Pucelle, that witch, that damnèd sorceress,
  Hath wrought this hellish mischief unawares,
40 That hardly we escaped the pride° of France.

                       Exit.

20 **practisants** companions in the stratagem   25 **to** comparable to
28 **Talbonites** followers of Talbot   31 **shine** it may it shine   33
Defer waste   35s.d. **excursion** sortie   40 **pride** finest warriors

*An alarum: excursions. Bedford, brought in sick in
a chair. Enter Talbot and Burgundy without: within
[La] Pucelle, Charles [the Dauphin], Bastard,
[Alençon,] and Reignier on the walls.*

Pucelle. Good morrow, gallants!° Want ye corn for
　　bread?
　I think the Duke of Burgundy will fast
　Before he'll buy again at such a rate.
　'Twas full of darnel;° do you like the taste?

Burgundy. Scoff on, vile fiend and shameless
　　courtesan!°　　　　　　　　　　　　　　　　　　45
　I trust ere long to choke thee with thine own
　And make thee curse the harvest of that corn.

Dauphin. Your grace may starve perhaps before that
　　time.

Bedford. O, let no words, but deeds, revenge this
　　treason!

Pucelle. What will you do, good gray-beard? Break
　　a lance,　　　　　　　　　　　　　　　　　　50
　And run a-tilt° at death within a chair?

Talbot. Foul fiend of France, and hag of all despite,°
　Encompassed° with thy lustful paramours!°
　Becomes it thee to taunt his valiant age
　And twit° with cowardice a man half dead?　　55
　Damsel,° I'll have a bout with you again,
　Or else let Talbot perish with this shame.

Pucelle. Are ye so hot,° sir? Yet, Pucelle, hold thy
　　peace;
　If Talbot do but thunder, rain will follow.

　　　　[The English] whisper together in council.

　God speed the parliament! who shall be the
　　Speaker?°　　　　　　　　　　　　　　　　　60

---

41 **gallants** gentlemen　44 **darnel** weeds　45 **courtesan** prostitute
50–51 **Break . . . a-tilt** joust, combat　52 **of all despite** full of malice　53 **Encompassed** surrounded　53 **paramours** lovers　55 **twit**
chide　56 **Damsel** girl　58 **hot** angry　60 **Speaker** presiding officer

Talbot. Dare ye come forth and meet us in the field?

Pucelle. Belike° your lordship takes us then for fools,
To try if that our own be ours or no.

Talbot. I speak not to that railing Hecate,°
65   But unto thee, Alençon, and the rest.
Will ye, like soldiers, come and fight it out?

Alençon. Signior,° no.

Talbot. Signior, hang! base muleters° of France!
Like peasant foot-boys° do they keep the walls
70   And dare not take up arms like gentlemen.

Pucelle. Away, captains! let's get us from the walls;
For Talbot means no goodness by his looks.
Good-bye, my lord! we came but to tell you
That we are here.   *Exeunt from the walls.*

75   *Talbot.* And there will we be too, ere it be long,
Or else reproach be Talbot's greatest fame.
Vow, Burgundy, by honor of thy house,
Pricked on° by public wrongs sustained in France,
Either to get the town again or die.
80   And I, as sure as English Henry lives
And as his father here was conqueror,
As sure as in this late-betrayèd town
Great Cordelion's° heart was burièd,
So sure I swear to get° the town or die.

85   *Burgundy.* My vows are equal partners with thy vows.

Talbot. But, ere we go, regard° this dying prince,
The valiant Duke of Bedford. Come, my lord,
We will bestow you in some better place,
Fitter for sickness and for crazy° age.

90   *Bedford.* Lord Talbot, do not so dishonor me;
Here will I sit before the walls of Rouen

62 **Belike** perhaps   64 **railing Hecate** abusive witch (after Hecate,
goddess of sorcery)   67 **Signior** sir   68 **muleters** mule-drivers
69 **foot-boys** boy-servants   78 **Pricked on** provoked   83 **Cordelion's** King Richard the Lion-Hearted's   84 **get** retake   86 **regard**
behold   89 **crazy** infirm, decrepit

And will be partner of your weal or woe.°

Burgundy. Courageous Bedford, let us now persuade
  you.

Bedford. Not to be gone from hence, for once I read
  That stout Pendragon° in his litter° sick   *95*
  Came to the field and vanquishèd his foes.
  Methinks I should revive the soldiers' hearts,
  Because I ever found them as myself.

Talbot. Undaunted spirit in a dying breast!
  Then be it so: heavens keep old Bedford safe!   *100*
  And now no more ado, brave Burgundy,
  But gather we our forces out of hand
  And set upon our boasting enemy.

      [*Exeunt all but Bedford and his Attendants.*]

*An alarum: excursions.° Enter Sir John Falstaff
          and a Captain.*

Captain. Whither away, Sir John Falstaff, in such
  haste?

Falstaff. Whither away? To save myself by flight;   *105*
  We are like to have the overthrow° again.

Captain. What! Will you fly, and leave Lord Talbot?

Falstaff.   Ay,
  All the Talbots in the world, to save my life.

                                                Exit.

Captain. Cowardly knight, ill fortune follow thee!

                                                Exit.

*Retreat. Excursions. [La] Pucelle, Alençon, and
          Charles [the Dauphin enter and] fly.*

Bedford. Now, quiet soul, depart when heaven please,   *110*

92 **weal or woe** good or bad fortune   95 **Pendragon** Uther Pendragon, father of King Arthur   95 **litter** stretcher-bed   103s.d. **excursions** entries and exits of skirmishing troops   106 **have the overthrow** be defeated

For I have seen our enemies' overthrow.
What is the trust or strength of foolish man?
They that of late were daring with their scoffs
Are glad and fain° by flight to save themselves.

Bedford dies and is carried in by two in his chair.

An alarum. Enter Talbot, Burgundy, and the rest
[of their men].

115 *Talbot.* Lost, and recovered in a day again!
This is a double honor, Burgundy;
Yet heavens have glory for this victory!

Burgundy. Warlike and martial Talbot, Burgundy
Enshrines thee in his heart and there erects
120 Thy noble deeds as valor's monuments.

Talbot. Thanks, gentle duke. But where is Pucelle
now?
I think her old familiar° is asleep.
Now where's the Bastard's braves,° and Charles
his gleeks?°
What, all amort?° Rouen hangs her head for grief
125 That such a valiant company are fled.
Now will we take some order° in the town,
Placing therein some expert° officers,
And then depart to Paris to the king,
For there young Henry with his nobles lie.°

130 *Burgundy.* What wills Lord Talbot pleaseth Burgundy.

Talbot. But yet, before we go, let's not forget
The noble Duke of Bedford, late deceased,
But see his exequies° fulfilled in Rouen.
A braver soldier never couchèd° lance,
135 A gentler° heart did never sway° in court.
But kings and mightiest potentates must die,
For that's the end of human misery.   *Exeunt.*

---

114 **fain** eager   122 **familiar** servant demon   123 **braves** boasts
123 **gleeks** jests, scoffs   124 **amort** dejected   126 **take some order**
restore order   127 **expert** experienced   129 **lie** reside   133 **exe-
quies** funeral ceremonies   134 **couchèd** leveled for the assault   135
gentler nobler   135 **sway** prevail

Scene III. [*The plains near Rouen.*]

Enter Charles [the Dauphin], Bastard, Alençon, [La]
Pucelle, [and forces].

Pucelle. Dismay not, princes, at this accident,
  Nor grieve that Rouen is so recoverèd.
  Care is no cure, but rather corrosive,°
  For things that are not to be remedied.
  Let frantic° Talbot triumph for a while   5
  And like a peacock sweep along his tail;
  We'll pull° his plumes and take away his train,°
  If Dolphin and the rest will be but ruled.°

Dauphin. We have been guided by thee hitherto
  And of thy cunning had no diffidence;°   10
  One sudden foil° shall never breed distrust.

Bastard. Search out thy wit° for secret policies,
  And we will make thee famous through the world.

Alençon. We'll set thy statue in some holy place,
  And have thee reverenced like a blessèd saint.   15
  Employ thee° then, sweet virgin, for our good.

Pucelle. Then thus it must be; this doth Joan devise:°
  By fair persuasions mixed with sugared° words
  We will entice the Duke of Burgundy
  To leave the Talbot and to follow us.   20

Dauphin. Ay, marry, sweeting,° if we could do that,
  France were no place for Henry's warriors,

III.iii.3 **corrosive** a caustic drug   5 **frantic** raging   7 **pull** pluck
7 **train** (1) followers (2) equipment for battle   8 **ruled** guided (by
Joan)   10 **diffidence** lack of confidence   11 **foil** defeat   12 **Search
out thy wit** examine your mind   16 **Employ thee** apply your efforts   17 **devise** determine   18 **sugared** sweet-sounding   21 **sweeting** sweetheart

Nor should that nation boast it so with° us,
But be extirpèd° from our provinces.

Alençon. Forever-should they be expulsed° from
25   France
And not have title of° an earldom here.

Pucelle. Your honors shall perceive how I will work
To bring this matter to the wishèd end.

Drum sounds afar off.

Hark! by the sound of drum you may perceive
30   Their powers are marching unto Paris-ward.°

Here sound an English march.

There goes the Talbot, with his colors spread,°
And all the troops of English after him.

French march. [*Enter the Duke of Burgundy and
forces.*]
Now in the rearward comes the duke and his;
Fortune in favor° makes him lag behind.
35   Summon a parley; we will talk with him.

Trumpets sound a parley.

Dauphin. A parley with the Duke of Burgundy!

Burgundy. Who craves a parley with the Burgundy?

Pucelle. The princely Charles of France, thy
countryman.

Burgundy. What say'st thou, Charles? For I am
marching hence.

Dauphin. Speak, Pucelle, and enchant him with thy
40   words.

Pucelle. Brave Burgundy, undoubted hope of France!
Stay, let thy humble handmaid speak to thee.

Burgundy. Speak on, but be not over-tedious.

---

23 **boast it so with** lord it over   24 **extirpèd** rooted out   25 **expulsed**
driven out   26 **title of** claim to   30 **unto Paris-ward** toward Paris
31 **colors spread** banners unfurled   34 **in favor** to our advantage

Pucelle. Look on thy country, look on fertile France,
And see the cities and the towns defaced   45
By wasting ruin of the cruel foe,
As looks the mother on her lowly babe
When death doth close his tender-dying° eyes.
See, see the pining° malady of France;
Behold the wounds, the most unnatural wounds,   50
Which thou thyself hast given her woeful breast.
O, turn thy edgèd° sword another way;
Strike those that hurt, and hurt not those that help.
One drop of blood drawn from thy country's bosom
Should grieve thee more than streams of foreign
    gore.   55
Return thee therefore with a flood of tears,
And wash away thy country's stainèd° spots.

Burgundy. Either she hath bewitched me with her
    words,
Or nature makes me suddenly relent.

Pucelle. Besides, all French and France exclaims on°
    thee,   60
Doubting thy birth and lawful progeny.°
Who join'st thou with, but with a lordly° nation
That will not trust thee but for profit's sake?
When Talbot hath set footing° once in France
And fashioned thee° that instrument of ill,   65
Who then but English Henry will be lord,
And thou be thrust out like a fugitive?
Call we to mind, and mark but this for proof:
Was not the Duke of Orleans thy foe?
And was he not in England prisoner?   70
But when they heard he was thine enemy,
They set him free without his ransom paid,
In spite of Burgundy and all his friends.
See then, thou fight'st against thy countrymen

48 **tender-dying** prematurely dying   49 **pining** consuming   52
edgèd sharp   57 **stainèd** disgraceful   60 **exclaims on** cries out
against   61 **lawful progeny** legitimate parentage   62 **lordly** imperious, disdainful   64 **set footing** entered   65 **fashioned thee** made
you into

75 And join'st with them will be thy slaughter-men.°
    Come, come, return; return, thou wandering lord;
    Charles and the rest will take thee in their arms.

Burgundy. I am vanquishèd; these haughty° words of
    hers
    Have battered me like roaring cannon-shot,
80 And made me almost yield upon my knees.
    Forgive me, country, and sweet countrymen,
    And, lords, accept this hearty kind° embrace.
    My forces and my power of men° are yours.
    So farewell, Talbot; I'll no longer trust thee.

Pucelle. [*Aside*] Done like a Frenchman: turn and
85   turn again!°

Dauphin. Welcome, brave duke! thy friendship makes
    us fresh.°

Bastard. And doth beget new courage in our breasts.

Alençon. Pucelle hath bravely played her part in this,
    And doth deserve a coronet° of gold.

Dauphin. Now let us on, my lords, and join our
90   powers,
    And seek how we may prejudice° the foe.   *Exeunt.*

---

75 **slaughter-men** executioners   78 **haughty** loftily brave   82 **kind**
(1) friendly (2) of a kinsman   83 **my power of men** (1) my full complement of troops (?) (2) command over my troops   85 **turn and
turn again** change sides frequently   86 **makes us fresh** renews our
spirits   89 **coronet** a small crown worn on state occasions by members of the nobility   91 **prejudice** damage

Scene IV. [*Paris. The Palace.*]

*Enter the King, Gloucester, Winchester, York, Suf-
folk, Somerset, Warwick, Exeter, [Vernon, Basset,
and others]. To them, with his Soldiers, Talbot.*

Talbot. My gracious prince, and honorable peers,
  Hearing of your arrival in this realm,
  I have awhile given truce unto my wars
  To do my duty to my sovereign.
  In sign whereof, this arm, that hath reclaimed°   *5*
  To your obedience fifty fortresses,
  Twelve cities, and seven wallèd towns of strength,
  Beside five hundred prisoners of esteem,°
  Lets fall his sword before your highness' feet,
  And with submissive loyalty of heart   *10*
  Ascribes the glory of his conquest got
  First to my God and next unto your grace.

King. Is this the Lord Talbot, uncle Gloucester,
  That hath so long been resident in France?

Gloucester. Yes, if it please your majesty, my liege.°   *15*

King. Welcome, brave captain and victorious lord!
  When I was young (as yet I am not old)
  I do remember° how my father said
  A stouter champion never handled sword.
  Long since we were resolvèd of your truth,°   *20*
  Your faithful service, and your toil in war;
  Yet never have you tasted our reward
  Or been reguerdoned° with so much as thanks,

III.iv.5 **reclaimed** subdued   8 **esteem** good reputation in battle and
high birth (thus likely to command a profitable ransom) 15 **liege**
sovereign lord 18 **remember** (but Henry VI was only nine months
old when his father died) 20 **resolvèd of your truth** convinced of
your loyalty 23 **reguerdoned** repaid

Because till now we never saw your face.
25　Therefore, stand up, and for these good deserts
We here create you Earl of Shrewsbury,
And in our coronation take your place.

Sennet. Flourish. Exeunt. Manet° Vernon and Basset.

Vernon. Now, sir, to you, that were so hot° at sea,
Disgracing of° these colors that I wear
30　In honor of my noble Lord of York—
Dar'st thou maintain the former words thou
spak'st?

Basset. Yes, sir, as well as you dare patronage°
The envious barking of your saucy tongue
Against my lord the Duke of Somerset.

35　*Vernon.* Sirrah, thy lord I honor as he is.

Basset. Why, what is he? As good a man as York.

Vernon. Hark ye, not so: in witness,° take ye that.

Strikes him.

Basset. Villain, thou knowest the law of arms is such
That whoso draws a sword,° 'tis present° death,
40　Or else this blow should broach° thy dearest blood.
But I'll unto his majesty and crave°
I may have liberty to venge° this wrong.
When thou shalt see I'll meet thee to thy cost.

Vernon. Well, miscreant,° I'll be there as soon as
you,
45　And, after, meet you sooner than you would.

Exeunt.

27s.d. **Manet** remains (the Latin singular with a plural subject is
common in Elizabethan stage directions)　28 **hot** passionate　29
Disgracing of disparaging　32 **patronage** (1) maintain (2) defend
37 **in witness** as proof　39 **draws a sword** i.e., in a royal residence
39 **present** immediate　40 **broach** draw as with a tap　41 **crave**
beg　42 **venge** avenge　44 **miscreant** coward

ACT IV

Scene I. [*Paris. A hall of state.*]

Enter King, Gloucester, Winchester, York, Suffolk, Somerset, Warwick, Talbot, Exeter, Governor [of Paris and others].

Gloucester. Lord bishop, set the crown upon his head.

Winchester. God save King Henry, of that name the
    sixth!

Gloucester. Now, governor of Paris, take your oath,
    That you elect no other king but him;
    Esteem none friends but such as are his friends,   5
    And none your foes but such as shall pretend°
    Malicious practices° against his state:
    This shall ye do, so help you righteous God!

Enter Falstaff.

Falstaff. My gracious sovereign, as I rode from Calais
    To haste unto your coronation,   10
    A letter was delivered to my hands,
    Writ to your grace from th' Duke of Burgundy.

   Talbot. Shame to the Duke of Burgundy and thee!
     I vowed, base knight, when I did meet thee next,
5 To tear the garter° from thy craven's° leg,

                [Plucking it off.]

     Which I have done, because unworthily
     Thou wast installèd in that high degree.°
     Pardon me, princely Henry, and the rest:
     This dastard, at the battle of Poictiers,°
20 When but in all I was six thousand strong
     And that the French were almost ten to one,
     Before we met or that a stroke was given,
     Like to a trusty squire° did run away.
     In which assault we lost twelve hundred men;
25 Myself and divers gentlemen beside
     Were there surprised and taken prisoners.
     Then judge, great lords, if I have done amiss,
     Or whether that such cowards ought to wear
     This ornament of knighthood, yea or no.

30 *Gloucester.* To say the truth, this fact° was infamous
     And ill beseeming any common man,
     Much more a knight, a captain, and a leader.

   Talbot. When first this order was ordained, my lords,
     Knights of the Garter were of noble birth,
35 Valiant and virtuous, full of haughty° courage,
     Such as were grown to credit° by the wars;
     Not fearing death, nor shrinking for distress,°
     But always resolute in most extremes.°
     He then that is not furnished in this sort°
40 Doth but usurp the sacred name of knight,
     Profaning this most honorable order,
     And should (if I were worthy to be judge)

---

15 **garter** badge of the Order of the Garter, England's highest degree of knighthood   15 **craven's** coward's   17 **degree** dignity   19 **Poictiers** i.e., Patay (1429)   23 **trusty squire** (used contemptuously: a person of inferior character)   30 **fact** deed   35 **haughty** high 36 **credit** honorable reputation   37 **distress** adversity   38 **in most extremes** in the most difficult situations   39 **furnished in this sort** possessed of such qualities

Be quite degraded, like a hedge-born swain°
That doth presume to boast of gentle blood.

King. Stain to thy countrymen, thou hear'st
    thy doom!°   45
Be packing,° therefore, thou that wast a knight:
Henceforth we banish thee on pain of death.

                [Exit Falstaff.]

And now, Lord Protector, view the letter
Sent from our uncle Duke of Burgundy.

Gloucester. What means his grace, that he hath
    changed his style?°   50
No more but plain and bluntly, "To the king!"
Hath he forgot he is his sovereign?
Or doth this churlish superscription
Pretend° some alteration in good will?
What's here? "I have, upon especial cause,   55
Moved with compassion of my country's wrack,°
Together with the pitiful complaints
Of such as your oppression feeds upon,
Forsaken your pernicious faction
And joined with Charles, the rightful King of
    France."   60
O monstrous treachery! can this be so,
That in alliance, amity, and oaths,
There should be found such false dissembling
    guile?

King. What! doth my uncle Burgundy revolt?

Gloucester. He doth, my lord, and is become your foe.   65

King. Is that the worst this letter doth contain?

Gloucester. It is the worst, and all, my lord, he writes.

King. Why, then, Lord Talbot there shall talk with
    him

---

43 **hedge-born swain** low peasant   45 **doom** judgment, condemnation   46 **Be packing** begone   50 **style** form of address   54 **Pretend** signify   56 **wrack** misfortune

And give him chastisement for this abuse.
70   How say you, my lord; are you not content?

Talbot. Content, my liege? Yes, but that I am prevented,°
   I should have begged I might have been employed.

King. Then gather strength, and march unto him
   straight;
   Let him perceive how ill we brook° his treason
75   And what offense it is to flout his friends.

Talbot. I go, my lord, in heart desiring still
   You may behold confusion of your foes.   [*Exit.*]

Enter Vernon and Basset.

Vernon. Grant me the combat,° gracious sovereign.

Basset. And me, my lord, grant me the combat too.

80   *York.* This is my servant; hear him, noble prince.

Somerset. And this is mine; sweet Henry, favor him.

King. Be patient, lords, and give them leave to
   speak.
   Say, gentlemen, what makes you thus exclaim,
   And wherefore crave you combat? Or with whom?

Vernon. With him, my lord, for he hath done me
85   wrong.

Basset. And I with him, for he hath done me wrong.

King. What is that wrong whereof you both complain?
   First let me know, and then I'll answer you.

Basset. Crossing the sea from England into France,
90   This fellow here, with envious carping° tongue,
   Upbraided° me about the rose I wear,
   Saying, the sanguine° color of the leaves

---

71 **prevented** anticipated   74 **brook** bear with   78 **combat** trial by
arms   90 **carping**   fault-finding   91 **Upbraided**   reproached   92
sanguine blood-red

Did represent my master's blushing cheeks,
When stubbornly he did repugn° the truth
About a certain question in the law   *95*
Argued betwixt the Duke of York and him;
With other vile and ignominious terms;
In confutation of which rude reproach
And in defense of my lord's worthiness,
I crave the benefit of law of arms.°   *100*

Vernon. And that is my petition, noble lord:
For though he seem with forgèd quaint conceit°
To set a gloss upon° his bold intent,
Yet know, my lord, I was provoked by him,
And he first took exceptions at° this badge,   *105*
Pronouncing that the paleness of this flower
Bewrayed° the faintness of my master's heart.

York. Will not this malice, Somerset, be left?

Somerset. Your private grudge, my Lord of York, will
    out,
Though ne'er so cunningly you smother it.   *110*

King. Good Lord, what madness rules in brain-
    sick men,
When for so slight and frivolous a cause
Such factious emulations° shall arise!
Good cousins both, of York and Somerset,
Quiet yourselves, I pray, and be at peace.   *115*

York. Let this dissension first be tried by fight,
And then your highness shall command a peace.

Somerset. The quarrel toucheth° none but us alone;
Betwixt ourselves let us decide it then.

York. There is my pledge;° accept it, Somerset.   *120*

Vernon. Nay, let it rest where it began at first.

---

94 **repugn** resist   100 **benefit . . . arms** privilege of trial by combat
102 **forgèd quaint conceit** crafty manner of expression   103 **set a
gloss upon** veil in specious language   105 **took exceptions at** disap-
proved of   107 **Bewrayed** revealed   113 **emulations** contentions
118 **toucheth** concerns   120 **pledge** challenge (made by casting
down one's glove)

Basset. Confirm it so, mine honorable lord.

Gloucester. Confirm it so? Confounded be your strife!
    And perish ye with your audacious prate!°
125   Presumptuous vassals, are you not ashamed
    With this immodest° clamorous outrage
    To trouble and disturb the king and us?
    And you, my lords, methinks you do not well
    To bear with their perverse objections,
130   Much less to take occasion from their mouths
    To raise a mutiny betwixt yourselves.
    Let me persuade you take a better course.

Exeter. It grieves his highness. Good my lords, be
    friends.

King. Come hither, you that would be com-
    batants:
135   Henceforth I charge you, as you love our favor,
    Quite to forget this quarrel and the cause.
    And you, my lords, remember where we are:
    In France, amongst a fickle wavering nation;
    If they perceive dissension in our looks
140   And that within ourselves we disagree,
    How will their grudging stomachs° be provoked
    To wilful disobedience, and rebel!
    Beside, what infamy will there arise,
    When foreign princes shall be certified°
145   That for a toy,° a thing of no regard,
    King Henry's peers and chief nobility
    Destroyed themselves and lost the realm of France!
    O, think upon the conquest of my father,
    My tender years, and let us not forgo
150   That for a trifle that was bought with blood!
    Let me be umpire in this doubtful strife.
    I see no reason, if I wear this rose,

                [Putting on a red rose.]

    That anyone should therefore be suspicious

---

124 **prate** chatter 126 **immodest** arrogant 141 **grudging stomachs**
resentful dispositions 144 **certified** informed 145 **toy** trifle

I more incline to Somerset than York;
Both are my kinsmen, and I love them both.   *155*
As well they may upbraid me with my crown
Because, forsooth,° the King of Scots is crowned.
But your discretions° better can persuade
Than I am able to instruct or teach,
And therefore, as we hither came in peace,   *160*
So let us still continue peace and love.
Cousin of York, we institute your grace
To be our Regent in these parts of France;
And, good my Lord of Somerset, unite
Your troops of horsemen with his bands of foot,   *165*
And, like true subjects, sons of your progenitors,
Go cheerfully together and digest
Your angry choler° on your enemies.
Ourself, my Lord Protector, and the rest
After some respite will return to Calais;   *170*
From thence to England, where I hope ere long
To be presented, by your victories,
With Charles, Alençon, and that traitorous rout.°

> *Flourish. Exeunt. Manet York, Warwick,*
> *Exeter, Vernon.*

Warwick. My Lord of York, I promise you, the king
Prettily, methought, did play the orator.   *175*

York. And so he did, but yet I like it not,
In that he wears the badge of Somerset.

Warwick. Tush, that was but his fancy, blame him
not;
I dare presume, sweet prince, he thought no harm.

York. And if—I wish—he did. But let it rest;   *180*
Other affairs must now be managèd.

> *Exeunt. Manet Exeter.*

---

157 **forsooth** in truth (used derisively)   158 **discretions** lordships,
judgments   168 **choler** bile (according to earlier physiology, the
cause of anger or hot temper)   173 **rout** crowd

Exeter. Well didst thou, Richard, to suppress thy
    voice;
    For, had the passions of thy heart burst out,
    I fear we should have seen deciphered° there
185   More rancorous spite, more furious raging broils,
    Than yet can be imagined or supposed.
    But howsoe'er, no simple man that sees
    This jarring discord of nobility,
    This shouldering° of each other in the court,
190   This factious bandying° of their favorites,
    But that it doth presage some ill event.°
    'Tis much° when scepters are in children's hands,
    But more when envy breeds unkind division;°
    There comes the ruin, there begins confusion. *Exit.*

[Scene II.] *Before Bordeaux.*

Enter Talbot, with trump and drum.

Talbot. Go to the gates of Bordeaux, trumpeter;
    Summon their general unto the wall.
                     [Trumpet] sounds.

Enter General aloft [with others].

    English John Talbot, captains, calls you forth,
    Servant in arms to Harry King of England,
5   And thus he would: open your city gates,
    Be humble to us, call my sovereign yours
    And do him homage as obedient subjects,
    And I'll withdraw me and my bloody power.
    But, if you frown upon this proffered peace,
10   You tempt the fury of my three attendants,

---

184 **deciphered** revealed   189 **shouldering** jostling   190 **bandying**
contention   191 **presage some ill event** predict some evil outcome
192 **much** difficult   193 **unkind division** unnatural disunion

Lean Famine, quartering° Steel, and climbing Fire,
Who in a moment even° with the earth
Shall lay your stately and air-braving° towers,
If you forsake the offer of their love.

General. Thou ominous and fearful owl of death,°   *15*
Our nation's terror and their bloody scourge!
The period° of thy tyranny approacheth.
On us thou canst not enter but by death,
For, I protest, we are well fortified
And strong enough to issue out and fight.   *20*
If thou retire, the Dolphin, well appointed,°
Stands with the snares of war to tangle thee.
On either hand° thee there are squadrons pitched
To wall thee from the liberty of flight,
And no way canst thou turn thee for redress,°   *25*
But death doth front° thee with apparent spoil,°
And pale destruction meets thee in the face.
Ten thousand French have ta'en the sacrament°
To rive° their dangerous artillery
Upon no Christian soul but English Talbot.   *30*
Lo, there thou stand'st, a breathing valiant man,
Of an invincible unconquered spirit!
This is the latest° glory of thy praise
That I, thy enemy, due° thee withal,
For ere the glass that now begins to run   *35*
Finish the process of his sandy hour,
These eyes, that see thee now well colorèd,°
Shall see thee withered, bloody, pale, and dead.

                              Drum afar off.

Hark! hark! The Dolphin's drum, a warning bell,
Sings heavy° music to thy timorous soul,   *40*

IV.ii.11 **quartering** that cuts men into quarters   12 **even** level   13
air-braving skyscraping   15 **owl of death** (alluding to the owl as a
supposed harbinger of death or misfortune)   17 **period** end   21
appointed equipped   23 **hand** side of   25 **redress** relief   26 **front**
confront   26 **apparent spoil** obvious destruction   28 **ta'en the
sacrament** confirmed their oaths by receiving holy communion
29 **rive** burst   33 **latest** final   34 **due** endue   37 **well colorèd** of
healthy complexion   40 **heavy** doleful

    And mine shall ring thy dire departure out.

                     Exit [with his followers].

Talbot. He fables not,° I hear the enemy;
    Out, some light° horsemen, and peruse their wings.°
    O, negligent and heedless discipline!
45   How are we parked and bounded in a pale,°
    A little herd of England's timorous deer,
    Mazed with° a yelping kennel of French curs!
    If we be English deer, be then in blood,°
    Not rascal-like° to fall down with a pinch,°
50   But rather moody-mad;° and, desperate stags,
    Turn on the bloody° hounds with heads of steel
    And make the cowards stand aloof at bay.
    Sell every man his life as dear as mine,
    And they shall find dear° deer of us, my friends.
55   God and Saint George, Talbot and England's right,
    Prosper our colors in this dangerous fight! [*Exeunt.*]

[Scene III. *Plains in Gascony.*]

*Enter a Messenger that meets York. Enter York with
trumpet and many Soldiers.*

York. Are not the speedy scouts returned again
    That dogged° the mighty army of the Dolphin?

Messenger. They are returned, my lord, and give it
    out°
    That he is marched to Bordeaux with his power
5   To fight with Talbot. As he marched along,
    By your espials° were discoverèd

42 fables not does not speak falsely **43 light** lightly armed **43
peruse their wings** scout their flanks **45 parked . . . pale** surrounded and hemmed in by a fence **47 Mazed with** terrified by
48 in blood (1) in full vigor (2) in temper **49 rascal-like** like inferior deer **49 pinch** nip **50 moody-mad** furious in mood **51
bloody** bloodthirsty **54 dear** costly **IV.iii.2 dogged** tracked, closely
pursued **3 give it out** report **6 espials** spies

Two mightier troops than that the Dolphin led,
Which joined with him and made their march for
    Bordeaux.

York. A plague upon that villain Somerset,
    That thus delays my promisèd supply   *10*
    Of horsemen that were levied for this siege!
    Renownèd Talbot doth expect° my aid,
    And I am louted° by a traitor villain
    And cannot help the noble chevalier.°
    God comfort him in this necessity!   *15*
    If he miscarry,° farewell wars in France.

Enter another Messenger: [Sir William Lucy.]

Lucy. Thou princely leader of our English strength,
    Never so needful on the earth of France,
    Spur to the rescue of the noble Talbot,
    Who now is girdled with a waist of iron   *20*
    And hemmed about with grim destruction.
    To Bordeaux, warlike duke! to Bordeaux, York!
    Else, farewell Talbot, France, and England's honor.

York. O God, that Somerset, who in proud heart
    Doth stop my cornets,° were in Talbot's place!   *25*
    So should we save a valiant gentleman
    By forfeiting a traitor and a coward.
    Mad ire and wrathful fury makes me weep,
    That thus we die, while remiss traitors sleep.

Lucy. O, send some succor to the distressed lord!   *30*

York. He dies, we lose; I break my warlike word;
    We mourn, France smiles; we lose, they daily get;
    All long° of this vile traitor Somerset.

Lucy. Then God take mercy on brave Talbot's soul,
    And on his son young John, who two hours since   *35*
    I met in travel toward his warlike father!
    This seven years did not Talbot see his son,
    And now they meet where both their lives are done.

12 expect await   13 louted mocked   14 chevalier knight   16 miscarry be destroyed   25 stop my cornets withhold my squadrons of cavalry   33 long on account

York. Alas, what joy shall noble Talbot have
40   To bid his young son welcome to his grave?
    Away! vexation almost stops my breath,
    That sundered° friends greet in the hour of death.
    Lucy, farewell, no more my fortune can°
    But curse the cause° I cannot aid the man.
45   Maine, Blois, Poictiers, and Tours are won away,
    Long all of Somerset and his delay.

                   Exit [with his Soldiers].

Lucy. Thus, while the vulture of sedition
    Feeds in the bosom of such great commanders,
    Sleeping neglection° doth betray to loss
50   The conquest of our scarce-cold° conqueror,
    That ever living man of memory,
    Henry the Fifth. Whiles they each other cross,
    Lives, honors, lands, and all hurry to loss.

[Scene IV. *Other plains in Gascony.*]

*Enter Somerset with his army, [a Captain of Talbot's
with him].*

Somerset. It is too late, I cannot send them now;
    This expedition was by York and Talbot
    Too rashly plotted. All our general° force
    Might with a sally° of the very° town
5   Be buckled with. The over-daring Talbot
    Hath sullied all his gloss° of former honor
    By this unheedful, desperate, wild adventure;
    York set him on to fight and die in shame,
    That, Talbot dead, great York might bear the name.

---

42 **sundered** separated 43 **fortune can** circumstances enable me to
do 44 **cause** reason why 49 **neglection** negligence 50 **scarce-cold**
barely dead IV.iv.3 **general** whole 4 **sally** sudden outrush 4 **very**
itself 6 **gloss** luster

Captain. Here is Sir William Lucy, who with me   10
  Set from our o'er-matched° forçes forth for aid.

Somerset. How now, Sir William! whither were you
  sent?

Lucy. Whither, my lord? from bought and sold Lord
  Talbot;
  Who, ringed about with bold adversity,°
  Cries out for noble York and Somerset   15
  To beat assailing death from his weak regions;°
  And whiles the honorable captain there
  Drops bloody sweat from his war-wearied limbs,
  And in advantage ling'ring° looks for rescue,
  You, his false hopes, the trust of England's honor,   20
  Keep off aloof with worthless emulation.°
  Let not your private discord keep away
  The levied succors° that should lend him aid
  While he, renownèd noble gentleman,
  Yield up his life unto a world of odds: 25
  Orleans the Bastard, Charles, Burgundy,
  Alençon, Reignier compass him about,
  And Talbot perisheth by your default.

Somerset. York set him on, York should have sent
  him aid.

Lucy. And York as fast upon your grace exclaims,   30
  Swearing that you withhold his levied host,
  Collected for this expedition.

Somerset. York lies; he might have sent and had the
  horse!
  I owe him little duty, and less love,
  And take° foul scorn to fawn on him by sending.   35

Lucy. The fraud of England, not the force of France,
  Hath now entrapped the noble-minded Talbot;

11 **o'er-matched** outnumbered   14 **bold adversity** confident opponents   16 **regions** places   19 **in advantage ling'ring** (1) desperately clinging to every advantage (?) (2) while holding out on
advantageous ground (?)   21 **emulation** rivalry   23 **succors** rein-
forcements   35 **take** submit to

Never to England shall he bear his life,
But dies betrayed to fortune by your strife.

Somerset. Come, go; I will dispatch the horsemen
40   straight;
Within six hours they will be at his aid.

Lucy. Too late comes rescue, he is ta'en or slain,
For fly he could not, if he would have fled,
And fly would Talbot never though he might.

45 *Somerset.* If he be dead, brave Talbot, then adieu!

Lucy. His fame lives in the world, his shame in you.
                                                    Exeunt.

[Scene V. *The English camp near Bordeaux.*]

Enter Talbot and his son.

Talbot. O young John Talbot! I did send for thee
To tutor thee in stratagems of war,
That Talbot's name might be in thee revived
When sapless° age and weak unable° limbs
5   Should bring thy father to his drooping chair.°
But, O malignant and ill-boding stars!
Now thou art come unto a feast of death,
A terrible and unavoided° danger:
Therefore, dear boy, mount on my swiftest horse,
10   And I'll direct thee how thou shalt escape
By sudden flight. Come, dally not, be gone.

John. Is my name Talbot? And am I your son?
And shall I fly? O, if you love my mother,
Dishonor not her honorable name,
15   To make a bastard and a slave of me.

IV.v.4 **sapless** withered   4 **unable** powerless   5 **drooping chair** decline from vigor   8 **unavoided** unavoidable

    The world will say, he is not Talbot's blood,
    That basely fled when noble Talbot stood.

Talbot. Fly, to revenge my death, if I be slain.

John. He that flies so will ne'er return again.

Talbot. If we both stay, we both are sure to die.   20

John. Then let me stay, and, father, do you fly:
    Your loss is great, so your regard should be;
    My worth unknown, no loss is known in me.
    Upon my death the French can little boast;
    In yours they will, in you all hopes are lost.   25
    Flight cannot stain the honor you have won,
    But mine it will, that no exploit have done;
    You fled for vantage,° everyone will swear,
    But, if I bow,° they'll say it was for fear.
    There is no hope that ever I will stay   30
    If the first hour I shrink and run away.
    Here on my knee I beg mortality,°
    Rather than life preserved with infamy.

Talbot. Shall all thy mother's hopes lie in one tomb?

John. Ay, rather than I'll shame my mother's womb.   35

Talbot. Upon my blessing, I command thee go.

John. To fight I will, but not to fly the foe.

Talbot. Part of thy father may be saved in thee.

John. No part of him but will be shame in me.

Talbot. Thou never hadst renown, nor canst not lose
    it.   40

John. Yes, your renownèd name: shall flight abuse it?

Talbot. Thy father's charge° shall clear thee from that
    stain.

John. You cannot witness for me, being slain.
    If death be so apparent, then both fly.

28 **for vantage** to gain a tactical advantage   29 **bow** flee   32 **mortality** death   42 **charge** attack

45 *Talbot.* And leave my followers here to fight and die?
My age was never tainted with such shame.

John. And shall my youth be guilty of such blame?
No more can I be severed from your side
Than can yourself yourself in twain° divide.
50 Stay, go, do what you will, the like do I;
For live I will not, if my father die.

Talbot. Then here I take my leave of thee, fair son,
Born to eclipse° thy life this afternoon.
Come, side by side together live and die;
55 And soul with soul from France to heaven fly.
Exit [with Son].

[Scene VI. *A field of battle.*]

*Alarum: excursions, wherein Talbot's Son is hemmed
about, and Talbot rescues him.*

Talbot. Saint George and victory! fight, soldiers, fight!
The Regent hath with Talbot broke his word
And left us to the rage of France his sword.
Where is John Talbot? Pause, and take thy breath;
5 I gave thee life and rescued thee from death.

John. O, twice my father, twice am I thy son!
The life thou gav'st me first was lost and done,
Till with thy warlike sword, despite of° fate,
To my determined° time thou gav'st new date.

Talbot. When from the Dolphin's crest thy sword
10   struck fire,
It warmed thy father's heart with proud desire
Of bold-faced victory. Then leaden° age,
Quickened° with youthful spleen° and warlike rage,

49 **twain** two   53 **eclipse** end   IV.vi.8 **despite of** in spite of   9
determined predestined, fated   12 **leaden** spiritless   13 **Quickened**
animated   13 **spleen** high spirits, courage

Beat down Alençon, Orleans, Burgundy,
And from the pride of Gallia° rescued thee.   15
The ireful bastard Orleans, that drew blood
From thee, my boy, and had the maidenhood
Of thy first fight, I soon encounterèd,
And interchanging blows I quickly shed
Some of his bastard blood; and in disgrace   20
Bespoke him thus: "Contaminated, base,
And misbegotten blood I spill of thine,
Mean and right poor, for that pure blood of mine
Which thou didst force from Talbot, my brave
    boy."
Here,° purposing the Bastard to destroy,   25
Came in strong rescue. Speak, thy father's care,
Art thou not weary, John? How dost thou fare?
Wilt thou yet leave the battle, boy, and fly,
Now thou art sealed° the son of chivalry?
Fly, to revenge my death when I am dead;   30
The help of one stands me in little stead.
O, too much folly is it, well I wot,°
To hazard° all our lives in one small boat!
If I today die not with Frenchmen's rage,
Tomorrow I shall die with mickle° age.   35
By me they nothing gain and if I stay;
'Tis but the short'ning of my life one day.
In thee thy mother dies, our household's name,
My death's revenge, thy youth, and England's fame:
All these and more we hazard by thy stay;   40
All these are saved if thou wilt fly away.

John. The sword of Orleans hath not made me smart;
    These words of yours draw life-blood from my
        heart.
    On that advantage, bought with such a shame,
    To save a paltry life and slay bright fame,   45
    Before young Talbot from old Talbot fly,
    The coward horse that bears me fall and die!
    And like° me to the peasant boys of France,

15 **Gallia** France   25 **Here** i.e., here I   29 **sealed** authenticated
(by his deeds)   32 **wot** know   33 **hazard** gamble   35 **mickle** much,
advanced   48 **like** compare

To be shame's scorn and subject of mischance!°
50   Surely, by all the glory you have won,
And if I fly, I am not Talbot's son.
Then talk no more of flight, it is no boot;°
If son to Talbot, die at Talbot's foot.

Talbot. Then follow thou thy desperate sire of Crete,°
55   Thou Icarus; thy life to me is sweet;
If thou wilt fight, fight by thy father's side;
And, commendable proved, let's die in pride.°

                         Exit [with Son].

[Scene VII. *Another part of the field.*]

*Alarum: excursions. Enter old Talbot, led [by a
               Servant].*

Talbot. Where is my other life? Mine own is gone.
O, where's young Talbot? Where is valiant John?
Triumphant death, smeared with captivity,°
Young Talbot's valor makes me smile at thee.
5   When he perceived me shrink° and on my knee,
His bloody sword he brandished over me,
And like a hungry lion did commence
Rough deeds of rage and stern impatience,
But when my angry guardant° stood alone,
10   Tend'ring° my ruin and assailed of° none,
Dizzy-eyed° fury and great rage of heart
Suddenly made him from my side to start
Into the clust'ring battle° of the French,
And in that sea of blood my boy did drench

49 **subject of mischance** an example of unhappy fate   52 **boot** use
54 **sire of Crete** Daedalus (who made wings of feathers and wax on
which he and his son Icarus attempted to escape from King Minos
of Crete)   57 **pride** glory   IV.vii.3 **captivity** the blood of your
captives (?)   5 **shrink** give way   9 **guardant** protector   10 **Ten-
d'ring** tenderly caring for me in   10 **of** by   11 **Dizzy-eyed** giddy
13 **clust'ring battle** close-grouped battle formation

His over-mounting° spirit and there died,   15
My Icarus, my blossom, in his pride.

Enter [Soldiers,] with John Talbot, borne.

Servant. O my dear lord, lo, where your son is
    borne!

Talbot. Thou antic° death, which laugh'st us here to
    scorn,
Anon,° from thy insulting tyranny,.
Coupled in bonds of perpetuity,°   20
Two Talbots, wingèd through the lither° sky,
In thy despite shall 'scape mortality.
O thou, whose wounds become hard-favored°
    death,
Speak to thy father ere thou yield thy breath!
Brave Death by speaking, whether he will or no;   25
Imagine him a Frenchman and thy foe.
Poor boy! he smiles, methinks, as who should say,
"Had Death been French, then Death had died
    today."
Come, come and lay him in his father's arms;
My spirit can no longer bear these harms.   30
Soldiers, adieu! I have what I would have,
Now my old arms are young John Talbot's grave.
                                            Dies.

*Enter Charles [the Dauphin], Alençon, Burgundy,
    Bastard, and [La] Pucelle, [with forces].*

Dauphin. Had York and Somerset brought rescue in,
We should have found a bloody day of this.

Bastard. How the young whelp of Talbot's, raging
    wood,°   35
Did flesh his puny-sword° in Frenchmen's blood!

Pucelle. Once I encountered him, and thus I said:

15 **over-mounting** too highly aspiring   18 **antic** (1) grinning (2)
buffoon   19 **Anon** immediately   20 **of perpetuity** eternal   21 **lither**
yielding, pliant   23 **hard-favored** ugly-looking   35 **wood** mad   36
flesh his puny-sword initiate his untried sword in battle

"Thou maiden youth, be vanquished by a maid."
But, with a proud majestical high scorn,
40 He answered thus: "Young Talbot was not born
To be the pillage° of a giglot° wench."
So, rushing in the bowels°of the French,
He left me proudly, as unworthy fight.°

Burgundy. Doubtless he would have made a noble
knight.
45 See, where he lies inhearsèd° in the arms
Of the most bloody nurser° of his harms!

Bastard. Hew them to pieces, hack their bones
asunder,
Whose life was England's glory, Gallia's wonder.

Dauphin. O no, forbear! for that which we have fled
50 During the life, let us not wrong it dead.

Enter Lucy, [attended by a French Herald].

Lucy. Herald, conduct me to the Dolphin's tent,
To know who hath obtained the glory of the day.

Dauphin. On what submissive message art thou sent?

Lucy. Submission, Dolphin! 'Tis a mere French word;
55 We English warriors wot not what it means.
I come to know what prisoners thou hast ta'en
And to survey the bodies of the dead.

Dauphin. For prisoners ask'st thou? Hell our prison
is.°
But tell me whom thou seek'st.

60 *Lucy.* But where's the great Alcides° of the field,
Valiant Lord Talbot, Earl of Shrewsbury,
Created, for his rare success in arms,
Great Earl of Washford, Waterford, and Valence,
Lord Talbot of Goodrig and Urchinfield,
65 Lord Strange of Blackmere, Lord Verdun of Alton,

41 **pillage** plunder 41 **giglot** wanton 42 **bowels** midst 43 **un-worthy fight** not worthy of fighting with 45 **inhearsèd** enclosed as in a hearse 46 **nurser** fosterer 58 **Hell our prison is** i.e., we kill all our enemies 60 **Alcides** Hercules

Lord Cromwell of Wingfield, Lord Furnival of
      Sheffield,
The thrice-victorious Lord of Falconbridge,
Knight of the noble order of Saint George,
Worthy Saint Michael, and the Golden Fleece,°
Great Marshal to Henry the Sixth   70
Of all his wars within the realm of France?

Pucelle. Here's a silly stately style° indeed!
The Turk,° that two and fifty kingdoms hath,
Writes not so tedious a style as this.
Him that thou magnifi'st with all these titles   75
Stinking and fly-blown lies here at our feet.

Lucy. Is Talbot slain, the Frenchmen's only scourge,
Your kingdom's terror and black Nemesis?
O, were mine eyeballs into bullets turned,
That I in rage might shoot them at your faces!   80
O, that I could but call these dead to life,
It were enough to fright the realm of France!
Were but his picture left amongst you here,
It would amaze° the proudest of you all.
Give me their bodies, that I may bear them hence   85
And give them burial as beseems their worth.

Pucelle. I think this upstart is old Talbot's ghost,
He speaks with such a proud commanding spirit.
For God's sake, let him have him; to keep them
      here,
They would but stink and putrefy the air.   90

Dauphin. Go, take their bodies hence.

Lucy. I'll bear them hence, but from their ashes shall
      be reared
A phoenix° that shall make all France afeard.°

68–70 Saint George . . . Saint Michael . . . the Golden Fleece
chivalric orders of England, France, and the Holy Roman Empire
respectively   **72 stately style** imposing title   **73 the Turk** the Sultan
84 amaze stupefy, terrify   **93 phoenix** in mythology, an Arabian
bird that is resurrected from the ashes of its own funeral pyre   **93
afeard** afraid

Dauphin. So we be rid of them, do with him what
        thou wilt.
95   And **now** to Paris, in this conquering vein:°
        All will be ours, now bloody Talbot's slain.

                                        Exeunt.

95 **vein** mood

ACT V

[Scene I. *London. The palace.*]

Sennet. Enter King, Gloucester, and Exeter.

King. Have you perused the letters from the pope,
    The emperor, and the Earl of Armagnac?

Gloucester. I have, my lord, and their intent is this:
    They humbly sue unto your excellence
    To have a godly peace concluded of   5
    Between the realms of England and of France.

King. How doth your grace affect° their motion?

Gloucester. Well, my good lord, and as the only means
    To stop effusion of our Christian blood
    And stablish° quietness on every side.   10

King. Ay, marry, uncle, for I always thought
    It was both impious and unnatural
    That such immanity° and bloody strife
    Should reign among professors of° one faith.

Gloucester. Beside, my lord, the sooner to effect   15
    And surer bind this knot of amity,
    The Earl of Armagnac, near knit° to Charles,
    A man of great authority in France,

V.i.7 **affect** like   10 **stablish** establish   13 **immanity** monstrous
cruelty   14 **professors of** believers in   17 **near knit** closely bound
by blood relationship

Proffers his only daughter to your grace
20   In marriage, with a large and sumptuous dowry.

King. Marriage, uncle! alas, my years are young,
      And fitter is my study and my books
      Than wanton dalliance with a paramour.°
      Yet call th' ambassadors, and, as you please,
25   So let them have their answers every one:
      I shall be well content with any choice
      Tends to God's glory and my country's weal.

*Enter Winchester [in Cardinal's habit], and three Am-
      bassadors, [one of them a Legate°].*

Exeter. What! is my Lord of Winchester installed,
      And called unto a cardinal's degree?
30   Then I perceive that will be verified
      Henry the Fifth did sometime° prophesy:
      "If once he come to be a cardinal,
      He'll make his cap° co-equal with the crown."

King. My lords ambassadors, your several suits°
35   Have been considered and debated on.
      Your purpose is both good and reasonable,
      And therefore are we certainly resolved
      To draw conditions of a friendly peace,
      Which by my Lord of Winchester we mean
40   Shall be transported presently to France.

Gloucester. And for the proffer of my lord your mas-
            ter,°
      I have informed his highness so at large
      As,° liking of the lady's virtuous gifts,
      Her beauty and the value of her dower,°
45   He doth intend she shall be England's queen.

King. In argument and proof of which contract,
      Bear her this jewel, pledge of my affection.

---

23 wanton . . . paramour lascivious sport with a mistress   **27s.d.
Legate** representative of the Pope   **31 sometime** once   **33 cap** red
cardinal's skullcap   **34 several suits** individual requests   **41 master**
i.e., the Count of Armagnac   **43 As that**   **44 dower** marriage settlement

And so, my Lord Protector, see them guarded
And safely brought to Dover, wherein shipped,°
Commit them to the fortune of the sea.   50
    Exeunt [all but Winchester and the Legate].

Winchester. Stay, my Lord Legate; you shall first
    receive
The sum of money which I promisèd
Should be delivered to his Holiness
For clothing me in these grave ornaments.°

Legate. I will attend upon your lordship's leisure.   55

Winchester. [*Aside*] Now Winchester will not submit,
    I trow,
Or be inferior to the proudest peer.
Humphrey of Gloucester, thou shalt well perceive
That, neither in birth or for authority,
The bishop will be overborne by thee.   60
I'll either make thee stoop and bend thy knee,
Or sack this country with a mutiny.°   *Exeunt.*

[Scene II. *France. Plains in Anjou*].

*Enter Charles [the Dauphin], Burgundy, Alençon,
Bastard, Reignier, and Joan [la Pucelle, with forces].*

Dauphin. These news, my lords, may cheer our droop-
    ing spirits:
'Tis said the stout Parisians do revolt
And turn again unto the warlike French.

Alençon. Then march to Paris, royal Charles of
    France.
And keep not back your powers in dalliance.°   5

49 **shipped** embarked   54 **grave ornaments** symbols of high rank
62 **mutiny** rebellion   V.ii.5 **dalliance** idleness

Pucelle. Peace be amongst them, if they turn to us;
　　Else, ruin combat with their palaces!

Enter Scout.

Scout. Success unto our valiant general,
　　And happiness to his accomplices!

Dauphin. What tidings send our scouts? I prithee,
10　　speak.

Scout. The English army, that divided was
　　Into two parties, is now conjoined° in one,
　　And means to give you battle presently.

Dauphin. Somewhat too sudden, sirs, the warning is,
15　　But we will presently provide for them.

Burgundy. I trust the ghost of Talbot is not there;
　　Now he is gone, my lord, you need not fear.

Pucelle. Of all base passions, fear is most accursed.
　　Command the conquest, Charles, it shall be thine;
20　　Let Henry fret and all the world repine.°

Dauphin. Then on, my lords, and France be fortunate!
　　　　　　　　　　　　　　　　　　　Exeunt.

[Scene III. *Before Angiers.*]

Alarum. Excursions. Enter Joan la Pucelle.

Pucelle. The Regent° conquers, and the Frenchmen
　　fly.
　　Now help, ye charming° spells and periapts,°
　　And ye choice° spirits that admonish° me
　　And give me signs of future accidents.° *Thunder.*

12 **conjoined** united   20 **repine** complain   V.iii.1 **Regent** i.e., York
2 **charming** exercising magic power   2 **periapts** amulets   3 **choice**
excellent   3 **admonish** inform   4 **accidents** events

You speedy helpers, that are substitutes   5
Under the lordly monarch of the north,°
Appear and aid me in this enterprise.

Enter Fiends.

This speedy and quick appearance argues proof
Of your accustomed diligence to me.
Now, ye familiar spirits, that are culled°   10
Out of the powerful regions under earth,
Help me this once, that France may get° the field.
                    They walk, and speak not.
O, hold me not with silence over-long!
Where I was wont to feed you with my blood,
I'll lop a member° off and give it you   15
In earnest° of a further benefit,
So you do condescend to help me now.
                    They hang their heads.
No hope to have redress? My body shall
Pay recompense, if you will grant my suit.
                    They shake their heads.
Cannot my body nor blood-sacrifice   20
Entreat you to your wonted furtherance?°
Then take my soul; my body, soul, and all,
Before that England give the French the foil.°
                    They depart.
See, they forsake me! Now the time is come
That France must vail° her lofty plumèd crest   25
And let her head fall into England's lap.
My ancient° incantations are too weak,
And hell too strong for me to buckle with.
Now, France, thy glory droopeth to the dust. *Exit.*

Excursions. Burgundy and York fight hand to hand.
French fly, [pursued. York returns with La Pucelle
captive].

---

6 **monarch of the north** the devil (evil spirits were traditionally
thought to dwell in the regions of the north)   10 **culled** gathered
12 **get** win   15 **member** part of the body   16 **earnest** pledge   21
furtherance assistance   23 **the foil** defeat, repulse   25 **vail** lower
or take off in token of submission   27 **ancient** former

30 *York.* Damsel of France, I think I have you fast;
        Unchain your spirits now with spelling° charms
        And try if they can gain your liberty.
        A goodly prize, fit for the devil's grace!
        See, how the ugly witch doth bend her brows,
35   As if, with Circe,° she would change my shape!

    Pucelle. Changed to a worser shape thou canst not be.

    York. O, Charles the Dolphin is a proper man;
        No shape but his can please your dainty° eye.

    Pucelle. A plaguing° mischief light on Charles and
            thee!
40   And may ye both be suddenly surprised
        By bloody hands, in sleeping on your beds!

    York. Fell banning° hag, enchantress, hold thy
            tongue!

    Pucelle. I prithee, give me leave to curse awhile.

    York. Curse, miscreant, when thou comest to the
            stake.   *Exeunt.*

    Alarum. Enter Suffolk, with Margaret in his hand.

45 *Suffolk.* Be what thou wilt, thou art my prisoner.
                                        Gazes on her.
        O fairest beauty, do not fear nor fly!
        For I will touch thee but with reverent° hands;
        I kiss these fingers for eternal peace
        And lay them gently on thy tender side.
50   Who art thou? Say, that I may honor thee.

    Margaret. Margaret my name, and daughter to a
            king,
        The King of Naples, whosoe'er thou art.

    Suffolk. An earl I am, and Suffolk am I called.
        Be not offended, nature's miracle,

---

31 **spelling** spell-casting   35 **with Circe** like Circe (the sorceress in
the *Odyssey* who transformed men into beasts)   38 **dainty** fastidi-
ous   39 **plaguing** tormenting   42 **Fell banning** evil cursing   47
reverent respectful

Thou art allotted° to be ta'en by me: 55
So doth the swan her downy cygnets save,
Keeping them prisoner underneath her wings.
Yet if this servile usage° once offend,
Go and be free again as Suffolk's friend.

                      She is going.

O, stay! [*Aside*] I have no power to let her pass;   60
My hand would free her, but my heart says no.
As plays the sun upon the glassy° streams,
Twinkling another counterfeited° beam,
So seems this gorgeous beauty to mine eyes.
Fain would I woo her, yet I dare not speak;   65
I'll call for pen and ink, and write my mind.
Fie, De la Pole! disable° not thyself.
Hast not a tongue? Is she not here?
Wilt thou be daunted at a woman's sight?
Ay, beauty's princely majesty is such,   70
Confounds the tongue and makes the senses
    rough.°

Margaret. Say, Earl of Suffolk, if thy name be so,
    What ransom must I pay before I pass?
    For I perceive I am thy prisoner.

Suffolk. [*Aside*] How canst thou tell she will deny thy
    suit,   75
    Before thou make a trial of her love?

Margaret. Why speak'st thou not? What ransom must
    I pay?

Suffolk. [*Aside*] She's beautiful and therefore to be
    wooed;
    She is a woman, therefore to be won.

Margaret. Wilt thou accept of ransom, yea or no?   80

Suffolk. [*Aside*] Fond man, remember that thou hast
    a wife;
    Then how can Margaret be thy paramour?

---

55 **allotted** fated   58 **servile usage** unworthy treatment   62 **glassy**
smooth   63 **counterfeited** reflected   67 **disable** disparage   71 **rough**
dull

Margaret. I were best to leave him, for he will not
    hear.

Suffolk. [*Aside*] There all is marred; there lies a
    cooling card.°

85 *Margaret.* He talks at random; sure, the man is mad.

Suffolk. [*Still aside, but more loudly*] And yet a
    dispensation° may be had.

Margaret. And yet I would that you would answer
    me.

Suffolk. [*Aside*] I'll win this Lady Margaret. For
    whom?
    Why, for my king. [*Somewhat more loudly*] Tush,
    that's a wooden° thing!

90 *Margaret.* He talks of wood: it° is some carpenter.

Suffolk. [*Aside*] Yet so my fancy may be satisfied
    And peace establishèd between these realms.
    But there remains a scruple° in that too:
    For though her father be the King of Naples,
95   Duke of Anjou and Maine, yet is he poor,
    And our nobility will scorn the match.

Margaret. Hear ye, captain, are you not at leisure?

Suffolk. [*Aside*] It shall be so, disdain they ne'er so
    much:
    Henry is youthful and will quickly yield.
100   [*Aloud*] Madam, I have a secret to reveal.

Margaret. [*Aside*] What though I be enthralled?° he
    seems a knight,
    And will not any way dishonor me.

Suffolk. Lady, vouchsafe to listen what I say.

Margaret. [*Aside*] Perhaps I shall be rescued by the
    French,

---

84 **cooling card** something to cool my ardor   86 **dispensation** i.e.,
annulment of a previous marriage   89 **wooden** dull   90 **it** he   93
scruple difficulty   101 **enthralled** captured

And then I need not crave his courtesy.   *105*

Suffolk. Sweet madam, give me hearing in a cause.

Margaret. [*Aside*] Tush, women have been captivate
　　ere now.

Suffolk. Lady, wherefore talk you so?

Margaret. I cry you mercy,° 'tis but *quid* for *quo.*°

Suffolk. Say, gentle princess, would you not suppose   *110*
　　Your bondage happy, to be made a queen?

Margaret. To be a queen in bondage is more vile
　　Than is a slave in base servility,
　　For princes should be free.

Suffolk.　　　　　　　　And so shall you,
　　If happy England's royal king be free.   *115*

Margaret. Why, what concerns his freedom unto me?

Suffolk. I'll undertake to make thee Henry's queen,
　　To put a golden scepter in thy hand
　　And set a precious crown upon thy head,
　　If thou wilt condescend to be my—

Margaret.　　　　　　　　　　　　What?   *120*

Suffolk. His love.

Margaret. I am unworthy to be Henry's wife.

Suffolk. No, gentle madam, I unworthy am
　　To woo so fair a dame to be his wife,
　　And have no portion in° the choice myself.   *125*
　　How say you, madam, are ye so content?

Margaret. And if my father please, I am content.

Suffolk. Then call our captains and our colors forth.
　　And, madam, at your father's castle walls
　　We'll crave a parley, to confer with him.   *130*

---

109 cry you mercy beg your pardon　**109 quid for quo** even exchange, tit for tat　**125 no portion in** (1) no share in (2) nothing to
gain by

Sound [a parley.] Enter Reignier on the walls.

See, Reignier, see, thy daughter prisoner!

Reignier. To whom?

Suffolk.   To me.

Reignier.   Suffolk, what remedy?
I am a soldier and unapt° to weep
Or to exclaim on fortune's fickleness.

135 *Suffolk.* Yes, there is remedy enough, my lord:
Consent, and for thy honor give consent,
Thy daughter shall be wedded to my king,
Whom° I with pain° have wooed and won thereto,
And this her easy-held imprisonment
140 Hath gained thy daughter princely liberty.

Reignier. Speaks Suffolk as he thinks?

Suffolk.   Fair Margaret knows
That Suffolk doth not flatter, face,° or feign.

Reignier. Upon thy princely warrant, I descend
To give thee answer of thy just demand.

                                [Exit.]

145 *Suffolk.* And here I will expect° thy coming.

Trumpets sound. Enter Reignier.

Reignier. Welcome, brave earl, into our territories;
Command in Anjou what your honor pleases.

Suffolk. Thanks, Reignier, happy for° so sweet a
    child,
Fit to be made companion with a king.
150 What answer makes your grace unto my suit?

Reignier. Since thou dost deign to woo her little
    worth°
To be the princely bride of such a lord,
Upon condition I may quietly

133 **unapt** not ready   138 **Whom** i.e., Margaret   138 **pain** much
effort   142 **face** deceive   145 **expect** await   148 **for** in having   **151
her little worth** a lady of such modest rank and fortune

Enjoy mine own, the country Maine and Anjou,
Free from oppression or the stroke of war,   155
My daughter shall be Henry's, if he please.

Suffolk. That is her ransom; I deliver her,
And those two counties I will undertake
Your grace shall well and quietly enjoy.

Reignier. And I again, in Henry's royal name,   160
As deputy° unto that gracious king,
Give thee her hand, for sign of plighted faith.°

Suffolk. Reignier of France, I give thee kingly thanks
Because this is in traffic° of a king.
[*Aside*] And yet, methinks, I could be well content 165
To be mine own attorney° in this case.
[*Aloud*] I'll over then to England with this news,
And make this marriage to be solemnized.
So farewell, Reignier; set this diamond safe
In golden palaces, as it becomes.   170

Reignier. I do embrace thee, as I would embrace
The Christian prince, King Henry, were he here.

Margaret. Farewell, my lord; good wishes, praise, and
    prayers
Shall Suffolk ever have of Margaret.   *She is going.*

Suffolk. Farewell, sweet madam; but hark you,
    Margaret: 175
No princely commendations to my king?

Margaret. Such commendations as becomes a maid,
A virgin, and his servant, say to him.

Suffolk. Words sweetly placed and modestly di-
    rected.°
But, madam, I must trouble you again: 180
No loving token to his majesty?

Margaret. Yes, my good lord, a pure unspotted heart,
Never yet taint with love,° I send the king.

161 deputy i.e., Suffolk   162 plighted faith promise to marry   164
in traffic in negotiation   166 attorney pleader   179 directed uttered   183 taint with love tinged with immodest desire

Suffolk. And this withal.   *Kisses her.*

185 *Margaret.* That for thyself; I will not so presume
    To send such peevish tokens° to a king.

                    [*Exeunt Reignier and Margaret.*]

Suffolk. O, wert thou for myself! But, Suffolk, stay;
    Thou mayst not wander in that labyrinth;
    There Minotaurs° and ugly treasons lurk.
190 Solicit° Henry with her wondrous praise;
    Bethink thee on her virtues that surmount,
    And natural graces that extinguish° art;
    Repeat their semblance° often on the seas,
    That, when thou com'st to kneel at Henry's feet,
195 Thou mayst bereave° him of his wits with wonder.
                                            Exit.

[Scene IV. *Camp of the Duke of York in Anjou.*]

Enter York, Warwick, [and others].

York. Bring forth that sorceress condemned to burn.

    [*Enter La Pucelle, guarded, and a Shepherd.*]

Shepherd. Ah, Joan, this kills thy father's heart out-
        right!
    Have I sought° every country far and near,
    And now° it is my chance to find thee out,
    Must I behold thy timeless° cruel death?
    Ah, Joan, sweet daughter Joan, I'll die with thee!

---

186 **peevish tokens** foolish signs of affection   189 **Minotaurs** (alluding to the mythological monster of Crete, half-bull and half-
man, who was slain by Theseus)   190 **Solicit** allure   192 **extinguish** obscure by greater brilliancy   193 **Repeat their semblance**
remind yourself of their appearance   195 **bereave** dispossess
V.iv.3 **sought** searched   4 **now** now that   5 **timeless** untimely

Pucelle. Decrepit miser!° base ignoble wretch!
　I am descended of a gentler blood.
　Thou art no father nor no friend of mine.

Shepherd. Out, out!° My lords, and° please you, 'tis
　　not so.　　　　　　　　　　　　　　　　　　　　*10*
　I did beget her, all the parish knows;
　Her mother liveth yet, can testify
　She was the first fruit of my bachelorship.°

Warwick. Graceless! wilt thou deny thy parentage?

York. This argues what her kind of life hath been,　*15*
　Wicked and vile, and so her death concludes.

Shepherd. Fie, Joan, that thou wilt be so obstacle!°
　God knows thou art a collop° of my flesh,
　And for thy sake have I shed many a tear.
　Deny me not, I prithee, gentle Joan.　　　　　*20*

Pucelle. Peasant, avaunt!° You have suborned° this
　　man
　Of purpose to obscure° my noble birth.

Shepherd. 'Tis true, I gave a noble° to the priest
　The morn that I was wedded to her mother.
　Kneel down and take my blessing, good my girl.　*25*
　Wilt thou not stoop? Now cursèd be the time
　Of thy nativity! I would the milk
　Thy mother gave thee when thou suck'dst her
　　breast
　Had been a little ratsbane° for thy sake!
　Or else, when thou didst keep my lambs a-field,　*30*
　I wish some ravenous wolf had eaten thee!
　Dost thou deny thy father, cursèd drab?°
　O, burn her, burn her! hanging is too good.　*Exit.*

7 **miser** old wretch　10 **Out, out** alas　10 **and** if it　13 **first . . .
bachelorship** i.e., begotten out of wedlock (but the shepherd apparently is confused about the meaning of *bachelorship*)　17 **obstacle** obstinate (a malapropism)　18 **collop** piece　21 **avaunt** begone
21 **suborned** bribed　22 **obscure** conceal　23 **noble** gold coin
worth about ten shillings　29 **ratsbane** rat poison　32 **drab** prostitute

York. Take her away, for she hath lived too long,
35   To fill the world with vicious qualities.

Pucelle. First, let me tell you whom you have con-
    demned:
    Not me begotten of a shepherd swain
    But issued from the progeny of kings;
    Virtuous and holy, chosen from above,
40   By inspiration of celestial grace,
    To work exceeding miracles on earth.
    I never had to do with wicked spirits,
    But you, that are polluted with your lusts,
    Stained with the guiltless blood of innocents,
45   Corrupt and tainted with a thousand vices,
    Because you want the grace that others have,
    You judge it straight a thing impossible
    To compass° wonders but by help of devils.
    No, misconceivèd!° Joan of Arc hath been
50   A virgin from her tender infancy,
    Chaste and immaculate in very thought,
    Whose maiden blood, thus rigorously effused,°
    Will cry for vengeance at the gates of heaven.

York. Ay, ay; away with her to execution!

55 *Warwick.* And hark ye, sirs: because she is a maid,
    Spare for no° faggots, let there be enow;°
    Place barrels of pitch upon the fatal stake,
    That so her torture may be shortenèd.

Pucelle. Will nothing turn your unrelenting hearts?
60   Then, Joan, discover thine infirmity,°
    That warranteth by law to be thy privilege.
    I am with child, ye bloody homicides;
    Murder not then the fruit within my womb,
    Although ye hale° me to a violent death.

York. Now heaven forfend!° the holy maid with
65   child!

48 **compass** accomplish 49 **misconceivèd** deceived person 52
rigorously effused cruelly shed 56 **Spare for no** do not spare
56 **enow** enough 60 **discover thine infirmity** reveal your bodily un-
fitness 64 **hale** drag 65 **forfend** forbid

Warwick. The greatest miracle that e'er ye wrought.
  Is all your strict preciseness° come to this?

York. She and the Dolphin have been juggling;°
  I did imagine° what would be her refuge.°

Warwick. Well, go to;° we'll have no bastards live,   70
  Especially since Charles must father it.

Pucelle. You are deceived, my child is none of his,
  It was Alençon that enjoyed my love.

York. Alençon! that notorious Machiavel!°
  It dies, and if it had a thousand lives.   75

Pucelle. O, give me leave, I have deluded you:
  'Twas neither Charles nor yet the duke I named,
  But Reignier, king of Naples, that prevailed.°

Warwick. A married man! that's most intolerable.

York. Why, here's a girl!° I think she knows not well,   80
  There were so many, whom she may accuse.

Warwick. It's sign she hath been liberal and free.°

York. And yet, forsooth,° she is a virgin pure.
  Strumpet, thy words condemn thy brat and thee.
  Use no entreaty, for it is in vain.   85

Pucelle. Then lead me hence; with whom I leave my
     curse:
  May never glorious sun reflex° his beams
  Upon the country where you make abode,
  But darkness and the gloomy shade of death
  Environ you, till mischief and despair   90
  Drive you to break your necks or hang yourselves!
                  Exit, [*guarded*].

---

67 **preciseness** pretense of scrupulousness 68 **juggling** playing
tricks 69 **imagine** wonder 69 **refuge** excuse 70 **go to** come,
come 74 **Machiavel** intriguer (after Niccolò Machiavelli, author
of *The Prince*) 78 **prevailed** i.e., gained her love 80 **girl** wench
82 **liberal and free** (used ironically, since a lady was supposed to
have these qualities, without Joan's implied wantonness) 83 **forsooth** in truth 87 **reflex** reflect

York. Break thou in pieces and consume to ashes,
Thou foul accursèd minister° of hell.

Enter Cardinal [Beaufort, Bishop of Winchester].

Winchester. Lord Regent, I do greet your excellence
95   With letters of commission from the king.
For know, my lords, the states of Christendom,
Moved with remorse of° these outrageous broils,
Have earnestly implored a general peace
Betwixt our nation and the aspiring French,
100 And here at hand the Dolphin and his train°
Approacheth, to confer about some matter.

York. Is all our travail° turned to this effect?
After the slaughter of so many peers,
So many captains, gentlemen, and soldiers,
105 That in this quarrel have been overthrown
And sold their bodies for their country's benefit,
Shall we at last conclude effeminate peace?
Have we not lost most part of all the towns,
By treason, falsehood, and by treachery,
110 Our great progenitors had conquerèd?
O, Warwick, Warwick! I foresee with grief
The utter loss of all the realm of France.

Warwick. Be patient, York; if we conclude a peace,
It shall be with such strict and severe covenants°
115 As little shall the Frenchmen gain thereby.

*Enter Charles [the Dauphin], Alençon, Bastard,
Reignier, [and others].*

Dauphin. Since, lords of England, it is thus agreed
That peaceful truce shall be proclaimed in France,
We come to be informèd by yourselves
What the conditions of that league must be.

120 *York.* Speak, Winchester, for boiling choler chokes
The hollow passage of my poisoned° voice
By sight of these our baleful enemies.

93 **minister** agent   97 **remorse of** sorrow at   100 **train** retinue   102
travail labor, trouble   114 **covenants** conditions   121 **poisoned** sickened as though with poison

Winchester. Charles, and the rest, it is enacted thus:
    That, in regard King Henry gives consent,
    Of° mere compassion and of lenity,   *125*
    To ease your country of distressful war
    And suffer you to breathe in fruitful peace,
    You shall become true liegemen° to his crown.
    And, Charles, upon condition thou wilt swear
    To pay him tribute, and submit thyself,   *130*
    Thou shalt be placed as viceroy under him,
    And still enjoy thy regal dignity.

Alençon. Must he be then as shadow of himself?
    Adorn his temples with a coronet,
    And yet, in substance and authority,   *135*
    Retain but privilege of a private man?
    This proffer is absurd and reasonless.

Dauphin. 'Tis known already that I am possessed
    With more than half the Gallian territories,
    And therein reverenced for° their lawful king: *140*
    Shall I, for lucre° of the rest unvanquished,
    Detract so much from that prerogative°
    As to be called but viceroy of the whole?
    No, lord ambassador, I'll rather keep
    That which I have than, coveting for more,   *145*
    Be cast° from possibility of all.

York. Insulting Charles! hast thou by secret means
    Used intercession to obtain a league,°
    And, now the matter grows to compromise,
    Stand'st thou aloof upon comparison?°   *150*
    Either accept the title thou usurp'st,
    Of° benefit proceeding from our king
    And not of any challenge of desert,°
    Or we will plague thee with incessant wars.

Reignier. My lord, you do not well in obstinacy   *155*

---

125 **Of** out of   128 **liegemen** vassals   140 **reverenced for** honored
as   141 **lucre** gain   142 **prerogative** preeminence (as king)   146
cast driven   148 **league** alliance   150 **upon comparison** weighing
the odds   152 **Of** through   153 **challenge of desert** claim that it
is yours by right

To cavil° in the course of this contract:
If once it be neglected, ten to one
We shall not find like opportunity.

Alençon. To say the truth, it is your policy
160   To save your subjects from such massacre
And ruthless slaughters as are daily seen
By our proceeding in hostility;
And therefore take this compact of° a truce—
[*Aside*] Although you break it when your pleasure
    serves,

Warwick. How say'st thou, Charles? Shall our condi-
165   tion stand?

Dauphin. It shall;
Only reserved, you claim no interest
In any of our towns of garrison.

York. Then swear allegiance to his majesty,
170   As thou art knight, never to disobey
Nor be rebellious to the crown of England,
Thou, nor thy nobles, to the crown of England.

[*The Dauphin and French nobles give signs of fealty.*]

So, now dismiss your army when ye please;
Hang up your ensigns,° let your drums be still,
175   For here we entertain° a solemn peace.
                                        Exeunt.

[Scene V. *London. The royal palace.*]

Enter Suffolk in conference with the King, Gloucester,
and Exeter.

King. Your wondrous rare description, noble earl,
  Of beauteous Margaret hath astonished me.
  Her virtues, gracèd with external gifts,
  Do breed love's settled passions in my heart,
  And like as rigor° of tempestuous gusts   5
  Provokes° the mightiest hulk° against the tide,
  So am I driven by breath° of her renown
  Either to suffer shipwreck or arrive
  Where I may have fruition of her love.

Suffolk. Tush, my good lord, this superficial° tale   10
  Is but a preface of her worthy praise.
  The chief perfections of that lovely dame,
  Had I sufficient skill to utter them,
  Would make a volume of enticing lines,
  Able to ravish any dull conceit;°   15
  And, which is more, she is not so divine,
  So full replete with choice of all delights,
  But with as humble lowliness of mind
  She is content to be at your command;
  Command, I mean, of virtuous chaste intents,°   20
  To love and honor Henry as her lord.

King. And otherwise will Henry ne'er presume.
  Therefore, my Lord Protector, give consent
  That Margaret may be England's royal queen.

V.v.5 rigor violence **6 Provokes** drives on **6 hulk** ship **7 breath**
utterance **10 superficial** touching only the surface **15 ravish . . .**
conceit i.e., enchant even the dullest imagination **20 intents** intentions

25 *Gloucester*. So should I give consent to flatter° sin.
      You know, my lord, your highness is betrothed
      Unto another lady° of esteem.
      How shall we then dispense with that contract,
      And not deface your honor with reproach?

30 *Suffolk*. As doth a ruler with unlawful oaths,
      Or one that, at a triumph° having vowed
      To try his strength, forsaketh yet the lists°
      By reason of his adversary's odds.°
      A poor earl's daughter is unequal odds,
35   And therefore may be broke° without offense.

    Gloucester. Why, what, I pray, is Margaret more than
        that?
      Her father is no better than an earl,
      Although in glorious titles he excel.

    Suffolk. Yes, my lord, her father is a king,
40   The King of Naples and Jerusalem,
      And of such great authority in France
      As his alliance will confirm our peace
      And keep the Frenchmen in allegiance.

    Gloucester. And so the Earl of Armagnac may do
45   Because he is near kinsman unto Charles.

    Exeter. Beside, his wealth doth warrant a liberal
        dower,
      Where Reignier sooner will receive than give.

    Suffolk. A dower, my lords! disgrace not so your king,
      That he should be so abject, base, and poor,
50   To choose for wealth and not for perfect love.
      Henry is able to enrich his queen
      And not to seek a queen to make him rich.
      So worthless peasants bargain for their wives,
      As market men for oxen, sheep, or horse.
55   Marriage is a matter of more worth

25 **flatter** condone   27 **another lady** i.e., the daughter of the Earl
of Armagnac   31 **triumph** tournament   32 **lists** tournament ground
33 **odds** inferiority   35 **broke** i.e., the pledge of marriage may be
broken

Than to be dealt in by attorneyship;°
Not whom we will, but whom his grace affects,
Must be companion of his nuptial bed.
And therefore, lords, since° he affects her most,
Most of all these reasons bindeth us,   60
In our opinions she should be preferred.
For what is wedlock forcèd but a hell,
An age of discord and continual strife?
Whereas the contrary bringeth bliss,
And is a pattern of celestial peace.   65
Whom should we match with Henry, being a king,
But Margaret, that is daughter to a king?
Her peerless feature,° joinèd with her birth,
Approves° her fit for none but for a king.
Her valiant courage and undaunted spirit,   70
More than in women commonly is seen,
Will answer our hope in issue of a king;
For Henry, son unto a conqueror,
Is likely to beget more conquerors,
If with a lady of so high resolve   75
As is fair Margaret he be linked in love.
Then yield, my lords, and here conclude with me
That Margaret shall be queen, and none but she.

King. Whether it be through force of your report,
My noble Lord of Suffolk, or for that   80
My tender youth was never yet attaint°
With any passion of inflaming love,
I cannot tell; but this I am assured,
I feel such sharp dissension in my breast,
Such fierce alarums both of hope and fear,   85
As I am sick with working of my thoughts.
Take, therefore, shipping; post, my lord, to France;
Agree to any covenants, and procure
That Lady Margaret do vouchsafe to come
To cross the seas to England and be crowned   90
King Henry's faithful and anointed queen.

---

56 **attorneyship** proxy   59 **since** the fact that   68 **feature** comeli-
ness   69 **Approves** proves   81 **attaint** stained

For your expenses and sufficient charge,°
Among the people gather up a tenth.°
Be gone, I say, for, till you do return,
95 I rest° perplexèd with a thousand cares.
And you, good uncle, banish all offense;
If you do censure° me by what you were,
Not what you are, I know it will excuse
This sudden execution° of my will.
100 And so, conduct me where, from company,
I may revolve and ruminate° my grief.   *Exit.*

Gloucester. Ay, grief, I fear me, both at first and last.

Exit Gloucester [with Exeter].

Suffolk. Thus Suffolk hath prevailed, and thus he
goes,
As did the youthful Paris once to Greece,
105 With hope to find the like event° in love,
But·prosper better than the Trojan did.
Margaret shall now be queen, and rule the king;
But I will rule both her, the king, and realm. *Exit.*

FINIS

92 **sufficient charge** adequate money to meet costs   93 **tenth** (a
levy of a tenth of the value of personal property, collected to meet
unusual expenses such as a royal marriage)   95 **rest** remain   97
censure judge   99 **execution** carrying into effect   101 **revolve and
ruminate** consider and meditate upon   105 **event** result

Textual Note

The First Part of Henry the Sixth is preserved only in the Folio of 1623, the basis of the present edition. Though acted infrequently after Shakespeare's lifetime, apparently the drama was originally well received. In the epilogue to Shakespeare's *Henry V*, the Chorus asks the spectators to applaud this more recent work by reminding them of the company's earlier dramatizations of the reign of Henry VI:

> Which oft our stage hath shown; and for their sake,
> In your fair minds let this acceptance take.

It is even likely that in its earliest production *1 Henry VI* was the theatrical hit of the year. On March 3, 1592, the producer Philip Henslowe recorded in his diary that the first performance of a new (or refurbished) play called "harey the vj." had grossed £3.16s.8d., a sum indicating an exceptionally profitable opening. Over the next ten months this work was acted at least fourteen, perhaps fifteen, additional times. It may be that the patriotic theme appealed strongly to a London audience still exulting over the debacle of the Spanish Armada; for the heroic death of Lord Talbot in the fourth act, as Thomas Nashe wrote during the same year in *Pierce Penniless,* had been found deeply moving by "ten thousand spectators at least (at several times), who, in the tragedian that represents his person, imagine they behold him fresh bleeding."

The entry in Henslowe's diary and Nashe's allusion in his pamphlet to "Talbot (the terror of the French)" suggest that the play in question may have been *1 Henry VI*. Still, some doubt must remain whether this particular version was the same as that printed in the Folio, and whether Shakespeare had participated in its composition. With few exceptions, however, modern Shakespearean critics have assumed that *1 Henry VI* as we know it does come, along with the second and third parts of the trilogy, from Shakespeare's apprentice years as a playwright. In the absence of any positive evidence to the contrary, it thus seems reasonable to declare for late 1591 or early 1592 as the likeliest date of original composition for the play printed in the Folio and to presume that it is substantially, perhaps entirely, from the hand of Shakespeare.

The Folio is the only authority and affords a remarkably clear text, apart from a few baffling words and some apparently mangled lines of verse. In the present edition, therefore, the temptation to emend the original has been resisted as much as possible. Only two words to fill apparent lacunae have been supplied from consultation with the later Folios. These are *Nero* (I.iv.95) and *sir* (II.iv.-132). Both of these are bracketed in the text and their sources given in the notes below. Without editorial comment, punctuation and spelling have been modernized (though "Dolphin" is retained in the dialogue), names prefixed to speeches and appearing in stage directions expanded and regularized, act and scene divisions translated where the Folio gives them in Latin, and obvious typographical errors corrected.

In the few instances where lines of verse are improperly divided in the Folio, they have been rearranged; all such corrections are noted in the table below. Occasionally when the printers of the Folio may seem to have divided a single line into two verses, it is quite clear that the line was too long for the space available, and was simply broken at a clause, rather than at the end of the column. Because the stage directions in the original are on the whole clear and amply descriptive, they have been reproduced with a minimum of emendations and additions;

wherever changes have been made, they are enclosed in square brackets. In dividing acts and scenes the Folio is deficient: no scene divisions are given for Acts I and II; Act III is correctly divided into four scenes; Act IV is not only too long—since nothing but the final scene is left for Act V—but within it the scenes are also inaccurately divided. The act and scene divisions of the present edition are therefore those of the Globe text; wherever they differ from those of the Folio, they are enclosed in square brackets. The table that follows includes emendations and corrections of the Folio text. The altered reading appears first, in italics; the original follows, in roman. Where a Folio reading is retained, but seems extremely dubious, the word is given in roman, and commentary or suggested emendation is placed within square brackets.

I.i.94 *Reignier* Reynold   96 *crownèd* crown'd   132 *vanward* Vauward

I.ii.30 *bred* breed   99 fine [so F, but later editors, following mention in Holinshed's *Chronicles* of a pattern of "five" fleurs-de-lis on the sword, emend to *five;* conceivably the *n* in F is a mistakenly inverted *u* (i.e., for *v*)]   103s.d. *la* de   113 *rites* rights   132 *enterèd* entred

I.iii.29 *Humphrey* Vmpheir

I.iv.10 Went [so F, but Tyrwhitt's conjecture *Wont* is accepted by some modern editors]   16–18 [two lines in F, but perhaps should be printed as three, divided after *watched, them,* and *longer*]   29 *ransomèd* ransom'd   69s.d. *fall* falls   95 *Nero* [not in F; conjectured by Malone from the Second Folio reading "and *Nero* like will" for "and like thee"]   101 *la* de

I.v.s.d. *la* de

I.vi.3 *la* de   6 garden [so F, but *were* in line 7 suggests that the intended reading may have been *gardens*]   29 *la* de

II.i.7 s.d. drums . . . march [so F, but sounding drums seems a most peculiar way of beginning a surprise attack]   29 *all together* altogether   77 [F reads *Exeunt* here, but the following stage direction renders the word superfluous]   77s.d. *an* a

II.ii.6 *center* Centure   20 *Arc* Acre   59 *Whispers* [printed at end of line in F]

II.iii.11–12 [printed as one line in F]

II.iv.s.d. *Vernon, and another Lawyer* and others   117 whipped [so F, but Second Folio and all subsequent editions read *wiped*]   132 *sir* [not in F; supplied by Second Folio]

II.v.121 s.d. *Exeunt . . . Mortimer* Exit   129 will [so F, though modern editors, following Theobald, conjecture *ill* (i.e., turn my injuries to my benefit)]

III.i.52–53 [most modern editions reassign line 52 to Somerset and line 53 to Warwick]   164 all [so F, but the word is superfluous for both sense and meter]   200 *lose* loose

III.ii.50–51 [printed as three (metrically defective) lines in F, divided after *gray-beard, death,* and *chair*]   59s.d. *The English* They   103s.d. *Exeunt . . . Attendants* Exit   123 *gleeks* glikes

IV.i.s.d. *Exeter . . . Paris* and Gouernor Exeter   173s.d. *Flourish* [apparently misplaced in F in s.d. that follows line 181]

IV.ii. *Before Bordeaux* [supplied by s.d. in F]   3 *calls* call   34 *due* dew   50 *moody-mad* moodie mad

IV.iii.20 *waist* waste

IV.iv.16 regions [so F, but most modern editors emend to *legions*]

IV.vi.18 *encounterèd* encountred

IV.vii.96 s.d. *Exeunt* Exit

V.i. *Scene I* Scena secunda

V.ii. *Scene II* Scena Tertia

V.iii.s.d. *la* de   44 *comest* comst   57 *her* his   179 *modestly* modestie   184s.d. *Kisses* Kisse   188, 195 *mayst* mayest   190 *wondrous* wonderous   192 *And* Mad

V.iv.s.d. *and others* Shepheard, Pucell [who obviously enter after line 1]   49 *Arc* Aire   58 *shortenèd* shortned   60 *discover* discouet   93 s.d. [placed in F after line 91]

V.v. *Scene V* Actus Quintus

The Sources of
Henry VI, Part One

For the plot of *1 Henry VI* Shakespeare drew upon at least four English chronicle histories. His chief sources are Edward Hall's *The Union of the Two Noble and Illustre Families of Lancaster and York* (1548) and the second edition of Raphael Holinshed's *Chronicles of England, Scotland, and Ireland* (1587). For a few details not found in Hall or Holinshed he also consulted the *Chronicles* of Robert Fabyan (1516) and Richard Grafton (1569), the latter substantially a reprint of Hall. Some of the best scenes in the play, however, such as the quarrel of the roses in the Temple Garden, appear to have been invented by the playwright himself.

Although Geoffrey Bullough in his *Narrative and Dramatic Sources of Shakespeare* inclines to Hall as the principal source, in many scenes *1 Henry VI* appears to follow more closely Holinshed's account, which is largely derived from Hall without the latter's invented orations, amplification of detail, and attempts at an eloquence commensurate with the grandeur of his theme. But since Shakespeare improvised so freely upon his source materials, in most episodes of the play it is not possible to determine whether his immediate inspiration is Hall or Holinshed.

In view of this uncertainty, I have decided mainly to quote from Holinshed, to whom Shakespeare turned frequently in composing several other plays based upon British and Scottish history, but to give the account of Talbot's death in Hall's words, so that the reader may gain some idea of the elevated style of the source upon which Shakespeare obviously relied for this particular episode. In order that the reader may also acquire some sense of Shakespeare's juggling of historical chronology to suit his dramatic purposes, the selections are printed below in the sequence in which they occur in Holinshed, with both the actual historical dates and the scenes to which they contribute indicated in square brackets prefixed to the quotations.

RAPHAEL HOLINSHED

from *Chronicles of England, Scotland, and Ireland* (1587)

[1422: I.i] After that death had bereft the world of
that noble prince King Henry the Fifth, his only son
Prince Henry, being of the age of nine months, or there-
abouts, with the sound of trumpets was openly proclaimed
King of England and France the thirtieth day of August,
by the name of Henry the Sixth; in the year of the world
five thousand three hundred eighty and nine, after the
birth of our Savior 1422, about the twelfth year of the
Emperor Frederick the Third, the fortieth and two, and
last, of Charles the Sixth, and the third year of Murdoch's
regiment (after his father Robert) governor of Scotland.
The custody of this young prince was appointed to
Thomas, Duke of Exeter, and to Henry Beaufort, Bishop
of Winchester. The Duke of Bedford was deputed Regent
of France, and the Duke of Gloucester was ordained Protector of England; who, taking upon him that office, called
to him wise and grave councillors, by whose advice he
provided and took order as well for the good government
of the realm and subjects of the same at home, as also
for the maintenance of the wars abroad, and further conquest to be made in France, appointing valiant and expert
captains, which should be ready when need required. Besides this, he gathered great sums of money to maintain

men of war, and left nothing forgotten that might advance
the good estate of the realm.

While these things were a-doing in England, the Duke
of Bedford, Regent of France, studied most earnestly, not
only to keep and well order the countries by King Henry
late conquered, but also determined not to leave off war
and travail, till Charles the Dauphin (which was now
afoot, because King Charles his father in the month of
October in this present year was departed to God) should
either be subdued, or brought to obeisance. And surely
the death of this King Charles caused alterations in
France. For a great many of the nobility which before,
either for fear of the English puissance, or for the love of
this King Charles (whose authority they followed) held
on the English part, did now revolt to the Dauphin, with
all endeavor to drive the English nation out of the French
territories. Whereto they were the more earnestly bent,
and thought it a thing of greater facility, because of King
Henry's young years; whom (because he was a child)
they esteemed not, but with one consent revolted from
their sworn fealty: as the recorder of the Englishmen's
battles with foreign nations very aptly doth note, saying:

> *Hic Franci puerum regem neglectui habentes*
> *Desciscunt, violatque fidem gens perfida sacro*
> *Consilio ante datam.*

[Here the French revolt, holding in scorn the boy king,
and this perfidious race violates allegiance hitherto
granted in holy council.]

The Duke of Bedford being greatly moved with these
sudden changes, fortified his towns both with garrisons of
men, munition, and victuals, assembled also a great army
of Englishmen and Normans, and so effectuously exhorted
them to continue faithful to their liege and lawful lord,
young King Henry, that many of the French captains willingly sware to King Henry fealty and obedience, by whose
example the communalty did the same. Thus the people
quieted, and the country established in order, nothing was
minded but war, and nothing spoken of but conquest.

The Dauphin, which lay the same time in the city of Poitiers, after his father's decease, caused himself to be proclaimed King of France, by the name of Charles the Seventh: and in good hope to recover his patrimony, with an haughty courage preparing war, assembled a great army; and first the war began by light skirmishes, but after it grew into main battles. . . .

[1425: I.iii] Somewhat before this season fell a great division in the realm of England, which of a sparkle was like to have grown to a great flame. For whether the Bishop of Winchester called Henry Beaufort, son to John, Duke of Lancaster, by his third wife, envied the authority of Humphrey, Duke of Gloucester, Protector of the realm; or whether the duke disdained at the riches and pompous estate of the bishop: sure it is that the whole realm was troubled with them and their partakers, so that the citizens of London were fain to keep daily and nightly watches, and to shut up their shops for fear of that which was doubted to have issued of their assembling of people about them. The Archbishop of Canterbury and the Duke of Coimbra, called the Prince of Portugal, rode eight times in one day between the two parties, and so the matter was stayed for a time. But the Bishop of Winchester, to clear himself of blame so far as he might, and to charge his nephew the Lord Protector with all the fault, wrote a letter to the Regent of France, the tenor whereof ensueth.

The Bishop of Winchester's Letter Excusatory.
Right high and mighty prince, and my right noble and, after one, lievest lord, I recommend me unto you with all my heart. And as you desire the welfare of the king, our sovereign lord, and of his realms of England and France, your own health, and ours also: so haste you hither. For by my truth, if you tarry, we shall put this land in adventure with a field; such a brother you have here, God make him a good man. For your wisdom knoweth that the profit of France standeth in the welfare of England, etc. Written in great haste on All Hallowen Even. By your true servant to my life's end, Henry Winchester.

The Duke of Bedford being sore grieved with these news, constituted the Earl of Warwick, which was lately come into France with six thousand men, his lieutenant in the French dominions and in the Duchy of Normandy; and so with a small company, he with the duchess his wife returned again over the seas into England, and the tenth day of January he was with all solemnity received into London, to whom the citizens gave a pair of basins of silver and gilt, and a thousand marks in money. Then from London he rode to Westminster and was lodged in the king's palace. [1426: III.i] The five and twentieth day of March after his coming to London, a parliament began at the town of Leicester, where the Duke of Bedford openly rebuked the lords in general, because that they in the time of war, through their privy malice and inward grudge, had almost moved the people to war and commotion, in which time all men ought or should be of one mind, heart, and consent: requiring them to defend, serve, and dread their sovereign lord King Henry, in performing his conquest in France, which was in manner brought to conclusion. In this parliament the Duke of Gloucester laid certain articles to the Bishop of Winchester his charge, the which with the answers hereafter do ensue, as followeth. . . .

. . . And when this was done [the rivals required to become reconciled by the arbitrators of their dispute], it was decreed by the same arbitrators that every each of my Lord of Gloucester, and Winchester, should take either other by the hand, in the presence of the king and all the parliament, in sign and token of good love and accord, the which was done, and the parliament adjourned till after Easter.

At this reconciliation, such as love peace rejoiced (sith it is a foul and pernicious thing for private men, much more for noblemen, to be at variance, sith upon them depend many in affections diverse, whereby factions might grow to the shedding of blood), though others, to whom contention and heartgrudge is delight, wished to see the uttermost mischief that might thereof ensue, which

is the utter overthrow and desolation of populous tribes,
even as with a little sparkle whole houses are many times
consumed to ashes, as the old proverb saith, and that
very well and aptly:

Sola scintilla perit haec domus aut domus illa.

[Gone is this house or that with a single spark.]

But when the great fire of this dissension between these
two noble personages was thus by the arbitrators (to their
knowledge and judgment) utterly quenched out, and laid
under board, all other controversies between other lords,
taking part with one party or the other, were appeased
and brought to concord, so that for joy the king caused a
solemn feast to be kept on Whitsunday; on which day he
created Richard Plantagenet, son and heir to the Earl of
Cambridge (whom his father at Southampton had put to
death, as before ye have heard) Duke of York, not foreseeing that this preferment should be his destruction, nor
that his seed should of his generation be the extreme end
and final conclusion. . . .

[1427: V.i] After that the Duke of Bedford had set all
things in good order in England, he took leave of the
king, and together with his wife returned into France, first
landing at Calais, where the Bishop of Winchester (that
also passed the seas with him) received the habit, hat,
and dignity of a cardinal, with all ceremonies to it appertaining: which promotion, the late k[ing] right deeply
piercing into the unrestrainable ambitious mind of the
man, that even from his youth was ever to check at the
highest, and also right well ascertained with what intolerable pride his head should soon be swollen under such a
hat, did therefore all his life long keep this prelate back
from that presumptuous estate. But now the king being
young and the Regent his friend, he obtained his purpose,
to his great profit, and the impoverishing of the spirituality
of this realm. For by a bull legatine, which he purchased
from Rome, he gathered so much treasure that no man

in manner had money but he: so that he was called the rich Cardinal of Winchester. . . .

[1428: I.iv] After this, in the month of September the earl came before the city of Orleans and planted his siege on the one side of the River of Loire; but before his coming, the Bastard of Orleans, the bishop of the city, and a great number of Scots, hearing of the earl's intent, made divers fortifications about the town and destroyed the suburbs, in which were twelve parish churches and four orders of friars. They cut also down all the vines, trees, and bushes within five leagues of the city, so that the Englishmen should have neither refuge nor succor.

After the siege had continued full three weeks, the Bastard of Orleans issued out of the gate of the bridge and fought with the Englishmen; but they received him with so fierce and terrible strokes, that he was with all his company compelled to retire and flee back into the city. But the Englishmen followed so fast, in killing and taking of their enemies, that they entered with them.

The bulwark of the bridge, with a great tower standing at the end of the same, was taken incontinently by the Englishmen, who behaved themselves right valiantly under the conduct of their courageous captain, as at this assault, so in divers skirmishes against the French, partly to keep possession of that which Henry the Fifth had by his magnanimity and puissance achieved, as also to enlarge the same. But all helped not. For who can hold that which will away? In so much that some cities by fraudulent practices, other some by martial prowess, were recovered by the French, to the great discouragement of the English and the appalling of their spirits; whose hope was now dashed partly by their great losses and discomfitures (as after you shall hear), but chiefly by the death of the late deceased Henry, their victorious king, as Chr[istopher] Ockland very truly and agreeably to the story noteth:

> *Delphinus comitesque eius fera proelia tentant,*
> *Fraude domi capiunt alias, virtute receptae*
> *Sunt urbes aliae quaedam, sublapsa refertur*

Anglum spes retro, languescere pectora dicas,
Quippe erat Henricus quintus, dux strenuus olim,
Mortuus: hinc damni gravior causa atque doloris.

[The Dauphin and his counts essay fierce battles:
through treachery they capture some cities at home,
through valor some other cities are recovered. The
hope of the English is reported to have declined; you
would say it languished in their breasts. To be sure,
Henry the Fifth, once an energetic leader, was dead:
hence more grievous the cause of the loss and the
sorrow.]

In this conflict, many Frenchmen were taken, but more
were slain, and the keeping of the tower and bulwark was
committed to William Glasdale, Esquire. By the taking of
this bridge the passage was stopped, that neither men nor
victuals could go or come by that way. After this, the earl
caused certain bulwarks to be made round about the town,
casting trenches between the one and the other, laying
ordnance in every place where he saw that any battery
might be devised. When they within saw that they were
environed with fortresses and ordnance, they laid gun
against gun, and fortified towers against bulwarks, and
within cast new rampiers, and fortified themselves as
strongly as might be devised.

The Bastard of Orleans and the Hire were appointed
to see the walls and watches kept, and the bishop saw
that the inhabitants within the city were put in good order,
and that victuals were not vainly spent. In the tower that
was taken at the bridge end (as before you have heard)
there was an high chamber, having a grate full of bars of
iron, by the which a man might look all the length of the
bridge into the city; at which grate many of the chief
captains stood many times, viewing the city and devising
in what place it was best to give the assault. They within
the city well perceived this tooting hole and laid a piece
of ordnance directly against the window.

It so chanced that the nine and fiftieth day after the
siege was laid the Earl of Salisbury, Sir Thomas Gargrave,

and William Glasdale, with divers other went into the said
tower, and so into the high chamber, and looked out at
the grate, and within a short space the son of the master-
gunner, perceiving men looking out at the window, took his
match (as his father had taught him who was gone down
to dinner) and fired the gun; the shot whereof brake, and
shivered the iron bars of the grate, so that one of the same
bars strake the earl so violently on the head, that it struck
away one of his eyes and the side of his cheek. Sir Thomas
Gargrave was likewise stricken and died within two days.

The earl was conveyed to Meung on Loire, where after
eight days he likewise departed this world, whose body
was conveyed into England with all funeral appointment,
and buried at Bisham by his progenitors, leaving behind
him an only daughter named Alice, married to Richard
Neville, son to Ralph, Earl of Westmorland, of whom
more shall be said hereafter. The damage that the realm
of England received by the loss of this noble man manifestly appeared, in that immediately after his death the
prosperous good luck which had followed the English
nation began to decline, and the glory of their victories
gotten in the parties beyond the sea fell in decay.

[1429: I.ii] In time of this siege at Orleans (French
stories say), the first week of March, 1428 [i.e., 1429],
unto Charles the Dauphin at Chinon, as he was in very
great care and study how to wrestle against the English
nation, by one Peter Baudricourt, captain of Vaucouleur
(made after Marshal of France by the Dauphin's creation) was carried a young wench of an eighteen years
old, called Joan Are [Arc], by name of her father (a sorry
shepherd) James of Are, and Isabel her mother, brought
up poorly in their trade of keeping cattle, born at Domremy (therefore reported by Bale: Joan Domremy) upon
Meuse in Lorraine within the diocese of Toul. Of favor
was she counted likesome, of person strongly made and
manly, of courage great, hardy, and stout withal, an un-
derstander of councils though she were not at them, great
semblance of chastity both of body and behavior, the
name of Jesus in her mouth about all her businesses,

humble, obedient, and fasting divers days in the week. A
person (as their books make her) raised up by power
divine only for succor to the French estate then deeply in
distress, in whom, for planting a credit the rather, first
the company that toward the Dauphin did conduct her,
through places all dangerous as holden by the English,
where she never was afore, all the way and by nighter-
tale safely did she lead; then at the Dauphin's sending by
her assignment, from Saint Katherine's Church of Fierbois
in Touraine (where she never had been and knew not) in
a secret place there among old iron, appointed she her
sword to be sought out and brought her, that with five
flower-de-lices was graven on both sides, wherewith she
fought and did many slaughters by her own hands. On
warfare rode she in armor cap-a-pie and mustered as a
man, before her an ensign all white, wherein was Jesus
Christ painted with a flower-de-lice in his hand.

Unto the Dauphin in his gallery when first she was
brought, and he shadowing himself behind, setting other
gay lords before him to try her cunning, from all the company with a salutation (that indeed mars all the matter)
she picked him out alone; who thereupon had her to the
end of the gallery, where she held him an hour in secret
and private talk that of his privy chamber was thought
very long, and therefore would have broken it off; but he
made them a sign to let her say on. In which (among
other) as likely it was, she set out unto him the singular
feats (forsooth) given her to understand by revelation
divine, that in virtue of that sword she should achieve,
which were: how with honor and victory she would raise
the siege at Orleans, set him in state of the crown of
France, and drive the English out of the country, thereby
he to enjoy the kingdom alone. Hereupon he heartened at
full, indeed appointed her a sufficient army with absolute
power to lead them, and they obediently to do as she
bade them. Then fell she to work, and first defeated the
siege at Orleans, by and by encouraged him to crown himself King of France at Rheims, that a little before from
the English she had won. Thus after pursued she many
bold enterprises to our great displeasure a two year to-

gether, for the time she kept in state until she were taken
and for heresy and witchery burned, as in particularities
hereafter followeth. But in her prime time she, armed
at all points like a jolly captain, rode from Poitiers to
Blois, and there found men of war, victuals, and munition ready to be conveyed to Orleans.

Here was it known that the Englishmen kept not so
diligent watch as they had been accustomed to do, and
therefore this maid (with other French captains) coming
forward in the dead time of the night, and in a great rain
and thunder entered into the city with all their victuals,
artillery, and other necessary provisions. The next day
the Englishmen boldly assaulted the town, but the Frenchmen defended the walls so as no great feat worthy of
memory chanced that day betwixt them, though the
Frenchmen were amazed at the valiant attempt of the
Englishmen, whereupon the Bastard of Orleans gave
knowledge to the Duke of Alençon in what danger the
town stood without his present help, who, coming within
two leagues of the city, gave knowledge to them within
that they should be ready the next day to receive him.

This accordingly was accomplished: for the Englishmen willingly suffered him and his army also to enter, supposing that it should be for their advantage to have so
great a multitude to enter the city, whereby their victuals
(whereof they within had great scarcity) might the sooner
be consumed. On the next day in the morning the Frenchmen all together issued out of the town, won by assault
the bastille of Saint Lô, and set it on fire. And after they
likewise assaulted the tower at the bridge foot, which was
manfully defended. But the Frenchmen (more in number)
at length took it, ere the Lord Talbot could come to the
succors, in the which William Glasdale the captain was
slain, with the Lord Moulins and Lord Poinings also.

The Frenchmen, puffed up with this good luck, fetched
a compass about and in good order of battle marched toward the bastille, which was in the keeping of the Lord
Talbot; the which upon the enemy's approach, like a captain without all fear or dread of that great multitude,
issued forth against them and gave them so sharp an

encounter that they, not able to withstand his puissance, fled (like sheep before the wolf) again into the city, with great loss of men and small artillery. Of Englishmen were lost in the two battles to the number of six hundred persons, or thereabout, though the French writers multiply this number of hundreds to thousands, as their manner is.

The Earl of Suffolk, the Lord Talbot, the Lord Scales, and other captains assembled together in council, and after causes showed to and fro, it was amongst them determined to leave their fortresses and bastilles, and to assemble in the plain field, and there to abide all the day, to see if the Frenchmen would issue forth to fight with them. This conclusion taken was accordingly executed, but when the Frenchmen durst not once come forth to show their heads, the Englishmen set fire of their lodgings and departed in good order of battle from Orleans. . . .

[1429: IV.i] All which [French lords] being once joined in one army, shortly after fought with the Lord Talbot (who had with him not past six thousand men) near unto a village in Beauce called Patay; at which battle the charge was given by the French so upon a sudden that the Englishmen had not leisure to put themselves in array after they had put up their stakes before their archers, so that there was no remedy but to fight at adventure. This battle continued by the space of three long hours; for the Englishmen, though they were overpressed with multitude of their enemies, yet they never fled back one foot till their captain the Lord Talbot was sore wounded at the back, and so taken.

Then their hearts began to faint, and they fled, in which flight were slain above twelve hundred, and forty taken, of whom the Lord Talbot, the Lord Scales, the Lord Hungerford, and Sir Thomas Rampston were chief. Divers archers, after they had shot all their arrows, having only their swords, defended themselves, and with help of some of their horsemen came safe to Meung. This overthrow, and specially the taking of the Lord Talbot, did not so much rejoice the Frenchmen, but it did as much abash the Englishmen, so that immediately thereupon the towns of

Janville, Meung, Fort, and divers other returned from the
English part and became French. From this battle departed without any stroke stricken Sir John Fastolfe, the
same year for his valiantness elected into the Order of
the Garter. But for doubt of misdealing at this brunt, the
Duke of Bedford took from him the image of Saint
George and his garter, though afterward by means of
friends and apparent causes of good excuse, the same
were to him again delivered against the mind of the Lord
Talbot. . . .

[1430–31: V.iii, iv] In the chase and pursuit [at Com-
piègne] was the Pucelle taken, with divers other, besides
those that were slain, which were no small number.
Divers were hurt also on both parts. Among the Englishmen, Sir John Montgomery had his arm broken and Sir
John Steward was shot into the thigh with a quarrel.

As before ye have heard somewhat of this damsel's
strange beginning and proceedings, so sith the ending of
all such miraclemongers doth (for the most part) plainly
decipher the virtue and power that they work, by her
shall ye be advertised what at last became of her; cast
your opinions as ye have cause. Of her lovers (the Frenchmen) reporteth one how in Compiègne thus besieged,
Guillaume de Flavie the captain, having sold her afore-
hand to the Lord of Luxembourg, under color of hasting
her with a band out of the town towards their king, for
him with speed to come and levy the siege there, so gotten
her forth he shut the gates after her, when anon by the
Burgundians set upon and overmatched in the conflict she
was taken; marry, yet (all things accounted) to no small
marvel how it could come so to pass, had she been of any
devotion or of true belief, and no false miscreant, but all
holy as she made it. For early that morning she gat her
to Saint James's Church, confessed her, and received her
Maker (as the book terms it), and after setting herself
to a pillar, many of the townsmen that with a five or six
score of their children stood about there to see her,
unto them quoth she: "Good children and my dear
friends, I tell you plainly one hath sold me. I am betrayed

and shortly shall be delivered to death. I beseech you, pray to God for me, for I shall never have more power to do service either to the king or to the realm of France again."

Saith another book, she was entrapped by a Picard captain of Soissons, who sold that city to the Duke of Burgundy, and he then put it over into the hands of the Lord of Luxembourg, so by that means the Burgundians approached and besieged Compiègne, for succor whereof as damsel Joan with her captains from Lagny was thither come, and daily to the English gave many a hot skirmish, so happened it on a day in an outsally that she made, by a Picard of the Lord of Luxembourg's band in the fiercest of her fight she was taken, and by him by and by to his lord presented, who sold her over again to the English, who for witchcraft and sorcery burnt her at Rouen. Tillet telleth it thus, that she was caught at Compiègne by one of the Earl of Lagny's soldiers, from him had to Beaurevoir Castle, where kept a three months, she was after for ten thousand pounds in money and three hundred pounds rent (all Tournois) sold into the English hands.

In which for her pranks so uncouth and suspicious, the lord regent by Peter Cauchon, Bishop of Beauvais (in whose diocese she was taken), caused her life and belief after order of law to be inquired upon and examined. Wherein found though a virgin, yet first shamefully her sex abominably in acts and apparel to have counterfeit mankind, and then all damnably faithless to be a pernicious instrument to hostility and bloodshed in devilish witchcraft and sorcery, sentence accordingly was pronounced against her. Howbeit upon humble confession of her iniquities, with a counterfeit contrition pretending a careful sorrow for the same, execution spared and all mollified into this: that from thenceforth she should cast off her unnatural wearing of man's habiliments and keep her to garments of her own kind, abjure her pernicious practices of sorcery and witchery, and have life and leisure in perpetual prison to bewail her misdeeds. Which to perform (according to the manner of abjuration) a solemn oath very gladly she took.

But herein (God help us) she, fully afore possessed of the fiend, not able to hold her in any towardness of grace, falling straightway into her former abominations (and yet seeking to eke out life as long as she might) stake not (though the shift were shameful) to confess herself a strumpet and (unmarried as she was) to be with child. For trial, the lord regent's lenity gave her nine months stay, at the end whereof she, found herein as false as wicked in the rest, an eight days after, upon a further definitive sentence declared against her to be relapsed and a renouncer of her oath and repentance, was she thereupon delivered over to secular power, and so executed by consumption of fire in the old market place at Rouen, in the selfsame stead where now Saint Michael's Church stands, her ashes afterward without the town walls shaken into the wind. . . .

These matters may very rightfully denounce unto all the world her execrable abominations, and well justify the judgment she had, and the execution she was put to for the same. A thing yet (God wot) very smally shadowed and less holpen by the very travail of the Dauphin, whose dignity abroad foully spotted in this point, that, contrary to the holy degree of a right Christian prince (as he called himself), for maintenance of his quarrels in war would not reverence to profane his sacred estate, as dealing in devilish practices with misbelievers and witches. . . .

[1435: III.iii; IV.i] But now to return to the communication at Arras, which after the departure of the English commissioners held betwixt the Frenchmen and Burgundians, till at length a peace was concluded, accorded, and sworn betwixt King Charles and Duke Philip of Burgundy, upon certain conditions, as in the French histories more plainly appeareth.

And after, the Duke of Burgundy, to set a veil before the King of England's eyes, sent Toison d'Or, his chief herald, to King Henry with letters, excusing the matter by way of information that he was constrained to enter in this league with K[ing] Charles by the daily outcries,

complaints, and lamentations of his people, alleging
against him that he was the only cause of the long con-
tinuance of the wars, to the utter impoverishing of his
own people and the whole nation of France. Therefore
sith he could not otherwise do, but partly to content his
own people, and chiefly to satisfy the request of the
whole general council, was in manner compelled for his
part to grow unto a peace and amity with King Charles.

He likewise wished that King Henry, upon reasonable
and honorable conditions of agreement offered, should
in no wise refuse the same; whereby the long continued
war at length might cease and take end, to the pleasure
of almighty God, which is the author of peace and unity;
and hereto he promised him his aid and furtherance, with
many gay words, which I pass over. The superscription
of this letter was thus: "To the high and mighty prince
Henry, by the grace of God King of England, his well-
beloved cousin"—neither naming him King of France,
nor his sovereign lord, according as (ever before that
time) he was accustomed to do. This letter was much
marveled at of the council after they had thoroughly
considered all the contents thereof, and they could not
but be much disquieted, so far forth that divers of them
offended so much with the untruth of the duke that they
could not temper their passions, but openly called him
traitor. . . .

[1435: III.ii] After the death of that noble prince the
Duke of Bedford, the bright sun in France toward Englishmen began to be cloudy and daily to darken; the
Frenchmen began not only to withdraw their obedience
by oath to the King of England but also took sword in
hand and openly rebelled. Howbeit all these mishaps
could not anything abash the valiant courages of the
English people; for they, having no mistrust in God and
good fortune, set up a new sail, began the war afresh,
and appointed for regent in France Richard, Duke of
York, son to Richard, Earl of Cambridge.

[1435: IV.iii] Although the Duke of York was worthy

(both for birth and courage) of this honor and preferment, yet so disdained of Edmund, Duke of Somerset,
being cousin to the king, that by all means possible he
sought his hindrance, as one glad of his loss and sorry
of his well doing; by reason whereof, ere the Duke of
York could get his dispatch, Paris and divers other of
the chiefest places in France were gotten by the French
king. The Duke of York, perceiving his evil will, openly
dissembled that which he inwardly minded, either of
them working things to the other's displeasure, till
through malice and division between them, at length by
mortal war they both were consumed, with almost their
whole lines and offspring.

[1441: III.ii] While the French king was in Guienne,
the Lord Talbot took the town of Couchet, and after
marched toward Gallardon, which was besieged by the
Bastard of Orleans, otherwise called the Earl of Dunois;
which earl hearing of the Lord Talbot's approach raised
his siege and saved himself. The Frenchmen a little before this season had taken the town of Évreux by treason
of a fisher. Sir Francis the Aragonois hearing of that
chance appareled six strong fellows like men of the
country, with sacks and baskets as carriers of corn and
victuals, and sent them to the Castle of Corneille, in
the which divers Englishmen were kept as prisoners, and
he with an ambush of Englishmen lay in a valley nigh
to the fortress.

The six counterfeit husbandmen entered the castle un-
suspected, and straight came to the chamber of the captain and, laying hands on him, gave knowledge to them
that lay in ambush to come to their aid. The which
suddenly made forth and entered the castle, slew and
took all the Frenchmen, and set the Englishmen at
liberty; which thing done, they set fire in the castle and
departed to Rouen with their booty and prisoners. This
exploit they had not achieved peradventure by force (as
haply they mistrusted), and therefore by subtlety and
deceit sought to accomplish it, which means to use in
war is tolerable, so the same war be lawful, though both

fraud and bloodshed otherwise be forbidden even by the instinct of nature to be put in practice and use, and that doth the poet insinuate in a proper sententious verse, saying:

Fraus absit, vacuas caedis habete manus.

[Away with treachery, keep your hands free of slaughter.]

[1441: III.i] But now to speak somewhat of the doings in England in the meantime. Whilst the men of war were thus occupied in martial feats, and daily skirmishes within the realm of France, ye shall understand that after the Cardinal of Winchester and the Duke of Gloucester were (as it seemed) reconciled either to other, yet the cardinal and the Archbishop of York ceased not to do many things without the consent of the king or of the duke, being (during the minority of the king) governor and Protector of the realm, whereas the duke (as good cause he had) greatly offended, thereupon in writing declared to the king wherein the cardinal and the archbishop had offended both his majesty and the laws of the realm. This complaint of the Duke of Gloucester was contained in four and twenty articles which chiefly rested in that the cardinal had from time to time, through his ambitious desire to surmount all others in high degrees of honor and dignity, sought to enrich himself, to the great and notorious hindrance of the king, as in defrauding him not only of his treasure, but also in doing and practicing things greatly prejudicial to his affairs in France, and namely by setting at liberty the King of Scots upon so easy conditions as the king's majesty greatly lost thereby. . . .

[1443: V.i] In this year died in Guienne the Countess of Comminges, to whom the French king and also the Earl of Armagnac pretended to be heir, insomuch that the earl entered into all the lands of the said lady. And because he knew the French king would not take the matter well, to have a Roland for an Oliver, he sent solemn

ambassadors to the King of England, offering him his
daughter in marriage with promise to be bound (beside
great sums of money, which he would give with her) to
deliver into the King of England's hands all such castles
and towns as he or his ancestors detained from him
within any part of the Duchy of Aquitaine, either by
conquest of his progenitors or by gift and deliverance of
any French king; and further to aid the same king with
money for the recovery of other cities within the same
duchy from the French king, or from any other person
that against King Henry unjustly kept and wrongfully
withholden them.

This offer seemed so profitable and also honorable to
King Henry and the realm that the ambassadors were
well heard, honorably received, and with rewards sent
home into their country. After whom were sent for the
conclusion of the marriage into Guienne Sir Edward Hull,
Sir Robert Ross, and John Grafton, Dean of St. Severin's,
the which (as all the chronographers agree) both concluded the marriage and by proxy affied the young lady.
The French king, not a little offended herewith, sent his
eldest son Louis, the Dauphin of Vienne, into Rouergue
with a puissant army which took the earl and his youngest son, with both his daughters, and by force obtained
the countries of Armagnac, L'Auvergne, Rouergue, and
Moulessonois [Limousin?], beside the cities Severac and
Cadeac, chasing the bastard of Armagnac out of his
countries, and so by reason hereof the concluded marriage was deferred, and that so long that it never took
effect, as hereafter it may appear. . . .

[1444–45: V.iii, v] In treating of this truce [between
England and France], the Earl of Suffolk, adventuring
somewhat upon his commission without the assent of his
associates, imagined that the next way to come to a
perfect peace was to contrive a marriage between the
French king's kinswoman, the Lady Margaret, daughter
to Reignier, Duke of Anjou, and his sovereign lord King
Henry. This Reignier, Duke of Anjou, named himself
King of Sicily, Naples, and Jerusalem, having only the

name and style of those realms without any penny, profit, or foot of possession. This marriage was made strange to the earl at the first, and one thing seemed to be a great hindrance to it, which was, because the King of England occupied a great part of the Duchy of Anjou and the whole County of Maine, appertaining (as was alleged) to King Reignier.

The Earl of Suffolk (I cannot say), either corrupted with bribes or too much affectioned to this unprofitable marriage, condescended that the Duchy of Anjou and the County of Maine should be delivered to the king, the bride's father, demanding for her marriage neither penny nor farthing; as who should say, that this new affinity passed all riches and excelled both gold and precious stones. And to the intent that of this truce might ensue a small concord, a day of interview was appointed between the two kings in a place convenient between Chartres and Rouen. When these things were concluded, the Earl of Suffolk with his company returned into England, where he forgat not to declare what an honorable truce he had taken, out of the which there was a great hope that a final peace might grow the sooner for that honorable marriage which he had concluded, omitting nothing that might extol and set forth the personage of the lady or the nobility of her kindred.

But although this marriage pleased the king and divers of his council, yet Humphrey, Duke of Gloucester, Protector of the realm, was much against it, alleging that it should be both contrary to the laws of God and dishonorable to the prince if he should break that promise and contract of marriage, made by ambassadors sufficiently thereto instructed, with the daughter of the Earl of Armagnac, upon conditions both to him and his realm as much profitable and honorable. But the duke's words could not be heard, for the earl's doings were only liked and allowed. So that for performance of the conclusions the French king sent the Earl of Vendôme, great master of his house, and the Archbishop of Rheims, first peer of France, and divers other into England, where they were honorably received; and after that the instruments were once sealed and delivered on both parts, the said ambassadors returned again into their countries with great gifts and rewards.

When these things were done the king, both for honor of his realm and to assure to himself more friends, created John Holland, Earl of Huntington, Duke of Exeter as his father was; Humphrey, Earl of Stafford, was made Duke of Buckingham; and Henry, Earl of Warwick, was elected to the title of Duke of Warwick, to whom the king also gave the castle of Bristol, with the isle of Jersey and Guernsey. Also the Earl of Suffolk was made Marquess of Suffolk, which marquess with his wife and many honorable personages of men and women richly adorned both with apparel and jewels, having with them many costly chariots and gorgeous horselitters, sailed into France for the conveyance of the nominated queen into the realm of England. For King Reignier, her father, for all his long style had too short a purse to send his daughter honorably to the king her spouse.

from *The Union of the Two Noble and Illustre Families of Lancaster and York* (1548)

[1453: IV.ii] When the Earl of Shrewsbury was thus according to his intent of all things furnished and adorned, first he fortified Bordeaux with Englishmen and victual; after that he rode into the country abroad, where he obtained cities and gat towns without stroke or dint of sword, for the poor and needy people being fatigate and weary with the oppression of their new landlords, rendered their towns before they were of them required, and beside this the towns and cities far distant from Bordeaux sent messengers to the Earl, promising to him both service and obeisance. And among other the town and castle of Châtillon in Perigord was to him delivered by the Frenchmen upon composition that they might with their lives safely depart; which town the earl strongly fortified both with men and ordnance. . . .

[IV.v–vii] [Upon learning of Talbot's approach a French force besieging Châtillon] . . . with all diligence left the siege and retired in good order into the place which they had trenched, ditched, and fortified with ordnance. They within the town, seeing the siege removed, sent out word to the Englishmen that the Frenchmen fled. The courageous earl, hearing these news and

fearing lest through long tarrying the birds might be flown
away, not tarrying till his footmen were come, set forward toward his enemies, which were in mind surely to
have fled, as they confessed afterward, if the fear of the
French king's rebuke, which was not far off, had not
caused them to tarry, and yet in this army were present
the marshal and great master of France, the Earl of
Ponthieu, the Seneschal of Poitou, the Lord Beziers,
and many valiant barons and knights. When the Englishmen were come to the place where the Frenchmen
were encamped, in the which (as Aeneas Silvius testi-
fieth) were three hundred pieces of brass, beside divers
other small pieces and subtle engines to the Englishmen unknown and nothing suspected, they lighted all
on foot, the Earl of Shrewsbury only except, which because of his age rode on a little hackney, and fought
fiercely with the Frenchmen, and got the entry of their
camp, and by fine force entered into the same. This
conflict continued in doubtful judgment of victory two
long hours, during which fight the lords of Montauban
and Hunaudières with a great company of Frenchmen
entered the battle and began a new field, and suddenly
the gunners, perceiving the Englishmen to approach near,
discharged their ordnance and slew three hundred persons near to the earl, who, perceiving the imminent
jeopardy and subtle labyrinth in which he and his people were enclosed and illaqueate, despising his own
safeguard and desiring the life of his entirely and well-
beloved son the Lord Lisle, willed, advertised, and
counseled him to depart out of the field and to save
himself. But when the son had answered that it was
neither honest nor natural for him to leave his father
in the extreme jeopardy of his life, and that he would
taste of that draught which his father and parent should
assay and begin, the noble earl and comfortable captain
said to him: "Oh, son, son, I thy father, which only
hath been the terror and scourge of the French people so many years, which hath subverted so many
towns, and profligate and discomfited so many of them
in open battle and martial conflict, neither can here

die for the honor of my country without great laud
and perpetual fame, nor fly or depart without perpetual
shame and continual infamy. But because this is thy
first journey and enterprise, neither thy flying shall redound to thy shame, nor thy death to thy glory; for
as hardy a man wisely flieth as a temerarious person
foolishly abideth; therefore the fleeing of me shall be
the dishonor, not only of me and my progeny, but
also a discomfiture to all my company; thy departure
shall save thy life and make thee able another time,
if I be slain, to revenge my death and to do honor to
thy prince and profit to his realm." But nature so
wrought in the son that neither desire of life nor thought
of security could withdraw or pluck him from his natural
father; who, considering the constancy of his child and
the great danger that they stood in, comforted his
soldiers, cheered his captains, and valiantly set upon his
enemies and slew of them more in number than he had
in his company. But his enemies, having a greater
company of men and more abundance of ordnance than
before had been seen in a battle, first shot him through
the thigh with a handgun, and slew his horse, and
cowardly killed him, lying on the ground, whom they
never durst look in the face while he stood on his feet;
and with him there died manfully his son the Lord
Lisle, his bastard son, Henry Talbot, and Sir Edward
Hull, elect to the noble Order of the Garter, and thirty
valiant personages of the English nation, and the Lord
Moulins was there taken prisoner with sixty other. The
residue of the English people fled to Bordeaux and
other places, whereof in the flight were slain above a
thousand persons. At this battle of Châtillon, fought the
thirteenth day of July in this year, ended his life John,
lord Talbot, and of his progeny the first Earl of Shrewsbury, after that he with much fame, more glory, and
most victory had for his prince and country, by the
space of twenty-four years and more, valiantly made
war and served the king in the parts beyond the sea;
whose corpse was left on the ground, and after was
found by his friends and conveyed to Whitchurch in

Shropshire, where it is intumulate. This man was to the French people a very scourge and a daily terror, in so much that as his person was fearful and terrible to his adversaries present, so his name and fame was spiteful and dreadful to the common people absent, in so much that women in France to fear their young children would cry, "The Talbot cometh! the Talbot cometh!"

Commentaries

HERMANN ULRICI

from *Shakspeare's Dramatic Art*

The *First Part* forms the real conclusion to *Henry V,*
for it is here that we have the termination of the war
which was there represented. It ends to the advantage
of France, and in the first place because the right, in
its ethico-historical significance, has changed sides. For
although the French people and the nobility do not prove
themselves better, simply more prudent and wiser by
experience, still, on the other hand, their arrogance and
thoroughly senseless vanity had apparently diminished,
and their esteem for their adversaries was already the
beginning of victory. On the other hand—and this is
the main point—England had lost her moral superiority.
In the very first introductory scene, we distinctly see
how it has degenerated, owing to the selfish intrigues
and quarrels of the nobility, in which the people also
have now become involved. Single features of the war
—for instance, Fastolfe's cowardly, ignominious flight—
prove that the people and the army are no longer animated by the old spirit. The play opens with the coffin

From *Shakspeare's Dramatic Art. History and Character of Shakspeare's Plays* by Dr. Hermann Ulrici. Translated by L. Dora Schmitz.
London: George Bell and Sons, 1876.

of Henry V lying in state, thus representing the grave of the English victories and conquests. These had necessarily to be lost, sooner or later, for it was a grand mistake, but nevertheless a mistake, to suppose that the England of the day could maintain a *lasting* supremacy over France. As long as the political and national energy of an independent country is not wholly broken, it cannot sink so far as to become a mere province of another. This error only maintained the semblance of truth for a short time, because of the moral weakness of the French people, and because of the heroic energy of Henry V. If France had again rallied, the conquest could not have been maintained even by a monarch more powerful than Henry VI, because, when more closely examined, it contained an unjust presumption, as unjust as every attempt to enslave the liberty of a man as long as he is morally capable of freedom. The same justice which had formerly weighed in England's favor, ultimately turns the scales against her.

As this unhappy termination of the war corresponds with the spirit and character of the whole trilogy, intimated by the above discussion, so we have it reflected in a peculiar coloring in the character, the doings and the fate of the Maid of Orleans. She is, as it were, the soul of the rekindled war on the French side, as Talbot represents it on that of England. With her appearance the fortune of war turns from England to France, because she succeeds in arousing the French nation to enthusiastic patriotism by faith in a higher and divine aid. The poet does not deny the existence of this higher aid, which is represented in Joan, but, as a true Englishman, he looks upon it as the aid of ungodly, demoniacal powers. The enthusiastic rise of the French nation with the appearance of Joan la Pucelle he considers as a stirring of the nightside of nature, as an interference of the evil principle. He therefore becomes untrue to himself, and sins against the principle of the historical drama, which demands strict impartiality for the inner motives and great turning points in the course of history. We have a proof of how this error—which

was as much an error against the laws of poetry—
takes its revenge, for the character of Joan is not only
untrue, but also unpoetical. From the very fact of
Shakspeare not being aware of this, and from his having here entirely followed the English view and the
English authorities in regard to the history of the time,
we might infer (even though it were not otherwise established) that the First Part of *Henry VI* is one of
Shakspeare's youthful works, written at a time when he
did not as yet possess a clear idea of what an historical drama should be, in order to be free from the faults
of blind patriotism and national prejudice. On the other
hand we have an excuse for the poet in the circumstance that Shakspeare's conception of the character of
Joan of Arc was quite in keeping with the opinions of
the English nation, nay, that it corresponded pretty
closely with the *general* opinion of the whole age to
which the history belongs. For an *historical* drama,
which represents its substance as actually *present*, ought
at the same time to depict the spirit and character of
the age in which it moves. And moreover it was one of
the features in the character of the age, that it was in-
capable of comprehending that which was great, pure,
and noble, nay, that what was good and beautiful could
not even keep itself quite pure. For Joan of Arc does
not appear quite pure even according to French authorities, nor according to our modern and more accurate
historical investigations. That she was inspired by a great
and beautiful thought before her appearance in public,
is intimated even by Shakspeare through the rumor
which he allows to precede her appearance, and his fault
is only in having merely intimated it, and in not having
given us a vivid representation of it. But Shakspeare
must certainly have had some object in introducing this
intimation; at all events it is in excellent keeping with
the spirit and ideal character of the whole trilogy, especially of the First Part. For if we follow this intimation,
we shall have to assume that Joan—in order to realize
her great and beautiful thought in *such a time,* i.e., when
she entered actively into the current of events—did give

herself up to the evil principle; whether she did this voluntarily, or was overpowered by it, is a point which the poet could justly leave undecided, as it was a matter of indifference to his purpose. In history, and hence in Shakspeare, she therefore fell the victim to the tragic fate which, like a fearful specter, wanders through the whole trilogy.

Joan's death, when conceived in this light, appears at the same time the organic contrast to that of the Earl of Salisbury [sic], of Lord Talbot and his son. Lord Talbot is obviously the noblest character in the whole play, a rough and vigorous knight; battle and war, self-devoted patriotism, knightly honor and bravery, these have constituted his entire life; all higher ideas seem beyond him; he knows how to win a battle, but not how to carry on a war; he is an excellent military captain, but no general, no chief, because, although valiant and even discreet and prudent (as is proved by his interview with the Countess of Auvergne), he does not possess either presence of mind, creative power, or a clear insight into matters. This, together with the roughness and harshness of his virtue, which has in it something of the rage of the lion, is his weak point, and proves the cause of his death. His power was not equal to the complicated circumstances and the depravity of the age; under the iron rod of chastisement, he became equally unbending and iron; he is the representative of the rage and ferocity of the war, to which he falls a victim because he is wholly absorbed in it and therefore unable to become the master in directing it. In such days, however, the honorable death of a noble character proves a blessing; victory and pleasure are found in death when life succumbs to the superior power of evil, to the weight and misery of a decline which affects both the nation and the state.

This is the special modification of the theme which is carried out throughout the play, the special task which the First Part has to solve, and to the solution of which the other parts have to contribute their share. Henry VI, who in himself is pious and innocent and by nature unimpassionate, is led by Suffolk's seductive arts to break his royal word and his already plighted troth, and to conclude his unfortunate marriage with Margaret of Anjou. Even he cannot keep himself pure, and, inasmuch as in youthful levity he follows his sensual desires, he himself lays the foundation of his subsequent unhappy life. Gloster's honest, high-minded, and truly patriotic nature is likewise carried away by party spirit and passion. The quarrel between him and the bishop of Winchester, which has also affected their retainers, the jealousy between Somerset and Richard of York, the powerlessness of old Bedford and Exeter—all this helps to bring about the death of Talbot, the impending and soon no longer inevitable destruction of all the better minds. The citizens and people do not as yet take any direct part in the dissensions of the nobility, the Mayor of London appears more in the light of a mediator, and a promoter of peace. Still some incidents, such as the brawls among the servingmen, the cowardliness of Fastolfe and his troops show that the people are already affected by the general state of corruption. In the following parts this, accordingly, is brought more prominently forward.

E. M. W. TILLYARD

from *Shakespeare's History Plays*

"The First Part of Henry VI"

I am fully in accord with a growing trend of belief that Shakespeare wrote this play. It is not in the least surprising if the style is hesitant and varied. If a young man attempts a big thing, a thing beyond his years, he will imitate others when his own invention flags. Some of the verse in this play, as in the rest of the tetralogy, is in the common, little differentiated dramatic idiom of the age: it is the sort of thing that just was being written. That Shakespeare should have had recourse to it was perfectly natural. Why should he, more than another poet, be expected to find himself instantaneously? No one disputes the authorship of Pope's *Pastorals* because they do not show the author's achieved and unmistakable genius throughout, or collects the truly Popean lines and conjectures that he added just these to a lost original. Such treatment is kept for Shakespeare. One cannot of course be sure that a manuscript which waited over thirty years for publication remained in every word or sentence as the poet penned it. But the editors of the First Folio thought the play to be Shakespeare's; and this is evidence that only something very solid on the other side should be

From *Shakespeare's History Plays* by E. M. W. Tillyard. London: Chatto and Windus, 1944; New York: Collier Books, 1962. Reprinted by permission of the publishers. Additional excerpts from this book appear in the Signet Classic edition of *3 Henry VI*.

allowed to gainsay. The evidence, apart from the First Folio, that is overwhelmingly on the side of Shakespeare's being the author is the masterly structure. None of his contemporary dramatists was capable of this. The steady political earnestness is further proof.

I cannot believe either that this part was written after the other two parts of *Henry VI*. The evidence for a later date is the entry in Henslowe's Diary for 3 March 1591-92 of *Henry VI* as "ne" or new. Alexander has argued that the entry probably refers to another play altogether. Quite apart from the greater immaturity of its style, in itself a strong argument for earlier date, the first part is a portion of a larger organism. The very difference of its structure from that of the second part is an essential and deliberate contrast within a total scheme, while characters, embryonic in the first part, develop in the second in full congruity with their embryonic character.

Nor can I agree with Alexander that the scenes at the end of the play of Suffolk fetching Margaret of Anjou are an afterthought designed to link the play closely with the next. They have the same function as the last scenes in the next two plays, which suggest the opening scenes of their successors. They *all* argue the organic nature of the whole tetralogy.

Apart from the queer reluctance to allow Shakespeare to have written ill or like other dramatists when he was immature, the chief reason why people have been hostile to Shakespeare's authorship is the way he treats Joan of Arc. That the gentle Shakespeare could have been so ungentlemanly as to make his Joan other than a saint was intolerable. This is precisely like arguing that Shakespeare could not have written *King John* because he does not mention Magna Carta. That England adopted the French opinion of Joan of Arc and saw the beginnings of our liberties in Magna Carta may have been excellent things; but these acts are comparatively recent, belonging to the "1066 and All That" phase of history, about which the Elizabethans knew nothing. To an Elizabethan, France did not mean saints, but instability, wars of religion,

political intrigue, with the Massacre of St. Bartholomew
the outstanding event. Not that moderns can enjoy the
way Shakespeare treats the French, Joan of Arc included. But he is just as bad (and with less excuse because older) in *Henry V*; and any argument, based on
Joan of Arc, against the Shakespearean authorship of *1
Henry VI* is just as pertinent to the later play. It is some
comfort to reflect that in his contribution to *Sir Thomas
More* Shakespeare treated the alien like an ordinary
human being. George Betts has said that expelling the
London aliens will be good for trade, and More replies:

> Grant them remov'd and grant that this your noise
> Had chid down all the majesty of England.
> Imagine that you see the wretched strangers,
> Their babies at their backs and their poor luggage,
> Plodding to th' ports and coasts for transportation—

But these were aliens who could be seen and heard,
and taken as individuals. Frenchmen in the mass were
judged by other standards.

The *First Part of Henry VI* is the work of an ambitious and reflective young man who has the power to
plan but not worthily to execute something great. His
style of writing lags behind the powerful imagination
that arranged the inchoate mass of historical material
into a highly significant order. The characters are well
thought out and consistent but they are the correct pieces
in a game moved by an external hand rather than self-
moving. Yet they come to life now and then and, in
promise, are quite up to what we have any right to expect from Shakespeare in his youth.

If this play had been called the *Tragedy of Talbot* it
would stand a much better chance of being heeded by a
public which very naturally finds it hard to remember
which part of *Henry VI* is which, and where Joan of
Arc or Jack Cade, or Margaret crowning York with a
paper crown, occur. And if we want something by which
to distinguish the play, let us by all means give it that
title. It is one that contains much truth, but not all. The
whole truth in this matter is that though the action re-

volves around Talbot, though he stands preeminently for
loyalty and order in a world threatened by chaos, he is
not the hero. For there is no regular hero either in this
or in any of the other three plays; its true hero being
England or Respublica after the fashion of the Morality
Play, as pointed out in the last section. It is therefore
truer to the nature of the separate plays that they should
be given colorless regal titles than that they should be
named after the seemingly most important characters or
events.

Along with the Morality hero goes the assumption of
divine interference. The theme of the play is the testing
of England, already guilty and under a sort of curse,
by French witchcraft. England is championed by a great
and pious soldier, Talbot, and the witchcraft is directed
principally at him. If the other chief men of England
had all been like him, he could have resisted and saved
England. But they are divided against each other, and
through this division Talbot dies and the first stage in
England's ruin and of the fulfillment of the curse is accomplished. Respublica has suffered the first terrible
wounds.

As so often happens in literature the things which
initially are the most troublesome prove to be the most
enlightening. The Joan episodes, unpleasant and hence
denied Shakespeare, are the clue to the whole plot. They
are hinted at right in the front of the play. In the first
scene Exeter, commenting on the funeral of Henry V,
says:

> What! shall we curse the planets of mishap
> That plotted thus our glory's overthrow?
> Or shall we think the subtle-witted French
> Conjurers and sorcerers, that afraid of him
> By magic verses have contriv'd his end?

One cannot understand the bearing of these lines on the
play without remembering how the influence of the stars
and witchcraft fitted into the total Elizabethan conception of the universe. Though these two things were
thought to be powerful in their effects and were dreaded,

they did not work undirected. God was ultimately in control, and the divine part of man, his reason and the freedom of his will, need not yield to them. Further, God used both stars and evil spirits to forward his own ends. Joan, then, is not a mere piece of fortuitous witchcraft, not a mere freakish emissary of Satan, but a tool of the Almighty, as she herself (though unconsciously) declares in her words to Charles after her first appearance.

> Assign'd am I to be the English scourge.

Who but God has assigned her this duty? True, if this line were unsupported, we might hesitate to make this full inference. But combined with the various cosmic references and the piety of Talbot, it is certain. For not only the first scene of the play, but the second scene (where Joan first appears) begins with a reference to the heavens. The first passage was quoted above; the Dauphin Charles begins the second scene:

> Mars his true moving, even as in the heavens
> So in the earth, to this day is not known:
> Late did he shine upon the English side;
> Now we are victors; upon us he smiles.

Not only do these words contrast significantly with Bedford's opening speech about the "bad revolted stars"; they combine with it in presenting the whole world order with God, the unmoved mover, directing it. And the full context of witchcraft is implied when Talbot before Orleans, already harassed by Joan's supernatural power, exclaims of the French:

> Well, let them practice and converse with spirits:
> God is our fortress, in whose conquering name
> Let us resolve to scale their flinty bulwarks.

A modern, who needs much working up to pay any real heed to witchcraft, is apt not to notice such a passage and to pass on faintly disgusted with Talbot for being not only a butcher but a prig: an Elizabethan, granted a generally serious context, would find Talbot's defiance apt and noble.

What were the sins God sought to punish? There had been a number, but the preeminent one was the murder of Richard II, the shedding of the blood of God's deputy on earth. Henry IV had been punished by an uneasy reign but had not fully expiated the crime; Henry V, for his piety, had been allowed a brilliant reign. But the curse was there; and first England suffers through Henry V's early death and secondly she is tried by the witch-craft of Joan.

Into the struggle between Talbot and Joan, which is the main motive of the play, is introduced the theme of order and dissension. The first scene presents the funeral of Henry V and declares the disaster of his death. Dissension appears through the high words between the bad ambitious Beaufort, Bishop of Winchester, and Humphrey Duke of Gloucester, honest but hot-tempered, the regent of England. Bad news from France follows. But the case of England is not hopeless. Bedford sets off at once for France, Gloucester takes charge at home.

The next scene is before Orleans. The French are in a mood of facile triumph. They will relieve the town, still besieged by Salisbury and the English. Though ten to one they are beaten back with loss and confusion. That, the poet makes us feel, is the natural order, God's order, provided England is true to herself. Then Joan enters, a dazzling blonde, claiming her beauty to be from the Virgin—

> And, whereas I was black and swart before,
> With those clear rays which she infus'd on me
> That beauty am I bless'd with which you see—

but of course owing it to the Devil. She fascinates Charles and ends by imposing on the French a discipline and an order which by nature is not theirs. That this order is bogus, a devilish not a divine one, is evident by the single combat Charles the Dauphin has with Joan to test her pretensions. He is beaten; and for a man to yield to a woman was a fundamental upsetting of degree.

Then, before a background of dissension in England,
the struggle between Talbot and Joan is worked out.
There are three episodes: Orleans, Rouen, Bordeaux.
Before Orleans Talbot's men melt before Joan's attack,
and, though he is dauntless, she relieves the town. The
French triumph. But now Bedford has arrived with
Burgundian allies: there is a new union on the English
side, and the town (quite unhistorically) is captured.
Talbot has kept up his heart and with united supporters
he triumphs. The pattern is repeated at Rouen. Through
a trick Joan wins the town for the French. Again Talbot
does not lose heart. He gets Burgundy to swear to capture
the town or die. Bedford, brought in on a litter and
near his death, insists on taking his share:

> Here will I sit before the walls of Roan[1]
> And will be partner of your weal or woe.

Union once more and it succeeds. The town is captured,
and Talbot emerges more strongly than ever the symbol
of true and virtuous order:

> Now will we take some order in the town,
> Placing therein some expert officers,
> And then depart to Paris to the king,
> For there young Henry with his nobles lie.

To which Burgundy, again showing the natural relation
of French to English, replies,

> What wills Lord Talbot pleaseth Burgundy.

Talbot then goes on to more proprieties:

> But yet, before we go, let's not forget
> The noble Duke of Bedford late deceas'd
> But see his exequies fulfill'd in Roan.

But Joan had not yet ceased to be the English scourge,

[1] A monosyllable: the Elizabethan form of Rouen (now, alas,
given up).

and Talbot was wrong in saying just before the above
lines,

> I think her old familiar is asleep.

In the next scene, outside Rouen, Joan cheers the
dispirited French leaders and says she has another plan:
she will detach Burgundy from the English alliance. Then,
in what must have been a most effective scene on the
Elizabethan stage, the English forces pass across in triumph with colors spread, headed by Talbot, on their way
to Paris. The Burgundians follow and Joan waylays them.
She addresses to their Duke those commonplaces about
avoiding civil war of which, ironically, England was even
then in such desperate need, for between the episodes of
Orleans and Rouen had come the quarrel between
Lancastrians and Yorkists in the Temple Garden and
Richard Plantagenet's resolve to claim the Duchy of
York:

> See, see the pining malady of France;
> Behold the wounds, the most unnatural wounds,
> Which thou thyself hast given her woeful breast.
> O, turn thy edged sword another way;
> Strike those that hurt and hurt not those that help.
> One drop of blood drawn from thy country's bosom
> Should grieve thee more than streams of foreign gore.

Excellent advice when applied to England; but to France,
where Massacres of St. Bartholomew were endemic, quite
perverse. With a speed, familiar to readers of contemporary Elizabethan drama or of *Savonarola Brown*,
Burgundy acquiesces and joins with the French. Joan,
with a cynicism that anticipates the Bastard of Falconbridge, exclaims:

> Done like a Frenchman: turn, and turn again!

Meanwhile Talbot, ignorant of Burgundy's defection,
arrives in Paris and does homage to Henry in the scene I
have already pointed to [in an earlier passage, not printed

in this selection] as epitomizing the principle of degree
and the way a kingdom should be ordered. Henry is
crowned, and immediately after comes the news of
Burgundy's defection. Talbot leaves at once to renew the
wars. But the court he leaves, that should have been his
base and his certainty, shows itself divided and weak.
Yorkist and Lancastrian refer their quarrels to the king,
who quite fails to grasp the ugliness of the situation,
frivolously chooses a red rose for himself with the words,

> I see no reason, if I wear this rose,
> That anyone should therefore be suspicious
> I more incline to Somerset than York,

and sets out to return to England, leaving Somerset and
York in divided command of all the forces except the
few that accompany Talbot. English division is now
acutely contrasted with French reconciliation. Exeter pronounces the choric comment that prepares for the
culminating catastrophe:

> No simple man that sees
> This jarring discord of nobility,
> This shouldering of each other in the court,
> This factious bandying of their favorites,
> But that it doth presage some ill event.
> 'Tis much when scepters are in children's hands,
> But more when envy breeds unkind division:
> There comes the ruin, there begins confusion.

From this there follows inevitably the final tragedy of
Talbot near Bordeaux. Twice he had resisted the machinations of Joan and triumphed; but then he was supported
by his own people. The third time, though he does all
he can, he perishes; for York and Somerset, to whom he
had sent for help, each refuses it for envy of the other.
Joan is not allowed to kill Talbot; that would be un-
seemly: he must die on heaps of French dead. After
his death she reports how his son had refused to fight her
("to be the pillage of a giglot wench") and insults over
his body. Lucy, who has come to learn the news, recites

the full list of Talbot's great titles; at which Joan exclaims:

> Here is a silly stately style indeed!
> The Turk, who two and fifty kingdoms hath,
> Writes not so tedious a style as this.
> Him that thou magnifi'st with all these titles
> Stinking and fly-blown lies here at our feet.

Joan, by God's permission and through the general col-
lapse of order among the English nobility, has dealt England a great blow. Having dealt it, and ceasing to be
God's tool, she loses her power. Her evil spirits desert
her, and she is captured and burnt for the wicked woman
she is. It is possible that we are meant to think that her
evil spells are transferred to another Frenchwoman,
Margaret of Anjou, who, at the end of the play, is allowed through the machinations of her would-be paramour, the unscrupulous Suffolk, to supplant the daughter
of the Earl of Armagnac, already affianced, in the affections of Henry VI. On the ominous note of this royal
perjury the play ends.

Such is the play's outline. There is no scene or episode
not mentioned above that does not reinforce one or
other of the main themes. Even the episode of Talbot
and the Countess of Auvergne serves to exalt the hero
as well as creating a legitimate diversion at a pause in
the action.

Shakespeare took great trouble over his plot, but his
emotions too were deeply stirred in his task. The gradual
but sure stages in Talbot's destruction express the painful
seriousness with which Shakespeare took the historical
theme. He also took trouble over the characters, but he
felt far less strongly about them. At least he made them
consistent, even if he did not give them a great deal of
life. For instance, Suffolk at his first appearance in the
Temple Garden (II.iv) shows himself both diplomatic
and unscrupulous. It is he who has brought the dispute
between Somerset and York from the hall into the privacy
of the garden:

> Within the Temple Hall we were too loud;
> The garden here is more convenient.

And, when asked his opinion on the legal point, he coolly says,

> Faith, I have been a truant in the law
> And never yet could frame my will to it;
> And therefore frame the law unto my will.

York is the true anticipation of the

> dogged York, that reaches at the moon

of the second part. He is violently ambitious, yet not rashly but obstinately and persistently: strong in all the regal qualities but goodness of heart. Gloucester is simply but sufficiently shown as the opposite of York: good-hearted but free-spoken to a fault. The contrast of their characters already prepares for the main motive of the next play.

Talbot and Joan are the most alive, for they both have a touch of breeziness, or hearty coarseness with which Shakespeare liked to furnish his most successfully practical characters. Joan's remarks on Burgundy's change of mind and on Talbot's dead body, quoted above, are examples. And this is Talbot's comment on Salisbury's dying wounds received before Orleans:

> Hear, hear how dying Salisbury doth groan!
> It irks his heart he cannot be reveng'd.
> Frenchmen, I'll be a Salisbury to you:
> Pucelle or puzzle, Dolphin or dogfish,
> Your hearts I'll stamp out with my horse's heels
> And make a quagmire of your mingled brains.
> Convey me Salisbury into his tent.

In Henry VI's character Shakespeare shows little interest. There is a strong religious feeling throughout the tetralogy that culminates in *Richard III,* but it is religion applied to the workings of history not the religious feelings in the mind of a poor king and a saint. Shakespeare stops short at the poor king, who is also pathetic; he omits the more interesting self-questionings of the same character in the *Mirror for Magistrates*.

For style, much of the play is a competent example of the dramatic norm of the period. As this:

> Crossing the sea from England into France,
> This fellow here with envious carping tongue
> Upbraided me about the rose I wear;
> Saying, the sanguine color of the leaves
> Did represent my master's blushing cheeks,
> When stubbornly he did repugn the truth
> About a certain question in the law
> Argu'd betwixt the Duke of York and him,
> With other vile and ignominious terms.
> In confutation of which rude reproach
> And in defense of my lord's worthiness
> I crave the benefit of law of arms.

But this is not the only way of writing. Once or twice the rhythm is unpleasantly lame, as when Joan says to Charles, about to try her in single combat,

> I am prepar'd. Here is my keen-edg'd sword,
> Deck'd with five flower-de-luces on each side,
> The which at Touraine, in Saint Katharine's churchyard,
> Out of a great deal of old iron I chose forth.

Such lameness is not so surprising when we refer the passage to its original in Holinshed:

> Then at the Dolphin's sending, by her assignment, from Saint Katharine's Church of Fierbois in Touraine (where she never had been and knew not) in a secret place there, among old iron, appointed she her sword to be sought out and brought her, that with five flower-delices was graven on both sides.

Shakespeare much later in his career was apt to be careless of rhythms when he paraphrased Holinshed. Besides, Holinshed is here reporting the French version of Joan's inspiration, and Shakespeare may be deliberately making

it ridiculous; just as, in general, he made the French talk
foolishly. Then sometimes there are outbursts of the turgid
or dulcet writing dear to the University Wits, to vary the
more sober norm of the play. The classical references,
profuse for a play on a historical theme, are in keeping
with these and form yet another link with *Titus Andronicus*. Here is Talbot's account of how the French treated
him in captivity:

> In open market-place produc'd they me,
> To be a public spectacle to all.
> Here, said they, is the terror of the French,
> The scarecrow that affrights our children so.
> Then broke I from the officers that led me
> And with my nails digg'd stones out of the ground
> To hurl at the beholders of my shame.
> My grisly countenance made others fly;
> None durst come near for fear of sudden death.
> In iron walls they deem'd me not secure.
> So great fear of my name 'mongst them was spread
> That they suppos'd I could rend bars of steel
> And spurn in pieces posts of adamant.

And for the dulcet style Suffolk's words to Margaret of
Anjou when he has captured her will do as illustration:

> Be not offended, nature's miracle,
> Thou are allotted to be ta'en by me:
> So doth the swan her downy cygnets save,
> Keeping them prisoner underneath her wings.
> Yet, if this servile usage once offend,
> Go and be free again as Suffolk's friend.
> O, stay! I have no power to let her pass;
> My hand would free her, but my heart says no.
> As plays the sun upon the glassy streams,
> Twinkling another counterfeited beam,
> So seems this gorgeous beauty to mine eyes.

When Shakespeare has to deal with his climax, the death
of Talbot, he wisely adds the formality of rhyme to the
heightened style of the University Wits. This is how Talbot describes his son's death:

> Triumphant Death, smear'd with captivity,
> Young Talbot's valor makes me smile at thee.
> When he perceiv'd me shrink and on my knee,
> His bloody sword he brandish'd over me,
> And like a hungry lion did commence
> Rough deeds of rage and stern impatience:
> But when my angry guardant stood alone,
> Tendering my ruin and assail'd of none,
> Dizzy-eyed fury and great rage of heart
> Suddenly made him from my side to start
> Into the clustering battle of the French;
> And in that sea of blood my boy did drench
> His over-mounting spirit and there died,
> My Icarus, my blossom, in his pride.

Shakespeare seems to have known that his power over words did not match the grandeur of conception contained in Talbot's death. So he resorted to the conventional, the formal, the stylized, as the best way out.

But in compensation, bits of imaginative writing show themselves at intervals throughout the play; and as much in the less dignified scenes as in the rest. That they are thus scattered is a strong argument for the whole play being Shakespeare's. Thus Reignier, commenting on English valor, uses the metaphor of the artificial figure of a man striking the hours of a clock with a hammer, as Shakespeare was to use it again with superb effect in *Richard III*:

> I think by some odd gimmers or device
> Their arms are set like clocks, still to strike on;
> Else ne'er could they hold out so as they do.

Again, Talbot, deserted by his men in front of Orleans, exclaims,

> My thoughts are whirled like a potter's wheel.

Shakespeare knows exactly what to make the servingmen of Gloucester and Winchester say, when they quarrel:

First Serv. Nay, if we be forbidden stones, we'll fall to it
with our teeth.
Second Serv. Do what ye dare, we are as resolute.

Talbot, offering terms to the French commanders in Bordeaux, gets beyond good melodrama and touches true grandeur:

> But, if you frown upon this proffer'd peace,
> You tempt the fury of my three attendants,
> Lean famine, quartering steel, and climbing fire;
> Who in a moment even with the earth
> Shall lay your stately and air-braving towers,
> If you forsake the offer of their love.

But it is rare for Shakespeare's execution to be thus equal to his theme; and the chief virtue of the play must reside in the vehement energy with which Shakespeare both shaped this single play and conceived it as an organic part of a vast design.

J. P. BROCKBANK

from *The Frame of Disorder—"Henry VI"*

The four plays about the Wars of the Roses were staged fully and in sequence, probably for the first time, in 1953. The experience was arresting and moving, testifying to the continuity of our own preoccupations with those of Tudor England; here, it seemed, was yet another historical instance of anarchy owed to innocence and order won by atrocity. The three parts of *Henry VI* express the plight of individuals caught up in a cataclysmic movement of events for which responsibility is communal and historical, not personal and immediate, and they reveal the genesis out of prolonged violence of two figures representing the ultimate predicament of man as a political animal—Henry and Richard, martyr and machiavel. But one would not wish to overstress whatever analogues there may be between the fifteenth century and the twentieth, since these might be proved quite as striking for ages other than our own. If we are now more sympathetically disposed toward Shakespeare's history plays than were the readers and audiences of seventy years ago, it is largely because we have more flexible ideas about the many possible forms that history might take.

From "The Frame of Disorder—*Henry VI*," by J. P. Brockbank, in *Stratford-upon-Avon Studies 3: Early Shakespeare*, eds. John Russell Brown and Bernard Harris. London: Edward Arnold (Publishers) Ltd., 1961. Reprinted by permission of the publishers. Additional excerpts from this book appear in the Signet Classic editions of *2 Henry VI* and *3 Henry VI*.

We are less dominated by the Positivist view that the truth is co-extensive with, and not merely consistent with, the facts. Contemporaries of Boswell-Stone were re-luctant to take seriously a vision of the past that made free with the data for purposes they took to be simply dramatic. Following the lead of Richard Simpson, critics began to read Shakespeare's histories as documents of Tudor England, addressed primarily to contemporary problems and not fundamentally curious about the past-ness of the past.[1] Now we are better placed to see them from the point of view represented, for instance, by R. G. Collingwood's *The Idea of History* and Herbert Butter-field's *Christianity and History,* putting a less exclusive stress on facts, and looking harder at the myths and hy-potheses used to interpret them—at ideas of providence, historical process, personal responsibility and the role of the hero. These are precisely the ideas that the playwright is fitted to explore and clarify, and Shakespeare's treat-ment of them is the most searching our literature has to offer. For Shakespeare was peculiarly sensitive to the subtle analogues between the world and the stage, between the shape of events and the shape of a play, be-tween the relationship of historical process to individuals and that of the playwright to his characters. He tried from the beginning to meet the urgent and practical problem of finding dramatic forms and conventions that would ex-press whatever coherence and order could be found in the "plots" of chronicle history. Where narrative and play are incompatible, it may be the record and it may be the art that is defective as an image of human life, and in the plays framed from English and Roman history it is pos-sible to trace subtle modulations of spectacle, structure and dialogue as they seek to express and elucidate the full potential of the source material. A full account would take in *The Tempest,* which is the last of Shakespeare's plays to be made out of historical documents and which has much to do with the rule of providence over the po-

[1] Richard Simpson, "The Politics of Shakespeare's History Plays," in *Trans. New Sh. Soc.* (1874). A similar approach is made by L. B. Campbell.

litical activities of man. But from these early plays alone
there is much to be learned about the vision and technique
of historical drama, and these are the plays that are submitted most rigorously to the test of allegiance to historical record.

Part 1 and the Pageantry of Dissension

We might begin by taking a famous passage of Nashe
as the earliest surviving critical comment on *Part 1*.[2]

> How would it have joyed brave *Talbot* (the terror of the
> French) to think that after he had lyne two hundred
> yeares in his Tombe, hee should triumphe againe on the
> Stage, and have his bones new embalmed with the teares
> of ten thousand spectators at least, (at severall times)
> who, in the Tragedian that represents his person, imagine
> they behold him fresh bleeding.

This, primarily, is the ritual experience Shakespeare
sought and won. He transposed the past of the tombs, the
"rusty brass" and the "worm-eaten books" into living
spectacle. Whatever else must be said about all three
plays, they keep this quality of epic mime and with it an
elementary power to move large audiences. There is, too,
something in Nashe's glance at those early performances
that chimes with Coleridge's observation that "in order
that a drama may be properly historical, it is necessary that
it should be the history of the people to whom it is
addressed."[3] Shakespeare's early histories are addressed
primarily to the audience's heroic sense of community, to
its readiness to belong to an England represented by its
court and its army, to its eagerness to enjoy a public show
celebrating the continuing history of its prestige and
power. This does not mean, however, that we must surrender these early plays to Joyce's remark that Shakespeare's "pageants, the histories, sail full-bellied on a tide

2 Quoted in E. K. Chambers, *Shakespeare* (1930), II, p. 188.
3 T. M. Raysor (ed.), *Coleridge's Shakespeare Criticism* (1930) I,
p. 138.

of Mafeking enthusiasm." In the more mature plays of
Henry IV the heroic sense of community will be challenged by the unheroic—by that range of allegiances
which binds us less to authority and the King than to each
other and to Falstaff; and the death of Hotspur is a more
complicated theatrical experience than that of Talbot in
Nashe's description. But the early histories too express
stresses and ironies, complexities and intricate perspectives beyond the reach of the condescensions usually
allowed them.

Even *Part 1* has its share. If this is a play more moving
to watch than to read it is because it makes the historical
facts eloquent through the language of pageantry. In a
way that Nashe does not sufficiently suggest, Shakespeare
exploits the poignant contrast between the past nostal-
gically apprehended through its monuments, and the past
keenly re-enacted in the present—between the past "en-
tombed" "and fresh-bleeding." The effect, which testifies
to the continuity of stage techniques with those of the
Tournament and the civic pageant, is felt immediately in
the first scene (where the mood of a cathedral entomb-
ment is mocked by the energies of the brawl), in the
scene of Bedford's death (III.ii), and, most distinctly, in
the death of Talbot (IV.vii). These are among the several episodes of *Henry VI* that are presented both as
"events"—as if they actually happened, the figures caught
up in them alive and free, and as "occasions"—happenings that have some symbolic significance, or are (in
retrospect) "inevitable" turning-points in the history.
Thus the scene of Talbot's and Lisle's death would, if perfectly executed, present the chronicled event with convincing documentary detail, in a style befitting the occasion—the fire of English chivalry glowing brightest before
it expires. The context ensures that Talbot stands at his
death for the martial glory of England, and Bordeaux for
the dominion of France. When the English and French
nobles meet over his corpse (IV.vii), the retrospective,
reflective mood and the instant, practical mood are sustained side by side; the first calling to mind the image of a
memorial tomb seen in the remote perspective of a later

time, and the second recalling us to the hard realities of the battlefield. Talbot is discovered dead with his son "enhearsed in his arms" (IV.vii.45), resembling a figure on a monument. Lucy's long intonement of Talbot's titles was taken at first or second hand from the inscription on Talbot's actual tomb at Rouen, and it retains its lapidary formality.[4] Joan's lines,

> Him that thou magnifiest with all these titles
> Stinking and fly-blown lies here at our feet.
>
> (IV.vii.75)

have been mocked for their documentary impropriety (fly-blown in two minutes!) but they serve to accent the recollection in the spectacle of a Tudor tomb. Beneath the effigy of the complete man in, as it were, painted marble finery, lies the image of the rotten corpse. Joan's jeer mediates between the mutability threnody and the return to the exigencies of battle; the action gets under way again—there is a body to dispose of.

While there are other opportunities to arrest the flux of events, they are not all of this kind. The changes in pace and shifts of perspective owe as much to the chronicle as to the techniques of pageantry. The essential events and the processes and energies that shape and direct them are transmitted into the spectacle with a high sense of responsibility to the chronicle vision.

The three parts of *Henry VI* coincide with three distinct phases of the history and show that Shakespeare did what he could to tease a form for each of the plays out of the given material. The first phase of Holinshed's version[5] reports about four hundred incidents in the French campaign, some perfunctorily and some with full solemnity. The siege of Orleans is the most conspicuous in both chronicle and play. Holinshed finds occasion to deploy his epic clichés, with the "Englishmen" behaving themselves

---

4 See J. Pearce, "An Earlier Talbot Epitaph," *Modern Language Notes* (1944), p. 327.

5 Pp. 585–625 in the 1587 ed. These are the "first phase" as they supply almost all the material of *Part 1*. *Part 2* uses pp. 622–43, and *Part 3* pp. 643–93.

"right valiantlie under the conduct of their couragious capteine" to keep and enlarge "that which Henrie the fift had by his magnanimite & puissance atchived" (*Hol.* [1587/1808], p. 161). But the accent changes to somber historical prophecy, marking the ineluctable, impersonal historical law:

> But all helped not. For who can hold that which will awaie: In so much that some cities by fraudulent practises, othersome by martial prowesse were recovered by the French, to the great discouragement of the English and the appalling of their spirits; whose hope was now dashed partlie by their great losses and discomfitures (as after you shall heare) but cheeflie by the death of the late deceassed Henrie their victorious king.

These opening pages license a chauvinistic battle-play framing an historical morality about the evil consequences of civil dissension. Here is Holinshed on the loss of a group of towns in 1451:

> Everie daie was looking for aid, but none came. And whie? Even bicause the divelish division that reigned in England, so incombred the heads of the noble men there, that the honor of the realme was cleerelie forgotten. (*Hol.*, p. 228)

The chronicled sources of disaster are more nakedly sprung in the play: the loss of the puissant and magnanimous Henry V, the hostile stars, the hard fortunes of war, the perverse skill of the French, the steady eclipse of English chivalry with the deaths of its aging heroes, and the corrosive quarrels and dynastic rivalries of the nobles at home. All this is manifest in the mere pantomime of *Part 1*—its force would be felt by the stone-deaf, and the routine of the play's rhetoric does much to accent and little to qualify, explore or challenge the basic simplicities of the history.

The originality of Shakespeare's accomplishments is in the shedding of all literary artifice except that which serves to express the temper and structure of the history.

The first scene, for instance, establishes at once that double perspective which controls the mood of the chronicle—the sense of being close to the event together with a sense of knowing its consequences. The messenger's long review of the calamities of thirty future years, spoken in the memorial presence of the dead Henry V, is a precise dramatic expression of the narrative's parenthesis, "as after you shall heare," of which many repetitions catch the effect of a remorseless historical law expounded by an omniscient commentator.

The symmetrical sallies and counter-sallies of the next hour of the pantomime express the fickle movement of Mars, so often moralized by Holinshed: "thus did things waver in doubtful balance betwixt the two nations English and French"; "thus oftentimes varied the chance of doubtful war"; "thus flowed the victory, sometimes on the one party, and sometimes on the other" (*Hol.*, pp. 172, 180, 192). So speaks the dramatic Dauphin:

> Mars his true moving, even as in the heavens
> So in the earth, to this day is not known:
> Late did he shine upon the English side;
> Now we are victors; upon us he smiles.
>
> (I.ii.1)

The literary commonplace carries the chronicle moral in a naïve rhetoric transparent enough to let the raw facts tell.

It is French cunning that most often conspires with Mars to confound the English. The sniping of Salisbury at Orleans exemplifies it in an arresting stage effect ready-made in Holinshed for upper stage (tarras) performance. But as Holinshed's data is otherwise scanty and undramatic, Shakespeare amplifies it by making the French instead of the English employ "counterfeit husbandmen" to capture Rouen (*Stone,* pp. 205–07). He betrays the chronicle detail in order to enforce one of its generalizations, for while on one occasion defending the use of fraud in lawful war, Holinshed habitually prefers honest violence—an impression strengthened in the play by the

rival characterizations of Joan and Talbot. Talbot's stratagem at Auvergne (II.iii) is not subtle-witted but represents the triumph of soldierly resourcefulness over French
and female craft.

While "martiall feates, and daily skirmishes" continue
in France, the play returns in four scenes to England and
conveys the essential Holinshed by keeping the civil
causes coincident with the military effects. Thus the
dramatic concurrence of the siege of Orleans and the
brawl outside the Tower of London (I.iii) directly expresses the chronicle point, "Through dissention at home,
all lost abroad" (*Hol.*, p. 228). The Gloster-Winchester
feud is elaborately chronicled and patience and some
skill go into Shakespeare's abbreviation of it. More important than his management of the intricate detail, however, is the strategic liberty taken with the facts in order
to reduce the formal reconciliation elaborately mounted
in the chronicle to a repetition of the earlier squabble, but
this time concluded with a reluctant, casual handshake;
the Mayor, the muttered asides, and the servants off to the
surgeon's and the tavern, demote the dignity of the event
(*Hol.*, p. 146).[6] That quarrel thus becomes representative
of those which Holinshed ascribes to "privie malice and
inward grudge," while the dynastic rivalry assumes by
contrast a status appropriate to its remoter origin and
more terrible consequence.

It is in his presentation of the struggle between Lancaster and York that Shakespeare does most to transcend
the temper and enrich the data of the chronicle. For in
the early pages of Holinshed the struggle is nowhere
clearly epitomized. There are only allusions to things that
will "hereafter more manifestlie appeare"; Henry, for instance, creates Plantagenet Duke of York, "not foreseeing
that this preferment should be his destruction, nor that
his seed should of his generation be the extreame end and
finall conclusion" (*Hol.*, p. 155; *Stone,* p. 223). Hence
Shakespeare's invention of four scenes which, through the
heraldic formality of their language, reveal the hidden

---

[6] Here it is Bedford who formally rebukes the quarrelsome lords;
the play's homely figure of the mayor is borrowed from Fabyan.

keenness and permanence of the dynastic conflict. The
only distinguished one—the Temple scene—is much in
the manner of *Richard II;* there is the same tension between ceremony and spleen:

> And that I'll prove on better men than Somerset,
> Were growing time once ripen'd to my will.
>
> (II.iv.98)

But the note is caught again in the scene of Mortimer's
death:

> Here dies the dusky torch of Mortimer,
> Choked with ambition of the meaner sort.
>
> (II.v.122)

The two scenes between Vernon and Basset (III.iv and
IV.i) extend the Roses dispute from the masters to the
"servants"; but unlike those other servants who "enter
with bloody pates" (III.i.85 SD) in pursuit of Winchester's and Gloster's causes, these conduct their quarrel
according to "the law of arms." Ceremony and savagery
are equally characteristic of chronicle taste, and in *Part 1*
a full range of types of dissension is displayed by the
mutations of the spectacle.

The labored and repetitious data of the chronicle are
clarified without undue simplification, with the audience required to dwell at leisure on episodes of mo-
mentous and lasting significance to the course of history.
The rhythm between pattern and process is maintained;
the play like the history must be both reflected upon
and lived through, its moral shape apprehended but its
clamor and hurly-burly wracking the nerves. But not all
the chronicle material is adroitly and happily assimilated.
Shakespeare's embarrassment as heir to the facts and
judgments of Holinshed is disconcertingly evident in his
treatment of Joan. Holinshed presents two versions; a
"French" one, stated at length but unsympathetically,
"that this Jone (forsooth) was a damsell divine" (*Hol.,*
p. 171; *Stone,* pp. 210–12); and an "English" one, owed
to Monstrelet, that she was "a damnable sorcerer

suborned by Satan" (*Hol.*, p. 172). Shakespeare pursues
the chronicle by making her a manifestly evil angel of
light, and as the trick of turning devil into seeming angel
was a Morality Play commonplace, a technique of presentation lay to hand.[7] But the figure was much easier to
accept under the old allegoric conventions of the
Morality Play that Shakespeare has all but discarded,
than under the new historical documentary ones he was
forging. In the early scenes the nice and nasty views
about Joan are credibly distributed between the French
and English,[8] but after allowing her to voice an authentic
French patriotism (winning Burgundy back to her cause)
Shakespeare capitulates and throws his French Daniel to
the English lions, "Done like a Frenchman: turne and
turne againe" (III.iii.85). Shakespeare—as an examination of the detail would show—does nothing to mask
and much to stress the tension between the rival images
of "Puzel" and "Pussel," the "high-minded strumpet" and
"the holy prophetess." Late in the play she is made to
speak a searching indictment of English hypocrisy (V.iv.
36ff.) whose barbs are not removed by the spectacle of
her converse with evil spirits.

The play ends with the patching of a false peace which
holds no promise of a renewed civil order, and whose
terms, born out of a silly flirtation, prefigure the final
loss of France. None of the many reconciliations have
any quality of goodwill, Shakespeare taking his tone
again from Holinshed:

> But what cause soever hindered their accord and unitie
> ... certeine it is, that the onelie and principal cause was,
> for that the God of peace and love was not among them,
> without whom no discord is quenched, no knot of con-
> cord fastened, no bond of peace confirmed, no distracted

---

[7] E.g., John Bale, *The Temptation of our Lord* (see *Works*, ed.
Farmer, p. 155), and *The Conflict of Conscience* (see Hazlitt-Dodsley,
Vol. VI, p. 35).

[8] The only mocking lines spoken of Joan by the French are
Alençon's at I.ii.119; the English messenger calls her "holy prophetess"
at I.iv.102.

minds reconciled, no true freendship mainteined. (*Hol.*,
p. 183)

Suffolk's courtship of Margaret (V.iii) prefaces a false
peace with a false love. To parody the absurdities of
political romance Shakespeare allows Suffolk the style
of a professional philanderer (one thinks of de Simier's
wooing of Elizabeth for Alençon) and compiles for him
"A volume of enticing lines" more felicitous than Lacy's
in *Friar Bacon and Friar Bungay;* but in Greene's play
the courtship is an engaging frolic merely, while here
the treacheries exercised in the politics of flirtation are
as sinister as they are amusing—the betrayal of trust
must have evil consequences in the harsh chronicle
setting.

Holinshed grieves that "the God of peace and love"
was not among the jarring nobles; but in a sense he was
—in the unfortunate person of King Henry—and Shakespeare is well aware of the irony. Henry is "too virtuous
to rule the realm of England," like Elidure, the comically
naïve King in the early chronicle-morality *Nobody and
Somebody,*[9] but Shakespeare makes the point unsmilingly.
In the *Henry VI* plays, virtue, through varying degrees of
culpable innocence, connives in its own destruction. Had
they been performed in the reign of Henry VII, when
the canonization of "Holy Harry" was still a point of
debate and his martyrdom a theme for civic spectacle,
those who thought the King an innocent might have appealed to the first two plays, and those who took him
for a saint, to the last. For as the plays advance, the
paradoxical plight of moral man under the rule of historical and political processes grows more disturbing until
it reaches something like a tragic solution.

---

[9] This play (edited by Richard Simpson for the Shakespeare Society)
treats the ups and downs of Elidure's reign with challenging irreverence.
The extant edition is of 1606, but the original may antedate *Henry VI.*

PHYLLIS RACKIN

Anti-Historians: *Women's Roles in Shakespeare's Histories*

Historiography is a major concern in Shakespeare's
plays. Characters repeatedly allude to history, past and
future, and define their actions as attempts to inscribe
their names in the historical record. Like their playwright,
these characters show an obsessive concern with the work
of the historian—the writing, reading, and preservation of
historical texts.

No woman is the protagonist in a Shakespearean historical play. Renaissance gender role definitions prescribed
silence as a feminine virtue, and Renaissance sexual mythology associated the feminine with body and matter as
opposed to masculine intellect and spirit. Renaissance
historiography constituted a masculine tradition, written
by men, devoted to the deeds of men, glorifying the
masculine virtues of courage, honor, and patriotism, and
dedicated to preserving the names of past heroes and re-
cording their patriarchal genealogies. Within that historical record, women had no voice.

The protagonists of Shakespeare's history plays, conceived both as subjects and as writers of history, were

From *Theatre Journal*, 37 (1985), 329–44. Reprinted by permission
of The Johns Hopkins University Press and Phyllis R. Rackin.

inevitably male. The women who do appear are typically defined as opponents and subverters of the historical and historiographical enterprise—in short, as antihistorians. But Shakespeare does give them a voice—a voice that challenges the logocentric, masculine historical record.[1] For the most part, and especially in his early histories, Shakespeare depicts male protagonists defending masculine historical projects against both female characters who threaten to obstruct those projects and feminine appeals to the audience that threaten to discredit them. In Shakespeare's later history plays those feminine voices become more insistent. They both threaten to invalidate the great, inherited historical myths that Shakespeare found in his historiographic sources and imply that before the masculine voice of history can be accepted as valid, it must come to terms with women and the subversive forces they represent. However, as soon as Shakespeare attempts to incorporate those feminine forces, marrying words and things, spirit and matter, historiography itself becomes problematic, no longer speaking with the clear, univocal voice of unquestioned tradition but re-presented as a dubious construct, always provisional, always subject to erasure and reconstruction, and never adequate to recover the past in full presence.

The pattern of masculine history writing and feminine subversion is probably clearest in *1 Henry VI*. Here Shakespeare defines the project of writing English history as an effort to preserve the legacy of English glory left by Henry V and associates it with the masculine, military struggle to secure English power in France. Michel Foucault's observation that the Greek epic "was intended to perpetuate the immortality of the hero" aptly characterizes Shakespeare's conception of history at this point in his career. In Foucault's view, the hero's death represents a kind of trade-off between the hero and his story: "if he was willing to die young, it was so that his life, consecrated and magnified by death, might pass into immortality."[2]

The process by which human mortality is translated into

textual immortality was a frequent theme for Renaissance theorists of historiography as well as for Shakespearean sonnets. However, a problem arises—as it did for historians during Shakespeare's own lifetime—when history, the second party to this trade, comes to be seen itself as subject to mutability. Various forces were conspiring in Shakespeare's time to compel a recognition that the historical past was not necessarily identical with the historiographic text. Faced with a growing sense of alienation from the past, a newly critical attitude toward texts, and an increasing reliance on physical remains to verify or refute verbal reports, the medieval union of history and myth was breaking down.[3] Written accounts of the past were no longer accepted as authentic simply because they existed. Like the Bible itself, historical writing no longer had a direct, unequivocal relation to truth. Translated into the vernacular, subjected to different interpretations from rival Christian sects, the Bible had become a problematic document in which alternative words contended to translate the meaning of the original text and alternative interpretations contended to explicate it. In a similar way, alternative accounts of historical events and opposed interpretations of their causes and significance threatened to disrupt each other's authority. Thus undermined, history loses its power to make the hero immortal. In such a case, the hero's death becomes meaningless, and heroism itself becomes impossible.

This is the problem dramatized in *1 Henry VI*. The play begins as history itself begins, with (or immediately following) the death of the hero. The opening scene depicts the funeral of Henry V, the legendary warrior-king who was, we are told, "too famous to live long" (I. i. 6);[4] and the entire play can be seen as a series of attempts on the part of the English to write a history that will preserve Henry's fame. That conflict begins in the opening scene when the audience (along with their countrymen on stage) are confronted with reports of French victories that threaten to erase Henry's name from the historical record as

surely as death has destroyed his body. Bedford's heroic
invocation of Henry's ghost, implying that the dead king
will occupy a place in history even more glorious than
Julius Caesar's, is interrupted mid-sentence by a messenger bringing news that eight French cities have been lost.

The French action—to erase the English record—
operates at two levels. Within the represented action, the
French fight to drive the English from their country. At
the rhetorical level, they attack both the English version
of history and the values it expresses with an earthy
iconoclasm that subverts the inherited notions of chivalric
glory invoked by the English. Talbot, the English champion, and Joan, his French antagonist, speak alternative
languages.[5] His language reifies glory, while hers is the
language of physical objects; and the play defines their
conflict as a contest between English words and French
things, between the historical record that Talbot wishes to
preserve and the physical reality that Joan invokes to discredit it. Shakespeare departs from his sources in having
Talbot bury Salisbury, one of the last English heroes of
the former age, in France. The real Salisbury was buried
in England, but Shakespeare's Talbot announces that he
will erect Salisbury's tomb in the "chiefest temple" of the
French, "Upon the which, that everyone may read, / Shall
be engraved the sack of Orleans, / The treacherous manner of his mournful death, / And what a terror he had
been to France" (II. ii. 14–17). Talbot's effort here, as in
his military campaign to secure Henry's French conquests,
is a struggle to leave an English historical record in
France.[6]

Shakespeare repeatedly calls attention to the fact that
the French champion is a woman, thereby defining the
conflict between England and France as a conflict between
masculine and feminine values—chivalric virtue vs. prag-
matic craft, historical fame vs. physical reality, patriarchal
age vs. subversive youth, high social rank vs. low, self vs.
other. "English Talbot" is a venerable gentleman who
fights according to the chivalric code. Joan is a youthful

peasant whose forces resort to craft, subterfuge, and modern weapons (a French boy sniper shoots the great Salisbury, and Joan recaptures Rouen by sneaking in, disguised as the peasant she really is, to admit the French army).

In addition to Joan, *1 Henry VI* includes two other female characters—the Countess of Auvergne and Margaret of Anjou. All three are French, and all three represent threats to the English protagonists and to the heroic values associated with history as the preserver of masculine fame and glory.[7] Like Joan, the Countess attacks Talbot; like Joan, she resorts to craft and stratagem; and like Joan she places her faith in physical reality over verbal report. The Countess says she wants to verify the reports of Talbot's glory by seeing his person: "Fain would mine eyes be witness with mine ears / To give their censures of these rare reports." What she sees—"a child, a silly dwarf . . . this weak and writhled shrimp," in short, Talbot's physical appearance—convinces her that "report is fabulous and false" (II. iii. 9–23).

The Countess's preference for physical evidence over historical report associates her with the French and female forces in the play as a threat to the project of writing English history. We see this conflict in its purest form after Talbot's death when Sir William Lucy calls for him in heroic language:

> But where's the great Alcides of the field,
> Valiant Lord Talbot, Earl of Shrewsbury,
> Created, for his rare success in arms,
> Great Earl of Washford, Waterford, and Valence,
> Lord Talbot of Goodrig and Urchinfield,
> Lord Strange of Blackmere, Lord Verdun of Alton,
> Lord Cromwell of Wingfield, Lord Furnival of Sheffield,
> The thrice-victorious Lord of Falconbridge,
> Knight of the noble order of Saint George,
> Worthy Saint Michael, and the Golden Fleece,
> Great Marshal to Henry the Sixth
> Of all his wars within the realm of France?

(IV. vii. 60–71)

Rejecting the grandiose pretentions of the string of titles Lucy bestows on Talbot and relying on material fact to debunk the titles and attack Lucy's language, Joan replies:

> Here's a silly stately style indeed!
> The Turk, that two and fifty kingdoms hath,
> Writes not so tedious a style as this.
> Him that thou magnifi'st with all these titles
> Stinking and fly-blown lies here at our feet.
> (IV. vii. 72–76)

Lucy describes Talbot as history was to describe him, decked in the titles that designate his patriarchal lineage and heroic military achievements. Joan, like the Countess, insists on physical fact, rejecting the masculine historical ideals and significance that Lucy's glorious names invoke.

Joan's reductive, nominalistic attack has an obvious appeal for an audience: her vigorous language, tied to the material facts of earth, threatens to topple the imposing formal edifice Lucy has constructed with his tower of names. But in this, the first of Shakespeare's English history plays, the subversive female voice is never allowed to prevail for more than a moment, and it is tempting to speculate that at least some in Shakespeare's audience may have realized that the glorious words of Lucy, unlike Joan's fictitious speech, take their authority from an enduring historical monument, Talbot's tomb at Rouen, where they were inscribed.[8]

In the case of the Countess, no more speculation is required. Shakespeare contrives Talbot's encounter with the Countess so that she, and the audience along with her, will be clearly instructed in the superiority of report over physical fact. Just before Talbot summons the hidden soldiers who will free him from her trap, he announces, "I am but shadow of myself: / You are deceived, my substance is not here" (II. iii. 50–51); and a minute later the Countess acknowledges that the verbal reports she doubted were really true. For the audience, Talbot's lines were doubly significant: a "shadow" was a common term for an actor, and in that sense the man who spoke those lines was quite literally "but a shadow" of the elusive Talbot, the emblem of lost historical presence, celebrated by historiographer and playwright, but never present in substance even to the Countess who thinks she has him captured in her castle. Relying as it does on physical presence, the reductive, French, female version of Talbot is always vulnerable to metadramatic attack, which invokes the ultimate fact of theatrical occasion to remind the audience that no actual physical presence is involved.

This reminder is important because the whole issue of physical presence vs. historical record, dramatized in *1 Henry VI* as a conflict between English men and French women, is central, not only to this particular play, but to the history play genre itself. Urging the value of English history plays, Thomas Nashe used Talbot as an example when he wrote that in these productions,

> our forefathers valiant acts (that have line long buried in rustie brass and worme-eaten books) are revived, and they themselves raised from the Grave of Oblivion. . . . How would it have joyed brave Talbot (the Terror of the French) to think that after he had lyne two hundred years in his tomb, he should triumph again on the stage, and have his bones new embalmed with the tears of ten thousand spectators who . . . imagine they behold him fresh bleeding.[9]

The audience, as Nashe reminds us, went to the play hoping to see those historical records brought to life and to make direct contact with the living reality that was celebrated but also obscured by the "worme-eaten" books of history.

For Shakespeare's audience, as for the characters in the play, Talbot's "glory [still] fill[ed] the world with loud report" (II. iii. 43). His mere name, like the name of God, is sufficient to rout the French soldiers (I. iv. 50;

II. i. 79–81). Although Talbot is finally killed, his glory survives his physical death. Like the Countess, Shakespeare's audience wanted to *see* the renowned Talbot, and like her, they were likely to be disappointed. Exploiting its own inadequacies to validate the historical record, the play instructs its audience along with the Countess that the sight they see on stage is only a "shadow" of Talbot— that history and renown portrayed him more truly than physical presence ever could. The masculine authority of history is thus sustained against the feminine challenge of physical presence as the play is revealed as a representation. Presence remains ineluctably absent—the elusive Other, that, like the feminine principle itself, must be suppressed in order to sustain the masculine historiographic narrative. The nominalist challenge posed by the women's appeals to physical fact is discredited by reminders that the drama contains no physical facts, and so the verbal construction of Talbot's glory survives.

In this context the scene of Talbot's death is instructive. A long contention between Talbot and his son—a son repeatedly addressed by his father as "Talbot," the father's own name—in which each urges the other to save his life by fleeing from battle and in which neither, of course, will flee ends with the death of both. Talbot's paternal solicitude and his son's filial devotion, along with their mutual devotion to honor, have insured that there will be no survivor to carry their name into the future. And yet the name will still survive, recorded in history books, alive in sixteenth-century memory and celebrated on Shakespeare's stage—stripped now of any living human referent but still potent and significant.

The argument that finally convinces Talbot to allow his son to stay with him and die in battle is the boy's claim that if he runs away, he will lose his patriarchal title and become "like . . . the peasant boys of France": "If I fly, I am not Talbot's son. . . . If son to Talbot, die at Talbot's foot" (IV. vi. 48–53). Talbot and his son both make the heroic choice described by Foucault, sacrificing their lives to preserve their heroic titles. In direct contrast, Shakespeare contrives Joan's final interview with her father to show her placing life above historical glory. We see her rejecting her father, revealed as a bastard, and finally claiming to be pregnant with yet another bastard, all in a futile effort to save her life (V. iv).

This final schematic contrast between the strong bond that unites the male Talbot and Joan's denial of her peasant father completes Shakespeare's picture of Talbot and Joan as opposites and connects the various terms in which their opposition has been defined—historian vs. antihistorian, noble man vs. peasant woman, realist vs. nominalist. As Kenneth Burke has pointed out, the medieval realist conception of language had strong affinities with the medieval feudal conception of the family, for both realism and feudalism treat "individuals as members of a group" or "tribe." In direct contrast, nominalism, the subversive movement in medieval philosophy, is "linguistically individualistic or atomistic," because it treats "groups as aggregates of individuals." Realism and feudalism both imply history because both involve what Burke calls "an *ancestral* notion." A realist conception of language holds that universals precede things and "give birth" to them.[10] Nominalism, like Joan, denies history because it denies the diachronic links that unite meaning and word like the successive generations of a great feudal family (the kind of family whose name the Talbots die to preserve). Drawing the same kinds of connections, R. Howard Bloch associates the story of Abelard's castration with the fact of Abelard's nominalism: just as Abelard's intellectual position disrupted the "intellectual genealogy" of words, so too is his own physical genealogy represented as disrupted.[11] And, although Bloch does not mention it, the castration, like the nominalism, also associates Abelard with the feminine.

Joan's sexual promiscuity, hinted from the first, is less obviously connected than her nominalism to her role as antihistorian, but it is connected nonetheless. Just as her

nominalism associates her with the Countess of Auvergne,
so her sexual promiscuity associates her with the third
Frenchwoman in the play, Margaret of Anjou, soon to
become the adulterous queen of Henry VI. Immediately
linked to Joan in the audience's eyes, Margaret is introduced by being led captive onto the stage at the same
time that Joan is led off it after her final capture. Moreover, we quickly learn in 2 *Henry VI* that the marriage
between Margaret and Henry threatens to erase history
itself:

> Fatal this marriage, canceling your fame,
> Blotting your names from books of memory,
> Razing the characters of your renown,
> Defacing monuments of conquered France,
> Undoing all, as all had never been.
>
> (I. i. 98–103)

Besides Joan, Margaret is the only woman who plays a
major part in the *Henry VI* plays and the only character
of either sex who appears in all four plays of the first
tetralogy. Margaret's disruptive role becomes increasingly
prominent as the story progresses and the world of the
plays sinks into chaos. A virago who defies her husband,
leads armies into battle, and gloats at the murder of an
innocent child, Shakespeare's Margaret has a "tiger's heart
wrapped in a woman's hide." Shakespeare follows Hall in
making her "a manly woman, usyng to rule and not to be
ruled," but he departs from his historiographic source in
making her an adulteress.[12]

Like Joan's sexual promiscuity, Margaret's adultery has
no real impact on the action of the *Henry VI* plays. In
both cases, the women's sexual transgressions seem almost
irrelevant—dramatically unnecessary attributes, at best
added to underscore their characterization as threats to
masculine honor, at worst gratuitous slanders, like the
slander by which a Renaissance woman who transgressed

in any way, even by excessive gossip and railing, was commonly characterized as a whore.

The women in Shakespeare's English history plays differ in virtue, strength, nationality, and social rank; and they speak with a variety of voices. But despite their many roles, they are never the central actors, and they differ only as the masculine project of writing history is conceived differently. In the world of history, women are inevitably alien, representatives of the unarticulated residue that eludes the men's historiographic texts and threatens their historical myths.

We can explain the subversive roles of women in Shakespeare's history plays in various ways. We can postulate that Shakespeare derived them from observation of real women. Joan Kelly has pointed out that early feminist writers, opposing their own experience to masculine texts, were "unremittingly critical of the authors—ancient, modern, even scriptural—at a time when the *auctores* were still *auctoritates* to many."[13] We can explain the subversive roles of Shakespeare's women as projection. Shakespeare, as a male writer of history that denied the feminine, may have expressed his anxiety about that denial by projecting it onto his female characters. We can say that Shakespeare's gift for imaginative sympathy or the logic of his structure forced him to cast his women as antihistorians, necessarily opposed to a masculine script designed to suppress their roles and silence their voices. But whatever explanation we choose to adopt, we come to the same conclusion: the women were antihistorians because they had to be. It was the only part they could play in the story the men had written.[14]

[1] See Linda Woodbridge, *Women and the English Renaissance: Literature and the Nature of Womankind, 1540–1620* (Urbana: University of Illinois Press, 1984),

p. 208: "Women's tongues are instruments of aggression or self-defense; men's are the tools of authority. In either case speech is an expression of authority; but male speech represents legitimate authority, while female speech attempts to usurp authority or rebel against it."

[2] Michel Foucault, "What is an Author," in *Textual Strategies: Perspectives in Post-Structuralist Criticism,* ed. Josué V. Harari (Ithaca: Cornell University Press, 1979), p. 142.

[3] Gabrielle M. Spiegel, "Genealogy: Form and Function in Medieval Historical Narrative," *History and Theory: Studies in the Philosophy of History,* 22 (1983), 43–53. See also Peter Burke, *The Renaissance Sense of the Past* (London: Edward Arnold, Ltd., 1969) and F. J. Levy, *Tudor Historical Thought* (San Marino, California: The Huntington Library, 1967).

[4] All citations of *Henry VI* are from this present edition.

[5] In *Henry V* the women will literally speak an alternative language. There Shakespeare departs from theatrical convention to write the women's lines in French, excluding them from the linguistic community that includes virtually all of the male characters—French as well as English—along with his English-speaking audience.

[6] David Riggs, *Shakespeare's Heroical Histories: Henry VI and Its Literary Tradition* (Cambridge: Harvard University Press, 1971), pp. 22–23; 100–113, shows how the conventions of the funeral oration are used to characterize Talbot as well as Salisbury and Henry V. Riggs argues convincingly that Talbot exemplifies "the aristocratic ideal of military service and gentle blood" that was disappearing at the very time when *Henry VI* was written and that Joan "epitomized the external forces that threaten[ed] that ideal."

[7] See David Bevington, "The Domineering Female in *1 Henry VI,*" *Shakespeare Studies,* 2 (1966), 51–58; and Sigurd Burckhardt, " 'I Am But Shadow of Myself': Ceremony and Design in *1 Henry VI,*" in *Shakespearean Meanings* (Princeton: Princeton University Press, 1968), pp. 47–77.

[8] Although Lucy is not mentioned in Shakespeare's chronicle sources, there was a historical Sir William Lucy who lived near Shakespeare's home and was three times Sheriff of Warwickshire in the time of Henry VI. It has been suggested that Shakespeare knew of him from local oral tradition. Perhaps there is a connection between the fact that Lucy was historical—although not historiographic—authority and the fact that he recites the words that really were inscribed on Talbot's tomb at Rouen even though they, like Lucy himself, were not recorded in Shakespeare's chronicle sources.

[9] Thomas Nashe, *Pierce Penilesse his Supplication to the Diuell* (1592), reprinted in E. K. Chambers, *The Elizabethan Stage,* Vol. IV (Oxford: The Clarendon Press, 1923), pp. 238–39.

[10] Kenneth Burke, "Realist Family and Nominalist Aggregate" and "Familiar Definition," both in *A Grammar of Motives* (Cleveland: Meridian Books, 1962), pp. 247–52 and 26–27.

[11] R. Howard Bloch, *Etymologies and Genealogies: A Literary Anthropology of the French Middle Ages* (Chicago: University of Chicago Press, 1983), p. 149. Bloch also cites a fourteenth-century Provençal author who developed an elaborate system of analogies between modes of paternity and modes of lexical derivation (p. 42).

[12] Edward Hall, *The Union of the Two Noble and Illustre Famelies of Lancastre and Yorke* (London, 1548–50), rpt. (London: J. Johnson *et al.,* 1809), p. 249. Robert Greene's famous attack on Shakespeare as a "Tygers hart wrapt in a Players hyde" (*Greens Groatsworth of Wit,* 1596, reprinted in Chambers, IV, 241) offers a tantalizing suggestion of identity between the gentle playwright described in Ben Jonson's *Discoveries* ("honest, and of an open, and free nature") and the wicked queen. Stephen Orgel, in a recent article ("Prospero's Wife," *Representations,* 8 [Fall 1984]) suggests that Prospero (who is generally recognized as a Shakespearean self-representation), in his claim to have raised the dead,

"has incorporated Ovid's witch, the wicked mother." Nowhere is Shakespeare/Prospero's claim more applicable than in the English history plays, and nowhere is Orgel's observation more suggestive. In those plays, Shakespeare incorporates the women and raises the dead in order to confute the historical record. And he does so with women's own weapons—lies (fictitious characters, dialogues, events) and materiality (stage spectacle), both of which he uses to oppose the written historiographic text.

[13] Joan Kelly, "Early Feminist Theory and the *Querelle des Femmes,* 1400–1789," *Signs* (Autumn 1982), 4–28. Kelly cites Christine de Pisan's *City of Women,* 1404 (translated into English, 1521, as *The Boke of the Cyte of Ladies*) as an example of this opposition of women's experience to men's texts: "Although you have seen such things in writing, you have not seen them with your eyes," says one of Christine's female speakers, addressing her in what Kelly calls "tones of modern empiricism, urging her to accept as true only what conformed to her (and other women's) experience." And, as Maureen Quilligan has reminded me, the problematic union of patriarchal authority and female sex embodied in Queen Elizabeth—who had herself been declared a bastard—provides a crucial contemporary context for Shakespeare's practice in his English history plays, and especially in *King John.*

[14] This paper was originally prepared for the University of Pennsylvania's Mellon Seminar on the Diversity of Language and the Structure of Power. I am indebted to the members of that seminar—especially to Lucienne Frappier-Mazur, Gwynne Kennedy, Maureen Quilligan, and Carroll Smith-Rosenberg—for their stimulating questions and suggestions.

LAWRENCE V. RYAN

"Henry VI" on Stage and Screen

Of specific dates for stagings of *King Henry VI* in
Shakespeare's lifetime no record exists. From March,
1592, through January, 1594, however, Philip Henslowe's
diary mentions receipts for sixteen performances of a
"ne[w]" play called "harey the vj," apparently Shakespeare's Part One, the most popular dramatic production
at Henslowe's Rose Theatre over that span of time. That
the third part of the trilogy had been staged by 1592 is
evident from Robert Greene's envious comments in his
Groats-vvorth of witte on the success of a certain "upstart"
dramatist, where a disparaging phrase about Shakespeare
as having a "Tygers hart wrapt in a Players hyde" echoes
the captured York's outburst at the cruelty of Queen
Margaret, "O tiger's heart wrapped in a woman's hide!"
(I. iv. 137). Part Three in fact must then have been on
the boards before 1595, the year in which was printed
The True Tragedie of Richard Duke of York, actually a
"bad" quarto of *3 Henry VI,* the title page of which states
that the play "was sundrie times acted by the Right Honourable the Earle of Pembrooke his servants." While there
is no similar reference to any early productions of *2 Henry
VI,* it too was published in an inferior quarto version in
1594, with the title *The First part of the Contention
betwixt the two famous Houses of Yorke and Lancaster.*
Yet apparently all three parts were popular with Eliza-

bethan audiences. Not only were the quartos of *2* and *3
Henry VI* reprinted twice (1600, 1619) before the issuing
of the First Folio in 1623, but in the same year as
Greene's diatribe appeared another pamphlet, Thomas
Nashe's *Pierce Penilesse his Supplication to the Divell*,
remarked

> How would it have joyed brave *Talbot* (the terror of the
> French) to thinke that after he had lyne two hundred
> yeares in his Tombe, hee should triumphe againe on
> the Stage, and have his bones newe embalmed with the
> teares of ten thousand spectators at least, (at severall
> times) who, in the Tragedian that represents his person,
> imagine they behold him fresh bleeding.

Nashe's "ten thousand spectators," though the figure may
be exaggerated, seems to allude to attendance at the several performances of the "harey the vj" put on by Henslowe during the first half of 1592, the consensus now
being that this drama was most likely the First Part of
Shakespeare's trilogy. It is generally assumed, therefore,
that all three parts of *Henry VI* had most likely been
produced by 1592.

The popularity of these plays in their author's own time
may have been due in part to his having invented a new
kind of drama about history, about a historical subject,
moreover, in which his contemporaries were intensely
interested. For Elizabethan audiences stood even closer in
time to their dynastic civil wars of the fifteenth century
than do Americans of today to their own traumatic and
divisive Civil War.

Still, from the close of the first Elizabethan Age to the
beginning of the second in the 1950s, productions of the
Henry VI plays, especially in authentic rather than in
drastically adapted and rewritten versions, appeared infrequently in the dramatic repertoire. After the Restoration
and the reopening of the theaters, John Crowne did write
adaptations of the Second and Third Parts, presented,
respectively, in early 1681 and early 1680 in the recently

built Duke's Theatre, Dorset Garden. In Crowne's hands, *2 Henry VI* became, as the 1681 title page reads, *Henry the Sixth, The First Part. With the Murder of Humphrey Duke of Glocester.* Crowne stitched his version up from Acts I-III of Shakespeare's play, omitting the later scenes dealing with Cade's and York's rebellions and stretching out those episodes dealing with the falls of Gloucester and Henry Beaufort by adding much, especially anti-papal, material to the portrait of the cardinal. Since the late years of Charles II's reign were the times of the "Popish Plots," the author may have thought his additions timely. The play, however, was unsuccessful, and Crowne claimed, most likely without grounds, that the authorities had suppressed it for an anti-Catholic bias that the king and his brother James would not have approved. In *The Misery of Civil-War* (1680) Crowne reattached Cade's rebellion from the fourth act of *2 Henry VI* to *3 Henry VI*, and again justifying himself, as he had in his earlier adaptation, on the grounds that he believed Shakespeare had written little of either play, added other scenes of his own devising. A couple of these center upon the amours of King Edward IV; another, in order to increase the pathos of Rutland's murder, portrays the young victim in a sad parting from his father York. As an instance of how foreign matter has often been retained in later productions of Shakespearean plays after such tampering has occurred, the Rutland-York parting invented by Crowne found its way into Theophilus Cibber's portmanteau version of *2 and 3 Henry VI* (1723) and into an adaptation of all three parts in which Edmund Kean appeared in 1817.

During the year 1723 two plays about Henry VI's reign were produced at the Drury Lane Theatre, Cibber's adaptation and Ambrose Philips' *Humfrey Duke of Gloucester, a Tragedy*. The latter, as a note to the reader in the printed version admits, retained only about thirty of Shakespeare's original lines and was really a new drama built around certain episodes that Philips admired in *2 Henry VI*. Cibber's adaptation, which appeared in five printings from *c.* 1722 to 1736, bears the title *An Historical Tragedy of the Civil Wars in the Reign of King Henry VI. (Being a Sequel to the Tragedy of Humfrey Duke of Gloucester: And an Introduction to the Tragical History of King Richard III.)* Its first act is drawn from the final scenes of *2 Henry VI*; its next two, from Acts I and II of *3 Henry VI*. Even more than Crowne in *The Misery of Civil-War,* Cibber in his final two acts makes much of amours, of the passion of Henry VI's son Prince Edward for Anne Clifford (later to be Richard III's reluctant bride), as well as of the Duke of Clarence's love for Anne's sister Elizabeth. A curious omission is an authentic scene which has proved to be particularly affecting in recent productions. Cibber did retain King Henry's soliloquy at Towton field, but he excised the moving speeches of a son who has killed his father and of a father who has killed his son in the battle. Although Cibber, unlike Philips, retained much of Shakespeare's poetry, in cutting and rearranging incidents he wrote in many linking passages and other lines of his own, a precedent that was to be followed even in what has probably been the most influential production of the trilogy mounted during this present century.

Alterations in these Shakespearean histories by eighteenth-century playwrights tended to make them conform to neo-classical notions about the importance of the unities and of dramatic decorum. In Philips' *Humfrey Duke of Gloucester,* for example, Eleanor Cobham is converted from Shakespeare's proud and ambitious duchess into a guiltless woman, an innocent victim of machinations by rivals at court, and thus a person toward whom Humfrey, in contrast with his characterization in Shakespeare's play, can enact the part of an unselfishly noble and supportive husband. Pathos is also increased, not only in the addition or augmentation of the love interest in certain adaptations, but also in scenes of tragic parting or death. Theophilus Cibber has young Clifford enter in time to swear to his mortally wounded father that he will avenge his death upon York, even though in Shakespeare's version Old

Clifford is already slain at the battle of St. Alban's before
the son comes onstage. Again, after Clifford has killed
Rutland at the battle of Wakefield, instead of the "bloody
napkin" with which York is taunted in *3 Henry VI,* Cibber
intensifies the pathos by having Queen Margaret and
Clifford bring the youth's corpse into the presence of his
about-to-be-murdered father. Finally, Cibber's and Philips'
adaptations, staged and published during a time of concern about stirrings on behalf of the exiled Stuarts, apparently were meant, as George C. Branam has suggested,
to point a "single moral" against the dangers of "faction
and uprising."

During the remainder of the eighteenth century, passages from the trilogy were sometimes inserted into adaptations of other Shakespearean plays, most strangely,
perhaps, in Tate Williamson's production of *Hamlet*
(1773), where lines from the deathbed scene of Cardinal
Beaufort in *2 Henry VI* are used to portray the agonized
last moments of King Claudius. Only three productions of
dramas based on these histories of Shakespeare, however,
appear to have been staged. A single performance of *1
Henry VI* that departed little from Shakespeare's version
did take place at Covent Garden on March 13, 1738.
Because it was done apart from any connection with the
latter two parts of the trilogy, the acting company retained
the scenes dealing with the wars in France, with the
Talbots and Joan of Arc, that are so frequently abridged
or omitted in modern performances.

The other known late eighteenth-century adaptations
were not produced in the London theater. In 1773–74
thirteen plays by Shakespeare were staged in Charleston,
South Carolina, including some version of *Henry VI.*
Finally, in 1795 Richard Valpy's *The Roses*; *or King
Henry the Sixth*; *an Historical Tragedy* was acted at
Reading School and printed in that city during the same
year. Because Valpy's work was an effort to give greater
unity of time and place to the action of *3 Henry VI,* he
defended the omission of scenes that he deemed out of

keeping with these neo-classical principles as well as with his own sense of what kind of behavior met standards of dramatic decorum.

On December 15, 1817, Edmund Kean played the leading role in Herman Merivale's *Richard Duke of York,* a pastiche of all three parts of the trilogy that incorporated matter taken from plays by Shakespeare's contemporaries George Chapman, John Marston, and John Webster. In its random selection of episodes from the Second and Third Parts and consequent lack of any sense of unity or real dramatic progression, Merivale's effort has been labeled by one critic "the worst mélange we have been called on to notice in the entire course of our history of Shakespearian alterations." Yet in spite of the shortcomings of the adaptation, a contemporary reviewer in the *European Magazine* reported that Kean was "in many scenes, unusually great" and noted that "the performance was well received by a more crowded house than we have witnessed this season."

After nearly two centuries of such liberties taken with Shakespeare's trilogy, a reviewer in the *Athenaeum* (April 30, 1864) was able to report "A Successful Revival" of *2 Henry VI* Presented at the Surrey Theatre in London in honor of the three hundredth anniversary of Shakespeare's birth, the revival enjoyed a dozen performances. The producer and leading actor, James Anderson, contrary to the prevailing scholarly opinion of the time that little of the play was actually Shakespearean, affirmed its authenticity and demonstrated with the performance that "it acts remarkably well and manifestly excites interest in the audience." Anderson thus established a precedent for those more recent directors who have tried to respect the integrity of the text in their productions. Although the actresses playing Queen Margaret and the Duchess of Gloucester were apparently not up to exhibiting the strength of those two leading female characters, Anderson himself was said to have carried off the roles of both York and the rebel Jack Cade "with great animation and spirit." In enacting

Cade's fatal duel with Alexander Iden. "Mr. Anderson threw considerable humour into it by indicating the weakness he suffered from a five days' fast, and buckling his belt tighter in order to strengthen himself for the task. He died boldly like a courageous rebel of the true English type, and won our respect even in his fall." In another celebration of the tercentenary of Shakespeare's birth, an adaptation of *Henry VI,* along with the rest of Shakespeare's two historical tetralogies, was staged at Weimar in 1864.

Twenty-five years were to elapse before any part of the trilogy was produced again. Then, on April 23, 1889, Osmond Tearle directed a revival of Charles Flower's abridgement of *1 Henry VI* in the Shakespeare Memorial Theatre at Stratford upon Avon, followed by a staging of *2 Henry VI,* directed by Frank R. Benson, in April, 1899. In 1906 Benson presented all three plays on successive days (May 2–4), the first director in modern times, and probably the first ever, to do so. In fact, from April 30 to May 5 of that year Benson produced, and along with his wife, Constance, acted leading parts in, all of Shakespeare's histories except *King John* and *King Henry VIII,* and these he had staged at Stratford earlier, in 1901 and 1902, respectively. In the *Henry VI* trilogy, Constance Benson always played Queen Margaret while her husband always chose for himself the most challenging male roles; namely, Talbot, Cardinal Beaufort, and Richard, Duke of Gloucester. For some time Benson had avoided this undertaking because he doubted that most of the histories would be profitable to stage and because they contained no dominant characters for him to portray, such as the two King Richards and Henry V. But his company was composed of skilled actors, and with the Bensons assuming major parts, the performances were successful. Except for his 1899 and 1906 productions, Benson avoided the other two parts of the trilogy and showed his preference for *2 Henry VI* by staging it by itself during the spring festivals at Stratford in 1901 and again in 1909. He and Constance found a number of its scenes particularly ad-

mirable. among them the quarrel between Duke Humphrey
and Cardinal Beaufort in the return from the hawking
scene (II.i) and the tender final parting of Margaret from
her lover Suffolk (III.ii). Because he viewed the dynastic
struggles in the trilogy as "practically a punishment, for a
war of greed and spoliation" against France, Benson offered an unusual interpretation of Joan la Pucelle's part in
1 Henry VI. Instead of Shakespeare's ambiguously depicted witch. Benson had the actress Tita Brand portray
the Maid of Orleans "as a heroine and not a minister of
hell." much to the chagrin of the critic Richard Dickins,
who wondered, if the role were to be so altered from the
clear intention of the text, why it should have been represented in the production at all. Curiously, in the only
other noteworthy British production of the play until after
the Second World War, the shortened version put on at
the Old Vic Theatre by Robert Atkins in 1923, Joan la
Pucelle also became less Shakespearean and more like the
sainted or heroic Joan of Lorraine honored by her own
countrymen and by such later playwrights as Schiller,
George Bernard Shaw, and Maxwell Anderson.

Except for a staging of all three parts, along with
Richard III, at the Pasadena Playhouse in California in
1937, no other notable productions of *Henry VI* until
after World War II have been recorded. That presentation
of all four plays in series was prophetic, perhaps, in at
least two ways. It anticipated the eventual assumption by
postwar producers that these histories, as a group and not
simply *Richard III*, are stageworthy and can attract audiences to successive performances of the individual parts.
Along with later experiments with such in-series production, it helped confirm the growing conviction among
scholars and critics, against the prevailing earlier assumption of collaborative authorship, that all three *Henry VI*
plays are the work of Shakespeare. Further, as R. W.
Chambers asserted, this experimental tetralogy "had probably had no parallel since Aeschylus wrote the trilogy of
which the *Persians* is the surviving fragment."

Since the 1950s, the *Henry VI* plays have attracted considerable attention and have been much more frequently staged, both in Great Britain and internationally. Early in that decade, two significant revivals occurred, one at Sir Barry Jackson's Repertory Theatre in Birmingham, England; the other, at the Shakespearean Festival Theater in Ashland, Oregon. At Birmingham, from 1951 to 1953, and in the latter year at the Old Vic in London, Douglas Seale put on all three parts, originally in the order *2* and *3 Henry VI* (1951 and 1952), and then in 1953 Part One in a truncated three-act version. The undertaking was a theatrical triumph and even led one critic to assert that it had proved Parts Two and Three to be superior as dramas to the ever-popular *Richard III*. Reviewers praised the effective stage settings, the pacing and fluidity of the action, and above all else the young members of the company for their strength and grace and for their ability to grasp the nature of a character and "sound the viol and woodwind and brass of the verse." Especially noteworthy were the performances of Edgar Wreford, Jack May, and Rosalind Boxall. Wreford's tour de force was to play both Dukes of Gloucester—in Part Two beginning as Humphrey and then, after the Protector's death, switching to the role of Richard Crookback. Jack May's development throughout the trilogy of the character of King Henry VI was judged by the reviewer in *The Times Educational Supplement* as "one of the finest things that have been seen in London since the war," while Rosalind Boxall's Queen Margaret, the first interpretation to give the character the prominence and force that Shakespeare's lines demand, was impressive as she grew from the young bride disillusioned in her royal match to the fierce and grieving queen and mother of Part Three. Finally, Seale's interpretation underscored Shakespeare's dramatic grasp of the tragic consequences of international and civil strife that probably accounts in large part for the increasing interest in the *Henry VI* plays among audiences in the unsettled latter half of this present century. Unfortunately, the effect achieved in these productions was diminished when, at the Old Vic in 1957, Seale put on a version truncated to fit into two nights of performance, omitting almost all of the First Part of the trilogy, and resulting in what a reviewer deplored as an unclear, "blood-soaked magma of rambling pageantry."

At about the same time as the Birmingham Repertory productions, Angus Bowmer, director of the Oregon Shakespearean Festival, decided to try staging all ten of Shakespeare's histories in the order of the kings' reigns, and to offer one of the plays during each summer season at Ashland. Except for minor cuts, the company presented the texts without tampering. It did so, as Bowmer observed in his autobiography, because of "a kind of zealous faith in Shakespeare as an effective man of the theatre whose scripts could be taken literally," along with a conviction that even his less polished earlier efforts "could create breath-taking excitement for a twentieth century audience." From 1953 to 1955, Bowmer produced the three parts of *Henry VI* in sequence, and by 1977 the pattern had been repeated twice more, making Ashland the only place where the complete trilogy has enjoyed so many separate productions. The three Ashland stagings of Part One, retaining the all-too-frequently-cut scenes from the French wars that had apparently so moved Shakespeare's original audiences, proved the theatrical effectiveness of those episodes, such as Talbot's encounter with the Countess of Auvergne and his exchange with his young son just before their fatal last battle with the French. In the 1975 Ashland production, moreover, the often-excised duel between Joan la Pucelle and Talbot (I. v) was staged in such a manner as to suggest effectively the beginning of the ascendancy of Joan's supernaturally derived powers over the doomed natural chivalry of her English adversary.

The two most widely acclaimed modern productions of the trilogy have been those by the Royal Shakespeare Company at Stratford in 1963–64 and 1977. They represent two contrasting approaches, both of which have strongly influenced subsequent stage and television versions. The earlier, directed by Peter Hall, John Barton, and Frank Evans, reworked the *Henry VI* plays and *Richard III* into three dramas with many original additions to the text by Barton. In the 1977 production, also for the Royal Shakespeare Company, the director, Terry Hands, decided instead to put on all of *Henry VI* as written, with only minor cuts and changes, and rather than concluding with a performance of *Richard III,* to introduce the trilogy with *Henry V.*

Under the general, and since often copied, label *The Wars of the Roses,* the three adapted, almost "new" plays presented at Stratford in 1963 were entitled *Henry VI, Edward IV,* and *Richard III.* In order to fit them into a single day, or at most two days, and to reduce the time for staging to something under ten hours, the directors, eliminated many of the minor characters and cut over half of the original texts. Then Barton added over 1,400 lines of his own to tighten the narrative structure, as well as to provide necessary transitions and logical coherence to the complicated action and relationships among the characters of the trilogy. He and Hall were working on the assumption that audiences would not come to see all of the plays as written, and that anyway many of their scenes were non-Shakespearean. The manufactured verse sounded so authentic that members of the audiences, including such an expert man of the theater as Robert Speaight, often were unable to distinguish the Shakespearean from the Bartonian touch, even though the program made clear that the modern interpolations were present. Surprisingly, although this *Henry VI* represented what J. C. Trewin called "one of the most drastic revisions of Shakespeare since the Restoration," neither he, nor most other critics and reviewers, were upset by what Hall and Barton had done, or "objected," as Dame Peggy Ashcroft wrote a few years afterward, "to what might have been considered a sacrilege." Shakespearean purists, while defending the viability of the trilogy as originally written, admitted that the adaptations were a stunning success. The consensus was that *The Wars of the Roses* had been up to that time the greatest of the Royal Shakespeare Company's achievements. So impressive, for instance, did Speaight find the *Henry VI* portions of this production, that to him *Richard III* "as a play seemed far less significant than what Peter Hall and John Barton between them had made of its precursors."

The thematic effect of the alterations to and of the manner of staging the plays was to present a political world of violence, bloodshed, and deceit in which men, and women, stop at almost nothing to justify and realize their personal ambitions. Even the settings that John Bury designed stressed that this was, as he remarked in a later interview, "a period of armour and a period of the sword: they were plays about warfare, about power, about danger. . . . And this was the image of the plays." In constructing the scenery, he therefore "built everything out of steel, or simulated steel" in order to suggest "a dangerous world, a terrible world, in which all these happenings fit." Besides the image of discord and martial violence suggested by the use of clanging metals, Bury evoked that of intrigue and of the rapid shiftings of power by placing in the set, as Trewin noted, "an enormous council table that . . . remained, though those who sat about it changed with frightening regularity." This kind of political emphasis in the production resulted in large measure from Peter Hall's professed radicalism, along with the influence on the directors of Jan Kott's notion of the interchangeability in Shakespeare of victims and executioners, and of Bertolt Brecht's technique of making political statements through distancing action in the theater. In fact, one reviewer likened *The Wars of the Roses* as an epic panorama on the disastrous effects of protracted warfare to Brecht's own *Mother Courage*.

Among the achievements of the Hall-Barton version was to bring out clearly the dramatic development of the characters of King Henry and Queen Margaret, as played by an award-winning actor and actress, David Warner and Peggy Ashcroft. Unlike the almost featureless, nearly imbecilic Henry of historical legend and of earlier productions and adaptations of Shakespeare's dramas, Warner showed the king as growing from youthful naiveté and subservience to the intriguers around him into a man of perception and personal intergrity entrapped in and lamenting a world of violence not of his own making. "Isolated and incompetent," wrote Speaight, "he still illuminated the folly of the strife he was unable to quell." But the individual triumph of the production was the performance of Peggy Ashcroft as Margaret of Anjou. In her introduction to the Folio Society edition of the trilogy (1967), Dame Peggy wrote that Henry's queen

> a Dark Lady if ever there was one—and prototype for Cressida, Cleopatra, Lady Macbeth—was Shakespeare's first 'heroine'—if such she can be called. . . . It takes four plays to make her one of the great female characters in Shakespeare—and the full-length portrait has been seen only in the 'Wars of the Roses' cycle—but she has facets that are not touched on in any other.

In Ashcroft's unforgettable portrayal, "a daring emotional performance revealing depths of unwilled and conflicting desires," Margaret developed from the romantically hopeful young bride of the king, lisping her English with a French accent, to the taunting, yet weeping, murderess of the captive York, and finally, in the third play, to the inconsolable prophetess of doom to her victim's now-dominant progeny. Speaight marveled at her ability to give this effect of aging and growth in complexity in the queen and called her portrayal "a great tragic creation."

In the same introduction, Dame Peggy made a comment that suggests one reason why the *Henry VI* plays have been found increasingly significant and have begun to be produced with increasing frequency in current times. Citing William Hazlitt's dismissal of the trilogy for depicting fifteenth-century England merely as "a perfect bear-garden," she countered his objection:

> Perhaps because we are more aware than ever before what a bear-garden the whole world is, we see in these plays a microcosm of so many of the violent and tragic conflicts of our own time. The romantic view of Shakespeare, popular with the Victorians and lasting almost to the first half of this century, has now changed, and we have become more aware of Shakespeare's political absorption and inspired interpretations of man's difficulty in governing himself and others.

The directors had also assumed that the plays would speak with relevance to modern audiences, who, as Hall later remarked, also are "living in the middle of a blood-soaked century."

Since the success of *The Wars of the Roses* at Stratford, the production has continued to influence stagings on the Continent and in North America. In 1965, at the Piccolo Teatro di Milano, Giorgio Strehler presented Shakespeare's violent and corrupt fifteenth-century world as an image for the wars, political intrigues, and revolutions of our contemporary age. In *Il Gioco dei Potenti,* based on the trilogy, with additions from other Shakespearean histories, Strehler took Brecht's concept of the Grand Mechanism of cyclical history to an extreme and startled the spectators by implying through the manner of his staging their own interchangeability with the actors playing out the political game before them. "The production style," remarked Samuel Leiter,

> resembled a slow and unending cinematic zoom-in. The audience and the stage were counterposed like two mirrors, producing an innumerable series of recessed reflections. The effect of such an extended metaphor was the complete diffusion of the borderlines merging illusion and reality.

Strehler also underscored the sinister and yet gamelike nature of political intrigue by juxtaposing with the opening scenes vignettes of children playing and singing: "The innocent children's games reflected a monstrous and dangerous game for power." Partly reworked, and translated into German as *Das Spiel der Mächtigen,* Strehler's version was performed again at the Salzburg Festival (1973) and at the Burgtheater in Vienna (1975). During the same year, at the Théâtre de France in Paris, Jean-Louis Barrault staged an adaptation of François-Victor Hugo's translation of the trilogy, intending by his interpretation to depict the rise of Renaissance power politics as the Middle Ages waned and to remind audiences of the tragic consequences attendant upon warfare and the play for political domination.

Productions directly influenced by *The Wars of the Roses* have also occurred at Stratford, Ontario (1966), at the New York (1970) and New Jersey (1983) Shakespeare Festivals, at the University of California, Berkeley (1987), and, in translations, on the Continent in Berlin (1965), in Stockholm and Mainz (both in 1983), and (Parts Two and Three only) at the Yerevan Theater in the Soviet Union (1981). Among other foreign-language stagings of all, or parts, or adaptations of the trilogy, though not all have been directly influenced by the Hall-Barton production, have been a *3 Henry VI* in Romania (1977), an adaptation of *3 Henry VI* along with *Richard III* at the Croatian National Theater in Zagreb (1978–79), and a revival of Hugo's translation of the trilogy at Montreuil (1980). *Kings,* a free adaptation of Hugo's version produced by Denis Llorca at Carcassonne (1978), at Creteil (1979) and at the Festival of Lyon (1980) proved to be, despite an "exuberance" that tended to "overwhelm" its French audiences, an "enthralling production." In a translation by Yushi Odashima, all three parts were enacted at Tokyo in 1982. In North America, besides the cyclical repetitions at Ashland, all or portions of the trilogy have been performed, at the Antioch College, Ohio (1953, 1981), Great Lakes (1967), Colorado (1967, 1969), Stratford, Ontario (1980), and University of Vermont (1983) Festivals, and at the Globe Playhouse in Los Angeles (1979–80) and the Yale School of Drama (1983).

This substantial number of stagings throughout the world, particularly in the case of several of those in the past decade, seems due to the impact not only of the Hall-Barton production but also of that directed by Terry Hands at Stratford, Newcastle upon Tyne, and London in 1977–78, and of the television versions released by the British Broadcasting Corporation early in 1983. In contrast with Hall and Barton, Hands and his colleagues proceeded under the assumption that *Henry VI* was completely Shakespearean; they had evolved, moreover, different kinds of staging and acting techniques from their immediate predecessors in the Royal Shakespeare Company. They conceived of the trilogy, Hands said, as a "single long play—like a TV serial or a serialized novel by Dickens," and they designed the staging "to give the maximum speed so that we could put the maximum of the text onto the stage." Although usually they offered the three parts on successive nights, on three or four occasions they enacted the whole trilogy in one day, a nine-hour marathon with breaks for lunch and dinner.

Hands' intent in respecting the original was "to put it all very crudely, very naively down on the stage—everything that was there, warts and all, in the hope that one or two of them would turn out to be beauty spots. There was something to learn." What the company did learn was that the plays as written were eminently actable and that many of the "warts" did turn out to be spots of authentic dramatic beauty. While the verse does not measure up to the poetry of later Shakespearean drama, the touch of the born playwright was recognizable in his creation of memorable scenes and characters. Even episodes that seemed at first irrational or bizarre turned out in actual staging to make sure dramatic sense, and not only did each part, each "inner play" in Hands' expression, contain great characters—Talbot, Joan, Cade, the three sons of York—but also in the "superplay" represented by all three parts, the personages of King Henry, Margaret, Warwick, and York turned out to be masterful creations by Shakespeare. Further, Alan Howard's and Helen Mirren's interpretations of the roles of the king and queen made the two of them more complex than they had appeared in any earlier stagings. Mirren played Margaret not as the bloodthirsty tigress or "she-wolf" but as a woman who, in spite of her own adulterous sensuality and insatiable ambition, remains loyal to and fights desperately for the cause of her spouse to the very end. Howard has been acclaimed for portraying the king not as ineptly feeble but as a person developing from the offspring of the heroic and politically astute Henry V who inherits his father's potential without being able to actualize it, into what Howard himself saw as "a revolutionary . . . so far ahead, so much deeper than anyone else that he is simply not able to lead people who are interested only in power." Henry's growth, as depicted by Howard, wrote one critic, gave "proof enough that the character was created by Shakespeare."

While Hands' experiment received much praise, not all reviewers were pleased by it. One claimed that retaining nearly all of the lines led to a certain "iambic plod" in the delivery of the speeches, another found Mirren and Howard "sometimes inadequate" in their performances, and the critical objection seems to have been that too great reverence for the text left the plays less entertaining than they might have been with judicious pruning out of supernumerary characters and minor scenes. Hall and Barton, objectors believed, by skillful excision and rearrangement, and by Barton's rewriting, had rendered the plots more coherent, if less Shakespearean. Hands' procedure, on the contrary, did bring out the richness of the characterizations in the plays. Despite its mixed critical reception, on the whole the 1977 *Henry VI* was acknowledged as a landmark in the history of production of the trilogy because it made even more convincing the emerging view that all of it was the work of Shakespeare and proved the theatrical viability of the text as written. The intention of the company had been to discover whether these assumptions were true and to encourage others who, having profited from whatever virtues and flaws may have appeared in the experiment, to present the plays without tailoring or adaptation. As Homer Swander wrote in rejoicing over this "rediscovery" of the trilogy, "We have at last found the play. We must now—against all the odds stacked so heavily against a work so vast—allow it to enter fully into the shared tradition, the active theatrical life."

In media other than the stage, *Henry VI* has been treated significantly only on television. No motion pictures have been made from the trilogy, although in 1955, when he starred in the film *Richard III*, Lawrence Olivier opened with the coronation of Edward IV from Part Three (V. vii) and interpolated into the scene lines from Richard's famous "Machiavel" soliloquy in III. ii of the same history. During the same year RAI, the Italian national radio network, broadcast all of the histories in translated versions, *Henry VI* in a form that compressed the three parts into a single play. In 1962 the Marlowe society made uncut studio recordings of all three parts. For television, four different productions have been made. In 1961, Peter Dews made for the BBC *An Age Of Kings*, a repertory series of fifteen one-hour plays based on Shakespeare's two tetralogies. This first transfer to the relatively new medium was not an unqualified success. Since the *Richard II-Henry V* sequence was presented first, the latter, less familiar tetralogy in this dramatic pageant of fifteenth-century British history failed to sustain a similar degree of interest. Further, compression of the plays to fit a rigid broadcast time schedule led to some injudicious cutting, the actors tended to speak their lines too rapidly for audience comprehension, and the director, apparently not quite certain how to exploit the medium of television, ended up with what were simply "filmed stage plays" rather than a more fluid kind of dramatization appropriate to the video screen. More successful was the televised Hall-Barton *Wars of the Roses,* produced by Michael Barry in three three-hour parts (April, 1965) with the principal actors—Ashcroft, Warner, Roy Dotrice, and Ian Holm—from the original cast. In 1982, Peter Benson and other actors made two-hour color videotapes of each of the *Henry VI* plays.

During January, 1983, as part of the BBC/*Time-Life* project of televising all of the Shakespearean canon, Jane Howell directed a "triumphant" *Henry VI.* She succeeded in combining "the resources of theatre and television," wrote the reviewer in the *Shakespeare Quarterly,* "with exceptional imagination, in the process demonstrating just how remarkable this trilogy is." Howell used an effective single set that adapted readily to the many changes of action and scene in the plays and that disintegrated symbolically over the course of the three parts to reflect the deteriorating fortunes of England. She was also blessed with a cast that formed an integrated ensemble, and she gave her actors firm direction. The principals handled the dialogue with greater assurance and suitability to the medium of television than had the cast in *An Age of Kings.* As Queen Margaret, Julia Foster was so effective that her performance "challenged . . . comparison" with that of Peggy Ashcroft in *The Wars of the Roses.* Finally, the production did greater justice to *1 Henry VI,* and to the too-often-diminished roles of Talbot and Joan la Pucelle, than had almost any preceding theatrical or television version on record.

Bibliographic Note: In preparing this essay, I have used numerous sources without direct acknowledgment. Besides Sir Barry Jackson's "On Producing 'Henry VI,' " reprinted with *2 Henry VI* in this edition, several other commen-

taries on productions of the trilogy are worth especial
mention here. For a brief general sketch of the staging of
Henry VI since the eighteenth century, see Arthur Colby
Sprague, *Shakespeare's Histories: Plays for the Stage*
(1964). A more detailed treatment of revivals and adaptations from the later seventeenth through the nineteenth
centuries is George C. D. Odell, *Shakespeare from
Betterton to Irving* (1920). Robert Speaight's *Shakespeare on the Stage: An Illustrated History of Shakespearean Performance* (1973) includes photographs, as
well as brief discussion, of some actors in and performances of the trilogy. David Addenbrooke, *The Royal
Shakespeare Company: The Peter Hall Years* (1974)
prints interviews with several of the principal figures involved in the Royal Shakespeare Company's 1963–64
production of *The Wars of the Roses.* Dame Peggy Ashcroft, in her introduction to the Folio Society edition of
the *Henry VI* plays (1967), defends the Hall-Barton
adaptations, while J. C. Trewin, *Going to Shakespeare*
(1978), argues that Sir Barry Jackson's Birmingham
Repertory revivals had proved the viability of the original
texts. Homer D. Swander extolled Terry Hands' nearly
uncut 1977 staging of the complete trilogy in "The Rediscovery of Henry VI," *Shakespeare Quarterly,* 29 (1978),
143–63, and G. K. Hunter, "The Royal Shakespeare
Company Plays *Henry VI,*" *Renaissance Drama,* 9 (1978,
publ. 1979), 91–108, contrasted the styles of the 1963
and 1977 productions. In *Drama and Society,* ed. James
Redmond (1979), David Daniell commented similarly in
"Opening the Text: Shakespeare's *Henry VI* Plays in
Performance." For a view of international stagings, see
Samuel L. Leiter, ed., *Shakespeare Around the Globe: A
Guide to Notable Postwar Revivals* (1986). An anthology
of essays that includes commentaries on televised versions
of the trilogy is *Shakespeare on Television,* eds. J. C.
Bulman and H. R. Coursen (1987). Peter Hall has
written introductions to the BBC televised versions of the
three plays constituting *The Wars of the Roses* (1970),

while John Wilders has done the same for, and Henry Fenwick has added notes on the productions of, each of the *Henry VI* plays in the BBC/*Time-Life* television performances (1983). Readers wishing to keep abreast of the ongoing theatrical history of the trilogy may turn to *Shakespeare Survey,* for British productions, and to *Shakespeare Quarterly,* for coverage of performances throughout the world.

William Shakespeare

HENRY VI, PART TWO

Edited by Arthur Freeman

Contents

Introduction

Shakespeare's *Henry VI, Part Two* may be his earliest surviving work; it may be the first adaptation by anyone of English history for the Elizabethan stage; and if it is neither, it still certainly remains among the three or four earliest both of the career and the genre, and as such the object of curious examination for centuries. But has the play value beyond curiosity and "importance," or virtues beyond nuggets of promise and flashes of the characteristic "easiness of expression and fluency of numbers" we identify in the body of Shakespeare's work? Rarely, we observe, does *Henry VI*—singly, doubly, or triply—come on the stage, and scarcely more often does a single part recommend itself to the modern reader who is not simply covering or re-covering *all* of Shakespeare, like an obstacle course. How good is the play? And more pointedly, perhaps, from what particular strengths does its excellence, if any, arise?

Unquestionably the poetry of *2 Henry VI* is no strong point. It ranges from inflated extreme:

> The gaudy, blabbing and remorseful day
> Is crept into the bosom of the sea,
> And now loud-howling wolves arouse the jades
> That drag the tragic melancholy night . . .
>
> (IV.i.1–4)

to slack plateau:

> And had I twenty times so many foes,
> And each of them had twenty times their power,

> All these could not procure me any scathe,
> So long as I am loyal, true and crimeless . . .
> (II.iv.60–63)

embracing along the way all sorts of weakness appropriate to the neophyte versifier: flatness, extravagance, redundancy, and unassimilated imitation. When Margaret lamely laments her enforced parting from the Duke of Suffolk, and the imminent death of Cardinal Beaufort,

> Ay me! What is this world! What news are these!
> But wherefore grieve I at an hour's poor loss,
> Omitting Suffolk's exile, my soul's treasure?
> Why only, Suffolk, mourn I not for thee,
> And with the southern clouds contend in tears . . . ?
> (III.ii.380–84)

her rhetoric is heavily indebted to Thomas Kyd's; likewise the "jades" are Marlowe's, and the "twenty . . . twenty" hyperbole a well-worn piece of stock from the Kyd-Marlowe-Greene warehouse of formulaic clichés. Often, indeed, *2 Henry VI* sounds so unlike the later Shakespeare and so much like his predecessors and mentors that scholars have sought another's hand in the text—either as collaborator, or as the unwitting source of Shakespeare's flagrant plagiary. Yet few would deny to Shakespeare the fine intensity of Young Clifford's battlefield imprecations (V.ii.31–65), the emotional accuracy of the bulk of III.ii, Margaret's farewell to Suffolk, or the wily and succinct logic of Warwick's apology for the commons, and the warning to King Henry (III.ii.242–269); and what seems less than the best in the play may as easily be explained in terms of uncertainty and inexperience as of fragmentary authorship. We cannot demand of Shakespeare in his twenties the consistency, control, and ease of the seasoned professional he was rapidly to become.

But what emerges preeminently from the play is the sure sense of theater, dramatic design, and skill in characterization which are such inalienable hallmarks of

Shakespeare's genius that even bardolatrous theatergoers of 1796 could without hesitation hiss a travesty like *Vortigern* (forged by W. H. Ireland) from the stage— not for its mawkish language and already tainted reputation, but for the lack of those attributes absolutely characteristic of the Genuine Remains. Ragged and faltering though its verse may occasionally be, *Henry VI* exemplifies the dramatic virtues of construction—continuity, tension, proportion, pace—which no playwright before Shakespeare had succeeded in uniting with a good sense of what interests an audience. Thinking of *2 Henry VI* as a playwright's play—an embryonic, germinal type— we can single out from it virtues of dramaturgy, aspects of craftsmanship which may illuminate for us what Shakespeare the playwright "began with" at the outset of a career in Elizabethan theater.

The peculiar problem facing a playwright who attempts a play based on chronicle history is that no very extravagant changes in plot may be introduced. All the more pressing are the demands on the playwright's skill as a shaper of story, selector of detail, imputer of motives; all the more difficult his task of making an arbitrary tract of historical time appear complete and self-sufficient, artistically independent from the events-leading-up and the sequel. Given the limitations of the source, the exigencies of factual history, as well as the prescribed slants Tudor chroniclers imposed on their material (King John a victim of papal interference, Richard III—the last Plantagenet—an ignominious tyrant, Richard II's overthrow fundamentally unjustified) and the necessity for treading lightly where political or social issues come into question, how does Shakespeare's artistry shape, structure, and implement the twenty-year history his play intends to convey? Most obviously, and first, by a compression of time, and a conflation of events. Facts remain facts, but their order may justifiably be varied: Eleanor's attainture may be laid to Queen Margaret's influence, although in fact it took place four years before the royal marriage; Peter's combat with his master the Armorer may be relocated at the time of York's displacement as regent of France, and associated—as in the chronicles it is not—with York's treason. Likewise, the long and repetitious subversion of Salisbury and Warwick, among other members of the nobility, which drags over years in Hall and Holinshed, may be reduced to a single scene (II.ii) and left firmly settled rather than tentative; and the long-smoldering hostilities between King Henry and York, all their intermittent battles, truces, accords, and new outbreaks, may be altered to a single continuing action in Act V, with a conclusion more "final" than history suggests. Thus twenty years of fits and starts in the Lancaster–York troubles appear all part of one rational sequence of events, impelled forward by the force of hindsight, the implied teleology of history itself, stripped of "irrelevant" excursions, like York's in and out of Ireland, and framed artificially by emphasis on fulfilled prophecy and culminatory violence. Like any dramatist restricted to a small repertory cast, Shakespeare dwells on individual confrontations rather than spectacular, massive, and realistic encounters to embody the historical action. Chosen pairs of antagonists, like chosen events, stand for the struggle at large: York duels anachronistically with Old Clifford as a representative of all the loyal nobility, and the company of factious schemers of I.i dwindle from eight to a soliloquizing York, as if to symbolize the disintegration of English union into rival, baronial interests. Another dramatic device insuring the illusion of continuity is Shakespeare's imputation of motives in certain matters the chronicles agree to leave haphazard: only a hint in Hall provides the suggestion, fully implemented by Shakespeare, of an intrigue between Suffolk and the Queen; and the ensuing suggestion that Somerset fills the same office is merely extrapolated from the first: there is no source for this in written history. Nor do the chroniclers provide any connection between Cade's uprising and the policy of York, whereas the play quite plausibly links Cade to the main action specifically as York's factor in Kent.

The illusion that history, in *2 Henry VI,* is self-contained and independent, that a "just period" has been imposed on the events described, once more is a function of dramatic management. We watch the Duke of York alter from a silent, politic, and guarded rival claimant, whose primary mode of self-expression is the ironic "aside" and the soliloquy (I.i., III.i), to an outspoken enemy of the crown who dares fling his defiance in the face of the Presence: the play thus provides a kind of emotional catharsis for York not wholly warranted by the chronicles, and which gives the impression of a retaliatory anger coming full circle from the implied past outrage and house-curse of Richard II's deposition. Paired against York's rise to action is King Henry's degeneration into helpless passivity: never martial, nor even authoritative in his office, he does flare up once in righteous fury against Suffolk, following the murder of Duke Humphrey —even if Warwick's unsubtle pressure must goad him to a firm stand—but by IV.viii, in the face of Yorkist defense, he has reached a nadir of despair and incompetence:

> Come wife, let's in, and learn to govern better;
> For yet may England curse my wretched reign.

By the end of Act V he remains scarcely a man, let alone King (*Queen.* What are you made of? You'll nor fight nor fly), and his death in the play's sequel seems a foregone conclusion. While York's forces, around Salisbury and Warwick, have snowballed into an irresistible front, King Henry's counselors, like the provinces of France, have fallen from him one by one; until like Lear alone on the heath with his fool, stripped of his entourage, King and Queen must flee the lost battle at the prompting of no more than the Young Clifford, last of the loyalists, bitter, pitiless, and a little mad. A more deliberate device, perhaps, for setting the just period on events in the play, is the satisfaction of a second of three prophecies made late in Act I: Somerset's death under the sign of the Castle, an alehouse in Saint Albans, seems to even up the score between Gloucester's family and their assailants— Suffolk for Gloucester (IV.i), and now Somerset for Eleanor.

Within the measure of the play, the period of the whole action, lodges a rhythmic pattern of interlocked impugnments—fortuitous falls, medieval "tragedies," if we wish, or inevitable consequences of one fatal, preliminary mistake. "The three *Henry VI* plays, and *Richard III*," writes Irving Ribner, "may be viewed as virtually a series of successive waves, in each of which one hero falls and another rises to replace him. The most significant of the falls are displayed as divine retribution for sin, but there are some also which seem to illustrate only an arbitrary and capricious fortune." Within *2 Henry VI* a parallel series may be distinguished: first Eleanor, then Humphrey, then Suffolk, then Lord Say, and finally Somerset are impugned, attainted, and done away with, as the barriers between King Henry and the raw malice of York one by one come down. Successive objects of blame for the loss of France—Humphrey by the peers, York by Somerset and Suffolk, Suffolk by Warwick, Salisbury, and the commons, Say by Jack Cade and his rebels, and Salisbury by York—suggest the harried administration of a losing enterprise firing manager after manager. And all comes about through the "fatal marriage" of Henry with Margaret, the "haught-stomached" mannish Queen of the chronicles, the amorous impatient designer of Part Two, the bloody avenger of Part Three, and the hideous Cassandra of *Richard III*. As France forms the unseen background for the historical tragedy, in Elizabethan terms, of Henry VI's reign, so France in the person of Margaret and the responsibility for mismanaging the wars forms the pretext of all the succeeding failures in the play. For the want of Anjou and Maine, Normandy is lost, for the want of Normandy, Gascony, for the want of all France, English popular solidarity and loyalty; and by all these interlocked disasters falls King Henry. France and its "blood-bespotted Neapolitan" Queen lurk like a Senecan curse behind the action of *2 Henry VI, 3 Henry VI,* and *Richard III,* a trilogy linked by themes of retribution and revenge, by generations of guilt accumulated by Lancastrians and Yorkists, until Henry Tudor can wipe clean the slate of Bosworth Field. But the triggering event of the chain, in Part Two, is the unsuitable, expensive marriage of French Margaret with English Henry, and the hateful articles thereby concluded.

A play lives in its characters. Samuel Johnson selected from *2 Henry VI* King Henry, Queen Margaret, Warwick, and Gloucester; but there are bits as well—Peter, Eleanor, Walter Whitmore, Cade—which an actor can render memorable. At the outset of the action, a triangle of major figures—Henry, Margaret, and Humphrey—dominates our attention, Margaret and the Protector vying for control of the pietistic, unworldly figurehead of a King. Now Humphrey, by sixteenth-century convention, is portrayed as charitable to a fault ("to dine at Duke Humphrey's table," an Elizabethan expression for "to go hungry," reflects the supposed self-impoverishment Gloucester's generosity drew upon himself), high-minded, confident, as Hall has it, in "his strong truth," and in "indifferent justice"—a victimized heifer or partridge, in Warwick's image, an unweaned calf, in Henry's, and a shepherd in Gloucester's own, to the lamblike King. Queen Margaret, again at Hall's suggestion, is equal in vehement ambition to the calm majesty and accustomed authority of her rival; and the traditional character of King Henry as a man "of a meek spirit, and a simple wit, preferring peace before war, rest before business, honesty before profit, and quietness before labor," is implemented by Shakespeare in scriptural terms, by larding the King's discourse with holy aphorisms, and revealing him ever more willing to comment helplessly upon an event—with eyes upraised, and hands clasped, as the adult portrait in the National Portrait Gallery depicts him—than to demand action. The interrelationship of these three main figures is never better exposed than in II.i, at the spurious miracle of cured blindness in Saint Albans. To a Townsman's announcement of "A miracle!" Henry reacts immediately with full credulity: "Now God be praised, etc.," and with a homely and pious *caveat:*

> Great is his comfort in this earthly vale,
> Although by sight his sin be multiplied.

Gloucester, meanwhile, seasons his admiration with the
skepticism of a good judge. Interrogation confirms his
suspicions, and with a bit of low comedy he administers
an unmasking. Now that Simpcox is revealed an impostor,
the King speaks again:

> O God, seest Thou this, and bearest so long?

Whereas Queen Margaret, in a reflection superbly revealing of her hardening nature, comments:

> It made me laugh to see the villain run.

Given the King's ineffectuality, it of course falls to
Gloucester to prescribe punishment; and as the case does
not warrant mercy (the Wife's plea, "Alas, sir, we did
it for pure need," appeals merely for pity, in a Stoical
sense) Gloucester's sentence is not unsevere. "By this
may be seen," says Foxe, "how Duke Humphrey had not
only an head to discern and dissever truth from forged
and feigned hypocrisy, but study also and diligence likewise was in him to reform that which was amiss." Shakespeare has retained the main point of the *exemplum,* but
simultaneously seized upon the occasion to underscore his
portraits of Henry and Margaret as well.

After the elimination of Gloucester, the "crutch" of the
King, our attention is shifted to those auguries of disintegration, the wrangling peers, the scheming Yorkists, pirates, and the anarchic rebels of Jack Cade. From the
decorum of the first scene, a courtly reception of the new
Queen, to the bloody holocaust of Act V, culminating in
the emergence of a new order of violent young men—
York's savage sons, the "foul, indigested lump" Richard,
and furious Clifford Junior—we are led by way of dissi-
dent nobles and lawless commoners, to an end no better
than what precedes it, but certainly less weak. After
Gloucester's death the focus of characterization moves
freely among the representative types of imperial decay,
pausing once for a curiously affecting last interview be-

tween Margaret and the Duke of Suffolk (III.ii.300 ff.).
Prior to this parting we have had little or no sympathy
for either party, but in the space of a hundred lines our
antagonism is severely shaken. It is a crude and unpre-
pared reversal, perhaps, but there are few examples in
the English drama before 1590 of anything at all like
Shakespeare's "shading" of characterization, or of his
insistence on keeping our judgment on the ultimate
worth of a man suspended until the tension of the
action involving him has relaxed. We have been encouraged to dislike Suffolk, but with III.ii we are not permitted to despise him; we are asked to reconsider our
earlier censure of both Queen and lover, and to imagine,
for a moment, the action of the play, favorable and un-
favorable to them, through their own eyes, as it affects
them, rather than as they affect it. This is a remarkable
achievement, in a somewhat primitive form, for a short
unexpected exchange. Analogous to it perhaps is the pity
evoked in us by the sight of Eleanor humbled—we may
think of Kent in the stocks or the dead Hotspur—or our
grudging admiration for the impolitic and noble arrogance
with which Suffolk meets his end; but these are simpler
dramatic formulas.

In its own time, and possibly in ours, the main attraction of the play as staged may well have been the comical
prose scenes of Cade's rebellion. Action is not lacking in
2 *Henry VI,* nor spectacle, what with witchcraft, trial
by combat, a false miracle, alarums and excursions, and
the excitement generated by York's open defiance and
Gloucester's bristling temper against Beaufort's; but the
Cade scenes bring to the stage as well an element, especially trenchant for Elizabethans, of sociopolitical commentary. Shakespeare's audiences were accustomed to
read into plays on past history lessons for the present,
and indeed contemporary playwrights were not blind to
the implications their histories raised. *Gorboduc* warned
of the evils of dividing a kingdom; *Richard II* of the
hazards of weak kingship (after Essex' rebellion in 1601,
and the ill-advised performance of *Richard II* on the eve

of the uprising, the Queen angrily remarked to William
Lambarde, "I am Richard II, know ye not that?"); and
2 Henry VI contains an action if anything more provoca-
tive than either of those. Presupposing a popular audience to watch a play dealing with popular revolt—one in
particular in which the rabble bears all before it for some
time—and considering that London in the early 1590's
was racked by insubordination and riot, one may imagine
how determined the authorities might be to assure themselves no matter or opinion expressed in such a scene of
such a play were "dangerous," and to be certain that any
moral extrapolated from the conclusion be perfectly in
accord with law, order, and the present regime. Thus episodes like Cade's rebellion and the rising of the masses in
Sir Thomas More (Shakespeare's putative revision for this
controversial play is reprinted in the source-appendix below) were composed under strict scrutiny, and carefully
reviewed by the Master of the Revels or his staff before
production could be permitted. Change a scene, omit a
scene, and shorten an address, "and not otherwise, at your
own perils," warns Edmund Tilney in his holograph comment extant on the manuscript of *Sir Thomas More:* the
recommendations of the authorities are specific, censorious, and peremptory.

Nothing in Shakespeare's career or works suggests that
he might find conscientious compliance with such strictures difficult. In fact the implicit conservatism of his political attitudes, so far as we can isolate them (a dangerous attempt, when speech and character must sometimes
be separated), made him ideal for the job of rewriting
a questioned passage of *More,* and evidently quite at ease
in the matter of Cade. In line either with official policy,
or his own predilections, or both, Shakespeare's Cade
scarcely resembles the "youngman of goodly stature and
pregnant wit," the "subtle captain," and audacious field-
general Hall portrays; rather he stands for rampant ignorance, executing a clerk for his ability to read and write,
and Lord Say, as much as for anything, for his cultural
accomplishment—whereas Hall's Cade took advantage

of sophistical doctrine, "teachers," and "privy school-masters" to suborn the men of Kent to his side in the struggle, and was witty enough to perceive the "dilatory plea" of Lord Say, to be tried by his peers—rather than anxious to kill him before his words might win away followers. True, in his curious fashion Hall does give a conflicting impression of Cade—as "covetous," a "mischievous head," and "a cruel tyrant"—almost in counterpoint with his more respectful estimate, but Shakespeare unquestionably was in command of information about Cade's nature which he chose not to use. Likewise, the character of Lord Say, which in Hall is made shifty and not a little cowardly, in Shakespeare is held up as maligned virtue and honesty personified, a very test case of Cade's anarchic administration, urging us to particular repugnance toward civil disobedience. And for reasons, at last, of leaving no loophole in the morality of rebellion, Shakespeare has also introduced the otherwise gratuitous episode of Iden's garden, a scene which well may bear cutting in a modern production. Iden himself remains an annoyingly loose end among disparate new faces in the last act: the man who pronounces himself loath to "live turmoilèd in the court" when he "may enjoy such quiet walks as these" in Kent (IV.x.17–18) seems within a few lines overjoyed to attend henceforth on King Henry at court: "May Iden live to merit such a bounty!"

"As narratives in verse," sums up Dr. Johnson, the *Henry VI* plays "are more happily conceived and more accurately finished than those of *King John, Richard II,* or the tragic scenes of *Henry IV* and *V*"—this "without regard to characters and incidents," in which they presumably are deficient; and of the three, adds Johnson, "I think the second the best." Taste since 1765 has perhaps downgraded the *Henry VI* plays, and scholarship has fastened so firmly on the bibliographical labyrinths they offer to explore, that seldom are they spoken of as literature, hence seldom staged, and hence seldom read. But it is almost fair to assert that the least of Shakespeare is better than all but the best of his early theatrical contemporaries, and *2 Henry VI*—a little clumsy and uneven, but fresh, and at times brilliant—deserves nowadays more than its canonical or compulsive moiety of readership.

ARTHUR FREEMAN
Boston University

The Second Part of Henry the Sixth, with the Death of the Good Duke Humphrey

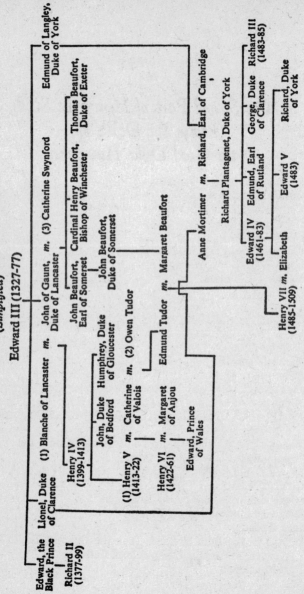

THE HOUSES OF LANCASTER AND YORK
(Simplified)

Edward III (1327-77)

Edward, the Black Prince

Richard II (1377-99)

Lionel, Duke of Clarence

John of Gaunt, Duke of Lancaster m. (1) Blanche of Lancaster (3) Catherine Swynford

Edmund of Langley, Duke of York

Henry IV (1399-1413)

John, Duke of Bedford

Humphrey, Duke of Gloucester

John Beaufort, Earl of Somerset

Cardinal Henry Beaufort, Bishop of Winchester

Thomas Beaufort, Duke of Exeter

(1) Henry V (1413-22) m. Catherine of Valois m. (2) Owen Tudor

John Beaufort, Duke of Somerset

Henry VI (1422-61) m. Margaret of Anjou

Edmund Tudor m. Margaret Beaufort

Edward, Prince of Wales

Anne Mortimer m. Richard, Earl of Cambridge

Richard Plantagenet, Duke of York

Henry VII (1485-1509) m. Elizabeth

Edward IV (1461-83)

Edmund, Earl of Rutland

George, Duke of Clarence

Richard III (1483-85)

Edward V (1483)

Richard, Duke of York

King Henry the Sixth
Humphrey, Duke of Gloucester, uncle to the King, and
    Protector
Cardinal Beaufort, Bishop of Winchester, great-uncle to
    the King
Richard Plantagenet, Duke of York
Edward
Richard, afterwards Richard III } his sons
Duke of Somerset
Humphrey, Duke of Buckingham
William de la Pole, Marquess (afterwards Duke) of Suffolk
Earl of Salisbury
Richard, Earl of Warwick, his son
Lord Clifford
Young Clifford, his son
Lord Say
Lord Scales
Sir Humphrey Stafford
Sir William Stafford, his brother
Sir John Stanley
Sir Matthew Goffe
Vaux
Lieutenant, Master, and Master's-Mate, Walter Whitmore,
    and two Gentlemen, prisoners with Suffolk
John Hum and John Southwell, priests, Roger Bolingbroke,
    a conjuror, and a Spirit
Thomas Horner, an armorer, and Peter Thump, his
    apprentice
Mayor of Saint Albans
Clerk of Chatham
Alexander Iden, a Kentish landowner
Saunder Simpcox, an impostor
Jack Cade
George Bevis, John Holland, Dick the Butcher, Smith the
    Weaver, Michael, all followers of Cade
Two Murderers

Queen Margaret
Eleanor, Duchess of Gloucester
Margery Jourdain, a witch
Wife of Simpcox

Two Petitioners, Beadle, Herald, Sheriff, Aldermen, three
    Neighbors of Horner, three Prentices; Falconers, Citi-
    zens, Guards, Soldiers, Messengers, Attendants

Scene: England]

The Second Part of Henry the Sixth, with the Death of the Good Duke Humphrey

ACT I

Scene I. [*London. The Palace.*]

Flourish°1 of trumpets: then hautboys.° Enter at one door King Henry the Sixth, and Humphrey, Duke of Gloucester, the Duke of Somerset, the Duke of Buckingham, Cardinal Beaufort, and others. Enter at the other door the Duke of York, and the Marquess of Suffolk, and Queen Margaret, and the Earl of Salisbury and Warwick.

Suffolk. As by your high imperial Majesty
I had in charge at my depart for France,
As procurator° to your Excellence,
To marry Princess Margaret for your Grace,
So in the famous ancient city, Tours,   5

---

1 The degree sign (°) indicates a footnote, which is keyed to the text by line number. Text references are printed in **boldface** type; the annotation follows in roman type.
I.i.s.d. Flourish fanfare   **s.d. hautboys** oboes   **3 procurator** deputy

In presence of the Kings of France and Sicil,
The Dukes of Orleans, Calaber,° Bretagne and
    Alençon,
Seven earls, twelve barons, and twenty reverend
    bishops,
I have performed my task and was espoused,
10 And humbly now upon my bended knee,
In sight of England and her lordly peers,
Deliver up my title in the Queen
To your most gracious hands, that are the sub-
    stance
Of that great shadow I did represent—
15 The happiest° gift that ever marquess gave,
The fairest queen that ever king received.

King. Suffolk, arise. Welcome, Queen Margaret:
I can express no kinder sign of love
Than this kind° kiss. O Lord, that lends me life,
20 Lend me a heart replete with thankfulness!
For Thou hast given me in this beauteous face
A world of earthly blessings to my soul,
If sympathy of love unite our thoughts.

Queen. Great King of England and my gracious lord,
25 The mutual conference° that my mind hath had,
By day, by night, waking, and in my dreams,
In courtly company or at my beads,
With you mine alderliefest° sovereign,
Makes me the bolder to salute my king
30 With ruder terms, such as my wit° affords
And overjoy of heart doth minister.°

King. Her sight did ravish, but her grace in speech,
Her words yclad° with wisdom's majesty,
Makes me from wond'ring fall to weeping joys,
35 Such is the fullness of my heart's content.
Lords, with one cheerful voice welcome my love,

7 Calaber location uncertain, but evidently *not* Calabria   15 hap-
piest most fortunate   18–19 kinder . . . kind more natural . . .
affectionate   25 mutual conference intimate conversation   28 al-
derliefest dearest of all   30 wit intelligence, understanding   31
minister provide   33 yclad clad (archaic)

All kneel. Long live Queen Margaret, England's hap-
     piness!

Queen. We thank you all.   *Flourish.*

Suffolk. My Lord Protector, so it please your Grace,
     Here are the articles of contracted peace   40
     Between our sovereign and the French King
         Charles,
     For eighteen months concluded by consent.

Gloucester. (Reads.) "Imprimis,° It is agreed be-
     tween the French King Charles, and William de la
     Pole, Marquess of Suffolk, ambassador for Henry   45
     King of England, that the said Henry shall espouse
     the Lady Margaret, daughter unto Reignier King
     of Naples, Sicilia and Jerusalem, and crown her
     Queen of England ere the thirtieth of May next
     ensuing. *Item,* That the duchy of Anjou and the   50
     county of Maine shall be released and delivered to
     the king her father"—   *Gloucester lets it fall.*

King. Uncle, how now?

Gloucester.   Pardon me, gracious lord;
     Some sudden qualm hath struck me at the heart,
     And dimmed mine eyes, that I can read no further.   55

King. Uncle of Winchester, I pray read on.

Cardinal. [*Reads*] "Item, It is further agreed between
     them, that the duchies of Anjou and Maine shall
     be released and delivered over to the King her
     father, and she sent over of the King of England's   60
     own proper° cost and charges, without having any
     dowry."

King. They please us well.
     Lord Marquess, kneel down: we here create thee
     First Duke of Suffolk, and girt thee with the sword.   65
     Cousin of York, we here discharge your Grace
     From being regent i' th' parts of France,

43 **Imprimis** in the first place   61 **proper** personal

Till term of eighteen months be full expired.
Thanks, uncle Winchester, Gloucester, York,
70 Buckingham, Somerset, Salisbury, and Warwick;
We thank you all for this great favor done,
In entertainment° to my princely queen.
Come, let us in, and with all speed provide
To see her coronation be performed.

> *Exit King, Queen, and Suffolk; and*
> *Gloucester stays all the rest.*

Gloucester. Brave peers of England, pillars of the
75   state,
To you Duke Humphrey must unload his grief—
Your grief, the common grief of all the land.
What! Did my brother Henry spend his youth,
His valor, coin, and people, in the wars?
80 Did he so often lodge in open field,
In winter's cold, and summer's parching heat,
To conquer France, his true inheritance?°
And did my brother Bedford° toil his wits,
To keep by policy° what Henry got?
85 Have you yourselves, Somerset, Buckingham,
Brave York, Salisbury, and victorious Warwick,
Received deep scars in France and Normandy?
Or hath mine uncle Beaufort and myself,
With all the learnèd council° of the realm,
90 Studied so long, sat in the council house
Early and late, debating to and fro
How France and Frenchmen might be kept in awe,
And had his Highness in his infancy
Crownèd in Paris in despite of foes?
95 And shall these labors and these honors die?
Shall Henry's conquest, Bedford's vigilance,
Your deeds of war and all our counsel die?
O peers of England, shameful is this league!
Fatal this marriage, canceling your fame,

---

72 **entertainment** welcome   82 **inheritance** i.e., by his marriage with
Katherine of Valois (see *Henry V*, V.ii.333)   83 **Bedford** John,
Duke of Bedford, the second of Henry IV's three sons   84 **policy**
political craft, statesmanship   89 **council** the privy council

Blotting your names from books of memory,   100
Razing the characters° of your renown,
Defacing monuments of conquered France,
Undoing all, as all had never been.

Cardinal. Nephew, what means this passionate dis-
    course,
This peroration with such circumstance?°   105
For France, 'tis ours; and we will keep it still.

Gloucester. Ay, uncle, we will keep it, if we can;
But now it is impossible we should.
Suffolk, the new-made duke that rules the roast,°
Hath given the duchy of Anjou and Maine   110
Unto the poor King Reignier, whose large style
Agrees° not with the leanness of his purse.

Salisbury. Now, by the death of Him that died for all,
These counties were the keys of Normandy!
But wherefore weeps Warwick, my valiant son?   115

Warwick. For grief that they are past recovery:
For, were there hope to conquer them again,
My sword should shed hot blood, mine eyes no
    tears.
Anjou and Maine! myself did win them both;
Those provinces these arms of mine did conquer: 120
And are the cities that I got with wounds
Delivered up again with peaceful words?
Mort Dieu!°

York. For Suffolk's duke, may he be suffocate
That dims the honor of this warlike isle!   125
France should have torn and rent my very heart
Before I would have yielded to this league.
I never read but England's kings have had
Large sums of gold and dowries with their wives;

---

101 **Razing the characters** effacing the written letters   105 **peroration with such circumstance** rhetorical discourse with so many
details or illustrations   109 **rules the roast** domineers (from the
proverbial expression "to rule the roast after one's own diet")
112 **Agrees** accords   123 **Mort Dieu** by God's death

130   And our King Henry gives away his own,
        To match with her that brings no vantages.°

Gloucester. A proper jest, and never heard before,
        That Suffolk should demand a whole fifteenth°
        For costs and charges in transporting her!
        She should have stayed in France, and sterved° in
135   France,
        Before—

Cardinal. My lord of Gloucester, now ye grow too
        hot:
        It was the pleasure of my lord the King.

Gloucester. My lord of Winchester, I know your
        mind;
140   'Tis not my speeches that you do mislike,
        But 'tis my presence that doth trouble ye.
        Rancor will out: proud prelate, in thy face
        I see thy fury. If I longer stay,
        We shall begin our ancient bickerings.
145   Lordings, farewell, and say, when I am gone,
        I prophesied France will be lost ere long.
                            Exit Gloucester.

Cardinal. So, there goes our Protector in a rage.
        'Tis known to you he is mine enemy.—
        Nay more, an enemy unto you all,
150   And no great friend, I fear me, to the King.
        Consider, lords, he is the next of blood,
        And heir apparent to the English crown:
        Had Henry got an empire by his marriage,
        And all the wealthy kingdoms of the west,
155   There's reason he should be displeased at it.
        Look to it, lords: let not his smoothing words
        Bewitch your hearts, be wise and circumspect.
        What though the common people favor him,
        Calling him "Humphrey, the good Duke of
        Gloucester,"
160   Clapping their hands, and crying with loud voice,

131 **vantages** profit   133 **fifteenth** tax of one-fifteenth part levied
on property   135 **sterved** (1) died (2) starved

"Jesu maintain your royal excellence!"
With "God preserve the good Duke Humphrey!"
I fear me, lords, for all this flattering gloss,
He will be found a dangerous Protector.

Buckingham. Why should he then protect our sov-
  ereign,   *165*
  He being of age to govern of himself?
  Cousin of Somerset, join you with me,
  And altogether with the Duke of Suffolk,
  We'll quickly hoise° Duke Humphrey from his
    seat.

Cardinal. This weighty business will not brook° delay;   *170*
  I'll to the Duke of Suffolk presently.°
                                      Exit Cardinal.

Somerset. Cousin of Buckingham, though Hum-
  phrey's pride
  And greatness of his place° be grief to us,
  Yet let us watch the haughty Cardinal.
  His insolence is more intolerable   *175*
  Than all the princes' in the land beside.
  If Gloucester be displaced, he'll be Protector.

  Buckingham. Or thou or° I, Somerset, will be Pro-
    tector,
  Despite Duke Humphrey or the Cardinal.
                        Exit Buckingham and Somerset.

Salisbury. Pride went before, Ambition follows him.   *180*
  While these do labor for their own preferment,
  Behoves° it us to labor for the realm.
  I never saw but Humphrey Duke of Gloucester
  Did bear him like a noble gentleman.
  Oft have I seen the haughty Cardinal,   *185*
  More like a soldier than a man o' th' church,
  As stout° and proud as he were lord of all,

169 **hoise** hoist   170 **brook** tolerate   171 **presently** immediately
173 **place** position   178 **Or . . . or** either . . . or   182 **Behoves** be-
hooves   187 **stout** fierce, arrogant

Swear like a ruffian and demean himself
Unlike the ruler of a commonweal.
190 Warwick, my son, the comfort of my age,
Thy deeds, thy plainness, and thy housekeeping,°
Hath won the greatest favor of the commons,
Excepting none but good Duke Humphrey:
And, brother York, thy acts in Ireland,
195 In bringing them to civil discipline,
Thy late exploits done in the heart of France,
When thou wert regent for our sovereign,
Have made thee feared and honored of the people:
Join we together for the public good,
200 In what we can, to bridle and suppress
The pride of Suffolk and the Cardinal,
With Somerset's and Buckingham's ambition;
And, as we may, cherish Duke Humphrey's deeds,
While they do tend° the profit of the land.

205 *Warwick.* So God help Warwick, as he loves the land,
And common profit of his country!

York. And so says York—[*aside*] for he hath greatest cause.

Salisbury. Then let's make haste away, and look unto
the main.°

Warwick. Unto the main! O father, Maine is lost,
210 That Maine which by main force Warwick did win,
And would have kept so long as breath did last!
Main chance, father, you meant, but I meant Maine,
Which I will win from France, or else be slain.
            Exit Warwick and Salisbury; manet° York.

York. Anjou and Maine are given to the French;
215 Paris is lost; the state of Normandy
Stands on a tickle point° now° they are gone:
Suffolk concluded on the articles,
The peers agreed, and Henry was well pleased

---

191 **housekeeping** hospitality   204 **tend** foster   208 **main** i.e., main
chance, a gambling term for the most important thing at stake
213s.d. **manet** remains (Latin)   216 **on a tickle point** in an unstable
position   216 **now** now that

To change two dukedoms for a duke's fair daughter.
I cannot blame them all—what is't to them?   220
'Tis thine they give away, and not their own.
Pirates may make cheap pennyworths of their
    pillage,°
And purchase friends, and give to courtesans,
Still reveling like lords till all be gone;
While as the silly° owner of the goods   225
Weeps over them and wrings his hapless hands,
And shakes his head and trembling stands aloof,
While all is shared and all is borne away,
Ready to sterve and dare not touch his own:
So York must sit, and fret, and bite his tongue,   230
While his own lands are bargained for and sold.
Methinks the realms of England, France, and Ire-
    land
Bear that proportion to my flesh and blood
As did the fatal brand Althaea° burned
Unto the Prince's heart of Calydon.°   235
Anjou and Maine both given unto the French?
Cold news for me, for I had hope of France,
Even as I have of fertile England's soil.
A day will come when York shall claim his own;
And therefore I will take the Nevils' parts   240
And make a show of love to proud Duke Hum-
    phrey,
And, when I spy advantage, claim the crown,
For that's the golden mark I seek to hit.
Nor shall proud Lancaster° usurp my right,
Nor hold the scepter in his childish fist,   245
Nor wear the diadem upon his head,
Whose church-like humors° fits not for a crown.
Then, York, be still awhile, till time do serve:
Watch thou and wake, when others be asleep,
To pry into the secrets of the state;   250

222 make . . . pillage squander recklessly what they steal   225 silly
pitiful   234 Althaea Althaea caused the death of her son, Meleager,
Prince of Calydon, by temperamentally burning a brand (log) upon
which the Fates had told her his life would depend   235 Prince's
. . . Calydon the Prince of Calydon's heart   244 Lancaster i.e.,
Henry VI   247 humors temperament

Till Henry surfeit in the joys of love,
With his new bride and England's dear-bought
    queen,
And Humphrey with the peers be fall'n at jars:°
Then will I raise aloft the milk-white rose,
255   With whose sweet smell the air shall be perfumed,
And in my standard bear the arms of York,
To grapple with the house of Lancaster;
And, force perforce,° I'll make him yield the
    crown,
Whose bookish° rule hath pulled fair England
    down.   *Exit York.*

[Scene II. *The Duke of Gloucester's house.*]

Enter Gloucester and his wife Eleanor.

Duchess. Why droops my lord, like over-ripened corn
Hanging the head at Ceres'° plenteous load?
Why doth the great Duke Humphrey knit his
    brows,
As frowning at the favors of the world?
5   Why are thine eyes fixed to the sullen° earth,
Gazing on that which seems to dim thy sight?
What seest thou there? King Henry's diadem,
Enchased° with all the honors of the world?
If so, gaze on, and grovel on thy face,
10 Until thy head be circled with the same.
Put forth thy hand, reach at the glorious gold.
What, is't too short? I'll lengthen it with mine;
And, having both together heaved it up,
We'll both together lift our heads to heaven,
15 And never more abase our sight so low
As to vouchsafe one glance unto the ground.

253 **at jars** to quarreling 258 **force perforce** willy-nilly 259 **book-ish** scholarly, i.e., inactive I.ii.2 **Ceres** the goddess of the harvest
5 **sullen** dull 8 **Enchased** adorned

Gloucester. O Nell, sweet Nell, if thou dost love thy
    lord,
    Banish the canker of ambitious thoughts:
    And may that thought, when I imagine ill
    Against my King and nephew, virtuous Henry,   *20*
    Be my last breathing in this mortal world!
    My troublous dreams this night° doth make me
    sad.

Duchess. What dreamed my lord? Tell me, and I'll
    requite it
    With sweet rehearsal of my morning's dream.°

Gloucester. Methought this staff, mine office-badge in
    court,   *25*
    Was broke in twain: by whom, I have forgot,
    But as I think, it was by th' Cardinal;
    And on the pieces of the broken wand
    Were placed the heads of Edmund Duke of Somer-
    set,
    And William de la Pole, first Duke of Suffolk.   *30*
    This was my dream: what it doth bode, God
    knows.

Duchess. Tut, this was nothing but an argument
    That he that breaks a stick of Gloucester's grove
    Shall lose his head for his presumption.
    But list to me, my Humphrey, my sweet Duke: *35*
    Methought I sat in seat of majesty
    In the cathedral church of Westminster,
    And in that chair where kings and queens were
    crowned;
    Where Henry and Dame Margaret kneeled to me,
    And on my head did set the diadem.   *40*

Gloucester. Nay, Eleanor, then must I chide outright:
    Presumptuous dame, ill-nurtured Eleanor,
    Art thou not second woman in the realm,
    And the Protector's wife, beloved of him?
    Hast thou not worldly pleasure at command   *45*

22 this night last night   24 morning's dream morning dreams were
reputed true

Above the reach or compass of thy thought?
And wilt thou still be hammering° treachery,
To tumble down thy husband and thyself
From top of honor to disgrace's feet?
50   Away from me, and let me hear no more!

Duchess. What, what, my lord! Are you so choleric°
With Eleanor, for telling but her dream?
Next time I'll keep my dreams unto myself,
And not be checked.

55 *Gloucester.* Nay, be not angry; I am pleased again.

Enter Messenger.

Messenger. My Lord Protector, 'tis his Highness'
     pleasure
You do prepare to ride unto Saint Albans,
Where as° the King and Queen do mean to hawk.°

Gloucester. I go. Come, Nell, thou wilt ride with us?

60 *Duchess.* Yes, my good lord, I'll follow presently.°
               Exit Gloucester [and Messenger].
Follow I must; I cannot go before,
While Gloucester bears this base and humble mind.
Were I a man, a duke, and next of blood,°
I would remove these tedious stumbling-blocks
65   And smooth my way upon their headless necks;
And, being a woman, I will not be slack
To play my part in Fortune's pageant.
Where are you there, Sir John? Nay, fear not, man,
We are alone; here's none but thee and I.

Enter Hum.

70 *Hum.* Jesus preserve your royal Majesty!

Duchess. What say'st thou, "majesty"? I am but Grace.

---

47 **hammering** devising   51 **choleric** angry   58 **Where as** where   58
hawk hunt with hawks   60 **presently** immediately   63 **next of
blood** i.e., the successor to the crown, if Henry VI dies without issue

Hum. But, by the grace of God, and Hum's advice,
  Your Grace's title shall be multiplied.°

Duchess. What say'st thou, man? Hast thou as yet
    conferred
  With Margery Jourdain, the cunning witch,   *75*
  With Roger Bolingbroke, the conjuror?
  And will they undertake to do me good?

Hum. This they have promisèd, to show your High-
    ness
  A spirit raised from depth of underground,
  That shall make answer to such questions   *80*
  As by your Grace shall be propounded him.

Duchess. It is enough: I'll think upon the questions.
  When from Saint Albans we do make return,
  We'll see these things effected to the full.
  Here, Hum, take this reward; make merry, man,   *85*
  With thy confederates in this weighty cause.

                              Exit Eleanor.

Hum. Hum must make merry with the Duchess' gold;
  Marry,° and shall. But, how now, Sir John Hum!
  Seal up your lips, and give no words but mum:
  The business asketh° silent secrecy.   *90*
  Dame Eleanor gives gold to bring the witch:
  Gold cannot come amiss, were she a devil.
  Yet have I gold flies from another coast°—
  I dare not say, from the rich Cardinal
  And from the great and new-made Duke of Suffolk. *95*
  Yet I do find it so—for, to be plain,
  They, knowing Dame Eleanor's aspiring humor,°
  Have hirèd me to undermine the Duchess
  And buzz these conjurations° in her brain.
  They say "A crafty knave does need no broker";   *100*
  Yet am I Suffolk and the Cardinal's broker.°
  Hum, if you take not heed, you shall go near

73 Your . . . multiplied a play on I Peter, i.2: "Grace and peace
be multiplied unto you"   88 Marry a mild oath, from "By the
Virgin Mary"   90 asketh requires   93 coast quarter   97 humor
temperament   99 conjurations incantations   101 broker agent, go-
between

To call them both a pair of crafty knaves.
Well, so it stands; and thus, I fear, at last
105 Hum's knavery will be the Duchess' wrack,°
And her attainture° will be Humphrey's fall.
Sort how it will, I shall have gold for all.   *Exit.*

[Scene III. *The palace.*]

*Enter three or four Petitioners; [Peter Thump],
the Armorer's man, being one.*

First Petitioner. My masters, let's stand close: my
Lord Protector will come this way by and by, and
then we may deliver our supplications in the quill.°

Second Petitioner. Marry, the Lord protect him, for
5   he's a good man, Jesu bless him!

Enter Suffolk and Queen.

Peter. Here 'a° comes, methinks, and the Queen with
him. I'll be the first, sure.

Second Petitioner. Come back, fool! this is the Duke
of Suffolk, and not my Lord Protector.

10 *Suffolk.* How now, fellow! wouldst anything with me?

First Petitioner. I pray, my lord, pardon me: I took
ye for my Lord Protector.

Queen. For my Lord Protector! Are your supplications to his lordship? Let me see them: what is
13   thine?

First Petitioner. Mine is, and't please your Grace,
against John Goodman, my Lord Cardinal's man,°
for keeping my house, and lands, and wife and all,
from me.

105 wrack ruin   106 attainture incrimination   I.iii.3 in the quill
in succession (?)   6 'a he   17 man agent, protégé

Suffolk. Thy wife too! that's some wrong, indeed.   20
What's yours? What's here? [*Reads*] "Against the
Duke of Suffolk, for enclosing the commons° of
Melford." How now, sir knave!

Second Petitioner. Alas, sir, I am but a poor petitioner of our whole township.   25

Peter. [*Giving his petition*] Against my master,
Thomas Horner, for saying that the Duke of York
was rightful heir to the crown.

Queen. What say'st thou? did the Duke of York say
he was rightful heir to the crown?   30

Peter. That my master was? No, forsooth: my master
said that he was, and that the King was an usurer.

Queen. An usurper, thou wouldst say.

Peter. Ay, forsooth, an usurper.

Suffolk. Who is there? (*Enter Servant.*) Take this fel- 35
low in, and send for his master with a pursuivant°
presently. We'll hear more of your matter before
the King.   *Exit* [*Servant with Peter*].

Queen. And as for you, that love to be protected
Under the wings of our Protector's grace,   40
Begin your suits anew, and sue to him.
                    Tear[*s*] *the supplication.*
Away, base cullions!° Suffolk, let them go.

All. Come, let's be gone.   *Exit.*

Queen. My Lord of Suffolk, say, is this the guise,°
Is this the fashions in the court of England?   45
Is this the government of Britain's isle,
And this the royalty of Albion's° King?
What! Shall King Henry be a pupil still
Under the surly Gloucester's governance?
Am I a queen in title and in style,°   50

22 enclosing the commons fencing off the public pasture   36 pur-
suivant warrant officer   42 cullions rascals   44 guise custom   47
Albion's England's   50 style name

And must be made a subject to a duke?
I tell thee, Pole, when in the city Tours
Thou ran'st a tilt° in honor of my love
And stol'st away the ladies' hearts of France,
55 I thought King Henry had resembled thee
In courage, courtship, and proportion:°
But all his mind is bent to holiness,
To number Ave-Maries on his beads;°
His champions° are the prophets and apostles,
60 His weapons holy saws° of sacred writ,
His study is his tilt-yard, and his loves
Are brazen images of canonized saints.
I would the College of the Cardinals
Would choose him Pope and carry him to Rome,
65 And set the triple crown° upon his head:
That were a state fit for his Holiness.

Suffolk. Madam, be patient: as I was cause
Your Highness came to England, so will I
In England work your Grace's full content.

Queen. Beside the haughty Protector, have we Beau-
70   fort
The imperious churchman, Somerset, Buckingham,
And grumbling York; and not the least of these
But can do more in England than the King.

Suffolk. And he of these that can do most of all
75 Cannot do more in England than the Nevils:
Salisbury and Warwick are no simple peers.

Queen. Not all these lords do vex me half so much
As that proud dame, the Lord Protector's wife:
She sweeps it through the court with troops of
      ladies,
80 More like an empress than Duke Humphrey's wife.
Strangers° in court do take her for the Queen:

53 ran'st a tilt competed in a tourney   56 proportion shape   58 number . . . beads say Rosaries   59 champions warriors chosen to represent him (chivalric term)   60 saws maxims, platitudes   65 triple crown the papal tiara   81 Strangers foreigners

She bears a duke's revenues on her back,
And in her heart she scorns our poverty.
Shall I not live to be avenged on her?
Contemptuous° base-born callet° as she is,   85
She vaunted 'mongst her minions° t'other day,
The very train of her worst wearing gown
Was better worth than all my father's lands,
Till Suffolk gave two dukedoms for his daughter.

Suffolk. Madam, myself have limed a bush° for her,   90
And placed a quire° of such enticing birds
That she will light to listen to the lays,°
And never mount to trouble you again.
So let her rest: and, madam, list to me,
For I am bold to counsel you in this: 95
Although we fancy not the Cardinal,
Yet must we join with him and with the lords,
Till we have brought Duke Humphrey in disgrace.
As for the Duke of York, this late complaint°
Will make but little for his benefit.   100
So, one by one, we'll weed them all at last,
And you yourself shall steer the happy° helm.

*Sound a sennet.° Enter King Henry, and the
Duke of York and the Duke of Somerset on both
sides of the King, whispering with him; and enter
Gloucester, Dame Eleanor, the Duke of Buckingham, Salisbury, the Earl of Warwick, and
the Cardinal of Winchester.*

King. For my part, noble lords, I care not which:
Or Somerset or York, all's one to me.

York. If York have ill demeaned himself in France,   105
Then let him be denayed° the regentship.

---

85 **Contemptuous** contemptible   85 **callet** trull   86 **minions** effeminate or female retainers (contemptuous)   90 **limed a bush** small
birds were trapped by smearing bird-lime (a sticky preparation of
holly-bark) over the twigs of bushes   91 **quire** (1) group (2) choir
92 **lays** songs   99 **this late complaint** i.e., Peter's   102 **happy** fortunate   102s.d.**sennet** phrase on the trumpet   106 **denayed** old
form of "denied"

Somerset. If Somerset be unworthy of the place,
  Let York be regent; I will yield to him.

Warwick. Whether your Grace be worthy, yea or no,
110 Dispute not that: York is the worthier.

Cardinal. Ambitious Warwick, let thy betters speak.

Warwick. The Cardinal's not my better in the field.

Buckingham. All in this presence are thy betters,°
  Warwick.

Warwick. Warwick may live to be the best of all.

Salisbury. Peace, son; and show some reason, Buck-
115   ingham,
  Why Somerset should be preferred in this.°

Queen. Because the King, forsooth, will have it so.

Gloucester. Madam, the King is old enough himself
  To give his censure.° These are no women's
    matters.

120 *Queen.* If he be old enough, what needs your Grace
  To be Protector of his Excellence?

Gloucester. Madam, I am Protector of the realm,
  And at his pleasure will resign my place.

Suffolk. Resign it then and leave thine insolence.
125 Since thou wert King—as who is King but thou?—
  The commonwealth hath daily run to wrack,
  The Dolphin° hath prevailed beyond the seas,
  And all the peers and nobles of the realm
  Have been as bondmen° to thy sovereignty.

Cardinal. The commons hast thou racked; the clergy's
130   bags
  Are lank and lean with thy extortions.

---

113 **betters** superiors in rank   116 **preferred in this** promoted to
this position   119 **censure** opinion, judgment   127 **Dolphin** Dauphin, eldest son of the King of France   129 **bondmen** slaves, serfs

Somerset. Thy sumptuous buildings and thy wife's
    attire
    Have cost a mass of public treasury.

Buckingham. Thy cruelty in execution
    Upon offenders hath exceeded law,   *135*
    And left thee to the mercy of the law.

Queen. Thy sale of offices and towns in France,
    If they were known, as the suspect° is great,
    Would make thee quickly hop without thy head.
        Exit Gloucester. [The Queen drops her fan.]
    Give me my fan! What, minion, can ye not?   *140*
        She gives the Duchess a box on the ear.
    I cry you mercy,° madam; was it you?

Duchess. Was't I! Yea, I it was, proud Frenchwoman:
    Could I come near your beauty with my nails,
    I'd set my ten commandments in your face.°

King. Sweet aunt, be quiet;° 'twas against her will.°   *145*

Duchess. Against her will, good King? Look to't, in
    time
    She'll hamper thee, and dandle thee like a baby.
    Though in this place most master° wear no
    breeches,
    She shall not strike Dame Eleanor unrevenged.
        Exit Eleanor.

Buckingham. Lord Cardinal, I will follow Eleanor,   *150*
    And listen after Humphrey, how he proceeds.
    She's tickled° now; her fury needs no spurs,
    She'll gallop far enough to her destruction.
        Exit Buckingham.

        Enter Gloucester.

Gloucester. Now, lords, my choler being over-blown
    With walking once about the quadrangle,   *155*

138 **suspect** suspicion   141 **cry you mercy** beg your pardon   144
set . . . face mark with fingernails   145 **quiet** calm   145 **against
her will** unwittingly   148 **most master** the greatest master; i.e., here
the wife rules the house   152 **tickled** provoked, touched

     I come to talk of commonwealth affairs.
     As for your spiteful false objections,°
     Prove them, and I lie open to the law:
     But God in mercy so deal with my soul,
160   As I in duty love my king and country!
     But to the matter that we have in hand:
     I say, my Sovereign, York is meetest° man
     To be your regent in the realm of France.

Suffolk. Before we make election, give me leave
165   To show some reason, of no little force,
     That York is most unmeet of any man.

York. I'll tell thee, Suffolk, why I am unmeet:
     First, for I cannot flatter thee in pride;°
     Next, if I be appointed for the place,
170   My Lord of Somerset will keep me here,
     Without discharge,° money, or furniture,°
     Till France be won into the Dolphin's hands.
     Last time, I danced attendance on his will
     Till Paris was besieged, famished, and lost.

175 *Warwick.* That can I witness; and a fouler fact°
     Did never traitor in the land commit.

Suffolk. Peace, headstrong Warwick!

Warwick. Image° of pride, why should I hold my
     peace?

     Enter [Horner, the] Armorer, and [Peter], his
     man, [both guarded].

Suffolk. Because here is a man accused of treason.
180   Pray God the Duke of York excuse himself!

York. Doth anyone accuse York for° a traitor?

King. What mean'st thou, Suffolk? Tell me. what are
     these?

---

157 **objections** accusations   162 **meetest** most suitable   168 **for . . .
pride** because I cannot entertain you sumptuously   171 **discharge**
payment of what he owes   171 **furniture** equipment (for war)   175
fact evil deed   178 **Image** embodiment, epitome   181 **for** as

Suffolk. Please it your Majesty, this is the man
  That doth accuse his master of high treason.
  His words were these: that Richard Duke of York   *185*
  Was rightful heir unto the English crown,
  And that your Majesty was an usurper.

King. Say, man, were these thy words?

Horner. And't shall please your Majesty, I never said
  nor thought any such matter! God is my witness,   *190*
  I am falsely accused by the villain.

Peter. By these ten bones,° my lords, he did speak
  them to me in the garret one night, as we were
  scouring my Lord of York's armor.

York. Base dunghill villain and mechanical,°   *195*
  I'll have thy head for this thy traitor's speech!
  I do beseech your royal Majesty,
  Let him have all the rigor of the law.

Horner. Alas, my lord, hang me if ever I spake the
  words! My accuser is my prentice;° and when I did   *200*
  correct him for his fault° the other day, he did vow
  upon his knees he would be even with me: I have
  good witness of this; therefore I beseech your
  Majesty, do not cast away an honest man for a
  villain's accusation.   *205*

King. Uncle, what shall we say to this in law?

Gloucester. This doom,° my lord, if I may judge:
  Let Somerset be regent o'er the French,
  Because in York this breeds suspicion.°
  And let these have a day appointed them   *210*
  For single combat,° in convenient° place,
  For he hath witness of his servant's malice.
  This is the law, and this Duke Humphrey's doom.

Somerset. I humbly thank your royal Majesty.

---

192 **ten bones** i.e., fingers   195 **mechanical** manual laborer, i.e.,
drudge   200 **prentice** apprentice   201 **fault** mistake   207 **doom**
sentence   209 **breeds suspicion** suggests doubt (of his loyalty)   211
single combat a duel   211 **convenient** appropriate

215 *Horner.* And I accept the combat willingly.

Peter. Alas, my lord, I cannot fight; for God's sake,
pity my case! The spite of man prevaileth against
me. O Lord, have mercy upon me! I shall never be
able to fight a blow. O Lord, my heart!

Gloucester. Sirrah,° or you must fight, or else be
220   hanged.

King. Away with them to prison; and the day of combat shall be the last of the next month. Come,
Somerset, we'll see thee sent away.

Flourish; exeunt.

[Scene IV. *A garden outside Gloucester's house,
before a tower.*]

Enter the witch [*Margaret Jourdain*], *the two
priests* [*Hum and Southwell,*] *and Bolingbroke*
[*the conjuror*].

Hum. Come, my masters; the Duchess, I tell you, expects performance of your promises.

Bolingbroke. Master Hum, we are therefore provided:° will her ladyship behold and hear our
5   exorcisms?°

Hum. Ay, what else? Fear° you not her courage.

Bolingbroke. I have heard her reported to be a
woman of an invincible spirit: but it shall be convenient, Master Hum, that you be by her aloft,
10   while we be busy below; and so, I pray you, go,
in God's name, and leave us. (*Exit Hum.*) Mother
Jourdain, be you prostrate and grovel on the earth;
John Southwell, read you; and let us to our work.

220 **Sirrah** contemptuous term of address   **I.iv.3–4 therefore pro-**
vided equipped for that   **5 exorcisms** ceremonies for expelling the
Devil (but here a malapropism for *raising* the Devil)   **6 Fear** doubt

Enter Duchess aloft, [Hum following].

Duchess. Well said, my masters; and welcome all. To
　this gear,° the sooner the better.　　　　　　　　　15

Bolingbroke. Patience, good lady; wizards know their
　times.
　Deep night, dark night, the silent° of the night,
　The time of night when Troy was set on fire,
　The time when screech-owls cry, and ban-dogs°
　　howl
　And spirits walk, and ghosts break up their graves—　20
　That time best fits the work we have in hand.
　Madam, sit you, and fear not: whom we raise
　We will make fast within a hallowed verge.°
　　　　　Here [they] do the ceremonies belonging,
　　　　　and make the circle; Bolingbroke or South-
　　　　　well reads, "Conjuro te, etc."° It thunders
　　　　　and lightens° terribly; then the Spirit riseth.

Spirit. Adsum.°

Margery Jourdain. Asnath,°　　　　　　　　　25
　By the eternal God, whose name and power
　Thou tremblest at, answer that I shall ask:
　For till thou speak, thou shalt not pass from hence.

Spirit. Ask what thou wilt. That I had said and done!

Bolingbroke. [*Consulting a paper*] First of the King:
　what shall of him become?　　　　　　　　　30

Spirit. The Duke yet lives that Henry shall depose,
　But him outlive, and die a violent death.°
　　　　　[*Southwell writes out the questions*
　　　　　　　　　and answers.]

Bolingbroke. What fates await the Duke of Suffolk?

15 **gear** business　17 **silent** silent time　19 **ban-dogs** fierce dogs
chained up　23 **hallowed verge** charmed circle　23s.d. **Conjuro te,
etc.** beginning of the incantation: "I conjure you . . ."　23s.d.
lightens makes lightning　24 **Adsum** here I am　25 **Asnath** obscure; possibly an anagram for "Sathan"　31–32 **The Duke . . .
death** a typically cryptic and ambiguous prophecy: either "The duke
who will depose Henry is now living," or "the duke Henry will
depose is now living." See lines 62–63

Spirit. By water shall he die, and take his end.

35 *Bolingbroke.* What shall befall the Duke of Somerset?

Spirit. Let him shun castles:
Safer shall he be upon the sandy plains
Than where castles mounted stand.
Have done, for more I hardly can endure.

Bolingbroke. Descend to darkness and the burning
40   lake!
False fiend, avoid!°
           Thunder and lightning; he sinks down again.

     *Enter the Duke of York and the Duke of Buck-
          ingham with their guard and break in.*

York. Lay hands upon these traitors and their trash.
Beldam, I think we watched you at an inch.°
What, madam, are you there? The King and com-
     monweal
45   Are deeply indebted for this piece of pains.°
My Lord Protector will, I doubt it not,
See you well guerdoned° for these good deserts.

Duchess. Not half so bad as thine to England's King,
Injurious° Duke, that threatest where's no cause.

Buckingham. True, madam, none at all: what call you
50   this?
Away with them! Let them be clapped up close,
And kept asunder. You, madam, shall with us.
Stafford, take her to thee.
           Exit Duchess above [*and Hum, guarded*].
We'll see your trinkets° here all forthcoming.
55 All, away!
           Exit [*Margery Jourdain, Southwell, and
           Bolingbroke, with the rest of the guard*].

41 **avoid** go hence 43 **at an inch** closely (enough) 45 **piece of
pains** masterpiece of service (ironic) 47 **guerdoned** rewarded 49
Injurious abusive 54 **trinkets** i.e., the conjuring apparatus, including Southwell's written record

York. Lord Buckingham, methinks you watched her
    well:
 A pretty plot, well chosen to build upon!
 Now, pray, my lord, let's see the devil's writ.
 What have we here?   *Reads.*
 "The Duke yet lives that Henry shall depose;   *60*
 But him outlive, and die a violent death."
 Why, this is just *"Aio te, Acacida,*
 Romanos vincere posse."° Well, to the rest:
 "Tell me what fate awaits the Duke of Suffolk?
 By water shall he die, and take his end.   *65*
 What shall betide the Duke of Somerset?
 Let him shun castles;
 Safer shall he be upon the sandy plains
 Than where castles mounted stand."
 Come, come, my lords, these oracles are hard,   *70*
 Hardly attained, and hardly° understood.
 The King is now in progress towards Saint Albans;
 With him, the husband of this lovely° lady.
 Thither goes these news, as fast as horse can carry
    them—
 A sorry breakfast for my Lord Protector.   *75*

Buckingham. Your Grace shall give me leave, my lord
    of York,
 To be the post,° in hope of his reward.

York. At your pleasure, my good lord. Who's within
    there, ho!

Enter a Servingman.

 Invite my Lords of Salisbury and Warwick
 To sup with me tomorrow night. Away!   *Exeunt.* *80*

62–63 **Aio . . . posse** from Ennius, the ambiguous response of the
Pythian oracle Apollo to King Pyrrhus, when Pyrrhus asked if he
would conquer Rome: either "I affirm that you, descendant of
Aeacus, can conquer the Romans," or "I affirm that the Romans
can conquer you, etc." 70–71 **hard . . . Hardly . . . hardly** obscure
. . . with difficulty . . . scarcely to be 73 **lovely** lovable 77 **post**
messenger

[ACT II

Scene I. *Saint Albans.*]

*Enter the King, Queen, with a hawk on her fist,
Gloucester, Cardinal, and Suffolk, with falconers
hallooing.*

Queen. Believe me, lords, for flying at the brook,°
    I saw not better sport these seven years' day:
    Yet, by your leave, the wind was very high;
    And, ten to one, old Joan had not gone out.°

5 *King.* But what a point,° my lord, your falcon made,
    And what a pitch° she flew above the rest!
    To see how God in all his creatures works!
    Yea, man and birds are fain of climbing high.

Suffolk. No marvel, and it like your Majesty,
10   My Lord Protector's hawks do tow'r so well:
    They know their master loves to be aloft,
    And bears his thoughts above his falcon's pitch.

Gloucester. My lord, 'tis but a base ignoble mind
    That mounts no higher than a bird can soar.

Cardinal. I thought as much: he would be above the
15   clouds.

II.i.1 **at the brook** i.e., at waterfowl   4 **ten ... out** the odds were
against this hawk (the Queen's?) flying   5 **point** position from
which to swoop   6 **pitch** altitude

64

Gloucester. Ay, my lord Cardinal, how think you by
  that?
  Were it not good your Grace could fly to heaven?

King. The treasury of everlasting joy.

Cardinal. Thy heaven is on earth; thine eyes and
  thoughts
  Beat on° a crown, the treasure of thy heart.   20
  Pernicious Protector, dangerous peer,
  That smooth'st it° so with King and commonweal!

Gloucester. What, Cardinal, is your priesthood grown
  peremptory?°
  Tantaene animis coelestibus irae?°
  Churchmen so hot? Good uncle, can you dote,°   25
  To hide such malice with such holiness?

Suffolk. No malice, sir; no more than well becomes
  So good a quarrel and so bad a peer.

Gloucester. As who, my lord?

Suffolk.   Why, as you, my lord,
  An't like your lordly Lord-Protectorship.   30

Gloucester. Why, Suffolk, England knows thine insolence.

Queen. And thy ambition, Gloucester.

King. I prithee peace,
  Good Queen, and whet not on these furious peers,
  For blessèd are the peacemakers on earth.   35

Cardinal. Let me be blessèd for the peace I make,
  Against this proud Protector, with my sword!

Gloucester. [*Aside*] Faith, holy uncle, would 'twere
  come to that!

Cardinal. [*Aside*] Marry, when thou dar'st.

20 **Beat on** harp on 22 **smooth'st it** flatters 23 **peremptory** overbearing 24 **Tantaene . . . irae** *Aeneid*, I,11: "So much anger in
heavenly souls?" 25 **can you dote?** are you so much a fool (as
to attempt)

Gloucester. [*Aside*] Make up no factious numbers for
40   the matter;°
    In thine own person answer thy abuse.

Cardinal. [*Aside*] Ay, where thou dar'st not peep:
    and if° thou dar'st,
    This evening, on the east side of the grove.

King. How now, my lords!

Cardinal.   Believe me, cousin Gloucester,
45   Had not your man put up the fowl° so suddenly,
    We had had more sport. [*Aside*] Come with thy
    two-hand sword.

Gloucester. True, uncle.

Cardinal. [*Aside*] Are ye advised?° The east side of
    the grove?

Gloucester. [*Aside*] Cardinal, I am with you.

King.   Why, how now, uncle Gloucester!

Gloucester. Talking of hawking; nothing else, my
50   lord.
    [*Aside*] Now, by God's mother, priest, I'll shave
    your crown for this.
    Or all my fence° shall fail.

Cardinal. [*Aside*] *Medice, teipsum*°—
    Protector, see to't well, protect yourself.

King. The winds grow high, so do your stomachs,°
55   lords.
    How irksome is this music to my heart!
    When such strings jar, what hope of harmony?
    I pray, my lords, let me compound° this strife.

---

40 Make . . . matter bring none of your own faction into the quarrel   **42 and if** if   **45 put up the fowl** flushed the game ("your man"
disrespectfully suggests King Henry)   **48 advised** agreed   **52 fence**
skill at swordplay   **53 Medice, teipsum** "physician, [cure] thyself"
55 stomachs tempers   **58 compound** compose

Enter one, crying "A miracle!"

Gloucester. What means this noise?
  Fellow, what miracle dost thou proclaim?   60

One. A miracle! a miracle!

Suffolk. Come to the King and tell him what miracle.

One. Forsooth, a blind man at Saint Alban's shrine,
  Within this half hour hath received his sight—
  A man that ne'er saw in his life before.   65

King. Now, God be praised, that to believing souls
  Gives light in darkness, comfort in despair!

*Enter the Mayor of Saint Albans and his brethren,
bearing the man [Saunder Simpcox] between two
in a chair, [Simpcox's Wife following].*

Cardinal. Here comes the townsmen, on° procession,
  To present your Highness with the man.

King. Great is his comfort in this earthly vale,   70
  Although by sight his sin be multiplied.°

Gloucester. Stand by, my masters: bring him near the
    King:
  His Highness' pleasure is to talk with him.

King. Good fellow, tell us here the circumstance,
  That we for thee may glorify the Lord.   75
  What, hast thou been long blind, and now restored?

Simpcox. Born blind, and't please your Grace.

Wife. Ay, indeed, was he.

Suffolk. What woman is this?

Wife. His wife, and't like your Worship.   80

Gloucester. Hadst thou been his mother, thou couldst
  have better told.

---

68 on in   71 Although . . . multiplied cf. John, ix.41: "If ye were
blind, ye would have no sin, but now ye say, We see: therefore
your sin remaineth"

King. Where wert thou born?

Simpcox. At Berwick in the north, and't like your
    Grace.

King. Poor soul, God's goodness hath been great to
    thee:
85 Let never day nor night unhallowed pass,
    But still° remember what the Lord hath done.

Queen. Tell me, good fellow, cam'st thou here by
    chance,
    Or of devotion, to this holy shrine?

Simpcox. God knows, of pure devotion, being called
90 A hundred times and oftener, in my sleep,
    By good Saint Alban; who said, "Simpcox, come,
    Come, offer at my shrine, and I will help thee."

Wife. Most true, forsooth; and many time and oft
    Myself have heard a voice to call him so.

Cardinal. What, art thou lame?

95 *Simpcox.*   Ay, God Almighty help me.

Suffolk. How cam'st thou so?

Simpcox.   A fall off of a tree.

Wife. A plum tree, master.

Gloucester.   How long hast thou been blind?

Simpcox. O, born so, master.

Gloucester.   What, and wouldst climb a tree?

Simpcox. But that° in all my life, when I was a youth.

100 *Wife.* Too true, and bought his climbing very dear.

Gloucester. 'Mass,° thou lov'dst plums well, that
    wouldst venture so.

86 still always   99 But that only once   101 'Mass by the mass

Simpcox. Alas, good master, my wife desired some
    damsons,
    And made me climb, with danger of my life.

Gloucester. [*Aside*] A subtle knave! But yet it shall
    not serve.
    Let me see thine eyes: wink° now: now open them.   *105*
    In my opinion yet thou see'st not well.

Simpcox. Yes, master, clear as day, I thank God and
    Saint Alban.

Gloucester. Say'st thou me so? What color is this
    cloak of?

Simpcox. Red, master; red as blood.

Gloucester. Why, that's well said. What color is my
    gown of?   *110*

Simpcox. Black, forsooth, coal-black, as jet.

King. Why, then, thou know'st what color jet is of?

Suffolk. And yet, I think, jet did he never see.

Gloucester. But cloaks and gowns, before this day, a
    many.

Wife. Never, before this day, in all his life!   *115*

Gloucester. Tell me, sirrah, what's my name?

Simpcox. Alas, master, I know not.

Gloucester. What's his name?

Simpcox. I know not.

Gloucester. Nor his?   *120*

Simpcox. No, indeed, master.

Gloucester. What's thine own name?

Simpcox. Saunder Simpcox, and if it please you,
    master.

105 wink close them

125 *Gloucester.* Then, Saunder, sit there, the lying'st knave
in Christendom. If thou hadst been born blind, thou
might'st as well have known all our names as thus
to name the several colors we do wear. Sight may
distinguish of colors, but suddenly to nominate°
130 them all, it is impossible. My lords, Saint Alban
here hath done a miracle—and would ye not think
his cunning to be great that could restore this
cripple to his legs again?

Simpcox. O master, that you could!

135 *Gloucester.* My masters of Saint Albans,
Have you not beadles° in your town,
And things called whips?

Mayor. Yes, my lord, if it please your Grace.

Gloucester. Then send for one presently.

140 *Mayor.* Sirrah, go fetch the beadle hither straight.
                    Exit [*an Attendant*].

Gloucester. Now fetch me a stool hither by and by.
[*They bring one.*] Now, sirrah, if you mean to save
yourself from whipping, leap me° over this stool
and run away.

145 *Simpcox.* Alas, master, I am not able to stand alone:
You go about to torture me in vain.

                Enter a Beadle with whips.

Gloucester. Well, sir, we must have you find your legs.
Sirrah beadle, whip him till he leap over that same
stool.

150 *Beadle.* I will, my lord. Come on, sirrah: off with your
doublet quickly.

---

129 nominate give them names   **136 beadles** minor parish officials,
entrusted with keeping order in church, and punishing petty offenders   **143 leap me** leap for me

Simpcox. Alas, master, what shall I do? I am not able
to stand.

> *After the Beadle hath hit him once, he
> leaps over the stool and runs away; and
> they follow and cry, "A miracle!"*

King. O God, seest Thou this, and bearest so long?

Queen. It made me laugh to see the villain run.   155

Gloucester. Follow the knave, and take this drab°
away.

Wife. Alas, sir, we did it for pure need.

Gloucester. Let them be whipped through every
market-town
Till they come to Berwick, from whence they came.
> *Exit [Mayor, Beadle, Wife, etc.].*

Cardinal. Duke Humphrey has done a miracle today.   160

Suffolk. True—made the lame to leap and fly away.

Gloucester. But you have done more miracles than I:
You made in a day, my lord, whole towns to fly.°

> *Enter Buckingham.*

King. What tidings with our cousin Buckingham?

Buckingham. Such as my heart doth tremble to un-
fold: 165
A sort of naughty persons, lewdly bent,°
Under the countenance and confederacy°
Of Lady Eleanor, the Protector's wife,
The ringleader and head of all this rout,
Have practiced dangerously against your state,   170
Dealing with witches and with conjurors,
Whom we have apprehended in the fact,°
Raising up wicked spirits from under ground,

---

156 **drab** whore   163 **You . . . fly** i.e., by presenting them to the
King of France   166 **sort . . . bent** group of worthless persons,
wickedly inclined   167 **countenance and confederacy** patronage
and participation   172 **in the fact** in the act

Demanding of° King Henry's life and death,
175   And other of your Highness' Privy Council,
As more at large your Grace shall understand.

Cardinal. [*Aside*] And so, my Lord Protector, by this
          means
Your lady is forthcoming° yet at London.
This news, I think, hath turned your weapon's edge;
180   'Tis like, my lord, you will not keep your hour.°

Gloucester. [*Aside*] Ambitious churchman, leave to
          afflict my heart:
Sorrow and grief have vanquished all my powers;
And, vanquished as I am, I yield to thee,
Or to the meanest groom.

185 *King.* O God, what mischiefs work the wicked ones,
Heaping confusion on their own heads thereby!

Queen. Gloucester, see here the tainture° of thy nest.
And look thyself be faultless, thou wert best.

Gloucester. Madam, for myself, to heaven I do appeal,
190   How I have loved my King and commonweal!
And for my wife, I know not how it stands.
Sorry I am to hear what I have heard;
Noble she is; but if she have forgot
Honor and virtue and conversed with such
195   As, like to pitch, defile nobility,
I banish her my bed and company,
And give her as a prey to law and shame,
That hath dishonored Gloucester's honest name.

King. Well, for this night we will repose us here:
200   Tomorrow toward London back again,
To look into this business thoroughly,
And call these foul offenders to their answers;
And poise the cause in Justice' equal scales,
Whose beam stands sure, whose rightful
          cause prevails.°   *Flourish. Exeunt.*

174 **Demanding of** inquiring about 178 **forthcoming** due for trial
180 **hour** appointment 187 **tainture** defilement 203–4 **poise** . . .
prevails balance the testimony in the scales of justice to see which
weighs more

[Scene II. *London. The Duke of York's garden.*]

Enter York, Salisbury, and Warwick.

York. Now, my good Lords of Salisbury and Warwick,
  Our simple supper ended, give me leave,
  In this close walk,° to satisfy myself
  In craving your opinion of my title,
  Which is infallible, to England's crown.   5

Salisbury. My lord, I long to hear it at full.

Warwick. Sweet York, begin: and if thy claim be good,
  The Nevils are thy subjects to command.

York. Then thus:
  Edward the Third, my lords, had seven sons: 10
  The first, Edward the Black Prince, Prince of Wales;
  The second, William of Hatfield; and the third,
  Lionel Duke of Clarence; next to whom
  Was John of Gaunt, the Duke of Lancaster;
  The fifth was Edmund Langley, Duke of York;   15
  The sixth was Thomas of Woodstock, Duke of
    Gloucester;
  William of Windsor was the seventh and last.
  Edward the Black Prince died before his father,
  And left behind him Richard, his only son,
  Who after Edward the Third's death reigned as King;   20
  Till Henry Bolingbroke, Duke of Lancaster,
  The eldest son and heir of John of Gaunt,
  Crowned by the name of Henry the Fourth,
  Seized on the realm, deposed the rightful king,
  Sent his poor queen to France, from whence she
    came,   25
  And him to Pomfret; where, as all you know,
  Harmless Richard was murdered traitorously.

II.ii.3 **close walk** private or concealed pathway

Warwick. Father, the Duke hath told the truth;
    Thus got the house of Lancaster the crown.

30 *York.* Which now they hold by force and not by right:
    For Richard, the first son's heir, being dead,
    The issue of the next son should have reigned.

Salisbury. But William of Hatfield died without an
    heir.

York. The third son, Duke of Clarence, from whose
    line
35 I claim the crown, had issue, Philippa, a daughter,
    Who married Edmund Mortimer, Earl of March;
    Edmund had issue, Roger Earl of March;
    Roger had issue, Edmund, Anne and Eleanor.

Salisbury. This Edmund, in the reign of Bolingbroke,
40 As I have read, laid claim unto the crown;
    And, but for Owen Glendower, had been King,
    Who kept him in captivity till he died.
    But to the rest.

York.   His eldest sister, Anne,
    My mother, being heir unto the crown,
45 Married Richard, Earl of Cambridge,
    Who was to Edmund Langley,
    Edward the Third's fifth son, the son.
    By her I claim the kingdom: she was heir
    To Roger Earl of March, who was the son
50 Of Edmund Mortimer, who married Philippa,
    Sole daughter unto Lionel, Duke of Clarence:
    So, if the issue of the elder son
    Succeed before the younger, I am King.

Warwick. What plain proceedings° is more plain than
    this?
55 Henry doth claim the crown from John of Gaunt,
    The fourth son; York claims it from the third.
    Till Lionel's issue fails, his should not reign:
    It fails not yet, but flourishes in thee,

54 **proceedings** order of events (in the pedigree)

And in thy sons, fair slips° of such a stock.
Then, father Salisbury, kneel we together,   60
And in this private plot be we the first
That shall salute our rightful sovereign
With honor of his birthright to the crown.

Both. [*Kneeling*] Long live our sovereign Richard,
    England's King!

York. We thank you, lords. But I am not your king   65
    Till I be crowned and that my sword be stained
    With heart-blood of the house of Lancaster;
    And that's not suddenly to be performed,
    But with advice° and silent secrecy.
    Do you as I do in these dangerous days: 70
    Wink at° the Duke of Suffolk's insolence,
    At Beaufort's pride, at Somerset's ambition,
    At Buckingham and all the crew of them,
    Till they have snared the shepherd of the flock,
    That virtuous prince, the good Duke Humphrey: 75
    'Tis that they seek, and they in seeking that
    Shall find their deaths, if York can prophesy.

Salisbury. My lord, break we off; we know your mind
    at full.

Warwick. My heart assures me that the Earl of War-
    wick
    Shall one day make the Duke of York a king.   80

York. And, Nevil, this I do assure myself:
    Richard shall live to make the Earl of Warwick
    The greatest man in England but the King. *Exeunt.*

---

59 **slips** shoots, cuttings   69 **advice** deliberation   71 **Wink** at close
your eyes to

[Scene III. *A hall of justice.*]

Sound trumpets. Enter King Henry, and the Queen, Gloucester, the Duke of Suffolk, and the Duke of Buckingham, the Cardinal, and the Duchess of Gloucester, led with the Officers; and then enter to them the Duke of York, and the Earls of Salisbury and Warwick.

King. Stand forth, Dame Eleanor Cobham, Gloucester's
    wife.
    In sight of God and us, your guilt is great:
    Receive the sentence of the law for sins
    Such as by God's book are adjudged to death.°
5   You four, from hence to prison back again;
    From thence unto the place of execution:
    The witch in Smithfield° shall be burnt to ashes,
    And you three shall be strangled on the gallows.
    You, madam, for you are more nobly born,
10   Despoilèd of your honor in your life,
    Shall, after three days' open penance done,
    Live in your country here in banishment,
    With Sir John Stanley, in the Isle of Man.

Duchess. Welcome is banishment, welcome were my
    death.

Gloucester. Eleanor, the law thou seest hath judgèd
15   thee:
    I cannot justify whom the law condemns.
                     [Exeunt the Duchess and the
                           other prisoners, guarded.]
    Mine eyes are full of tears, my heart of grief.
    Ah, Humphrey, this dishonor in thine age

II.iii.4 **God's . . . death** Exodus, xxii.18: "Thou shalt not suffer a witch to live"   7 **Smithfield** a place of public execution in east-central London, now the site of the wholesale meat markets

Will bring thy head with sorrow to the ground!
I beseech your Majesty, give me leave to go;　　20
Sorrow would° solace, and mine age would ease.

King. Stay, Humphrey Duke of Gloucester: ere thou go,
Give up thy staff: Henry will to himself
Protector be; and God shall be my hope,
My stay, my guide and lanthorn° to my feet.　　25
And go in peace, Humphrey, no less beloved
Than when thou wert Protector to thy King.

Queen. I see no reason why a king of years
Should be° to be protected like a child.
God and King Henry govern England's realm!　　30
Give up your staff, sir, and the King his realm.

Gloucester. My staff? Here, noble Henry, is my staff:
As willingly do I the same resign
As e'er thy father Henry made it mine;
And even as willingly at thy feet I leave it　　35
As others would ambitiously receive it.
Farewell, good King: when I am dead and gone,
May honorable peace attend thy throne.

　　　　　　　　　　　　　　　　Exit Gloucester.

Queen. Why, now is Henry King, and Margaret Queen;
And Humphrey Duke of Gloucester scarce himself,　　40
That bears so shrewd a maim:° two pulls° at once:
His lady banished, and a limb lopped off.
This staff of honor raught,° there let it stand
Where it best fits to be, in Henry's hand.

Suffolk. Thus droops this lofty pine and hangs his
　　sprays;　　45
Thus Eleanor's pride dies in her youngest days.

York. Lords, let him go. Please it your Majesty,
This is the day appointed for the combat,
And ready are the appellant and defendant,

---

21 **would** desires　25 **lanthorn** lantern (old form)　28–29 **king . . .
be** a king should be of age　41 **shrewd a maim** sharp or painful a
mutilation　41 **pulls** pluckings (as of fruit, or a branch)　43 **raught**
reached, attained (by us)

50   The armorer and his man, to enter the lists,
     So please your Highness to behold the fight.

Queen. Ay, good my lord: for purposely therefore
     Left I the court, to see this quarrel tried.

King. A God's name, see the lists and all things fit:
55   Here let them end it; and God defend the right!

York. I never saw a fellow worse bested,°
     Or more afraid to fight, than is the appellant,
     The servant of this armorer, my lords.

Enter at one door [Thomas Horner] the Armorer,
and his neighbors, drinking to him so much that
he is drunk; and he enters with a drum before
him and his staff with a sand-bag fastened to it;°
and at the other door his man, with a drum and
sand-bag, and Prentices drinking to him.

First Neighbor. Here, neighbor Horner, I drink to you
60   in° a cup of sack:° and fear not, neighbor, you
     shall do well enough.

Second Neighbor. And here, neighbor, here's a cup of
     charneco.°

Third Neighbor. And here's a pot of good double°
65   beer, neighbor: drink, and fear not your man.

Horner. Let it come; i'faith I'll pledge you all, and a
     fig for Peter!

First Prentice. Here, Peter, I drink to thee: and be not
     afeared.

70   *Second Prentice.* Here, Peter, here's a pint of claret
     wine for thee.

Third Prentice. And here's a quart for me; be merry,
     Peter, and fear not thy master: fight for credit of
     the prentices.

---

56 worse bested in worse circumstances **58s.d. staff with a sand-
bag fastened to it** a mock-weapon used in sporting combat **60 in**
with **60 sack** sweet sherry **63 charneco** a kind of port wine **64
double** extra strong

Peter. I thank you all, but I'll drink no more. Here, 73
Robin, and if I die, here I give thee my hammer;
and Will, thou shalt have my apron; and here,
Tom, take all the money that I have. O Lord bless
me, I pray God, for I am never able to deal with
my master, he hath learnt so much fence already. 80

Salisbury. Come, leave your drinking, and fall to
blows. Sirrah, what's thy name?

Peter. Peter, forsooth.

Salisbury. Peter? What more?

Peter. Thump. 85

Salisbury. Thump! then see thou thump thy master well.

Horner. Here's to thee, neighbor; fill all the pots again,
for before we fight, look you, I will tell you my
mind: for I am come hither, as it were, of my man's
instigation, to prove myself an honest man, and Peter 90
a knave: and so have at you, Peter, with downright
blows, as Bevis of Southampton fell upon Ascapart.°

York. Dispatch; this knave's tongue begins to double.°
Sound trumpets; alarum to the combattants!°
They fight, and Peter strikes him down.

Horner. Hold, Peter, hold! I confess, I confess treason. 95
He dies.

York. Take away his weapon. Fellow, thank God, and
the good wine in thy master's way.

Peter. O God, have I overcome mine enemies in this
presence?° O Peter, thou hast prevailed in right!

King. Go, take hence that traitor from our sight; 100
For by his death we do perceive his guilt:
And God in justice hath revealed to us

---

92 **Bevis . . . Ascapart** a legendary English knight and his adversary,
a giant thirty feet high; a pun may have been intended on the name
of an actor, Bevis, playing the part of Horner   93 **double** stutter
94 **Sound . . . combattants** given as York's line in F (Q omits) but
possibly intended as a stage direction   99 **presence i.e.,** of the King

The truth and innocence of this poor fellow,
Which he had thought to have murdered wrongfully.
105 Come, fellow, follow us for thy reward.

                    Sound a flourish; exeunt.

                [Scene IV. *A street.*]

            Enter Gloucester and his men,
                in mourning cloaks.

Gloucester. Thus sometimes hath the brightest day a
        cloud;
    And after summer evermore succeeds
    Barren winter with his wrathful nipping cold:
    So cares and joys abound, as seasons fleet.
    Sirs, what's o'clock?

5 *Servant.*   Ten, my lord.

Gloucester. Ten is the hour that was appointed me
    To watch the coming of my punished duchess:
    Uneath° may she endure the flinty streets,
    To tread them with her tender-feeling feet.
10 Sweet Nell, ill can thy noble mind abrook°
    The abject° people gazing on thy face
    With envious° looks, laughing at thy shame,
    That erst° did follow thy proud chariot-wheels
    When thou didst ride in triumph through the streets.
15 But, soft!° I think she comes, and I'll prepare
    My tear-stained eyes to see her miseries.

II.iv.8 **Uneath** with difficulty   10 **abrook** tolerate   11 **abject** despicable   12 **envious** malicious   13 **erst** formerly   15 **soft** stay,
hold (exclamation)

*Enter Duchess of Gloucester barefoot, and a
white sheet about her, with a wax candle in her
hand, and verses written on her back and pinned
on; and accompanied with the Sheriffs of London
and Sir John Stanley, and Officers, with bills and
halberds.°*

Servant. So please your Grace, we'll take her from the
sheriff.

Gloucester. No, stir not, for your lives; let her pass by.

Duchess. Come you, my lord, to see my open shame?
Now thou dost penance too. Look how they gaze!   20
See how the giddy multitude do point,
And nod their heads, and throw their eyes on thee!
Ah, Gloucester, hide thee from their hateful looks,
And, in thy closet pent up, rue my shame,
And ban° thine enemies, both mine and thine.   25

Gloucester. Be patient, gentle Nell; forget this grief.

Duchess. Ah, Gloucester, teach me to forget myself!
For whilst I think I am thy married wife
And thou a prince, Protector of this land,
Methinks I should not thus be led along,   30
Mailed° up in shame, with papers on my back,
And followed with a rabble that rejoice
To see my tears and hear my deep-fet° groans.
The ruthless flint doth cut my tender feet,
And when I start, the envious° people laugh   35
And bid me be advisèd how I tread.
Ah, Humphrey, can I bear this shameful yoke?
Trowest thou that e'er I'll look upon the world
Or count them happy that enjoys the sun?
No; dark shall be my light and night my day;   40
To think upon my pomp shall be my hell.
Sometime I'll say, I am Duke Humphrey's wife,

16s.d. **bills and halberds** long, ax-headed weapons 25 **ban** curse
31 **Mailed** wrapped (hawking term) 33 **deep-fet** deep-fetched, profound 35 **envious** malicious

And he a prince, and ruler of the land:
Yet so he ruled and such a prince he was
45 As he stood by whilst I, his forlorn duchess,
Was made a wonder and a pointing-stock
To every idle rascal follower.
But be thou mild and blush not at my shame,
Nor stir at nothing, till the ax of death
50 Hang over thee, as, sure, it shortly will;
For Suffolk—he that can do all in all
With her that hateth thee and hates us all—
And York, and impious Beaufort, that false priest,
Have all limed bushes° to betray thy wings;
55 And fly thou how thou canst, they'll tangle thee.
But fear not thou, until thy foot be snared,
Nor never seek prevention° of thy foes.

Gloucester. Ah, Nell, forbear! Thou aimest all awry.
I must offend before I be attainted;°
60 And had I twenty times so many foes,
And each of them had twenty times their power,
All these could not procure me any scathe,°
So long as I am loyal, true and crimeless.
Wouldst have me rescue thee from this reproach?
65 Why, yet thy scandal were not wiped away,
But I in danger for the breach of law.
Thy greatest help is quiet, gentle Nell:
I pray thee, sort° thy heart to patience;
These few days' wonder° will be quickly worn.

Enter a Herald.

Herald. I summon your Grace to his Majesty's Parlia-
70 ment,
Holden at Bury the first of this next month.

Gloucester. And my consent ne'er asked herein before?
This is close° dealing. Well, I will be there.
Exit Herald.

---

54 **limed bushes** smeared with a sticky substance (a means of catching birds) 57 **prevention** remedy by anticipation 59 **attainted** condemned 62 **scathe** damage 68 **sort** adapt 69 **few days' wonder** spectacle, sensation 73 **close** secret

My Nell, I take my leave: and, master sheriff,
Let not her penance exceed the King's commission.   75

Sheriff. And't please your Grace, here my commission
stays,
And Sir John Stanley is appointed now
To take her with him to the Isle of Man.

Gloucester. Must you, Sir John, protect my lady here?

Stanley. So am I given in charge, may't please your
Grace.   80

Gloucester. Entreat her not the worse in that I pray
You use her well. The world may laugh again;
And I may live to do you kindness if
You do it her: and so, Sir John, farewell.

Duchess. What, gone, my lord, and bid me not farewell?   85

Gloucester. Witness my tears, I cannot stay to speak.
                    Exit Gloucester [*and Serving-men*].

Duchess. Art thou gone too? All comfort go with thee!
For none abides with me: my joy is death—
Death, at whose name I oft have been afeared,
Because I wished this world's eternity.   90
Stanley, I prithee go, and take me hence;
I care not whither, for I beg no favor;
Only convey me where thou art commanded.

Stanley. Why, madam, that is to the Isle of Man,
There to be used according to your state.   95

Duchess. That's bad enough, for I am but reproach:
And shall I then be used reproachfully?

Stanley. Like to a duchess, and Duke Humphrey's
lady:
According to that state° you shall be used.

99 state dignity

100 *Duchess.* Sheriff farewell, and better than I fare,°
     Although thou hast been conduct° of my shame.

    Sheriff. It is my office; and madam, pardon me.

    Duchess. Ay, ay, farewell; thy office is discharged.
     Come, Stanley, shall we go?

    Stanley. Madam, your penance done, throw off this
105   sheet,
     And go we to attire you for our journey.

    Duchess. My shame will not be shifted° with my sheet:
     No, it will hang upon my richest robes,
     And show itself, attire me how I can.
110   Go, lead the way; I long to see my prison.

                           Exeunt.

---

100 **better than I fare** fare better than I   101 **conduct** guide   107 **shifted** play on "shift," i.e., smock, what Eleanor is wearing

[ACT III

Scene I. *The Abbey at Bury St. Edmunds.*]

Sound a Sennet. Enter King, Queen, Cardinal, Suffolk, York, Buckingham, Salisbury and War-wick [and Attendants] to the Parliament.

King. I muse my Lord of Gloucester is not come:
'Tis not his wont to be the hindmost man,
Whate'er occasion keeps him from us now.

Queen. Can you not see? Or will ye not observe
The strangeness of his altered countenance?   5
With what a majesty he bears himself,
How insolent of late he is become,
How proud, how peremptory, and unlike himself?
We know the time since he was mild and affable,
And if we did but glance a far-off look,   10
Immediately he was upon his knee,
That all the court admired him for submission.
But meet him now, and, be it in the morn,
When everyone will give the time of day,
He knits his brow and shows an angry eye   15
And passeth by with stiff unbowèd knee,
Disdaining duty that to us belongs.
Small curs are not regarded when they grin,°
But great men tremble when the lion roars;
And Humphrey is no little man in England.   20
First note that he is near you in descent,

III.i.18 grin bare their teeth

And should you fall, he is the next will mount.
Me seemeth then it is no policy,
Respecting° what a rancorous mind he bears,
25   And his advantage following your decease,
That he should come about your royal person
Or be admitted to your Highness' Council.
By flattery hath he won the commons' hearts,
And when he please to make commotion,
30   'Tis to be feared they all will follow him.
Now 'tis the spring, and weeds are shallow-rooted;
Suffer them now, and they'll o'ergrow the garden,
And choke the herbs for want of husbandry.
The reverent care I bear unto my lord
35   Made me collect° these dangers in the Duke.
If it be fond,° call it a woman's fear—
Which fear if better reasons can supplant,
I will subscribe,° and say I wronged the Duke.
My Lord of Suffolk, Buckingham, and York,
40   Reprove° my allegation, if you can,
Or else conclude my words effectual.°

Suffolk. Well hath your Highness seen into this duke;
And had I first been put to speak my mind,
I think I should have told your Grace's tale.
45   The Duchess by his subornation,
Upon my life, began her devilish practices:
Or if he were not privy to° those faults,
Yet, by reputing of his high descent,
As next the King he was successive heir,
50   And such high vaunts of his nobility,
Did instigate the bedlam° brain-sick Duchess
By wicked means to frame our sovereign's fall.
Smooth runs the water where the brook is deep,
And in his simple show he harbors treason.
55   The fox barks not when he would steal the lamb.
No, no, my sovereign; Gloucester is a man
Unsounded yet, and full of deep deceit.

23–24 **no policy,**/**Respecting** unwise, considering   35 **collect** i.e., as
if by weeding   36 **fond** foolish   38 **subscribe** agree   40 **Reprove**
disprove   41 **effectual** pertinent, conclusive   47 **privy to** ac-
quainted with   51 **bedlam** crazy

Cardinal. Did he not, contrary to form of law,
  Devise strange deaths for small offenses done?

York. And did he not, in his Protectorship,   60
  Levy great sums of money through the realm
  For soldiers' pay in France, and never sent it?
  By means whereof the towns each day revolted.

Buckingham. Tut, these are petty faults to faults un-
    known,
  Which time will bring to light in smooth Duke
    Humphrey.   65

King. My lords, at once: the care you have of us,
  To mow down thorns that would annoy our foot,
  Is worthy praise: but, shall I speak my conscience,
  Our kinsman Gloucester is as innocent
  From meaning treason to our royal person   70
  As is the sucking lamb or harmless dove.
  The Duke is virtuous, mild, and too well given
  To dream on evil, or to work my downfall.

Queen. Ah, what's more dangerous than this fond
    affiance!°
  Seems he a dove? His feathers are but borrowed,   75
  For he's disposèd as the hateful raven.
  Is he a lamb? His skin is surely lent him,
  For he's inclined as is the ravenous wolves.
  Who cannot steal a shape, that means deceit?
  Take heed, my lord: the welfare of us all   80
  Hangs on the cutting short that fraudful man.

Enter Somerset.

Somerset. All health unto my gracious sovereign!

King. Welcome, Lord Somerset. What news from
    France?

Somerset. That all your interest in those territories
  Is utterly bereft you: all is lost.   85

74 **fond affiance** foolish trust

King. Cold news, Lord Somerset: but God's will be
     done!

York. [*Aside*] Cold news for me; for I had hope of
     France
          As firmly as I hope for fertile England.°
          Thus are my blossoms blasted in the bud,
90   And caterpillars eat my leaves away;
          But I will remedy this gear° ere long,
          Or sell my title for a glorious grave.

Enter Gloucester.

Gloucester. All happiness unto my lord the King!
          Pardon, my liege, that I have stayed° so long.

Suffolk. Nay, Gloucester, know that thou art come
95   too soon,
          Unless thou wert more loyal than thou art:
          I do arrest thee of high treason here.

Gloucester. Well, Suffolk, thou shalt not see me
          blush,
          Nor change my countenance for this arrest:
100   A heart unspotted is not easily daunted.
          The purest spring is not so free from mud
          As I am clear from treason to my sovereign.
          Who can accuse me? Wherein am I guilty?

York. 'Tis thought, my lord, that you took bribes of
          France,°
105   And, being Protector, stayed the soldiers' pay;
          By means whereof his Highness hath lost France.

Gloucester. Is it but thought so? What are they that
          think it?
          I never robbed the soldiers of their pay,
          Nor ever had one penny bribe from France.
110   So help me God, as I have watched the night,
          Ay, night by night, in studying good for England!

87–88 **Cold . . . England** almost a literal repetition of I.i.238–39
91 **gear** business 94 **stayed** delayed 104 **France** the King of
France

That doit° that e'er I wrested from the King,
Or any groat I hoarded to my use,
Be brought against me at my trial-day!
No; many a pound of mine own proper store,°   *115*
Because I would not tax the needy commons,
Have I dispursèd° to the garrisons,
And never asked for restitution.

Cardinal. It serves you well, my lord, to say so much.

Gloucester. I say no more than truth, so help me God!   *120*

York. In your Protectorship you did devise
Strange tortures for offenders, never heard of,
That° England was defamed by tyranny.

Gloucester. Why, 'tis well known that whiles I was
    Protector
Pity was all the fault that was in me: *125*
For I should melt at an offender's tears,
And lowly words were ransom for their fault.
Unless it were a bloody murderer,
Or foul felonious thief that fleeced poor passen-
    gers,°
I never gave them condign° punishment.   *130*
Murder indeed, that bloody sin, I tortured
Above the felon or what° trespass else.

Suffolk. My lord, these faults are easy, quickly an-
    swered;
But mightier crimes are laid unto your charge,
Whereof you cannot easily purge yourself.   *135*
I do arrest you in his Highness' name,
And here commit you to my Lord Cardinal
To keep, until your further time of trial.

King. My lord of Gloucester, 'tis my special hope
That you will clear yourself from all suspense.° *140*
My conscience tells me you are innocent.

---

112 **doit** Dutch coin of minimal value   115 **proper store** personal
possession   117 **dispursèd** disbursed   123 **That** so that   129 **passengers** travelers   130 **condign** deserved   132 **what** whatever   140
suspense suspicion

Gloucester. Ah, gracious lord, these days are danger-
　　　ous:
　　　Virtue is choked with foul ambition,
　　　And charity chased hence by rancor's hand;
145　Foul subornation is predominant,
　　　And equity exiled your Highness' land.
　　　I know their complot° is to have my life,
　　　And if my death might make this island happy,
　　　And prove the period° of their tyranny,
150　I would expend it with all willingness.
　　　But mine is made the prologue to their play:
　　　For thousands more, that yet suspect no peril,
　　　Will not conclude their plotted tragedy.
　　　Beaufort's red sparkling eyes blab his heart's malice,
155　And Suffolk's cloudy brow his stormy hate;
　　　Sharp Buckingham unburthens with his tongue
　　　The envious load that lies upon his heart;
　　　And doggèd York, that reaches at the moon,
　　　Whose overweening arm I have plucked back,
160　By false accuse doth level at° my life.
　　　And you, my sovereign lady, with the rest,
　　　Causeless have laid disgraces on my head,
　　　And with your best endeavor have stirred up
　　　My liefest° liege to be mine enemy.
165　Ay, all of you have laid your heads together—
　　　Myself had notice of your conventicles°—
　　　And all to make away my guiltless life.
　　　I shall not want° false witness to condemn me,
　　　Nor store of treasons to augment my guilt;
170　The ancient proverb will be well effected:
　　　"A staff is quickly found to beat a dog."

Cardinal. My liege, his railing is intolerable.
　　　If those that care to keep your royal person
　　　From treason's secret knife and traitors' rage
175　Be thus upbraided, chid, and rated at,°

---

147 **complot** plot　149 **period** end, limit　160 **level at** aim at　164
liefest dearest　166 **conventicles** meetings　168 **want** lack　175
rated at inveighed against

And the offender granted scope of speech,
'Twill make them cool in zeal unto your Grace.

Suffolk. Hath he not twit our sovereign lady here
With ignominious words, though clerkly couched,°
As if she had subornèd some to swear   *180*
False allegations to o'erthrow his state?

Queen. But I can give the loser leave to chide.

Gloucester. Far truer spoke than meant: I lose indeed;
Beshrew the winners, for they played me false!
And well such losers may have leave to speak.   *185*

Buckingham. He'll wrest the sense° and hold us here
all day.
Lord Cardinal, he is your prisoner.

Cardinal. Sirs, take away the Duke, and guard him
sure.

Gloucester. Ah, thus King Henry throws away his
crutch
Before his legs be firm to bear his body.   *190*
Thus is the shepherd beaten from thy side,
And wolves are gnarling° who shall gnaw thee first.
Ah, that my fear were false! Ah, that it were!
For, good King Henry, thy decay° I fear.
                    Exit Gloucester [guarded].

King. My lords, what to your wisdoms seemeth best, *195*
Do or undo, as if ourself were here.

Queen. What, will your Highness leave the Parliament?

King. Ay, Margaret; my heart is drowned with grief,
Whose flood begins to flow within mine eyes,
My body round engirt with misery: *200*
For what's more miserable than discontent?
Ah, uncle Humphrey, in thy face I see
The map of honor, truth, and loyalty;

---

179 **ignominious . . . couched** infamous words, although learnedly
(i.e., cleverly) phrased   186 **wrest the sense** distort the meaning (of
what we say)   192 **gnarling** snarling   194 **decay** downfall

And yet, good Humphrey, is the hour to come
205 That e'er I proved thee false or feared thy faith?
What louring star now envies thy estate,
That these great lords, and Margaret our Queen
Do seek subversion° of thy harmless life?
Thou never didst them wrong, nor no man wrong:
210 And as the butcher takes away the calf,
And binds the wretch, and beats it when it strays,
Bearing it to the bloody slaughter-house,
Even so remorseless have they borne him hence;
And as the dam runs lowing up and down,
215 Looking the way her harmless young one went,
And can do nought but wail her darling's loss,
Even so myself bewails good Gloucester's case
With sad unhelpful tears, and with dimmed eyes
Look after him and cannot do him good,
220 So mighty are his vowèd enemies.
His fortunes I will weep, and 'twixt each groan
Say "Who's a traitor? Gloucester he is none."
              Exit King, Salisbury, and Warwick.

Queen. Free° lords, cold snow melts with the sun's hot
    beams.
Henry my lord is cold in great affairs,
225 Too full of foolish pity; and Gloucester's show°
Beguiles him as the mournful crocodile
With sorrow snares relenting passengers,°
Or as the snake, rolled in a flow'ring bank,
With shining checkered slough, doth sting a child
230 That for the beauty thinks it excellent.
Believe me, lords, were none more wise than I—
And yet herein I judge mine own wit good—
This Gloucester should be quickly rid the world,
To rid us from the fear we have of him.

235 *Cardinal.* That he should die is worthy policy,°

---

208 **subversion** overthrow 223 **Free** noble, magnanimous 225
show outward appearance 227 **passengers** travelers 235 **is worthy
policy** deserves shrewd planning

But yet we want a color° for his death:
'Tis meet° he be condemned by course of law.

Suffolk. But in my mind that were no policy:
     The King will labor still to save his life,
     The commons haply rise, to save his life;   *240*
     And yet we have but trivial argument,
     More than mistrust, that shows him worthy death.

York. So that, by this, you would not have him die.

Suffolk. Ah, York, no man alive so fain° as I!

York. [*Aside*] 'Tis York that hath more reason for his
     death.   *245*
     [*Aloud*] But my Lord Cardinal, and you, my Lord
     of Suffolk,
     Say as you think, and speak it from your souls:
     Were't not all one, an empty eagle were set
     To guard the chicken from a hungry kite,°
     As place Duke Humphrey for the King's Protector?   *250*

Queen. So,° the poor chicken should be sure of death.

Suffolk. Madam, 'tis true; and were't not madness,
     then,
     To make the fox surveyor° of the fold?
     Who being° accused a crafty murderer,
     His guilt should be but idly posted over,°   *255*
     Because his purpose is not executed.°
     No: let him die, in that he is a fox,
     By nature proved an enemy to the flock,
     Before his chaps° be stained with crimson blood,
     As Humphrey proved by reasons to my liege.°   *260*
     And do not stand on quillets° how to slay him:
     Be it by gins,° by snares, by subtlety,
     Sleeping or waking, 'tis no matter how,

---

236 **color** pretext (perhaps punning on "collar," i.e., hangman's
noose)   237 **meet** appropriate   244 **fain** willingly   249 **kite** bird of
prey   251 **So** if so   253 **surveyor** overseer   254 **Who being** whoever has been   255 **posted over** hurried past   256 **executed** accomplished   259 **chaps** jaws   260 **As . . . liege** i.e., above, lines 191–94
261 **quillets** fine distinctions, quibbles   262 **gins** traps

So he be dead; for that is good deceit
265 Which mates° him first that first intends deceit.

Queen. Thrice-noble Suffolk, 'tis resolutely spoke.

Suffolk. Not resolute, except so much° were done;
    For things are often spoke and seldom meant:
    But that my heart accordeth with my tongue,
270 Seeing the deed is meritorious,°
    And to preserve my sovereign from his foe,
    Say but the word, and I will be his priest.°

Cardinal. But I would have him dead, my Lord of
        Suffolk,
    Ere you can take due orders for a priest:
275 Say you consent and censure well° the deed,
    And I'll provide his executioner;
    I tender so° the safety of my liege.

Suffolk. Here is my hand, the deed is worthy doing.

Queen. And so say I.

280 *York.* And I: and now we three have spoke it,
    It skills not greatly who impugns our doom.°

                Enter a Post.

Post. Great lords, from Ireland am I come amain,°
    To signify that rebels there are up,°
    And put the Englishmen unto the sword.
285 Send succors, lords, and stop the rage betime,°
    Before the wound do grow uncurable;
    For, being green,° there is great hope of help.

Cardinal. A breach that craves a quick expedient stop!
    What counsel give you in this weighty cause?

290 *York.* That Somerset be sent as regent thither.

---

265 **mates** checkmates, suppresses   267 **except so much** unless as
much   270 **meritorious** worthy reward (esp. in a religious sense,
from God)   272 **be his priest** i.e., kill him   275 **censure well** approve of   277 **I tender so** I am so solicitous of   281 **It . . . doom**
it matters little who disapproves of our decision   282 **amain** in
haste   283 **up** up in arms   285 **betime** in time, rapidly   287 **green**
fresh

'Tis meet that lucky ruler be employed;
Witness the fortune he hath had in France.

Somerset. If York, with all his far-fet° policy,
Had been the regent there instead of me,
He never would have stayed in France so long.   *295*

York. No, not to lose it all, as thou hast done.
I rather would have lost my life betimes°
Than bring a burden of dishonor home
By staying there so long till° all were lost.
Show me one scar charactered° on thy skin: *300*
Men's flesh preserved so whole do seldom win.

Queen. Nay then, this spark will prove a raging fire,
If wind and fuel be brought to feed it with!
No more, good York; sweet Somerset, be still:
Thy fortune, York, hadst thou been regent there,   *305*
Might happily° have proved far worse than his.

York. What, worse than nought? Nay, then a shame
take all!

Somerset. And in the number thee, that wishest shame!

Cardinal. My Lord of York, try what your fortune is.
Th' uncivil kerns° of Ireland are in arms   *310*
And temper° clay with blood of Englishmen.
To Ireland will you lead a band of men,
Collected choicely, from each county some,
And try your hap against the Irishmen?

York. I will, my lord, so please his Majesty.   *315*

Suffolk. Why, our authority is his consent,
And what we do establish he confirms:
Then, noble York, take thou this task in hand.

York. I am content: provide me soldiers, lords,
Whiles I take order for mine own affairs.   *320*

---

293 **far-fet** far-fetched, i.e., deep   297 **betimes** early   299 **staying
. . . till** delaying or temporizing there until   300 **charactered** inscribed   306 **happily** by chance   310 **kerns** light-armed Irish footsoldiers   311 **temper** moisten (as with mortar)

Suffolk. A charge, Lord York, that I will see performed.
But now return we to the false Duke Humphrey.

Cardinal. No more of him; for I will deal with him
That henceforth he shall trouble us no more.
325   And so break off: the day is almost spent;
Lord Suffolk, you and I must talk of that event.

York. My Lord of Suffolk, within fourteen days
At Bristow° I expect my soldiers;
For there I'll ship them all for Ireland.

330 *Suffolk.* I'll see it truly done, my Lord of York.
                    Exeunt. Manet York [alone].

York. Now, York, or never, steel thy fearful thoughts,
And change misdoubt to resolution:
Be that thou hop'st to be, or what thou art
Resign to death; it is not worth th' enjoying.
335   Let pale-faced fear keep with the mean-born man,
And find no harbor in a royal heart.
Faster than spring-time show'rs comes thought on
          thought,
And not a thought but thinks on dignity.°
My brain more busy than the laboring spider
340   Weaves tedious° snares to trap mine enemies.
Well, nobles, well: 'tis politicly done,
To send me packing with an host of men:
I fear me you but warm the starvèd snake,
Who, cherished in your breasts, will sting your hearts.
345   'Twas men I lacked, and you will give them me:
I take it kindly; yet be well assured
You put sharp weapons in a madman's hands.
Whiles I in Ireland nourish a mighty band,
I will stir up in England some black storm
350   Shall blow ten thousand souls to heaven or hell;
And this fell° tempest shall not cease to rage
Until the golden circuit° on my head,
Like to the glorious sun's transparent beams,

---

328 **Bristow** Bristol   338 **dignity** rank   340 **tedious** laborious, intricate   351 **fell** evil   352 **circuit** circle (crown)

Do calm the fury of this mad-bred flaw.°
And, for a minister of my intent,   355
I have seduced a headstrong Kentishman,
John Cade of Ashford,
To make commotion, as full well he can,
Under the title of John Mortimer.
In Ireland have I seen this stubborn Cade   360
Oppose himself against a troop of kerns,
And fought so long, till that his thighs with darts
Were almost like a sharp-quilled porpentine;°
And, in the end being rescued, I have seen
Him caper upright like a wild Morisco,°   365
Shaking the bloody darts as he° his bells.
Full often, like a shag-haired crafty kern,
Hath he conversèd with the enemy,
And undiscovered come to me again
And given me notice of their villainies.   370
This devil here shall be my substitute;
For that John Mortimer, which now is dead,
In face, in gait, in speech, he doth resemble:
By this I shall perceive the commons' mind,
How they affect° the house and claim of York.   375
Say he be taken, racked, and torturèd:
I know no pain they can inflict upon him
Will make him say I moved him to those arms.
Say that he thrive, as 'tis great like he will:
Why, then from Ireland come I with my strength   380
And reap the harvest which that rascal sowed.
For Humphrey being dead, as he shall be,
And Henry put apart, the next for me.   *Exit.*

---

354 **flaw** squall of wind   363 **porpentine** porcupine   365 **Morisco**
Moorish, or morris-dancer; the dance is performed in grotesque
attire with bells attached to the legs   366 **he** i.e., the dancer   375
affect favor, approve

[Scene II. *Bury St. Edmunds. A room of state.*]

*Enter two or three running over the stage, from
the murder of Gloucester.*

First Murderer. Run to my Lord of Suffolk; let him
    know
We have dispatched the Duke, as he commanded.

Second Murderer. O that it were to do! What have we
    done?
Didst ever hear a man so penitent?

Enter Suffolk.

5 *First Murderer.* Here comes my lord.

Suffolk. Now, sirs, have you dispatched this thing?

First Murderer. Ay, my good lord, he's dead.

Suffolk. Why, that's well said. Go, get you to my house;
    I will reward you for this venturous deed.
10 The King and all the peers are here at hand.
Have you laid fair the bed? Is all things well,
According as I gave directions?

First Murderer. 'Tis, my good lord.

Suffolk. Away, be gone.   *Exeunt [Murderers].*

*Sound trumpets. Enter the King, the Queen,
Cardinal, Buckingham, Somerset,
with Attendants.*

15 *King.* Go, call our uncle to our presence straight;
Say we intend to try his Grace today,
If he be guilty, as 'tis publishèd.

Suffolk. I'll call him presently, my noble lord.   *Exit.*

King. Lords, take your places; and I pray you all,
　　Proceed no straiter° 'gainst our uncle Gloucester　　20
　　Than from true evidence of good esteem,
　　He be approved° in practice culpable.

Queen. God forbid any malice should prevail,
　　That faultless may condemn a nobleman!
　　Pray God he may acquit him of suspicion!　　25

King. I thank thee, Meg; these words content me much.

Enter Suffolk.

　　How now! Why look'st thou pale? Why tremblest
　　　　thou?
　　Where is our uncle? What's the matter, Suffolk?

Suffolk. Dead in his bed, my lord; Gloucester is dead.

Queen. Marry, God forfend!°　　30

Cardinal. God's secret judgment: I did dream tonight
　　The Duke was dumb and could not speak a word.
　　　　　　　　　　　　　King sounds.°

Queen. How fares my lord? Help, lords, the King is
　　　　dead!

Somerset. Rear up his body; wring° him by the nose.

Queen. Run, go, help, help! O Henry, ope thine eyes!　　35

Suffolk. He doth revive again; madam, be patient.

King. O heavenly God!

Queen.　　　　　　　　　How fares my gracious lord?

Suffolk. Comfort, my sovereign; gracious Henry, com-
　　fort.

King. What, doth my Lord of Suffolk comfort me?
　　Came he right now to sing a raven's note,　　40
　　Whose dismal tune bereft my vital pow'rs,
　　And thinks he that the chirping of a wren,

III.ii.20 **straiter** more strictly　　**22 approved** proven　　**30 forfend** forbid　　**32.s.d. sounds** swoons　　**34 wring** squeeze (a method of restor-
ing circulation)

By crying comfort from a hollow breast,
Can chase away the first-conceivèd sound?
45 Hide not thy poison with such sugared words;
Lay not thy hands on me; forbear, I say!
Their touch affrights me as a serpent's sting.
Thou baleful messenger, out of my sight!
Upon thy eyeballs murderous tyranny
50 Sits in grim majesty to fright the world.
Look not upon me, for thine eyes are wounding.
Yet do not go away; come, basilisk,°
And kill the innocent gazer with thy sight:
For in the shade of death I shall find joy,
55 In life but double death, now Gloucester's dead.

Queen. Why do you rate° my Lord of Suffolk thus?
Although the Duke was enemy to him,
Yet he most Christian-like laments his death:
And for myself, foe as he was to me,
60 Might liquid tears or heart-offending groans
Or blood-consuming sighs recall his life,
I would be blind with weeping, sick with groans,
Look pale as primrose with blood-drinking sighs,
And all to have the noble Duke alive.
65 What know I how the world may deem of me?
For it is known we were but hollow friends:
It may be judged I made the Duke away;
So shall my name with slander's tongue be wounded,
And princes' courts be filled with my reproach.
70 This get I by his death: ay me, unhappy!
To be a queen, and crowned with infamy!

King. Ah, woe is me for Gloucester, wretched man!

Queen. Be woe for me, more wretched than he is.
What, dost thou turn away and hide thy face?
75 I am no loathsome leper; look on me.
What! Art thou, like the adder, waxen° deaf?
Be poisonous too, and kill thy forlorn Queen.
Is all thy comfort shut in Gloucester's tomb?

52 basilisk a mythical reptile, supposedly able to kill with its eyes
56 rate berate 76 waxen grown

Why, then, Dame Margaret was ne'er thy joy.
Erect his statuë and worship it,   *80*
And make my image but an alehouse sign.
Was I for this nigh wracked upon the sea
And twice by awkward° wind from England's bank
Drove back again unto my native clime?
What boded this, but well forewarning wind   *85*
Did seem to say "Seek not a scorpion's nest,
Nor set no footing on this unkind shore?"
What did I then, but cursed the gentle gusts
And he that loosed them forth their brazen° caves,
And bid them blow towards England's blessèd shore,   *90*
Or turn our stern upon a dreadful rock?
Yet Aeolus° would not be a murderer,
But left that hateful office unto thee.
The pretty vaulting° sea refused to drown me,
Knowing that thou wouldst have me drowned on
   shore   *95*
With tears as salt as sea, through thy unkindness;
The splitting rocks cow'red in the sinking sands,
And would not dash me with their ragged sides,
Because thy flinty heart, more hard than they,
Might in thy palace perish Margaret.   *100*
As far as I could ken° thy chalky cliffs,
When from thy shore the tempest beat us back,
I stood upon the hatches in the storm,
And when the dusky sky began to rob
My earnest-gaping sight of thy land's view,   *105*
I took a costly jewel from my neck—
A heart° it was, bound in with diamonds—
And threw it towards thy land: the sea received it,
And so I wished thy body might my heart:
And even with this I lost fair England's view,   *110*
And bid mine eyes be packing with my heart,
And called them blind and dusky spectacles,°
For losing ken of Albion's wishèd coast.

---

83 **awkward** adverse   89 **brazen** extremely strong   92 **Aeolus** god
of winds   94 **vaulting** bounding   101 **ken** discern   107 **heart** heart-
shaped gemstone   112 **spectacles** organs of sight, or instruments,
like spyglasses

How often have I tempted Suffolk's tongue,
115 The agent of thy foul inconstancy,
To sit and witch° me, as Ascanius did
When he to madding° Dido would unfold
His father's acts, commenced in burning Troy!
Am I not witched like her? Or thou not false like
  him?
120 Ay me, I can° no more! Die, Margaret,
For Henry weeps that thou dost live so long.

*Noise within. Enter Warwick, Salisbury and
many Commons.*

Warwick. It is reported, mighty sovereign,
That good Duke Humphrey traitorously is murdered
By Suffolk and the Cardinal Beaufort's means.
125 The commons, like an angry hive of bees
That want their leader, scatter up and down,
And care not who they sting in his revenge.
Myself have calmed their spleenful° mutiny,
Until they hear the order of his death.

130 *King.* That he is dead, good Warwick, 'tis too true;
But how he died God knows, not Henry.
Enter his chamber, view his breathless corpse,
And comment then upon his sudden death.

Warwick. That shall I do, my liege. Stay, Salisbury,
135 With the rude multitude till I return.
    *[Exeunt Warwick to the inner chamber,°
    and Salisbury with the Commons.]*

King. O Thou that judgest all things, stay my thoughts,
My thoughts, that labor to persuade my soul
Some violent hands were laid on Humphrey's life!
If my suspect° be false, forgive me, God,
140 For judgment only doth belong to Thee.
Fain would I go to chafe his paly° lips

---

116 **witch** bewitch 117 **madding** becoming mad 120 **can** am capable of 128 **spleenful** eager, angry 135 s.d. **inner chamber** see textual note to III.ii 139 **suspect** suspicion 141 **paly** pale

With twenty thousand kisses, and to drain
Upon his face an ocean of salt tears,
To tell my love unto his dumb deaf trunk,
And with my fingers feel his hand unfeeling: *145*
But all in vain are these mean obsequies;
And to survey his dead and earthy image,
What were it but to make my sorrow greater?

> *Warwick [from within] draws the curtains and*
> *shows Gloucester in his bed.*

Warwick. Come hither, gracious sovereign, view this
body.

King. That is to see how deep my grave is made;   *150*
For with his soul fled all my wordly solace,
For, seeing him, I see my life in death.

Warwick. As surely as my soul intends to live
With that dread King that took our state upon him
To free us from His Father's wrathful curse,   *155*
I do believe that violent hands were laid
Upon the life of this thrice-famèd Duke.

Suffolk. A dreadful oath, sworn with a solemn tongue!
What instance gives Lord Warwick for his vow?

Warwick. See how the blood is settled in his face.   *160*
Oft have I seen a timely-parted ghost,°
Of ashy semblance, meager,° pale, and bloodless,
Being° all descended to the laboring heart,
Who,° in the conflict that it holds with death,
Attracts the same° for aidance 'gainst the enemy;   *165*
Which° with the heart there cools, and ne'er re-
turneth
To blush and beautify the cheek again.
But see, his face is black and full of blood,
His eyeballs further out than when he lived,
Staring full ghastly like a strangled man;   *170*

---

161 **timely-parted ghost** dead man who died naturally   162 **meager**
thin   163 **Being** i.e., the blood being   164 **Who** i.e., the heart   165
the same i.e., the blood   166 **Which** i.e., the blood

His hair upreared, his nostrils stretched with
    struggling;
His hands abroad displayed, as one that grasped
And tugged for life, and was by strength subdued.
Look, on the sheets his hair, you see, is sticking;
175 His well-proportioned beard made rough and rugged,
Like to the summer's corn by tempest lodged.°
It cannot be but he was murdered here:
The least of all these signs were probable.°

Suffolk. Why, Warwick, who should do the Duke to
    death?
180 Myself and Beaufort had him in protection;
And we, I hope, sir, are no murderers.

Warwick. But both of you were vowed Duke Hum-
    phrey's foes,
And you, forsooth, had the good Duke to keep:
'Tis like you would not feast him like a friend,
185 And 'tis well seen he found an enemy.

Queen. Then you, belike, suspect these noblemen
As guilty of Duke Humphrey's timeless° death?

Warwick. Who finds the heifer dead, and bleeding fresh,
And sees fast by a butcher with an ax,
190 But will suspect 'twas he that made the slaughter?
Who finds the partridge in the puttock's° nest,
But may imagine how the bird was dead,
Although the kite soar with unbloodied beak?
Even so suspicious is this tragedy.

Queen. Are you the butcher, Suffolk? Where's your
195   knife?
Is Beaufort termed a kite? Where are his talons?

Suffolk. I wear no knife to slaughter sleeping men;
But here's a vengeful sword, rusted with ease,
That shall be scourèd in his rancorous heart
200 That slanders me with murder's crimson badge.

176 **lodged** beaten flat   178 **probable** indicative (of murder)   187
timeless untimely   191 **puttock's** kite's

Say, if thou dar'st, proud Lord of Warwickshire,
That I am faulty in Duke Humphrey's death.
Exit Cardinal [and others].

Warwick. What dares not Warwick, if false Suffolk
  dare him?

Queen. He dares not calm his contumelious° spirit
  Nor cease to be an arrogant controller,°   *205*
  Though Suffolk dare him twenty thousand times.

Warwick. Madam, be still—with reverence may I say—
  For every word you speak in his behalf
  Is slander to your royal dignity.

Suffolk. Blunt-witted lord, ignoble in demeanor!   *210*
  If ever lady wronged her lord so much,
  Thy mother took into her blameful bed
  Some stern° untutored churl; and noble stock
  Was graft with crab-tree slip, whose fruit thou art,
  And never of the Nevils' noble race.   *215*

Warwick. But that the guilt of murder bucklers° thee,
  And I should rob the deathsman of his fee,
  Quitting thee thereby of ten thousand shames,
  And that my sovereign's presence makes me mild,
  I would, false murd'rous coward, on thy knee   *220*
  Make thee beg pardon for thy passèd speech,
  And say it was thy mother that thou meant'st,
  That thou thyself wast born in bastardy;
  And after all this fearful homage done,
  Give thee thy hire and send thy soul to hell,   *225*
  Pernicious blood-sucker of sleeping men!

Suffolk. Thou shalt be waking while I shed thy blood,
  If from this presence thou dar'st go with me.

Warwick. Away even now, or I will drag thee hence:
  Unworthy though thou art, I'll cope with thee,   *230*
  And do some service to Duke Humphrey's ghost.
Exeunt [Suffolk and Warwick].

---

204 **contumelious** slanderous 205 **controller** censorious critic, de-
tractor 213 **stern** rough 216 **bucklers** shields

King. What stronger breastplate than a heart untainted!
    Thrice is he armed that hath his quarrel just,
    And he but naked, though locked up in steel,
235   Whose conscience with injustice is corrupted.

                        A noise within.

Queen. What noise is this?

         Enter Suffolk and Warwick,
          with their weapons drawn.

King. Why, how now, lords! Your wrathful weapons
    drawn
    Here in our presence? Dare you be so bold?
    Why, what tumultuous clamor have we here?

240 *Suffolk.* The trait'rous Warwick, with the men of Bury,
    Set all upon me, mighty sovereign.

            Enter Salisbury.

Salisbury. [*To the Commons without*] Sirs, stand apart:
    the King shall know your mind.
    Dread Lord, the commons send you word by me,
    Unless Lord Suffolk straight be done to death,
245   Or banishèd fair England's territories,
    They will by violence tear him from your palace,
    And torture him with grievous ling'ring death.
    They say, by him the good Duke Humphrey died;
    They say, in him they fear your Highness' death;
250   And mere° instinct of love and loyalty,
    Free from a stubborn opposite° intent,
    As being thought to contradict your liking,
    Makes them thus forward in his banishment.
    They say, in care of your most royal person,
255   That if your Highness should intend to sleep,
    And charge that no man should disturb your rest
    In pain of your dislike, or pain of death,
    Yet, notwithstanding such a strait° edict,
    Were there a serpent seen, with forkèd tongue,
260   That slyly glided towards your Majesty,

250 **mere** pure   251 **opposite** antagonistic   258 **strait** strict

It were but necessary you were waked;
. Lest, being suffered° in that harmful slumber,
The mortal worm° might make the sleep eternal.
And therefore do they cry, though you forbid,
That they will guard you, whe'r° you will or no,　　265
From such fell° serpents as false Suffolk is;
With whose envenomèd and fatal sting
Your loving uncle, twenty times his worth,
They say, is shamefully bereft of life.

Commons within. An answer from the King, my Lord
　　of Salisbury!　　270

Suffolk. 'Tis like° the commons, rude unpolished
　　hinds,°
Could send such message to their sovereign:
But you, my lord, were glad to be employed,
To show how quaint° an orator you are.
But all the honor Salisbury hath won　　275
Is, that he was the Lord Ambassador
Sent from a sort° of tinkers to the King.

[Commons] within. An answer from the King, or we
　　will all break in!

King. Go, Salisbury, and tell them all from me,
I thank them for their tender loving care;　　280
And had I not been cited° so by them,
Yet did I purpose as they do entreat;
For sure, my thoughts do hourly prophesy
Mischance unto my state by Suffolk's means.
And therefore, by His Majesty I swear,　　285
Whose far unworthy deputy I am,
He shall not breathe infection in this air
But three days longer, on the pain of death.
　　　　　　　　　　　　　Exit Salisbury.

Queen. O Henry, let me plead for gentle° Suffolk!

---

262 **suffered** allowed to continue　263 **mortal worm** deadly snake
265 **whe'r** whether　266 **fell** cruel　271 **like** likely　271 **hinds** boors
274 **quaint** clever, fine　277 **sort** group　281 **cited** incited, urged
289 **gentle** noble

290 *King.* Ungentle° queen, to call him gentle Suffolk!
      No more, I say: if thou dost plead for him,
      Thou wilt but add increase unto my wrath.
      Had I but said, I would have kept my word;
      But when I swear, it is irrevocable.
295   [*To Suffolk*] If after three days' space thou here be'st
         found
      On any ground that I am ruler of,
      The world shall not be ransom for thy life.
      Come, Warwick, come, good Warwick, go with me;
      I have great matters to impart to thee.

                              Exit King and Warwick.
                              Manet Queen and Suffolk.

300 *Queen.* Mischance and sorrow go along with you!
      Heart's discontent and sour affliction
      Be playfellows to keep you company!
      There's two of you; the Devil make a third!
      And threefold vengeance tend upon your steps!

305 *Suffolk.* Cease, gentle Queen, these execrations,
      And let thy Suffolk take his heavy leave.

    Queen. Fie, coward woman and soft-hearted wretch!
      Hast thou not spirit to curse thine enemy?

    Suffolk. A plague upon them! Wherefore should I curse
         them?
310   Would curses kill, as doth the mandrake's groan,°
      I would invent as bitter searching° terms,
      As curst, as harsh, and horrible to hear,
      Delivered strongly through my fixèd teeth,
      With full as many signs of deadly hate,
315   As lean-faced Envy in her loathsome cave.
      My tongue should stumble in mine earnest words;
      Mine eyes should sparkle like the beaten flint;
      Mine hair be fixed an° end, as one distract;°

---

290 Ungentle unkind, harsh   **310 mandrake's groan** the mandrake
is a poisonous plant, its forked root shaped like two human legs;
when uprooted it supposedly groaned like a human, the sound
being fatal to any hearer   **311 searching** cutting, lancing (as in
surgery)   **318 an** on   **318 distract** distracted, mad

Ay, every joint should seem to curse and ban:°
And even now my burdened heart would break,   *320*
Should I not curse them. Poison be their drink!
Gall, worse than gall, the daintiest that they taste!
Their sweetest shade a grove of cypress° trees!
Their chiefest prospect murd'ring basilisks!°
Their softest touch as smart as lizards' stings!   *325*
Their music frightful as the serpent's hiss,
And boding screech-owls make the consort° full!
All the foul terrors in dark-seated hell—

Queen. Enough, sweet Suffolk; thou torment'st thyself;
And these dread curses, like the sun 'gainst glass,   *330*
Or like an overchargèd gun, recoil,
And turns the force of them upon thyself.

Suffolk. You bade me ban, and will you bid me leave?
Now, by the ground that I am banished from,
Well could I curse away a winter's night,   *335*
Though standing naked on a mountain top,
Where biting cold would never let grass grow,
And think it but a minute spent in sport.

Queen. O, let me entreat thee cease. Give me thy hand,
That I may dew it with my mournful tears;   *340*
Nor let the rain of heaven wet this place,
To wash away my woeful monuments.
O, could this kiss be printed in thy hand,
That thou mightst think upon these° by the seal,
Through whom a thousand sighs are breathed for
    thee!   *345*
So, get thee gone, that I may know my grief;
'Tis but surmised whiles thou art standing by,
As one that surfeits thinking on a want.
I will repeal thee, or, be well assured,
Adventure° to be banishèd myself: *350*
And banishèd I am, if but from thee.
Go, speak not to me; even now be gone.

---

319 **curse and ban** formally excommunicate   323 **cypress** traditionally grown in graveyards   324 **basilisks** mythical reptiles thought
to kill by a glance   327 **consort** group of musicians   344 **these**
i.e., these lips   350 **Adventure** venture

O, go not yet! Even thus two friends condemned
Embrace and kiss and take ten thousand leaves,
355   Loather a hundred times to part than die.
Yet now farewell, and farewell life with thee!

Suffolk. Thus is poor Suffolk ten times banishèd;
Once by the King, and three times thrice by thee.
'Tis not the land I care for, wert thou thence;
360   A wilderness is populous enough,
So Suffolk had thy heavenly company:
For where thou art, there is the world itself,
With every several° pleasure in the world,
And where thou art not, desolation.
365   I can no more: live thou to joy thy life;
Myself to joy in nought but that thou liv'st.

Enter Vaux.

Queen. Whither goes Vaux so fast? What news, I
    prithee?

Vaux. To signify unto his Majesty
That Cardinal Beaufort is at point of death;
370   For suddenly a grievous sickness took him,
That makes him gasp, and stare, and catch the air,
Blaspheming God, and cursing men on earth.
Sometime he talks as if Duke Humphrey's ghost
Were by his side; sometime he calls the King,
375   And whispers to his pillow, as to him,
The secrets of his overchargèd soul:
And I am sent to tell his Majesty
That even now he cries aloud for him.

Queen. Go tell this heavy message to the King.
                     Exit [Vaux].
380   Ay, me! What is this world! What news are these!
But wherefore grieve I at an hour's poor loss,
Omitting Suffolk's exile, my soul's treasure?
Why only, Suffolk, mourn I not for thee,
And with the southern clouds contend in tears,

363 several single

Theirs for the earth's increase,° mine for my sor-
    rows?   *385*
Now get thee hence: the King, thou know'st, is
    coming;
If thou be found by me, thou art but dead.

Suffolk. If I depart from thee I cannot live;
And in thy sight to die, what were it else
But like a pleasant slumber in thy lap?   *390*
Here could I breathe my soul into the air,
As mild and gentle as the cradle-babe
Dying with mother's dug between its lips;
Where, from thy sight, I should be raging mad,
And cry out for thee to close up mine eyes,   *395*
To have thee with thy lips to stop my mouth:
So shouldst thou either turn my flying soul,
Or I should breathe it so into thy body,
And then it lived in sweet Elysium.
To die by thee were but to die in jest;   *400*
From thee to die were torture more than death:
O, let me stay, befall what may befall!

Queen. Away! Though parting be a fretful corrosive,°
It is applièd to a deathful wound.
To France, sweet Suffolk: let me hear from thee;   *405*
For wheresoe'er thou art in this world's globe,
I'll have an Iris° that shall find thee out.

Suffolk. I go.

Queen. And take my heart with thee. *She kisseth him.*

Suffolk. A jewel, locked into the wofull'st cask   *410*
That ever did contain a thing of worth.
Even as a splitted bark, so sunder we:
This way fall I to death.   *Exit Suffolk.*

Queen.   This way for me.
    Exit Queen.

---

385 **increase** fruition   403 **corrosive** caustic remedy   407 **Iris**
Juno's messenger, and goddess of the rainbow

[Scene III. *A bedchamber.*]

Enter the King, Salisbury, and Warwick; and then the curtains be drawn, and the Cardinal is discovered in his bed, raving and staring as if he were mad.

King. How fares my lord? Speak, Beaufort, to thy
    sovereign.

Cardinal. If thou be'st Death, I'll give thee England's
    treasure,
  Enough to purchase such another island,
  So thou wilt let me live, and feel no pain.

5 *King.* Ah, what a sign it is of evil life,
  Where death's approach is seen so terrible!

Warwick. Beaufort, it is thy sovereign speaks to thee.

Cardinal. Bring me unto my trial when you will.
  Died he not in his bed? Where should he die?
10 Can I make men live, whe'r they will or no?
  O, torture me no more! I will confess.
  Alive again? Then show me where he is:
  I'll give a thousand pound to look upon him.
  He hath no eyes, the dust hath blinded them.
15 Comb down his hair; look, look! It stands upright,
  Like lime-twigs° set to catch my wingèd soul.
  Give me some drink, and bid the apothecary
  Bring the strong poison that I bought of him.

King. O thou eternal Mover of the heavens,
20 Look with a gentle eye upon this wretch!
  O, beat away the busy meddling fiend

III.iii.16 **lime-twigs** twigs smeared with bird-lime

That lays strong siege unto this wretch's soul
And from his bosom purge this black despair!

Warwick. See how the pangs of death do make him
grin.°

Salisbury. Disturb him not, let him pass peaceably.   *25*

King. Peace to his soul, if God's good pleasure be.
Lord Cardinal, if thou think'st on heaven's bliss,
Hold up thy hand, make signal of thy hope.
                              The Cardinal dies.
He dies, and makes no sign. O God, forgive him!

Warwick. So bad a death argues° a monstrous life.   *30*

King. Forbear to judge, for we are sinners all.
Close up his eyes and draw the curtain close;
And let us all to meditation.   *Exeunt.*

24 grin bare his teeth, grimace   30 argues suggests, betokens

[ACT IV

Scene I. *The Coast of Kent.*]

*Alarum. Fight at sea. Ordnance goes off. And
then enter the Lieutenant of the ship, and the
Master, and the Master's Mate, and the Duke of
Suffolk, disguised, and others with him, and
Walter Whitmore.*

Lieutenant.° The gaudy, blabbing and remorseful day
  Is crept into the bosom of the sea,
  And now loud-howling wolves arouse the jades°
  That drag the tragic melancholy night;
5 Who, with their drowsy, slow, and flagging wings
  Clip° dead men's graves, and from their misty jaws
  Breathe foul contagious darkness in the air.
  Therefore bring forth the soldiers of our prize,
  For whilst our pinnace anchors in the Downs°
10 Here shall they make their ransom on the sand,
  Or with their blood stain this discolored shore.
  Master, this prisoner freely give I thee;
  And thou that art his mate, make boot of° this;
  The other, Walter Whitmore, is thy share.

First Gentleman. What is my ransom, master? Let me
15 know.

IV.i.1 **Lieutenant** "Captain" in Q: i.e., the military commander
of the pirate ship   3 **jades** horses (contemptuous)   6 **Clip** embrace,
hover over   9 **Downs** bay area off the Kentish coast   13 **make
boot of** profit by

114

Master. A thousand crowns, or else lay down your head.

Mate. And so much shall you give, or off goes yours.
                    [*The prisoners react adversely.*]

Lieutenant. What! Think you much to pay two thou-
    sand crowns,
And bear the name and port° of gentlemen?
Cut both the villains' throats; for die you shall: *20*
The lives of those which we have lost in fight
Be counterpoised with such a petty sum!

First Gentleman. I'll give it, sir; and therefore spare my
    life.

Second Gentleman. And so will I, and write home for
    it straight.

Whitmore. [*To Suffolk*] I lost mine eye in laying the
    prize aboard,   *25*
And therefore to revenge it shalt thou die;
And so should these, if I might have my will.

Lieutenant. Be not so rash: take ransom, let him live.

Suffolk. Look on my George;° I am a gentleman.
Rate me at what thou wilt, thou shalt be paid.   *30*

Whitmore. And so am I: my name is Walter Whitmore.
How now! Why starts thou? What, doth death af-
    fright?

Suffolk. Thy name affrights me, in whose sound is death.
A cunning man did calculate my birth,°
And told me that by "water"° I should die: *35*
Yet let not this make thee be bloody-minded;
Thy name is Gaultier, being rightly sounded.

Whitmore. Gaultier or Walter, which it is I care not.
Never yet did base dishonor blur our name,
But with our sword we wiped away the blot.   *40*

---

19 **port** style, stature   29 **George** insignia or badge of the Order of
the Garter, showing Saint George on horseback   34 **calculate my
birth** cast my horoscope   35 **water** "Walter" is pronounced "water,"
and occasionally so spelled in Q and F

Therefore, when merchant-like I sell revenge,
Broke be my sword, my arms torn and defaced,
And I proclaimed a coward through the world!

Suffolk. Stay, Whitmore, for thy prisoner is a prince,
45   The Duke of Suffolk, William de la Pole.

Whitmore. The Duke of Suffolk, muffled up in rags?

Suffolk. Ay, but these rags are no part of the Duke:
Jove sometime went disguised, and why not I?

Lieutenant. But Jove was never slain, as thou shalt be.

50   *Suffolk.* Obscure and lousy swain, King Henry's blood,
The honorable blood of Lancaster,
Must not be shed by such a jaded groom.°
Hast thou not kissed thy hand and held my stirrup?
Bare-headed plodded by my foot-cloth° mule,
55   And thought thee happy when I shook my head?
How often hast thou waited at my cup,
Fed from my trencher, kneeled down at the board,
When I have feasted with Queen Margaret?
Remember it, and let it make thee crest-fall'n,
60   Ay, and allay this thy abortive° pride:
How in our voiding lobby° hast thou stood
And duly waited for my coming forth.
This hand of mine hath writ in thy behalf,
And therefore shall it charm thy riotous tongue.

Whitmore. Speak, Captain, shall I stab the forlorn
65   swain?°

Lieutenant. First let my words stab him, as he hath me.

Suffolk. Base slave, thy words are blunt, and so art
thou.

Lieutenant. Convey him hence and on our long-boat's
side
Strike off his head.

52 **groom** low, ignoble fellow   54 **foot-cloth** ornamented with elaborate hangings, as in processions and tourneys   60 **abortive** monstrous, untimely   61 **voiding lobby** waiting-room   65 **forlorn swain**
wretched (a) fellow (b) lover (of the Queen)

Suffolk.   Thou dar'st not, for thy own.

Lieutenant. Yes, Poole!

Suffolk.   Poole?°   70

Lieutenant. Ay, kennel,° puddle, sink, whose filth
    and dirt
Troubles the silver spring where England drinks.
Now will I dam up this thy yawning mouth
For swallowing the treasure of the realm;
Thy lips, that kissed the Queen, shall sweep the
    ground;   75
And thou that smil'dst at good Duke Humphrey's
    death
Against the senseless winds shalt grin in vain,
Who in contempt shall hiss at thee again.
And wedded be thou to the hags of hell,
For daring to affy° a mighty lord   80
Unto the daughter of a worthless king,
Having neither subject, wealth, nor diadem.
By devilish policy art thou grown great
And like ambitious Sylla° overgorged
With gobbets of thy mother's bleeding heart.   85
By thee Anjou and Maine were sold to France,
The false revolting Normans thorough° thee
Disdain to call us lord, and Picardy
Hath slain their governors, surprised our forts,
And sent the ragged soldiers wounded home.   90
The princely Warwick, and the Nevils all,
Whose dreadful swords were never drawn in vain,
As hating thee, are rising up in arms;
And now the house of York, thrust from the crown
By shameful murder of a guiltless king   95
And lofty proud encroaching tyranny,
Burns with revenging fire, whose hopeful colors

70 Poole . . . Poole puns on "to poll" (shave the head, as for execution), "pool" (cesspool), and "Pole" (de la Pole) 71 kennel gutter 80 affy betroth 84 Sylla i.e., Sulla, dictator of Rome, who
proscribed and persecuted followers of his rival Marius. Rome
(and for Suffolk, England) is represented as the "mother," and the
victims (e.g., Gloucester) as "gobbets" 87 thorough through (old
form)

Advance our half-faced sun,° striving to shine,
Under the which is writ *Invitis nubibus*.°
100   The commons here in Kent are up in arms;
And, to conclude, reproach and beggary
Is crept into the palace of our King,
And all by thee. Away! Convey him hence.

Suffolk. O that I were a god, to shoot forth thunder
105   Upon these paltry, servile, abject drudges!
Small things make base men proud: this villain here,
Being captain of a pinnace, threatens more
Than Bargulus the strong Illyrian pirate.°
Drones suck not eagles' blood, but rob bee-hives:
110   It is impossible that I should die
By such a lowly vassal as thyself.
Thy words move rage and not remorse in me.

Lieutenant. Ay, but my deeds shall stay thy fury soon.

Suffolk. I go of message from the Queen to France;°
115   I charge thee waft me safely cross the Channel.

Whitmore. Come, Suffolk, I must waft thee to thy
death.

Suffolk. Pene gelidus timor occupat artus:° it is thee I
fear.

Whitmore. Thou shalt have cause to fear before I leave
thee.
What, are ye daunted now? Now will ye stoop?

120 *First Gentleman.* My gracious lord, entreat him, speak
him fair.

Suffolk. Suffolk's imperial tongue is stern and rough,
Used to command, untaught to plead for favor.
Far be it we should honor such as these

---

98 **Advance our half-faced sun** raise high our insignia, the sun
emerging from clouds (Edward III's personal badge)   99 **Invitis
nubibus** "in spite of the clouds"   108 **Bargulus . . . pirate** Bargalus
or Bardulis, a pirate in Greek waters mentioned by Cicero   114
France i.e., the King of France   117 **Pene . . . artus** "chill fear
almost seizes my limbs": source unidentified, possibly a corrupt recollection of *Aeneid*, VII, 446

With humble suit: no, rather let my head
Stoop to the block than these knees bow to any,   *125*
Save to the God of heaven, and to my King;
And sooner dance upon a bloody pole
Than stand uncovered to the vulgar groom.
True nobility is exempt from fear:
More can I bear than you dare execute.   *130*

Lieutenant. Hale him away, and let him talk no more.

Suffolk. Come, soldiers, show what cruelty ye can,
That this my death may never be forgot.
Great men oft die by vile besonians:°
A Roman sworder° and banditto slave   *135*
Murdered sweet Tully;° Brutus' bastard hand°
Stabbed Julius Caesar; savage islanders
Pompey the Great; and Suffolk dies by pirates.
                    Exit Walter with Suffolk.

Lieutenant. And as for these whose ransom we have set,
It is our pleasure one of them depart: *140*
Therefore come you with us and let him go.
                    Exit Lieutenant, and the rest;
                    manet the First Gentleman.

        Enter Walter [Whitmore] with the body
        [of Suffolk].

Whitmore. There let his head and lifeless body lie,
    Until the Queen his mistress bury it.   *Exit Walter.*

First Gentleman. O barbarous and bloody spectacle!
    His body will I bear unto the King: *145*
    If he revenge it not, yet will his friends;
    So will the Queen, that living held him dear.
                    [Exit, with Suffolk's body.]

---

134 **besonians** base fellows, wretches   135 **sworder** gladiator   136
Tully Cicero   136 **Brutus' bastard hand** a false tradition held that
Brutus was Caesar's bastard son

[Scene II. *Blackheath.*]

Enter Bevis and John Holland.°

Bevis. Come, and get thee a sword, though máde of a
lath:° they have been up° these two days.

Holland. They have the more need to sleep now, then.

Bevis. I tell thee, Jack Cade the clothier means to
5   dress the commonwealth, and turn it, and set a new
nap upon it.

Holland. So he had need, for 'tis threadbare. Well, I
say, it was never merry world in England since
gentlemen came up.°

10 *Bevis.* O miserable age! virtue is not regarded in han-
dicraftsmen.

Holland. The nobility think scorn to go in leather
aprons.

Bevis. Nay, more, the King's Council are no good work-
15   men.

Holland. True: and yet it is said, "Labor in thy vocation"; which is as much to say as, "Let the magis-
trates° be laboring men"; and therefore should we
be magistrates.

20 *Bevis.* Thou hast hit it: for there's no better sign of a
brave mind than a hard hand.

Holland. I see them! I see them! There's Best's son,
the tanner of Wingham.

IV.ii.s.d. **Bevis and John Holland** actors in the company: see note
to II.iii.92   1–2 **sword . . . lath** a mock-weapon, as employed by
soldier-clowns in the early Tudor plays   2 **up** i.e., up in arms   9
came up came into fashion   17–18 **magistrates** rulers, administrators

Bevis. He shall have the skins of our enemies, to make
  dog's-leather° of.   25

Holland. And Dick the butcher.

Bevis. Then is sin struck down like an ox, and iniqui-
  ty's throat cut like a calf.

Holland. And Smith the weaver.

Bevis. Argo,° their thread of life is spun.   30

Holland. Come, come, let's fall in with them.

  *Drum. Enter Cade, Dick [the] Butcher, Smith
  the Weaver, and a Sawyer, with infinite numbers.*

Cade. We John Cade, so termed of our supposed
  father—

Dick. [Aside] Or rather, of stealing a cade° of herrings.

Cade. For our enemies shall fall° before us, inspired   35
  with the spirit of putting down kings and princes
  . . . Command silence.

Dick. Silence!

Cade. My father was a Mortimer—

Dick. [Aside] He was an honest man, and a good brick-   40
  layer.

Cade. My mother a Plantagenet—

Dick. [Aside] I knew her well; she was a midwife.

Cade. My wife descended of the Lacies—

Dick. [Aside] She was indeed a pedlar's daughter, and   45
  sold many laces.

Smith. [Aside] But now of late, not able to travel with
  her furred pack,° she washes bucks° here at home.

25 **dog's-leather** leather for gloves   30 **Argo** corruption of Latin
ergo = therefore   34 **cade** barrel of five hundred   35 **fall** pun on
Latin sense of "Cade" (*cadere,* to fall)   47–48 **travel with her
furred pack** (1) travel with a fur knapsack, as a pedlar (2) labor as
a prostitute   48 **washes bucks** (1) does rough laundry (2) absolves
cuckolds (by making them "even" with their wives)

Cade. Therefore am I of an honorable house.

50 *Dick.* [*Aside*] Ay, by my faith, the field is honorable;
and there was he born, under a hedge: for his father
had never a house but the cage.°

Cade. Valiant I am.

Smith. [*Aside*] 'A must needs, for beggary is valiant.

55 *Cade.* I am able to endure much.

Dick. [*Aside*] No question of that; for I have seen him
whipped three market-days together.

Cade. I fear neither sword nor fire.

Smith. [*Aside*] He need not fear the sword, for his
60   coat is of proof.°

Dick. [*Aside*] But methinks he should stand in fear of
fire, being burnt i' th' hand° for stealing of sheep.

Cade. Be brave, then; for your captain is brave, and
vows reformation. There shall be in England seven
65   halfpenny loaves sold for a penny; the three-hooped
pot shall have ten hoops;° and I will make it felony
to drink small beer. All the realm shall be in common,° and in Cheapside° shall my palfry go to
grass; and when I am King, as King I will be—

70 *All.* God save your Majesty!

Cade. I thank you, good people—there shall be no
money; all shall eat and drink on my score;° and I
will apparel them all in one livery, that they may
agree like brothers, and worship me their lord.

75 *Dick.* The first thing we do, let's kill all the lawyers.

Cade. Nay, that I mean to do. Is not this a lamentable

---

52 **cage** a temporary prison for vagabonds and harlots, commonly
set up in marketplaces   60 **of proof** (1) reliable (2) wellworn   62
burnt i' th' hand with the letter "T," for "thief"   65–66 **three-
hooped . . . hoops** i.e., the quart measure will contain three quarts
67–68 **in common** held communally   68 **Cheapside** elegant com-
mercial district of London   72 **on my score** at my expense

thing, that of the skin of an innocent lamb should
be made parchment? That parchment, being scrib-
bled o'er, should undo a man? Some say the bee
stings; but I say, 'tis the bee's wax: for I did but   *80*
seal once to a thing, and I was never mine own
man° since. How now! who's there?

Enter a Clerk, [led by others].

Smith. The clerk of Chatham: he can write and read,
and cast accompt.°

Cade. O monstrous!   *85*

Smith. We took him setting of boys' copies.°

Cade. Here's a villain!

Smith. H'as a book in his pocket with red letters in't.

Cade. Nay, then, he is a conjuror.

Dick. Nay, he can make obligations,° and write court-   *90*
hand.°

Cade. I am sorry for't: the man is a proper man, of
mine honor; unless I find him guilty, he shall not
die. Come hither, sirrah, I must examine thee: what
is thy name?   *95*

Clerk. Emmanuel.

Dick. They use to write it on the top of letters:° 'twill
go hard with you.

Cade. Let me alone. Dost thou use to write thy name?
Or hast thou a mark° to thyself, like an honest   *100*
plain-dealing man?

Clerk. Sir, I thank God, I have been so well brought
up that I can write my name.

81–82 **mine own man** my own master   84 **accompt** account   86
setting of boys' copies teaching schoolchildren to write   90 **obligations** bonds   90–91 **court-hand** formal legal script   97 **They . . .
letters** "Emmanuel" ("God with us") was often prefixed to formal
letters, deeds, etc.   100 **mark** i.e., an "X"

All. He hath confessed: away with him! He's a villain
105   and a traitor.

Cade. Away with him, I say! Hang him with his pen
and ink-horn about his neck.

> *Exit one with the Clerk.*

> *Enter Michael.*

Michael. Where's our general?

Cade. Here I am, thou particular° fellow.

110 *Michael.* Fly, fly, fly! Sir Humphrey Stafford and his
brother are hard by, with the King's forces.

Cade. Stand, villain, stand, or I'll fell thee down. He
shall be encountered with a man as good as himself:
he is but a knight, is 'a?

115 *Michael.* No.

Cade. To equal him, I will make myself a knight presently. [*Kneels.*] Rise up Sir John Mortimer. [*Rises.*]
Now have at him!

> *Enter Sir Humphrey Stafford and his Brother,*
> *with [a Herald], drum and Soldiers.*

Stafford. Rebellious hinds, the filth and scum of Kent,
120   Marked for the gallows: lay your weapons down.
Home to your cottages, forsake this groom!
The King is merciful, if you revolt.°

Brother. But angry, wrathful, and inclined to blood,
If you go forward: therefore yield, or die.

125 *Cade.* As for these silken-coated slaves, I pass° not.
It is to you, good people, that I speak,
Over whom, in time to come, I hope to reign:
For I am rightful heir unto the crown.

Stafford. Villain, thy father was a plasterer,
130   And thou thyself a shearman,° art thou not?

---

109 **particular** private (pun on "general")   122 **revolt** turn (against
Cade)   125 **pass** care   130 **shearman** worker with cloth

Cade. And Adam was a gardener.

Brother. And what of that?

Cade. Marry, this: Edmund Mortimer, Earl of March,
  Married the Duke of Clarence' daughter, did he not?

Stafford. Ay, sir.   135

Cade. By her he had two children at one birth.

Brother. That's false.

Cade. Ay, there's the question; but I say, 'tis true:
  The elder of them, being put to nurse,
  Was by a beggar-woman stol'n away,   140
  And, ignorant of his birth and parentage,
  Became a bricklayer when he came to age:
  His son am I; deny it, if you can.

Dick. Nay, 'tis too true; therefore he shall be king.

Smith. Sir, he made a chimney in my father's house,   145
  and the bricks are alive at this day to testify it; therefore deny it not.

Stafford. And will you credit this base drudge's words,
  That speaks he knows not what?

All. Ay, marry, will we; therefore get ye gone.   150

Brother. Jack Cade, the Duke of York hath taught you
  this.

Cade. [*Aside*] He lies, for I invented it myself.—Go
  to, sirrah, tell the King from me, that, for his father's
  sake, Henry the Fifth, in whose time boys went to   155
  span-counter° for French crowns, I am content he
  shall reign; but I'll be Protector over him.

Dick. And furthermore, we'll have the Lord Say's head
  for selling the Dukedom of Maine.

Cade. And good reason: for thereby is England   160

---

156 **span-counter** a game played with marbles close up to the opponents; figuratively close combat

mained,° and fain to go with a staff, but that my
puissance holds it up. Fellow kings, I tell you that
that Lord Say hath gelded the commonwealth, and
made it an eunuch: and more than that, he can
165 speak French; and therefore he is a traitor.

Stafford. O gross and miserable ignorance!

Cade. Nay, answer, if you can: the Frenchmen are our
enemies; go to, then, I ask but this: can he that
speaks with the tongue of an enemy be a good
170 counselor, or no?

All. No, no, and therefore we'll have his head.

Brother. Well, seeing gentle words will not prevail,
Assail them with the army of the King.

Stafford. Herald, away; and throughout every town
175 Proclaim them traitors that are up with Cade;
That those which fly before the battle ends
May, even in their wives' and children's sight,
Be hanged up for example at their doors:
And you that be the King's friends, follow me.
Exit [Staffords and their forces].

180 *Cade.* And you that love the commons, follow me.
Now show yourselves men; 'tis for liberty.
We will not leave one lord, one gentleman:
Spare none but such as go in clouted shoon;°
For they are thrifty honest men and such
185 As would, but that they dare not, take our parts.

Dick. They are all in order and march toward us.

Cade. But then are we in order when we are most out
of order. Come, march forward. *[Exeunt.]*

---

161 **mained** maimed (variant spelling)   183 **clouted shoon** hobnailed
boots

[Scene III. *Another part of Blackheath.*]

*Alarums to the fight, wherein both the Staffords
are slain. Enter Cade and the rest.*

Cade. Where's Dick, the butcher of Ashford?

Dick. Here, sir.

Cade. They fell before thee like sheep and oxen, and
thou behav'dst thyself as if thou hadst been in thine
own slaughter-house: therefore thus will I reward   5
thee, the Lent shall be as long again as it is; and
thou shalt have a license to kill° for a hundred
lacking one.°

Dick. I desire no more.

Cade. And, to speak truth, thou deserv'st no less. [*He*   10
puts on Sir Humphrey's armor.] This monument
of the victory will I bear; and the bodies shall be
dragged at my horse heels till I do come to London,
where we will have the Mayor's sword borne before us.   15

Dick. If we mean to thrive and do good, break open
the jails and let out the prisoners.

Cade. Fear not that, I warrant thee. Come, let's march
towards London.   *Exeunt.*

IV.iii.7 **license to kill** only infirm persons were permitted to eat
meat during Lent, and favored butchers specially licensed to kill
for them   7–8 **hundred lacking one** i.e., ninety-nine years, the usual
term of a lease

127

[Scene IV. *London. The palace.*]

*Enter the King with a supplication, and the
Queen with Suffolk's head, the Duke of Buckingham and the Lord Say.*

Queen. [*Aside*] Oft have I heard that grief softens the
    mind
    And makes it fearful and degenerate:
    Think therefore on revenge, and cease to weep.
    But who can cease to weep and look on this?
5   Here may his head lie on my throbbing breast;
    But where's the body that I should embrace?

Buckingham. What answer makes your Grace to the
    rebels' supplication?

King. I'll send some holy bishop to entreat;
10   For God forbid so many simple souls
    Should perish by the sword! And I myself,
    Rather than bloody war shall cut them short,
    Will parley with Jack Cade their General.
    But stay, I'll read it over once again.

Queen. [*Aside*] Ah, barbarous villains! Hath this lovely
15   face
    Ruled, like a wandering planet° over me,
    And could it not enforce them to relent,
    That were unworthy to behold the same?

King. Lord Say, Jack Cade hath sworn to have thy
    head.

20 *Say.* Ay, but I hope your Highness shall have his.

King. How now, madam!

IV.iv.16 **wandering planet** i.e., the star under which one is born,
astrologically

128

Still lamenting and mourning for Suffolk's death?
I fear me, love, if that I had been dead,
Thou wouldest not have mourned so much for me.

Queen. No, my love, I should not mourn, but die for
thee.   25

Enter a Messenger.

King. How now! What news? Why com'st thou in
such haste?

Messenger. The rebels are in Southwark: fly, my
lord!
Jack Cade proclaims himself Lord Mortimer,
Descended from the Duke of Clarence' house,
And calls your Grace usurper openly,   30
And vows to crown himself in Westminster.
His army is a ragged multitude
Of hinds and peasants, rude and merciless:
Sir Humphrey Stafford and his brother's death
Hath given them heart and courage to proceed.   35
All scholars, lawyers, courtiers, gentlemen,
They call false caterpillars° and intend their death.

King. O graceless men! They know not what they do.

Buckingham. My gracious lord, retire to Killingworth,°
Until a power be raised to put them down.   40

Queen. Ah, were the Duke of Suffolk now alive,
These Kentish rebels would be soon appeased!

King. Lord Say, the traitors hateth thee;
Therefore away with us to Killingworth.

Say. So might your Grace's person be in danger.   45
The sight of me is odious in their eyes:
And therefore in this city will I stay,
And live alone as secret as I may.

---

37 **caterpillars** parasites (a common figure for capitalistic oppressors)
39 **Killingworth** Kenilworth Castle

Enter another Messenger.

Second Messenger. Jack Cade hath gotten London
    Bridge!
50   The citizens fly and forsake their houses;
    The rascal people, thirsting after prey,
    Join with the traitor, and they jointly swear
    To spoil° the city and your royal court.

Buckingham. Then linger not, my lord; away, take
    horse.

King. Come, Margaret: God, our hope, will succor
55   us.

Queen. My hope is gone, now Suffolk is deceased.°

King. Farewell, my lord: trust not the Kentish rebels.

Buckingham. Trust nobody, for fear you be betrayed.

Say. The trust I have is in mine innocence,
60   And therefore am I bold and resolute.   *Exeunt.*

[Scene V. *London. The Tower.*]

Enter Lord Scales upon the Tower, walking.
Then enters two or three Citizens below.

Scales. How now! Is Jack Cade slain?

First Citizen. No, my lord, nor likely to be slain; for
    they have won the Bridge, killing all those that
    withstand them: the Lord Mayor craves aid of your
5   honor from the Tower to defend the city from the
    rebels.

Scales. Such aid as I can spare you shall command,
    But I am troubled here with them myself:

53 **spoil** despoil   56 **My . . . deceased** (a possible "aside")

The rebels have assayed to win the Tower.
But get you to Smithfield, and gather head,   10
And thither I will send you Matthew Goffe.
Fight for your King, your country and your lives;
And so farewell, for I must hence again.

Exeunt.

[Scene VI. *London. Cannon Street.*]

*Enter Jack Cade and the rest, and strikes his
sword on London Stone.*

Cade. Now is Mortimer lord of this city. And here,
sitting upon London Stone, I charge and command
that, of the city's cost, the pissing-conduit° run
nothing but claret wine this first year of our reign.
And now henceforward it shall be treason for any   5
that calls me other than Lord Mortimer.

Enter a Soldier, running.

Soldier. Jack Cade! Jack Cade!

Cade. Knock him down there.   *They kill him.*

Smith. If this fellow be wise, he'll never call ye Jack
Cade more: I think he hath a very fair warning.   10

Dick. My lord, there's an army gathered together in
Smithfield.

Cade. Come, then, let's go fight with them: but first,
go and set London Bridge on fire; and if you can,
burn down the Tower too. Come, let's away.   15

Exeunt Omnes.

IV.vi.3 **pissing-conduit** an open gutter of drinking-water in London,
derisively so termed

[Scene VII. *London. Smithfield.*]

Alarums. Matthew Goffe is slain, and all the rest.
Then enter Jack Cade, with his company.

Cade. So, sirs: now go some and pull down the
Savoy; others to th' Inns of Court; down with them
all.

Dick. I have a suit unto your lordship.

5 *Cade.* Be it a lordship, thou shalt have it for that
word.

Dick. Only that the laws of England may come out
of your mouth.

Holland. [*Aside*] Mass, 'twill be sore law, then; for he
10 was thrust in the mouth with a spear, and 'tis not
whole yet.

Smith. [*Aside*] Nay, John, it will be stinking law; for
his breath stinks with eating toasted cheese.

Cade. I have thought upon it; it shall be so. Away,
15 burn all the records of the realm: my mouth shall
be the parliament of England.

Holland. [*Aside*] Then we are like to have biting°
statutes, unless his teeth be pulled out.

Cade. And henceforward all things shall be in com-
20 mon.

Enter a Messenger.

Messenger. My lord, a prize, a prize! Here's the Lord
Say, which sold the towns in France; he that made

IV.vii.17 **biting** severe

132

us pay one and twenty fifteens,° and one shilling
to the pound, the last subsidy.

Enter George, with the Lord Say.

Cade. Well, he shall be beheaded for it ten times. Ah,   25
thou say, thou serge, nay, thou buckram° lord, now
art thou within point-blank of our jurisdiction
regal! What canst thou answer to my Majesty
for ⟩ giving up of Normandy unto Mounsieur
Basimecu,° the Dolphin of France? Be it known   30
unto thee by these presence,° even the presence of
Lord Mortimer, that I am the besom° that must
sweep the court clean of such filth as thou art.
Thou hast most traitorously corrupted the youth
of the realm in erecting a grammar school: and   35
whereas before, our forefathers had no other books
but the score and the tally, thou hast caused printing to be used, and contrary to the King, his crown
and dignity, thou hast built a paper-mill.° It will
be proved to thy face that thou hast men about   40
thee that usually talk of a noun and a verb, and
such abhominable° words as no Christian ear can
endure to hear. Thou hast appointed justices of
peace, to call poor men before them about matters
they were not able to answer. Moreover, thou hast   45
put them in prison, and because they could not
read° thou hast hanged them, when, indeed, only
for that cause they have been most worthy to live.
Thou dost ride on a foot-cloth,° dost thou not?

---

23 **one and twenty fifteens** taxes (a gross exaggeration)   26 **say . . .
serge . . . buckram** puns on Lord Say's name: say is a silk cloth,
resembling serge; serge a serviceable but less elegant material; and
buckram a coarse linen stiffened with glue, commonly used in making theatrical properties   30 **Basimecu** pseudo-French pun on *baise
mon cul* = "kiss my backside"   30–31 **Be . . . presence** play on the
formal beginning of documents, *Noverint universi per praesentes*
("Be it known unto all by these presents")   32 **besom** broom
37–39 **printing . . . paper-mill** (flagrant anachronisms, perhaps in-
tentionally humorous)   42 **abhominable** possibly a pun on *"ad
hominem"*   46–47 **because they could not read** refers to the legal
exemption from hanging and other penalties ("benefit of clergy")
which Latin-reading offenders could claim   49 **foot-cloth** horse or
mule decorated for a procession

50 *Say.* What of that?

Cade. Marry, thou ought'st not to let thy horse wear
    a cloak, when honester men than thou go in their
    hose and doublets.

Dick. And work in their shirt too as myself, for ex-
55 ample, that am a butcher.

Say. You men of Kent—

Dick. What say you of Kent?

Say. Nothing but this: 'tis *bona terra, mala gens.*°

Cade. Away with him, away with him! He speaks
60 Latin.

Say. Hear me but speak, and bear me where you will.
    Kent, in the *Commentaries* Caesar writ,
    Is termed the civil'st place of all this isle:
    Sweet is the country, because full of riches;
65 The people liberal, valiant, active, wealthy;
    Which makes me hope you are not void of pity.
    I sold not Maine, I lost not Normandy,
    Yet to recover them would lose my life.
    Justice with favor have I always done;
    Prayers and tears have moved me, gifts could
70 never.
    When have I aught exacted at your hands,
    But to maintain the King, the realm, and you?
    Large gifts have I bestowed on learnèd clerks,°
    Because my book° preferred me to the King,
75 And seeing ignorance is the curse of God,
    Knowledge the wing wherewith we fly to heaven,
    Unless you be possessed with devilish spirits,
    You cannot but forbear to murder me:
    This tongue hath parleyed unto foreign kings
80 For your behoof°—

Cade. Tut, when struck'st thou one blow in the field?

---

58 **bona terra, mala gens** good land, bad inhabitants   73 **clerks**
scholars   74 **book** learning   80 **behoof** behalf

Say. Great men have reaching hands: oft have I
    struck
  Those that I never saw, and struck them dead.

George. O monstrous coward! What, to come behind
  folks?   85

Say. These cheeks are pale for watching for your
  good.

Cade. Give him a box o' th' ear and that will make
  'em red again.

Say. Long sitting to determine poor men's causes
  Hath made me full of sickness and diseases.   90

Cade. Ye shall have a hempen caudle then and the
  help of hatchet.°

Dick. Why dost thou quiver, man?

Say. The palsy, and not fear, provokes me.

Cade. Nay, he nods at us, as who should say, "I'll be   95
  even with you." I'll see if his head will stand
  steadier on a pole, or no: take him away, and be-
  head him.

Say. Tell me: wherein have I offended most?
  Have I affected wealth or honor? Speak!   100
  Are my chests filled up with extorted gold?
  Is my apparel sumptuous to behold?
  Whom have I injured, that ye seek my death?
  These hands are free from guiltless blood-shed-
    ding,°
  This breast from harboring foul deceitful thoughts.   105
  O, let me live!

Cade. [*Aside*] I feel remorse in myself with his
  words; but I'll bridle it: he shall die, and it be but

91–92 Ye . . . hatchet you will be first hanged (a "caudle" is a
curative gruel, a "hempen caudle" a euphemism for hanging) and
then beheaded 104 guiltless blood-shedding shedding guiltless
blood

for pleading so well for his life.— Away with him!
He has a familiar° under his tongue; he speaks not
a° God's name. Go, take him away, I say, and
strike off his head presently; and then break into
his son-in-law's house, Sir James Cromer, and
strike off his head, and bring them both upon two
poles hither.

All. It shall be done.

Say. Ah, countrymen! If when you make your
prayers,
God should be so obdurate as yourselves,
How would it fare with your departed souls?
And therefore yet relent, and save my life.

Cade. Away with him! And do as I command ye.
                                    [*Say is led away.*]
The proudest peer in the realm shall not wear a
head on his shoulders, unless he pay me tribute;
there shall not a maid be married, but she shall pay
to me her maidenhead ere they have it: men shall
hold of me *in capite;*° and we charge and command that their wives be as free as heart can wish
or tongue can tell.

Dick. My lord, when shall we go to Cheapside and
take up commodities upon our bills?°

Cade. Marry, presently.

All. O, brave!

Enter one with the heads.

Cade. But is not this braver? Let them kiss one another, for they loved well when they were alive.
Now part them again, lest they consult about the
giving up of some more towns in France. Soldiers,
defer the spoil of the city until night: for with these

110 **familiar** demonic attendant of a witch   111 **a** in   126 **in capite**
in chief, the legal term for holding property direct from the King,
at the "head" of the state   130 **take . . . bills** (1) borrow money
from usurers with promissory notes (2) pillage property with our
weapons

borne before us, instead of maces, will we ride
through the streets; and at every corner have them
kiss. Away!   *Exit [all].* 140

[Scene VIII. *Southwark.*]

Alarum and retreat.
Enter again Cade and all his rabblement.

Cade. Up Fish Street! Down Saint Magnus' Corner!
Kill and knock down! Throw them into Thames!
(*Sound a parley.*) What noise is this I hear? Dare
any be so bold to sound retreat or parley, when I
command them kill?   5

Enter Buckingham and old Clifford.

Buckingham. Ay, here they be that dare and will
    disturb thee:
Know, Cade, we come ambassadors from the King
Unto the commons whom thou hast misled,
And here pronounce free pardon to them all
That will forsake thee and go home in peace.   10

Clifford. What say ye, countrymen? Will ye relent,
And yield to mercy whilst 'tis offered you,
Or let a rebel lead you to your deaths?
Who loves the King and will embrace his pardon,
Fling up his cap, and say "God save his Majesty!"   15
Who hateth him and honors not his father,
Henry the Fifth, that made all France to quake,
Shake he his weapon at us and pass by.

All. God save the King! God save the King!

Cade. What, Buckingham and Clifford, are ye so   20
brave? And you, base peasants, do ye believe him?
Will you needs be hanged with your pardons about
your necks? Hath my sword therefore broke

through London gates, that you should leave me
25   at the White Hart in Southwark?° I thought ye
would never have given out these arms till you had
recovered your ancient freedom: but you are all
recreants and dastards, and delight to live in slavery
to the nobility. Let them break your backs with
30   burdens, take your houses over your heads, ravish
your wives and daughters before your faces. For
me, I will make shift for one; and so, God's curse
light upon you all!

All. We'll follow Cade, we'll follow Cade!

35   *Clifford.* Is Cade the son of Henry the Fifth,
That thus you do exclaim you'll go with him?
Will he conduct you through the heart of France,
And make the meanest of you earls and dukes?
Alas, he hath no home, no place to fly to;
40   Nor knows he how to live but by the spoil,
Unless by robbing of your friends and us.
Were't not a shame, that whilst you live at jar,°
The fearful French, whom you late vanquishèd,
Should make a start o'er seas and vanquish you?
45   Methinks already in this civil broil
I see them lording it in London streets,
Crying *"Villiago!"*° unto all they meet.
Better ten thousand base-born Cades miscarry
Than you should stoop unto a Frenchman's mercy.
50   To France, to France! and get what you have lost:
Spare England, for it is your native coast.
Henry hath money, you are strong and manly;
God on our side, doubt not of victory.

All. A Clifford! A Clifford! We'll follow the King and
55   Clifford.

Cade. Was ever feather so lightly blown to and fro as
this multitude? The name of Henry the Fifth hales
them to an hundred mischiefs and makes them

IV.viii.25 **White Hart in Southwark** inn where Cade lodged ("White
Hart" puns on pale, or cowardly, heart)   42 **at jar** quarreling   47
Villiago villain, coward (Spanish or Italian)

leave me desolate. I see them lay their heads together to surprise me. My sword make way for me,   60
for here is no staying: in despite of the devils and
hell, have through the very middest of you! And
heavens and honor be witness that no want of resolution in me, but only my followers' base and
ignominious treasons, makes me betake me to my   65
heels.

> *He runs through them with his staff,*
> *and flies away.*

Buckingham. What, is he fled? Go some, and follow
   him;
And he that brings his head unto the King
Shall have a thousand crowns for his reward.

> *Exeunt some of them.*

Follow me, soldiers: we'll devise a mean   70
To reconcile you all unto the King.

> *Exeunt omnes.*

[Scene IX. *Kenilworth Castle.*]

Sound trumpets. Enter King, Queen, and
Somerset, on the terrace.

King. Was ever king that joyed an earthly throne,
   And could command no more content than I?
   No sooner was I crept out of my cradle
   But I was made a king, at nine months old.
   Was never subject longed to be a king   5
   As I do long and wish to be a subject.

Enter Buckingham and [old] Clifford.

Buckingham. Health and glad tidings to your
   Majesty!

King. Why, Buckingham, is the traitor Cade surprised?
Or is he but retired to make him strong?

Enter multitudes, with halters about their necks.

Clifford. He is fled, my lord, and all his powers do
10   yield,
       And humbly thus, with halters° on their necks,
       Expect your Highness' doom, of life or death.

King. Then, heaven, set ope thy everlasting gates,
       To entertain° my vows of thanks and praise!
15   Soldiers, this day have you redeemed your lives
       And showed how well you love your Prince and
          country:
       Continue still in this so good a mind,
       And Henry, though he be infortunate,
       Assure yourselves, will never be unkind:
20   And so, with thanks and pardon to you all,
       I do dismiss you to your several countries.°

All. God save the King! God save the King!

Enter a Messenger.

Messenger. Please it your Grace to be advertisèd°
       The Duke of York is newly come from Ireland,
25   And with a puissant and a mighty power
       Of gallowglasses° and stout kerns°
       Is marching hitherward in proud array,
       And still proclaimeth, as he comes along,
       His arms are only to remove from thee
30   The Duke of Somerset, whom he terms a traitor.

King. Thus stands my state, 'twixt Cade and York
          distressed,
       Like to a ship, that having 'scaped a tempest,
       Is straightway calmed, and boarded with° a pirate.
       But now is Cade driven back, his men dispersed;
35   And now is York in arms to second him.
       I pray thee, Buckingham, go and meet him,

IV.ix.11 **halters** nooses (a symbol of complete submission) 14 **entertain** receive 21 **countries** counties, areas 23 **advertised** informed 26 **gallowglasses** heavily armed Irish footsoldiers 26 **kerns** light-armed troops 33 **with** by

And ask him what's the reason of these arms.
Tell him I'll send Duke Edmund to the Tower,
And, Somerset, we will commit thee thither,
Until his army be dismissed from him.   40

Somerset. My lord,
 I'll yield myself to prison willingly,
 Or unto death, to do my country good.

King. In any case, be not too rough in terms,
 For he is fierce, and cannot brook hard language.   45

Buckingham. I will, my lord; and doubt not so to deal
 As all things shall redound unto your good.

King. Come, wife, let's in, and learn to govern better;
 For yet may England curse my wretched reign.
                              Flourish. Exeunt.

[Scene X. *Kent. Iden's garden.*]

Enter Cade.

Cade. Fie on ambitions! Fie on myself, that have a
 sword, and yet am ready to famish! These five days
 have I hid me in these woods and durst not peep
 out, for all the country is laid° for me; but now
 am I so hungry that if I might have a lease of my   5
 life for a thousand years I could stay no longer.
 Wherefore, on a brick wall have I climbed into this
 garden, to see if I can eat grass, or pick a sallet°
 another while, which is not amiss to cool a man's
 stomach° this hot weather. And I think this word°   10
 "sallet" was born to do me good: for many a time,
 but for a sallet, my brainpan had been cleft with

IV.x.4 **laid** set with traps   8 **sallet** (1) salad (2) iron helmet   9–10
cool a man's stomach (1) satisfy a man's hunger and thirst (2)
pacify a man's anger   10 **word** pun on "wort," i.e., medicinal or
edible herb

a brown bill;° and many a time, when I have been
dry and bravely marching, it hath served me in-
15 stead of a quart pot to drink in; and now the word
"sallet" must serve me to feed on.

Enter [Alexander] Iden.

Iden. Lord, who would live turmoilèd in the court,
And may enjoy such quiet walks as these?
This small inheritance my father left me
20 Contenteth me, and worth° a monarchy.
I seek not to wax great by others' waning,
Or gather wealth, I care not with what envy:
Sufficeth that I have maintains my state,
And sends the poor well pleasèd from my gate.

25 *Cade.* Here's the lord of the soil come to seize me for
a stray, for entering his fee-simple without leave.°
Ah, villain, thou wilt betray me, and get a thousand
crowns of the King by carrying my head to him:
but I'll make thee eat iron like an ostrich, and
30 swallow my sword like a great pin, ere thou and
I part.

Iden. Why, rude companion,° whatsoe'er thou be,
I know thee not; why then should I betray thee?
Is't not enough to break into my garden,
35 And like a thief to come to rob my grounds,
Climbing my walls in spite of me the owner,
But thou wilt brave° me with these saucy terms?

Cade. Brave thee! Ay, by the best blood that ever
was broached, and beard thee° too. Look on me
40 well: I have eat no meat these five days; yet, come
thou and thy five men, and if I do not leave you
all as dead as a doornail, I pray God I may never
eat grass more.

---

13 brown bill halberd used by constables   **20 worth** is worth
25–26 Here's ... leave the absolute owner ("lord of the soil") of an
estate ("fee-simple") was entitled to impound any stray animal
which wandered accidentally over the bounds of the property   **32
companion** fellow (derogatory)   **37 brave** challenge   **39 beard thee**
defy you to your face

Iden. Nay, it shall ne'er be said, while England
    stands,
   That Alexander Iden, an esquire of Kent,   45
   Took odds° to combat a poor famished man.
   Oppose thy steadfast-gazing eyes to mine,
   See if thou canst outface me with thy looks;
   Set limb to limb, and thou art far the lesser:
   Thy hand is but a finger to my fist,   50
   Thy leg a stick comparèd with this truncheon;
   My foot shall fight with all the strength thou hast;
   And if mine arm be heavèd in the air,
   Thy grave is digged already in the earth.
   As for words, whose greatness answers words,   55
   Let this my sword report what speech forbears.

Cade. By my valor, the most complete champion that
   ever I heard! Steel, if thou turn the edge, or cut
   not out the burly-boned clown in chines° of beef
   ere thou sleep in thy sheath, I beseech God on my   60
   knees thou mayst be turned to hobnails.
                    They fight, and Cade falls down.
   O, I am slain! Famine and no other hath slain
   me: let ten thousand devils come against me, and
   give me but the ten meals I have lost, and I'd defy
   them all. Wither, garden, and be henceforth a   65
   burying-place to all that do dwell in this house,
   because the unconquered soul of Cade is fled.

Iden. Is't Cade that I have slain, that monstrous
    traitor?
   Sword, I will hallow thee for this thy deed,
   And hang thee o'er my tomb when I am dead: 70
   Ne'er shall this blood be wipèd from thy point,
   But thou shalt wear it as a herald's coat,
   To emblaze° the honor that thy master got.

Cade. Iden, farewell, and be proud of thy victory.
   Tell Kent from me, she hath lost her best man,   75

---

46 **Took odds** relied on help   59 **chines** portion of flesh surround-
ing the backbone   73 **emblaze** emblazon, set forth (as in a coat
of arms)

and exhort all the world to be cowards: for I, that
never feared any, am vanquished by famine, not
by valor.   *Dies.*

 Iden. How much thou wrong'st me, heaven be my
  judge.
 Die, damnèd wretch, the curse of her that bare
30   thee:
 And as I thrust thy body in with my sword,
 So wish I I might thrust thy soul to hell.
 Hence will I drag thee headlong° by the heels
 Unto a dunghill which shall be thy grave,
35 And there cut off thy most ungracious head,
 Which I will bear in triumph to the King,
 Leaving thy trunk for crows to feed upon.
           Exit.

83 **headlong** head downwards

[ACT V

Scene I. *Fields between London and Saint Albans.*]

*Enter York, and his army of Irish, with
drum and colors.*

York. From Ireland thus comes York to claim his
    right,
  And pluck the crown from feeble Henry's head.
  Ring, bells, aloud; burn, bonfires, clear and bright,
  To entertain great England's lawful king.
  Ah, *sancta majestas!°* Who would not buy thee
    dear?   5
  Let them obey that knows not how to rule;
  This hand was made to handle nought but gold.
  I cannot give due action to my words,
  Except a sword or scepter balance it:
  A scepter shall it have, have I a soul,   10
  On which I'll toss the fleur-de-luce° of France.

Enter Buckingham.

  Whom have we here? Buckingham, to disturb me?
  The King hath sent him, sure: I must dissemble.

Buckingham. York, if thou meanest well, I greet thee
    well.

V.i.5 **sancta majestas** holy majesty (Ovid) **11 fleur-de-luce** fleur-de-
lys, the heraldic emblem of French kings

York. Humphrey of Buckingham, I accept thy greet-
15   ing.
Art thou a messenger, or come of pleasure?

Buckingham. A messenger from Henry, our dread
          liege,
To know the reason of these arms in peace;
Or why thou, being a subject as I am,
20   Against thy oath and true allegiance sworn,
Should raise so great a power without his leave,
Or dare to bring thy force so near the court.

York. [*Aside*] Scarce can I speak, my choler is so
          great.
O, I could hew up rocks and fight with flint,
25   I am so angry at these abject° terms;
And now, like Ajax Telamonius,
On sheep or oxen could I spend my fury.°
I am far better born than is the King,
More like a king, more kingly in my thoughts:
30   But I must make fair weather yet awhile,
Till Henry be more weak and I more strong.
[*Aloud*] Buckingham, I prithee, pardon me,
That I have given no answer all this while;
My mind was troubled with deep melancholy.
35   The cause why I have brought this army hither
Is to remove proud Somerset from the King,
Seditious to his Grace, and to the state.

Buckingham. That is too much presumption on thy
          part:
But if thy arms be to no other end,
40   The King hath yielded unto thy demand:
The Duke of Somerset is in the Tower.

York. Upon thine honor, is he prisoner?

Buckingham. Upon mine honor, he is prisoner.

York. Then, Buckingham, I do dismiss my pow'rs.

25 **abject** degrading   26–27 **like Ajax . . . fury** Ajax, son of Tela-
mon, in a mad rage over being denied an honor, slaughtered a flock
of sheep and then killed himself

Soldiers, I thank you all; disperse yourselves;   *45*
Meet me tomorrow in Saint George's Field,
You shall have pay and everything you wish.
And let my sovereign, virtuous Henry,
Command my eldest son, nay, all my sons,
As pledges of my fealty and love;   *50*
I'll send them all as willing as I live:
Lands, goods, horse, armor, anything I have,
Is his to use, so° Somerset may die.

Buckingham. York, I commend this kind° submission:
We twain will go into his Highness' tent.   *55*

      Enter King and Attendants.

King. Buckingham, doth York intend no harm to us,
That thus he marcheth with thee arm in arm?

York. In all submission and humility
York doth present himself unto your Highness.

King. Then what intends these forces thou dost bring?   *60*

York. To heave the traitor Somerset from hence,
And fight against that monstrous rebel Cade,
Who since I heard to be discomfited.

      Enter Iden, with Cade's head.

Iden. If one so rude and of so mean condition
May pass into the presence of a king,   *65*
Lo, I present your Grace a traitor's head,
The head of Cade, whom I in combat slew.

King. The head of Cade! Great God, how just art
    Thou!
O, let me view his visage, being dead,
That living wrought me such exceeding trouble.   *70*
Tell me, my friend, art thou the man that slew him?

Iden. I was, an't like your Majesty.

King. How art thou called? And what is thy degree?

Iden. Alexander Iden, that's my name;
75   A poor esquire of Kent, that loves his King.

Buckingham. So please it you, my lord, 'twere not amiss
    He were created knight for his good service.

King. Iden, kneel down. [*He kneels.*] Rise up a knight.
    We give thee for reward a thousand marks,
80   And will that thou henceforth attend on us.

Iden. May Iden live to merit such a bounty,
    And never live but true unto his liege!

Enter Queen and Somerset.

King. See, Buckingham, Somerset comes with th'
    Queen:
    Go, bid her hide him quickly from the Duke.

85 *Queen.* For thousand Yorks he shall not hide his head,
    But boldly stand and front° him to his face.

York. How now! Is Somerset at liberty?
    Then, York, unloose thy long-imprisoned thoughts,
    And let thy tongue be equal with thy heart.
90   Shall I endure the sight of Somerset?
    False King, why hast thou broken faith with me,
    Knowing how hardly° I can brook abuse?
    King did I call thee? No, thou art not King,
    Not fit to govern and rule multitudes,
95   Which dar'st not, no, nor canst not rule a traitor.
    That head of thine doth not become a crown;
    Thy hand is made to grasp a palmer's staff,°
    And not to grace an awful princely scepter.
    That gold must round engirt these brows of mine,
100   Whose smile and frown, like to Achilles' spear,
    Is able with the change to kill and cure.°
    Here is a hand to hold a scepter up

---

86 front confront   **92 how hardly** with what difficulty   **97 palmer's staff** insignia of the returned pilgrim, hence emblem of piety   **100–1 like . . . cure** Telephus, wounded by Achilles' spear, was supposedly cured by the application of its rust

And with the same to act controlling laws.
Give place: by heaven, thou shalt rule no more
O'er him whom heaven created for thy ruler.   *105*

Somerset. O monstrous traitor! I arrest thee, York,
Of capital treason 'gainst the King and crown:
Obey, audacious traitor; kneel for grace.

York. Wouldst have me kneel? First let me ask of
    these,°
If they can brook I bow a knee to man.   *110*
Sirrah, call in my sons to be my bail:
                                    [*Exit Attendant.*]
I know ere they will have me go to ward,°
They'll pawn their swords for my enfranchisement.

Queen. Call hither Clifford; bid him come amain,
To say if that the bastard boys of York   *115*
Shall be the surety for their traitor father.
                                    [*Exit Attendant.*]

York. O blood-bespotted Neapolitan,°
Outcast of Naples, England's bloody scourge!
The sons of York, thy betters in their birth,
Shall be their father's bail; and bane to those   *120*
That for my surety will refuse the boys!

            Enter Edward and Richard.

See where they come: I'll warrant they'll make it
    good.

            Enter Clifford and his Son.

Queen. And here comes Clifford to deny their bail.

Clifford. (*Kneels to Henry*) Health and all happiness
    to my lord the King!

York. I thank thee, Clifford: say, what news with thee? *125*

----

109 **these** i.e., the troops   112 **to ward** into custody   117 **Neapoli-**
tan traditionally murderous and fond of intrigue. Although Margaret was French, her father claimed the throne of Naples (cf.
I.i.47–48)

Nay, do not fright us with an angry look:
We are thy sovereign, Clifford, kneel again;
For thy mistaking so, we pardon thee.

Clifford. This is my King, York, I do not mistake;
130 But thou mistakes me much to think I do.
To Bedlam° with him! Is the man grown mad?

King. Ay, Clifford; a bedlam° and ambitious humor
Makes him oppose himself against his King.

Clifford. He is a traitor; let him to the Tower,
135 And chop away that factious pate of his.

Queen. He is arrested, but will not obey;
His sons, he says, shall give their words for him.

York. Will you not, sons?

Edward. Ay, noble father, if our words will serve.

140 *Richard.* And if words will not, then our weapons shall.

Clifford. Why, what a brood of traitors have we here!

York. Look in a glass, and call thy image so.
I am thy King, and thou a false-heart traitor.
Call hither to the stake my two brave bears,
145 That with the very shaking of their chains
They may astonish° these fell-lurking° curs:
Bid Salisbury and Warwick come to me.

Enter the Earls of Warwick and Salisbury.

Clifford. Are these thy bears? We'll bait thy bears to
death,
And manacle the bear'ard° in their chains,
150 If thou dar'st bring them to the baiting place.

Richard. Oft have I seen a hot o'erweening cur
Run back and bite, because he was withheld;
Who, being suffered,° with° the bear's fell paw

131 **Bedlam** Bethlehem Hospital in London, where insane persons
were confined   132 **bedlam** crazy   146 **astonish** terrify   146 **fell-
lurking** balefully skulking   149 **bear'ard** bear-ward, the keeper of
bears intended for baiting in the ring   153 **suffered** loosed   153
with i.e., struck with

Hath clapped his tail between his legs and cried:
And such a piece of service will you do,   155
If you oppose yourselves to match Lord Warwick.

Clifford. Hence, heap of wrath, foul indigested° lump,
As crooked in thy manners as thy shape!

York. Nay, we shall heat you thoroughly anon.

Clifford. Take heed, lest by your heat you burn yourselves.   160

King. Why, Warwick, hath thy knee forgot to bow?
Old Salisbury, shame to thy silver hair,
Thou mad misleader of thy brain-sick son!
What, wilt thou on thy death-bed play the ruffian,
And seek for sorrow with thy spectacles?°   165
O, where is faith? O, where is loyalty?
If it be banished from the frosty head,
Where shall it find a harbor in the earth?
Wilt thou go dig a grave to find out war,
And shame thine honorable age with blood?   170
Why art thou old, and want'st° experience?
Or wherefore dost abuse° it, if thou hast it?
For shame! In duty bend thy knee to me,
That bows unto the grave with mickle° age.

Salisbury. My lord, I have considered with myself   175
The title of this most renownèd duke,
And in my conscience do repute his Grace
The rightful heir to England's royal seat.

King. Hast thou not sworn allegiance unto me?

Salisbury. I have.   180

King. Canst thou dispense with° heaven for such an
oath?

Salisbury. It is great sin to swear unto a sin,
But greater sin to keep a sinful oath.

---

157 **indigested** shapeless   165 **spectacles** organs of sight   171
want'st lack   172 **abuse** misuse   174 **mickle** much, great   181
dispense with come to terms with

Who can be bound by any solemn vow
185 To do a murd'rous deed, to rob a man,
To force a spotless virgin's chastity,
To reave° the orphan of his patrimony,
To wring the widow from her customed right,°
And have no other reason for this wrong
190 But that he was bound by a solemn oath?

Queen. A subtle traitor needs no sophister.°

King. Call Buckingham, and bid him arm himself.

York. Call Buckingham, and all the friends thou hast,
I am resolved for death or dignity.

195 *Clifford.* The first I warrant thee, if dreams prove true.

Warwick. You were best to go to bed and dream again,
To keep thee from the tempest of the field.

Clifford. I am resolved to bear a greater storm
Than any thou canst conjure up today;
200 And that I'll write upon thy burgonet,°
Might I but know thee by thy housèd badge.°

Warwick. Now, by my father's badge, old Nevil's crest,
The rampant bear chained to the ragged staff,
This day I'll wear aloft my burgonet,
205 As on a mountain top the cedar shows
That keeps his leaves in spite of any storm,
Even to affright thee with the view thereof.

Clifford. And from thy burgonet I'll rend thy bear
And tread it under foot with all contempt,
210 Despite the bear'ard that protects the bear.

Young Clifford. And so to arms, victorious father,
To quell the rebels and their complices.

Richard. Fie! Charity, for shame! Speak not in spite,
For you shall sup with Jesu Christ tonight.

---

187 **reave** bereave, rob   188 **customed right** i.e., of part of her
husband's estate for life   191 **sophister** cunning spokesman   200
burgonet helmet   201 **housèd badge** emblem of the family

Young Clifford. Foul stigmatic,° that's more than thou
 canst tell.   215

Richard. If not in heaven, you'll surely sup in hell.
            Exeunt.

[Scene II. *Saint Albans.*]

Enter Warwick.

Warwick. Clifford of Cumberland, 'tis Warwick calls:
 And if thou dost not hide thee from the bear,
 Now, when the angry trumpet sounds alarum,
 And dead men's cries do fill the empty air,
 Clifford, I say, come forth and fight with me! 5
 Proud northern lord, Clifford of Cumberland,
 Warwick is hoarse with calling thee to arms.

Enter York.

How now, my noble lord! What, all afoot?

York. The deadly-handed Clifford slew my steed,
 But match to match I have encountered him, 10
 And made a prey for carrion kites and crows
 Even of the bonny beast he loved so well.

Enter Clifford.

Warwick. Of one or both of us the time is come.

York. Hold, Warwick, seek thee out some other chase,°
 For I myself must hunt this deer to death. 15

Warwick. Then, nobly, York; 'tis for a crown thou
 fight'st.
 As I intend, Clifford, to thrive today,
 It grieves my soul to leave thee unassailed.
          Exit Warwick.

215 **stigmatic** branded criminal, hence a deformed person (branded
by God, as if in punishment) V.ii.14 **chase** game

Clifford. What seest thou in me, York? Why dost thou
    pause?

20 *York.* With thy brave bearing should I be in love,
    But that thou art so fast mine enemy.

Clifford. Nor should thy prowess want praise and
    esteem,
    But that 'tis shown ignobly, and in treason.

York. So let it help me now against thy sword,
25   As I in justice and true right express it.

Clifford. My soul and body on the action both!

York. A dreadful lay!° Address° thee instantly.
                    Alarums, and they fight, and
                    York kills Clifford.

Clifford. La fin couronne les œuvres.°   [*Dies.*]

York. Thus war hath given thee peace, for thou art
    still.
30 Peace with his soul, heaven, if it be thy will!
                           Exit York.

Enter Young Clifford.

Young Clifford. Shame and confusion! All is on the
    rout;
    Fear frames disorder, and disorder wounds
    Where it should guard. O war, thou son of hell,
    Whom angry heavens do make their minister,
35   Throw in the frozen bosoms of our part
    Hot coals of vengeance! Let no soldier fly.
    He that is truly dedicate to war
    Hath no self-love; nor he that loves himself
    Hath not essentially, but by circumstance,°
    The name of valor. [*Sees his dead father.*] O, let the
40   vile world end,
    And the premisèd° flames of the last day

---

27 lay wager 27 Address prepare 28 La . . . œuvres "the end
crowns the work" 39 not . . . circumstance not by nature, but by
accident 41 premisèd predestined

Knit earth and heaven together!
Now let the general trumpet blow his blast,
Particularities° and petty sounds
To cease! Wast thou ordained, dear father,   45
To lose thy youth in peace, and to achieve
The silver livery of advisèd age,
And, in thy reverence and thy chair-days, thus
To die in ruffian battle? Even at this sight
My heart is turned to stone: and while 'tis mine,   50
It shall be stony. York not our old men spares;
No more will I their babes: tears virginal
Shall be to me even as the dew to fire,
And beauty, that the tyrant oft reclaims,
Shall to my flaming wrath be oil and flax.   55
Henceforth I will not have to do with pity:
Meet I an infant of the house of York,
Into as many gobbets will I cut it
As wild Medea young Absyrtus did:°
In cruelty will I seek out my fame.   60
Come, thou new ruin of old Clifford's house:
As did Aeneas old Anchises bear,
So bear I thee upon my manly shoulders;
But then Aeneas bare a living load,
Nothing so heavy as these woes of mine.   65
          Exit Young Clifford with his father.

*Enter the Duke of Somerset and Richard fighting,
and Richard kills him under the sign of the Castle,
in Saint Albans.*

Richard. So, lie thou there;
For underneath an alehouse' paltry sign,
The Castle in Saint Albans, Somerset
Hath made the wizard famous in his death.
Sword, hold thy temper; heart, be wrathful still: 70
Priests pray for enemies, but princes kill.   *Exit.*

44 **Particularities** trifles   59 **As . . . did** Medea, fleeing with Jason
from Colchis, murdered her brother Absyrtus and cut the body into
pieces, so that her father would be delayed in his pursuit

Fight. Excursions.° Enter King, Queen,
and others.

Queen. Away, my lord! You are slow; for shame,
away!

King. Can we outrun the heavens? Good Margaret,
stay.

Queen. What are you made of? You'll nor fight nor
fly:
75   Now is it manhood, wisdom, and defense,
To give the enemy way, and to secure us
By what we can, which can no more but fly.

Alarum afar off.

If you be ta'en, we then should see the bottom
Of all our fortunes: but if we haply scape—
80   As well we may, if not through your neglect—
We shall to London get, where you are loved
And where this breach now in our fortunes made
May readily be stopped.

Enter [Young] Clifford.

Young Clifford. But that my heart's on future mischief
set,
85   I would speak blasphemy ere bid you fly:
But fly you must; uncurable discomfit°
Reigns in the hearts of all our present parts.
Away, for your relief, and we will live
To see their day and them our fortune give.
90   Away, my lord, away!   *Exeunt.*

71s.d. **Excursions** turbulent action   86 **discomfit** defeat

[Scene III. *Fields near Saint Albans.*]

Alarum. Retreat. Enter York, Richard, Warwick,
and Soldiers, with drum and colors.

York. Of Salisbury, who can report of him,
　　That winter lion, who in rage forgets
　　Agèd contusions and all brush of time,
　　And, like a gallant in the brow of youth,
　　Repairs him with occasion?° This happy day   5
　　Is not itself, nor have we won one foot,
　　If Salisbury be lost.

Richard.　　　　My noble father,
　　Three times today I holp° him to his horse,
　　Three times bestrid° him; thrice I led him off,
　　Persuaded him from any further act: 10
　　But still, where danger was, still there I met him;
　　And like rich hangings in a homely house,
　　So was his will in his old feeble body.
　　But, noble as he is,'look where he comes.

Enter Salisbury.

　　Now, by my sword, well hast thou fought today.   15

Salisbury. By th' mass, so did we all. I thank you,
　　　　Richard:
　　God knows how long it is I have to live,
　　And it hath pleased Him that three times today
　　You have defended me from imminent death.
　　Well, lords, we have not got that which we have:°   20
　　'Tis not enough our foes are this time fled,
　　Being opposites of such repairing nature.°

V.iii.5 **Repairs him with occasion** revives with opportunity　8 **holp**
helped　9 **bestrid** straddled (to defend)　20 **we have not got that**
which we have we have not secured what we have acquired　22 **re-**
pairing nature powers of recovery

157

York. I know our safety is to follow them;
For, as I hear, the King is fled to London,
To call a present court of Parliament.
Let us pursue him ere the writs go forth.
What says Lord Warwick? Shall we after them?

Warwick. After them! Nay, before them, if we can.
Now, by my hand, lords, 'twas a glorious day:
Saint Albans battle won by famous York
Shall be eternized in all age to come.
Sound drum and trumpets, and to London all:
And more such days as these to us befall!   *Exeunt.*

FINIS

Textual Note

In 1594 appeared an anonymous quarto (Q) entitled
"THE/First part of the Con-/tention betwixt the two
famous Houses of Yorke/and Lancaster, with the death
of the good/Duke Humphrey:/And the banishment and
death of the Duke of/*Suffolke*, and the Tragicall end of
the proud Cardinall/of *Winchester*, with the notable Rebel-
lion/of *Iacke Cade:/And the Duke of Yorkes first claime
unto the/Crowne*," consisting of some 2200 lines which
parallel closely and occasionally match the 1623 Folio
(F) text of *2 Henry VI*. Considered as an independent
play, Q is shorter, cruder, and vastly inferior in language
and characterization to F, but its relationship to the "finished" work offers an interesting problem. As early as
1734 it was theorized, by Lewis Theobald, that Q represents a primitive version of the play later revised by
Shakespeare and published. In 1787 Edmond Malone,
taking Greene's famous slur on the "upstart crow" (see
Prefatory Remarks, pp. viii–ix) to imply plagiarism on
Shakespeare's part, suggested that Greene, and Peele, or
possibly (1821) Marlowe, were the original authors of
The Contention and its companion piece, *The True Tragedie of Richard Duke of Yorke* (1595), which bears a
similar relation to *3 Henry VI*.

In the late 1920's, however, with the studies of Peter
Alexander (*Shakespeare's Henry VI and Richard III*,
1929) and Madeleine Doran (*Henry VI*, 1928), a different explanation was advanced: that Q is actually a
mutilated and wholly derivative "bad" version of the

"good" text preserved in the Folio; that it derives, like many other unauthorized Elizabethan quartos, from a memorial reconstruction of the acted play—possibly by the bit-player who took the parts of the Armorer, the Spirit, the Mayor, Vaux, and Scales. In support of this explanation it has been shown that Q contains frequent echoes of unrelated contemporary plays such as Marlowe's *Edward II,* and *Arden of Feversham,* as if the "reporter" who furnished the copy to the typesetter were fleshing out what he had memorized imperfectly with scraps of the rest of his repertory. The F text is relatively free of such contaminations.

Some modern scholars (Feuillerat, Prouty, J. D. Wilson) argue for a return to the "revision" theory, but the consensus opposes them. Good summaries of the conflicting evidence, and a discussion of the complications compounded by the third quarto (1619) of *The Contention,* may be found in G. B. Evans' review of Prouty's *The Contention and Shakespeare's '2 Henry VI'* (*JEGP,* LIII [1954], 628–37) and J. G. McManaway, "*The Contention* and *2 Henry VI,*" *Wiener Beiträge zur Englischen Philologie,* LXV (1957), 143–154.

As a "bad" quarto, the textual utility of Q is slight, except in its stage directions, which are frequently fuller than those of F (e.g., I. i. 52 s.d., which occurs only in Q). In some passages, however (e.g., II. i. 125 ff., II. iii. 58 s.d. ff.) the F editors appear to have used slices of Q as printer's copy, possibly when the holograph script they employed primarily was defective or illegible; and in such instances the F text is likely to be mediocre, or misaligned (I. i. 64–65), and Q readings may be preferable. Basically the copy for F seems to have been an author's manuscript or "foul papers," but there is evidence as well of a theatrical bookkeeper's interpolations and cuts.

This edition follows F except where indicated in the following; stage directions derived from Q are so designated. Editorial additions are set off in square brackets; spelling, punctuation, and capitalization have been modernized; and names in speech prefixes and stage directions (e.g., Duke Humphrey *alias* Gloucester, Winchester *alias*

Beaufort *alias* Cardinal) regularized. In a few instances
verse has been slightly rearranged. The following list of
significant departures from F gives the reading of the
present text in italics, followed by a bracketed [Q] if the
quarto provides the reading, and the F text, *literatim*, in
roman.

I.i. s.d. *Enter . . . Warwick* [Q] Enter King, Duke Humfrey, Salisbury, Warwicke, and Beauford on the one side. The Queene, Suffolke, Yorke, Somerset, and Buckingham, on the other 52 s.d.
[Q] F omits 58 duchies [Q gives "Duches"] Dutchesse 64-65
create thee/First [Q] create thee the first 74 s.d. *Gloucester . . .
rest* [Q] Manet the rest 93 *had* hath 178 *Protector* [Q] Protectors
251 *surfeit in the* surfetting in 256 *in* [Q] in in

I.ii.60 s.d. follows line 59 [F, Q] 69 s.d. *Hum* [Q and chronicles]
Hume

I.iii.13 *For* To 31 *That my master was?* That my Mistresse was?
32 *usurer* Vsurper 33-34 [Q] F omits 102 s.d. *sound* Exit. Sound
102 s.d. *Enter . . . Winchester* [Q] Enter the King, Duke Humfrey,
Cardinall, Buckingham, Yorke, Salisbury, Warwicke, and the
Duchesse 144 *I'd* [Q] I could 152 *fury* Fume

I.iv.25 *Asnath* Asmath 36-38 Q prints as prose; probably a corruption of original octosyllabic couplets 41 s.d. *He sinks down
again* [Q] Exit Spirit 53 s.d. [Q] F omits 62-63 *Aio . . . posse* Aio
Aeacida Romanos vincere posso 70-71 *hard . . . understood* [Hib-
bard conj.] hardly attain'd,/And hardly vnderstood

II.i. s.d. *with a hawk on her fist* [Q] F omits 25-26 *Good uncle,
can you dote,/To hide such malice with such holiness?* [Cairncross
conj.] Good Vnkle hide such mallice:/With such Holynesse can you
doe it? 30 *Lord-Protectorship* Lords Protectorship 39-40 between these lines Q inserts the following: "*Humphrey*. Dare. I tell
thee Priest, Plantagenets could neuer brooke the dare./*Card*. I am
Plantagenet as well as thou, and sonne to Iohn of Gaunt./*Humph*.
In Bastardie./*Cardin*. I scorne thy words" 46-48 F gives all these
lines to Gloucester 71 *by sight* by his sight 91 *Simpcox* Symon
107 *Alban* Albones 125-33 Q gives as prose; F, following the
text of Q, aligns haphazardly as verse 132 *his* [Q] it 140-51 here
F again follows the Q copy, which is aligned roughly as verse, yet
prints these lines as prose. Probably they were verse originally, but
so corrupt now that no plausible restoration of arrangement can be
attempted

II.ii.35 *Philippa* Phillip 47 *son, the son* Sonnes Sonne 50 *Philippa*
Phillip

II.iii.s.d. *Enter . . . Warwick* [Q] Enter the King and State, with
Guard, to banish the Duchesse   3 *sins* sinne   66 *i'faith I'll* [Q]
yfaith, and Ile   69 *afeared* [Q] afraid   70–72 *Second Prentice . . .
a quart for me* [Q] F omits; and as F provides only two prentices,
Second Prentice speaks the line here given to Third Prentice   75–77
I thank . . . my apron [Q] I thanke you all: drinke, and pray for me,
I pray you, for I thinke I haue taken my last Draught in this World.
Here *Robin*, and if I dye, I giue thee my Aporne; and *Will*, thou shalt
haue my Hammer   87–92 *Here's . . . Ascapart* [Q] Masters, I am
come hither as it were vpon my Mans instigation, to proue him a
Knaue, and my selfe an honest man: and touching the Duke of
Yorke, I will take my death, I neuer meant him any ill, nor the King,
nor the Queene: and therefore *Peter* haue at thee with a downe-right
blow   95 s.d. [Q] F omits

II.iv.16 s.d. *Enter . . . halberds* [Q] Enter the Duchesse in a white
Sheet, and a Taper burning in her hand, with the Sherife and Officers
73 s.d. [Q] F omits

III.i.222 s.d. *Exit . . . Warwick* [Q] Exit

III.ii. s.d. *Enter . . . Gloucester* [F] Here Q actually stages the murder on the inner stage, where Gloucester's body, concealed by curtains, remains throughout the scene: "Then the Curtaines being
drawne, Duke *Humphrey* is discouered in his bed, and two men
lying on his brest and smothering him in his bed. And then enter the
Duke of *Suffolke* to them." But the F stage directions here, and at
III.ii.148 below, appear to intend eliminating this use of the inner
stage: thus "Bed put forth" rather than "*Warwicke* drawes the curtaines and showes Duke *Humphrey* in his bed," and the lines of ex-
planatory dialogue (III.ii.1–4) not found in Q. The Q staging, however, seems more efficient and theatrical, and has been partially retained in this text   14 s.d. *Buckingham* [Q] Suffolke   26 *Meg* Nell
79 *Margaret* Elianor   100 *Margaret* Elianor   116 *witch* watch
120 *Margaret* Elinor   121 s.d. *Salisbury* [Q] F omits   148 s.d. *Warwick . . . bed* [Q] Bed put forth [following line 146 in F]   202 s.d.
Exit Cardinal [Q] F omits   265 *whe'r* where   288 s.d. *Exit Salisbury* [Q] F omits   299 *Exit . . . Suffolk* [Q] Exit   366 *to* no   409
s.d. *She kisseth him* [Q] F omits   413 s.d. *Exit Suffolk . . . Exit
Queen* [Q] Exeunt [follows 413 in F]

III.iii. s.d. *and then . . . mad* [Q] to the Cardinal in bed [for the dis-
crepancy compare III.ii. s.d. above]   10 *whe'r* [Q whether] where
28 s.d. *The Cardinal dies* [Q] F omits

IV.i. s.d. *And then . . . Whitmore* [Q with emendation from "Cap-
taine" to "Lieutenant"] Enter Lieutenant, Suffolke, and others   6
Clip Cleape   48 *Jove . . . I* [Q] F omits   50 *Obscure . . . blood* F
assigns this line to the Lieutenant; Q to Suffolk   70 *Poole . . . Poole*

[Q] Lieu[tenant]. Poole, Sir Poole? Lord   77 *shalt* shall   86
mother's bleeding Mother-bleeding   94 *are* and   114 *Ay . . . soon*
[Q] F omits   117 *Whitmore* Lieu. Water: W   118 *Pene* Pine   133
Come . . . can F assigns to the Lieutenant

IV.ii.35 *fall* faile   83 *Chatham* [Q Chattam] Chartam   100 *an* a

IV.iv.24 *wouldest* would'st   58 *be betrayed* betraid

IV.v.2–6 *No . . . rebels* F and Q print as verse

IV.vi.s.d. *sword* [Q] staffe   9 *Smith* But[cher] [i.e., Dick]

IV.vii.26 *serge* Surge   49 *on* [Q] in   72 *But* Kent   91 *caudle*
Candle

IV.viii.13 *rebel* rabble   66s.d. *He . . . away* [Q] Exit

IV.ix.33 *calmed* calme

IV.x.21 *waning* warning   27 *Ah* a   60 *God* [Q] Ioue   61s.d. *They
. . . down* [Q] Heere they Fight

V.i.109 *these* thee   111 *sons* sonne   113 *for* of   122s.d. *and his
son* [Q] F omits   124s.d. *(Kneels to Henry.)* [Q] F omits   194 *or*
and

V.ii.27s.d. *Alarums . . . Clifford* [Q] F omits   28 *œuvres* eumenes
30s.d. *Exit York* [Q] F omits   65s.d. *Exit . . . father* [Q] F omits
65s.d. *Enter Somerset . . . Albans* [Q] Enter Richard, and Somerset
to fight   71s.d. *Exit* [Q] F omits

V.iii.15 *Now . . . today* F assigns to Salisbury

The Date and the Sources of
Henry VI, Part Two

The Date. Despite the consecutive titles provided by the Folio editors for *Henry VI*, Parts One, Two and Three, it is probable that Parts Two and Three originally constituted a two-part play, and that Part One had an independent conception and existence in the contemporary repertory. Early quartos (See the Textual Note) designated Part Two *The First Part of the Contention between the Two Famous Houses of York and Lancaster*, and Part Three *The True Tragedy of Richard, Duke of York;* and subsequently a piratical quarto of 1619 combined the two (still ignoring Part One) as *The Whole Contention*.

Scholarly opinion, however, is divided on the question of precedence: did the composition proceed chronologically, with Part One first, followed by a double play on subsequent events, or was Part One, with its emphasis on action and adventure, worked up *after* Parts Two–Three, to capitalize upon their evident popularity? Certain inconsistencies of plot and characterization suggest, if anything, the latter alternative—much as *The First Part of Jeronimo*, or "Spain's Comedy," evidently postdated the immensely popular *Spanish Tragedy* of Thomas Kyd—but all we can be moderately sure of is that the three parts do not constitute an intentional trilogy. And as it is not certain that Part One preceded the two-part play, we can accept as established that *2 Henry VI* is the earliest defi-

nitely datable play of Shakespeare, and as such, a monument of precocious accomplishment.

Because of Robert Greene's attack (September, 1592)
on the new actor-playwright Shakespeare (Prefatory Remarks, pp. viii–ix), playing on a phrase of *3 Henry VI*,
and our knowledge of a plague inhibition during the summer, we can date the composition and performance of
Parts Two–Three earlier than June 23, 1592. The publication of the second edition of Holinshed's *Chronicles* (1587)
may provide an early limit of date; but apparent echoes
of Part Three in an especially allusive history play, *The
Troublesome Reign of King John* (published 1591), tend
to set back the date of Parts Two–Three to 1591 or 1590
or even earlier. Hence, whether Part One or Parts Two–
Three are what Henslowe terms "harey the vi" in March,
1592, has little effect on our dating-estimate of Parts
Two–Three; 1590–91 is a good enough guess, and possibly
thus renders *2 Henry VI* the earliest known "modern"
play concerned primarily with English history.

The Sources. Shakespeare's main source appears to
have been either the York-Lancaster chronicle of Edward
Hall (1542; 1548; 1550), or of Hall's publisher Richard
Grafton (*A Chronicle at Large*, 1569), which are often
indistinguishable, due to Grafton's cheerful and exten-
sive plagiarism of his predecessors. Raphael Holinshed's
Chronicles (2nd ed., 1587), which Shakespeare certainly
knew, may also have contributed some supplementary
matter, or transmitted portions of Hall's text (for like
Grafton, Holinshed borrowed liberally: compare the passages cited by Brockbank, in the Commentaries, from
Holinshed, with the originals, given below, from Hall).
The story of Simpcox appears first in Sir Thomas More's
Dialogue . . . of the Veneration and Worship of Images
(1529), subsequently in Grafton, but is also to be found
in the extremely popular *Acts and Monuments* of the
martyrologist John Foxe (1563; 1570; 1576; 1583;
quoted here from the 1583 edition). Traces of Robert
Fabyan's *Chronicle* (1516 *et seq.*), the versified *Mirror*

for Magistrates (1559 ed., for the death of Suffolk), and John Hardyng's verse *Chronicle* (1543, another of Grafton's "sources") may or may not be indentifiable in Shakespeare's text; but the primary original, in one form or another, remains Hall (see Lucille King, "The Use of Hall's Chronicles in the Folio and Quarto Texts of *Henry VI*," *Philological Quarterly*, XIII [1934], 321–32).

A most interesting analogue to the Cade scenes is found in the supposedly Shakespearean revision of Anthony Munday's *Sir Thomas More* [?1593–?1601], a play surviving only in manuscript, crabbed and partially defective, and unpublished until 1844. The passage reproduced below in modernized English (following W. W. Greg, ed., *The Book of Sir Thomas More* [London: The Malone Society, 1911]) has frequently been ascribed to Shakespeare on stylistic and paleographic grounds, many scholars considering this scrap of manuscript to be holograph, and the only extant specimen, thus, save signatures, of Shakespeare's own handwriting. (For a summary of the controversy, see R. C. Bald, *"The Booke of Sir Thomas More* and its Problems," *Shakespeare Survey 2* [1949], pp. 44–61.) Only in the Cade sequence of *2 Henry VI* and in *Sir Thomas More*, if indeed both are his work, did Shakespeare treat at large the issues raised by popular insurrection—a most ticklish subject for any playwright to explore (as the heavy censorship of *More* testifies), and one most topical in the disturbed early 1590's. The political point of view, at once conservative and considerate, inherent in More's pacification of the unruly mob and in the Cade episodes of *Henry VI* seems suggestively consistent.

EDWARD HALL

from *The Union of the Two Noble and Illustre Families of Lancaster and York*

[Despite the Duke of Gloucester's accusations against Cardinal Beaufort] the matter was winked at, and dallied out, and nothing said to it. . . . [Thereafter] divers secret attempts were advanced forward this season [1440] against the noble Duke Humphrey of Gloucester, afar off, which in conclusion came so near, they bereft him both life and land. . . . For first this year, Dame Eleanor Cobham, wife to the said Duke, was accused of treason, for that she, by sorcery and enchantment, intended to destroy the King, to th' intent to advance and to promote her husband to the crown: upon this she was examined in Saint Stephen's Chapel before the Bishop of Canterbury, and there by examination convict and judged, to do open penance in three open places within the city of London, and after that adjudged to perpetual prison in the Isle of Man, under the keeping of Sir John Stanley, Knight. At the same season were arrested as aiders and counselors to the said Duchess Thomas Southwell, priest and canon of Saint Stephen's in Westminster, John Hum, priest, Roger Bolingbroke, a cunning necromancer, and Margery Jourdain, surnamed the Witch of Eye, to

whose charge it was laid that they, at the request of the
Duchess, had devised an image of wax representing the
King, which by their sorcery a little and little consumed,
intending thereby in conclusion to waste and destroy the
King's person, and so bring him to death; for the which
treason they were adjudged to die, and so Margery
Jourdain was brent in Smithfield, and Roger Bolingbroke was drawn and quartered at Tyburn, taking upon
his death that there was never no such thing by them
imagined; John Hum had his pardon, and Southwell
died in the Tower before execution. The Duke of
Gloucester took all these things patiently, and said
little. . . .

[Suffolk and other English noblemen] came to the
city of Tours in Touraine, where they were honorably
received, both of the French King, and of the King of
Sicil. Where the Marquess of Suffolk, as procurator to
King Henry, espoused the said lady in the church of Saint
Martin's. At which marriage were present the father and
mother of the bride, the French King himself, which
was uncle to the husband, and the French Queen also,
which was aunt to the wife; there were also the Dukes of
Orleans, of Calaber, of Alençon, and of Bretagne, seven
earls, twelve barons, twenty bishops, beside knights and
gentlemen. There were triumphant jousts, costly feasts,
and delicate banquets; but all pleasure hath an end, and
every joy is not continual: so that after these high
solemnities finished, and these honorable ceremonies
ended, the Marquess had the Lady Margaret to him delivered, which in great estate he conveyed through Normandy to Dieppe, and so transported her into England,
where she landed at Portsmouth in the month of April
[1445]. This woman excelled all other, as well in beauty
and favor as in wit and policy, and was in stomach and
courage more like to a man than a woman. Soon after
her arrival she was conveyed to the town of Southwick
in Hampshire, where she with all nuptial ceremonies was
coupled in matrimony to King Henry the sixth of that
name. After which marriage she was with great triumph
conveyed to London, and so to Westminster, where,

upon the thirtieth day of May, she with all solemnity thereunto appertaining, was crowned Queen of this noble realm of England. . . .

This marriage seemed to many both infortunate and unprofitable to the realm of England, and that for many causes. First, the King with her had not one penny, and for the fetching of her the Marquess of Suffolk demanded a whole fifteen, in open Parliament; also, for her marriage the Duchy of Anjou, the city of Mans, and the whole country of Maine were delivered and released to King Regnier her father, which countries were the very stays and backstands to the Duchy of Normandy. Furthermore, for this marriage the Earl of Armagnac took such great displeasure that he became utter enemy to the realm of England, and was the chief cause that the Englishmen were expulsed out of the whole Duchy of Aquitaine, and lost both the countries of Gascoigne and Guyenne. But most of all, it should seem that God with this matrimony was not content. For after this spousage the King's friends fell from him, both in England and in France, the lords of his realm fell in division amongst themselves, the commons rebelled against their sovereign lord and natural prince, fields [i.e. battles] were foughten, many thousand slain, and finally the King deposed, and his son slain, and this queen sent home again with as much misery and sorrow as she was received with pomp and triumph. . . .

[Fearing a new outbreak in France] the King called his high court of Parliament, in the which above all things it was concluded diligently to foresee that Normandy should be well furnished and strongly defended, before the term of the truce should be expired: for it was openly known that the French King was ready in all things to make open war, if no peace or abstinence of war were agreed or concluded. For which consideration money was granted, men were appointed, and a great army gathered together; and the Duke of Somerset was appointed Regent of Normandy, and the Duke of York thereof discharged. . . .

This year [1446] an armorer's servant of London ap-

pealed his master of treason, which offered to be tried
by battle. At the day assigned, the friends of the master
brought him malmsey and *aqua vitae* to comfort him
withal; but it was the cause of his and their discomfort:
for he poured in so much that when he came into the
place in Smithfield where he should fight, both his wit
and strength failed him; and so he, being a tall and a
hardy personage, overladed with hot drinks, was vanquished of his servant, being but a coward and a wretch;
whose body was drawn to Tyburn, and there hanged
and beheaded.

During the time of this truce or abstinence of war,
while there was nothing to vex or trouble the minds of
men, within the realm a sudden mischief and a long
discord sprang out suddenly, by the means of a woman:
for King Henry, which reigned at this time, was a man
of a meek spirit and of a simple wit, preferring peace
before war, rest before business, honesty before profit,
and quietness before labor. And to the intent that all
men might perceive that there could be none more
chaste, more meek, more holy, nor a better creature, in
him reigned shamefastness, modesty, integrity, and patience to be marveled at, taking and suffering all losses,
chances, displeasures, and such worldly torments in good
part and with a patient manner, as though they had
chanced by his own fault or negligent oversight. Yet he
was governed of them whom he should have ruled, and
bridled of such whom he sharply should have spurred.
He gaped not for honor, nor thirsted for riches, but
studied only for the health of his soul, the saving whereof
he esteemed to be the greatest wisdom, and the loss
thereof the extremest folly that could be. But on the
other part, the Queen his wife was a woman of great
wit, and yet of no greater wit than of haught stomach,
desirous of glory and covetous of honor, and of reason,
policy, counsel, and other gifts and talents of nature
belonging to a man, full and flowing; of wit and wiliness
she lacked nothing, nor of diligence, study, and business
she was not unexpert; but she had one point of a very
woman: for often time, when she was vehement and

fully bent in a matter, she was suddenly like a weather-
cock mutable and turning. This woman, perceiving that
her husband did not frankly rule as he would, but did
all thing by th' advice and counsel of Humphrey, Duke
of Gloucester, and that he passed not much on the
authority and governance of the realm, determined with
herself to take upon her the rule and regiment both of
the King and his kingdom, and to deprive and evict out
of all rule and authority the said Duke, then called the
Lord Protector of the realm; lest men should say and
report that she had neither wit nor stomach, which would
permit and suffer her husband, being of perfect age and
man's estate, like a young scholar or innocent pupil to
be governed by the disposition of another man. This
manly woman, this courageous queen ceased not to
prosecute forthwith her invented imagination and pre-
pensed purpose, but practiced daily the furtherance of
the same. And although this invention first came of her
own high mind and ambitious courage, yet it was furthered and set forward by such as of long time had
borne malice to the Duke for declaring their untruth,
as you before have heard. Which venomous serpents and
malicious tigers persuaded, incensed, and exhorted the
Queen to look well upon the expenses and revenues of
the realm, and thereof to call an accompt: affirming
plainly that she should evidently perceive that the Duke
of Gloucester had not so much advanced and preferred
the commonwealth and public utility, as his own private
things and peculiar estate. . . .

The Queen, persuaded and encouraged by these means
. . . excluded the Duke of Gloucester from all rule and
governance, not prohibiting such as she knew to be his
mortal enemies to invent and imagine causes and griefs
against him, of the which divers writers affirm the
Marquess of Suffolk and the Duke of Buckingham to
be the chief, not unprocured by the Cardinal of Winchester, and the Archbishop of York. Divers articles
both heinous and odious were laid to his charge in open
council, and in especial one, that he had caused men
adjudged to die to be put to other execution than the

law of the land had ordered or assigned: for surely the
Duke, being very well learned in the law civil, detesting
malefactors and punishing their offenses, gat great malice
and hatred of such as feared to have condign reward for
their ungracious acts and mischievous doings. Although
the Duke, not without great laud and praise, sufficiently
answered to all things to him objected, yet because his
death was determined, his wisdom little helped, nor his
truth smally availed: but of this unquietness of mind he
delivered himself, because he neither thought of death,
nor of condemnation to die, such affiance had he in
his strong truth, and such confidence had he in indifferent justice. But his capital enemies and mortal foes,
fearing that some tumult and commotion might arise if
a prince so well beloved of the people should be openly
executed and put to death, determined to trap and undo
him, or [i.e., ere] he thereof should have knowledge or
warning. So, for the furtherance of their purpose, a Parliament was summoned to be kept at Bury, whither resorted all the peers of the realm, and amongst them the
Duke of Gloucester, which on the second day of the session was, by the lord Beaumont, then High Constable
of England, accompanied by the Duke of Buckingham,
and other, arrested, apprehended, and put in ward, and
all his servants sequestered from him; and thirty-two of
the chief of his retinue were sent to diverse prisons, to
the great admiration [i.e., astonishment] of the common people. The Duke, the night after his imprisonment,
was found dead in his bed, and his body showed to the
lords and commons as though he had died of a palsy
or impostume [i.e., festering abscess]: but all indifferent
persons well knew that he died of no natural death, but
of some violent force. Some judged him to be strangled;
some affirm that a hot spit was put in at his fundament;
other write that he was stifled or smoldered between
two featherbeds. After whose death, none of his servants
(although they were arraigned and attainted) were put
to death: for the Marquess of Suffolk, when they should
have been executed, showed openly their pardon; but
this doing appeased not the grudge of the people, which

said that the pardon of the servants was no amends for murdering of their master.

[In 1448, at Queen Margaret's prompting, Suffolk was made a Duke. York now began to declare himself] After the deposition or rather the destruction of the good Duke of Gloucester, and the exaltation and advancement of this glorious [i.e., vainglorious] man, Richard Duke of York, being greatly allied by his wife to the chief peers and potentates of the realm, over and beside his own progeny and great consanguinity, perceiving the King to be a ruler not ruling, and the whole burden of the realm to depend in the ordinances of the Queen and the Duke of Suffolk, began secretly to allure to his friends of the nobility, and privately declared to them his title and right to the crown. . . .

During these doings, Henry Beaufort, Bishop of Winchester, and called "the rich Cardinal," departed out of this world, and was buried at Winchester. This man was son to John of Gaunt, Duke of Lancaster, descended of an honorable lineage, but born in baste [i.e., bastardy]; more noble of blood than notable in learning, haught in stomach and high in countenance, rich above measure of all men, and to few liberal, disdainful to his kin and dreadful to his lovers, preferring money before friendship, many things beginning and none performing. His covetous [i.e., covetousness] insatiable and hope of long life made him both to forget God, his prince, and himself, in his latter days: for Doctor John Baker, his privy counselor and his chaplain, wrote that he, lying on his death bed, said these words: "Why should I die, having so much riches? If the whole realm would save my life, I am able either by policy to get it, or by riches to buy it. Fie, will not Death be hired, nor will money do nothing? When my nephew of Bedford died, I thought myself half up the wheel; but when I saw mine other nephew of Gloucester deceased, then I thought myself to be equal with kings, and so thought to increase my treasure in hope to have worn a triple crown. But I see now the world faileth me, and so I am deceived; praying you all to pray for me" . . . .

[Rumors of discord among the English nobility prompted new outbreaks in Normandy and Gascony] It was not enough, the realm of England this season thus to be vexed and unquieted with the business of Normandy, but also a new rebellion began in Ireland, to the great displeasure of the King and his Council: for repressing whereof, Richard Duke of York, with a convenient number of men, was sent thither as lieutenant to the King, which not only appeased the fury of the wild and savage people there, but also gat him such love and favor of the country and the inhabitants that their sincere love and friendly affection could never be separated from him and his lineage. . . .

[Meanwhile (July, 1450) the Duke of Somerset in Normandy] partly to please the townsmen [of Caen], but more desirous to please the Duchess his wife, made an agreement with the French King that he would render the town, so that he and all his might depart in safeguard with all their goods and substance: which offer the French King gladly accepted and allowed, knowing that by force he might lenger have longed for the strong town than to have possessed the same so soon. After this conclusion taken, Sir Davy Hall, with diverse other of his trusty friends, departed to Cherburg, and from thence sailed into Ireland to the Duke of York, making relation to him of all these doings: which thing kindled so great a rancor in his heart and stomach that he never left persecuting of the Duke of Somerset till he had brought him to his fatal point, and extreme confusion. . . .

[Finally all Normandy was lost to the French. Some allege that during the struggle] the Duke of Somerset, for his own peculiar profit, kept not half his number of soldiers, and put their wages in his purse. These be men's imaginations and conjectures, but surely the loss of it was the domestical division within the realm, every great man desiring rather to be revenged on his foe at home than on his outward enemy. . . .

For while these conquests were obtained in the parts beyond the sea with sword, spear, and target, by the adversaries of the Englishmen, three mischievous captains

[i.e., "inward grudge," "adulation," and "disdain of lascivious sovereignty"] set the people of the realm (as well
of the nobility, as of the mean sort) in a civil war and
intestine division. . . . [They] began to make exclamation
against the Duke of Suffolk, affirming him to be the only
cause of the delivery of Anjou and Maine, the chief pro-
curer of the death of the good Duke of Gloucester, the
very occasion of the loss of Normandy, the most swallower-
up and consumer of the King's treasure (by reason whereof,
the wars in France were not maintained), the expeller
from the King of all good and virtuous counselors, and
the bringer-in and advancer of· vicious persons, common
enemies, and apparent adversaries to the public wealth:
so that the Duke was called in every man's mouth a traitor,
a murderer, a robber of the King's treasure, and worthy
to be put to most cruel punishment. . . .

[Suffolk was imprisoned in the Tower, but soon released.
Whereupon, at the next Parliament] the commons of the
lower house, not forgetting their old grudge, beseeched
the King that such persons as assented to the release of
Anjou and deliverance of Maine might be extremely punished and tormented: and to be privy to this face, they
accused as principal the Duke of Suffolk, with John,
Bishop of Salisbury, and Sir James Fynes, Lord Say, and
divers other. When King Henry perceived that the commons were thus·stomached and bent against the Queen's
darling William Duke of Suffolk, he plainly saw that
neither glozing would serve, nor dissimulation could appease the continual clamor of the importunate commons:
wherefore, to begin a short pacification in so long a broil,
first he sequestered the Lord Say, being Treasurer of
England, and other the Duke's adherents, from their
offices and authority, and after banished and put in exile
the Duke of Suffolk, as the abhorred toad and common
nuisance of the realm of England, for the term of five
years: meaning by this exile to appease the furious rage
of the outrageous [i.e., outraged] people; and, that pacified, to revocate him into his old estate, as the Queen's
chief friend and counselor. But fortune would not that
this flagitious person should so escape: for when he shipped

in Suffolk, intending to be transported into France, he was encountered with a ship of war appertaining to the Duke of Exeter, the Constable of the Tower in London, called Nicholas of the Tower. The captain of the same bark with small fight entered into the Duke's ship, and perceiving his person present, brought him to Dover Road, and there, on the one side of a cockboat, caused his head to be stricken off, and left his body with the head upon the sands of Dover; which corse was there found by a chaplain of his, and conveyed to Wingfield College in Suffolk, and there buried. This end had William de la Pole, first Duke of Suffolk, as men judge by God's punishment: for above all things he was noted to be the very organ, engine, and devisor of the destruction of Humphrey, the good Duke of Gloucester, and so the blood of the innocent man was with his dolorous death recompensed and punished. . . .

[Meanwhile, from Ireland, York had set in motion many conspiracies] and to set open the flood-gates of these devices, it was thought necessary to cause some great commotion and rising of the people to be made against the King: so that if they prevailed, then had the Duke of York and his complices their appetite and desire. And because the Kentishmen be impatient in wrongs, disdaining of too much oppression, and ever desirous of new change and newfangleness, the overture of this matter was put forth first in Kent. And to th' intent that it should not be known that the Duke of York or his friends were the cause of the sudden rising, a certain youngman of a goodly stature and pregnant wit was enticed to take upon him the name of John Mortimer, although his name were John Cade—and not for a small policy, thinking that by that surname the line and lineage of the assistant house of the Earl of March, which were no small number, should be to him both adherent and favorable. This captain, not only suborned by teachers but also enforced by privy schoolmasters, assembled together a great company of tall [i.e., brave] personages, assuring them that their attempt was both honorable to God and the King, and also profitable to the commonwealth; promising them that if either by force or by policy they might once take the King, the Queen, and other their counselors into their hands and governance, that they would honorably entreat [i.e., deal with] the King, and so sharply handle his counselors that neither fifteens should hereafter be demanded, nor once any impositions or tax should be spoken of. These persuasions, with many other fair promises of liberty (which the common people more affect and desire, rather than reasonable obedience and due conformity) so animated the Kentish people that they, with their captain above named, in good order of battle (not in great number) came to the plain of Blackheath, between Eltham and Greenwich. . . . Whereupon the King assembled a great army, and marched toward them. . . .

The subtle captain named Jack Cade, intending to bring the King farther within the compass of his net, brake up his camp and retired backward to the town of Sevenoaks in Kent, and there, expecting his prey, encamped himself and made his abode. The Queen, which bare the rule, being of his retreat well advertised, sent Sir Humphrey Stafford, Knight, and William his brother, with many other gentlemen, to follow the chase of the Kentishmen, thinking that they had fled; but verily they were deceived: for at the first skirmish both the Staffords were slain, and all their company shamefully discomfited. . . .

When the Kentish captain, or the covetous Cade, had thus obtained victory and slain the two valiant Staffords, he appareled himself in their rich armor, and so with pomp and glory returned again toward London: in which retreat divers idle and vagabond persons resorted to him from Sussex and Surrey, and from other parts, to a great number. Thus this glorious captain, compassed about and environed with a multitude of evil, rude, and rustical persons, came again to the plain of Blackheath, and there strongly encamped himself; to whom were sent by the King the Archbishop of Canterbury and Humphrey, Duke of Buckingham, to commune with him of his griefs and requests. These lords found him sober in communication, wise in disputing, arrogant in heart, and stiff in his opinion, and by no ways possible to be persuaded to dissolve his

army, except the King in person would come to him and
assent to all things which he should require. These lords,
perceiving the willful pertinacy and manifest contumacy
of this rebellious javelin, departed to the King, declaring
to him his temerarious and rash words and presumptuous
requests. The King somewhat hearing and more marking
the sayings of this outrageous losel [i.e., scoundrel], and
having daily report of the concourse and access of people
which continually resorted to him, doubting as much his
familiar servants as his unknown subjects (which spared
not to speak that the Captain's cause was profitable for
the commonwealth), departed in all haste to the Castle
of Killingworth in Warwickshire, leaving only behind him
the Lord Scales, to keep the Tower of London. The Captain, being advertised of the King's absence, came first
into Southwark, and there lodged at the White Hart, prohibiting to all men murder, rape, or robbery; by which
color he allured to him the hearts of the common people.
But after that he entered into London, and cut the ropes
of the drawbridge, striking his sword on London Stone,
saying, "Now is Mortimer lord of this city," and rode in
every street like a lordly captain. And after a flattering
declaration made to the Mayor of the city of his thither
coming, he departed again into Southwark. And upon the
third day of July he caused Sir James Fynes, Lord Say,
and Treasurer of England, to be brought to the Guildhall
of London and there to be arraigned: which, being before
the King's justices put to answer, desired to be tried by
his peers, for the longer delay of his life. The Captain,
perceiving his dilatory plea, by force took him from the
officers and brought him to the Standard in Cheap, and
there, before his confession ended, caused his head to be
cut off and pitched it on a high pole, which was openly
borne before him through the streets. And this cruel tyrant,
not content with the murder of the Lord Say, went to Mile
End and there apprehended Sir James Cromer, then shrieve
of Kent, and son-in-law to the said Lord Say, and him,
without confession or excuse heard, caused there likewise to be headed and his head to be fixed on a pole;
and with these two heads this bloody butcher entered into

the city again, and in despite caused them in every street kiss together, to the great detestation of all the beholders. . . .

He also put to execution in Southwark divers persons, some for infringing his rules and precepts, because he would be seen indifferent; other he tormented of his old acquaintance, lest they should blaze and declare his base birth and lousy lineage, disparaging him from his usurped surname of Mortimer, for the which he thought and doubted not both to have friends aud fautors [i.e., partisans] both in London, Kent, and Essex. The wise mayor and sage magistrates of the city of London, perceiving themselves neither to be sure of goods, nor of life well warranted, determined with fear to repell and expulse this mischievous head and his ungracious company. And because Lord Scales was ordained Keeper of the Tower, with Matthew Gough, the often-named captain in Normandy (as you have heard before), they purposed to make them privy both of their intent and enterprise. The Lord Scales promised them his aid, and Matthew Gough was by him appointed to assist the Mayor and the Londoners, because he was both of manhood and experience greatly renowned and noised. So the captains of the city appointed took upon them in the night to keep the Bridge of London, prohibiting the Kentishmen either to pass or approach. The rebels, which never soundly slept, for fear of sudden chances, hearing the Bridge to be kept and manned, ran with great haste to open their passage, where between both parts was a fierce and cruel encounter. Matthew Gough, more expert in martial feats than the other chieftains of the city, perceiving the Kentishmen better to stand to their tackling than his imagination expected, advised his company no further to proceed toward Southwark till the day appeared, to the intent that the citizens, hearing where the place of the jeopardy rested, might occur [i.e., encounter] their enemies, and relieve their friends and companions. But this counsel came to small effect: for the multitude of the rebels drave the citizens from the stoops [i.e., posts] at the bridge foot to the drawbridge, and began to set fire in divers houses. Alas, what sorrow it was to

behold that miserable chance: for some, desiring to eschew
the fire, leapt on his enemy's weapon, and so died; fearful
women, with children in their arms, amazed and appalled,
leapt into the river; other, doubting how to save themself
between fire, water, and sword, were in their houses suffocate and smoldered. Yet the captains, nothing regarding
these chances, fought on the drawbridge all the night
valiantly, but, in conclusion, the rebels gat the drawbridge,
and drowned many, and slew John Sutton, Alderman,
and Robert Heysand, a hardy citizen, with many other,
beside Matthew Gough, a man of great wit, much experience in feats of chivalry, the which in continual wars had
valiantly served the King and his father in the parts beyond the sea. . . . This hard and sore conflict endured
on the bridge till nine of the clock in the morning in doubtful chance, and fortune's balance; for some time the Londoners were beat back to the stoops at Saint Magnus'
Corner, and suddenly again the rebels were repulsed and
driven back to the stoops in Southwark, so that both parts,
being faint, weary, and fatigate, agreed to desist from fight,
and to leave battle till the next day, upon condition that
neither Londoners should pass into Southwark, nor Kentishmen into London.

After this abstinence of war agreed, the lusty Kentish
captain, hoping on more friends, brake up the jails of the
King's Bench and Marshalsea, and set at liberty a swarm
of gallants both meet for his service and apt for his enterprise. The Archbishop of Canterbury, being then Chancellor of England, and for his surety lying in the Tower
of London, called to him the Bishop of Winchester, which,
also for fear, lurked at Haliwell. These two prelates seeing
the fury of the Kentish people, by reason of their beating
back, to be mitigate and minished, passed the River of
Thames from the Tower into Southwark, bringing with
them, under the King's Great Seal, a general pardon unto
all the offenders, which they caused to be openly proclaimed and published. Lord, how glad the poor people
were of this pardon (the more so than of the great Jubilee
of Rome), and how they accepted the same! In so much
that the whole multitude, without bidding farewell to their

captain, retired the same night, every man to his own home, as men amazed and stricken with fear. But John Cade, desperate of succors, which by the friends of the Duke of York were to him promised, and seeing his company thus without his knowledge suddenly depart, mistrusting the sequel of the matter, departed secretly, in habit disguised, into Sussex. But all his metamorphosis or transfiguration little prevailed: for, after a proclamation made, that whosoever could apprehend the said Jack Cade should have for his pain a thousand marks, many sought for him, but few espied him, till one Alexander Iden, Esquire, of Kent, found him in a garden, and there in his defense manfully slew the caitiff Cade, and brought his dead body to London, whose head was set on London Bridge....

After this commotion the King himself came into Kent, and there sat in judgment upon the offenders; and if he had not mitigated his justice with mercy and compassion, more than five hundred by the law had been justly put to execution. But he considered both their fragility and innocency, and how they with perverse people were seduced and deceived; and so punished the stubborn heads, and delivered the ignorant and miserable people, to the great rejoicing of all his subjects. . . .

[Whereupon the Duke of York] minding no lenger to dream in his weighty matter, nor to keep secret his right and title, returned out of Ireland, and came to London in the Parliament time, where he deliberately consulted with his especial friends: as John, Duke of Norfolk, Richard, Earl of Salisbury, and Lord Richard his son, which after was Earl of Warwick, Thomas Courtney, Earl of Devonshire, and Edward Brooke, Lord Cobham, a man of great wit and much experience: requiring them both of advice and counsel, how he might without spot of treason or color of usurpation set forth his title and obtain his right.

After long consultation, it was thought expedient first to seek some occasion, and pick some quarrel to the Duke of Somerset, which ruled the King, ordered the realm, and most might do with the Queen; whom the commons, for the loss of Normandy, worse than a toad or scorpion hated, disdained, and execrated. . . .

[Subsequently York] with help of his friends assembled a great army in the marches of Wales, publishing openly that the cause of his motion was for the public wealth of the realm, and great profit of the commons; which fair-told tale allured to him much people, as well of the chivalry as of the mean sort. The King, much astonished with this sudden commotion, by the advice of his Council raised a great host, and marched forward toward the Duke; but he, being of his approach credibly advised by his espials, diverted from the King's way, and took his journey toward London. And having knowledge that he might not be suffered with his army to pass through London, he crossed over the Thames at Kingston Bridge, and so set forth toward Kent, where he knew that he had both friends and good willers; and there, on Brent Heath, a mile from Dartford and ten miles from London, he embattled himself, and encamped his army very strongly, both with trenches and artillery. The King, being thereof advertised, with great diligence brought his army to Blackheath, and there pitched his tents. While both th' armies lay thus embattled, the King, by th' advice of his Council, sent the Bishops of Winchester and Ely to the Duke, both to know what was the cause of so great a tumult, and also to make a concord, if the requests of the Duke and his company seemed to them consonant to reason, or profitable to the people. The Duke, hearing the message of the two bishops, either doubting the variable chance of mortal battle, or looking for a better occasion or a more lucky day, answered the prelates that his coming was neither to damnify the King, neither in honor, nor in person, nor yet any good man; but his intent was to remove from him certain evil-disposed persons of his Council, which were the bloodsuckers of the nobility, the pollers [i.e., shearsmen] of the clergy, and oppressors of the poor people: amongst whom he chiefly named Edmund, Duke of Somerset, whom if the King would commit to ward, to answer to such articles as against him should in open Parliament be both proponed and proved, he promised not only to dissolve his army and dispatch his people, but also offered himself, like an obedient subject, to come to the King's presence, and to do

him true and faithful service, according to his truth and
bounden duty. When the messengers were returned with
this reasonable answer, the King, perceiving that without
great bloodshed he could not bridle the Duke of York,
nor without war he could not appease the furious rage of
the common people, being once set on fire, except he followed their minds and granted their requests, caused the
Duke of Somerset to be committed to ward, as some say
(or to keep himself privy in his own house, as other write),
till the fury of the people were somewhat assuaged and
pacified. Which thing done, the Duke of York the first day
of March dissolved his army and brake up his camp, and
came to the King's tent, where, beside his expectation,
and contrary to the promise made by the King, he found
the Duke of Somerset set at large and at liberty: whom
the Duke of York boldly accused of treason, of bribery,
oppression, and many other crimes. The Duke of Somerset
not only made answer to the Duke's objections, but also
accused him of high treason toward the King his sovereign
lord, affirming that he and his fautors and complices had
consulted together how to obtain the crown and scepter
of the realm. By means of which words the King removed
straight to London, and the Duke of York as a prisoner
rode before him, and so was kept a while. . . . [A Council was called to decide between Somerset and York, but]
while the Council treated of saving or losing of this dolorous Duke of York, a rumor sprang throughout London
that Edward, Earl of March, son and heir apparent to the
said Duke, a young prince of great wit and much stomach,
accompanied with a strong army of Marchmen, was coming toward Lond[on]; which tidings sore appalled the
Queen and the whole Council. . . .

[Faced at the same time with trouble in Gascony, the
Council] lest this dissension between two persons might
be the let of outward conquest, set the Duke of York at
liberty, and permitted him to return to his castle of Wig-
more in the marches of Wales, where he studied both how
to displease his enemies and to obtain his purpose. And
so by means of the absence of the Duke of York, which
was in this manner banished the court and the King's

presence, the Duke of Somerset rose up in high favor with the King and the Queen, and his word only ruled, and his voice was only heard. . . .

When foreign war and outward battles were brought to an end and final conclusion, domestical discord and civil dissension began again to renew and arise within the realm of England . . . for the Duke of York, which sore gaped and more thirsted for the superiority and preeminence, studied, devised, and practiced all ways and means by the which he might attain to his pretensed purpose and long-hoped desire. And amongst all imaginations, one seemed most necessary for his purpose, which yet again was to stir and provoke the malice of all the people against the Duke of Somerset. . . . When the Duke of York saw men's appetites, and felt well their minds, he chiefly entertained two Richards, and both Nevils, the one of Salisbury, the other of Warwick being Earl, the first the father, the second the son. . . . This Richard [of Warwick] was not only a man of marvelous qualities and fecundious fashions, but also, from his youth, by a certain practice or natural inclination, so set them forward with witty and gentle demeanor to all persons of high and low degree, that among all sorts of people he obtained great love, much favor, and more credence. . . .

When the Duke of York had fastened his chain between these two strong and robustious pillars, he with his friends so seriously wrought and so politicly handled his business that the Duke of Somerset was arrested in the Queen's great chamber, and sent to the Tower of London, where he, without great solemnity, kept a doleful Christmas; against whom in open Parliament were laid diverse and heinous articles of high treason, as well for the loss of Normandy as for the late mischance which happened in Guyenne. The King at this time was sick at Clarendon, and so conveyed to London, by reason whereof no final determination proceeded in this great and weighty cause; but it was put in suspense till the next assembly of the high court of Parliament. During which time the King, either of his own mind or by the Queen's procurement, caused the Duke of Somerset to be set at liberty: by which

doing grew great envy and displeasure between the King
and divers of his lords, and in especial between the Duke
of York and the King's lineage. And to aggravate more
the malice new begun, the Queen, which then ruled the
roast and bare the whole rule, caused the Duke of Somerset to be preferred to the captainship of Calais, wherewith
not only the commons but also many of the nobility
were greatly grieved and offended: saying that he had lost Normandy, and so would he do Calais. The Duke of York
and his adherents, perceiving that neither exhortation
served, nor accusements prevailed against the Duke of
Somerset, determined to revenge their quarrel and obtain
their purpose by open war and martial adventure, and
no lenger to sleep in so weighty a business. So he, being
in the marches of Wales associate with his especial friends,
the Earls of Salisbury and Warwick, the Lord Cobham,
and other, assembled an army, and gathered a great power,
and like warlike persons marched toward London. The
Londoners, hearing of so great a multitude coming toward
their city, were greatly astonied and much abashed: for
every person considered his own part, that either with-
holding with the one side, or being contrariant to the other,
or meddling with no part, he should incur indignation or
displeasure. The King, being credibly informed of the
great army coming toward him, assembled an host, intending to meet with the Duke in the north part, because he
had too many friends about the city of London; and for
that cause, with great speed and small luck, he being
accompanied with the Dukes of Somerset and Buckingham, th' Earls of Stafford, Northumberland, and Wiltshire,
with the Lord Clifford and divers other barons, departed
out of Westminster the twentieth day of May toward the
town of Saint Albans: of whose doings the Duke of York
being advertised by his espials, with all his power coasted
the countries, and came to the same town the third day
next ensuing. The King, hearing of their approaching, sent
to him messengers, straightly charging and commanding
him, as an obedient subject, to keep the peace, and not,
as an enemy to his natural country, to murder and slay
his own countrimen and proper nation. While King Henry,

more desirous of peace than of war, was sending forth his
orators at the one end of the town, the Earl of Warwick
with the Marchmen entered at the other gate of the town
and fiercely set on the King's forward, and them shortly
discomfited. Then came the Duke of Somerset and all the
other lords, with the King's power, which fought a sore
and a cruel battle, in the which many a tall man lost his
life; but the Duke of York sent ever fresh men to succor
the weary, and put new men in the places of the hurt
persons, by which only policy the King's army was profligate and dispersed, and all the chieftains of the field
almost slain and brought to confusion. For there died
under the sign of the Castle Edmund, Duke of Somerset,
who long before was warned to eschew all castles, and
beside him lay Henry, the second Earl of Northumberland,
Humphrey, Earl of Stafford, son to the Duke of Buckingham, John Lord Clifford, and eight thousand men and
more. Humphrey Duke of Buckingham, being wounded,
and James Butler, Earl of Wiltshire and Ormond, seeing
fortune's louring chance, left the King post alone, and
with a great number fled away. This was th' end of the
first battle at Saint Albans, which was fought on Thursday
before the feast of Pentecost, being the twenty-third day
of May in this thirty-third year of the King's reign. . . .

JOHN FOXE

from *Acts and Monuments of Martyrs*

In the young days of this King Henry the Sixth, being
yet under the governance of Duke Humphrey his Protector, there came to Saint Albans a certain beggar with
his wife, and there was walking about the town begging
five or six days before the King's coming thither, saying
he was born blind and never saw in his life, and was
warned in his dream that he should come out of Berwick,
where he said he had ever dwelled, to seek Saint Alban;
and that he had been at his shrine and had not been
holpen, and therefore he would go and seek him at some
other place: for he had heard some say, since he came,
that Saint Alban's body should be at Cologne—and indeed
such a contention hath there been, but of truth, as I am
surely informed, he lieth here at Saint Albans, saving some
relics of him, which there they show shrined. But to tell
you forth, when the King was comen, and the town full,
suddenly this blind man at Saint Alban's shrine had his
sight again, and a miracle solemnly rung, and *Te Deum*
sung, so that nothing was talked of in all the town but
this miracle. So happened it then that Duke Humphrey
of Gloucester, a man no less wise than also well learned,
having great joy to see such a miracle, called the poor
man unto him; and first showing himself joyous of God's

glory, so showed in the getting of his sight, and exhorting him to meekness, and to no ascribing of any part of the worship to himself, nor to be proud of the people's praise, which would call him a good and godly man thereby, at last he looked well upon his eyne [i.e., eyes], and asked whether he could see nothing at all in all his life before. And when as well his wife as himself affirmed fastly no, then he looked advisedly upon his eyen again, and said, "I believe you very well, for me thinketh ye cannot see well yet."

"Yes, sir," quod he, "I thank God and His holy martyr I can see now as well as any man." "Ye can?" quod the Duke; "What color is my gown?" Then anon the beggar told him. "What color," quoth he, "is this man's gown?" He told him also, and so forth, without any sticking, he told him the names of all the colors that could be showed him. And when the Duke saw that, he bade him walk traitor, and made him to be set openly in the stocks: for though he could have seen suddenly by miracle the difference between divers colors, yet he could not by the sight so suddenly tell the names of all these colors, except he had known them before, no more than the names of all the men that he should suddenly see.

By this it may be seen how Duke Humphrey had not only an head to discern and dissever truth from forged and feigned hypocrisy, but study also and diligence likewise was in him to reform that which was amiss.

[ANTHONY MUNDAY, WILLIAM SHAKESPEARE (?), *et al.*]

from *Sir Thomas More**

[After considerable provocation, the yeomen and apprentices of London are in a state of insurrection, crying down especially the government policy of allowing aliens ("strangers") to seek employment and do business in England.]

Enter Lincoln, Doll, Clown, George Betts, Williamson, others; and a sergeant-at-arms.

Lincoln. Peace, hear me! He that will not see a red herring at a Harry-groat,° butter at elevenpence a pound, meal at nine shillings a bushel, and beef at four nobles a stone, list to me.

5 *George Betts.* It will come to that pass if strangers be suffered. Mark him.

Lincoln. Our country is a great eating country: *argo,*° they eat more in our country than they do in their own.

---

* Not a source, but an analogue, perhaps by Shakespeare. See page 167. 2 Harry-groat small coin minted in Henry VIII's reign 7 argo corruption of Latin *ergo,* i.e., "therefore": compare *2 Henry VI,* IV.ii.30

Betts, Clown. By a halfpenny loaf a day, troy weight.   10

Lincoln. They bring in strange roots, which is merely
to the undoing of poor prentices: for what's a sorry
parsnip to a good hart?

Williamson. Trash, trash: they breed sore eyes, and
'tis enough to infect the city with the palsy.   15

Lincoln. Nay, it has infected it with the palsy: for
these bastards of dung—as you know, they grow
in dung—have infected us, and it is our infection
will make the city shake, which partly comes
through the eating of parsnips.   20

Clown, Betts. True: and pumpions° together.

Sergeant. What say ye to the mercy of the King?
Do ye refuse it?

Lincoln. You would have us upon th' hip, would you?
No, marry, do we not: we accept of the King's   25
mercy, but we will show no mercy upon the strangers.

Sergeant. You are the simplest things that ever stood
In such a question.

Lincoln. How say ye now, prentices? Prentices simple!   30
Down with him!
All. Prentices simple! Prentices simple!

    Enter the Lord Mayor, Surrey, Shrewsbury,
      [and Thomas More].

Mayor. Hold! In the King's name, hold!

Surrey. Friends, masters, countrymen—

Mayor. Peace, how, peace! I charge you, keep the   35
peace!

Shrewsbury. My masters, countrymen—

Williamson. The noble Earl of Shrewsbury: let's
hear him.

21 **pumpions** pumpkins

40 *Betts.* We'll hear the Earl of Surrey.

Lincoln. The Earl of Shrewsbury.

Betts. We'll hear both.

All. Both, both, both, both!

Lincoln. Peace, I say, peace! Are you men of wisdom,
45 or what are you?

Surrey. What you will have them; but not men of
wisdom.

All. We'll not hear my lord of Surrey, no, no, no, no,
no! Shrewsbury, Shrewsbury!

More. Whiles they are o'er the bank of their obedience,
Thus will they bear down all things.

50 *Lincoln.* Shrieve° More speaks: shall we hear Shrieve

More speak?

Doll. Let's hear him: 'a keeps a plentiful shrievaltry,
and 'a made my brother° Arthur Watchins Sergeant
55 Safe's yeoman: let's hear Shrieve More.

All. Shrieve More, More, More, Shrieve More!

More. Even by the rule you have among yourselves,
Command still audience.

All. Surrey, Surrey!

60 *All.* More, More!

Lincoln, Betts. Peace, peace, silence, peace!

More. You that have voice and credit with the number,
Command them to a stillness.

Lincoln. A plague on them, they will not hold their
65 peace: the devil cannot rule them.

More. Then what a rough and riotous charge have
you,

51 Shrieve sheriff   54 brother brother-in-law

To lead those that the devil cannot rule!
Good masters, hear me speak.

Doll. Ay, by th' mass will we, More: th' art a good
housekeeper, and I thank thy good worship for my   70
brother, Arthur Watchins.

All. Peace, peace.

More. Look what° you do offend you cry upon,
    That is, the peace: not [one] of you here present,
    Had there such fellows lived when you were babes,   75
    That could have topped the peace, as now you
        would,
    The peace wherein you have till now grown up
    Had been ta'en from you; and the bloody times
    Could not have brought you to the state of men.
    Alas, poor things, what is it you have got,   80
    Although we grant you get the thing you seek?

Betts. Marry, the removing of the strangers, which
cannot choose but much advantage the poor handi-
crafts° of the city.

More. Grant them removed, and grant that this your
        noise   85
    Hath chid down all the majesty of England:
    Imagine that you see the wretched strangers,
    Their babies at their backs, and their poor luggage,
    Plodding to th' ports and coasts for transportation,
    And that you sit as kings in your desires,   90
    Authority quite silenced by your brawl,
    And you in ruff of your opinions clothed,
    What had you got? I'll tell you: you had taught
    How insolence and strong hand should prevail,
    How order should be quelled; and by this pattern   95
    Not one of you should live an agèd man:
    For other ruffians, as their fancies wrought,
    With self-same hand, self reasons, and self right,

73 'Look what whatever, that which   83-84 handicrafts craftsmen

Would shark on you; and men, like ravenous fishes,
100   Would feed on one another.

Doll. Before God, that's as true as the Gospel.

Lincoln. Nay, this° a sound fellow, I tell you: let's
   mark him.

More. Let me set up before your thoughts, good
   friends,
105   One supposition, which, if you will mark,
   You shall perceive how horrible a shape
   Your innovation° bears: first, 'tis a sin
   Which oft th' Apostle° did forwarn us of,
   Urging obedience to authority—
110   And 'twere no error if I told you all
   You were in arms 'gainst G[od . . .]°

All. Marry, God forbid that!

More. Nay, certainly you are:
   For to the King God hath His office lent,
115   Of dread, of justice, power, and command,
   Hath bid him rule, and willed you to obey;
   And, to add ampler majesty to this,
   He hath not only lent the King His figure,
   His throne and sword, but given him His own name,
120   Calls him a god on earth. What do you then,
   Rising 'gainst him that God Himself installs,
   But rise 'gainst God? What do you to your souls
   In doing this? O, desperate as you are,
   Wash your foul minds with tears, and those same
      hands
125   That you like rebels lift against the peace,
   Lift up for peace; and your unreverent knees,
   Make them your feet, to kneel to be forgiven!
   Tell me but this: what rebel captain,
   As mutinies are incident,° by his name

---

102 **this** 'tis   107 **innovation** rebellion   108 **th' Apostle** i.e., Saint
Paul   111 **G[od . . .]** MS defective   129 **incident** commonplace

Can still the rout? Who will obey a traitor?   130
Or how can well that proclamation sound
When there is no addition but a rebel
To qualify° a rebel? You'll put down strangers,
Kill them, cut their throats, possess their houses,
And lead the majesty of law in leam°   135
To slip° him like a hound. Say now the King
(As he is clement, if th' offender mourn)
Should so much come to short of° your great
    trespass
As but to banish you, whither would you go?
What country, by the nature of your error,   140
Should give you harbor? Go you to France or
    Flanders,
To any German province, Spain, or Portugal—
Nay, anywhere that not adheres to England—
Why, you must needs be strangers. Would you
    be pleased
To find a nation of such barbarous temper,   145
That, breaking out in hideous violence,
Would not afford you an abode on earth,
Whet their detested knives against your throats,
Spurn you like dogs—and like as if that God
Owed° not nor made not you, nor that the elements 150
Were not all appropriate to your comforts,
But chartered unto them—what would you think
To be thus used? This is the strangers' case;
And this your mountainish inhumanity.

All. Faith, 'a says true: let's us do as we may be done 155
    by.

Lincoln. We'll be ruled by you, Master More, if you'll
    stand our friend to procure our pardon.

More. Submit you to these noble gentlemen,
    Entreat their mediation to the King,   160
    Give up yourself to form, obey the magistrate,
    And there's no doubt but mercy may be found,
    If you so seek it.

133 **qualify** control 135 **leam** leash 136 **slip** unleash 138 **short of** make light of, underestimate 150 **Owed** acknowledged

Commentaries

SAMUEL JOHNSON

from *The Plays of William Shakespeare* (1765)

The three parts of *Henry VI* are suspected, by Mr. Theobald, of being supposititious, and are declared, by Dr. Warburton, to be "certainly not Shakespeare's." Mr. Theobald's suspicion arises from some obsolete words; but the phraseology is like the rest of our author's style, and single words, of which however I do not observe more than two, can conclude little.

Dr. Warburton gives no reason, but I suppose him to judge upon deeper principles and more comprehensive views, and to draw his opinion from the general effect and spirit of the composition, which he thinks inferior to the other historical plays.

From mere inferiority nothing can be inferred; in the productions of wit there will be inequality. Sometimes judgment will err, and sometimes the matter itself will defeat the artist. Of every author's works one will be the best, and one will be the worst. The colors are not equally pleasing, nor the attitudes equally graceful, in all the pictures of Titian or Reynolds.

Dissimilitude of style and heterogeneousness of sentiment, may sufficiently show that a work does not really belong to the reputed author. But in these plays no such marks of spuriousness are found. The diction, the versification, and the figures, are Shakespeare's. These plays, considered, without regard to characters and incidents, merely as narratives in verse, are more happily conceived and more accurately finished than those of *King John, Richard II,* or the tragic scenes of *Henry IV* and *V.* If we take these plays from Shakespeare, to whom shall they be given? What author of that age had the same easiness of expression and fluency of numbers?

Having considered the evidence given by the plays themselves, and found it in their favor, let us now enquire what corroboration can be gained from other testimony. They are ascribed to Shakespeare by the first editors, whose attestation may be received in questions of fact, however unskillfully they superintended their edition. They seem to be declared genuine by the voice of Shakespeare himself, who refers to the second play in his epilogue to *Henry V* and apparently connects the first act of *Richard III* with the last of the third part of *Henry VI.* If it be objected that the plays were popular, and therefore he alluded to them as well known; it may be answered, with equal probability, that the natural passions of a poet would have disposed him to separate his own works from those of an inferior hand. And indeed if an author's own testimony is to be overthrown by speculative criticism, no man can be any longer secure of literary reputation.

Of these three plays I think the second the best. The truth is, that they have not sufficient variety of action, for the incidents are too often of the same kind; yet many of the characters are well discriminated. King Henry, and his queen, King Edward, the Duke of Gloucester, and the earl of Warwick, are very strongly and distinctly painted.

The old copies of the two latter parts of *Henry VI* and of *Henry V* are so apparently imperfect and mutilated, that there is no reason for supposing them the first drafts of Shakespeare. I am inclined to believe them copies taken by some auditor who wrote down, during the representation, what the time would permit, then perhaps filled up some of his omissions at a second or third hearing, and when he had by this method formed something like a play, sent it to the printer.

SIR BARRY JACKSON

On Producing "Henry VI"

[The Birmingham Repertory Theatre produced
2 Henry VI on 3 April 1951, and *3 Henry VI* on
1 April 1952. The latter was taken to the Old Vic
on 21 July 1952. *Editor.*]

Over a lengthy period of playgoing it is inevitable that
certain productions of the classics make more lasting
effect than others. This may be due to superlative rendering or, and I think more probably, the frame of mind of
the spectator, who by some chance happens to be in a
receptive key or mood to receive the play's message. Of
the whole chronological sequence of Shakespeare's histories given at Stratford-upon-Avon by F. R. Benson in
1906, it was the unknown Second Part of *King Henry VI*
that made the greatest impression on my mind. To see
all the histories in succession was the experience of a lifetime, and, under present conditions, very unlikely to be
repeated. Benson and his company had all the histories

From *Shakespeare Survey 6*, ed. Allardyce Nicoll. Cambridge: The University Press, 1953, pp. 49–52. Reprinted by permission of the publisher.

excepting the three parts of *Henry VI* in their repertoire:
no existing company of artists can claim so much, and it
was of unimaginable help in presenting the entire cycle
to have only the Trilogy to rehearse and prepare from
scratch. To embark upon the project with a blank sheet
would prove a superhuman task. Nowadays, the only practical method, as with Benson, would be to build up the
histories over a course of years with a permanent company. As modern theatrical activities are, in the main,
opposed to team work, the chances of ever witnessing the
entire chronology in order must remain beyond possibility.

Ambition is inherent to all of us, and my own is that the
Birmingham Repertory Theatre shall share with the
Shakespeare Memorial Theatre and Old Vic the honor
and duty of having given its public the whole Shakespearian canon. During its thirty-eight years, the number
presented at the Birmingham Repertory Theatre is now
twenty-seven, many of which have had more than one
production. The conditions of the theater, an intimate-
sized auditorium with a company of young artists, who
make up in zest and loyalty for what they may lack in
their more publicized comrades, is to me the ideal line of
attack required for the poet's plays. They all demand
youthful vigor and drive. Some of the subtleties, the
results of age and experience, may be missing, but I
willingly sacrifice these for forthright exposition. There
comes a time when subtleties of production and star
mannerisms grow to such proportion that the main theme
vanishes into oblivion. When all is said and done, the
plays were written at speed and speedily put before their
public. That the lines have such profound significance is
the accident of sheer inspiration. It has been my good
fortune to hear some of the most famous of bygone actors
in their interpretation of Hamlet. Every possible shade
of thought was expressed. All that was lacking was the
author's explicit direction that Hamlet was an under-
graduate and, in appearance, precisely like Rosencrantz
and Guildenstern. The tragedy had become a vehicle for
the exploitation of an artist of quality and no longer the
unfolding of the interplay of passionate story-telling—that

inherent demand of the public which is the magical touch-
stone of the drama in all its diverse forms.

Here we have the main reason for the neglect of the
Trilogy. That the work is ill-shaped, lacking the cohesion
brought of practice, a spate of events viewed from a wide
angle, may be added cause for neglect, but there is little
doubt in my mind that the basic reason is the omission
of one or two star roles and the inclusion of a number of
interesting ones. Typical is the fact that when Charles
Kean decided to present the play he seized upon one
character, the Duke of York, extracted everything appertaining to that one role, making it a "star" part, and
pieced the various bits together in the hope of molding
one complete historical play in which he alone could
shine. The result, as might be expected, was dire failure,
as indeed I think must be the fate of any attempt, no
matter how skillful, to boil down or condense the Trilogy
for dramatic presentation.

The dissection of the text and the implication that it is
not entirely Shakespeare's I must leave to the scholars in
their cloistered nooks, but what is as clear as daylight from
the practical view of stage production is that the author was
a dramatist of the first rank, though perhaps immature.
If the author was not Shakespeare, I can only regret that
the writer in question did not give us more examples of
his genius. In short, *Henry VI* is eminently actable.

Whilst Charles Kean detected the importance of the
incidents connected with York, why has no major actress
ever discovered the tremendous character of Margaret of
Anjou, surely one of the greatest feminine roles in the
whole gallery? In quantity, if not in quality, she surpasses
her direct successor, Lady Macbeth, who has no such
torrents of venomous rhetoric with its reiteration of simile
to the tempestuous sea. (Incidentally, do not these references, so different from any previous ones, hint at
Shakespeare's personal knowledge of the equinoctial gales
at sea?) Margaret emerges as a gigantic character and her
appearance to curse again in *Richard III* is made a
hundredfold more comprehensible with the knowledge of
her place in the forerunning plays. It is by no means easy

to imagine the groundlings accepting her railings in
Richard III without any clue to the reasons which inspired them. And then there is the slight reference in
Part III to Warwick's daughter, the Lady Anne, who
becomes so important in the later play. It is dubious
whether the ordinary playgoer of today, seeing *Richard III,*
knows whose burial rites she is attending. I mention these
two instances to suggest that the original audiences were
made aware of the Plantagenet sequence as a whole.

The histories, other than the Trilogy, are fairly well
known. It has fallen to the lot of the Birmingham Repertory Theatre with its limited—in some views, fortunately
limited—resources to revive interest in Parts II and III
after too many years of neglect, years in which the main
concern with the plays has been the question of authorship in scholarly circles. The experiment, as I have already
indicated, proved beyond doubt that the author was a
dramatist of no mean stature. The primary duty of the
playwright, to portray events to his audience and show the
reaction of his characters to such events, is demonstrated
again and again. It is in incidents known to the spectator,
but unknown to the characters, that the attraction of
drama lies. In preparing the texts of *2* and *3 Henry VI* for
modern performance, certain practical and, indeed, physical aspects have to be taken into consideration. An
audience can become at least physically, if not mentally,
wearied if it is asked to sit much longer than an hour or
so. Intervals are, therefore, essential, as presumably they
were in the poet's day, though present-day technique of
breaking the thread of a play with an eye to eager anticipation has also to be considered when fixing them. In
Part II, the limitations of the Birmingham Repertory
Theatre enforced one interval after Act III, scene iii, the
death of Beaufort, and regretfully, following Act IV, scene
i. To have opened the latter half with the execution of
Suffolk would have entailed a much larger company of
players than the theater could afford. Beyond the omission of this scene, no drastic alterations were necessary.
In Part III, the sequence of short scenes, including the
fights—so baffling to all producers—which form the

greater part of Act IV, were blue-penciled and some lesser passages omitted. Regardless of such cuts and excluding the usual interval times, Part II played for 2 hours and 43 minutes, and Part III for 2 hours and 41 minutes, despite the intimate character of the theater. The conveyance of sound in a large auditorium always takes longer than in a smaller. I repeat, the impact of Shakespearian drama in an intimate house is intensified beyond belief.

Although Shakespeare was too experienced a man of the theater to make demands which cannot be fulfilled, the histories offer a few puzzles to the modern stage. The greatest of these problems is the presentation of the endless "alarms, excursions and battles." I have little doubt that originally these were very rough and ready affairs as the apology for "the vasty fields of France" in *Henry V* denotes. But as the artists, like all men of their time, were accustomed to the use of weapons, the duels must have been exhibitions of skill, a tradition that appears to have obtained up to the early nineteenth century. On the presentation of battles, there is much to be said for the small stage, since the bigger the acting area the more unwieldy the problem. Numbers, inevitably limited in any case, merely add to the complications. The disposal of the fallen, too, is no easy matter; so the fewer the better. Decapitations are best committed to the shadows, though in the Cade scenes of Part II, the stage direction respecting the head of Lord Say being brought in adds considerably to the dramatic tension. Nevertheless, as with the battles, the line between the risible and the serious is of such infinitesimal breadth that the reaction of the audience can never be foretold. Part III contains two stage directions which created problems for the producer. Although the author directs that York shall be crowned with a paper crown, there is not the slightest indication as to its origin. Paper crowns are not usually part of the impedimenta of battlefields. Where and how was it obtained? Eventually, the producer, Douglas Seale (the Wakefield scenes having been drawn into one) gave young Rutland an accompanying boy jester wearing a paper crown. The boy is killed at the same time as Rutland and, his body being left on the stage, Margaret takes the crown from his head. The other direction is the entrance of a son who has killed his father and a father who has killed his son. Though we know that family cleavages of such a tragic nature occurred in Germany during our own lifetime and that the parricides were not even accidental, Shakespeare's directions, when read, easily raise a smile. Rather than run the risk of a laugh in the audience, we discussed omitting the incident altogether. The poet's infallible intuition, however, proved right. The scene was retained, but treated as a static tableau: it shone out away and above the violent episodes with which it is surrounded and threw more light on the horror of civil war than all the scenes of wasteful bloodshed. The still figures of the father and son speaking quietly and unemotionally, as though voicing the thoughts that strike the saintly, sad King's conscience, presented a moment of calm and terrible reflection. The final scene also presented a problem. It is a very sketchy affair on which to end an almost melodramatic play. In an effort to strengthen it and, at the same time, to hint at things to come, after Edward's final couplet ending: "And here I hope begins our lasting joy," Richard was left on the stage to deliver the first lines of the opening soliloquy of Richard III, his voice being finally submerged by the fanfares and bells marking his brother's supposedly permanent triumph.

Perhaps the most important aspect of staging the Trilogy is the textual arrangement. We admit that cuts are essential so that the conventions of timing, required and expected by modern audiences, can be fulfilled. My own experience proves that having made such deletions as are deemed necessary, the proposed acting text should be submitted to a mind trained in academic study. Such approval will prevent irreparable blunders which can only draw obloquy on the producer's head. This has been a personal rule throughout my career, and guidance and advice have always been forthcoming, service for which I now record most grateful thanks. A young producer should be wary of incurring academic wrath by high-handed treatment of the classical works. The scholars will always respond with enthusiasm; they will never let him down and he will avoid many pitfalls.

The neglect of the Trilogy in present-day performance may well be due to a not infrequently expressed opinion that the public has little interest in the Shakespearian histories beyond those affording star roles. The rarity of revivals of Parts II and III may possibly account for the undeniable success achieved with the Birmingham public and those who came from afar to witness them. There is small doubt in my mind, however, that other revivals will follow elsewhere. How their undeniable theatricality has escaped attention is as perplexing as it is surprising, but I myself and my company at Birmingham regard it as an honor to have rescued at least these two plays from what was seemingly oblivion.

J. P. BROCKBANK

from *The Frame of Disorder—"Henry VI"*

Part 2: the Sacrifice of Gloster and the Dissolution of Law

There is much in *Part 2* to remind us that we are witnessing the education of a tragic playwright. Shakespeare assimilates and puts to the test theological, political and moral outlooks which, however ugly and pitiless, seem to meet with unsentimental honesty the recorded facts of human experience. *Part 1* could not end in the manner of an heroic tragedy, for the history confronted Shakespeare with the fact that society somehow survives the deaths of its heroes and the conditions for its survival must go on being renewed—a point that tells again in *Julius Caesar*. *Part 1* concludes by establishing the minimal and provisional terms of survival—the death of Joan and the marriage bargain, but the historical facts allow no revival in *Part 2* of the austere, soldierly virtues

From "The Frame of Disorder—*Henry VI*," by J. P. Brockbank, in *Stratford-upon-Avon Studies 3: Early Shakespeare*, eds. John Russell Brown and Bernard Harris. London: Edward Arnold (Publishers) Ltd., 1961. Reprinted by permission of the publishers. Additional excerpts from this book appear in the Signet Classic editions of *1 Henry VI* and *3 Henry VI*.

that supply the moral positives of the first part—Talbot will be displaced by Gloster.

From one point of view the second and third plays share the same structural frame, supplied by Holinshed in passages such as this:

> But most of all it would seeme, that God was displeased with this marriage: for after the confirmation thereof, the kings freends fell from him, both in England and in France, the lords of his realme fell at division, and the commons rebelled in such sort, that finallie after manie fields foughten, and manie thousands of men slaine, the king at length was deposed, and his sonne killed, and this queene sent home againe, with as much miserie and sorrow as she was received with pompe and triumphe: such is the instabilitie of worldlie felicitie, and so wavering is false flattering fortune. Which mutation and change of the better for the worse could not but nettle and sting hir with pensiveness, yea and any other person whatsoever, that having beene in good estate, falleth into the contrarie. (*Hol.*, p. 208)

In their unabashed drift from God's displeasure to the waverings of fortune Holinshed's pieties are characteristic of chronicle theology. The subtler medieval distinctions between the will of God and the waywardness of Fortune are lost, but the dominant ideas remain, and they are crucial to an understanding of Shakespeare's tetralogy, and more particularly, of the role of Queen Margaret. The chronicle is enlisting Old Testament theology to rationalize the processes of history: when the land is sinful, God's judgment recoils upon it, and evil must be atoned by blood sacrifice. Shakespeare makes fullest use of Margaret to exemplify this moral order; through the span of the plays she is in turn its agent, victim and oracle. It is in *Richard III* that Shakespeare's ironic questioning of the chronicle providence is most telling, when Margaret, disengaged from the action but brought to the court in the teeth of historical fact, is made the malignant prophetess of God's displeasure, and Clarence

is allowed to protest with humane eloquence against the
theology of his murderers (I. iv. 171–265). In the *Henry
VI* plays the chronicle theology is exposed to a different
kind of test—that of the chronicle's own political ide-
ology.

The chronicles were more ready to accept the tragic-
religious solution of social disorder as a past and finished
process than as an omnipresent law. They wrote in a
tradition which had quietly assimilated the mundane,
realistic attitudes for which Machiavelli was to become
the most persuasive apologist; and whenever they write
with an eye on the prospect of Tudor security, they show
themselves sympathetic to the "machiavellian" solution
—stability imposed by strong authority. Hence their
strictures on the "overmuch mildness" of a Henry found
"too soft for governor of a kingdom," and hence the
coolness with which they recognize the peace and pros-
perity of the later part of Edward IV's reign,[1] which
owed more to the King's military ability and popularity
(however limited) with nobility and commons, than to
his integrity as Rightful King and Servant of God. Shakespeare's most decisive criticism of the chronicle is his
virtual suppression of the temporary recovery under Edward, thus making his moral of peace at the end of
Richard III distinctly less "machiavellian" than it appears
in Holinshed—peace returns by God's ordinance only
when the forces of evil are quite expended. The kind of
dramatic thinking about history that makes Shakespeare's
plays does not prove hospitable to the kind of uncritical
good sense that allows the chroniclers to shift from one
scale of values to another. In *Henry VI* the sacrificial
idea, which makes catastrophe a consequence of sin, is
sharply challenged by the "machiavellian" idea that
makes it a consequence of weakness.

While this range of problems is entertained in *Part 2*
about the plight of the King himself, the unique form
of the play is yielded by the martyrdom of Gloster. The

---

[1] Hall's titles pass from the "troublesome season" of Henry VI to the
"prosperous reign" of Edward IV. Shakespeare's judgment of Edward is
harsher than that of any of the chroniclers.

play climbs to one crisis—a central point in the third act where the killing of Gloster calls out the strongest statement of the moral-political positives; and it falls to a second—where the battle of St. Albans occasions the most powerful poetry of negation.

It opens with a "Flourish of Trumpets: Then Hoboyes" announcing Margaret with chronicled "pompe and triumph," but almost at once, as he lets the paper fall and addresses his "peroration with such circumstance" to the assembled peers, it is Gloster who dominates the theater, assuming his representative and symbolic role. Like Gaunt in *Richard II,* he recollects the chivalry of the past and epitomizes a political wisdom alienated in the dramatic "present." But there is none of the spiritual and physical malaise that complicates the figure of Gaunt, no sterility or decay. Gaunt's prophecy is the "ague's privilege"— his approaching death calls out his honesty; but Gloster is vigorous and defiant, and his honesty brings about his death. If the Gaunt study is the more penetrating exploration of the relation of moral strength to political impotence, this version of Gloster is the shrewder study of heroic virtue.

Holinshed says that Gloster's praise should be undertaken by writers of "large discourse," and notes (as he takes over the Tudor legend) the "ornaments of his mind," his "feats of chivalry," "gravity in counsell" and "soundness of policy" (*Hol.,* p. 211; *Stone,* pp. 250, 265). Together with his magnanimity Holinshed finds a love of the commons and a devotion to the public good. With so strong a lead from the chronicle Shakespeare makes Gloster's qualities both personal and symbolic. In the first two acts he comes to stand for the rule of law and for the integrity of nobility and commons—the conditions of social order that cease to prevail the moment he is murdered. Holinshed is outspoken about the destruction of the rule of law: "while the one partie sought to destroie the other, all care of the common-wealth was set aside, and justice and equitie clearelie exiled" (*Hol.,* p. 237). But his moral is untied to any single incident, and Shakespeare gives it greater dramatic force by linking it specifically with the destiny of Gloster. The chronicle supplied hint enough:

> Suerlie the duke, verie well learned in the law civill, detesting malefactors, and punishing offenses in severitie of justice, gat him hatred of such as feared condigne reward for their wicked dooings. And although the duke sufficientlie answered to all things against him objected; yet, because his death was determined, his wisedome and innocencie nothing availed. (*Hol.*, p. 211; *Stone*, pp. 250, 265)

In the chronicle Gloster's learning in civil law takes the form of a wearisome passion for litigation. In the play he is first the severe executor of Justice and then its patient, vicarious victim.

As Protector he prescribes the judicial combat between Horner and his prentice, and replaces York by Somerset in France: "This is the Law, and this Duke Humfreyes doom" (I. iii. 213). When Eleanor is banished he again speaks the formal language of his office: "the Law thou seest hath judged thee, I cannot justifie whom the Law condemnes" (II. iii. 16). Too much in this manner would have been wearing, but Shakespeare traces in Gloster the humane impulses from which and for which the Law should speak. His practical genius for improvising justice is exemplified in the mock-miracle of St. Albans (II. i), it delights the dramatic townsmen as much as the theater audience, making Humphrey the shrewd, popular hero respected and "beloved of the commons." The King's piety gives place to laughter, displaying his curiously mixed qualities of ingenuousness and insight; and the scene concludes with an elegant exchange of sarcasms, a timely reminder that Suffolk and Beaufort are jealous of Gloster's public virtues.

Shakespeare makes less use in *Part 2* of the heraldic and pageant devices which accent the pattern of *Part 1*, and fuller use of the specifically dramatic techniques of the Morality play and English Seneca. Borrowing as much of the chronicle language as he can, he illuminates the historical event by casting it into a Morality perspective:

> Ah, gracious lord, these days are dangerous:
> Virtue is choked with foul ambition
> And charity chased hence by rancor's hand;
> Foul subornation is predominant
> And equity exiled your Highness' land.
>
> (III.i. 142)

"Justice and equitie clearelie exiled," says Holinshed (p. 237). But the Morality abstractions are in their turn tempered by the immediate interest in people that Shakespeare learned from his attempts to make historical facts dramatically convincing.

The private man is never for long masked by the public figure. Gloster speaks of his condemned Duchess in tones admirably poised between personal feeling and the decorum of his office (II. i. 189), and he speaks from his office unequivocally when she is led from the court (II. ii. 16). But as soon as she is gone, his eyes "full of teares," he asks the King's permission to leave, and for the first time we learn that Shakespeare's Gloster (not the chroniclers') is an old man; the personal pathos is heightened and we are reminded that honor is the prerogative of a fading generation. When he next appears, as looker-on at Eleanor's penance, the scene enlarges into a mutability threnody, including the conventional *Mirror for Magistrates* image of summer giving place to barren winter, and the chronicle sentiment about the irony of personal misfortune—"To think upon my pomp, shall be my hell" (II. iv. 41). But it remains an event in the London streets. The picture of Eleanor's humiliation (however deserved) confesses the cruelty of,

> The abject people gazing on thy face,
> With envious looks, laughing at thy shame.   (II.iv.11)

The intensely passive philosophy of Gloster meeting the frustrated malice of his Duchess foreshadows the

second scene of *Richard II*, but Gaunt puts jaded faith
in the principle of non-resistance to an anointed king,
while Gloster's more naïve faith is in the integrity of the
law: "I must offend, before I be attainted" (II. iv. 59).
His trial scene (III. i) takes on a symbolic quality.
Henry's reaction to it, undescribed in the chronicles, is
used in the play to disclose the natural sympathy between
the King's impotent saintliness and Gloster's political and
personal integrity:

> Ah, uncle Humphrey, in thy face I see
> The map of honor, truth, and loyalty . . .
> And as the butcher takes away the calf,
> And binds the wretch, and beats it when it strays,
> Bearing it to the bloody slaughter-house,
> Even so remorseless have they borne him hence.
>
> (III.i.202)

Gloster's murder is a piece of politic butchery at the
center of the "plotted tragedy" of the conspirators who
are credited with a perverse skill in making an unnatural
offense taste of expediency and practical wisdom: "But
yet we want a Color for his death," and " 'Tis meet he
be condemned by course of Law" (III. i. 234).

We are not made witnesses to the actual murder, but
Gloster's strangled body is exhibited in a sort of verbal
close-up, a remarkable passage, which throws an unusual
stress on physical horror (III. ii. 160 ff.). By this device
a frightening spectacular force is given to the dominant
historical and tragic idea of the play. By a staged metaphor now, "Virtue is choked with foul ambition," and
the play's mime displays the historical cause-and-effect,
by which the murder of Gloster issues in the Cade rebellion. The strangled body lies on the stage while the
commons "like an angry hive of bees" beat upon the
doors.

But his death, as Gloster says himself, is but the prologue to the plotted tragedy. Shakespeare is exposing a
period of English history when atrocities became part
of the routine of public life and stayed so for some twenty

years. Hence his knowledge, if not experience, of the arts of English Seneca becomes relevant to his own art as dramatic historian. It is perhaps no accident that at this point of the narrative Holinshed refers us to "maister Foxe's book of acts and monuments" (*Hol.*, p. 212). No reader of Foxe could be easily startled by the *Thyestes*, the *Troades*, or *Titus Andronicus*. And in the central acts of *Part 2* we can observe the confluence of the Senecan dramatic tradition, with its ruthless retributive morality, and the Christian (or Hebraic) cult of *Vindicta Dei*. These acts present not only what Foxe calls "the cruel death or martyrdom of the Good Duke of Glocester" but also "the judgement of God upon them which persecuted the Duke" (*Foxe* [1583], p. 706). But Shakespeare is not uncritical of the myth behind the grim theocratic drama that features the deaths of Suffolk and Winchester. Although he allows some of his characters to enjoy a complacent relish in witnessing or executing the interventions of the wrath of God, the audience is not allowed to share it. All the acts of retribution in this play and the next are invested in an atmosphere of evil —the images sickening and grotesque:

> And thou that smil'dst at good Duke Humphrey's death
> Against the senseless winds shall grin in vain.
>
> (IV. i. 76)

Suffolk's death is an act of lynch law, and one of several similar happenings which is at once a satisfying act of retribution, and therefore a recognition of the chronicle "Providence"; and "a barbarous and bloody spectacle" (IV. i. 174) and therefore a moral and aesthetic challenge to the validity of that Providence. In his presentation of the Cardinal's death (III. iii), however, and in his insinuations of the causal chain of prophecy, omen, curse, imprecation and dream, Shakespeare does stage the pitiless pageant of Holinshed and Foxe—*Vindicta Dei* works through revenge figures, through the worm of conscience (as plastic as a tapeworm) and through "chance" contingencies. But so much (were it not for

the tightness of the organization) might have been within
the range of Peele or Greene. Shakespeare's play is distinguished by its understanding of the tragic rhythm of
political history.

At first glance it might seem that Shakespeare's treatment of the Cade rebels is less sympathetic than Holinshed's. The chronicle Cade is "of goodlie stature and
right pregnant wit"; his "fair promises of reformation"
and his "Complaint of the Commons of Kent" are responsible and sensible (*Hol.,* p. 222); and his tactics at
the start are admirably humane. Why then the comic
but bloody spectacle of the fourth act of *Part 2?* Brents
Stirling[2] suggests that Shakespeare was aligning himself
with those who most severely judged the rioting Brown-
ists and Anabaptists of his own day, and claims a specific
parallel between the dramatic Cade and Hacket, a riot
leader convicted in 1591. But Hacket was a far grosser
fanatic than the Cade of the play (out of spiritual zeal
he bit off a man's nose and swallowed it), and in any
case there is evidence that Shakespeare deliberately
avoided giving any religious savor to the rebellion; it
might have been quite otherwise had he delayed the
Cardinal's death for a scene or two. It has been said
too that Shakespeare coarsened his stage mobs from
personal antipathy, and no doubt he had an eye for outrages in the London streets, a nose for the sour breath
of the plebeians and an ear for riotous chop-logic; but
at no point in any play do they pervert Shakespeare's
objectivity of judgment or his rich human sympathies.

To understand the Cade scenes we must recognize that
Shakespeare distorts Holinshed's account of the rebellion
itself merely in order to emphasize its place in a larger
and more significant movement of historical cause and
effect. The rebellion is offered as an evil consequence
of misrule, specifically of the misrule of Suffolk. The
fuse is touched early, when Suffolk tears the petitions of
the innocent, conscientious citizens (I. iii. 41). But the
petitioners, voicing their bewildered, nervous protests,

---

[2] *The Populace in Shakespeare* (1949), pp. 101 ff.

the apprentices of the Peter Thump scenes, and the crowd at St. Albans, while they make up the "populace" are not yet the "mob." The mob emerges at the moment of Gloster's death, when the people are compelled, through lack of a law-giver, through the total breakdown of the constitutional rule of order, to take the law into their own hands. The "populace" with a just grievance is by the exercise of violence transformed into the "mob," executors of lynch law. At first they are free from a "stubborn opposite intent" (III. ii. 251), but finally, "thirsting after prey" (IV. iv. 51), they are capable of a full range of atrocities.

The violence is not merely self-generated; all that York stands for in the way of destructive political purpose is right behind the reprisals of Smithfield. Nor are the reprisals quite arbitrary. Since Gloster is the dramatic symbol of regular administration of the law, and unquestioning faith in its authority, it is no accident that Shakespeare focused the iconoclasm of the rioters upon the agents and monuments of the civil law. To do so he turned back in the chronicle to the Tyler rebellion in the reign of *Richard II* and borrowed just those touches which furthered his purpose—the killing of the lawyers, the destruction of the Savoy and the Inns of Court, and the burning of the records of the realm.[8] It is significant too that Lord Say, the "treasurer of England" in 1450, is merged with the Lord Chief Justice beheaded by Tyler in 1381; his stage martyrdom (IV. vii) is that of a humane judge—thus obliquely repeating the point about Gloster.

Holinshed tells how the rising was subdued by Canterbury and Winchester bringing to Southwark a pardon from the King (*Hol.*, p. 226; *Stone*, p. 280). In the play the bishops figure only momentarily, in a soft-hearted plan of Henry's (IV. iv. 9), and Shakespeare abstains from giving to Lord Say the role he allows Sir Thomas in comparable circumstances in *Sir Thomas More*,

---

[3] See Stone, pp. 271, 277–78, for the relevant chronicle passages

quietening the people by authoritative eloquence (II. iv.
62–177). Although Lord Say has a comparable dignity,

> The trust I have is in mine innocence,
> And therefore am I bold and resolute,
>   (IV.iv.59)

he shares the vulnerability of Gloster as well as his integrity, and his head soon dances on a pole. Stafford
tries abuse (IV. ii. 117), but that fails too, and it is left
to Buckingham and Clifford to restore their version of
"order" (IV. viii). In place of the leisured approach of
two prelates, gathering exhausted citizens about them,
Shakespeare offers the murderous rabblement, their full
cry silenced by a trumpet and by the appearance of two
leading soldiers with their body-guards. The pardon,
garbled by Buckingham (IV. viii. 9), is not made a
factor in the peace. Clifford steps in with a sharply different appeal, invocating, as Shakespeare puts it elsewhere, the ghost of Henry V. Cade brutally reminds the
people that they have still to recover their "ancient
freedom," but his brand of demagoguery is surpassed by
the fine irrelevance of Clifford's patriotic exhortation—as
from soldier to soldiers, from one Englishman to another.
The oratory is not endorsed by the situation in the play
(no French invasion threatens) but its effect is to canalize
destructive energy along a track less threatening to the
Nobles of England—profitable indeed, and as Shakespeare shows in *Henry V,* even glorious in its own way.
But *Henry V* touches the heroic through its setting of a
tiny group of English against terrible odds; here the mob
yell of "A Clifford! A Clifford! We'll follow the King
and Clifford" (IV. viii. 54–55), is ironically close in spirit
to the "Kill and knock down" of the scene's opening.
The true interpretation of these events is voiced by the
only figure on the stage who is not implicated any longer,
in Cade's: "Was ever feather so lightly blown to and fro,
as this multitude? The name of Henry the Fifth hales
them to an hundred mischiefs and makes them leave me
desolate" (IV. viii. 56–59). Cade is seen for what he is,

but when he is chased off stage by his followers, there is a strong impression that he is victimized. The blood lust of the mob has been diverted but not sublimated.

In accents reminiscent of his apostrophe on Horner's death (II. iii. 100), Henry acknowledges the gruesome gift of Cade's head: "The head of Cade? Great God, how just art Thou?" (V. i. 68). There is this recognition that God's spirit showed itself in the dispersal of the rebels, not in the tide of rebellion; in the killing of Cade, not in his subornation. But Henry's outlook is of a piece with his isolation and impotence. Cade's death is not much more than a marginal note (IV. x); it occurs when he is alone and starving and cannot have the central significance that Henry's piety attributes to it. Iden, the yeoman in the garden and Cade's killer, is (as E. M. W. Tillyard puts it) a "symbol of degree," one who "seeks not to wax great by others' waning"; but he is a formal symbol, mechanically put together out of the chronicle, and can only appear as a "representative figure" to King Henry himself in a scene which Shakespeare is careful not to put last. As it is, the silence of the stage garden is not allowed to still the audience's memory of the clamor of Southwark; the internecine violence of the rebellion is carried through, across the recessed interludes, to the battlefield of St. Albans, where Clifford himself speaks the most terrible of Shakespeare's pronouncements about war (V. ii. 31 ff.).

Thus the moral of the last part of the play is not the simple-minded one of the *Mirror for Magistrates* which tells "How Jack Cade traitorously rebelling against his King, was for his treasons and cruel doings worthily punished."[4] It is assimilated into a firm comprehensive structure, a version of political and historical tragedy that will serve later as the ground of *Julius Caesar*—another play which moves through the plotting and execution of an assassination, through the generation of lynch law in the streets, to the deflection of that violence into civil war.

---

4 *Mirror*, ed. L. B. Campbell (1938), p. 171.

William Shakespeare

HENRY VI, PART THREE

Edited by Milton Crane

Contents

Introduction

From 1642 until late in the nineteenth century no performances of the uncontaminated Shakespearean dramas [2 and 3 Henry VI] seem to have taken place; and then only in one revival in London of Part Two and one at Stratford of both parts. In the present century they met with similar neglect. In America the plays have suffered even more nearly total oblivion.[1]

Thus wrote C. B. Young, less than fifteen years ago. But the whirligig of time, as Malvolio among others discovered, brings in his revenges. In the past ten years more persons have seen the three parts of *Henry VI* than had ever seen any one of the plays in all the centuries of their existence. The British Broadcasting Corporation has twice filmed and exhibited these plays (once in a cycle with *Richard II*, *Richard III*, *1 and 2 Henry IV*, and *Henry V*, under the general title *An Age of Kings;* and once with *Richard III* alone). Both these cycles have been shown widely in Great Britain, Canada, and the United States. In addition, *Henry VI*, in parts or as a trilogy, has been performed at Stratford-upon-Avon, at Stratford, Ontario, and at Stratford, Connecticut, and was performed at the two latter festivals as recently as the summer of 1966.

How is one to explain so striking a revival of interest? Or, more strictly speaking, how is one to explain this

---

1 "The Stage History of *King Henry VI, Parts II and III*," *The Third Part of King Henry VI*, ed. John Dover Wilson, The New Shakespeare (Cambridge, 1952), pp. xxxix–xl.

unprecedented wave of enthusiasm for plays that historically have had many more detractors than admirers—for
plays, indeed, that have only in recent years been generally accepted as Shakespeare's? The *Henry VI* cycle
has been roundly criticized, over the centuries, as 'prentice work, a primitive and violent chronicle of blood, of
interest only to scholars. Not that anything like a critical
consensus can be said to exist—*Richard III,* which has
often been deplored by the judicious for its bloody melodrama, has even more often run a close second in popularity to *Hamlet.* Nor should this be a cause for astonish-
ment; *Richard III,* like *3 Henry VI,* shares many of the
most notorious (and popular) qualities of television
drama.

For, though the framework of *Henry VI* is serious,
moral, and didactic—a history, on the one hand, of
France's efforts to free herself from English domination
and, on the other, of the hideous social and political convulsions that we call the Wars of the Roses—these annals
of an age of anarchy are full of thrilling and gruesome
details calculated to delight the heart of a groundling:
the rise and fall of the witch Joan of Arc; the rebellion
and death of Jack Cade; the sorcery of the Duchess of
Gloucester; the baiting and murder of the Duke of York,
the young Earl of Rutland, the Prince of Wales, and the
unfortunate King Henry himself. And, of course, the
whole bloody feud of York and Lancaster is Shakespeare's
inspired anticipation of the Western movie. One must not,
therefore, be astonished that Shakespeare's Grand Guignol
has retained its power to charm, particularly younger
spectators.

Obviously the history plays are by no means alone in
appealing to the audience's appetite for violence and excitement. *3 Henry VI* is hardly more gratifying in this
respect than *Macbeth* or *King Lear,* not to speak of the
matchless *Titus Andronicus,* in many respects Shakespeare's most shocking creation. Shakespeare pays a high
price, however, for the monstrous effects that he lovingly
devises for the latter play: it is the danger that the audience's *frisson* may dissolve into helpless laughter, as when

Titus enjoins the mutilated Lavinia, "Bear thou my hand, sweet wench, between thy teeth."

Titus Andronicus and *3 Henry VI* are alike in another important respect: until recent years, they were little known to either the common reader or the common playgoer. Granted that neither is a great monument of Shakespeare's art, both are nevertheless consistently interesting and lively works by a gifted professional playwright; their structure is clear and straightforward, and they provide gratifying roles for leading actors and actresses. For the more sophisticated, *3 Henry VI* reserves yet another reward—that of watching the early development of a major character, Richard III, from his beginnings as a strong, courageous, admittedly brutal, but not yet frankly villainous figure to the monster who will meet deserved destruction on Bosworth Field.

Civil war is, as it were, the expression in political terms of the anarchic, heedless, and all but suicidal rage that consumes, at one time or another, most of the leading characters of these plays. The scene in which Henry overhears the monologues of the son who has killed his father and of the father who has killed his son, ending in their formal but deeply moving lament, has been often and justly praised; in its terrible anonymity, this masque of death seems to come straight out of a morality play. The fact that these miserable men have unwittingly murdered and robbed their own kin is but another manifestation of the infernal forces that the Yorkists and Lancastrians have ignorantly loosed upon an appalled and helpless populace.[2]

2 This celebrated scene merits our attention for other reasons as well. It seems clear that it bears a significant relation to Sackville and Norton's *Gorboduc* (1561), one of the most explicit warnings directed to Elizabeth and designed to persuade her to take steps to avoid the danger of civil war. Miss Joan Rees has with justice pointed out (in "A Passage in 'Henry VI, Part 3'," *Notes and Queries*, 199 [May, 1954], 195–196) that the traditional attribution to Hall's *Chronicle* of the major influence on Shakespeare in the composition of this scene ("This conflict was in maner vnnaturall, for in it the sonne fought against the father, the brother against the brother, the nephew against the vncle, and the tenaūt against his lord . . ." [Hall, p. 256]) probably requires drastic modification. In the concluding and summarizing speech of Eubulus in *Gorboduc*, the following passage appears:

All right and lawe shall cease . . .

Willard Farnham has brilliantly summarized the cumulative impact of the three parts of *Henry VI*:

Throughout the trilogy we follow the ill-fated kingship of Henry, but the most constant theme is England torn

> The wiues shall suffer rape, the maides defloured,
> And children fatherlesse shall weepe and waile.
> With fire and sworde thy natiue folke shall perishe.
> One kinsman shall bereaue an-others life;
> The father shall vnwitting slay the sonne;
> The sonne shall slay the sire and know it not. . . .
>   (V.ii.204, 209–214)

Miss Rees goes on to say:

Amongst the touches which give to the last two acts of *Gorboduc* a greater vitality than is to be found in the first three, is a passage in Eubulus's speech in Act V scene 2 1. 180 to the end . . . in which he describes, with an almost lyrical intensity, the horrors of civil war. This passage . . . stands out even today and it is obvious that, because of its passionate realisation of its subject, it would be even more potent to an audience for whom the danger of civil war loomed large. . . . It may be that Hall's chronicle is at the back of this speech but the treatment of the theme in *Gorboduc* because it is so vividly realised is perhaps more likely to have stirred an imaginative response in Shakespeare than the cooler record of the chronicle. More elements of Shakespeare's scene are present in the *Gorboduc* lines than in the Hall passage: the double episode of father killing son and son father; the idea that they acted in ignorance (Shakespeare's line 69, the son's words, "Pardon me, God, I knew not what I did!" echo "The sonne shall slay the sire and know it not"); the emphasis on the personal tragedy in the lives affected which the *Gorboduc* speech goes on to stress further and which Hall subordinates to consideration of "the puyssance of thys realme". In addition, the whole context of the passage in *Gorboduc*, with its bitter recognition that:

> These are the plages, when murder is the meane
> To make new heires unto the royall crowne

is close to the theme of the Henry VI trilogy and might therefore be of especial interest to Shakespeare.

It might also be noted that the situation described in Eubulus's lines and in Shakespeare's scene has no parallel in *Gorboduc* as a whole. The moralizing and generalizing message of this *raisonneur*'s speech, directed at Elizabeth, is a warning against civil war, not a definition of the dangerous consequences of failing to name an heir in time.

Finally, despite the admitted importance of Hall's influence on Shakespeare's history plays, is it not highly probable that Shakespeare, in his early days as a tragic dramatist and a writer of history plays, should have looked back three decades to the honorable ancestor of all English tragedies and history plays? From this time forth, *Gorboduc* will be restricted to academic interest, at best; but for a moment it provided the young Shakespeare with a valuable suggestion.

by civil war. Coming and going upon the scene are men
and women who hope to profit by the bitter animosities
of the struggle, who have their little day of rising ambition and success, and who quickly fall. The civil war is
a forced draft fanning all those fires of worldly aspiration
which the ascetic tragedy of the Middle Ages sought to
quench. It favors all the criminal propensities in ambitious humanity. England as pictured under its influence is
very much like the world pictured by medieval Contempt, a trackless forest filled with wild beasts and robbers, where the struggle for place is merely madness with
horrible accompaniments. Sometimes the good man falls
(Humphrey, Duke of Gloucester); sometimes the evil
(Suffolk, destroyer of Gloucester). Henry himself is in
it all, yet not of it all. He is a spiritual opposite to those
around him who have lusts for power and domination;
he loves peace and he has manly pity for suffering. He is
hardly drawn as a weak man, and he is certainly not
drawn as basely or miserably weak. He is simply a king
who cannot use the strong hand of domination because
brutality repels him. The ironical result is that cruel
things happen in his realm which might never have happened if he had been willing to use cruelty on his own
account in taking the reins of government—Duke Humphrey's murder, for example.[3]

Although, to be sure, mankind throughout its history
has denounced all war as a plague, civil war has by common consent been the form most deeply dreaded—as *3
Henry VI* makes clear—for setting fathers, brothers, and
sons against one another. Moreover, not only does all
semblance of reason vanish when every man sets his face
against every other man, but the fear persists (and experience seems to bear it out) that whatever peace may be
concluded will be at best illusory and of short duration.

A kind of war that violates all normal expectations may
well lead, not illogically, to the destruction of the very

---

[3] *The Medieval Heritage of Elizabethan Tragedy* (Berkeley, 1936),
pp. 385–386.

fabric of society. Even among warlords—perhaps one should say, especially among warlords—the one virtue that is most greatly honored is loyalty. It is the supreme political virtue. But in the world of Henry VI loyalty is the exception, not the rule. Part 3 begins with Henry's pusillanimous acceptance of the Duke of York as his heir apparent (provided that Henry is permitted to occupy the throne in peace as long as he lives) in place of his legitimate son and heir, the Prince of Wales. Here the theme of betrayal is sounded, and most disgracefully, with a father's cowardly disinheritance of his blameless son. Shakespeare is skillfully preparing us for the ever-increasing violence of Margaret's mood and her determination to wreak a terrible revenge on the Yorkists.

Betrayal is soon heaped on betrayal. In II.i, a few short speeches by Richard suffice to persuade his father, the Duke of York, to break his oath to Henry and to prepare a conspiracy to unseat him. But before the Duke can begin to organize his plot, he learns that Margaret with twenty thousand men intends to besiege him in his castle; and so he is relieved of any moral dilemma that may have troubled him. In due course, the captured Duke is murdered by Margaret and Young Clifford, after they have tormented him with a paper crown and a handkerchief dipped in his son Rutland's blood. *"Vae victis!"* is the only principle of war that these ferocious antagonists recognize. York's death, strictly speaking, proceeds immediately from unspeakable brutality, though ultimately from treachery; but the distinction can interest only a logician. The savagery with which each party uses the other is such as to call in question the pretensions to chivalric ideals of all these gently born butchers.

The baiting and slaughter of York is paralleled in II.vii by that of Clifford, who falls into the hands of the Yorkists moments before he dies of the wounds he has received at Towton. But his enemies, not yet aware that he is dead, play out a grisly comedy in which they threaten the dead man with torture, mockingly call on him to repent, and at last cut off his head to fix on York gates in place of their father's.

Meanwhile the problem of loyalty is elaborated in III.i. Henry is recognized and taken prisoner by two keepers, who pride themselves on their loyalty to Edward:

> You are the king King Edward hath deposed;
> And we his subjects sworn in all allegiance
> Will apprehend you as his enemy.
>
> (III.i.69–71)

Henry attempts, unsuccessfully, to argue himself free:

> I was anointed king at nine months old;
> My father and my grandfather were kings,
> And you were sworn true subjects unto me:
> And tell me, then, have you not broke your oaths?
>
> (III.i.76–79)

The First Keeper knows an argument worth two of Henry's:

> No;
> For we were subjects but while you were king.
>
> (III.i.80–81)

The futility and absurdity of this disputation are expressed in Henry's rueful conclusion: "Such is the lightness of you common men" (III.i.89), though the unspoken point is clear enough: the keepers attempt to find ways to rationalize their yielding to the rule of might, whereas their betters (with rare exceptions) feel no compunctions whatever.

Richard's great set piece (III.ii.124–195) announces his grand design to win the crown for himself once he has seen "the lustful Edward's titles buried" and has disposed of

> Clarence, Henry, and his son young Edward,
> And all the unlooked-for issue of their bodies. . . .

He concludes with a self-revelation for which nothing thus far in the trilogy has prepared us:

> Why, I can smile, and murder whiles I smile,
> And cry "Content" to that which grieves my heart,

> And wet my cheeks with artificial tears,
> And frame my face to all occasions.
> I'll drown more sailors than the mermaid shall:
> I'll slay more gazers than the basilisk;
> I'll play the orator as well as Nestor,
> Deceive more slily than Ulysses could,
> And, like a Sinon, take another Troy.
> I can add colors to the chameleon,
> Change shapes with Proteus for advantages,
> And set the murderous Machiavel to school.
> Can I do this, and cannot get a crown?
> Tut, were it farther off, I'll pluck it down.
>   (III.ii.182–195)

Richard is the incomparable symbol of treachery and
deceit in all forms: cant, hypocrisy, corruption, secret
murder, usurpation. His last act in *3 Henry VI*, after murdering Henry in the Tower, is to give his brother Edward's
infant son what he himself calls a Judas kiss.

In this world of traitors Richard is supreme but by no
means unique. In III.iii Warwick arrives at the French
court to negotiate the marriage of Edward with Bona,
King Lewis's sister. But Warwick has been betrayed by
the womanizer Edward, whose passions have triumphed
over his sense of *Realpolitik* and have led him to marry
Lady Elizabeth Grey; furious at his loss of face, Warwick
promptly changes sides, and Lewis avenges the slight to
his sister by according Margaret the aid she has so far
sought in vain.

As the play approaches its climax, the Lancastrian
forces move up under their leaders: Oxford, Montague,
Somerset, and Clarence. "Wind-changing Warwick" con-
fidently awaits Clarence's formal greeting, but now the
most dramatic moment of treachery arrives: Warwick's
son-in-law, subverted by Richard, contemptuously takes
the red rose from his hat and throws it at Warwick, pro-
claiming his return to the Yorkist party. But worse lies
ahead. Edward, in his triumph, proclaims an amnesty for
Prince Edward, and there seems to be no reason to doubt
the sincerity of this chivalrous offer. The young prince,
however, tactlessly speaks his mind to his enemies, and,

before the eyes of Margaret, is stabbed to death by Edward, Richard, and Clarence, precisely as young Rutland was stabbed by Clifford, and York by Clifford and Margaret. Each step in this blood feud proceeds inexorably from the preceding one. The anguished Margaret, witnessing her son's death, entreats Richard: "O, kill me too!" and Richard seems of a mind to grant her request. But Edward, belatedly aware of what he has done, stays him: "Hold, Richard, hold; for we have done too much" (V.v.42).

Meanwhile Richard, who has left the scene of carnage with a berserker's cry: "The Tower! The Tower!", is ensuring that Henry, who has of course long since ceased to play any but a choric role in the descending action of the tragedy, will not live to see his prophecies fulfilled. Richard, in the full exercise of his powers as king-maker and king-destroyer, affords us a foretaste of his masterworks of villainy in *Richard III*. What the audience does not yet know is that the demi-devil Richard—whose great speeches of self-revelation in *3 Henry VI* are stylistically and dramatically of a piece with the fantastic unmasking speech of Aaron the Moor in *Titus Andronicus*—will presently reveal himself to be one of Shakespeare's most remarkable and most accomplished humorists. Indeed, one can hardly account for the popularity of *Richard III*, and particularly for the allure of Richard himself, except by invoking the hero-villain's devastating charm, which is compounded of enchanting audacity and a disarming and cynical refusal to take himself altogether seriously. In this, as in all else, he is a master dissembler and actor, and as such fittingly inherits not only the crown but the play itself.

Perhaps inevitably, one is inclined to think of the three parts of *Henry VI* as forming a whole, unified by themes, character, and structural devices. The degree of unity in these plays is, however, dangerously easy to exaggerate. The characters whose lives and fortunes link the three parts —King Henry, Margaret, and Richard, Duke of Gloucester—play significant roles in each of the parts, but their

personalities change and develop. Thus Henry begins as
an immature, saintly, love-besotted figure; becomes more
saintly and more ineffectual; and dies a victim of the
fiendlike Richard after making some abortive efforts to
regain command of the Lancastrian forces. He is a consistent character, whose life and death set a standard of
Christian charity and idealism that permits us to judge
the savagery and brutality of the world into which he has
been unfortunate enough to be born. On the other hand,
the fact that the reign of Henry was an unmitigated disaster was perfectly clear to every Tudor historian and
moralist, and men who lived in the last decade—or, indeed, any decade—of Elizabeth's reign had no difficulty in
applying the meaning of this disaster to their own situation. (The Queen herself was by no means the last to
draw such historical parallels. "Know ye not that I am
Richard the Second?" she demanded, after Essex's followers had caused Shakespeare's *Richard II* to be revived on
the eve of their leader's ill-fated rebellion.)

Henry's pitiful efforts to exculpate himself in *3 Henry
VI* (I.i) when his enemies the Yorkists taunt him for
having lost the lands won by his heroic father, the great
Henry V, recall that terrible piece of folk wisdom from
Ecclesiastes: "Woe to thee, O land, when thy king is a
child!" Admittedly it was not the infant Henry but his
Protector, the "good Duke" Humphrey of Gloucester,
who bore the responsibility for the loss of France. But
the judgment of history, however unfairly, inevitably seeks
the nearest scapegoat; and the judgment is found against
Henry, in whose name the follies were committed. (Henry
passes in silence, of course, over his wedding gift of Anjou
and Maine to his father-in-law Reignier [René], King of
Naples. These provinces, much more than the lands lost
by war, were fresh affronts in the minds of the Yorkists
and the chief subject of their reproaches to Henry.)

Henry's queen, Margaret, likewise undergoes trans-
formation in the course of the trilogy. She appears first in
1 Henry VI, in one of the concluding scenes of the play,
as the prisoner of Suffolk, whom she has already bewitched. She is a little too practical and matter-of-fact to

be entirely believable as the demure and lovely maid that
she seems to her infatuated captor; she already suggests
something of the judgment that Hall was to pass on her:

> This woman excelled all others as well in beautie and
> fauor, as in wit and pollicie, and was of stomack and
> corage, more like to a man, then a woman.[4]

And she finds little difficulty in accommodating herself to
her situation as the captive of the apologetic Suffolk:
"Tush, women have been captivate ere now" (V.iii.107).
In fact, the entire interview between Margaret and Suffolk
often seems to hesitate on the edge of comedy.

The Margaret of *2 Henry VI,* on the other hand, is a
virago and a meddler in matters of state, who shamelessly
takes Suffolk as her lover and contrives the downfall of
the Duchess of Gloucester and the murder of the Duke.
In *3 Henry VI* she becomes the infernal Ate in good
apparel, a murderess who with her own hand plunges the
sword into the captive York. The order of nature being
so violently disturbed, it follows that Margaret's punishment must be equally terrible. This is the measure of what
has happened to England in the course of Shakespeare's
trilogy: the weakness, uncertainty, and confusion of Part
One give way to the deep social disorders signaled by
the peasant rebellion of Part Two and ultimately to the
total anarchy of Part Three. Now the time is near for the
inferno over which Richard III will reign until he is
overthrown by Richmond, who will rule as Henry VII.
Hall thus sums up the restoration of order by the first
Tudor:

> Although by this eleccion of wyse and graue councel-
> lers all thinges semed to be brought to a good & perfight
> conclusion, yet there lacked a wrest to the harpe to set
> all the strynges in a monacorde and tune which was the
> matrimony to be fineshed betwene the kynge and the
> lady Elizabeth daughter to kyng Edward, which lyke a
> good prynce accordyng to his othe and promes, he did

---

4 Hall, *Chronicle,* ed. Sir Henry Ellis (London, 1809), p. 205.

both solempnise and cõsummate in brief tyme after, that is to saye on the xviij daye of Ianuary. By reason of whiche mariage peace was thought to discende oute of heauẽ into England, consideryng that the lynes of Lancastre & Yorke, being both noble families equivalẽt in ryches, fame and honour, were now brought into one knot and connexed together, of whose two bodyes one heyre might succede, which after their tyme should peaceably rule and enioye the whole monarchy and realme of England.[5]

Such, then, was the fragile peace and unity that emerged from the "long jars" (Ben Jonson's words) of York and Lancaster. Small wonder that Shakespeare, like many another Elizabethan, was far more deeply impressed and dismayed, in retrospect, by the holocaust of the Wars of the Roses than by its resolution. Small wonder, too, that Elizabeth thought nothing more important than the avoidance, by policy, trimming, or coercion, of such civil wars as Shakespeare has memorably re-created in this trilogy of *Henry VI.*

MILTON CRANE
The George Washington University

[5] *Ibid.,* pp. 424–425.

The Third Part of
Henry the Sixth,
with the Death of
the Duke of York

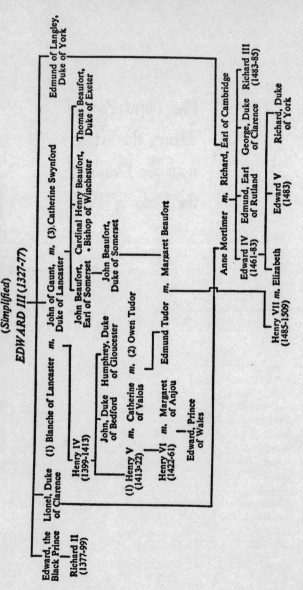

THE HOUSES OF LANCASTER AND YORK
(Simplified)

[*Dramatis Personae*

King Henry the Sixth
Edward, Prince of Wales, his son
Lewis XI, King of France
Duke of Somerset
Duke of Exeter
Earl of Oxford
Earl of Northumberland
Earl of Westmoreland
Lord Clifford
Richard Plantagenet, Duke of York
Edward, Earl of March, afterwards King
   Edward IV
Edmund, Earl of Rutland
George, afterwards Duke of Clarence
Richard, afterwards Duke of Gloucester
} his sons
Duke of Norfolk
Earl of Warwick
Marquess of Montague
Earl of Pembroke
Lord Hastings
Lord Stafford
Sir John Mortimer
Sir Hugh Mortimer
} uncles to the Duke of York
Henry, Earl of Richmond, a youth
Lord Rivers, brother to Lady Grey
Sir William Stanley
Sir John Montgomery
Sir John Somerville
Tutor to Rutland

37

Mayor of York and Aldermen
Mayor of Coventry
Lieutenant of the Tower
A Nobleman
Two Keepers
A Huntsman
A Son that has killed his father
A Father that has killed his son
The French Admiral
Queen Margaret
Lady Elizabeth Grey, afterwards Queen to Edward IV
Bona, sister to the French Queen

Soldiers, Attendants, Messengers, Watchmen, etc.
Scene: England and France]

The Third Part of
HENRY THE SIXTH

ACT I

Scene I. [*London. The Parliament House.*]

Alarum.°1 *Enter Plantagenet* [*the Duke of York*],
Edward, Richard, Norfolk, Montague, Warwick,
and Soldiers.

Warwick. I wonder how the King escaped our hands?

York. While we pursued the horsemen of the North,
He slily stole away, and left his men;
Whereat the great Lord of Northumberland,
Whose warlike ears could never brook° retreat,   5
Cheered up the drooping army; and himself,
Lord Clifford, and Lord Stafford all abreast
Charged our main battle's° front, and, breaking in,
Were by the swords of common soldiers slain.

Edward. Lord Stafford's father, Duke of Buckingham,   10
Is either slain or wounded dangerous.°

---

1 The degree sign (°) indicates a footnote, which is keyed to the
text by line number. Text references are printed in **boldface** type;
the annotation follows in roman type.
I.i.s.d. **Alarum** trumpet call to arms   5 **brook** endure   8 **battle's**
army's   11 **dangerous** dangerously

I cleft his beaver° with a downright blow;
That this is true, father, behold his blood.

                      [*Shows his bloody sword.*]

Montague. And, brother, here's the Earl of Wiltshire's
     blood,
15   Whom I encountered as the battles joined.

Richard. Speak thou for me, and tell them what I did.
         [*Throws down the Duke of Somerset's head.*]

York. Richard hath best deserved of all my sons.
     But is your Grace dead, my Lord of Somerset?

Norfolk. Such hope have all the line of John of
     Gaunt!°

20 *Richard.* Thus do I hope to shake King Henry's head.

Warwick. And so do I, victorious Prince of York.
     Before I see thee seated in that throne
     Which now the house of Lancaster usurps,
     I vow by heaven these eyes shall never close.
25   This is the palace of the fearful° King,
     And this the regal seat. Possess it, York;
     For this is thine and not King Henry's heirs'.

York. Assist me, then, sweet Warwick, and I will;
     For hither we have broken in by force.

30 *Norfolk.* We'll all assist you. He that flies shall die.

York. Thanks, gentle Norfolk; stay by me, my lords;
     And, soldiers, stay and lodge by me this night.

                         They go up.°

Warwick. And when the King comes, offer him no
     violence,
     Unless he seek to thrust you out perforce.

35 *York.* The Queen this day here holds her parliament,

---

12 **beaver** visor   19 **Such . . . Gaunt!** may all of the line of John of
Gaunt have such hope (ironical; though emendation of *hope* to
hap [fate] is plausible)   25 **fearful** timorous   32 s.d. **go up** i.e., to
the chair of state, presumably toward the rear of the stage

But little thinks we shall be of her council.
By words or blows here let us win our right.

Richard. Armed as we are, let's stay within this house.

Warwick. The bloody parliament shall this be called,
Unless Plantagenet, Duke of York, be King,   40
And bashful Henry deposed, whose cowardice
Hath made us by-words to our enemies.

York. Then leave me not, my lords. Be resolute;
I mean to take possession of my right.

Warwick. Neither the King, nor he that loves him best,   45
The proudest he that holds up° Lancaster,
Dares stir a wing, if Warwick shake his bells.°
I'll plant Plantagenet, root him up who dares.
Resolve thee, Richard; claim the English crown.
          [*York seats himself in the throne.*]

*Flourish.° Enter King Henry, Clifford, Northumber-
land, Westmoreland, Exeter, and the rest.*

King Henry. My lords, look where the sturdy rebel
sits,   50
Even in the chair of state. Belike° he means,
Backed by the power of Warwick, that false peer,
To aspire unto the crown and reign as king.
Earl of Northumberland, he slew thy father,
And thine, Lord Clifford; and you both have vowed
revenge   55
On him, his sons, his favorites, and his friends.

Northumberland. If I be not, heavens be revenged on
me!

Clifford. The hope thereof makes Clifford mourn in
steel.°

Westmoreland. What, shall we suffer° this? let's pluck
him down.
My heart for anger burns; I cannot brook° it.   60

46 **holds up** supports   47 **bells** falcon's bells   49 s.d. **Flourish** trumpet fanfare   51 **Belike** apparently   58 **steel** armor   59 **suffer** allow
60 **brook** endure

King Henry. Be patient, gentle° Earl of Westmoreland.

Clifford. Patience is for poltroons,° such as he.
    He durst not sit there, had your father lived.
    My gracious lord, here in the parliament
65   Let us assail the family of York.

Northumberland. Well hast thou spoken, cousin.°
    Be it so.

King Henry. Ah, know you not the city favors them,
    And they have troops of soldiers at their beck?

Exeter. But when the Duke is slain, they'll quickly fly.

King Henry. Far be the thought of this from Henry's
70   heart,
    To make a shambles° of the Parliament House!
    Cousin of Exeter, frowns, words, and threats
    Shall be the war that Henry means to use.
    Thou factious° Duke of York, descend my throne,
75   And kneel for grace and mercy at my feet.
    I am thy sovereign.

York.   I am thine.

Exeter. For shame, come down; he made thee Duke
    of York.

York. It was my inheritance, as the earldom was.

Exeter. Thy father was a traitor to the crown.

80 *Warwick.* Exeter, thou art a traitor to the crown
    In following this usurping Henry.

Clifford. Whom should he follow but his natural king?

Warwick. True, Clifford; that's Richard Duke of
    York.

King Henry. And shall I stand, and thou sit in my
    throne?

85 *York.* It must and shall be so: content thyself.

61 gentle noble   62 **poltroons** cowards   66 **cousin** kinsman   71
shambles slaughterhouse   74 **factious** rebellious

Warwick. Be Duke of Lancaster; let him be King.

Westmoreland. He is both King and Duke of Lan-
　　caster;
　　And that the Lord of Westmoreland shall maintain.

Warwick. And Warwick shall disprove it. You forget
　　That we are those which chased you from the field　　*90*
　　And slew your fathers, and with colors° spread
　　Marched through the city to the palace gates.

Northumberland. Yes, Warwick, I remember it to my
　　grief,
　　And, by his soul, thou and thy house shall rue it.

Westmoreland. Plantagenet, of thee and these thy
　　sons,　　*95*
　　Thy kinsmen and thy friends, I'll have more lives
　　Than drops of blood were in my father's veins.

Clifford. Urge it no more, lest that, instead of words,
　　I send thee, Warwick, such a messenger
　　As shall revenge his° death before I stir.　　*100*

Warwick. Poor Clifford; how I scorn his worthless
　　threats!

York. Will you we show our title° to the crown?
　　If not, our swords shall plead° it in the field.

King Henry. What title hast thou, traitor, to the
　　crown?
　　Thy father was, as thou art, Duke of York;　　*105*
　　Thy grandfather, Roger Mortimer, Earl of March.
　　I am the son of Henry the Fifth,
　　Who made the Dolphin° and the French to stoop°
　　And seized upon their towns and provinces.

Warwick. Talk not of France, sith° thou hast lost it
　　all.　　*110*

---

91 colors flags　　**100 his** i.e., my father's　　**102 title** legal right　　**103
plead** defend　　**108 Dolphin** Dauphin　　**108 stoop** yield　　**110 sith**
since

King Henry. The Lord Protector° lost it, and not I.
When I was crowned I was but nine months old.

Richard. You are old enough now, and yet° methinks
you lose.
Father, tear the crown from the usurper's head.

115 *Edward.* Sweet father, do so; set it on your head.

Montague. Good brother, as thou lov'st and honorest
arms,
Let's fight it out and not stand° caviling thus.

Richard. Sound drums and trumpets, and the King
will fly.

York. Sons, peace!

King Henry. Peace, thou! and give King Henry leave
120   to speak.

Warwick. Plantagenet shall speak first. Hear him,
lords;
And be you silent and attentive too,
For he that interrupts him shall not live.

King Henry. Think'st thou that I will leave my kingly
throne,
125   Wherein my grandsire and my father sat?
No: first shall war unpeople this my realm;
Ay, and their colors, often borne in France,
And now in England to our heart's great sorrow,
Shall be my winding-sheet. Why faint° you, lords?
130   My title's good, and better far than his.

Warwick. Prove it, Henry, and thou shalt be King.

King Henry. Henry the Fourth by conquest got the
crown.

York. 'Twas by rebellion against his king.

111 **Lord Protector** Humphrey, Duke of Gloucester   113 **yet** even
now   117 **stand** waste time   129 **faint** lose heart

King Henry. [*Aside*] I know not what to say; my title's
　　weak.——
　　Tell me, may not a king adopt an heir?　　*135*

York. What then?

King Henry. And if° he may, then am I lawful king;
　　For Richard, in the view of many lords,
　　Resigned the crown to Henry the Fourth,
　　Whose heir my father was, and I am his.　　*140*

York. He rose against him, being his sovereign,
　　And made him to resign his crown perforce.

Warwick. Suppose, my lords, he did it unconstrained,
　　Think you 'twere prejudicial to his crown?

Exeter. No; for he could not so resign his crown　　*145*
　　But that the next heir should succeed and reign.

King Henry. Art thou against us, Duke of Exeter?

Exeter. His is the right, and therefore pardon me.

York. Why whisper you, my lords, and answer not?

Exeter. My conscience tells me he is lawful king.　　*150*

King Henry. [*Aside*] All will revolt from me, and turn
　　to him.

Northumberland. Plantagenet, for all the claim thou
　　lay'st,
　　Think not that Henry shall be so deposed.

Warwick. Deposed he shall be, in despite of all.

Northumberland. Thou art deceived. 'Tis not thy
　　Southern power,°　　*155*
　　Of Essex, Norfolk, Suffolk, nor of Kent,
　　Which makes thee thus presumptuous and proud,
　　Can set the Duke up in despite of me.

Clifford. King Henry, be thy title right or wrong,

137 And if if　　155 power army

160 Lord Clifford vows to fight in thy defense:
May that ground gape and swallow me alive,
Where I shall kneel to him that slew my father!

King Henry. O Clifford, how thy words revive my
heart!

York. Henry of Lancaster, resign thy crown.
165 What mutter you, or what conspire you, lords?

Warwick. Do right unto this princely Duke of York,
Or I will fill the house with armèd men,
And over the chair of state, where now he sits,
Write up his title with usurping blood.
*He stamps with his foot, and the Soldiers show
themselves.*

King Henry. My Lord of Warwick, hear but one
170 word:
Let me for this my lifetime reign as king.

York. Confirm the crown to me and to mine heirs,
And thou shalt reign in quiet while thou liv'st.

King Henry. I am content. Richard Plantagenet,
175 Enjoy the kingdom after my decease.

Clifford. What wrong is this unto the Prince your son?

Warwick. What good is this to England and himself!

Westmoreland. Base, fearful, and despairing Henry!

Clifford. How hast thou injured both thyself and us!

180 *Westmoreland.* I cannot stay to hear these articles.°

Northumberland. Nor I.

Clifford. Come, cousin, let us tell the Queen these
news.

Westmoreland. Farewell, faint-hearted and degenerate
king,
In whose cold blood no spark of honor bides.

180 **articles** terms of agreement

Northumberland. Be thou a prey unto the house of
　　York,
　　And die in bands° for this unmanly deed!　　　*185*

Clifford. In dreadful war mayst thou be overcome,
　　Or live in peace abandoned and despised!
　　　　　　[Exeunt Northumberland, Clifford and
　　　　　　　　　　　　　　　　Westmoreland.]

Warwick. Turn this way, Henry, and regard them not.

Exeter. They seek revenge, and therefore will not
　　yield.　　　*190*

King Henry. Ah, Exeter!

Warwick.　　　　　　Why should you sigh, my lord?

King Henry. Not for myself, Lord Warwick, but my
　　son,
　　Whom I unnaturally shall disinherit.
　　But be it as it may. [*To York*] I here entail°　　　*195*
　　The crown to thee and to thine heirs for ever;
　　Conditionally, that here thou take an oath
　　To cease this civil war; and, whilst I live,
　　To honor me as thy king and sovereign;
　　And neither by treason nor hostility
　　To seek to put me down and reign thyself.　　　*200*

York. This oath I willingly take and will perform.
　　　　　　　　　　[Comes from the throne.]

Warwick. Long live King Henry! Plantagenet, em-
　　brace him.

King Henry. And long live thou and these thy for-
　　ward° sons!

York. Now York and Lancaster are reconciled.

Exeter. Accursed be he that seeks to make them foes!　*205*
　　　　　　Sennet.° Here they come down.

---

186 **bands** bonds　195 **entail** settle, bestow (as property)　203 **for-**
ward eager　205 **s.d. Sennet** trumpet call signaling the approach or
departure of processions

York. Farewell, my gracious lord; I'll to my castle.

Warwick. And I'll keep London with my soldiers.

Norfolk. And I to Norfolk with my followers.

Montague. And I unto the sea from whence I came.

[*Exeunt York and his sons, Warwick, Norfolk, and
    Montague, with their Soldiers, and Attendants.*]

210 *King Henry.* And I with grief and sorrow to the court.

Enter the Queen [*Margaret, and Edward the Prince of
    Wales*].

Exeter. Here comes the Queen, whose looks bewray°
    her anger.
    I'll steal away.

King Henry.   Exeter, so will I.

Queen Margaret. Nay, go not from me. I will follow
    thee.

King Henry. Be patient, gentle Queen, and I will stay.

Queen Margaret. Who can be patient in such ex-
215   tremes?
    Ah, wretched man! Would I had died a maid,
    And never seen thee, never borne thee son,
    Seeing thou hast proved so unnatural a father!
    Hath he deserved to lose his birthright thus?
220 Hadst thou but loved him half so well as I,
    Or felt that pain which I did for him once,
    Or nourished him as I did with my blood,
    Thou wouldst have left thy dearest heart-blood
        there,
    Rather than have made that savage duke thine heir
225 And disinherited thine only son.

Prince. Father, you cannot disinherit me.
    If you be King, why should not I succeed?

211 **bewray** reveal

King Henry. Pardon me, Margaret. Pardon me, sweet
 son.
 The Earl of Warwick and the Duke enforced me.

Queen Margaret. Enforced thee? Art thou King, and
 wilt be forced?   *230*
 I shame to hear thee speak. Ah, timorous wretch!
 Thou hast undone thyself, thy son, and me;
 And giv'n unto the house of York such head°
 As thou shalt reign but by their sufferance.°
 To entail him and his heirs unto the crown, *235*
 What is it, but to make thy sepulcher,
 And creep into it far before thy time?
 Warwick is Chancellor and the lord of Calais;
 Stern Falconbridge commands the Narrow Seas;°
 The Duke is made Protector of the realm; *240*
 And yet shalt thou be safe? Such safety finds
 The trembling lamb environèd with wolves.
 Had I been there, which am a silly° woman,
 The soldiers should have tossed me on their pikes
 Before I would have granted° to that act. *245*
 But thou preferr'st thy life before thine honor:
 And seeing thou dost, I here divorce myself
 Both from thy table, Henry, and thy bed,
 Until that act of parliament be repealed
 Whereby my son is disinherited. *250*
 The Northern lords, that have forsworn thy colors,
 Will follow mine, if once they see them spread;
 And spread they shall be, to thy foul disgrace
 And utter ruin of the house of York.
 Thus do I leave thee. Come, son, let's away. *255*
 Our army is ready; come, we'll after them.

King Henry. Stay, gentle Margaret, and hear me
 speak.

Queen Margaret. Thou hast spoke too much already;
 get thee gone.

---

233 **head** advantage 234 **sufferance** permission 239 **Narrow Seas**
English Channel 243 **silly** helpless 245 **granted** assented

King Henry. Gentle son Edward, thou wilt stay with
    me?

260 *Queen Margaret.* Ay, to be murdered by his enemies.

Prince. When I return with victory from the field,
    I'll see your Grace: till then I'll follow her.

Queen Margaret. Come, son, away; we may not linger
    thus.   [*Exeunt Queen Margaret and the Prince.*]

King Henry. Poor Queen! how love to me and to her
    son
265 Hath made her break out into terms of rage!
    Revenged may she be on that hateful Duke,
    Whose haughty spirit, wingèd with desire,
    Will cost° my crown, and like an empty eagle
    Tire° on the flesh of me and of my son!
270 The loss of those three lords torments my heart.
    I'll write unto them and entreat them fair.°
    Come, cousin, you shall be the messenger.

Exeter. And I, I hope, shall reconcile them all.
                          Exeunt.

[Scene II. *Sandal Castle, near Wakefield,
in Yorkshire.*]

Flourish. Enter Richard, Edward, and Montague.

Richard. Brother, though I be youngest, give me leave.

Edward. No, I can better play the orator.

Montague. But I have reasons strong and forcible.

---

268 **cost** (with pun on *coast* = attack)   269 **Tire** prey or feed rave-
nously upon   271 **entreat them fair** treat them courteously

Enter the Duke of York.

York. Why, how now, sons and brother! at a strife?
　What is your quarrel? How began it first?　　　　　　*5*

Edward. No quarrel, but a slight contention.°

York. About what?

Richard. About that which concerns your Grace and
　us—
　The crown of England, father, which is ⁻yours.

York. Mine, boy? Not till King Henry be .dead.　　*10*

Richard. Your right depends not on his life or death.

Edward. Now you are heir; therefore enjoy it now.
　By giving the house of Lancaster leave to breathe,
　It will outrun you, father, in the end.

York. I took an oath that he should quietly reign.　　*15*

Edward. But for a kingdom any oath may be broken.
　I would break a thousand oaths to reign one year.

Richard. No; God forbid your Grace should be
　forsworn.°

York. I shall be, if I claim by open war.

Richard. I'll prove the contrary, if you'll hear me
　speak.　　　　　　　　　　　　　　　　　　　*20*

York. Thou canst not, son; it is impossible.

Richard. An oath is of no moment, being not took
　Before a true and lawful magistrate,
　That hath authority over him that swears:
　Henry had none, but did usurp the place;　　　　　*25*
　Then, seeing 'twas he that made you to depose,°
　Your oath, my lord, is vain and frivolous.°
　Therefore, to arms! And, father, do but think
　How sweet a thing it is to wear a crown,
　Within whose circuit is Elysium　　　　　　　　　*30*

I.ii. 6 **contention** dispute　18 **forsworn** perjured　26 **depose** take an
oath　27 **vain and frivolous** worthless and insufficient

And all that poets feign° of bliss and joy.
Why do we linger thus? I cannot rest
Until the white rose that I wear be dyed
Even in the lukewarm blood of Henry's heart.

35　*York.* Richard, enough; I will be King, or die.
Brother, thou shalt to London presently,°
And whet on Warwick to this enterprise.
Thou, Richard, shalt to the Duke of Norfolk,
And tell him privily of our intent.
40　You, Edward, shall unto my Lord Cobham,
With whom the Kentishmen will willingly rise.
In them I trust; for they are soldiers,
Witty,° courteous, liberal,° full of spirit.
While you are thus employed, what resteth° more,
45　But that I seek occasion how to rise,
And yet the King not privy to my drift,°
Nor any of the house of Lancaster?

Enter [a Messenger] Gabriel.°

But stay! What news? Why com'st thou in such
post?°

Messenger. The Queen with all the Northern earls
and lords
50　Intend here to besiege you in your castle:
She is hard by with twenty thousand men;
And therefore fortify your hold,° my lord.

York. Ay, with my sword. What! think'st thou that
we fear them?
Edward and Richard, you shall stay with me;
55　My brother Montague shall post to London.
Let noble Warwick, Cobham, and the rest,
Whom we have left protectors of the King,
With pow'rful policy° strengthen themselves,
And trust not simple Henry nor his oaths.

31 **feign** relate in fiction　36 **presently** at once　43 **Witty** wise
43 **liberal** generous, gentlemanly　44 **resteth** remains　46 **drift** aim
47 s.d. **Gabriel** (probably not the name of the messenger, but of
Gabriel Spencer, the actor who played the part)　48 **post** haste
52 **hold** stronghold　58 **policy** secret plans

Montague. Brother, I go. I'll win them, fear° it not:　*60*
　　And thus most humbly I do take my leave.
　　　　　　　　　　　　　　Exit Montague.

　　Enter [Sir John] Mortimer and [Sir Hugh]
　　　　　　　　his Brother.

York. Sir John and Sir Hugh Mortimer, mine uncles,
　　You are come to Sandal in a happy° hour;
　　The army of the Queen mean to besiege us.

Sir John. She shall not need, we'll meet her in the field.　*65*

York. What, with five thousand men?

Richard. Ay, with five hundred, father, for a need.°
　　A woman's general. What should we fear?
　　　　　　　　　　　　　　A march afar off.

Edward. I hear their drums: let's set our men in order,
　　And issue forth and bid them battle straight.°　*70*

York. Five men to twenty! Though the odds be great,
　　I doubt not, uncle, of our victory.
　　Many a battle have I won in France,
　　When as the enemy hath been ten to one.
　　Why should I not now have the like success?　*75*
　　　　　　　　　　　　　　Alarum. Exeunt.

　　[Scene III. *Field of battle between Sandal Castle*
　　　　　　　　and Wakefield.]

　　　　　Enter Rutland and his Tutor.

Rutland. Ah, whither shall I fly to 'scape their hands?
　　Ah, tutor, look where bloody Clifford comes!

　　　　Enter Clifford [and Soldiers].

Clifford. Chaplain, away! thy priesthood saves thy life.

60 **fear** doubt　63 **happy** fortunate　67 **for a need** if necessary, i.e.,
if so many are needed　70 **straight** at once

As for the brat of this accursèd duke,
5   Whose father slew my father, he shall die.

Tutor. And I, my lord, will bear him company.

Clifford. Soldiers, away with him!

Tutor. Ah, Clifford, murder not this innocent child,
Lest thou be hated both of God and man!
           Exit [*dragged off by Soldiers*].

10 *Clifford.* How now! Is he dead already? Or is it fear
That makes him close his eyes? I'll open them.

Rutland. So looks the pent-up lion o'er the wretch
That trembles under his devouring paws;
And so he walks, insulting° o'er his prey,
15   And so he comes, to rend his limbs asunder.
Ah, gentle Clifford, kill me with thy sword
And not with such a cruel threat'ning look.
Sweet Clifford, hear me speak before I die.
I am too mean° a subject for thy wrath;
20   Be thou revenged on men, and let me live.

Clifford. In vain thou speak'st, poor boy; my father's
blood
Hath stopped the passage where thy words should
enter.

Rutland. Then let my father's blood open it again.
He is a man, and, Clifford, cope with him.

25 *Clifford.* Had I thy brethren here, their lives and thine
Were not revenge sufficient° for me;
No, if I digged up thy forefathers' graves
And hung their rotten coffins up in chains,
It could not slake mine ire, nor ease my heart.
30   The sight of any of the house of York
Is as a Fury to torment my soul;
And till I root out their accursèd line
And leave not one alive, I live in hell.
Therefore—

I.iii. 14 **insulting** exulting   19 **mean** unworthy   26 **sufficient** (as
often in Shakespeare, *-ient* is here disyllabic)

Rutland. O, let me pray before I take my death!
　To thee I pray. Sweet Clifford, pity me!   35

Clifford. Such pity as my rapier's point affords.

Rutland. I never did thee harm. Why wilt thou slay
　me?

Clifford. Thy father hath.

Rutland.   But 'twas ere I was born.
　Thou hast one son. For his sake pity me,   40
　Lest in revenge thereof, sith° God is just,
　He be as miserably slain as I.
　Ah, let me live in prison all my days;
　And when I give occasion of offense,
　Then let me die, for now thou hast no cause.   45

Clifford. No cause?
　Thy father slew my father. Therefore die.
　　　　　　　　　　　　　　　　　　[*Stabs him.*]

Rutland. Di faciant laudis summa sit ista tuae!°
　　　　　　　　　　　　　　　　　　[*Dies.*]

Clifford. Plantagenet! I come, Plantagenet!
　And this thy son's blood cleaving to my blade   50
　Shall rust upon my weapon, till thy blood,
　Congealed with this, do make me wipe off both.
　　　　　　　　　　　　　　　　　　Exit.

41 sith since   48 Di . . . tuae! Ovid, Heroides ii.66 (Phyllis to Demo-
phoon): The gods grant that this may be the peak of thy glory!

[Scene IV. *Another part of the field.*]

Alarum. Enter Richard, Duke of York.

York. The army of the Queen hath got° the field:
My uncles both are slain in rescuing me;
And all my followers to the eager foe
Turn back° and fly, like ships before the wind
5   Or lambs pursued by hunger-starvèd wolves.
My sons, God knows what hath bechancèd° them:
But this I know, they have demeaned° themselves
Like men born to renown by life or death.
Three times did Richard make a lane to me,
10 And thrice cried "Courage, father! fight it out!"
And full as oft came Edward to my side,
With purple° falchion,° painted to the hilt
In blood of those that had encountered him:
And when the hardiest warriors did retire,
Richard cried, "Charge! and give no foot of
15   ground!"
And cried, "A crown, or else a glorious tomb!
A scepter, or an earthly sepulcher!"
With this, we charged again: but out,° alas!
We budged° again, as I have seen a swan
20 With bootless° labor swim against the tide
And spend her strength with overmatching waves.
                    A short alarum within.
Ah, hark! The fatal° followers do pursue,
And I am faint, and cannot fly their fury.
And were I° strong, I would not shun their fury.

I.iv.1 **got** won   4 **Turn back** turn their backs   6 **bechancèd** happened to   7 **demeaned** behaved   12 **purple** red, i.e., with blood
12 **falchion** curved sword   18 **out** (interjection expressing regret)
19 **budged** flinched   20 **bootless** unavailing   22 **fatal** destined   24
And were I if I were

56

The sands are numbered that makes° up my life. 25
Here must I stay, and here my life must end.

Enter the Queen [Margaret], Clifford,
Northumberland, the young Prince [of Wales],
and Soldiers.

Come, bloody Clifford, rough Northumberland,
I dare your quenchless fury to more rage.
I am your butt,° and I abide° your shot.

Northumberland. Yield to our mercy, proud Plantage-
    net. 30

Clifford. Ay, to such mercy as his ruthless arm,
With downright payment showed unto my father.
Now Phaëton hath tumbled from his car,°
And made an evening at the noontide prick.°

York. My ashes, as the phoenix, may bring forth 35
A bird that will revenge upon you all;
And in that hope I throw mine eyes to heaven,
Scorning whate'er you can afflict me with.
Why come you not? what? multitudes, and fear?

Clifford. So cowards fight when they can fly no
    further; 40
So doves do peck the falcon's piercing talons;
So desperate thieves, all hopeless of their lives,
Breathe out invectives 'gainst the officers.

York. O Clifford, but bethink thee once again,
And in thy thought o'errun° my former time; 45
And, if thou canst for blushing, view this face,
And bite thy tongue,° that slanders him with
    cowardice
Whose frown hath made thee faint and fly ere this!

25 **makes** (the singular form of the verb is often used with a plural
subject) 29 **butt** a mark set up for archers to shoot at 29 **abide**
endure 33 **Phaëton . . . car** (the son of Phoebus Apollo was killed
while trying to drive his father's chariot) 34 **noontide prick** mark
on a sundial face indicating noon 45 **o'errun** review 47 **bite thy
tongue** keep silent

Clifford. I will not bandy with thee word for word,
50 But buckler° with thee blows, twice two for one.

Queen Margaret. Hold, valiant Clifford! For a thousand causes
    I would prolong awhile the traitor's life.
    Wrath makes him deaf: speak thou, Northumberland.

Northumberland. Hold, Clifford! Do not honor him so much
55 To prick thy finger, though to wound his heart.
    What valor were it, when a cur doth grin,°
    For one to thrust his hand between his teeth,
    When he might spurn° him with his foot away?
    It is war's prize to take all vantages;°
60 And ten to one is no impeach of° valor.
        [*They lay hands on York, who struggles.*]

Clifford. Ay, ay, so strives the woodcock with the gin.°

Northumberland. So doth the cony° struggle in the net.

York. So triumph° thieves upon their conquered booty;
    So true men yield, with robbers so o'er-matched.

Northumberland. What would your Grace have done
65 unto him now?

Queen Margaret. Brave warriors, Clifford and Northumberland,
    Come, make him stand upon this molehill here
    That raught° at mountains with outstretchèd arms,
    Yet parted but the shadow with his hand.
70 What, was it you that would be England's king?
    Was't you that reveled in our parliament,
    And made a preachment of your high descent?
    Where are your mess° of sons to back you now?

50 **buckler** grapple in combat   56 **grin** show his teeth   58 **spurn**
kick   59 **vantages** opportunities   60 **impeach of** detraction from
61 **gin** trap   62 **cony** rabbit (metaphorically, a gull or dupe)   63 **triumph** exult   68 **raught** reached   73 **mess** set of four

The wanton Edward, and the lusty George?
And where's that valiant crookback prodigy,° 75
Dicky your boy, that with his grumbling voice
Was wont to cheer his dad in mutinies?
Or, with the rest, where is your darling, Rutland?
Look, York, I stained this napkin° with the blood
That valiant Clifford, with his rapier's point, 80
Made issue from the bosom of the boy;
And if thine eyes can water for his death,
I give thee this to dry thy cheeks withal.
Alas, poor York! but that I hate thee deadly,
I should lament thy miserable state. 85
I prithee grieve, to make me merry, York.
What, hath thy fiery heart so parched thine entrails°
That not a tear can fall for Rutland's death?
Why art thou patient, man? Thou shouldst be mad;
And I, to make thee mad, do mock thee thus. 90
Stamp, rave, and fret, that I may sing and dance.
Thou wouldst be fee'd,° I see, to make me sport.
York cannot speak, unless he wear a crown.
A crown for York! and, lords, bow low to him.
Hold you his hands whilst I do set it on. 95
            [*Puts a paper crown on his head.*]
Ay, marry,° sir, now looks he like a king!
Ay, this is he that took King Henry's chair
And this is he was his adopted heir.
But how is it that great Plantagenet
Is crowned so soon, and broke his solemn oath? 100
As I bethink me, you should not be King
Till our King Henry had shook hands with death.
And will you pale° your head in Henry's glory,
And rob his temples of the diadem,
Now in his life, against your holy oath? 105
O, 'tis a fault too too unpardonable!
Off with the crown, and with the crown his head!
And whilst we breathe, take time to do him dead.

Clifford. That is my office, for my father's sake.

75 **prodigy** monster   79 **napkin** handkerchief   87 **entrails** (thought
of as the seat of sympathy)   92 **fee'd** paid   96 **marry** (a mild oath,
from "By the Virgin Mary")   103 **pale** enclose, encircle

Queen Margaret. Nay, stay. Let's hear the orisons he
110   makes.

York. She-wolf of France, but worse than wolves of
            France,
        Whose tongue more poisons than the adder's tooth!
        How ill-beseeming is it in thy sex
        To triumph like an Amazonian trull°
115   Upon their woes whom fortune captivates!
        But that thy face is vizard-like,° unchanging,
        Made impudent with use of evil deeds,
        I would assay, proud queen, to make thee blush.
        To tell thee whence thou cam'st, of whom derived,
        Were shame enough to shame thee, wert thou not
120   shameless.
        Thy father bears the type° of King of Naples,
        Of both the Sicils° and Jerusalem,
        Yet not so wealthy as an English yeoman.
        Hath that poor monarch taught thee to insult?
125   It needs not, nor it boots° thee not, proud queen,
        Unless the adage must be verified,
        That beggars mounted run their horse to death.
        'Tis beauty that doth oft make women proud;
        But God he knows thy share thereof is small.
130   'Tis virtue that doth make them most admired;
        The contrary doth make thee wondered at.
        'Tis government° that makes them seem divine;
        The want thereof makes thee abominable.
        Thou art as opposite to every good
135   As the Antipodes are unto us,
        Or as the South to the Septentrion.°
        O tiger's heart wrapped in a woman's hide!°
        How couldst thou drain the lifeblood of the child,
        To bid the father wipe his eyes withal,
140   And yet be seen to bear a woman's face?
        Women are soft, mild, pitiful, and flexible;
        Thou stern, obdurate, flinty, rough, remorseless.

114 **trull** prostitute   116 **vizard-like** masklike   121 **type** title   122 **both the Sicils** Naples and Sicily   125 **boots** avails   132 **government** self-control   136 **Septentrion** North   137 **O . . . hide!** (parodied by Robert Greene in *A Groatsworth of Wit* [1592])

Bid'st thou me rage? Why, now thou hast thy wish.
Wouldst have me weep? Why, now thou hast thy
    will.
For raging wind blows up incessant showers,   145
And when the rage allays the rain begins.
These tears are my sweet Rutland's obsequies,
And every drop cries vengeance for his death,
'Gainst thee, fell° Clifford, and thee, false French-
    woman.

Northumberland. Beshrew° me, but his passions
    moves me so   150
That hardly can I check my eyes from tears.

York. That face of his the hungry cannibals
Would not have touched, would not have stained
    with blood;
But you are more inhuman, more inexorable,
O, ten times more, than tigers of Hyrcania.°   155
See, ruthless queen, a hapless father's tears:
This cloth thou dipp'd'st in blood of my sweet boy,
And I with tears do wash the blood away.
Keep thou the napkin, and go boast of this;
And if thou tell'st the heavy story right,   160
Upon my soul, the hearers will shed tears;
Yea, even my foes will shed fast-falling tears
And say "Alas, it was a piteous deed!"
There, take the crown, and, with the crown, my
    curse;
And in thy need such comfort come to thee   165
As now I reap at thy too cruel hand!
Hard-hearted Clifford, take me from the world.
My soul to heaven, my blood upon your heads!

Northumberland. Had he been slaughterman to all
    my kin,
I should not for my life but weep with him   170
To see how inly° sorrow gripes° his soul.

---

149 fell fierce, savage   150 Beshrew curse   155 Hyrcania region of
the Caspian Sea   171 inly inwardly   171 gripes grieves

Queen Margaret. What! weeping-ripe,° my Lord
     Northumberland?
  Think but upon the wrong he did us all,
  And that will quickly dry thy melting tears.

Clifford. Here's for my oath! here's for my father's
175   death!   [*Stabs him.*]

Queen Margaret. And here's to right our gentlehearted
     king!   [*Stabs him.*]

York. Open Thy gate of mercy, gracious God!
  My soul flies through these wounds to seek out
     Thee.   [*Dies.*]

Queen Margaret. Off with his head, and set it on York
     gates,
180 So York may overlook the town of York.
                              Flourish. Exeunt.

172 **weeping-ripe** ready to weep

[ACT II

Scene I. *A plain near Mortimer's Cross in Herefordshire.*]

A march. Enter Edward, Richard, and their Power.°

Edward. I wonder how our princely father 'scaped,
   Or whether he be 'scaped away or no
   From Clifford's and Northumberland's pursuit.
   Had he been ta'en, we should have heard the news;
   Had he been slain, we should have heard the news;   5
   Or had he 'scaped, methinks we should have heard
   The happy tidings of his good escape.
   How fares my brother? Why is he so sad?°

Richard. I cannot joy, until I be resolved°
   Where our right valiant father is become.°   10
   I saw him in the battle range about
   And watched him how he singled Clifford forth.°
   Methought° he bore him in the thickest troop
   As doth a lion in a herd of neat,°
   Or as a bear, encompassed round with dogs,   15
   Who having pinched° a few and made them cry,
   The rest stand all aloof, and bark at him.
   So fared our father with his enemies;

II.i.s.d. **Power** army   8 **sad** serious   9 **resolved** freed from doubt
10 **Where . . . is become** where . . . has gone   12 **singled . . . forth**
selected (for hunting)   13 **Methought** it seemed to me   14 **neat**
cattle   16 **pinched** nipped

So fled his enemies my warlike father:
20　Methinks 'tis prize enough to be his son.
See how the morning opes her golden gates,
And takes her farewell of the glorious sun!
How well resembles it the prime of youth,
Trimmed like a younker° prancing to his love!

25　*Edward.* Dazzle mine eyes,° or do I see three suns?

Richard. Three glorious suns, each one a perfect sun;
Not separated with the racking° clouds,
But severed in a pale clear-shining sky.
See, see! they join, embrace, and seem to kiss,
30　As if they vowed some league inviolable:
Now are they but one lamp, one light, one sun.
In this the heaven figures° some event.

Edward. 'Twas wondrous strange, the like yet never
heard of.
I think it cites° us, brother, to the field,
35　That we, the sons of brave Plantagenet,
Each one already blazing by our meeds,°
Should notwithstanding join our lights together
And overshine the earth as this the world.
Whate'er it bodes, henceforward will I bear
40　Upon my target° three fair-shining suns.°

Richard. Nay, bear three daughters. By your leave I
speak it,
You love the breeder° better than the male.

Enter one blowing [a horn].

But what art thou, whose heavy looks foretell
Some dreadful story hanging on thy tongue?

45　*Messenger.* Ah, one that was a woeful looker-on
Whenas the noble Duke of York was slain,
Your princely father and my loving lord!

---

24 **younker** young man　25 **Dazzle mine eyes** are my eyes dazzled
27 **racking** driving　32 **figures** prefigures　34 **cites** calls　36 **meeds**
merits　40 **target** shield　40 **suns** (pun on "sons")　42 **breeder**
childbearer ·

Edward. O, speak no more, for I have heard too
  much.

Richard. Say how he died, for I will hear it all.

Messenger. Environèd he was with many foes,   50
  And stood against them, as the hope of Troy°
  Against the Greeks that would have entered Troy.
  But Hercules himself must yield to odds;
  And many strokes, though with a little ax,
  Hews down and fells the hardest-timbered oak.   55
  By many hands your father was subdued;
  But only slaughtered by the ireful arm
  Of unrelenting Clifford and the Queen,
  Who crowned the gracious Duke in high despite,°
  Laughed in his face, and when with grief he wept,   60
  The ruthless Queen gave him, to dry his cheeks,
  A napkin steepèd in the harmless blood
  Of sweet young Rutland, by rough Clifford slain;
  And after many scorns, many foul taunts,
  They took his head, and on the gates of York   65
  They set the same; and there it doth remain,
  The saddest spectacle that e'er I viewed.

Edward. Sweet Duke of York, our prop to lean upon,
  Now thou art gone, we have no staff, no stay.°
  O Clifford, boist'rous° Clifford! thou hast slain   70
  The flow'r of Europe for his chivalry;
  And treacherously hast thou vanquished him,
  For hand to hand he would have vanquished thee.
  Now my soul's palace is become a prison.
  Ah, would she break from hence, that this my body   75
  Might in the ground be closèd up in rest!
  For never henceforth shall I joy again;
  Never, O never, shall I see more joy.

Richard. I cannot weep; for all my body's moisture
  Scarce serves to quench my furnace-burning heart;   80
  Nor can my tongue unload my heart's great burden,
  For selfsame wind° that I should speak withal

51 the hope of Troy i.e., Hector   59 high despite haughty contempt
69 stay support   70 boist'rous savage   82 wind breath

Is kindling coals that fires all my breast,
And burns me up with flames that tears would
    quench.
85 To weep is to make less the depth of grief.
Tears, then, for babes; blows and revenge for me!
Richard, I bear thy name; I'll venge thy death,
Or die renownèd by attempting it.

Edward. His name that valiant duke hath left with
    thee;
90 His dukedom and his chair with me is left.

Richard. Nay, if thou be that princely eagle's bird,°
Show thy descent by gazing 'gainst the sun:
For chair and dukedom, throne and kingdom say;
Either thàt is thine, or else thou wert not his.

*March. Enter Warwick, Marquess Montague,
    and their Army.*

Warwick. How now, fair lords! What fare?° What
95   news abroad?°

Richard. Great Lord of Warwick, if we should re-
    compt°
Our baleful news, and at each word's deliverance
Stab poniards in our flesh till all were told,
The words would add more anguish than the
    wounds.
100 O valiant lord, the Duke of York is slain!

Edward. O Warwick, Warwick! that Plantagenet
Which held thee dearly as his soul's redemption,
Is by the stern Lord Clifford done to death.

Warwick. Ten days ago I drowned these news in tears,
105 And now, to add more measure° to your woes,
I come to tell you things sith° then befall'n.
After the bloody fray at Wakefield fought,
Where your brave father breathed his latest gasp,
Tidings, as swiftly as the posts° could run,

91 **bird** child (the eagle, king of birds, was said to gaze at the sun)
95 **What fare?** what cheer?   95 **abroad** in the world   96 **recompt**
recount 105 **measure** quantity 106 **sith** since 109 **posts** messengers

Were brought me of your loss and his depart.   *110*
I, then in London, keeper of the King,
Mustered my soldiers, gathered flocks of friends,
And very well appointed,° as I thought,
Marched toward Saint Albans to intercept the
    Queen,
Bearing the King in my behalf° along;°   *115*
For by my scouts I was advertisèd°
That she was coming with a full intent
To dash° our late decree in parliament
Touching King Henry's oath and your succession.
Short tale to make, we at Saint Albans met,   *120*
Our battles° joined, and both sides fiercely fought:
But whether 'twas the coldness of the King,
Who looked full gently on his warlike Queen,
That robbed my soldiers of their heated spleen;°
Or whether 'twas report of her success;   *125*
Or more than common fear of Clifford's rigor,°
Who thunders to his captives blood and death,
I cannot judge: but, to conclude with truth,
Their weapons like to lightning came and went;
Our soldiers', like the night-owl's lazy flight,   *130*
Or like an idle thresher with a flail,
Fell gently down, as if they struck their friends.
I cheered them up with justice of our cause,
With promise of high pay and great rewards;
But all in vain; they had no heart to fight,   *135*
And we in them no hope to win the day;
So that we fled; the King unto the Queen;
Lord George your brother, Norfolk and myself,
In haste, post-haste, are come to join with you;
For in the marches° here we heard you were,   *140*
Making another head° to fight again.

Edward. Where is the Duke of Norfolk, gentle War-
    wick?

113 appointed equipped   115 in my behalf for my advantage   115
along stretched out   116 advertisèd informed   118 dash frustrate
121 battles main forces   124 spleen passion   126 rigor cruelty
140 marches borderlands (of Wales)   141 Making another head
gathering another force

And when came George from Burgundy to England?

Warwick. Some six miles off the Duke is with the
soldiers;
145   And for your brother, he was lately sent
From your kind aunt, Duchess of Burgundy,
With aid of soldiers to this needful war.

Richard. 'Twas odds,° belike, when valiant Warwick
fled.
Oft have I heard his praises in pursuit,
150   But ne'er till now his scandal of retire.°

Warwick. Nor now my scandal, Richard, dost thou
hear;
For thou shalt know this strong right hand of mine
Can pluck the diadem from faint Henry's head,
And wring the awful° scepter from his fist,
155   Were he as famous and as bold in war
As he is famed for mildness, peace, and prayer.

Richard. I know it well, Lord Warwick. Blame me
not.
'Tis love I bear thy glories makes me speak.
But in this troublous time what's to be done?
160   Shall we go throw away our coats of steel,
And wrap our bodies in black mourning gowns,
Numb'ring our Ave-Maries° with our beads?
Or shall we on the helmets of our foes
Tell° our devotion with revengeful arms?
165   If for the last, say ay, and to it, lords.

Warwick. Why, therefore Warwick came to seek you
out,
And therefore comes my brother Montague.
Attend° me, lords. The proud insulting Queen,
With Clifford and the haught° Northumberland,
170   And of their feather many moe° proud birds,

---

148 odds inequality (of forces)   **150 scandal of retire** disgraceful
imputation of retreat   **154 awful** awe-inspiring   **162 Ave-Maries**
prayers   **164 Tell** count   **168 Attend** hear   **169 haught** haughty
170 moe more (old form)

Have wrought the easy-melting King like wax.
He swore consent to your succession,
His oath enrollèd° in the parliament;
And now to London all the crew are gone,
To frustrate both his oath and what beside   175
May make against the house of Lancaster.
Their power, I think, is thirty thousand strong.
Now, if the help of Norfolk and myself,
With all the friends that thou, brave Earl of March,
Amongst the loving Welshmen canst procure,   180
Will but amount to five and twenty thousand,
Why, via!° to London will we march amain,
And once again bestride our foaming steeds,
And once again cry "Charge!" upon our foes,
But never once again turn back and fly.   185

Richard. Ay, now methinks I hear great Warwick
    speak.
Ne'er may he live to see a sunshine day
That cries "Retire," if Warwick bid him stay.

Edward. Lord Warwick, on thy shoulder will I lean,
And when thou fail'st—as God forbid the hour!—   190
Must Edward fall, which peril heaven forfend!°

Warwick. No longer Earl of March, but Duke of
    York.
The next degree° is England's royal throne;
For King of England shalt thou be proclaimed
In every borough as we pass along;   195
And he that throws not up his cap for joy
Shall for the fault° make forfeit of his head.
King Edward, valiant Richard, Montague,
Stay we no longer, dreaming of renown,
But sound the trumpets, and about our task.   200

Richard. Then, Clifford, were thy heart as hard as
    steel,
As thou hast shown it flinty by thy deeds,
I come to pierce it, or to give thee mine.

173 **enrollèd** recorded on a parchment roll   182 **via!** away!   191
forfend forbid   193 **degree** step   197 **fault** offense

Edward. Then strike up, drums! God and Saint George
    for us!

           Enter a Messenger.

205 *Warwick.* How now? What news?

Messenger. The Duke of Norfolk sends you word by
    me,
    The Queen is coming with a puissant° host;
    And craves your company for speedy counsel.

Warwick. Why then it sorts.° Brave warriors, let's
    away.   *Exeunt omnes.°*

          [Scene II. *Before York.*]

Flourish. Enter the King, the Queen, Clifford, North-
umberland, and [the] Young Prince [of Wales], with
        Drum and Trumpets.

Queen Margaret. Welcome, my lord, to this brave°
    town of York.
    Yonder's the head of that arch-enemy
    That sought to be encompassed with your crown.
    Doth not the object° cheer your heart, my lord?

King Henry. Ay, as the rocks cheer them that fear
5   their wrack.°
    To see this sight, it irks my very soul.
    Withhold revenge, dear God! 'Tis not my fault,
    Nor wittingly have I infringed my vow.

Clifford. My gracious liege, this too much lenity
10   And harmful pity must be laid aside.
    To whom do lions cast their gentle looks?

207 **puissant** powerful   209 **it sorts** it is fitting   209 **omnes** all
(Latin)   II.ii.1 **brave** splendid   4 **object** sight   5 **wrack** shipwreck

Not to the beast that would usurp their den.
Whose hand is that the forest bear doth lick?
Not his that spoils° her young before her face.
Who 'scapes the lurking serpent's mortal sting?   15
Not he that sets his foot upon her back.
The smallest worm will turn, being trodden on.
And doves will peck in safeguard of their brood.
Ambitious York did level° at thy crown,
Thou smiling while he knit his angry brows: 20
He, but a duke, would have his son a king,
And raise his issue like a loving sire;
Thou, being a king, blest with a goodly son,
Didst yield consent to disinherit him,
Which argued° thee a most unloving father.   25
Unreasonable° creatures feed their young;
And though man's face be fearful to their eyes,
Yet, in protection of their tender° ones,
Who hath not seen them, even with those wings
Which sometime they have used with fearful flight,   30
Make war with him that climbed unto their nest,
Offering their own lives in their young's defense?
For shame, my liege! Make them your precedent!
Were it not pity that this goodly boy
Should lose his birthright by his father's fault,   35
And long hereafter say unto his child,
"What my great-grandfather and grandsire got
My careless father fondly° gave away"?
Ah, what a shame were this! Look on the boy;
And let his manly face, which promiseth   40
Successful fortune, steel thy melting heart
To hold thine own and leave thine own with him.

King Henry. Full well hath Clifford played the orator,
Inferring° arguments of mighty force.
But, Clifford, tell me, didst thou never hear   45
That things ill got had ever bad success?°
And happy always was it for that son
Whose father for his hoarding went to hell?

14 **spoils** carries off   19 **level** aim   25 **argued** proved   26 **Unrea-**
sonable not endowed with reason   28 **tender** young, beloved
38 **fondly** foolishly   44 **Inferring** adducing   46 **success** outcome

I'll leave my son my virtuous deeds behind;
50 And would my father had left me no more!
    For all the rest is held at such a rate
    As brings a thousand-fold more care to keep
    Than in possession any jot of pleasure.
    Ah, cousin York, would thy best friends did know
55 How it doth grieve me that thy head is here!

Queen Margaret. My lord, cheer up your spirits; our foes
      are nigh,
    And this soft courage° makes your followers faint.
    You promised knighthood to our forward son.
    Unsheathe your sword, and dub him presently.°
60 Edward, kneel down.

King Henry. Edward Plantagenet, arise a knight;
    And learn this lesson: Draw thy sword in right.

Prince. My gracious father, by your kingly leave,
    I'll draw it as apparent° to the crown,
65 And in that quarrel use it to the death.

Clifford. Why, that is spoken like a toward° prince.

                Enter a Messenger.

Messenger. Royal commanders, be in readiness;
    For with a band of thirty thousand men
    Comes Warwick, backing of the Duke of York,
70 And in the towns, as they do march along,
    Proclaims him king, and many fly to him.
    Darraign° your battle, for they are at hand.

Clifford. I would your Highness would depart the
      field.
    The Queen hath best success when you are absent.

Queen Margaret. Ay, good my lord, and leave us to
75   our fortune.

King Henry. Why, that's my fortune too; therefore I'll
      stay.

---

57 **soft courage** faint-heartedness 59 **presently** immediately 64
apparent heir apparent 66 **toward** bold 72 **Darraign** set in order

Northumberland. Be it with resolution, then, to fight.

Prince. My royal father, cheer these noble lords
    And hearten those that fight in your defense:
    Unsheathe your sword, good father; cry "Saint
        George!"   80

March. Enter Edward, Warwick, Richard, Clarence,°
    Norfolk, Montague, and Soldiers.

Edward. Now, perjured Henry, wilt thou kneel for
        grace,
    And set thy diadem upon my head,
    Or bide the mortal fortune of the field?

Queen Margaret. Go rate° thy minions, proud insult-
        ing boy!
    Becomes it thee to be thus bold in terms   85
    Before thy sovereign and thy lawful king?

Edward. I am his king, and he should bow his knee.
    I was adopted heir by his consent;
    Since when, his oath is broke; for, as I hear,
    You, that are King, though he do wear the crown,   90
    Have caused him, by new act of parliament,
    To blot out me, and put his own son in.

Clifford. And reason too!
    Who should succeed the father but the son?

Richard. Are you there, butcher? O, I cannot speak!   95

Clifford. Ay, Crookback, here I stand to answer thee,
    Or any he the proudest of thy sort.

Richard. 'Twas you that killed young Rutland, was it
        not?

Clifford. Ay, and old York, and yet not satisfied.

Richard. For God's sake, lords, give signal to the fight. 100

Warwick. What say'st thou, Henry? Wilt thou yield
        the crown?

---

80 s.d. (thus the Folio; in fact, George is not created Duke of Clarence until II, vi, 104)   84 **rate** drive away by chiding

Queen Margaret. Why, how now, long-tongued War-
wick! Dare you speak?
When you and I met at Saint Albans last,
Your legs did better service than your hands.

Warwick. Then 'twas my turn to fly, and now
105   'tis thine.

Clifford. You said so much before, and yet you fled.

Warwick. 'Twas not your valor, Clifford, drove me
thence.

Northumberland. No, nor your manhood that durst
make you stay.

Richard. Northumberland, I hold thee reverently.
110   Break off the parley; for scarce I can refrain
The execution of my big-swol'n heart
Upon that Clifford, that cruel child-killer.

Clifford. I slew thy father. Call'st thou him a child?

Richard. Ay, like a dastard and a treacherous coward,
115   As thou didst kill our tender brother Rutland;
But ere sun set I'll make thee curse the deed.

King Henry. Have down with words, my lords, and
hear me speak.

Queen Margaret. Defy them then, or else hold close
thy lips.

King Henry. I prithee, give no limits to my tongue:
120   I am a king, and privileged to speak.

Clifford. My liege, the wound that bred this meeting
here
Cannot be cured by words. Therefore be still.

Richard. Then, executioner, unsheathe thy sword.
By Him that made us all, I am resolved°
125   That Clifford's manhood lies upon his tongue.

Edward. Say, Henry, shall I have my right, or no?

124 resolved convinced

A thousand men have broke their fasts today
That ne'er shall dine unless thou yield the crown.

Warwick. If thou deny, their blood upon thy head!
For York in justice puts his armor on.   130

Prince. If that be right which Warwick says is right,
There is no wrong, but everything is right.

Richard. Whoever got° thee, there thy mother stands;
For well I wot thou hast thy mother's tongue.

Queen Margaret. But thou art neither like thy sire nor
        dam,   135
But like a foul misshapen stigmatic,°
Marked by the Destinies to be avoided,
As venom toads, or lizards' dreadful stings.

Richard. Iron of Naples, hid with English gilt,
Whose father bears the title of a king—   140
As if a channel° should be called the sea—
Sham'st thou not, knowing whence thou art ex-
        traught,°
To let thy tongue detect° thy base-born heart?

Edward. A wisp of straw were worth a thousand
        crowns,
To make this shameless callet° know herself.   145
Helen of Greece was fairer far than thou,
Although thy husband may be Menelaus;
And ne'er was Agamemnon's brother wronged
By that false woman as this King by thee.
His father reveled in the heart of France,   150
And tamed the King, and made the Dolphin°
        stoop;°
And had he matched according to his state,
He might have kept that glory to this day;
But when he took a beggar to his bed,
And graced thy poor sire with his bridal-day,   155
Even then that sunshine brewed a show'r for him,

133 **got** begot   136 **stigmatic** deformed one   141 **channel** gutter
142 **extraught** descended   143 **detect** reveal   145 **callet** scold, trull
151 **Dolphin** Dauphin   151 **stoop** yield

That washed his father's fortunes forth of° France,
And heaped sedition on his crown at home.
For what hath broached° this tumult but thy pride?
160 Hadst thou been meek, our title still° had slept;
And we, in pity of the gentle King,
Had slipped° our claim until another age.

   Clarence. But when we saw our sunshine made thy
      spring,
And that thy summer bred us no increase,
165 We set the ax to thy usurping root;
And though the edge hath something hit ourselves,
Yet, know thou, since we have begun to strike,
We'll never leave till we have hewn thee down,
Or bathed thy growing with our heated bloods.

170 *Edward.* And, in this resolution, I defy thee;
Not willing any longer conference,°
Since thou deniest the gentle King to speak.
Sound trumpets! Let our bloody colors wave!
And either victory, or else a grave.

175 *Queen Margaret.* Stay, Edward.

   Edward. No, wrangling woman, we'll no longer stay.
These words will cost ten thousand lives this day.
                      Exeunt omnes.

---

157 **forth of** out of   159 **broached** started   160 **still** always   162
slipped not asserted   171 **longer conference** further discussion

[Scene III. *A field of battle between Towton and Saxton, in Yorkshire.*]

Alarum. Excursions. Enter Warwick.

Warwick. Forspent° with toil, as runners with a race,
  I lay me down a little while to breathe;°
  For strokes received, and many blows repaid,
  Have robbed my strong-knit sinews of their
    strength,
  And spite of spite° needs must I rest awhile.   5

Enter Edward, running.

Edward. Smile, gentle heaven! or strike, ungentle°
  death!
  For this world frowns, and Edward's sun is clouded.

Warwick. How now, my lord! What hap? What hope
  of good?

Enter Clarence.

Clarence. Our hap° is loss, our hope but sad despair;
  Our ranks are broke, and ruin follows us.   10
  What counsel give you? Whither shall we fly?

Edward. Bootless° is flight. They follow us with wings,
  And weak we are and cannot shun pursuit.

Enter Richard.

Richard. Ah, Warwick, why hast thou withdrawn thy-
  self?
  Thy brother's blood the thirsty earth hath drunk,   15
  Broached° with the steely point of Clifford's lance;
  And in the very pangs of death he cried,

II.iii.1 **Forspent** exhausted 2 **breathe** rest 5 **spite of spite** come
what may 6 **ungentle** ignoble 9 **hap** (1) fortune (2) hope 12
Bootless useless 16 **Broached** pierced

Like to a dismal° clangor heard from far,
"Warwick, revenge! Brother, revenge my death!"
20 So, underneath the belly of their steeds,
That stained their fetlocks in his smoking° blood,
The noble gentleman gave up the ghost.

Warwick. Then let the earth be drunken with our
        blood!
I'll kill my horse, because I will not fly.
25 Why stand we like soft-hearted women here,
Wailing our losses, whiles the foe doth rage,
And look upon,° as if the tragedy
Were played in jest by counterfeiting actors?
Here on my knee I vow to God above,
30 I'll never pause again, never stand still,
Till either death hath closed these eyes of mine
Or fortune given me measure of revenge.

Edward. O Warwick, I do bend my knee with thine
And in this vow do chain my soul to thine!
35 And ere my knee rise from the earth's cold face,
I throw my hands, mine eyes, my heart to thee,
Thou setter up and plucker down of kings,
Beseeching thee (if with thy will it stands)°
That to my foes this body must be prey,
40 Yet that thy brazen gates of heaven may ope,
And give sweet passage to my sinful soul!
Now, lords, take leave until we meet again,
Where'er it be, in heaven or in earth.

Richard. Brother, give me thy hand; and, gentle War-
        wick,
45 Let me embrace thee in my weary arms.
I, that did never weep, now melt with woe
That winter should cut off our springtime so.

Warwick. Away, away! Once more, sweet lords, fare-
        well.

Clarence. Yet let us all together to our troops,

18 **dismal** boding disaster   21 **smoking** steaming   27 **look upon**
look on   38 **stands** agrees

And give them leave to fly that will not stay,   50
And call them pillars that will stand to us;
And, if we thrive, promise them such rewards
As victors wear at the Olympian games:
This may plant courage in their quailing breasts;
For yet is hope of life and victory.   55
Forslow° no longer! Make we hence amain!

                                    Exeunt.

[Scene IV. *Another part of the field.*]

Excursions. Enter Richard and Clifford.

Richard. Now, Clifford, I have singled thee alone.
Suppose this arm is for the Duke of York,
And this for Rutland, both bound to revenge
Wert thou environed with a brazen wall.

Clifford. Now, Richard, I am with thee here alone.   5
This is the hand that stabbed thy father York,
And this the hand that slew thy brother Rutland;
And here's the heart that triumphs° in their death
And cheers these hands that slew thy sire and
    brother
To execute the like upon thyself;   10
And so have at thee!°

          They fight. Warwick comes. Clifford flies.
Richard. Nay, Warwick, single out some other chase.
For I myself will hunt this wolf to death.

                                    Exeunt.

56 Forslow delay II.iv.8 triumphs exults 11 have at thee defend
yourself

[Scene V. *Another part of the field.*]

Alarum. Enter King Henry alone.

King Henry. This battle fares like to the morning's
    war,
    When dying clouds contend with growing light,
    What time the shepherd, blowing of his nails,°
    Can neither call it perfect day nor night.
5   Now sways it this way, like a mighty sea
    Forced by the tide to combat with the wind.
    Now sways it that way, like the selfsame sea
    Forced to retire by fury of the wind.
    Sometime the flood prevails, and then the wind;
10   Now one the better, then another best;
    Both tugging to be victors, breast to breast,
    Yet neither conqueror nor conquerèd:
    So is the equal poise° of this fell war.
    Here on this molehill will I sit me down.
15   To whom God will, there be the victory!
    For Margaret my queen, and Clifford too,
    Have chid me from the battle, swearing both
    They prosper best of all when I am thence.
    Would I were dead, if God's good will were so!
20   For what is in this world but grief and woe?
    O God! methinks it were a happy life,
    To be no better than a homely swain;°
    To sit upon a hill, as I do now,
    To carve out dials quaintly,° point by point,
25   Thereby to see the minutes how they run—
    How many makes the hour full complete,
    How many hours brings about° the day,

II.v.3 **of his nails** on his fingers   13 **poise** weight (as in the scales
of a balance)   22 **swain** shepherd   24 **quaintly** ingeniously   27
brings about completes

How many days will finish up the year,
How many years a mortal man may live;
When this is known, then to divide the times—   30
So many hours must I tend my flock,
So many hours must I take my rest,
So many hours must I contemplate,
So many hours must I sport myself,
So many days my ewes have been with young,   35
So many weeks ere the poor fools will ean,°
So many years ere I shall shear the fleece.
So minutes, hours, days, months, and years,
Passed over to the end they were created,
Would bring white hairs unto a quiet grave.   40
Ah, what a life were this! how sweet! how lovely!
Gives not the hawthorn-bush a sweeter shade
To shepherds looking on their silly° sheep,
Than doth a rich embroidered canopy
To kings that fear their subjects' treachery?   45
O, yes, it doth! a thousand-fold it doth!
And to conclude, the shepherd's homely curds,
His cold thin drink out of his leather bottle,
His wonted sleep under a fresh tree's shade,
All which secure° and sweetly he enjoys,   50
Is far beyond a prince's delicates,°
His viands sparkling in a golden cup,
His body couchèd in a curious° bed,
When care, mistrust, and treason waits on him.

*Alarum. Enter a Son that hath killed his Father, at
one door; and [later] a Father that hath killed
his Son at another door.*

Son. Ill blows the wind that profits nobody.   55
This man, whom hand to hand I slew in fight,
May be possessèd with some store of crowns;
And I, that haply° take them from him now,
May yet, ere night, yield both my life and them
To some man else, as this dead man doth me.   60

36 **ean** bring forth lambs   43 **silly** helpless   50 **secure** free from
care 51 **delicates** delicacies 53 **curious** exquisite 58 **haply** by
chance

Who's this? O God! it is my father's face,
Whom in this conflict I, unwares,° have killed.
O heavy times, begetting such events!
From London by the King was I pressed forth;
65 My father, being the Earl of Warwick's man,
Came on the part° of York, pressed by his master;
And I, who at his hands received my life,
Have by my hands of life bereavèd him.
Pardon me, God! I knew not what I did.
70 And pardon, father, for I knew not thee!
My tears shall wipe away these bloody marks;
And no more words till they have flowed their fill.

King Henry. O piteous spectacle! O bloody times!
Whiles lions war and battle for their dens,
75 Poor harmless lambs abide their enmity.
Weep, wretched man! I'll aid thee tear for tear;
And let our hearts and eyes, like civil war,
Be blind with tears, and break o'ercharged with
    grief.

Enter Father, bearing of his Son.

Father. Thou that so stoutly hath resisted me,
80 Give me thy gold, if thou hast any gold;
For I have bought it with an hundred blows.
But let me see: is this our foeman's face?
Ah, no, no, no! It is mine only son!
Ah, boy, if any life be left in thee,
85 Throw up thine eye! See, see what show'rs arise,
Blown with the windy tempest of my heart
Upon thy wounds, that kills mine eye and heart!
O, pity, God, this miserable age!
What stratagems,° how fell, how butcherly,
90 Erroneous,° mutinous and unnatural,
This deadly quarrel daily doth beget!
O boy, thy father gave thee life too soon,
And hath bereft thee of thy life too late!°

62 **unwares** unawares   66 **part** party, side   89 **stratagems** violent
deeds   90 **Erroneous** criminal   93 **late** recently

King Henry. Woe above woe! grief more than com-
    mon grief!
  O that my death would stay these ruthful° deeds!   *95*
  O, pity, pity, gentle heaven, pity!
  The red rose and the white are on his face,
  The fatal colors of our striving houses:
  The one his purple blood right well resembles;
  The other his pale cheeks, methinks, presenteth: *100*
  Wither one rose, and let the other flourish!
  If you contend, a thousand lives must wither.

Son. How will my mother for a father's death
  Take on with me and ne'er be satisfied!

Father. How will my wife for slaughter of my son   *105*
  Shed seas of tears and ne'er be satisfied!

King Henry. How will the country for these woeful
  chances
  Misthink° the King and not be satisfied!

Son. Was ever son so rued a father's death?

Father. Was ever father so bemoaned his son?   *110*

King Henry. Was ever king so grieved for subject's
  woe?
  Much is your sorrow; mine ten times so much.

Son. I'll bear thee hence, where I may weep my fill.
                    [Exit with the body.]

Father. These arms of mine shall be thy winding-
  sheet;
  My heart, sweet boy, shall be thy sepulcher,   *115*
  For from my heart thine image ne'er shall go;
  My sighing breast shall be thy funeral bell;
  And so obsequious° will thy father be,
  Even for the loss of thee, having no more,
  As Priam was for all his valiant sons.   *120*

---

95 **ruthful** lamentable   108 **Misthink** think ill of   118 **obsequious**
dutiful (particularly toward the dead)

I'll bear thee hence; and let them fight that will,
For I have murdered where I should not kill.
Exit [with the body].

King Henry. Sad-hearted men, much overgone° with
    care,
Here sits a king more woful than you are.

*Alarums. Excursions. Enter the Queen [Margaret],
    the Prince [of Wales], and Exeter.*

125 *Prince.* Fly, father, fly! for all your friends are fled
And Warwick rages like a chafèd bull:
Away! for death doth hold us in pursuit.

Queen Margaret. Mount you, my lord, towards Ber-
    wick post amain.°
Edward and Richard, like a brace of greyhounds
130 Having the fearful flying hare in sight,
With fiery eyes sparkling for very wrath,
And bloody steel grasped in their ireful hands,
Are at our backs; and therefore hence amain!°

Exeter. Away! for vengeance comes along with them:
135 Nay, stay not to expostulate; make speed!
Or else come after. I'll away before.

King Henry. Nay, take me with thee, good sweet
    Exeter.
Not that I fear to stay, but love to go
Whither the Queen intends. Forward, away!
Exeunt.

123 **overgone** overcome   128, 133 **amain** with full speed

[Scene VI. *Another part of the field.*]

A loud alarum. Enter Clifford, wounded.

Clifford. Here burns my candle out; ay, here it dies,
　　Which, whiles it lasted, gave King Henry light.
　　O Lancaster! I fear thy overthrow
　　More than my body's parting with my soul.
　　My love and fear glued° many friends to thee, 　　　　5
　　And now I fall, thy tough commixtures° melts,
　　Impairing Henry, strength'ning misproud° York.
　　And whither fly the gnats but to the sun?
　　And who shines now but Henry's enemies? 　　　　　10
　　O Phoebus, hadst thou never given consent
　　That Phaëthon should check thy fiery steeds,
　　Thy burning car never had scorched the earth!
　　And, Henry, hadst thou swayed° as kings should
　　　　do,
　　Or as thy father and his father did, 　　　　　　　15
　　Giving no ground unto the house of York,
　　They never then had sprung like summer flies;
　　I and ten thousand in this luckless realm
　　Had left no mourning widows for our death;
　　And thou this day hadst kept thy chair in peace. 　　20
　　For what doth cherish weeds but gentle air?
　　And what makes robbers bold but too much lenity?
　　Bootless are plaints, and cureless are my wounds;
　　No way to fly, nor strength to hold out flight;
　　The foe is merciless, and will not pity; 　　　　　25
　　For at their hands I have deserved no pity.
　　The air hath got into my deadly wounds,
　　And much effuse° of blood doth make me faint.

II.vi.5 **My love and fear glued** both love and fear of me attached
6 **commixtures** compound　7 **misproud** arrogant　14 **swayed** ruled
28 **effuse** pouring out

85

Come, York and Richard, Warwick and the rest;
30   I stabbed your fathers' bosoms; split my breast.

                             [*Faints.*]

Alarum and retreat. Enter Edward, Warwick, Richard,
     and Soldiers; Montague and Clarence.

Edward. Now breathe we,° lords: good fortune bids
    us pause,
    And smooth the frowns of war with peaceful looks.
    Some troops pursue the bloody-minded Queen,
    That led calm Henry, though he were a king,
35   As doth a sail, filled with a fretting gust,
    Command° an argosy° to stem the waves.
    But think you, lords, that Clifford fled with them?

Warwick. No, 'tis impossible he should escape;
    For, though before his face I speak the words,
40   Your brother Richard marked him for the grave:
    And whereso'er he is, he's surely dead.

                    Clifford groans [*and dies*].

Edward. Whose soul is that which takes her heavy
    leave?

Richard. A deadly groan, like life and death's de-
    parting.°

Edward. See who it is: and, now the battle's ended,
45   If friend or foe, let him be gently used.

Richard. Revoke that doom° of mercy, for 'tis Clif-
    ford;
    Who not contented that he lopped the branch
    In hewing Rutland when his leaves put forth,
    But set his murdering knife unto the root
50   From whence that tender spray did sweetly spring:
    I mean our princely father, Duke of York.

Warwick. From off the gates of York fetch down the
    head,

---

31 Now breathe we now let us rest   36 Command compel   36 argosy merchant vessel of the largest size and burden   43 departing separation   46 doom sentence

Your father's head, which Clifford placèd there;
Instead whereof let this supply the room:°
Measure for measure must be answerèd.   35

Edward. Bring forth that fatal screech-owl to our
    house,
That nothing sung but death to us and ours.
Now death shall stop his dismal threat'ning sound
And his ill-boding tongue no more shall speak.

Warwick. I think his understanding is bereft.°   60
Speak, Clifford, dost thou know who speaks to
    thee?
Dark cloudy death o'ershades his beams of life,
And he nor sees nor hears us what we say.

Richard. O, would he did! and so perhaps he doth:
'Tis but his policy to counterfeit,   65
Because he would avoid such bitter taunts
Which in the time of death he gave our father.

Clarence. If so thou think'st, vex° him with eager°
    words.

Richard. Clifford, ask mercy and obtain no grace.

Edward. Clifford, repent in bootless penitence.   70

Warwick. Clifford, devise excuses for thy faults.

Clarence. While we devise fell tortures for thy faults.

Richard. Thou didst love York, and I am son to York.

Edward. Thou pitied'st Rutland, I will pity thee.

Clarence. Where's Captain Margaret, to fence° you
    now?   75

Warwick. They mock thee, Clifford. Swear as thou
    wast wont.

Richard. What! not an oath? Nay, then the world goes
    hard

54 **room** place   60 **his understanding is bereft** he is deprived of his
understanding   68 **vex** torment   68 **eager** sharp   75 **fence** protect

When Clifford cannot spare his friends an oath.
I know by that he's dead; and, by my soul,
80 If this right hand would buy two hours' life,
That I in all despite might rail at him,
This hand should chop it off, and with the issuing
    blood
Stifle the villain whose unstanchèd thirst
York and young Rutland could not satisfy.

Warwick. Ay, but he's dead. Off with the traitor's
85   head,
And rear° it in the place your father's stands.
And now to London with triumphant march,
There to be crownèd England's royal king:
From whence shall Warwick cut the sea to France,
90 And ask the Lady Bona for thy queen.
So shalt thou sinew both these lands together;
And, having France thy friend, thou shalt not dread
The scattered foe that hopes to rise again;
For though they cannot greatly sting to hurt,
95 Yet look to have them buzz to offend thine ears.

First will I see the coronation.
And then to Brittany I'll cross the sea,
To effect this marriage, so it please my lord.
Edward. Even as thou wilt, sweet Warwick, let it be;
100 For in thy shoulder do I build my seat,
And never will I undertake the thing
Wherein thy counsel and consent is wanting.
Richard, I will create thee Duke of Gloucester;
And George, of Clarence: Warwick, as ourself,°
105 Shall do and undo as him pleaseth best.

Richard. Let me be Duke of Clarence, George of
    Gloucester;
For Gloucester's dukedom is too ominous.°

Warwick. Tut, that's a foolish observation.
Richard, be Duke of Gloucester. Now to London,
110 To see these honors in possession.   *Exeunt.*

86 **rear** erect 104 **ourself** (note the royal "we") 107 **For . . . ominous** (refers to the disgrace and murder of Humphrey, Duke of Gloucester, Lord Protector; see *2 Henry VI*)

[ACT III

Scene I. *A forest in the North of England.*]

Enter [two Keepers] with cross-bows in their hands.

First Keeper. Under this thick-grown brake° we'll
    shroud° ourselves;
  For through this laund° anon the deer will come,
  And in this covert° will we make our stand,°
  Culling° the principal of all the deer.

Second Keeper. I'll stay above the hill, so both may
    shoot.   *5*

First Keeper. That cannot be; the noise of thy cross-
    bow
  Will scare the herd, and so my shoot is lost.
  Here stand we both, and aim we at the best;°
  And, for° the time shall not seem tedious,
  I'll tell thee what befell me on a day   *10*
  In this self° place where now we mean to stand.

Second Keeper. Here comes a man, let's stay till he
    be past.

III.i.1 **brake** thicket **1 shroud** conceal **2 laund** glade **3 covert**
thicket 3 **stand** hiding place **4 Culling** picking out 8 **at the best**
as well as we can **9 for** so that 11 **self** same

Enter the King [Henry, disguised] with a prayer-book.

King Henry. From Scotland am I stol'n, even of pure
        love,
    To greet mine own land with my wishful sight.
15   No, Harry, Harry, 'tis no land of thine;
    Thy place is filled, thy scepter wrung from thee,
    Thy balm   washed   off   wherewith   thou   wast
        anointed:
    No bending knee will call thee Caesar now,
    No humble suitors press to speak for right,
20   No, not a man comes for redress of° thee;
    For how can I help them, and not myself?

First Keeper. Ay, here's a deer whose skin's a keeper's
        fee!
    This is the quondam° king; let's seize upon him.

King Henry. Let me embrace thee, sour Adversity,
25   For wise men say it is the wisest course.

Second Keeper. Why linger we? let us lay hands upon
        him.

First Keeper. Forbear awhile; we'll hear a little more.

King Henry. My queen and son are gone to France for
        aid;
    And, as I hear, the great commanding Warwick
30   Is thither gone, to crave the French king's sister
    To wife for Edward. If this news be true,
    Poor queen and son, your labor is but lost;
    For Warwick is a subtle orator,
    And Lewis a prince soon won with moving words.
35   By this account, then, Margaret may win him;
    For she's a woman to be pitied much.
    Her sighs will make a batt'ry° in his breast;
    Her tears will pierce into a marble heart;
    The tiger will be mild whiles she doth mourn;
40   And Nero will be tainted with remorse

20 of from   **23 quondam** former   **37 batt'ry** bombardment

To hear and see her plaints, her brinish tears.
Ay, but she's come to beg, Warwick, to give;
She on his left side, craving aid for Henry,
He on his right, asking a wife for Edward.
She weeps, and says her Henry is deposed;   *45*
He smiles, and says his Edward is installed;
That she (poor wretch) for grief can speak no
    more;
Whiles Warwick tells his title, smooths the wrong,
Inferreth arguments of mighty strength,
And in conclusion wins the King from her,   *50*
With promise of his sister, and what else,
To strengthen and support King Edward's place.
O Margaret, thus 'twill be; and thou (poor soul)
Art then forsaken, as thou went'st forlorn!

Second Keeper. Say, what art thou that talk'st of kings
    and queens?   *55*

King Henry. More than I seem, and less than I was
    born to:
A man at least, for less I should not be;
And men may talk of kings, and why not I?

Second Keeper. Ay, but thou talk'st as if thou wert a
    king.

King Henry. Why, so I am (in mind) and that's
    enough.   *60*

Second Keeper. But, if thou be a king, where is thy
    crown?

King Henry. My crown is in my heart, not on my
    head;
Not decked with diamonds and Indian stones,
Nor to be seen. My crown is called content:
A crown it is that seldom kings enjoy.   *65*

Second Keeper. Well, if you be a king crowned with
    content,
Your crown content and you must be contented
To go along with us; for (as we think)

You are the king King Edward hath deposed;
70   And we his subjects sworn in all allegiance
Will apprehend you as his enemy.

King Henry. But did you never swear, and break an
oath?

Second Keeper. No, never such an oath; nor will not
now.

King Henry. Where did you dwell when I was King
of England?

Second Keeper. Here in this country, where we now
75   remain.

King Henry. I was anointed king at nine months old;
My father and my grandfather were kings,
And you were sworn true subjects unto me:
And tell me, then, have you not broke your oaths?

80   *First Keeper.* No;
For we were subjects but while you were king.

King Henry. Why, am I dead? Do I not breathe a
man?
Ah, simple men, you know not what you swear!
Look, as I blow this feather from my face,
85   And as the air blows it to me again,
Obeying with my wind when I do blow,
And yielding to another when it blows,
Commanded always by the greater gust—
Such is the lightness of you common men.
90   But do not break your oaths; for of that sin
My mild entreaty shall not make you guilty.
Go where you will, the King shall be commanded;
And be you kings, command, and I'll obey.

First Keeper. We are true subjects to the king, King
Edward.

95   *King Henry.* So would you be again to Henry,
If he were seated as King Edward is.

First Keeper. We charge you, in God's name, and the
    King's,
  To go with us unto the officers.

King Henry. In God's name, lead. Your king's name
    be obeyed:
  And what God will, that let your king perform;   *100*
  And what he will, I humbly yield unto.

                            Exeunt.

[Scene II. *London. The Palace.*]

*Enter King Edward, [Richard, Duke of] Gloucester,
[George, Duke of] Clarence, Lady [Elizabeth] Grey.*

King Edward. Brother of Gloucester, at Saint Albans
    field
  This lady's husband, Sir Richard Grey, was slain,
  His land then seized on by the conqueror.
  Her suit is now to repossess those lands;
  Which we in justice cannot well deny,°   *5*
  Because in quarrel of the house of York
  The worthy gentleman did lose his life.

Richard. Your Highness shall do well to grant her
    suit;
  It were dishonor to deny it her.

King Edward. It were no less; but yet I'll make a
    pause.   *10*

Richard. [*Aside to Clarence*] Yea, is it so?
  I see the lady hath a thing to grant,
  Before the King will grant her humble suit.

Clarence. [*Aside to Richard*] He knows the game:
    how true he keeps the wind!°

15 *Richard.* [*Aside to Clarence*] Silence!

King Edward. Widow, we will consider of your suit;
    And come some other time to know our mind.

Lady Grey. Right gracious lord, I cannot brook°
    delay:
    May it please your Highness to resolve me now,
20   And what your pleasure is shall satisfy me.

Richard. [*Aside to Clarence*] Ay, widow? then I'll
    warrant° you all your lands,
    And if what pleases him shall pleasure you.
    Fight closer, or, good faith, you'll catch a blow.

Clarence. [*Aside to Richard*] I fear her not, unless she
    chance to fall.

Richard. [*Aside to Clarence*] God forbid that! for he'll
25   take vantages.°

King Edward. How many children hast thou, widow?
    tell me.

Clarence. [*Aside to Richard*] I think he means to beg
    a child of her.

Richard. [*Aside to Clarence*] Nay then, whip me: he'll
    rather give her two.

Lady Grey. Three, my most gracious lord.

Richard. [*Aside to Clarence*] You shall have four, if
30   you'll be ruled by him.

King Edward. 'Twere pity they should lose their
    father's lands.

Lady Grey. Be pitiful, dread lord, and grant it then.

---

14 keeps the wind (metaphor from hunting) keeps to the windward
side of the game **18 brook** endure **21 warrant** guarantee **25
take vantages** take advantage of opportunities

King Edward. Lords, give us leave: I'll try this widow's wit.°

Richard. [*Aside to Clarence*] Ay, good leave have you; for you will have leave,
  Till youth take leave and leave you to the crutch.°   35
                  [*Richard and Clarence withdraw.*]

King Edward. Now tell me, madam, do you love your children?

Lady Grey. Ay, full as dearly as I love myself.

King Edward. And would you not do much to do them good?

Lady Grey. To do them good, I would sustain some harm.

King Edward. Then get your husband's lands, to do them good.   40

Lady Grey. Therefore I came unto your Majesty.

King Edward. I'll tell you how these lands are to be got.

Lady Grey. So shall you bind me to your Highness' service.

King Edward. What service wilt thou do me, if I give them?

Lady Grey. What you command, that rests in me° to do.   45

King Edward. But you will take exceptions to my boon.°

Lady Grey. No, gracious lord, except I cannot do it.

King Edward. Ay, but thou canst do what I mean to ask.

---

33 **wit** intelligence   34–35 **for . . . crutch** for you will take liberties until youth departs and leaves you infirm   45 **rests in me** is in my power   46 **boon** favor

Lady Grey. Why, then I will do what your grace
     commands.

Richard. [*Aside to Clarence*] He plies her hard; and
50   much rain wears the marble.

Clarence. [*Aside to Richard*] As red as fire! Nay, then
     her wax must melt.

Lady Grey. Why stops my lord? shall I not hear my
     task?

King Edward. An easy task; 'tis but to love a king.

Lady Grey. That's soon performed, because I am a
     subject.

King Edward. Why, then, thy husband's lands I freely
55   give thee.

Lady Grey. I take my leave with many thousand
     thanks.

Richard. [*Aside to Clarence*] The match is made; she
     seals it with a curtsy.

King Edward. But stay thee, 'tis the fruits of love I
     mean.

Lady Grey. The fruits of love I mean, my loving
     liege.

60   *King Edward.* Ay, but, I fear me, in another sense.
     What love, think'st thou, I sue so much to get?

Lady Grey. My love till death, my humble thanks,
     my prayers;
     That love which virtue begs and virtue grants.

King Edward. No, by my troth, I did not mean such
     love.

Lady Grey. Why, then you mean not as I thought you
65   did.

King Edward. But now you partly may perceive my
     mind.

Lady Grey. My mind will never grant what I perceive
  Your Highness aims at, if I aim aright.

King Edward. To tell thee plain, I aim to lie with thee.

Lady Grey. To tell you plain, I had rather lie in
  prison.   *70*

King Edward. Why, then thou shalt not have thy
  husband's lands.

Lady Grey. Why, then mine honesty° shall be my
  dower;
  For by that loss I will not purchase them.

King Edward. Therein thou wrong'st thy children
  mightily.

Lady Grey. Herein your Highness wrongs both them
  and me.   *75*
  But, mighty lord, this merry inclination
  Accords not with the sadness of my suit.°
  Please you dismiss me, either with "ay" or "no."

King Edward. Ay, if thou wilt say "ay" to my request;
  No, if thou dost say "no" to my demand.   *80*

Lady Grey. Then, no, my lord. My suit is at an end.

Richard. [*Aside to Clarence*] The widow likes him
  not, she knits her brows.

Clarence. [*Aside to Richard*] He is the bluntest wooer
  in Christendom.

King Edward. [*Aside*] Her looks doth argue her re-
  plete with modesty;
  Her words doth show her wit incomparable;   *85*
  All her perfections challenge° sovereignty:
  One way or other, she is for a king;
  And she shall be my love, or else my queen—

---

72 honesty chastity   77 sadness of my suit seriousness of my request   86 challenge lay claim to

[*aloud*] Say that King Edward take thee for his
queen?

Lady Grey. 'Tis better said than done, my gracious
90   lord:
I am a subject fit to jest withal,
But far unfit to be a sovereign.

King Edward. Sweet widow, by my state I swear to
thee
I speak no more than what my soul intends;
95   And that is, to enjoy thee for my love.

Lady Grey. And that is more than I will yield unto.
I know I am too mean° to be your queen,
And yet too good to be your concubine.

King Edward. You cavil, widow: I did mean, my
queen.

Lady Grey. 'Twill grieve your Grace my sons should
100   call you father.

King Edward. No more than when my daughters call
thee mother.
Thou art a widow, and thou hast some children;
And, by God's Mother, I, being but a bachelor,
Have other some:° why, 'tis a happy° thing
105   To be the father unto many sons.
Answer no more, for thou shalt be my queen.

Richard. [*Aside to Clarence*] The ghostly° father now
hath done his shrift.

Clarence. [*Aside to Richard*] When he was made a
shriver, 'twas for shift.°

King Edward. Brothers, you muse what chat we two
have had.

Richard. The widow likes it not, for she looks very
110   sad.

97 **mean** low in rank   104 **other some** others   104 **happy** fortunate
107 **ghostly** spiritual   108 **for shift** (1) to serve a purpose (2) for a
woman's undergarment

King Edward. You'd think it strange if I should marry
      her.

Clarence. To who, my lord?

King Edward.   Why, Clarence, to myself.

Richard. That would be ten days' wonder at the least.

Clarence. That's a day longer than a wonder lasts.°

Richard. By so much is the wonder in extremes.   *115*

King Edward. Well, jest on, brothers. I can tell you
      both
  Her suit is granted for her husband's lands.

                Enter a Nobleman.

Nobleman. My gracious lord, Henry your foe is taken,
  And brought your prisoner to your palace gate.

King Edward. See that he be conveyed unto the
      Tower: *120*
  And go we, brothers, to the man that took him,
  To question of his apprehension.°
  Widow, go you along. Lords, use her honorably.
                    Exeunt. Manet° Richard.

Richard. Ay, Edward will use women honorably.
  Would he were wasted, marrow, bones and all,   *125*
  That from his loins no hopeful branch may spring,
  To cross me from the golden time I look for!
  And yet, between my soul's desire and me—
  The lustful Edward's title burièd—
  Is Clarence, Henry, and his son young Edward,   *130*
  And all the unlooked-for° issue of their bodies,
  To take their rooms, ere I can place myself:
  A cold premeditation for my purpose!
  Why then, I do but dream on sovereignty;
  Like one that stands upon a promontory,   *135*
  And spies a far-off shore where he would tread,

114 **That's . . . lasts** (proverbially a wonder lasts only nine days)
122 **apprehension** arrest 123 s.d. **Manet** remains (Latin) 131 **unlooked-for** (1) unforeseen (2) undesired

Wishing his foot were equal with his eye,
And chides the sea that sunders him from thence,
Saying, he'll lade° it dry to have his way:

140 So do I wish the crown, being so far off;
And so I chide the means that keeps me from it;
And so (I say) I'll cut the causes off,
Flattering me with impossibilities.
My eye's too quick, my heart o'erweens too much,°

145 Unless my hand and strength could equal them.
Well, say there is no kingdom then for Richard:
What other pleasure can the world afford?
I'll make my heaven in a lady's lap,
And deck my body in gay ornaments

150 And witch° sweet ladies with my words and looks.
O miserable thought! and more unlikely
Than to accomplish° twenty golden crowns!
Why, Love forswore° me in my mother's womb:
And, for° I should not deal in her soft laws,

155 She did corrupt frail Nature with some bribe,
To shrink mine arm up like a withered shrub;
To make an envious° mountain on my back,
Where sits deformity to mock my body;
To shape my legs of an unequal size;

160 To disproportion me in every part,
Like to a chaos,° or an unlicked bear-whelp
That carries no impression like the dam.
And am I then a man to be beloved?
O monstrous fault,° to harbor such a thought!

165 Then, since this earth affords no joy to me,
But to command, to check, to o'erbear such
As are of better person° than myself,
I'll make my heaven to dream upon the crown,
And, whiles I live, t' account this world but hell,

170 Until my misshaped trunk that bears this head
Be round impalèd with a glorious crown.
And yet I know not how to get the crown,

---

139 lade bail   144 o'erweens too much is too presumptuous
150 witch bewitch   152 accomplish obtain   153 forswore abjured
154 for so that   157 envious spiteful   161 chaos shapeless mass
164 fault error   167 person appearance

For many lives stand between me and home:°
And I—like one lost in a thorny wood,
That rends the thorns and is rent with the thorns,   *173*
Seeking a way and straying from the way,
Not knowing how to find the open air,
But toiling desperately to find it out—
Torment myself to catch the English crown:
And from that torment I will free myself,   *180*
Or hew my way out with a bloody ax.
Why, I can smile, and murder whiles I smile,
And cry "Content" to that which grieves my heart,
And wet my cheeks with artificial tears,
And frame my face to all occasions.   *185*
I'll drown more sailors than the mermaid shall;
I'll slay more gazers than the basilisk;°
I'll play the orator as well as Nestor,
Deceive more slily than Ulysses could,
And, like a Sinon,° take another Troy.   *190*
I can add colors to the chameleon,
Change shapes with Proteus° for advantages,
And set the murderous Machiavel° to school.
Can I do this, and cannot get a crown?
Tut, were it farther off, I'll pluck it down.   *Exit.* *195*

---

173 home my goal   **187 basilisk** fabulous reptile, said to kill by its
look and breath   **190 Sinon** Greek warrior who devised the stratagem of the wooden horse, by which the Greeks ultimately captured
and destroyed Troy   **192 Proteus** sea-deity who assumed various
forms   **193 Machiavel** Niccolò Machiavelli, author of *The Prince*
(1513), whose name became synonymous with sinister intrigue and
the worship of power

[Scene III. *France. The King's Palace.*]

*Flourish. Enter Lewis the French King, his sister
Bona, his Admiral, called Bourbon; Prince Edward,
Queen Margaret, and the Earl of Oxford. Lewis sits,
and riseth up again.*

King Lewis. Fair Queen of England, worthy Margaret,
　　Sit down with us: it ill befits thy state
　　And birth, that thou shouldst stand while Lewis
　　　doth sit.

Queen Margaret. No, mighty King of France: now
　　　Margaret
5　　Must strike her sail° and learn awhile to serve
　　Where kings command. I was (I must confess)
　　Great Albion's° Queen in former golden days;
　　But now mischance hath trod my title down,
　　And with dishonor laid me on the ground;
10　Where I must take like seat unto my fortune,
　　And to my humble seat conform myself.

King Lewis. Why, say, fair Queen, whence springs
　　　this deep despair?

Queen Margaret. From such a cause as fills mine eyes
　　　with tears
　　And stops my tongue, while heart is drowned in
　　　cares.

15　*King Lewis.* Whate'er it be, be thou still like thyself,
　　And sit thee by our side. (*Seats her by him.*) Yield
　　　not thy neck
　　To Fortune's yoke, but let thy dauntless mind
　　Still ride in triumph over all mischance.

III.iii.5 **strike her sail** humble herself　7 **Albion** ancient name of
Britain

Be plain, Queen Margaret, and tell thy grief;
It shall be eased, if France can yield relief.   20

Queen Margaret. Those gracious words revive my
    drooping thoughts
And give my tongue-tied sorrows leave to speak.
Now, therefore, be it known to noble Lewis,
That Henry, sole possessor of my love,
Is of a king become a banished man,   25
And forced to live in Scotland a forlorn;°
While proud ambitious Edward, Duke of York,
Usurps the regal title and the seat
Of England's true-anointed lawful King.
This is the cause that I, poor Margaret,   30
With this my son, Prince Edward, Henry's heir,
Am come to crave thy just and lawful aid;
And if thou fail us, all our hope is done.
Scotland hath will to help, but cannot help;
Our people and our peers are both misled,   35
Our treasure seized, our soldiers put to flight,
And, as thou seest, ourselves in heavy° plight.

King Lewis. Renownèd Queen, with patience calm the
    storm,
While we bethink a means to break it off.°

Queen Margaret. The more we stay, the stronger
    grows our foe.   40

King Lewis. The more I stay,° the more I'll succor
    thee.

Queen Margaret. O, but impatience waiteth on° true
    sorrow.
And see where comes the breeder of my sorrow!

Enter Warwick.

King Lewis. What's he approacheth boldly to our
    presence?

---

26 a forlorn a forlorn man   37 heavy sad   39 break it off end it
41 stay (with pun on the meaning "support")   42 waiteth on accompanies

Queen Margaret. Our Earl of Warwick, Edward's
45   greatest friend.

King Lewis. Welcome, brave Warwick! What brings
thee to France?   *He descends. She ariseth.*

Queen Margaret. [*Aside*] Ay, now begins a second
storm to rise,
For this is he that moves both wind and tide.

Warwick. From worthy Edward, King of Albion,
50   My lord and sovereign, and thy vowèd friend,
I come, in kindness and unfeignèd love,
First, to do greetings to thy royal person;
And then to crave a league of amity;
And lastly, to confirm that amity
55   With nuptial knot, if thou vouchsafe to grant
That virtuous Lady Bona, thy fair sister,
To England's King in lawful marriage.

Queen Margaret. [*Aside*] If that go forward, Henry's
hope is done.

Warwick. (*Speaking to Bona*) And, gracious madam,
in our king's behalf,
60   I am commanded, with your leave and favor,°
Humbly to kiss your hand, and with my tongue
To tell the passion° of my sovereign's heart;
Where fame,° late ent'ring at his heedful ears,
Hath placed thy beauty's image and thy virtue.

Queen Margaret. King Lewis and Lady Bona, hear
65   me speak,
Before you answer Warwick. His demand
Springs not from Edward's well-meant honest love,
But from deceit, bred by necessity;
For how can tyrants° safely govern home,
70   Unless abroad they purchase° great alliance?
To prove him tyrant this reason may suffice,
That Henry liveth still; but were he dead,
Yet here Prince Edward stands, King Henry's son.

60 **leave and favor** kind permission   62 **passion** suffering   63 **fame**
rumor   69 **tyrants** usurpers   70 **purchase** obtain

Look, therefore, Lewis, that by this league and
  marriage
Thou draw not on thy danger and dishonor;   *75*
For though usurpers sway the rule awhile,
Yet heavens are just, and time suppresseth wrongs.

Warwick. Injurious Margaret!

Prince.   And why not Queen?

Warwick. Because thy father Henry did usurp;
And thou no more art Prince than she is Queen.   *80*

Oxford. Then Warwick disannuls° great John of
  Gaunt,
Which did subdue the greatest part of Spain;
And, after John of Gaunt, Henry the Fourth,
Whose wisdom was a mirror° to the wisest;
And, after that wise prince, Henry the Fifth,   *85*
Who by his prowess conquerèd all France:
From these our Henry lineally descends.

Warwick. Oxford, how haps it, in this smooth dis-
  course,
You told not how Henry the Sixth hath lost
All that which Henry the Fifth had gotten?   *90*
Methinks these peers of France should smile at
  that.
But for the rest: you tell° a pedigree
Of threescore and two years—a silly° time
To make prescription° for a kingdom's worth.

Oxford. Why, Warwick, canst thou speak against thy
  liege,   *95*
Whom thou obeyèdst thirty and six years,
And not bewray° thy treason with a blush?

Warwick. Can Oxford, that did ever fence° the right,
Now buckler° falsehood with a pedigree?
For shame! leave Henry, and call Edward king.   *100*

---

81 **disannuls** again cancels 84 **mirror** model 92 **tell** (1) relate
(2) count 93 **silly** scanty 94 **prescription** claim 97 **bewray** reveal
98 **fence** defend 99 **buckler** shield

Oxford. Call him my king by whose injurious doom°
    My elder brother, the Lord Aubrey Vere,
    Was done to death? and more than so, my father,
    Even in the downfall of his mellowed years,
105   When nature brought him to the door of death?
    No, Warwick, no; while life upholds this arm,
    This arm upholds the house of Lancaster.

Warwick. And I the house of York.

King Lewis. Queen Margaret, Prince Edward, and
    Oxford,
110   Vouchsafe, at our request, to stand aside,
    While I use further conference with Warwick.
                     They stand aloof.

Queen Margaret. Heavens grant that Warwick's words
    bewitch him not!

King Lewis. Now, Warwick, tell me, even upon thy
    conscience,
    Is Edward your true king? for I were loath
115   To link with him that were not lawful chosen.

Warwick. Thereon I pawn my credit and mine honor.

King Lewis. But is he gracious° in the people's eye?

Warwick. The more that Henry was unfortunate.

King Lewis. Then further, all dissembling set aside,
120   Tell me for truth the measure of his love
    Unto our sister Bona.

Warwick.   Such it seems
    As may beseem a monarch like himself.
    Myself have often heard him say and swear
    That this his love was an eternal plant,
125   Whereof the root was fixed in virtue's ground,
    The leaves and fruit maintained with beauty's sun,
    Exempt from envy, but not from disdain,
    Unless the Lady Bona quit° his pain.

101 **injurious doom** unjust sentence   117 **gracious** favored, popular
128 **quit** requite

King Lewis. Now, sister, let us hear your firm resolve.

Bona. Your grant, or your denial, shall be mine: 130
    Yet I confess that often ere this day
                    (Speaks to Warwick),
    When I have heard your king's desert recounted,
    Mine ear hath tempted judgment to desire.

King Lewis. Then, Warwick, thus: our sister shall be
    Edward's;
    And now forthwith shall articles be drawn   135
    Touching the jointure° that your king must make,
    Which with her dowry shall be counterpoised.
    Draw near, Queen Margaret, and be a witness
    That Bona shall be wife to the English king.

Prince. To Edward, but not to the English king.   140

Queen Margaret. Deceitful Warwick! it was thy device
    By this alliance to make void my suit:
    Before thy coming Lewis was Henry's friend.

King Lewis. And still is friend to him and Margaret:
    But if your title to the crown be weak,   145
    As may appear by Edward's good success,
    Then 'tis but reason that I be released
    From giving aid which late I promisèd.
    Yet shall you have all kindness at my hand
    That your estate requires and mine can yield.   150

Warwick. Henry now lives in Scotland at his ease,
    Where having nothing, nothing can he lose.
    And as for you yourself, our quondam° queen,
    You have a father able to maintain you,
    And better 'twere you troubled him than France.   155

Queen Margaret. Peace, impudent and shameless
    Warwick, peace,
    Proud setter up and puller down of kings!
    I will not hence, till with my talk and tears
    (Both full of truth) I make King Lewis behold

136 jointure marriage settlement   **153 quondam** former

160   Thy sly conveyance° and thy lord's false love;
       For both of you are birds of selfsame feather.
                              Post blowing a horn within.

King Lewis. Warwick, this is some post to us or thee.

                    Enter the Post.

Post. (*Speaks to Warwick*) My lord ambassador,
       these letters are for you,
       Sent from your brother, Marquess Montague;
       (*To Lewis*) These from our King unto your
165   Majesty;
       (*To Margaret*) And, madam, these for you; from
       whom I know not.   *They all read their letters.*

Oxford. I like it well that our fair Queen and mistress
       Smiles at her news, while Warwick frowns at his.

Prince. Nay, mark how Lewis stamps, as he were
170   nettled.
       I hope all's for the best.

King Lewis. Warwick, what are thy news? and yours,
       fair Queen?

Queen Margaret. Mine, such as fill my heart with
       unhoped joys.

Warwick. Mine, full of sorrow and heart's discontent.

King Lewis. What! has your king married the Lady
       Grey?
175   And now, to soothe your forgery and his,
       Sends me a paper to persuade me patience?
       Is this th' alliance that he seeks with France?
       Dare he presume to scorn us in this manner?

Queen Margaret. I told your Majesty as much before:
180   This proveth Edward's love and Warwick's honesty!

---

160 **conveyance** (1) transfer of property (here, Lewis's promise of
aid) (2) trickery

Warwick. King Lewis, I here protest, in sight of
    heaven,
  And by the hope I have of heavenly bliss,
  That I am clear from this misdeed of Edward's,
  No more my king, for he dishonors me,
  But most himself, if he could see his shame.   *185*
  Did I forget that by the house of York
  My father came untimely to his death?
  Did I let pass th' abuse done to my niece?
  Did I impale° him with the regal crown?
  Did I put Henry from his native right?   *190*
  And am I guerdoned° at the last with shame?
  Shame on himself! for my desert is honor:
  And to repair my honor lost for him,
  I here renounce him and return to Henry.
  My noble Queen, let former grudges pass,   *195*
  And henceforth I am thy true servitor:
  I will revenge his wrong to Lady Bona
  And replant Henry in his former state.

Queen Margaret. Warwick, these words have turned
    my hate to love;
  And I forgive and quite forget old faults,   *200*
  And joy that thou becom'st King Henry's friend.

Warwick. So much his friend, ay, his unfeignèd
    friend,
  That, if King Lewis vouchsafe to furnish us
  With some few bands of chosen soldiers,
  I'll undertake to land them on our coast   *205*
  And force the tyrant from his seat by war.
  'Tis not his new-made bride shall succor him:
  And as for Clarence, as my letters tell me,
  He's very likely now to fall from him,
  For matching° more for wanton lust than honor,   *210*
  Or than for strength and safety of our country.

Bona. Dear brother, how shall Bona be revenged
  But by thy help to this distressèd queen?

189 **impale** encircle   191 **guerdoned** rewarded   210 **matching** marrying

Queen Margaret. Renownèd prince, how shall poor
    Henry live,
215   Unless thou rescue him from foul despair?

Bona. My quarrel and this English queen's are one.

Warwick. And mine, fair Lady Bona, joins with yours.

King Lewis. And mine with hers, and thine, and
    Margaret's.
    Therefore at last I firmly am resolved
220   You shall have aid.

Queen Margaret. Let me give humble thanks for all
    at once.

King Lewis. Then, England's messenger, return in
    post,°
    And tell false Edward, thy supposèd king,
    That Lewis of France is sending over masquers°
225   To revel it with him and his new bride:
    Thou seest what's passed, go fear° thy king withal.

Bona. Tell him, in hope he'll prove a widower shortly,
    I'll wear the willow garland° for his sake.

Queen Margaret. Tell him, my mourning weeds° are
    laid aside,
230   And I am ready to put armor on.

Warwick. Tell him from me that he hath done me
    wrong,
    And therefore I'll uncrown him ere't be long.
    There's thy reward. Be gone.   *Exit Post.*

King Lewis.   But, Warwick,
    Thou and Oxford, with five thousand men,
235   Shall cross the seas, and bid false Edward battle;
    And, as occasion serves,° this noble Queen
    And Prince shall follow with a fresh supply.
    Yet, ere thou go, but answer me one doubt,
    What pledge have we of thy firm loyalty?

222 **post** haste   224 **masquers** performers   226 **fear** (verb) frighten
228 **willow garland** sign of disappointed love   229 **weeds** garments
236 **serves** is opportune

Warwick. This shall assure my constant loyalty,   240
  That if our Queen and this young Prince agree,
  I'll join mine eldest daughter and my joy
  To him forthwith in holy wedlock bands.

Queen Margaret. Yes, I agree, and thank you for
    your motion.°
  Son Edward, she is fair and virtuous,   245
  Therefore delay not, give thy hand to Warwick;
  And, with thy hand, thy faith irrevocable,
  That only Warwick's daughter shall be thine.

Prince. Yes, I accept her, for she well deserves it;
  And here, to pledge my vow, I give my hand.   250
                    He gives his hand to Warwick.

King Lewis. Why stay we now? These soldiers shall
    be levied,
  And thou, Lord Bourbon, our High Admiral,
  Shall waft them over with our royal fleet.
  I long till Edward fall° by war's mischance,
  For mocking marriage with a dame of France.   255
                    Exeunt. Manet° Warwick.

Warwick. I came from Edward as ambassador,
  But I return his sworn and mortal foe:
  Matter of marriage was the charge he gave me,
  But dreadful war shall answer his demand.°
  Had he none else to make a stale° but me?   260
  Then none but I shall turn his jest to sorrow.
  I was the chief that raised him to the crown,
  And I'll be chief to bring him down again;
  Not that I pity Henry's misery,
  But seek revenge on Edward's mockery.   *Exit.* 265

[ACT IV

Scene I. *London. The Palace.*]

Enter Richard, Clarence, Somerset, and Montague.

Richard. Now tell me, brother Clarence, what think
  you
Of this new marriage with the Lady Grey?

Hath not our brother made a worthy choice?

Clarence. Alas, you know 'tis far from hence to
  France!
5   How could he stay till Warwick made return?

Somerset. My lords, forbear this talk; here comes the
  King.

Richard. And his well-chosen bride.

Clarence. I mind to tell him plainly what I think.

*Flourish. Enter King Edward, Lady Grey [as Queen],
Pembroke, Stafford, Hastings, [and others]. Four
  stand on one side and four on the other.*

King Edward. Now, brother of Clarence, how like
  you our choice,
10   That you stand pensive, as half malcontent?°

Clarence. As well as Lewis of France, or the Earl of
  Warwick,

IV.i.10 **malcontent** discontented, dissatisfied
112

Which are so weak of courage and in judgment
That they'll take no offense at our abuse.°

King Edward. Suppose they take offense without a
　　cause:
They are but Lewis and Warwick; I am Edward,　　*15*
Your King and Warwick's, and must have my will.

Richard. And shall have your will, because our King.
　　Yet hasty marriage seldom proveth well.

King Edward. Yea, brother Richard, are you offended
　　too?

Richard. Not I.　　　　　　　　　　　　　　　*20*
No, God forbid that I should wish them severed
Whom God hath joined together; ay, and 'twere pity
To sunder them that yoke so well together.

King Edward. Setting your scorns and your mislike
　　aside,
Tell me some reason why the Lady Grey　　　　　*25*
Should not become my wife and England's Queen.
And you too, Somerset and Montague,
Speak freely what you think.

Clarence. Then this is mine opinion, that King Lewis
Becomes your enemy for mocking him　　　　　　*30*
About the marriage of the Lady Bona.

Richard. And Warwick, doing what you gave in
　　charge,
Is now dishonorèd by this new marriage.

King Edward. What if both Lewis and Warwick be
　　appeased
By such invention as I can devise?　　　　　　　*35*

Montague. Yet, to have joined with France in such
　　alliance

13 abuse deceit

Would more have strengthened this our common-
    wealth
'Gainst foreign storms than any home-bred mar-
    riage.

40 *Hastings.* Why, knows not Montague that of itself
    England is safe, if true within itself?

Montague. But the safer when 'tis backed with France.

Hastings. 'Tis better using France than trusting
    France:
Let us be backed with God and with the seas
Which He hath given for fence impregnable,
45 And with their helps only° defend ourselves;
In them and in ourselves our safety lies.

Clarence. For this one speech Lord Hastings well
    deserves
To have the heir of the Lord Hungerford.

King Edward. Ay, what of that? It was my will and
    grant;
50 And for this once my will shall stand for law.

Richard. And yet methinks your Grace hath not done
    well,
To give the heir and daughter of Lord Scales
Unto the brother of your loving bride.
She better would have fitted me or Clarence;
55 But in your bride you bury brotherhood.

Clarence. Or else you would not have bestowed the
    heir
Of the Lord Bonville on your new wife's son,
And leave your brothers to go speed° elsewhere.

King Edward. Alas, poor Clarence! Is it for a wife
60 That thou art malcontent? I will provide thee.

Clarence. In choosing for yourself, you showed your
    judgment,
Which being shallow, you shall give me leave

45 **only** alone   58 **speed** prosper

To play the broker° in mine own behalf;
And to that end I shortly mind to leave you.

King Edward. Leave me or tarry, Edward will be
   King,   65
And not be tied unto his brother's will.

Queen Elizabeth. My lords, before it pleased his
   Majesty
To raise my state to title of a queen,
Do me but right, and you must all confess
That I was not ignoble of descent;   70
And meaner° than myself have had like fortune.
But as this title honors me and mine,
So your dislikes, to whom I would be pleasing,
Doth cloud my joys with danger and with sorrow.

King Edward. My love, forbear to fawn upon their
   frowns.   75
What danger or what sorrow can befall thee,
So long as Edward is thy constant friend
And their true sovereign, whom they must obey?
Nay, whom they shall obey, and love thee too,
Unless they seek for hatred at my hands;   80
Which if they do, yet will I keep thee safe,
And they shall feel the vengeance of my wrath.

Richard. [*Aside*] I hear, yet say not much, but think
   the more.

Enter a Post.

King Edward. Now, messenger, what letters or what
   news
From France?   85

Post. My sovereign liege, no letters; and few words,
But such as I, without your special pardon,°
Dare not relate.

King Edward. Go to,° we pardon thee. Therefore, in
   brief,

63 **play the broker** act as go-between   71 **meaner** persons of lower
rank   87 **pardon** permission   89 **Go to** (exclamation of impatience)

Tell me their words as near as thou canst guess
90   them.
    What answer makes King Lewis unto our letters?

Post. At my depart, these were his very words:
    "Go tell false Edward, thy supposèd King,
    That Lewis of France is sending over masquers
95   To revel it with him and his new bride."

King Edward. Is Lewis so brave?° Belike he thinks
    me Henry.
    But what said Lady Bona to my marriage?

Post. These were her words, uttered with mild
    disdain:
    "Tell him, in hope he'll prove a widower shortly,
100   I'll wear the willow garland for his sake."

King Edward. I blame not her, she could say little less;
    She had the wrong. But what said Henry's queen?
    For I have heard that she was there in place.

Post. "Tell him," quoth she, "my mourning weeds
    are done,
105   And I am ready to put armor on."

King Edward. Belike she minds to play the Amazon.
    But what said Warwick to these injuries?°

Post. He, more incensed against your Majesty
    Than all the rest, discharged me with these words:
110   "Tell him from me that he hath done me wrong,
    And therefore I'll uncrown him ere't be long."

King Edward. Ha! durst the traitor breathe out so
    proud words?
    Well, I will arm me, being thus forewarned.
    They shall have wars and pay for their presumption.
115   But say, is Warwick friends with Margaret?

Post. Ay, gracious sovereign. They are so linked in
    friendship

96 **brave** defiant   107 **injuries** insults

That young Prince Edward marries Warwick's
daughter.

Clarence. Belike° the elder; Clarence will have the
younger.
Now, brother king, farewell, and sit you fast,
For I will hence to Warwick's other daughter,   120
That, though I want° a kingdom, yet in marriage
I may not prove inferior to yourself.
You that love me and Warwick, follow me.
          Exit Clarence, and Somerset follows.

Richard. [*Aside*] Not I:
My thoughts aim at a further matter. I   125
Stay not for the love of Edward, but the crown.

King Edward. Clarence and Somerset both gone to
Warwick!
Yet am I armed against the worst can happen;
And haste is needful in this desp'rate case.
Pembroke and Stafford, you in our behalf   130
Go levy men, and make prepare for war.
They are already, or quickly will be, landed.
Myself in person will straight follow you.
          Exeunt Pembroke and Stafford.
But, ere I go, Hastings and Montague,
Resolve my doubt. You twain, of all the rest,   135
Are near to Warwick by blood and by alliance.
Tell me if you love Warwick more than me.
If it be so, then both depart to him;
I rather wish you foes than hollow friends.
But if you mind to hold your true obedience,   140
Give me assurance with some friendly vow,
That I may never have you in suspect.

Montague. So God help Montague as he proves true!

Hastings. And Hastings as he favors Edward's cause!

King Edward. Now, brother Richard, will you stand
by us?   145

118 **Belike** probably   121 **want** lack

Richard. Ay, in despite of all that shall withstand you.

King Edward. Why, so! then am I sure of victory.
Now therefore let us hence, and lose no hour,
Till we meet Warwick with his foreign pow'r.

                           Exeunt.

                [Scene II. *A plain in Warwickshire.*]

      Enter Warwick and Oxford in England, with
                French Soldiers.

Warwick. Trust me, my lord, all hitherto° goes well;
The common people by numbers swarm to us.

        Enter Clarence and Somerset.

But see where Somerset and Clarence comes!
Speak suddenly,° my lords, are we all friends?

5   *Clarence.* Fear not that,° my lord.

Warwick. Then, gentle Clarence, welcome unto War-
      wick;
And welcome, Somerset: I hold it cowardice
To rest° mistrustful where a noble heart
Hath pawned° an open hand in sign of love.
10   Else might I think that Clarence, Edward's brother,
Were but a feignèd friend to our proceedings:
But welcome, sweet Clarence; my daughter shall be
      thine.
And now what rests but, in night's coverture,°
Thy brother being carelessly encamped,
15   His soldiers lurking in the towns about,
And but attended by a simple guard,

IV.ii.1 **hitherto** thus far   4 **suddenly** at once   5 **Fear not that** do
not doubt it   8 **rest** remain   9 **pawned** pledged   13 **in night's
coverture** under cover of night

We may surprise and take him at our pleasure?
Our scouts have found the adventure very easy:
That as Ulysses and stout° Diomede
With sleight° and manhood stole to Rhesus' tents,   20
And brought from thence the Thracian fatal
    steeds,°
So we, well covered with the night's black mantle,
At unawares may beat down Edward's guard
And seize himself. I say not, slaughter him,
For I intend but only to surprise him.   2⟨
You that will follow me to this attempt,
Applaud the name of Henry with your leader.

> *They all cry, "Henry!"*

Why, then, let's on our way in silent sort.°
For Warwick and his friends, God and Saint
    George!   *Exeunt.*

[Scene III. *Edward's camp, near Warwick.*]

Enter three Watchmen, to guard the King's tent.

First Watchman. Come on, my masters, each man
    take his stand.
The King by this° is set him down to sleep.

Second Watchman. What, will he not to bed?

First Watchman. Why, no; for he hath made a solemn
    vow
Never to lie and take his natural rest   ⟨
Till Warwick or himself be quite suppressed.

---

19 stout valiant 20 sleight trickery 19–21 That as Ulysses . . .
fatal steeds *Iliad,* X. (because an oracle had said that Troy could not
be taken if Rhesus' horses grazed on Trojan plains, the Greeks sent
Ulysses and Diomede to capture the horses before they reached
Troy) 28 in silent sort silently IV.iii.2 by this by this time

Second Watchman. Tomorrow then belike shall be
     the day,
     If Warwick be so near as men report.

Third Watchman. But say, I pray, what nobleman is
     that
10   That with the King here resteth in his tent?

First Watchman. 'Tis the Lord Hastings, the King's
     chiefest friend.

Third Watchman. O, is it so? But why commands the
     King
     That his chief followers lodge in towns about him,
     While he himself keeps° in the cold field?

Second Watchman. 'Tis the more honor, because more
15   dangerous.

Third Watchman. Ay, but give me worship° and
     quietness;
     I like it better than a dangerous honor.
     If Warwick knew in what estate he° stands,
     'Tis to be doubted° he would waken him.

First Watchman. Unless our halberds° did shut up his
20   passage.

Second Watchman. Ay, wherefore else guard we his
     royal tent,
     But to defend his person from night-foes?

*Enter Warwick, Clarence, Oxford, Somerset, and
     French Soldiers, silent all.*

Warwick. This is his tent; and see where stand his
     guard.
     Courage, my masters! honor now or never!
25   But follow me, and Edward shall be ours.

First Watchman. Who goes there?

Second Watchman. Stay, or thou diest!

14 keeps lives   16 worship ease and dignity   18 he i.e., the King
19 doubted suspected   20 halberds battle-axes on poles

Warwick and the rest cry all, "Warwick! Warwick!"
and set upon the Guard, who fly, crying, "Arm!
arm!", Warwick and the rest following them.

The Drum playing and Trumpet sounding, enter War-
wick, Somerset, and the rest, bringing the King out in
his gown, sitting in a chair. Richard and Hastings
flies over the stage.

Somerset. What are they that fly there?

Warwick. Richard and Hastings. Let them go. Here is
   The Duke.

King Edward. The Duke! Why, Warwick, when we
   parted,   *30*
   Thou call'dst me King.

Warwick.   Ay, but the case is altered:
   When you disgraced me in my embassade,°
   Then I degraded you from being King,
   And come now to create you Duke of York.
   Alas, how should you govern any kingdom,   *35*
   That know not how to use ambassadors,
   Nor how to be contented with one wife,
   Nor how to use your brothers brotherly,
   Nor how to study for the people's welfare,
   Nor how to shroud yourself from enemies?   *40*

King Edward. Yea, brother of Clarence, art thou here
   too?
   Nay, then I see that Edward needs must down.
   Yet, Warwick, in despite of all mischance,
   Of thee thyself and all thy complices,
   Edward will always bear himself as King: *45*
   Though fortune's malice overthrow my state,°
   My mind exceeds the compass° of her wheel.

Warwick. Then, for his mind,° be Edward England's
   King: *Takes off his crown.*
   But Henry now shall wear the English crown,

---

32 **embassade** ambassadorial errand   46 **state** sovereignty   47 **com-**
pass range   48 **for his mind** i.e., in Edward's mind (but not otherwise)

50 And be true king indeed, thou but the shadow.
    My Lord of Somerset, at my request,
    See that forthwith Duke Edward be conveyed
    Unto my brother, Archbishop of York.
    When I have fought with Pembroke and his fellows,
55 I'll follow you, and tell what answer
    Lewis and the Lady Bona send to him.
    Now, for a while farewell, good Duke of York.
                              They lead him out forcibly.

King Edward. What fates impose, that men·must
        needs abide;
    It boots not to resist both wind and tide.   *Exeunt.*

60 *Oxford.* What now remains, my lords, for us to do
    But march to London with our soldiers?

Warwick. Ay, that's the first thing that we have to do,
    To free King Henry from imprisonment
    And see him seated in the regal throne.   *Exeunt.*

[Scene IV. *London. The Palace.*]

Enter Rivers and Lady Grey [*as Queen*].

Rivers. Madam, what makes you in this sudden
        change?°

Queen Elizabeth. Why, brother Rivers, are you yet to
        learn
    What late misfortune is befall'n King Edward?

Rivers. What, loss of some pitched battle against War-
        wick?

Queen Elizabeth. No, but the loss of his own royal
5   person.

IV.iv.1 **Madam ... change?** What is the cause of this sudden change
in you?

Rivers. Then is my sovereign slain?

Queen Elizabeth. Ay, almost slain, for he is taken
          prisoner,
     Either betrayed by falsehood° of his guard
     Or by his foe surprised at° unawares;
     And, as I further have to understand,   10
     Is new committed to the Bishop of York,
     Fell Warwick's brother and by that our foe.

Rivers. These news, I must confess, are full of grief;
     Yet, gracious madam, bear it as you may:
     Warwick may lose, that now hath won the day.   15

Queen Elizabeth. Till then fair hope must hinder life's
          decay.
     And I the rather wean me from despair
     For love of Edward's offspring in my womb.
     This is it that makes me bridle passion
     And bear with mildness my misfortune's cross.   20
     Ay, ay, for this I draw in many a tear
     And stop the rising of blood-sucking sighs,
     Lest with my sighs or tears I blast or drown
     King Edward's fruit, true heir to th' English crown.

Rivers. But, madam, where is Warwick then become?°   25

Queen Elizabeth. I am informèd that he comes
          towards London,
     To set the crown once more on Henry's head.
     Guess thou the rest; King Edward's friends must
          down.
     But, to prevent° the tyrant's violence—
     (For trust not him that hath once broken faith)   30
     I'll hence forthwith unto the sanctuary,
     To save at least the heir of Edward's right.
     There shall I rest secure from force and fraud.
     Come, therefore, let us fly while we may fly.
     If Warwick take us we are sure to die.   *Exeunt.*   35

---

8 falsehood treachery   **9 surprised at** captured   **25 where . . . become** what has become of Warwick   **29 prevent** forestall

[Scene V. *A park near Middleham Castle in Yorkshire.*]

Enter Richard, Lord Hastings, and Sir William Stanley.

Richard. Now, my Lord Hastings and Sir William Stanley,
Leave off to wonder why I drew you hither,
Into this chiefest thicket of the park.
Thus stands the case: you know our King, my brother,
5 Is prisoner to the Bishop here, at whose hands
He hath good usage and great liberty,
And often but attended with weak guard,
Comes hunting this way to disport himself.
I have advertised° him by secret means
10 That if about this hour he make this way
Under the color° of his usual game,
He shall here find his friends with horse and men
To set him free from his captivity.

Enter King Edward and a Huntsman with him.

Huntsman. This way, my lord, for this way lies the game.°

King Edward. Nay, this way, man! See where the
15 huntsmen stand.
Now, brother of Gloucester, Lord Hastings, and the rest,
Stand you thus close,° to steal the Bishop's deer?

Richard. Brother, the time and case requireth haste:
Your horse stands ready at the park-corner.

IV.v.9 **advertised** informed   11 **color** pretext   14 **game** quarry   17
close concealed

124

King Edward. But whither shall we then?

Hastings.   To Lynn, my lord,   *20*
   And ship from thence to Flanders.

Richard. Well guessed, believe me; for that was my
   meaning.

King Edward. Stanley, I will requite thy forwardness.°

Richard. But wherefore stay° we? 'tis no time to talk.

King Edward. Huntsman, what say'st thou? wilt thou
   go along?   *25*

Huntsman. Better do so than tarry and be hanged.

Richard. Come then, away; let's ha' no more ado.

King Edward. Bishop, farewell. Shield thee from Warwick's frown
   And pray that I may repossess the crown.   *Exeunt.*

[Scene VI. *London. The Tower.*]

*Flourish. Enter King Henry the Sixth, Clarence, War-
wick, Somerset, young Henry [Earl of Richmond],
Oxford, Montague, and Lieutenant [of the
Tower].*

King Henry. Master Lieutenant, now that God and
   friends
   Have shaken Edward from the regal seat
   And turned my captive state to liberty,
   My fear to hope, my sorrows unto joys,
   At our enlargement° what are thy due fees?   *5*

Lieutenant. Subjects may challenge° nothing of their
   sovereigns;

23 **forwardness** zeal   24 **stay** delay   IV.vi.5 **enlargement** liberation
6 **challenge** demand

But, if an humble prayer may prevail,
I then crave pardon of your Majesty.

King Henry. For what, Lieutenant? for well using me?
10 Nay, be thou sure I'll well requite thy kindness
For that it made my imprisonment a pleasure;
Ay, such a pleasure as incagèd birds
Conceive when after many moody thoughts
At last by notes of household harmony
15 They quite forget their loss of liberty.
But, Warwick, after God, thou set'st me free,
And chiefly therefore I thank God and thee;
He was the author, thou the instrument.
Therefore, that I may conquer Fortune's spite
20 By living low,° where Fortune cannot hurt me,
And that the people of this blessèd land
May not be punished with my thwarting stars,°
Warwick, although my head still wear the crown,
I here resign my government to thee,
25 For thou art fortunate in all thy deeds.

Warwick. Your Grace hath still° been famed for°
      virtuous;
And now may seem as wise as virtuous,
By spying and avoiding Fortune's malice,
For few men rightly temper° with the stars:
30 Yet in this one thing let me blame your Grace,
For choosing me when Clarence is in place.°

Clarence. No, Warwick, thou art worthy of the sway,°
To whom the heavens in thy nativity°
Adjudged an olive branch and laurel crown,
35 As likely to be blest in peace and war;
And therefore I yield thee my free consent.

Warwick. And I choose Clarence only for Protector.

King Henry. Warwick and Clarence, give me both
      your hands:

20 **low** humbly   22 **thwarting stars** ill fortune   26 **still** always
26 **famed for** reputed   29 **temper** blend, accord   31 **in place**
present   32 **sway** power   33 **nativity** horoscope

Now join your hands, and with your hands your
　　hearts,
That no dissension hinder government:　　　　　40
I make you both Protectors of this land,
While I myself will lead a private life,
And in devotion spend my latter days,
To sin's rebuke and my Creator's praise.

Warwick. What answers Clarence to his sovereign's
　　will?　　　　　　　　　　　　　　　　　45

Clarence. That he consents, if Warwick yield consent,
For on thy fortune I repose myself.°

Warwick. Why, then, though loath, yet must I be con-
　　tent:
We'll yoke together, like a double shadow
To Henry's body, and supply his place;　　　　50
I mean, in bearing weight of government,
While he enjoys the honor and his ease.
And, Clarence, now then it is more than needful
Forthwith that Edward be pronounced a traitor,
And all his lands and goods be confiscate.　　　55

Clarence. What else? And that succession be deter-
　　mined.

Warwick. Ay, therein Clarence shall not want his
　　part.°

King Henry. But, with the first of all your chief affairs,
Let me entreat (for I command no more)
That Margaret your queen and my son Edward　　60
Be sent for, to return from France with speed;
For, till I see them here, by doubtful fear
My joy of liberty is half eclipsed.

Clarence. It shall be done, my sovereign, with all
　　speed.

King Henry. My Lord of Somerset, what youth is that,　　65
Of whom you seem to have so tender care?

---

47 repose myself rely　　**57 want his part** lack his share

Somerset. My liege, it is young Henry, Earl of Rich-
    mond.

King Henry. Come hither, England's hope. (*Lays his
    hand on his head.*) If secret powers
Suggest but truth to my divining thoughts,
70 This pretty lad will prove our country's bliss.
His looks are full of peaceful majesty,
His head by nature framed to wear a crown,
His hand to wield a scepter, and himself
Likely in time to bless a regal throne.
75 Make much of him, my lords, for this is he
Must help you more than you are hurt by me.

              Enter a Post.

Warwick. What news, my friend?

Post. That Edward is escapèd from your brother,
    And fled, as he hears since, to Burgundy.

80 *Warwick.* Unsavory news! but how made he escape?

Post. He was conveyed° by Richard Duke of Glouces-
    ter
And the Lord Hastings, who attended° him
In secret ambush on the forest side
And from the Bishop's huntsmen rescued him;
85 For hunting was his daily exercise.

Warwick. My brother was too careless of his charge.
    But let us hence, my sovereign, to provide
    A salve for any sore that may betide.
    Exeunt. Manet° Somerset, Richmond, and Oxford.

Somerset. My lord, I like not of this flight of Edward's,
90 For doubtless Burgundy will yield him help,
And we shall have more wars before't be long.
As Henry's late presaging prophecy
Did glad my heart with hope of this young Rich-
    mond,

---

81 **conveyed** stolen away 82 **attended** waited for 88 s.d. **Manet**
remains (the Latin singular is often used in Elizabethan directions
with a plural subject)

So doth my heart misgive me, in these conflicts
What may befall him, to his harm and ours: 95
Therefore, Lord Oxford, to prevent the worst,
Forthwith we'll send him hence to Brittany,
Till storms be past of civil enmity.

Oxford. Ay, for if Edward repossess the crown,
'Tis like that Richmond with the rest shall down.   100

Somerset. It shall be so; he shall to Brittany.
Come, therefore, let's about it speedily.   *Exeunt.*

[Scene VII. *Before York.*]

*Flourish. Enter [King] Edward, Richard, Hastings,
and Soldiers.*

King Edward. Now, brother Richard, Lord Hastings,
    and the rest,
Yet thus far Fortune maketh us amends,
And says that once more I shall interchange
My wanèd state for Henry's regal crown.
Well have we passed and now repassed the seas   5
And brought desirèd help from Burgundy.
What then remains, we being thus arrived
From Ravenspurgh haven before the gates of York,
But that we enter, as into our dukedom?

Richard. The gates made fast! Brother, I like not this. 10
For many men that stumble at the threshold
Are well foretold that danger lurks within.

King Edward. Tush, man, abodements° must not now
    affright us:
By fair or foul means we must enter in,
For hither will our friends repair° to us.   15

IV.vii.13 **abodements** omens   15 **repair** come

Hastings. My liege, I'll knock once more to summon
them.

*Enter, on the walls, the Mayor of York and his
Brethren.*

Mayor. My lords, we were forewarnèd of your com-
ing,
And shut the gates for safety of ourselves;
For now we owe allegiance unto Henry.

King Edward. But, Master Mayor, if Henry be your
20   king,
Yet Edward at the least is Duke of York.

Mayor. True, my good lord; I know you for no less.

King Edward. Why, and I challenge nothing but my
dukedom,
As being well content with that alone.

25   *Richard.* But when the fox hath once got in his nose,
He'll soon find means to make the body follow.

Hastings. Why, Master Mayor, why stand you in a
doubt?
Open the gates; we are King Henry's friends.

Mayor. Ay, say you so? the gates shall then be opened.
He descends [with the Aldermen].

30   *Richard.* A wise stout° captain, and soon persuaded!

Hastings. The good old man would fain that all were
well,
So 'twere not long of° him; but being entered,
I doubt not, I, but we shall soon persuade
Both him and all his brothers unto reason.

Enter the Mayor and two Aldermen, [below].

King Edward. So, Master Mayor: these gates must
35   not be shut

30 **stout** valiant (here ironic)   32 **long of** because of

But in the night or in the time of war.
What! fear not, man, but yield me up the keys;
                    Takes his keys.

For Edward will defend the town and thee,
And all those friends that deign to follow me.

March. Enter Montgomery, with Drum and Soldiers.

Richard. Brother, this is Sir John Montgomery,   40
  Our trusty friend, unless I be deceived.

King Edward. Welcome, Sir John! But why come you
    in arms?

Montgomery. To help King Edward in his time of
    storm,
  As every loyal subject ought to do.

King Edward. Thanks, good Montgomery. But we
    now forget   45
  Our title to the crown and only claim
  Our dukedom till God please to send the rest.

Montgomery. Then fare you well, for I will hence
    again:
  I came to serve a king and not a duke.
  Drummer, strike up, and let us march away.   50
                    The Drum begins to march.

King Edward. Nay stay, Sir John, awhile, and we'll
    debate
  By what safe means the crown may be recovered.

Montgomery. What talk you of debating? in few
    words,
  If you'll not here proclaim yourself our King,
  I'll leave you to your fortune and be gone   55
  To keep them back that come to succor you.
  Why shall we fight, if you pretend° no title?

Richard. Why, brother, wherefore stand you on nice
    points?°

---

57 **pretend** claim   58 **nice points** subtle distinctions.

King Edward. When we grow stronger, then we'll
    make our claim;

60   Till then, 'tis wisdom to conceal our meaning.

Hastings. Away with scrupulous wit! Now arms must
    rule.

Richard. And fearless minds climb soonest unto
    crowns.
    Brother, we will proclaim you out of hand;
    The bruit° thereof will bring you many friends.

65 *King Edward.* Then be it as you will; for 'tis my right,
    And Henry but usurps the diadem.

Montgomery. Ay, now my sovereign speaketh like
    himself;
    And now will I be Edward's champion.

Hastings. Sound trumpet; Edward shall be here pro-
    claimed.
70   Come, fellow-soldier, make thou proclamation.
                        Flourish. Sound.

Soldier. Edward the Fourth, by the grace of God, King
    of England and France, and Lord of Ireland, &c.°

Montgomery. And whosoe'er gainsays King Edward's
    right,
    By this I challenge him to single fight.
                Throws down his gauntlet.

75 *All.* Long live Edward the Fourth!

King Edward. Thanks, brave Montgomery; and thanks
    unto you all:
    If fortune serve me, I'll requite this kindness.
    Now, for this night, let's harbor here in York;
    And when the morning sun shall raise his car°
80   Above the border of this horizon,
    We'll forward towards Warwick and his mates;
    For well I wot° that Henry is no soldier.

64 bruit rumor   **71–72 Edward . . . &c.** (this is the only prose passage in the play. The use of prose here represents the language of
proclamations, official documents, and formal statements)   **79 car**
chariot (of Phoebus Apollo)   **82 wot** know

Ah, froward° Clarence! how evil it beseems thee,
To flatter Henry and forsake thy brother!
Yet, as we may, we'll meet both thee and Warwick.   *85*
Come on, brave soldiers. Doubt not of the day,
And, that once gotten, doubt not of large pay.
                                    Exeunt.

[Scene VIII. *London.*
The Bishop of London's Palace.]

Flourish. Enter the King [Henry], Warwick,
Montague, Clarence, Oxford, and Exeter.

Warwick. What counsel, lords? Edward from Belgia,
With hasty Germans and blunt° Hollanders,
Hath passed in safety through the Narrow Seas,
And with his troops doth march amain° to London;
And many giddy people flock to him.   *5*

King Henry. Let's levy men, and beat him back again.

Clarence. A little fire is quickly trodden out;
Which, being suffered,° rivers cannot quench.

Warwick. In Warwickshire I have true-hearted friends,
Not mutinous in peace, yet bold in war;   *10*
Those will I muster up: and thou, son Clarence,
Shalt stir up in Suffolk, Norfolk and in Kent,
The knights and gentlemen to come with thee.
Thou, brother Montague, in Buckingham,
Northampton, and in Leicestershire shalt find   *15*
Men well inclined to hear what thou command'st.
And thou, brave Oxford, wondrous well beloved,
In Oxfordshire shalt muster up thy friends.
My sovereign, with the loving citizens,

---

83 **froward** rebellious   IV.viii.2 **blunt** rude   4 **amain** with full speed
8 **suffered** allowed (to grow)

20 Like to his island girt in with the ocean,
Or modest Dian° circled with her nymphs,
Shall rest in London till we come to him.
Fair lords, take leave and stand not to reply.
Farewell, my sovereign.

King Henry. Farewell, my Hector, and my Troy's true
25   hope.

Clarence. In sign of truth, I kiss your Highness' hand.

King Henry. Well-minded° Clarence, be thou fortunate!

Montague. Comfort, my lord! and so I take my leave.

Oxford. And thus I seal my truth and bid adieu.

30 *King Henry.* Sweet Oxford, and my loving Montague,
And all at once, once more a happy farewell.

Warwick. Farewell, sweet lords; let's meet at
Coventry.
          Exeunt [all but King Henry and Exeter].

King Henry. Here at the palace will I rest awhile.
Cousin of Exeter, what thinks your lordship?
35 Methinks the power that Edward hath in field
Should not be able to encounter mine.

Exeter. The doubt° is that he will seduce the rest.

King Henry. That's not my fear. My meed° hath got
me fame.
I have not stopped mine ears to their demands,
40 Nor posted off° their suits with slow delays.
My pity hath been balm to heal their wounds,
My mildness hath allayed their swelling griefs,
My mercy dried their water-flowing tears.
I have not been desirous of their wealth
45 Nor much oppressed them with great subsidies,°
Nor forward of° revenge, though they much erred.

21 **Dian** Diana, goddess of chastity   27 **Well-minded** well-disposed
37 **doubt** fear   38 **meed** merit, worth   40 **posted off** postponed
45 **subsidies** taxes   46 **forward of** eager for

Then why should they love Edward more than me?
No, Exeter, these graces challenge grace;°
And when the lion fawns upon the lamb,
The lamb will never cease to follow him.   50
    Shout within, "A Lancaster! A Lancaster!"°

Exeter. Hark, hark, my lord! what shouts are these?

    Enter [King] Edward, [Richard,] and his Soldiers.

King Edward. Seize on the shamefaced° Henry, bear
    him hence;
And once again proclaim us King of England.
You are the fount that makes small brooks to flow.
Now stops thy spring; my sea shall suck them dry   55
And swell so much the higher by their ebb.
Hence with him to the Tower. Let him not speak.
    Exit [some] with King Henry.
And, lords, towards Coventry bend we our course,
Where peremptory° Warwick now remains:
The sun shines hot; and, if we use delay,   60
Cold biting winter mars our hoped-for hay.

Richard. Away betimes, before his forces join,
And take the great-grown traitor unawares.
Brave warriors, march amain° towards Coventry.
                                        Exeunt.

---

48 graces challenge grace virtues claim favor   **50 s.d. A . . . Lancaster!** (so in F. Many editors read: "A York! A York!" as signaliz-
ing entrance of King Edward)   **52 shamefaced** modest, bashful   **59
peremptory** overbearing   **64 amain** swiftly

[ACT V.

Scene I. *Coventry*.]

Enter Warwick, the Mayor of Coventry, two
Messengers, and others upon the walls.

Warwick. Where is the post that came from valiant
   Oxford?
   How far hence is thy lord, mine honest fellow?

First Messenger. By this° at Dunsmore, marching
   hitherward.

Warwick. How far off is our brother Montague?
5   Where is the post that came from Montague?

Second Messenger. By this° at Daintry, with a puissant
   troop.

         Enter [Sir John] Somerville.

Warwick. Say, Somerville, what says my loving son?
   And, by thy guess, how nigh is Clarence now?

Somerville. At Southam I did leave him with his
   forces,
10   And do expect him here some two hours hence.
                              [*Drum heard.*]

Warwick. Then Clarence is at hand; I hear his drum.

Somerville. It is not his, my lord. Here Southam lies.
   The drum your Honor hears marcheth from Warwick.

V.i.3,6 **By this** by this time

136

Warwick. Who should that be? Belike, unlooked-for
  friends.

Somerville. They are at hand, and you shall quickly
  know.   15

   March. Flourish. Enter [King] Edward, Richard,
               and Soldiers.

King Edward. Go, trumpet,° to the walls, and sound
  a parle.

Richard. See how the surly Warwick mans the wall!

Warwick. O unbid spite! Is sportful° Edward come?
  Where slept our scouts, or how are they seduced,
  That we could hear no news of his repair?°   20

King Edward. Now, Warwick, wilt thou ope the city
  gates,
  Speak gentle words and humbly bend thy knee,
  Call Edward King, and at his hands beg mercy?
  And he shall pardon thee these outrages.

Warwick. Nay, rather, wilt thou draw thy forces
  hence,   25
  Confess who set thee up and plucked thee down,
  Call Warwick patron and be penitent?
  And thou shalt still remain the Duke of York.

Richard. I thought, at least, he would have said "the
  King";
  Or did he make the jest against his will?   30

Warwick. Is not a dukedom, sir, a goodly gift?

Richard. Ay, by my faith, for a poor earl to give!
  I'll do thee service for so good a gift.

Warwick. 'Twas I that gave the kingdom to thy
  brother.

King Edward. Why then 'tis mine, if but by Warwick's
  gift.   35

Warwick. Thou art no Atlas for so great a weight;
16 **trumpet** trumpeter   18 **sportful** wanton   20 **repair** return

And, weakling, Warwick takes his gift again,
And Henry is 'my king, Warwick his subject.

King Edward. But Warwick's king is Edward's
prisoner;
40   And, gallant Warwick, do but answer this:
What is the body when the head is off?

Richard. Alas, that Warwick had no more forecast,°
But, whiles he thought to steal the single ten,°
The king was slily fingered from the deck!
45   You left poor Henry at the Bishop's palace,
And ten to one you'll meet him in the Tower.

King Edward. 'Tis even so. Yet you are Warwick
still.

Richard. Come, Warwick, take the time.° Kneel down,
kneel down!
Nay, when?° Strike° now, or else the iron cools.

50   *Warwick.* I had rather chop this hand off at a blow,
And with the other fling it at thy face,
Than bear so low a sail to strike to thee.°

King Edward. Sail how thou canst, have wind and
tide thy friend,
This hand, fast wound about thy coal-black hair,
55   Shall, whiles thy head is warm and new cut off,
Write in the dust this sentence with thy blood,
"Wind-changing Warwick now can change no
more."

Enter Oxford, with Drum and Colors.

Warwick. O cheerful colors! see where Oxford comes!

Oxford. Oxford, Oxford, for Lancaster!
              [*He and his forces enter the city.*]

60   *Richard.* The gates are open, let us enter too.

---

42 **forecast** foresight   43 **single ten** mere ten (not a court card)
48 **take the time** seize the opportunity   49 **when** (exclamation of
impatience)   49 **Strike** (1) act (i.e., while the iron is hot) (2) yield
52 **bear . . . thee** be so humble as to surrender to you

King Edward. So other foes may set upon our backs.
  Stand we in good array, for they no doubt
  Will issue out again and bid us battle.
  If not, the city being but of small defense,
  We'll quickly rouse° the traitors in the same.   65

Warwick. O, welcome, Oxford! for we want thy help.

  Enter Montague, with Drum and Colors.

Montague. Montague, Montague, for Lancaster!
            [*He and his forces enter the city.*]

Richard. Thou and thy brother both shall buy this
            treason
  Even with the dearest blood your bodies bear.

King Edward. The harder matched, the greater vic-
            tory: 70
  My mind presageth happy gain and conquest.

  Enter Somerset, with Drum and Colors.

Somerset. Somerset, Somerset, for Lancaster!
            [*He and his forces enter the city.*]

Richard. Two of thy name, both Dukes of Somerset,
  Have sold their lives unto the house of York;
  And thou shalt be the third, if this sword hold.   75

  Enter Clarence, with Drum and Colors.°

Warwick. And lo, where George of Clarence sweeps
            along,

---

65 rouse flush (as an animal from its lair)   **75 s.d.** (at this point
Q introduces the following dialogue and business:

Warwick. And loe where *George* of *Clarence* sweepes
  Along, of power enough to bid his brother battell.
Clarence. Clarence, Clarence, for *Lancaster.*
Edward. Et tu Brute, wilt thou stab *Cæsar* too?
  A parlie sirra to *George* of Clarence.
  Sound a Parlie, and *Richard* and *Clarence* whispers togither, and
then Clarence takes his red Rose out of his hat and throwes it at
Warwike.

This passage, and especially the stage direction, follows closely
the account in the chronicles of both Hall and Holinshed of
Clarence's final change of allegiance.)

Of force enough to bid his brother battle;
With whom an upright zeal to right prevails
More than the nature of a brother's love!
80   Come, Clarence, come! Thou wilt, if Warwick call.

Clarence. Father of Warwick, know you what this
        means?   [*Takes his red rose out of his hat.*]°
Look here, I throw my infamy at thee.
I will not ruinate my father's house,
Who gave his blood to lime° the stones together,
And set up Lancaster. Why, trowest thou,° War-
85   wick,
That Clarence is so harsh, so blunt, unnatural,
To bend the fatal instruments of war
Against his brother and his lawful king?
Perhaps thou wilt object° my holy oath.
90   To keep that oath were more impiety
Than Jephthah, when he sacrificed his daughter.°
I am so sorry for my trespass made
That, to deserve well at my brother's hands,
I here proclaim myself thy mortal foe,
95   With resolution, wheresoe'er I meet thee
(As I will meet thee, if thou stir abroad)
To plague thee for thy foul misleading me.
And so, proud-hearted Warwick, I defy thee,
And to my brother turn my blushing cheeks.
100 Pardon me, Edward! I will make amends;
And, Richard, do not frown upon my faults,
For I will henceforth be no more unconstant.

King Edward. Now welcome more, and ten .times
        more beloved,
Than if thou never hadst deserved our hate.

Richard. Welcome, good Clarence! This is brother-
105   like.

Warwick. O passing° traitor, perjured and unjust!

81 s.d. **Takes . . . hat** i.e., removes the symbol of his allegiance **to**
the House of Lancaster   84 **lime** join with mortar   85 **trowest**
thou do you think   89 **object** invoke   91 **Jephthah . . . daughter**
(see Judges xi.30)   106 **passing** extreme

King Edward. What, Warwick, wilt thou leave the
　　town, and fight?
　　Or shall we beat the stones about thine ears?

Warwick. Alas, I am not cooped° here for defense!
　　I will away towards Barnet presently,°　　　　　　110
　　And bid thee battle, Edward, if thou dar'st.

King Edward. Yes, Warwick, Edward dares, and
　　leads the way.
　　Lords, to the field. Saint George and victory!
　　　　　　Exeunt [King Edward and his company].
　　　　　　March. Warwick and his company follows.

[Scene II. *A field of battle near Barnet.*]

*Alarum and excursions. Enter [King] Edward,
　bringing forth Warwick wounded.*

King Edward. So, lie thou there! Die thou, and die our
　　fear!
　　For Warwick was a bug° that feared° us all.
　　Now, Montague, sit fast!° I seek for thee,
　　That Warwick's bones may keep thine company.
　　　　　　　　　　　　　　　　　　　Exit.

Warwick. Ah, who is nigh? Come to me, friend or foe,　　5
　　And tell me who is victor, York or Warwick.
　　Why ask I that? My mangled body shows,
　　My blood, my want of strength, my sick heart
　　　shows,
　　That I must yield my body to the earth
　　And, by my fall, the conquest to my foe.　　　　　　10
　　Thus yields the cedar to the ax's edge,
　　Whose arms gave shelter to the princely eagle,

---

109 **cooped** prepared　110 **presently,** immediately　V.ii.2 **bug** bug-
bear　2 **feared** terrified　3 **sit fast** watch out

Under whose shade the ramping° lion slept,
Whose top-branch overpeered Jove's spreading
    tree°
15 And kept low shrubs from winter's pow'rful wind.
These eyes, that now are dimmed with death's
    black veil,
Have been as piercing as the mid-day sun
To search the secret treasons of the world.
The wrinkles in my brows, now filled with blood,
20 Were likened oft to kingly sepulchers;
For who lived king but I could dig his grave?
And who durst smile when Warwick bent his brow?
Lo, now my glory smeared in dust and blood!
My parks, my walks, my manors that I had,
25 Even now forsake me, and of all my lands
Is nothing left me but my body's length.
Why, what is pomp, rule, reign, but earth and dust?
And, live we how we can, yet die we must.

Enter Oxford and Somerset.

Somerset. Ah, Warwick, Warwick! wert thou as we
    are,
30 We might recover all our loss again!
The Queen from France hath brought a puissant
    power.
Even now we heard the news. Ah, couldst thou fly!

Warwick. Why, then I would not fly. Ah, Montague,
If thou be there, sweet brother, take my hand,
35 And with thy lips keep in my soul awhile!
Thou lov'st me not; for, brother, if thou didst,
Thy tears would wash this cold congealèd blood
That glues my lips and will not let me speak.
Come quickly, Montague, or I am dead.

Somerset. Ah, Warwick! Montague hath breathed his
40   last,
And to the latest gasp cried out for Warwick
And said "Commend me to my valiant brother."
And more he would have said, and more he spoke,

13 **ramping** rearing   14 **Jove's spreading tree** the oak

Which sounded like a cannon in a vault,
That mought° not be distinguished; but at last   45
I well might hear, delivered with a groan,
"O, farewell, Warwick!"

Warwick. Sweet rest his soul! Fly, lords, and save
    yourselves;
For Warwick bids you all farewell, to meet in
    heaven.   [*Dies.*]

Oxford. Away, away, to meet the Queen's great
    power!   *Here they bear away his body.*   50
                                        Exeunt.

· [Scene III. *Another part of the field.*]

*Flourish. Enter King Edward in triumph,
with Richard, Clarence, and the rest.*

King Edward. Thus far our fortune keeps an upward
    course
And we are graced with wreaths of victory.
But, in the midst of this bright-shining day
I spy a black, suspicious, threat'ning cloud
That will encounter with our glorious sun°   5
Ere he attain his easeful western bed.
I mean, my lords, those powers that the Queen
Hath raised in Gallia have arrived° our coast,
And, as we hear, march on to fight with us.

Clarence. A little gale will soon disperse that cloud   10
And blow it to the source from whence it came.
Thy very beams will dry those vapors up,
For every cloud engenders not a storm.

45 mought might   V.iii.5 sun badge of York   8 arrived landed on

Richard. The Queen is valued° thirty thousand strong,

15   And Somerset, with Oxford, fled to her:
If she have time to breathe, be well assured
Her faction will be full as strong as ours.

King Edward. We are advertised° by our loving friends
That they do hold their course toward Tewksbury.
20   We, having now the best at Barnet field,
Will thither straight,° for willingness rids way;°
And, as we march, our strength will be augmented
In every county as we go along.
Strike up the drum. Cry "Courage!" and away.

Exeunt.

[Scene IV. *Plains near Tewksbury.*]

Flourish. March. Enter the Queen [Margaret], young [Prince] Edward, Somerset, Oxford, and Soldiers.

Queen Margaret. Great lords, wise men ne'er sit and wail their loss,
But cheerly seek how to redress their harms.
What though the mast be now blown overboard,
The cable broke, the holding-anchor° lost,
5   And half our sailors swallowed in the flood?
Yet lives our pilot still. Is't meet° that he
Should leave the helm, and like a fearful lad
With tearful eyes add water to the sea,
And give more strength to that which hath too much,
10   Whiles, in his moan, the ship splits on the rock,

---

14 **valued** estimated 18 **advertised** informed 21 **straight** at once
21 **rids** way covers ground quickly V.iv.4 **holding-anchor** sheet
anchor (largest of ship's anchors) 6 **Is't meet** is it suitable

Which industry° and courage might have saved?
Ah, what a shame! ah, what a fault were this!
Say Warwick was our anchor. What of that?
And Montague our topmast. What of him?
Our slaughtered friends the tackles; what of these?   15
Why, is not Oxford here another anchor?
And Somerset another goodly mast?
The friends of France our shrouds and tacklings?
And, though unskilful, why not Ned and I
For once allowed the skilful pilot's charge?°   20
We will not from the helm to sit and weep,
But keep our course (though the rough wind say
   no)
From shelves and rocks that threaten us with wrack.
As good to chide the waves as speak them fair.
And what is Edward but a ruthless sea?   25
What Clarence but a quicksand of deceit?
And Richard but a ragged fatal rock?
All these the enemies to our poor bark.
Say you can swim—alas, 'tis but a while!
Tread on the sand—why, there you quickly sink!   30
Bestride the rock—the tide will wash you off,
Or else you famish: that's a threefold death.
This speak I, lords, to let you understand,
If case some one of you would fly from us,
That there's no hoped-for mercy with the brothers   35
More than with ruthless waves, with sands and
   rocks.
Why, courage then! What cannot be avoided
'Twere childish weakness to lament or fear.

Prince. Methinks a woman of this valiant spirit
   Should, if a coward heard her speak these words,   40
   Infuse his breast with magnanimity,
   And make him, naked,° foil a man at arms.
   I speak not this as doubting any here;
   For did I but suspect a fearful man,
   He should have leave to go away betimes,   45
   Lest in our need he might infect another

11 **industry** labor   20 **charge** duty   42 **naked** unarmed

And make him of like spirit to himself.
If any such be here (as God forbid!)
Let him depart before we need his help.

50 *Oxford.* Women and children of so high a courage,
And warriors faint! why, 'twere perpetual shame.
O brave young prince! thy famous grandfather°
Doth live again in thee: long mayst thou live
To bear his image° and renew his glories!

55 *Somerset.* And he that will not fight for such a hope,
Go home to bed, and, like the owl by day,
If he arise, be mocked and wondered at.

Queen Margaret. Thanks, gentle Somerset. Sweet Oxford, thanks.

Prince. And take his thanks that yet hath nothing else.

Enter a Messenger.

60 *Messenger.* Prepare you, lords, for Edward is at hand
Ready to fight; therefore be resolute.

Oxford. I thought no less: it is his policy°
To haste thus fast, to find us unprovided.

Somerset. But he's deceived; we are in readiness.

Queen Margaret. This cheers my heart, to see your
65 forwardness.

Oxford. Here pitch our battle; hence we will not
budge.

*Flourish and march. Enter [King] Edward,
Richard, Clarence, and Soldiers.*

King Edward. Brave followers, yonder stands the
thorny wood,
Which, by the heavens' assistance and your
strength,
Must by the roots be hewn up yet ere night.
70 I need not add more fuel to your fire,

52 **grandfather** Henry V   54 **image** likeness   62 **policy** craft

For well I wot ye blaze to burn them out.
Give signal to the fight, and to it, lords!

Queen Margaret. Lords, knights, and gentlemen, what
    I should say
My tears gainsay; for every word I speak,
Ye see I drink the water of my eye.   75
Therefore, no more but this: Henry, your sovereign,
Is prisoner to the foe; his state usurped,
His realm a slaughterhouse, his subjects slain,
His statutes canceled, and his treasure spent;
And yonder is the wolf that makes this spoil.°   80
You fight in justice. Then, in God's name, lords,
Be valiant, and give signal to the fight.
    Alarum. Retreat. Excursions. Exeunt.

[Scene V. *Another part of the field.*]

Flourish. Enter [*King*] *Edward, Richard, Clarence,*
    [*and Soldiers; with*] *Queen* [*Margaret*], *Oxford,*
    Somerset [*as prisoners*].

King Edward. Now here a period of° tumultuous
    broils.
Away with Oxford to Hames Castle straight.°
For Somerset, off with his guilty head.
Go bear them hence. I will not hear them speak.

Oxford. For my part, I'll not trouble thee with words.   5

Somerset. Nor I, but stoop with patience to my for-
    tune.   *Exeunt* [*Oxford and Somerset, guarded*].

Queen Margaret. So part we sadly in this troublous
    world,
To meet with joy in sweet Jerusalem.

---

80 spoil destruction   V.v.1 a period of an end to   2 straight immediately

King Edward. Is proclamation made, that who finds
    Edward
10 Shall have a high reward, and he his life?

Richard. It is: and lo, where youthful Edward comes!

King Edward. Bring forth the gallant, let us hear him
    speak.

           Enter the Prince [Edward].

What! Can so young a thorn begin to prick?
Edward, what satisfaction° canst thou make
15 For bearing arms, for stirring up my subjects,
And all the trouble thou hast turned me to?

Prince. Speak like a subject, proud ambitious York!
Suppose that I am now my father's mouth;
Resign thy chair, and where I stand kneel thou,
20 Whilst I propose the selfsame words to thee,
Which, traitor, thou wouldst have me answer to.

Queen Margaret. Ah, that thy father had been so
    resolved!

Richard. That you might still have worn the petticoat,
And ne'er have stol'n the breech° from Lancaster.

25 *Prince.* Let Aesop fable in a winter's night;
His currish° riddles sorts not with this place.

Richard. By heaven, brat, I'll plague ye for that word.

Queen Margaret. Ay, thou wast born to be a plague
    to men.

Richard. For God's sake, take away this captive scold.

30 *Prince.* Nay, take away this scolding crookback rather.

King Edward. Peace, wilful boy, or I will charm° your
    tongue.

Clarence. Untutored lad, thou art too malapert.°

14 **satisfaction** amends 24 **breech** breeches 26 **currish** (because
Aesop was sometimes thought to be a hunchback, because the fables
talk of animals, and because their morality resembles that of Cynic
[from a Greek word for "dog"] philosophy) 31 **charm** silence
32 **malapert** impudent

Prince. I know my duty; you are all undutiful:
Lascivious Edward, and thou perjured George,
And thou misshapen Dick, I tell ye all   35
I am your better, traitors as ye are:
And thou usurp'st my father's right and mine.

King Edward. Take that, the likeness of this railer
here.   *Stabs him.*

Richard. Sprawl'st thou? Take that, to end thy agony.
                                     Richard stabs him.

Clarence. And there's for twitting me with perjury.   40
                                     Clarence stabs him.

Queen Margaret. O, kill me too!

Richard. Marry,° and shall.   *Offers to kill her.*

King Edward. Hold, Richard, hold; for we have done
too much.

Richard. Why should she live, to fill the world with
words?

King Edward. What! doth she swoon? use means for
her recovery.   45

Richard. Clarence, excuse me to the King my brother;
I'll hence to London on a serious matter:
Ere ye come there, be sure to hear some news.

Clarence. What? what?

Richard. The Tower, the Tower! ·   *Exit.* 50

Queen Margaret. O Ned, sweet Ned! speak to thy
mother, boy!
Canst thou not speak? O traitors! murderers!
They that stabbed Caesar shed no blood at all,
Did not offend, nor were not worthy blame,
If this foul deed were by to equal it.   55
He was a man; this (in respect)° a child,
And men ne'er spend their fury on a child.

42 **Marry** indeed (light oath, from "By Mary")   56 **in respect in**
comparison

What's worse than murderer, that I may name it?
No, no, my heart will burst, and if I speak!
60 And I will speak, that so my heart may burst.
Butchers and villains! bloody cannibals!
How sweet a plant have you untimely cropped!
You have no children, butchers! If you had,
The thought of them would have stirred up re-
morse:
65 But if you ever chance to have a child,
Look in his youth to have him so cut off
As, deathsmen, you have rid this sweet young
prince!

King Edward. Away with her! Go bear her hence
perforce.

Queen Margaret. Nay, never bear me hence! Dispatch
me here.
70 Here sheathe thy sword, I'll pardon thee my death:
What, wilt thou not? Then, Clarence, do it thou.

Clarence. By heaven, I will not do thee so much ease.

Queen Margaret. Good Clarence, do! Sweet Clarence,
do thou do it!

Clarence. Didst thou not hear me swear I would not
do it?

Queen Margaret. Ay, but thou usest to forswear thy-
75 self.
'Twas sin before, but now 'tis charity.
What wilt thou not? Where is that devil's butcher,
Hard-favored° Richard? Richard, where art thou?
Thou art not here. Murder is thy alms-deed.
80 Petitioners for blood thou ne'er put'st back.°

King Edward. Away, I say. I charge ye bear her
hence.

Queen Margaret. So come to you and yours, as to this
prince!   *Exit Queen.*

---

78 **Hard-favored** ugly   80 **put'st back** refuse

King Edward. Where's Richard gone?

Clarence. To London, all in post;° and, as I guess,
  To make a bloody supper in the Tower.   85

King Edward. He's sudden° if a thing comes in his
    head.
  Now march we hence, discharge the common sort
  With pay and thanks, and let's away to London,
  And see our gentle Queen how well she fares:
  By this,° I hope, she hath a son for me.   *Exeunt.*   90

[Scene VI. *London. The Tower.*]

Enter [*King*] *Henry the Sixth and Richard, with the
  Lieutenant* [*of the Tower*], *on the walls.*

Richard. Good day, my lord. What, at your book so
    hard?

King Henry. Ay, my good lord—"my lord," I should
    say rather.
  'Tis sin to flatter. "Good" was little better.
  "Good Gloucester" and "good devil" were alike,
  And both preposterous;° therefore, not "good
    lord."   5

Richard. Sirrah,° leave us to ourselves: we must con-
    fer.   [*Exit Lieutenant.*]

King Henry. So flies the reckless shepherd from the
    wolf;
  So first the harmless sheep doth yield his fleece,

84 **all in post** in haste   86 **sudden** swift in action   90 **By this** by
this time   V.vi.5 **preposterous** an inversion of the natural order
6 **Sirrah** (form of address used to an inferior)

And next his throat unto the butcher's knife.

10   What scene of death hath Roscius° now to act?

Richard. Suspicion always haunts the guilty mind;
The thief doth fear each bush an officer.

King Henry. The bird that hath been limèd° in a
          bush,
With trembling wings misdoubteth° every bush;

15   And I, the hapless male to one sweet bird,
Have now the fatal object in my eye
Where my poor young was limed, was caught and
          killed.°

Richard. Why, what a peevish fool was that of Crete,
That taught his son the office° of a fowl!

20   And yet, for all his wings, the fool was drowned.

King Henry. I, Daedalus; my poor boy, Icarus;
Thy father, Minos, that denied our course;°
The sun that seared the wings of my sweet boy
Thy brother Edward, and thyself the sea

25   Whose envious gulf° did swallow up his life.
Ah, kill me with thy weapon, not with words!
My breast can better brook thy dagger's point
Than can my ears that tragic history.
But wherefore dost thou come? Is't for my life?

30   *Richard.* Think'st thou I am an executioner?

King Henry. A persecutor, I am sure, thou art:
If murdering innocents be executing,
Why, then thou art an executioner.

Richard. Thy son I killed for his presumption.

King Henry. Hadst thou been killed when first thou
35   didst presume,

10 **Roscius** great Roman actor (d. 62 B.C.) 13 **limèd** caught with
bird-lime (a sticky substance smeared on twigs) 14 **misdoubteth**
mistrusts 15–17 **And I . . . killed,** i.e., I, the father of one sweet
child, have in my eye the death-dealing substance by which my son
was trapped and slain 19 **office** function 22 **denied our course**
barred our way 25 **gulf** whirlpool

Thou hadst not lived to kill a son of mine.
And thus I prophesy, that many a thousand,
Which now mistrust no parcel of my fear,
And many an old man's sigh and many a widow's,
And many an orphan's water-standing° eye—   *40*
Men for their sons, wives for their husbands,
Orphans for their parents' timeless° death—
Shall rue the hour that ever thou wast born.
The owl shrieked at thy birth—an evil sign;
The night-crow cried, aboding° luckless time;   *45*
Dogs howled, and hideous tempest shook down trees;
The raven rooked her° on the chimney's top,
And chatt'ring pies° in dismal discords sung.
Thy mother felt more than a mother's pain,
And yet brought forth less than a mother's hope,   *50*
To wit, an indigested and deformèd lump,
Not like the fruit of such a goodly tree.
Teeth hadst thou in thy head when thou wast born,
To signify thou cam'st to bite the world;
And, if the rest be true which I have heard,   *55*
Thou cam'st—

Richard. I'll hear no more. Die, prophet, in thy
speech.   *Stabs him.*
For this, amongst the rest, was I ordained.

King Henry. Ay, and for much more slaughter after
this.
O God forgive my sins, and pardon thee!   *Dies.*   *60*

Richard. What? Will the aspiring blood of Lancaster
Sink in the ground? I thought it would have mounted.
See how my sword weeps for the poor King's death!
O may such purple tears be alway shed
From those that wish the downfall of our house!   *65*

40 **water-standing** flooded with tears   42 **timeless** untimely   45 **aboding** foreboding   47 **rooked her** squatted   48 **pies** magpies

If any spark of life be yet remaining,
Down, down to hell; and say I sent thee thither—
                              Stabs him again.
I, that have neither pity, love, nor fear.
Indeed, 'tis true that Henry told me of;
70   For I have often heard my mother say
I came into the world with my legs forward.
Had I not reason, think ye, to make haste
And seek their ruin that usurped our right?
The midwife wondered, and the women cried
75   "O Jesus bless us, he is born with teeth!"
And so I was, which plainly signified
That I should snarl and bite and play the dog.
Then, since the heavens have shaped my body so,
Let hell make crook'd my mind to answer° it.
80   I have no brother, I am like no brother;
And this word "love," which graybeards call
      divine,
Be resident in men like one another
And not in me: I am myself alone.
Clarence, beware. Thou keep'st me from the light;
85   But I will sort a pitchy day for thee;°
For I will buzz abroad° such prophecies
That Edward shall be fearful of his life,
And then, to purge his fear, I'll be thy death.
King Henry and the Prince his son are gone:
90   Clarence, thy turn is next, and then the rest,
Counting myself but bad till I be best.
I'll throw thy body in another room
And triumph, Henry, in thy day of doom.
                              Exit [with the body].

79 **answer** correspond to   85 **I . . . thee** I shall arrange a black future for you   86 **buzz abroad** spread

[Scene VII. *London. The Palace.*]

*Flourish. Enter King [Edward], Queen [Elizabeth],
Clarence, Richard, Hastings, [a] Nurse [with the
young Prince], and Attendants.*

King Edward. Once more we sit in England's royal
    throne,
Repurchased with the blood of enemies.
What valiant foemen, like to autumn's corn,
Have we mowed down in tops of all their pride!
Three Dukes of Somerset, threefold renowned   5
For hardy and undoubted champions;
Two Cliffords, as° the father and the son,
And two Northumberlands—two braver men
Ne'er spurred their coursers° at the trumpet's
    sound;
With them, the two brave bears,° .Warwick and
    Montague,   10
That in their chains fettered the kingly lion
And made the forest tremble when they roared.
Thus have we swept suspicion° from our seat
And made our footstool of security.
Come hither, Bess, and let me kiss my boy.   15
Young Ned, for thee, thine uncles and myself
Have in our armors watched° the winter's night,
Went all afoot in summer's scalding heat,
That thou mightst repossess the crown in peace:
And of our labors thou shalt reap the gain.   2(

Richard. [*Aside*] I'll blast his harvest, if your head
    were laid,°
For yet I am not looked on in the world.

V.vii.7 **as** namely   9 **coursers** horses   10 **bears** (alluding to the
family emblem)   13 **suspicion** anxiety   17 **watched** stayed awake
21 **laid** i.e., in the grave

This shoulder was ordained so thick to heave,
And heave it shall some weight, or break my back.
25 Work thou the way, and that shalt execute.

King Edward. Clarence and Gloucester, love my
    lovely queen;
And kiss your princely nephew, brothers both.

Clarence. The duty that I owe unto your majesty
I seal upon the lips of this sweet babe.

King Edward. Thanks, noble Clarence; worthy
30 brother, thanks.

Richard. And, that I love the tree from whence thou
    sprang'st,
Witness the loving kiss I give the fruit.
[*Aside*] To say the truth, so Judas kissed his
    master,
And cried, "All hail!" whenas he meant all harm.

35 *King Edward.* Now am I seated as my soul delights,
Having my country's peace and brothers' loves.

Clarence. What will your Grace have done with
    Margaret?
Reignier, her father, to the King of France
Hath pawned the Sicils and Jerusalem,
40 And hither have they sent it for her ransom.

King Edward. Away with her, and waft her hence
    to France!
And now what rests° but that we spend the time
With stately triumphs,° mirthful comic shows,
Such as befits the pleasure of the court?
45 Sound drums and trumpets! Farewell sour annoy!
For here, I hope, begins our lasting joy.
                              Exeunt omnes.
                    FINIS

---

42 rests remains   **43 triumphs** public processions

Textual Note

Henry VI, Part Three, has come down to us in two major texts: the so-called "Bad Quarto" (actually a "Bad Octavo"), called Q—*The true Tragedie of Rich-ard / Duke of Yorke, and the death of / good King Henrie the Sixt, / with the whole contention betweene / the two Houses Lancaster / and Yorke, as it was sundrie times / acted by the Right Honoura- / ble the Earle of Pem- / brooke his seruants*—and the First Folio of 1623 (called F). Q, which is about two-thirds the length of F and imperfect in numerous respects, was published in 1595 by P[eter] S[hort] for Thomas Millington. The copy was not entered in the Stationers' Register. Q was long considered (principally on the authority of the noted eighteenth-century editor Edmond Malone) to be the source of Shakespeare's play; but in the past four decades there has come into fairly general acceptance the view that Q represents a reported version (perhaps by the actors who played Warwick and Clifford) of the text of an early production of the play that was later printed as F. Such, at any rate, is the opinion of the most important modern editors of the play (A. S. Cairncross, John Dover Wilson, George Lyman Kittredge, and Peter Alexander, among others). The technical studies that were largely responsible for tipping the balance in favor of this view include J. S. Smart: *Shakespeare: Truth and Tradition* (1928); Madeleine Doran: *Henry VI, Parts II and III* (1928); and Peter Alexander: *Shakespeare's Henry VI and Richard III* (1929). A. S. Cairncross's introductions to his Arden editions of *Henry VI, Part Two,* and *Henry VI, Part Three,* summarize much useful information bearing on the relation between *Henry VI, Part Two,* and *The First Part of the Contention betwixt the two famous Houses of Yorke and Lancaster* . . . and between *Henry VI, Part Three,* and *The true Tragedie of Richard Duke of Yorke.*

Apart from the initial *"Actus Primus. Scœna Prima,"* no act or scene divisions appear in F, and none at all appear in Q. The act and scene divisions in the present edition are those of the Globe edition. All divisions and stage directions that have been added are enclosed in square brackets.

A number of the stage directions in Q, like stage directions in other Shakespeare quartos, reflect stage business in actual performance, for example:

> Enter *Richard* Duke of Yorke, The Earle of *Warwicke, The Duke of* Norffolke, *Marquis Montague, Edward Earle of March, Crookeback Richard,* and the yong *Earle of Rutland,* with Drumme and Souldiers, with white Roses in their hats.[1]

> Sound a Parlie, and *Richard* and *Clarence* whispers togither, and then Clarence takes his red Rose out of his hat, and throws it at *Warwike.*[2]

> Alarmes to the battell, *Yorke* flies, then the chambers be discharged. Then enter the king, *Cla.* & *Glo.* & the rest, & make a great shout, and crie, for *Yorke,* for *Yorke,* and then the *Queene* is taken, & the prince, & *Oxf.* & *Sum.* and then found and enter all againe.[3]

In the second direction quoted above, some effort has obviously been made to motivate Clarence's betrayal of Warwick—for which F does nothing to prepare us—and the stage business here echoes the accounts in the chronicles. Another stage direction of interest is at III.i, which

---

[1] W. W. Greg, ed., *The True Tragedy of Richard Duke of York (Henry the Sixth, Part III).* Shakespeare Quarto Facsimiles No. 11 (Oxford, 1958), Sig. A2.
[2] *Ibid.,* Sig. E2.
[3] *Ibid.,* Sig. E4.

reads: "Enter Sinklo, and Humfrey, with Crosse-bowes in their hands." (The Quarto reads: "Enter two keepers with bow and arrowes.") The names Sinklo and Humfrey appear to be those of actors in Shakespeare's company—John Sincler, and Humphrey Jeffes—incorporated into the text by error. Possibly Shakespeare wrote the names as he composed, possibly a prompter added them to the company's copy. "Gabriel" in the stage direction at I.ii.47 is probably a similar error, naming the actor Gabriel Spencer.

Speech prefixes have been silently regularized, and the position of a few stage directions slightly altered. The following list includes emendations and corrections of F. In each case, the altered reading appears first, in italics; the original reading follows, in roman. When the alteration is derived from Q, that fact is indicated.

I.i.69 *Exeter* [Q] Westm. 105 *Thy* [Q] My 259 *stay with* [Q] stay 261 *from* [Q] to 273 s.d. *Exeunt* Exit
I.ii.24 *Enter [a Messenger]* [Q] Enter 75 s.d. *Exeunt* Exit
I.iv.180 *Exeunt* Exit
II.i.113 *And very well appointed, as I thought* [Q; F omits] 131 *an idle* [Q] a lazie 158 *makes* make 182 *amain* [Q; F omits]
II.ii.89–92 *Since . . . in* [F assigns to Clarence] 133 *Richard* [Q] War. 172 *deniest* [Q] denied'st
II.v.119 *Even* Men
II.vi.44 *See who it is* [Q; F gives to Richard] 60 *his* [Q] is
III.i.s.d. *Enter two Keepers* [Q] Enter Sinklo, and Humfrey 12 *Second Keeper* Sink. [i.e., First Keeper] 18 *wast* was 24 *thee, sour Adversity* the sower Aduersaries 55 *thou that* [Q] thou
III.ii.123 *honorably* [Q] honourable
III.iii.124 *eternal* [Q] externall 156 *peace* [added in F2] 228 *I'll* [Q] I
IV.i.89–90 [three lines in F, ending *thee, words, them*] 93 *thy* [Q] the
IV.ii.15 *towns* Towne
IV.iii.64 s.d. *Exeunt* exit
IV.iv.17 *wean* waine
IV.v.4 *stands* stand 8 *Comes* Come 12 *ship* shipt
IV.vi.55 *be confiscate* confiscate
IV.viii.s.d. *Exeter* Somerset
V.i.75 s.d. (see note in text) 78 *an* in
V.v.s.d. *Clarence . . . prisoners* Queene, Clarence, Oxford, Somerset 78 *butcher* butcher Richard 90 s.d. *Exeunt* Exit
V.vii.5 *renowned* [Q] Renowne 30 *King Edward* Cla. 30 *Thanks* [Q] Thanke 38 *Reignier* Reynard

The Sources of
Henry VI, Part Three

Shakespeare drew on two principal sources for *Henry VI, Part Three,* as he had done earlier for *Parts One* and *Two*. These were two of the major historical works of sixteenth-century England: Edward Hall's chronicle (*The Union of the two noble and illustre Famelies of Lancaster & Yorke . . .* [1548]; modern edition, H. Ellis [1809]) and the second edition [1587] of Raphael Holinshed's *Chronicles of England, Scotlande, and Irelande;* modern edition, H. Ellis, 6 volumes [1807–8], and several abridged editions, notably W. G. Boswell-Stone, *Shakspere's Holinshed* [1896] and Allardyce and Josephine Nicoll, edd., *Holinshed's Chronicle as used in Shakespeare's Plays* [1927]. Shakespeare's indebtedness to Holinshed has of course long been recognized, but modern scholarship has tended to emphasize ever more strongly the importance of Hall's work, both as a direct influence on Shakespeare and as an indirect influence through Holinshed.

All the chroniclers are, to say the least, exceedingly casual about borrowing from one another's work; and when they copy hastily or carelessly, as they not infrequently do, the modern reader's best hope of recovering his author's original meaning is to compare the text with that of an earlier chronicle. Students of Shakespeare are likely to find most interesting and helpful, among the earlier chronicles, *The Brut or The Chronicles of England,* ed. Friedrich W. D. Brie, Part I, Early

English Text Society, Original Series 131, 1906 (reprinted 1960), and Part II, Original Series 136, 1908; Polydore Vergil's *English History* (Henry VI, Edward IV, and Richard III), ed. Sir Henry Ellis, The Camden Society, Volume 21, 1844; and Ranulph Higden's *Polychronicon,* translated by John Trevisa (the chronicle completed to 1461 by William Caxton, who published the *Polychronicon* in 1482); modern edition, Churchill Babington and Reverend J. R. Lumby, 9 volumes, 1865–86.

"Hall's chief importance," E. M. W. Tillyard has well observed, "is that he is the first English chronicle-writer to show in all its completeness that new moralising of history which came in with the waning of the Middle Ages, the weakening of the Church, and the rise of nationalism. And the special literary importance of this feat is to have introduced a sense of drama into his manner of expression . . . the sense of the moral concatenation of great events: moral as against psychological drama."[1] The subject of Hall's chronicle was the union of the houses of Lancaster and York, a union which was achieved only after England had suffered the convulsions of civil war, the memory and fear of which haunt Shakespeare's plays as they haunted Elizabethan Englishmen. Disunion came in with Henry Bolingbroke; union was restored by Henry VII and Henry VIII (Hall calls the latter "the vndubitate flower and very heire of both the sayd linages"). The history of the intervening years, as Tillyard and others have noted, may be read in the titles of Hall's chapters:

 i. The vnquiet tyme of kyng Hēry the Fowerth.
 ii. The victorious actes of kyng Henry the v.
 iii. The troubleous season of kyng Henry the vi.
 iiii. The prosperous reigne of kyng Edward the iiij.
 v. The pitifull life of kyng Edward the v.
 vi. The tragicall doynges of kyng Richard the iij.
 vii. The politike gouernaunce of kyng Henry the vij.
 viii. The triumphant reigne of king Henry the viij.[2]

---

1 *Shakespeare's History Plays* (London, 1944), p. 42.
2 Hall's *Chronicle* (1809 edition), p. viii.

Throughout his history plays Shakespeare repeatedly expounded these few essential ideas: that evil must be punished and expiated, that goodness will be rewarded, that piety cannot prevail unless conjoined with strength (thus the ineffectual saintliness of Henry VI is sharply contrasted with the more muscular Christianity of Henry V). Both Hall and Holinshed provided Shakespeare with clear and vivid portraits of his principal characters; and Shakespeare, as usual, missed no significant hint, no illuminating detail, in the chronicles. At the same time, he adroitly combined and abridged his materials so as to heighten dramatic effect. Thus, both Hall and Holinshed describe how Clifford caused a paper crown to be set on the severed head of Richard, Duke of York. Shakespeare, in contrast, makes the scene in which Queen Margaret, Clifford, and the other Lancastrians actually torment and kill York (I.iv) one of the most powerful episodes of this harrowing play.

EDWARD HALL

from *The Union of the Two Noble and Illustre Families of Lancaster and York* (1548)*

[1454–55] After this victory [first battle of St. Albans] obtained by the Duke of York and his companions, he remembered that oftentimes he had declared and divulged abroad the only cause of his war to be for the advancement of the public wealth and to set the realm in a more commodious estate and a better condition. Wherefore, he using all lenity, mercy, and bounteousness, would not once touch or apprehend the body of King Henry, whom he might both have slain and utterly destroyed, considering that he had him in his ward and governance, but with great honor and due reverence conveyed him to London, and so to Westminster, to which place was summoned and appointed a great assembly of three estates, commonly called a Parliament, which began the ninth day of July, in the which session the Duke of Gloucester was openly declared a true prince, both to the King and the realm. Beside this, it was enacted that no person should either judge or report any point of untruth of the Duke of York, the Earls of Salisbury and Warwick, for coming in warlike manner against the King at St. Albans, considering that their attempt and enterprise was only to see the King's person in safeguard

---

* Page references in parentheses are to Hall's *Chronicle*, ed. Sir Henry Ellis (London, 1809).

and sure keeping, and to put and aliene [alienate] from him the public oppressors of the commonwealth, by whose misgovernance his life might be in hazard and his authority hang in a very small thread. In which Parliament also the Duke of York was made Protector of the Realm and the Earl of Salisbury was appointed to be Chancellor, and had the great seal to him delivered; and the Earl of Warwick was elected to the office of the Captain of Calais and the territories of the same. As this device was politicly invented, so was the sequel thereof to the first authors, both honorable and profitable, if Fortune's ship had sailed all one way. For by this practice the whole rule and regiment of the whole realm consisted only in the heads and orders of the Duke and the Chancellor, and all the warlike affairs and business rested principally in the Earl of Warwick, and so amongst them it was agreed that King Henry should still reign, in name and dignity but neither in deed nor in authority: not minding either to depose or destroy the said King, lest they might suddenly provoke and stir the fury and ire of the common people against them: which for his holiness of life and abundant clemency was of the simple sort much favored and highly esteemed. After which authority given, these three persons ruled the realm and did all things after their own discretions (which without battle or manslaughter might have easily deprived the said King both of life and land). And first they removed from the Privy Council all such persons as the King loved, or the Queen favored, putting in their places men of their sect and confederacy, and changing officers throughout the realm at their will and disposition, so that the old spoken proverb here took place: New lords, new laws: such lips, such lettuce. And yet in all their rule I find no mention made of differing justice, or of their polling, or their bribery, as was openly proved by such as governed before their time, saving that they took out of the sanctuary of Westminster John Holland, Duke of Exeter, being repugnant to the order taken and concluded in the last Parliament, and conveyed him to Pomfret Which taking out was accounted an execrable and a damnable offense, of divers of the spiritualty, and especially of the Abbot of Westminster and his monks, and this is the most spot that was (as I could read) ever most to be cast in the Duke's fame, during his protectorship or of his counsel. (p. 233)

[1460–61] After long arguments made, and deliberate consultation had among the peers, prelates, and commons of the realm, upon the vigil of All Saints it was condescended and agreed by the three estates for so much as King Henry had been taken as King by the space of thirty-eight years and more, that he should enjoy the name and title of King and have possession of the realm during his life natural. And if he either died or resigned, or forfeited the same, for infringing any point of this concord, then the said crown and authority royal should immediately be devolved to the Duke of York, if he then lived, or else to the next heir of his line or lineage, and that the Duke from thenceforth should be Protector and Regent of the land, provided always that if the King did closely or apertly [covertly or overtly] study or go about to break or alter this agreement, or to compass or imagine the death or destruction of the said Duke or his blood, then he [was] to forfeit the crown, and the Duke of York to take it. These articles, with many other, were not only written, sealed, and sworn by the two parties, but also were enacted in the high court of Parliament, for joy whereof, the King having in his company the said Duke, rode to the cathedral church of St. Paul, within the city of London, and there on the day of All Saints went solemnly with the diadem on his head, in procession, and was lodged a good space after in the bishop's palace near to the said church. And upon the Saturday next ensuing Richard, Duke of York, was by the sound of a trumpet solemnly proclaimed heir apparent to the crown of England and Protector of the Realm. . . .

The Duke of York well knowing that the Queen would spurn and impugn the conclusions agreed and taken in this Parliament caused her and her son to be sent for by the King; but she, being a manly woman, using to rule and not to be ruled, and thereto counseled by the Dukes of Exeter and Somerset, not only denied to come but also assembled together a great army, intending to take the King by fine force out of the lords' hands and to set them to a new school. The Protector, lying in London, having perfect knowledge of all these doings, assigned the Duke of Norfolk and the Earl of Warwick, his trusty friends, to be about the King, and he, with the Earls of Salisbury and Rutland, with a convenient company, departed out of London the second day of December northward, and sent to the Earl of March, his eldest son, to follow him with all his power. The Duke by small journeys came to his castle of Sandal, beside Wakefield, on Christmas Eve, and there began to assemble his tenants and friends. The Queen, being thereof ascertained, determined to couple with him while his power was small and his aid not come. And so, having in her company the Prince her son, the Dukes of Exeter and Somerset, the Earl of Devonshire, the Lord Clifford, the Lord Ross, and in effect all the lords of the north party, with eighteen thousand men, or as some write twenty-two thousand, marched from York to Wakefield and bade base to [challenged] the Duke, even before his castle; he, having with him not fully five thousand persons, determined incontinent to issue out and to fight with his enemies, and although Sir Davy Halle, his old servant and chief counselor, advised him to keep his castle and to defend the same with his small number till his son the Earl of March were come with his power of Marchmen and Welsh soldiers, yet he would not be counseled, but in a great fury said, "A Davy, a Davy, hast thou loved me so long and now wouldst have me dishonored!" . . . The Duke of York with his people descended down the hill in good order and array and was suffered to pass forward, toward the main battle. But when he was in the plain ground between his castle and the town of Wakefield, he was environed on every side, like a fish in a net, or a deer in a buckstall, so that he, manfully fighting, was within half an hour slain and dead, and his whole army discomfited. . . . (pp. 249–250) While this

battle was in fighting, a priest called Sir Robert Aspall,
chaplain and schoolmaster to the young Earl of Rutland,
second son to the above-named Duke of York, scarce
of the age of twelve years, a fair gentleman and a maiden-
like person, perceiving that flight was more safeguard
than tarrying, both for him and his master, secretly
conveyed the Earl out of the field, by the Lord Clifford's
band, toward the town; but ere he could enter into a
house he was by the said Lord Clifford espied, followed,
and taken, and by reason of his apparel demanded what
he was. The young gentleman, dismayed, had not a word
to speak, but knelt on his knees imploring mercy and
desiring grace, both with holding up his hands and making dolorous countenance, for his speech was gone for
fear. "Save him," said his chaplain, "for he is a prince's
son and peradventure may do you good hereafter." With
that word, the Lord Clifford marked him and said: "By
God's blood, thy father slew mine, and so will I do
thee and all thy kin," and with that word stuck the Earl
to the heart with his dagger, and bade his chaplain bear
the Earl's mother and brother word what he had done
and said. In this act the Lord Clifford was accounted a
tyrant, and no gentleman. . . . This cruel Clifford and
deadly bloodsucker, not content with this homicide, or
childkilling, came to the place where the dead corpse of
the Duke of York lay, and caused his head to be stricken
off, and set on it a crown of paper, and so fixed it on
a pole, and presented it to the Queen, not lying far from
the field, in great despite and much derision, saying:
"Madame, your war is done, here is your king's ransom," at which present was much joy and great rejoicing, but many laughed then that sore lamented after,
as the Queen herself, and her son; and many were glad
then of other men's deaths, not knowing that their own
were near at hand, as the Lord Clifford, and other. But
surely man's nature is so frail that things passed be
soon forgotten, and mischiefs to come be not foreseen.
After this victory by the Queen and her party obtained,
she caused the Earl of Salisbury with all the other prisoners to be sent to Pomfret and there to be beheaded,

and sent all their heads, and the Duke's head of York,
to be set upon poles over the gate of the city of York,
in despite of them and their lineage: whose children
shortly revenged their fathers' quarrel, both to the
Queen's extreme perdition and the utter undoing of her
husband and son. This end had the valiant lord Richard
Plantagenet, Duke of York. . . . (p. 251) What should I
declare . . . how the counties adjoining to London daily
repaired to see, aid, and comfort this lusty prince and
flower of chivalry [Edward, Earl of March] as he in whom
the hope of their joy and the trust of their quietness only
then consisted. This wise and prudent noble man, perceiving the most part of the realm to be to him friendly and
adherent, minding to take time when time served, called a
great council both of lords spiritual and temporal and to
them repeated the title and right that he had to the realm
and dignity royal, rehearsing the articles of the agreement
not only concluded between King Henry and his noble
father, Richard, Duke of York, by their writings signed
and sealed, but also corroborated and confirmed by
authority of the high court of Parliament, the breaches
whereof he neither forgot nor omitted undeclared. After
the lords had considered and weighed his title and declaration, they determined by authority of the said council for
as much as King Henry, contrary to his oath, honor, and
agreement, had violated and infringed the order taken and
enacted in the last Parliament, and also because he was
insufficient to rule the realm, and inutile [useless] to the
commonwealth, and public profit of the poor people, he
was therefore by the aforesaid authority deprived and
dejected of all kingly honor and regal sovereignty. And
incontinent Edward, Earl of March, son and heir to
Richard, Duke of York, was by the lords in the said council assembled named, elected, and admitted for King and
governor of the realm, on which day the people of the
Earl's party, being in their muster in St. John's Field, and
a great number of the substantial citizens there assembled,
to behold their order: suddenly the Lord Fauconberg,
which took the musters, wisely declared to the multitude
the offenses and breaches of the late agreement done and

perpetrated by King Henry VI and demanded of the people whether they would have the said King Henry to rule and reign any longer over them. To whom they with a whole voice answered, nay, nay. Then he asked them if they would serve, love, and obey the Earl of March as their earthly prince and sovereign lord. To which question they answered, yea, yea, crying, King Edward, with many great shouts and clapping of hands. . . . (p. 253)

. . . The Lord Clifford, either for heat or pain, putting off his gorget, suddenly with an arrow (as some say) without an head, was striken into the throat, and incontinent rendered his spirit, and the Earl of Westmoreland's brother and all his company almost were there slain, at a place called Dintingdale, not far from Towton. This end had he, which slew the young Earl of Rutland, kneeling on his knees: whose young son Thomas Clifford was brought up with a shepherd, in poor habit and dissembled behavior, ever in fear, to publish his lineage or degree, till King Henry VII obtained the crown and got the diadem, by whom he was restored to his name and possessions. . . . (p. 255)

[1463–64] But now consider the old proverb to be true that saith that marriage is destiny. For during the time that the Earl of Warwick was . . . in France, concluding a marriage for King Edward, the King, being on hunting in the forest of Wychwood beside Stony Stratford, came for his recreation to the manor of Grafton, where the Duchess of Bedford sojourned, then wife to Sir Richard Woodville, Lord Rivers, on whom then was attending a daughter of hers, called Dame Elizabeth Grey, widow of Sir John Grey, knight, slain at the last battle of St. Albans, by the power of King Edward. This widow, having a suit to the King, either to be restored by him to something taken from her, or requiring him of pity to have some augmentation to her living, found such grace in the King's eyes that he not only favored her suit but much more fancied her person, for she was a woman more of formal countenance than of excellent beauty, but yet of such beauty and favor that with her sober demeanor, lovely looking, and feminine smiling (neither too wanton nor too humble) beside her tongue so eloquent, and her wit so pregnant, she was able to ravish the mind of a mean person, when she allured and made subject to her the heart of so great a king. After that King Edward had well considered all the lineaments of her body and the wise and womanly demeanor that he saw in her, he determined first to attempt if he might provoke her to be his sovereign lady, promising her many gifts and fair rewards, affirming farther, that if she would thereunto condescend, she might so fortune of his paramour and concubine to be changed to his wife and lawful bedfellow, which demand she so wisely and with so covert speech answered and refused, affirming that as she was for his honor far unable to be his spouse and bedfellow, so for her own poor honesty she was too good to be either his concubine or sovereign lady; that where he was a little before heated with the dart of Cupid, he was now set all on a hot burning fire, what for the confidence that he had in her perfect constancy and the trust that he had in her constant chastity, and without any farther deliberation, he determined with himself clearly to marry with her, after that asking counsel of them which he knew neither would nor once dared impugn his concluded purpose.

But the Duchess of York his mother letted [hindered] it as much as in her lay, alleging a precontract made by him with the Lady Lucy, and diverse other lets [obstacles], all which doubts were resolved and all things made clear and all cavilings avoided. And so, privily in a morning, he married her at Grafton, where he first fancied her visage.

[1464–65] And in the next year after, she was with great solemnity crowned Queen at Westminster. Her father also was created Earl Rivers, and made High Constable of England; her brother, Lord Anthony, was married to the sole heir of Thomas, Lord Scales, and by her he was Lord Scales. . . . Albeit this marriage, at the first appearance, was very pleasant to the King, but more joyous to the Queen and profitable to her blood, which were so highly exalted, yea and so suddenly promoted, that all the nobility more marveled than allowed this sudden rising and swift elevation: Yet whoso will mark the sequel of this story shall manifestly perceive what murder, what misery, and what trouble ensued by reason of this marriage; for it cannot be denied but for this marriage King Edward was expelled [from] the realm and dared not abide. And for this marriage was the Earl of Warwick and his brother miserably slain. By this marriage were King Edward's two sons declared bastards, and in conclusion deprived of their lives. And finally, by this marriage the Queen's blood was confounded, and utterly in manner destroyed. So that men did afterward divine that either God·was not contented nor yet pleased with this matrimony, or else that he punished King Edward in his posterity, for the deep dissembling and covert cloaking with his faithful friend the Earl of Warwick. But such conjectures, for the most part, be rather more of men's fantasies than of divine revelation. When this marriage was once blown abroad, foreign kings and princes marveled and mused at it; noble men detested and disdained it; the common people grudged and murmured at it, and all with one voice said that his unadvised wooing, hasty loving, and too speedy marriage were neither meet for him, being a king, nor consonant to the honor of so high an estate. The French King and his Queen were not a little discontent (as I cannot blame them) to have their sister first demanded and then granted, and in conclusion rejected, and apparently mocked without any cause reasonable. Wherefore shortly to appease her dolor they married her to Gian Galeazzo, Duke of Milan, where she lived in great felicity. But when the Earl of Warwick had perfect knowledge by the letters of his trusty friends that King Edward had gotten him a new wife and that all that he had done with King Lewis in his embassy for the conjoining of this new affinity was both frustrate and vain, he was earnestly moved and sore chafed with the chance, and thought it necessary that King Edward should be deposed from his crown and royal dignity as an inconstant prince, not worthy of such a kingly office. All men for the most part agree that this marriage was the only cause why the Earl of Warwick bore a grudge and made war on King Edward. Others affirm that there were other causes, which, added to this, made the fire to flame, which before was but a little smoke. For after that King Edward had obtained his kingdom (as it was then thought) by the only help and mean of the Earl of Warwick, he began to suspect, yea, and to doubt him, fearing lest he being in such authority and estimation of the people as he well might work him pleasure or displeasure, when he thereunto were minded, wherefore he thought it convenient a little and a little to pluck away and diminish the power and authority which he and his predecessors had given to the Earl, to the intent that he then might do at his pleasure, both at home and in outward parts, without fear or dread, without check or taunt, whatsoever to his own mind seemed most convenient. By this a man may see that often it chanceth that friends for one good turn will not render another, nor yet remember a great gratuity and benefit in time of necessity to them showed and exhibited; but for kindness they show unkindness, and for great benefits received, with great displeasure they do recompense. Of this the Earl of Warwick was nothing ignorant, which, although he had looked for better thanks and more ample benefits at King Edward's hands, yet he thought it best to dissemble the matter till such a time were come as he might find the King without strength, and then to imbraid [upbraid] him with the pleasure that he had done for him. And farther it erreth not from the truth that King Edward did attempt a thing once in the Earl's house which was much against the Earl's honesty (whether he would have deflowered his daughter or his niece, the certainty was not for both their honors openly known) for surely such a thing was attempted by King Edward, which loved well both to look and to feel fair damsels. But whether the injury that the Earl thought he had taken at King Edward's hands, or the disdain of authority that the Earl had under the King, was the cause of dissolution of their amity and league, truth it is that the privy intentions in their hearts broke into so many small pieces that England, France, and Flanders could never join them again during their natural lives. . . . (pp. 264–265)

[1467–68] The Earl of Warwick, being a man of a great wit, far casting, and many things vigilantly foreseeing, either perceived by other, or had perfect knowledge of himself, that the Duke of Clarence bore not the best will to King Edward his brother (as he did not indeed), thought first to prove him afar off, as it were in a problem, and after to open to him (if he saw him flexible to his purpose) the secret imaginations of his stomach, thinking that if he might by policy or promise allure the Duke to his party, that King Edward should be destitute of one of his best hawks when he had most need to make a flight. So at time and place convenient, the Earl began to complain to the Duke of the ingratitude and doubleness of King Edward, saying that he had neither handled him like a friend nor kept promise with him according as the estate of a prince required. The Earl had not half told his tale but the Duke in a great fury answered, "Why, my lord, think you to have him kind to you that is unkind and unnatural to me being his own brother, think you that friendship will make him keep promise where neither nature nor kindred in any wise can provoke or move him to favor his own blood? Think you that he will exalt and promote his cousin or ally which little careth for the fall or confusion of his own line and lineage? This you know well enough, that the heir of the Lord Scales he hath married to his wife's brother, the heir also of the Lord Bonville and Harrington, he hath given to his wife's son, and the heir of the Lord Hungerford he hath granted to the Lord Hastings: three marriages more meeter for his two brethren and kin than for such new foundlings as he hath bestowed them on. But by sweet St. George I swear, if my brother of Gloucester would join with me, we would make him know that we were all three one man's sons, of one mother and one lineage descended, which should be more preferred and promoted than strangers of his wife's blood."

When the Earl of Warwick had heard the Duke's words, he had that which he both sore thrusted and lusted for, and then began boldly to disclose to the Duke his intent and purpose even at the full, requiring him to take part with him and to be one of the attempted confederacy. And lest the Duke might think that the matter was lightly and uncircumspectly begun, he declared to him how warily, how secretly, how speedily all things concerning this purpose had been compassed, studied, and foreseen, requiring him in so great and urgent a cause both to take pain and travail and also to study with all circumspection and foreseeing how these things thus begun might be brought to a certainty and a final conclusion. And the rather to win the Duke's heart the Earl, beside divers and many fair promises made to the Duke, offered him his eldest daughter (being of ripe age and elegant stature) in marriage, with the whole halfedele [half-share] of his wife's inheritance. The Duke, at the persuasion and request of the Earl, promised to do all things which he would or could concerning their strange and dangerous affairs; they first determined to sail to Calais, of the which town the Earl was Chief Captain, where his wife and two daughters then sojourned, whom to visit, the Duke of Clarence being in amours, had no small affection. But the Earl, continually remembering the purpose that he was set on, thought to begin and kindle the fire of his ungracious conjuration (which so many years vexed and unquieted the realm of England) before his departure, wherefore he appointed his brethren the Archbishop and the Marquess that they should by some mean in his absence stir up new commotion or rebellion in the County of York and other places adjacent: so that this civil war should seem to all men to have been begun without his assent or knowledge (he being in the parts of beyond the sea). . . . (pp. 271–272)

[1470] While these lords [the Earl of Warwick, the Duke of Clarence, Jasper, Earl of Pembroke, and John, Earl of Oxford] were . . . in the French court, there landed at Calais a damsel belonging to the Duchess of Clarence (as she said) which made Monsieur de Vauclair believe that she was sent from King Edward to the Earl of Warwick with a plain overture and declaration of peace. Of the which tidings Vauclair was very glad for the Earl's sake, whom he thought (by this peace) to be restored to all his old possessions . . . and dignities. But he was sore by this damsel deceived, for her message (as it after proved) was the beginning of the Earl's confusion. For she persuaded the Duke of Clarence that it was neither natural nor honorable to him either to condescend or take part against the house of York (of which he was lineally descended) and to set up again the house of Lancaster, which lineage of the house of York was not only by the whole Parliament of the realm declared to be the very and indubitable heirs of the kingdom, but also King Henry VI and his blood affirmed the same, and thereupon made a composition, which of record appeareth. Farthermore, she declared that the marriage with the Earl's daughter with Prince Edward was for none other cause but to make the Prince King, and clearly to extinguish all the house of York, of whom the Duke himself was one, and next heir to the crown, after his eldest brother and his children. These reasons, and the marriage of the Prince to the Earl's daughter, so sank in the Duke's stomach that he promised at his return not to be so an extreme enemy to his brother as he was taken for, which promise afterward he did not forget. With this answer the damsel departed into England, the Earl of Warwick thereof being clearly ignorant. . . . (p. 281)

[1470–71] In this season Jasper, Earl of Pembroke, went into Wales to visit his county of Pembroke, where he found Lord Henry, son to his brother Edmund, Earl of Richmond, having not fully ten years of his age complete, which was kept in manner like a captive, but well and honorably educated, and in all kind of civility brought up, by the Lady Herbert, late wife to William, Earl of Pembroke, beheaded at Banbury. . . . This Lord Henry was he that, after King Richard, brother to King Edward, was vanquished and overthrown, obtained the crown and regality of this realm, whom we ought to believe to be sent from God, and of him only to be provided a king, for to extinguish both the factions and parties of King Henry VI and King Edward IV (which had almost brought the nobility of this realm to a final destruction and an utter decay) considering that he, once exalted to that dignity, nothing more minded, nor to any one thing more his study applied. This Henry was born of Margaret, the only daugh-

ter and heir to John the first Duke of Somerset, then not
being fully of thirteen years of age. The which Lady Margaret, although she were after conjoined in marriage with
Lord Henry, son to Humphrey, Duke of Buckingham, and
after to Thomas Stanley, Earl of Derby, both being lusty
and of age meet for generation, yet afterward she brought
forth no more fruit, as though she had done her part
sufficiently, for to have borne one man child, and the same
to be a king. Jasper, Earl of Pembroke, took this child,
being his nephew, out of the custody of the Lady Herbert,
and at his return he brought the child to London to King
Henry VI, whom, when the King had a good space by
himself secretly beholden and marked both his wit and his
likely towardness, he said to such princes as were then with
him: "Lo, surely this is he to whom both we and our
adversaries leaving the possession of all things shall hereafter give room and place." So this holy man showed
before the chance that this should happen, that this Earl
Henry so ordained by God should in time to come (as he
did indeed) have and enjoy the kingdom and the whole
rule of the realm. (p. 287)

[1471] . . . Upon the twelfth day of October [the Earl
of Warwick] rode to the Tower of London, which was to
him without resistance delivered, there took King Henry
VI out of the ward, where he before was kept, and was
brought to the King's lodging and there served according
to his degree. And the twenty-fifth day of the said month,
the Duke of Clarence, accompanied with the Earls of
Warwick, Shrewsbury, and the Lord Stanley, and other
lords and gentlemen, some for fear, and some for love,
and some only to gaze at the wavering world, resorted with
a great company to the Tower of London, and from thence
with great pomp brought King Henry VI, appareled in a
long gown of blue velvet, through the high streets of London to the cathedral church of St. Paul, the people on the
right hand and on the left hand rejoicing and crying God
save the King, as though all thing had succeeded as they
would have it, and when he had offered as kings use to
do, he was conveyed to the palace of the Bishop of London, and there kept his household like a king.

King Henry VI thus readepted [recovered] (by the means only of the Earl of Warwick) his crown and dignity royal, in the year of Our Lord 1471, newly after so many overthrows beginning to reign, likely within short space to fall again, and to taste more of his accustomed captivity and usual misery. This ill chance and misfortune, by many men's opinion, happened to him because he was a man of no great wit, such as men commonly call an innocent man, neither a fool, neither very wise, whose study always was more to excel other in godly living and virtuous example than in worldly regiment or temporal dominion, insomuch that, in comparison to the study and delectation that he had to virtue and godliness, as little regarded but in manner despised all worldly power and temporal authority, which seldom follow or seek after such persons as from them fly or disdain to take them. But his enemies ascribed all this to his coward stomach, affirming that he was a man apt to no purpose nor meet for any enterprise, were it never so small. But whosoever despiseth or dispraiseth that which the common people allow and marvel at is often taken of them for a mad and indiscreet person, but notwithstanding the vulgar opinion, he that followeth, loveth, and embraceth the contrary doth prove both sad and wise (verifying Solomon's proverb) the wisdom of this world is foolishness before God, affirming that the kingdom which Henry IV his grandfather wrongfully got and unjustly possessed against King Richard II and his heirs could not by very divine justice long continue in that injurious stock. And that therefore God, by his divine Providence, punished the offense of the grandfather in the son's son. . . . (pp. 285–286)

[1471–72] . . . The Earl [of Warwick] considering that King Edward did daily increase his power (as a running river by going more and more augmenteth) thought it most necessary for him to give him battle with speed, and thereupon . . . called together his army, and in all haste sent for the Duke of Clarence to join with him which had conscribed, and assembled together a great host about London. But when he perceived that the Duke lingered, and did all things negligently, as though he were in doubt of war or peace, he then began somewhat to suspect that that Duke was of his brethren corrupted and lately changed, and therefore without delay marched forward toward Coventry, to the intent to set upon his enemies. In the mean season, King Edward came to Warwick, where he found all the people departed, and from thence with all diligence advanced his power toward Coventry, and in a plain by the city he pitched his field. And the next day after that he came thither, his men were set forward, and marshaled in array, and he valiantly bade the Earl battle: which mistrusting that he should be deceived by the Duke of Clarence (as he was indeed) kept himself close within the walls. And yet he had perfect word that the Duke of Clarence came forward toward him with a great army, King Edward being also thereof informed, raised his camp, and made toward the Duke. And lest that there might bethought some fraud to be cloaked between them, the King set his battles in an order as though he would fight without any longer delay, the Duke did likewise. When each host was in sight of the other, Richard, Duke of Gloucester, brother to them both, as though he had been made arbiter between them, first rode to the Duke, and with him communed very secretly: from him he came to King Edward, and with like secretness so used him that in conclusion no unnatural war but a fraternal amity was concluded and proclaimed, and then, leaving all army and weapon aside, both the brethren lovingly embraced, and familiarly communed together. It was no marvel that the Duke of Clarence, with so small persuasion and less exhorting, turned from the Earl of Warwick's party, for as you have heard before, this merchandise was labored, conducted, and concluded by a damsel, when the Duke was in the French court, to the Earl's utter confusion.

After this, King Edward caused to be proclaimed that the Duke and all that came with him should be taken as his true friends, without fraud or ill suspicion. But this notwithstanding, it seemeth that God did neither forgive nor forget to punish the Duke with condign punishment for violating and breaking his oath solemnly and advisedly taken and made to the Earl of Warwick, for God not many years after suffered him like a perjured person to die a cruel and a strange death.

Then was it concluded amongst the three brethren to attempt the Earl of Warwick, if by any fair means he might be reconciled or by any promise allured to their party: To whom the Duke of Clarence sent divers of his secret friends, first to excuse him of the act that he had done, secondarily to require him to take some good end now while he might with King Edward.

When the Earl had heard patiently the Duke's message, Lord, how he detested and accursed him, crying out on him that he, contrary to his oath, promise, and fidelity, had shamefully turned his face from his confederates and allies. But to the Duke's messengers he gave more other answer but this, that he had liefer be always like himself than like a false and a perjured duke, and that he was fully determined never to leave war till either he had lost his own natural life, or utterly extinguished and put under his foes and enemies. . . . (p. 293)

When the day began to spring, the trumpets blew courageously and the battle fiercely began, archers first shot, and billmen then followed, King Edward, having the greater number of men, valiantly set on his enemies. The Earl, on the other side, remembering his ancient fame and renown, manfully withstood him. This battle on both sides was sore fought and many slain. . . . The Earl of Warwick, after long fight, wisely did perceive his men to be overpressed with the multitude of his adversaries; wherefore he caused new men to relieve them that fought in the forward, by reason of which succor King Edward's party gave a little back (which was the cause that some lookers-on, and no fighters, galloped to London, saying that the Earl had won the field) which thing when King Edward did perceive, he with all diligence sent fresh men to their succor.

If the battle were fierce and deadly before, now it was crueler, more bloody, more fervent and fiery, and yet they had fought from morning almost to noon without any party getting advantage of the other. King Edward, being weary of so long a conflict, and willing to see an end, caused a great crew of fresh men (which he had for this only policy kept all day in store) to set on their enemies, in manner being weary and fatigued; but although the Earl saw these new succors of fresh and new men to enter the battle, being nothing afraid but hoping of the victory (knowing perfectly that there was all King Edward's power), comforted his men being weary, sharply quickening and earnestly desiring them with hardy stomachs to bear out this last and final brunt of the battle, and that the field was even at an end. But when his soldiers, being sore wounded, wearied with so long a conflict, did give little regard to his words, he being a man of a mind invincible rushed into the midst of his enemies, where he (adventured so far from his own company, to kill and slay his adversaries, that he could not be rescued) was in the midst of his enemies struck down and slain. The Marquess Montague, thinking to succor his brother, which he saw was in great jeopardy, and yet in hope to obtain the victory, was likewise overthrown and slain. After the Earl was dead, his party fled and many were taken, but not one man of name, nor of nobility.

Some authors write that this battle was fought so near hand that King Edward was constrained to fight his own person, and fought as sore as any man of his party, and that the Earl of Warwick, which was wont ever to ride on horseback from place to place, from rank to rank, comforting his men, was now advised by the Marquess his brother to relinquish his horse, and try the extremity by hand strokes, which if he had been on his horseback might fortune to have escaped.

This end had Richard Nevill, Earl of Warwick, whose stout stomach and invincible courage, after so many strange fortunes and perilous chances by him escaped caused death before he came to any old age privily to steal on him and with his dart to take from him all worldly and mundane affections. But death did one thing that life could not do, for by death he had rest, peace, quietness, and tranquillity, which his life ever abhorred and could not suffer nor abide. On both parties were slain at this battle (Barnet) more than ten thousand men. . . .(p. 296)

[1470–71] . . . When the Queen was come to Tewkesbury, and knew that King Edward followed her with his horsemen at the very back, she was sore abashed, and wonderfully amazed and determined in herself to fly into Wales to Jasper, Earl of Pembroke. But the Duke of Somerset, willing in no wise to fly backward . . . determined there to tarry, to take such fortune as God should send, being in his own mind, and so fixed in a fair park, adjoining to the town, he pitched his field against the will and consent of many other captains which would that he should have drawn aside for a while till the Earl of Pembroke with his army were with him associate, but his will served for his reason, and so the chance followed. The Duke of Somerset, intending to abide the battle like a politic warrior, trenched his camp round about of such an altitude, and so strongly, that his enemies by no means . . . could make any entry, and farther perceiving that his party could never escape without battle, determined there to see the final end of his good or ill chance, wherefore he marshaled his host in this manner: he and the Lord John of Somerset, his brother, led the forward; the middleward was governed by the Prince under the conduct of the Lord of St. John and Lord Wenlock (whom King Edward had highly before preferred and promoted to the degree of a baron). The rearward was put in the rule of the Earl of Devonshire.

When all these battles [armies] were thus ordered and placed, the queen and her son Prince Edward rode about the field, encouraging their soldiers, promising to them (if they did show themselves valiant against their enemies) great rewards and high promotions, innumerable gain of the spoil and booty of their adversaries, and above all other fame and renown through the whole realm. King Edward likewise, which the day before was come within a mile of Tewkesbury, put his brother the Duke of Gloucester in the forward; and himself in the middleward; the Lord Marquess and the Lord Hastings led the rearward. The Duke of Gloucester, which lacked no policy, valiantly with his battle assaulted the trench of the Queen's camp, whom the Duke of Somerset with no less courage defended; the Duke of Gloucester, for a very politic purpose, with all his men recoiled back. The Duke of Somerset, perceiving that, like a knight more courageous than circumspect, came out of his trench, with his whole battle, and followed the chase, not doubting but the Prince and the Lord Wenlock with the middleward had followed just at his back. But whether the Lord Wenlock dissembled the matter for King Edward's sake, or whether his heart served him not, still he stood looking on. The Duke of Gloucester, taking the advantage that he adventured for, turned again face to face to the Duke of Somerset's battle, which (nothing less thinking on than of the return) were within a small season shamefully discomfited. The Duke of Somerset, seeing his unfortunate chance, returned to the middleward, where he, seeing the Lord Wenlock standing still, after he had reviled him and called him traitor with his ax he struck the brains out of his head. The Duke of Gloucester entered the trench, and after him the King, where, after no long conflict, the Queen's party went almost all to wreck, for the most part were slain. Some fled for succor in the thick of the park, some into the monastery, some into other places. The Queen was found in her chariot almost dead for sorrow, the Prince was apprehended and kept close by Sir Richard Crofts; the Duke of Somerset and the Lord Prior of St. John's were by force taken prisoners, and many other also. In the field and chase were slain Lord John of Somerset, the Earl of Devonshire . . . and three thousand other.

After the field ended, King Edward made a proclamation that whosoever could bring Prince Edward to him alive or dead should have an annuity of one hundred pounds during his life, and the Prince's life to be saved. Sir Richard Crofts, a wise and a valiant knight, nothing mistrusting the King's former promise, brought forth his prisoner Prince Edward, being a goodly feminine and a well-featured young gentleman, whom when King

Edward had well advised, he demanded of him how he
dared so presumptuously enter into his realm with ban-
ner displayed. The Prince, being bold of stomach and
of a good courage, answered, saying, "To recover my
father's kingdom and inheritance, from his father and
grandfather to him, and from him, after him, to me
lineally devolved." At which words King Edward said
nothing, but with his hand thrust him from him (or,
as some say, struck him with his gauntlet), whom incontinent they that stood about, which were George,
Duke of Clarence, Richard, Duke of Gloucester, Thomas,
Marquess Dorset, and William, Lord Hastings, suddenly
murdered and piteously slaughtered. The bitterness of
which murder some of the actors after in their latter days
tasted and assayed by the very rod of justice and punishment of God. His body was humbly interred with the
other simple corpses in the church of the monastery of
the Black Monks in Tewkesbury. This was the last civil
battle that was fought in King Edward's days, which was
gotten the third day of May, in the tenth year of his
reign, and in the year of Our Lord 1471, then being
Saturday. And on the Monday next ensuing was Edmund,
Duke of Somerset. . . . and twelve other knights and
gentlemen beheaded in the marketplace at Tewkesbury.

Queen Margaret like a prisoner was brought to London, where she remained till King Reignier her father
ransomed her with money, which sum (as the French
writers affirm) he borrowed of King Lewis XI, and because he was not of power nor ability to repay so great
a duty, he sold to the French King and his heirs the
kingdoms of Naples and both the Sicilies, with the county
of Provence, which is the very title that King Charles VII
made when he conquered the realm of Naples. After
the ransom paid, she was conveyed into France with
small honor, which with so great triumph and honorable entertainment was the pomp above all pride received into this realm twenty-eight years before. And
where in the beginning of her time she lived like a
Queen, in the middle she ruled like an empress, toward
the end she was vexed with trouble, never quiet nor in

peace, and in her very extreme age she passed her days
in France, more like a death than a life, languishing and
mourning in continual sorrow, not so much for herself
and her husband, whose ages were almost consumed and
worn, but for the loss of Prince Edward her son (whom
she and her husband thought to leave, both overliver
[survivor] of their progeny and also of their kingdom),
to whom in this life nothing could be either more dis-
pleasing or grievous. . . .

When King Edward had appeased, by the means
afore rehearsed, his kingdom and people, to the intent
that there should insurge hereafter no new commotion
within the realm again, he made a journey into Kent,
and there sat in judgment on such as in the last tumultuous business took part with bastard Fauconberg, where
many were (not unworthy) straitly punished and ransomed, which business once performed, to the intent
that all men might see apparently that indubitable peace
was come into the realm, and that all fear of exterior
hostility was banished and exiled forever, poor King
Henry VI, a little before deprived of his realm and imperial crown, was now in the Tower of London de-
spoiled of his life and all worldly felicity by Richard,
Duke of Gloucester (as the constant fame [rumor] ran)
which, to the intent that King Edward his brother should
be clear out of all secret suspicion of sudden invasion,
murdered the said King with a dagger. But whosoever
was the mankiller [murderer] of this holy man, it shall
appear that both the murderer and the consenter had
condign and not undeserved punishment for their bloody
stroke and butcherly act. And because they had now no
enemies risen on whom they might revenge themselves,
as you shall hereafter perceive, they exercised their
cruelty against their own selves; and with their proper
blood imbrued and polluted their own hands and members. . . . (pp. 300–301)

King Henry was of stature goodly, of body slender, to
which proportion all other members were correspondent:
his face beautiful, in the which continually was resident
the bounty of mind with which he was inwardly endowed.

He did abhor of his own nature all the vices, as well of the body as of the soul, and from his very infancy he was of honest conversation and pure integrity, no knower of evil, and a keeper of all goodness, a despiser of all things which be wont to cause the minds of mortal men to slide, fall, or appaire [be impaired]. Beside this, patience was so radicate in his heart that of all the injuries to him committed (which were no small number) he never asked vengeance nor punishment but for that rendered to Almighty God, his creator, hearty thanks, thinking that by this trouble and adversity his sins were to him forgotten and forgiven. What shall I say that this good, this gentle, this meek, this sober and wise man did declare and affirm that those mischiefs and miseries, partly, came to him for his own offense and wherefore he little or nothing esteemed or in any wise did torment or macerate himself whatsoever dignity, what honor, what state of life, what child, what friend he had lost or missed, but if it did but sound an offense toward God, he looked on that, and not without repentance both mourned and sorrowed for it. These and other like offices of holiness caused God to work miracles for him in his lifetime (as old men said). By reason whereof King Henry VII, not without cause, sued to Julius, Bishop of Rome, to have him canonized, as other saints be; but the fees of canonizing of a king were of so great a quantity at Rome (more than the canonizing of a bishop or a prelate, although he sat in St. Peter's chair) that the said King thought it more necessary to keep his money at home, for the profit of his realm and country rather than to impoverish his kingdom for the gaining of a new holiday of St. Henry, remitting to God the judgment of his will and intent. This King Henry was of a liberal mind, and especially to such as loved good learning and them whom he saw profit in any virtuous science he heartily favored and embraced, wherefore he first helped his own young scholars to attain to discipline, and for them he founded a solemn school at Eton, a town next to Windsor, in the which he hath established an honest college of sad priests, with a great number of children which be there, of his cost frankly and freely taught the eruditaments and rules of grammar. Besides this, he edified a princely college, in the University of Cambridge, called the King's College, for the further erudition of such as were brought up in Eton, which, at this day, so flourisheth in all kinds, as well of literature as of tongues, that above all other it is worthy to be called the Prince of Colleges. (pp. 303–304)

Commentaries

SAMUEL JOHNSON

from *The Plays of William Shakespeare* (1765)

This play is only divided from the former for the convenience of exhibition; for the series of action is continued without interruption, nor are any two scenes of any play more closely connected than the first scene of this play with the last of the former.

ACT I. SCENE iii. [I. i. 236]
> *What is it but to make thy Sepulcher.*

The Queen's reproach is founded on a position long received among politicians, that the loss of a King's power is soon followed by loss of life.

ACT I. SCENE iv. [I. ii. 22–3]
> *An oath is of no moment, being not took*
> *Before a true and lawful magistrate.*

The obligation of an oath is here eluded by very
despicable sophistry. A lawful magistrate alone has the
power to exact an oath, but the oath derives no part
of its force from the magistrate. The plea against the
obligation of an oath obliging to maintain an usurper,
taken from the unlawfulness of the oath itself in the
foregoing play, was rational and just.

ACT 1. SCENE iv. [I. ii. 49–50]
> *The Queen, with all the Northern Earls and Lords,*
> *Intend here to besiege you in your castle.*

I know not whether the author intended any moral
instruction, but he that reads this has a striking admoni-
tion against that precipitancy by which men often use
unlawful meáns to do that which a little delay would
put honestly in their power. Had York stayed but a few
moments he had saved his cause from the stain of perjury.

ACT I. SCENE vi. [I. iv. 132]
> *'Tis government that makes them* [i.e.women] *seem divine...*

Government, in the language of that time, signified
evenness of temper, and decency of manners.

ACT II. SCENE i. [II. i. 48]
> EDWARD. *Oh, speak no more!*

The generous tenderness of Edward, and savage fortitude of Richard, are well distinguished by their different
reception of their father's death.

ACT II. SCENE ii. [II. i. 130–2]
> *Our soldiers, like the night-owl's lazy flight,*
> *Or like a lazy thrasher with a flail,*
> *Fell gently down.*

This image [of the night owl] is not very congruous to

the subject, nor was it necessary to the comparison, which is happily enough completed by the thresher.

ACT II. SCENE vi. [II. v. 21 foll.]
> *O God! methinks it were a happy life*
> *To be no better than a homely swain.*

This speech is mournful and soft, exquisitely suited to the character of the king, and makes a pleasing interchange, by affording, amidst the tumult and horror of the battle, an unexpected glimpse of rural innocence and pastoral tranquillity.

ACT III. SCENE i. [III. i. 17] *Thy balm washt off.*

It is common in these plays to find the same images, whether jocular or serious, frequently recurring.

ACT III. SCENE ii. [III. ii. 16 foll.]

This is a very lively and spritely dialogue [between King Edward and Lady Grey]; the reciprocation is quicker than is common in Shakespeare.

ACT III. SCENE iii. [III. ii. 161]   *Unlick'd bear-whelp.*

It was an opinion which, in spite of its absurdity, prevailed long, that the bear brings forth only shapeless lumps of animated flesh, which she licks into the form of bears. It is now well known that the whelps of a bear are produced in the same state with those of other creatures.

ACT III. SCENE iii. [III. ii. 166–7]
> *To o'erbear such*
> *As are of better person than myself.*

Richard speaks here the language of nature. Whoever is stigmatized with deformity has a constant source of envy in his mind, and would counterbalance by some other superiority these advantages which they feel themselves to want. Bacon remarks that the deformed are commonly daring, and it is almost proverbially observed that they are ill-natured. The truth is, that the deformed, like all other men, are displeased with inferiority, and endeavor to gain ground by good or bad means, as they are virtuous or corrupt.

ACT III. SCENE v. [III. iii. 127]   *Exempt from envy.*

Envy is always supposed to have some fascinating or blasting power, and to be out of the reach of envy is therefore a privilege belonging only to great excellence.

ACT IV. SCENE i. [IV. i. 42–3]
    HASTINGS. *'Tis better using* France, *than trusting* France.
         Let us be back'd with God, and with the seas.

This has been the advice of every man who in any age understood and favored the interest of England.

ACT IV. SCENE i. [IV. i. 56]
    You would not have bestow'd the heir.

It must be remembered that till the restoration the heiresses of great estates were in the wardship of the king, who in their minority gave them up to plunder, and afterwards matched them to his favorites. I know not when liberty gained more than by the abolition of the court of wards.

ACT IV. SCENE vii. [IV. vi. 29]
    Few men rightly temper with the stars.

I suppose the meaning is, that few men conform their temper to their destiny, which King Henry did, when finding himself unfortunate he gave the management of public affairs to more prosperous hands.

ACT IV. SCENE vii. [IV. vi. 70]
    This pretty lad will prove our country's bliss.

He was afterwards Henry VII. A man who put an end to the civil war of the two houses, but not otherwise remarkable for virtue. Shakespeare knew his trade. Henry VII was Grandfather to Queen Elizabeth, and the King from whom James inherited.

ACT V. SCENE iii. [v. ii. 24–5]

> *My parks, my walks, my manors that I had,*
> *Ev'n now forsake me.*

Cedes coëmptis saltibus, et domo, Villâque. Horace.

This mention of his *parks* and *manors* diminishes the pathetic effect of the foregoing lines.

ACT V. SCENE vi. [v. iv. 67 foll]

This scene is ill-contrived, in which the king and queen appear at once on the stage at the head of opposite armies. It had been easy to make one retire before the other entered.

ACT V. SCENE vi. [v. v. 51]

> QUEEN. *Oh* Ned, *sweet* Ned!

The condition of this warlike queen would move compassion could it be forgotten that she gave York, to wipe his eyes in his captivity, a handkerchief stained with his young child's blood.

The three parts of *Henry VI* are suspected, by Mr. Theobald, of being supposititious, and are declared, by Dr. Warburton, to be *certainly not* Shakespeare's. Mr. Theobald's suspicion arises from some obsolete words; but the phraseology is like the rest of our author's style, and single words, of which however I do not observe more than two, can conclude little.

Dr. Warburton gives no reason, but I suppose him to judge upon deeper principles and more comprehensive views, and to draw his opinion from the general effect and spirit of the composition, which he thinks inferior to the other historical plays.

From mere inferiority nothing can be inferred; in the productions of wit there will be inequality. Sometimes judgment will err, and sometimes the matter itself will defeat the artist. Of every author's works one will be the best, and one will be the worst. The colors are not equally pleasing, nor the attitudes equally graceful, in all the pictures of Titian or Reynolds.

Dissimilitude of style and heterogeneousness of sentiment may sufficiently show that a work does not really belong to the reputed author. But in these plays no such marks of spuriousness are found. The diction, the versification, and the figures are Shakespeare's. These plays, considered, without regard to characters and incidents, merely as narratives in verse, are more happily conceived and more accurately finished than those of *King John, Richard II,* or the tragic scenes of *Henry IV* and *V.* If we take these plays from Shakespeare, to whom shall they be given? What author of that age had the same easiness of expression and fluency of numbers?

Having considered the evidence given by the plays themselves, and found it in their favor, let us now enquire what corroboration can be gained from other testimony. They are ascribed to Shakespeare by the first editors, whose attestation may be received in questions of fact, however unskillfully they superintended their edition. They seem to be declared genuine by the voice of Shakespeare himself, who refers to the second play in his epilogue to *Henry V* and apparently connects the first act of *Richard III* with the last of the third part of *Henry VI.* If it be objected that the plays were popular, and therefore he alluded to them as well known; it may be answered, with equal probability, that the natural passions of a poet would have disposed him to separate his own works from those of an inferior hand. And indeed if an author's own testimony is to be overthrown by speculative criticism, no man can be any longer secure of literary reputation.

Of these three plays I think the second the best. The truth is, that they have not sufficient variety of action, for the incidents are too often of the same kind; yet many of the characters are well discriminated. King Henry, and his queen, King Edward, the Duke of Gloucester, and the Earl of Warwick, are very strongly and distinctly painted.

The old copies of the two latter parts of *Henry VI* and of *Henry V* are so apparently imperfect and mutilated that there is no reason for supposing them the first drafts of Shakespeare. I am inclined to believe them copies taken by some auditor who wrote down, during the representation, what the time would permit, then perhaps filled up some of his omissions at a second or third hearing, and when he had by this method formed something like a play, sent it to the printer.

J. P. BROCKBANK

from *The Frame of Disorder—"Henry VI"*

Part 3 and the Shape of Anarchy

The tragic alignments of *Part 3* are declared on the
St. Albans battlefield. Henry prefigures the sacrificial
victim, suspended between action and inaction—he will
"nor fight nor fly" (V. ii. 74). Richard of York is the
agent of that political realism that is born in *Part 2* to
flourish in the later plays; he is the calculating joker
and the killer who despises the law of arms, rejoicing in
the superstitious prophecy by which he slaughters Somerset underneath "an ale-house' paltry sign," and he states
the harsh moral assumption that makes for anarchy in
Part 3

> Sword, hold thy temper; heart, be wrathful still:
> Priests pray for enemies, but princes kill.
>
> (V. ii. 71)

Clifford, Richard's antagonist in fact and symbol, is
not a "machiavel" but a nihilist, recognizing the virtues
of chivalry and order but dedicated to the defilement of

From "The Frame of Disorder—*Henry VI*," by J. P. Brockbank, in
Stratford-upon-Avon Studies 3: Early Shakespeare, eds. John Russell
Brown and Bernard Harris. London: Edward Arnold (Publishers) Ltd.,
1961. Reprinted by permission of the publishers. This is the third (and
last) portion of Mr. Brockbank's essay. The first portion is printed in
the Signet Classic edition of *1 Henry VI*, the second in the Signet
Classic edition of *2 Henry VI*.

both. Some disturbance of the text and inconsistency of fact suggest that his key speech (V. ii. 31–65), provoked by York's killing of the elder Clifford, was written during or immediately after the composition of *Part 3*, and set back into *Part 2* to offer intimations of the violence to come.[1] Its opening lines are powerfully symbolic:

> Shame and confusion! all is on the rout;
> Fear frames disorder, and disorder wounds
> Where it should guard.
>
>   (V. ii. 31)

They refer literally to the sort of confusion sometimes reported in the chronicles, where men are led to kill their friends instead of their enemies. But Shakespeare abstains from specifying the kind of disorder; by not limiting the connotation of "disorder," "frame" and "confusion" he keeps the abstract force of the words and makes the image immense and the idea metaphysically reverberant. In the next lines war is both the son of hell and the minister of heaven, ideas from Holinshed transmuted into a searching and disturbing rhetoric:

> O war, thou son of hell,
> Whom angry heavens do make their minister,
> Throw in the frozen bosoms of our part
> Hot coals of vengeance!

But while the speech epitomizes scattered groups of chronicle ideas, it keeps the urgency of the battlefield and it charges its destructive generalizations about war with heroic resolution:

> Let no soldier fly.
> He that is truly dedicate to war
> Hath no self-love, nor he that loves himself
> Hath not essentially but by circumstance
> The name of valor.

[1] In *3HVI* I.i.9, the elder Clifford is said by York, his stage killer, to have been slain by common soldiers. Since *2HVI* v.ii. and *3HVI* I.iii are both indebted to a passage in Hall (see *Stone*, p. 297) it is possible that Shakespeare revised the earlier scene to motivate Clifford's killing of Rutland.

The simple idea that the true soldier does not nurse his
life is transformed with measured, emphatic finality, into
an absolute acceptance of an ideal of nihilistic self-
sacrifice. The nihilism that follows outreaches the St.
Albans situation and assumes cosmic scale:

> O, let the vile world end,
> And the premised flames of the last day
> Knit earth and heaven together!
> Now let the general trumpet blow his blast,
> Particularities and petty sounds
> To cease!

The lines glance with magnificent assurance from the
image of the last judgment to the dead figure of old
Clifford, to age and wisdom in time of peace:

> Wast thou ordain'd, dear father,
> To lose thy youth in peace, and to achieve
> The silver livery of advised age,
> And in thy reverence and in thy chair-days, thus
> To die in ruffian battle?

There is a suddenly gathering intimacy, and then, out
of the personal pathos, a regeneration of the mood of
total war:

> Even at this sight
> My heart is turn'd to stone: and while 'tis mine,
> It shall be stony.

The rare accomplishment of Clifford's speech should
not blind us to its organic function in the plays. It is
simply the most lucid and telling expression of one range
of anarchic impulses at large in the tetralogy. The other
range, which does as much or more to precipitate anarchy,
is represented in the emergence of the Richards of York
and Gloster. In the play as history, Richard of York is
isolated from the rival barons by his greater political
know-how. But, equally important, in the play as theatrical
entertainment he is isolated by his privileged relationship with the audience. The politician is from the chronicle; the soliloquizer is from the dramatic conventions of

the Morality-play, and the key to Shakespeare's success is the intimate connection that he found between the two. The main fact about the chronicler York is that he takes his opportunities skillfully because, unlike the unreflective opportunists among his peers, he anticipates, calculates, and prepares the ground. His "attempt," says Holinshed, "was politicly handled," "secretly kept" and his purpose "ready" before it was "openly published" (*Hol.*, p. 212; *Stone,* p. 255). If all that York stands for in history is to be properly conveyed in the play, his emergence when "mischief breaks out" must take his enemies by surprise. But it must not take the audience by surprise; hence Shakespeare introduces short conspiratorial scenes to put fellow Yorkists *partly* "in the know" (the colloquialism fits the mood), and adds a number of soliloquies to put the audience wholly in the know. The soliloquy given to York at *Part 2* (I. i. 209) becomes the first experiment in the form to be turned to such advantage in *Richard III;* it enlists the audience's sympathy against the "others," exploits its readiness to take a low view of human nature and be brutally realistic about politics. In this first soliloquy York voices the muscular chronicle judgment that critics have sometimes taken for Shakespeare's definitive verdict on Henry:

> And force perforce I'll make him yield the crown,
> Whose bookish rule hath pull'd fair England down.
> (Pt. 2, I. i. 253)

But the rough verbal shoulder-shrugging of York is precisely expressive of the factious energy which does most to pull down fair England. A second soliloquy, in the same manner, sets York, "the laboring spider," behind the inception of the Cade rebellion (Pt. 2, V. i. 1).

In a passage of reflection on "the tragicall state of this land under the rent regiment of King Henrie," Holinshed speaks of the "sundrie practices" which "imbecilled" the "prerogative" of the King, and wonders at the pitched battles, which he divides into two groups, that were fought over and about him (*Hol.*, p. 272–3). Shakespeare keeps the outline and emphasizes the distinction between the military and political sources of catastrophe. The first two acts deal with the battles of 1460–61, when Henry had that "naked name of king"; the third and fourth acts are dominantly political, and about the chicanery of the nobles with their rival kings; and the last presents the campaigns of 1471, in which politics and war are indistinguishable. Once again one is struck in performance by the expressive force of the mere dumb show and noise (witness the stage directions); kings and crowns are treated as stage properties to enforce the chronicle moral about contempt for sovereignty, and Warwick is made quite literally the setter-up and plucker-down of kings (e.g., IV. iii). The pantomime is as skillful in the political scenes. The scene in the French court (III. iii), for instance, where Margaret has won the support of King Lewis, only to lose it to Warwick who comes as ambassador from Edward, becomes a superb exercise in the acrobatics of diplomacy, when letters are at last brought from Edward about the Bona marriage.

For the greater part of the third play Shakespeare is content to follow Holinshed in making his characters public masks, without intimately felt life, and therefore hardly seeming responsible for what they do. He tightens the sequence of atrocities, telescopes time, and eliminates all rituals of government, until the stage action and reaction appear yet more savagely mechanical than in the chronicle. So long as the characterization is neutral the first tetralogy displays a barbarous providence ruling murderous automatons whose reactions are predictable in terms of certain quasi-Hobbesian assumptions about human nature: when argument fails men resort to force; when an oath is inconvenient they break it; their power challenged, they retort with violence; their power subdued they resort to lies, murder or suicide; their honor impugned, they look for revenge; their enemies at their mercy, they torture and kill them; and if a clash of loyalties occurs they resolve it in the interest of their own survival. Such might be the vision of the play's pantomime, but its dimensions are not confined to its pantomime and to its shallower rhetoric. The anarchic, egocentric impulses are not presented as the inescapable laws of human nature; they are at most manifestations of forces that automatically take over when the constraints of government are withheld. Law and order cease to prevail when men cease to believe in them, and the process by which this comes about is explored in the play's dominant characters.

The figures of Clifford and York, who, in *Part 2,* personalize two kinds of anarchic skepticism—the soldier's nihilism and the politician's realism—are displaced in *Part 3* by the more significant contrast between Richard of Gloster and King Henry. With obvious propriety these are chosen to characterize the moral tensions which give meaning to the deep chaos of the last phase of the reign. But the crimes of the Roses Wars are so multiple and their agents so numerous that Shakespeare could not attempt, even if at this early date it were within his power, the comprehensively intimate exploration of evil he undertakes in *Macbeth,* and he allows himself only that measure of intimate soliloquy and address which will accord with the conventions of historical pageant.

In the first two plays the chronicle myth of a King absurdly and irrelevantly virtuous can just about pass muster, and in the first scene of *Part 3,* Henry's virtue is still associated with impotence; his war of "frowns, words, and threats" is disarmed by his readiness to concede the Yorkist claims, by the wry defection of Exeter (unwarranted by the history), and by the Robin Hood trickery of Warwick; his conscience-stricken asides carry as little conviction as his military posturing, and one feels the *gaucherie* is the playwright's as well as the character's. In the next phase, however, Shakespeare's tragic art wins distinction from the ferocity of the material and Henry assumes a stature outside the chronicle compass.

Both the finer qualities of Henry's virtue and the intensity of Richard of Gloster's virulence spring from Shakespeare's treatment of the Battle of Wakefield. Conventional heroic ideals cannot survive the battle, which turns on two blasphemies of chivalry—the killing of the prince and the degradation of the mock king. Clifford's

slaughter of Rutland (I. iii), in calculated contempt of
the Priest and the law of arms, is a repudiation of the
myth that expects from every "gentleman" in battle the
virtues of the lion. The values apt to an heroic battle play
are displaced by those prevailing in parts of English
Seneca; in Heywood's *Thyestes,* for example, where "ire
thinks nought unlawful to be done," "Babes be murdered ill" and "bloodshed lies the land about" (I. i.
79–89). Shakespeare gives the revenge motive a great
political significance by relating it to the dynastic feud
for which Clifford is not alone responsible.

Anarchism, Shakespeare had learned from the Cade
scenes, is more dramatic when it is iconoclastic, and the
next Wakefield outrage, the paper crowning (I. iv),
mutilates the idols of Knighthood, Kingship, Womanhood,
and Fatherhood. In making a ritual of the atrocity Shakespeare imitates the history—the scene is a formal set
piece because it was so staged by its historical performers.
Holinshed tells how the Lancastrians made obeisance and
cried, "Haile, king without rule"—"as the Jewes did
unto Christ" (*Hol.* p. 269; *Stone,* p. 299). Although
Shakespeare suppresses the open blasphemy, he keeps the
crucifixion parallel with the line, "Now looks he like a
King" (I. iv. 96), and, more significantly, by combining
the mockery reported in one of a choice of chronicle
accounts with the paper-coronation in another (*Hol.,* p.
268; *Stone,* p. 299). He takes little liberty with the
chronicle, moreover, when he makes the stage-managed
historical ceremony into an ordered, antiphonal combat
of words, with Northumberland presiding, as it were, in
the rhetorical lists. In spite of the controlling formality
the language moves on several planes between gnomic
generalization, " 'Tis government that makes them seem
divine, The want thereof makes thee abominable" (I. iv.
132); stylized feeling, "Oh tiger's heart wrapt in a
woman's hide! How could'st thou drain the life-blood of
the child" (I. iv. 137); plain, personal pathos, "This
cloth thou dip'dst in blood of my sweet boy" (I. iv. 157);
and colloquial venom, "And where's that valiant crookback prodigy, Dicky, your boy, that with his grumbling

voice Was wont to cheer his dad in mutinies?" In the blinding scene of *King Lear* the same changes will be rung in a richer peal, but there is enough in the Wakefield scene's counterpoint of reflection and feeling to tax the resources of its actors.

Henry is not made witness to the event. He is allowed the dignity of total isolation, and when he comes to the stage molehill at Towton (II. v), it is to speak the most moving of Shakespeare's comments on the civil wars. Shakespeare is less fully engaged when he writes about the objectives of the battle as seen by the participants than by its futility as it appears to a suffering observer. Hall had felt a similar need to withdraw into reflection:

> This conflict was in maner unnaturall, for in it the sonne fought agaynst the father, the brother agaynst the brother, the Nephew agaynst the Uncle, and the tenaunt 'agaynst hys Lorde, which slaughter did sore and much weaken the puyssance of this realme. (1548/1809, p. 256)

In *Gorboduc* and in Daniel's *Civil Wars* the commonplace is retailed with a complacent omniscience damaging to living language.[2] But by attributing it to the King in the course of battle Shakespeare is able to quicken it with personal feeling; beneath the ceremonious surface we again sense the pulse and surge of events.

The hint for the opening lines is one of Hall's "ebb and flow of battle" clichés (*Stone,* p. 306), but Shakespeare insinuates rarer images of the peaceful, symmetrical rhythms of nature—"the morning's war" and "the shepheard blowing of his nails," and after touching the conflicts inherent in nature, arrests the movement of battle in that of the sea—"the equal poise of this fell war." A glance at the humor and pathos of Henry's isolation (Margaret and Clifford have chid him from the battle), with a touch of wry exhaustion ("Would I were dead, if God's good will were so"), offers assurance of Shakespeare's gift for "reliving the past," and the sequent lines of exquisite pastoral seem to re-create the convention out

---

[2] The peroration of *Gorboduc* and the first stanza of *The Civil Wars.*

of the kind of human experience which underlies it. An alarum returns us to the battle and to a glimpse of its victims in another statuesque mirror scene in which blood and pallor are made heraldic (II. v. 97 ff.). Once again the feeling for the past is the cathedral-pavement sort, not the chronicle sort; it is at once a refreshing and a potentially devitalizing mood, and after a hundred and twenty lines Shakespeare pulls us out of it and lets the pantomime get under way again.

The authority of Henry's commentary on Towton is sufficiently memorable to help vindicate the innocence of the speech he makes before the keepers arrest him: "My pity hath been balm to heal their wounds. My mildness hath allay'd their swelling griefs, My mercy dry'd their water-flowing tears" (IV. viii. 41 ff.). From this and a few other passages in the plays it would be possible to present Henry as the center of a moral parable whose lineaments are traced in Thomas Elyot's *The Governour*. The King, says Elyot, must be merciful, but too much *Clementia* is a sickness of mind; as soon as any offend him the King should "immediately strike him with his most terrible dart of vengeance." But the occasions when Henry seems guilty of an excess of virtue are rare, and he is at his most impressive when he is martyred in his last scene of *Part 3*, not when he tries to throw his weight about in the first. The Wakefield battle once fought, moreover, "the terrible dart of vengeance" is lost to the armory of virtue. Henry's bemused and disappointed faith in the political efficacy of mercy, pity, peace, and love does not deserve the editorial mockery it has received—"characteristically effeminate" and "smug complacency."[3] Henry's virtue may be defective but Shakespeare commands from his audience a full reverence for it when, at the moment of his extermination, the King confronts his ultimate antagonist, Richard of Gloster.

Richard is introduced as York's heroic soldier son, but in his first characteristic speech of length (II. i. 79 ff.) he becomes the bitter, unchivalrous avenger—a reaction

[3] See notes to IV. viii. 38–50 in Hart's Arden and Wilson's New Cambridge editions.

to the Messenger's report of Wakefield which seems instinctive and inevitable. But Richard not only reacts to events (all the barons do that) he also becomes the conscious embodiment of all the drives—moral, intellectual, and physical—that elsewhere show themselves only in the puppetry. Translating into theatrical terms, we might say that when he takes the stage for his first exercise of the soliloquy prerogative he inherits from York (at the end of III. ii), his language shows him capable of playing the part of York, Clifford, Edward, Margaret, or Warwick. All their energies are made articulate: the doggedness of York "that reaches at the moon" and the same eye for the glitter of the Marlovian crown; the dedication to evil which characterizes Clifford; the prurience of Edward; the decorated and ruthless rhetoric of Margaret; and Warwick's gifts of king-maker, resolute "to command, to check, to overbear." Shakespeare has him use the fantastic lore about his birth to admirable effect: it strengthens the impression of blasphemy against love and fertility, makes deformity license depravity, and, most important, allegorizes the birth of a political monster in the present by recalling that of a physical monster in the past, "like to a chaos or an unlick'd bear-whelp." But it is not all specifically birth imagery—about Richard having teeth and the dogs howling. The sense of violent struggle, of unnatural energies breaking free, is best caught in lines that are not explicitly about birth at all:

> And I—like one lost in a thorny wood,
> That rends the thorns and is rent with the thorns,
> Seeking a way and straying from the way;
> Not knowing how to find the open air,
> But toiling desperately to find it out—
> Torment myself to catch the English crown:
> And from that torment I will free myself,
> Or hew my way out with a bloody ax.
>
> (III. ii. 74)

It is from the kennel of England's womb that his hellhound is to bite itself free. At the end of the soliloquy Richard promises the audience a performance more en-

tertaining than any heroic fantasy or medieval Trojan
legend; he will outplay all politic dissemblers, "add colors
to the chameleon," "change shapes with Proteus" and
"set the *murtherous* Machivill to school." The ground is
prepared for *Richard III,* where for three acts the comic
idiom will dominate the tragic, with politics a kings' game
best played by cunning actors.

But the continuity with the mood of *Richard III* is
deliberately fractured and the tragic mode made to dominate the comic in the scene of Henry's death. The King
opposes Richard's tongue and sword with a moral force
that Shakespeare makes all but transcendent and the
"scene of death" that "Roscius"—the actor and devil
Richard—performs at last, comes near to a tragic con-
summation. Yet the qualifications "all but" and "comes
near" are, after all, necessary. The brute facts of history
will not allow a satisfying tragic outcome; Shakespeare
cannot pretend that the martyrdom of an innocent king
appeased the appetite of providence or exhausted the
sophisticated savagery that Richard stands for.

Nor can Hall's dynastic myth be enlisted to reassure
us that all will be well when the White Rose is wedded
to the Red—that will only be possible at the end of
Richard III when, in a kind of postscript to the complete
tetralogy, Richmond will step into the Elizabethan present
and address an audience sufficiently remote from Henry's
reign. As it is, the plays of *Henry VI* are not, as it were,
haunted by the ghost of Richard II, and the catastrophes
of the civil wars are not laid to Bolingbroke's charge;
the catastrophic virtue of Henry and the catastrophic evil
of Richard are not an inescapable inheritance from the
distant past but are generated by the happenings we are
made to witness.

The questioning of the ways of God and the roles of
good and evil in English history will be reopened in
Richard III, but in the interim *Part 3* ends, as tragedies
remotely derived from fertility rites of course should,
with some elaborate imagery of autumn reaping. It is
fitting that Richard should be standing by to blast the
harvest and to boast himself a Judas.

E. M. W. TILLYARD

from *Shakespeare's History Plays*

The second part had showed us the murder of Duke
Humphrey of Gloucester, the rise of York, the destruction of two of Humphrey's murderers and the enmity
of the two survivors, York and Queen Margaret. Through
these happenings the country had been brought to the
edge of chaos. In the third part Shakespeare shows us
chaos itself, the full prevalence of civil war, the perpetra-
tion of one horrible deed after another. In the second
part there had remained some chivalric feeling. At the
battle of St. Albans York says to Clifford,

> With thy brave bearing should I be in love,
> But that thou art so fast mine enemy.

And Clifford answers,

> Nor should thy prowess want praise and esteem,
> But that 'tis shown ignobly and in treason.

But in the third part all the decencies of chivalric warfare
are abandoned. Young Clifford kills the twelve-year-old
Rutland at Wakefield. The three sons of York successively
stab Prince Edward, son of Henry VI, taken prisoner at
Tewkesbury. At Towton is displayed the supreme and

From *Shakespeare's History Plays* by E. M. W. Tillyard. London:
Chatto and Windus, 1944. Reprinted by permission of the publishers and
Mr. Stephen Tillyard. Another passage from this book appears in the
Signet Classic edition of *Henry VI, Part One*.

traditional picture of chaos, the denial of all chivalric
pieties, a father killing and robbing a son and a son
killing and robbing a father. Here is the culminating
expression of the horrors and wickedness of civil war.

In such a welter of crime the part of heaven is mainly
to avenge. And Shakespeare is extremely punctilious in
furnishing a crime to justify every disaster. Indeed his
lavishness tends to monotony. Edward IV, for instance,
commits three major crimes, any one of which was
enough to imperil himself and his posterity. He encouraged his father, York, to go back on his oath of loyalty
to Henry VI in return for the reversion of the crown;
he promised the Mayor of York that he had returned
to England to claim his dukedom and not the crown;
and he stabbed his prisoner the young prince Edward.
There is, however, sufficient reference to the positive
principles of order for us not to forget the less immediate
and more beneficent workings of heaven. It is Henry VI
who is the chief instrument of their expression. Whereas
in the second part he was conspicuous for his weakness,
he is now more conspicuous by his high principles and
his humanity. At Towton, as described above, he set
up the miniature order of the shepherd's life against the
major chaos of battle. In front of York he protests
against the brutality of the head of his dead enemy York
being set up on the walls. And it is he and no one else
who blesses the boy Richmond and, as if divinely inspired, prophesies a rescue through him from the present
ills:

> Come hither, England's hope. If secret powers
> Suggest but truth to my divining thoughts,
> This pretty lad will prove our country's bliss.
> His looks are full of peaceful majesty,
> His head by nature fram'd to wear a crown,
> His hand to wield a scepter, and himself
> Likely in time to bless a regal throne.
> Make much of him, my lords, for this is he
> Must help you more than you are hurt by me.

Warwick's dying soliloquy at Barnet is full of the tradi-

tional commonplaces associated with degree. Speaking
of himself he says:

> Thus yields the cedar to the ax's edge,
> Whose arms gave shelter to the princely eagle,
> Under whose shade the ramping lion slept,
> Whose top branch overpeer'd Jove's spreading tree
> And kept low shrubs from winter's powerful wind.

Warwick is thinking of his own power in making and
unmaking kings. He is not the oak, the king of trees, but
a cedar overtopping the oak; and he refers to a whole
sequence of primates in the chain of being: God or Jove
in heaven, the king on earth, the lion among beasts, the
eagle among birds, and the oak among plants.

With chaos as his theme it was not likely that Shakespeare would wish to cast this play into the clear patterns
of the first and second parts. Indeed, formlessness of a
sort was as necessary to his purposes here as the wide-
scattered geography of *Antony and Cleopatra* was to the
imperial setting of that play. But unfortunately with the
relaxation of form goes a decline of vitality. Shakespeare
had a great mass of chronicle matter to deal with and
he failed to control it; or rather in paring it to manageable length he fails to make it significant. The third part
of *Henry VI* is Shakespeare's nearest approach to the
Chronicle Play. There are indeed splendid things in it,
but they are rather islands sticking out of a sea of medi-
ocrity than hills arising from the valleys or undulations
of an organic landscape. In the intermediate passages
Shakespeare is either tired or bored: or perhaps both.
He may have been tired because he had already sustained
his theme of civil dissension so long; he may have been
bored because he was even then absorbed in the character of Richard and anxious to write the play to which
he gave his name. He may too have disliked repeating
himself; yet felt too much committed to a certain kind
of play to be able to fashion something quite new. Thus
he entirely omits one of his master themes in the previous
play: the character of the good king. But he cannot escape giving more examples of fierce noblemen exchanging

high words. And in plotting out cause and effect, in consonance with his loyalty to Hall and the *Mirror for Magistrates,* whereas in the other two plays he worked freely and with enthusiasm, he now repeats himself from a sense of duty. In the second scene of the play, which as a whole is a good example of this routine repetition, there is something factitious in the way York and his sons incriminate themselves by deciding to go back on York's oath to allow Henry the throne during his life- time, as if Shakespeare were deliberately fashioning the moral justification of York's terrible punishment at Wake- field immediately after. Another sign that Shakespeare's interest in cause and effect had worn a little thin is that he misses one of the big things in Hall. Act IV Scene 7, where Edward IV returning from France after his deposi- tion tries to obtain entry into the town of York, is not very emphatic. The Mayor of York from the ramparts says he cannot let him in because he now owes allegiance to Henry. Edward says that he is claiming only his duke- dom not his crown:

> Why, and I challenge nothing but my dukedom,
> As being well content with that alone.

In Hall Edward takes an oath; and the breaking of this oath is one of the major motives of the disasters that happened to England. Through his perjury Edward set- tled the fate of his two sons. Shakespeare takes care to incriminate Edward, but through several crimes, none of them particularly emphatic. In his sense of drama he here falls far behind Hall.

It would be tedious and fruitless to recount the vast course of the plot covering almost the whole of the Wars of the Roses, but I will describe the matters that Shakespeare really had at heart, and conjecture how he put the play together.

Shakespeare wanted to give his picture of civil chaos and to prepare for his next play. But he was committed, as a dramatic chronicler of history, to including a very big body of material. In his two first plays, not having included more matter than suited him, he was able to organize it into two well-proportioned wholes. But he paid for it by being left with a large and scarcely manageable residue. He spent himself on two great scenes of civil war, the battles of Wakefield and Towton, and on building up the character of Richard in the second half of his play. Into the gaps he fitted the bulk of his stuff as best he could. It is possible, however, that he tried to give some vague shape to the play through a hierarchy in the characters. Though the pirated version named the play after the Duke of York, he is not the chief character, for he is killed in the first act; nor are his sons, Edward and Richard, though all necessary preparations are made for Richard to become so in the next play. The chief characters are the instigators of the two kings who figure in the play, Margaret wife of Henry VI and Warwick on whose backing the sons of York rely. Such plot as there is (mere chronicling apart) consists in the emergence of these two as the truly dominant persons in the civil war, their opposition and varying fortunes, their unexpected reconciliation, and their final defeat largely through the expanding genius of Richard Duke of Gloucester. If these two characters were sufficiently emphasized, the play as a whole might not act too badly.

The two early battle scenes are greater affairs than anything in the earlier parts. The first, Wakefield, where York is captured, crowned with a paper crown by Queen Margaret, and murdered, enjoyed contemporary fame. Against the general trend of the play the printer of the pirated version of 1595 called it the *True Tragedy of Richard Duke of York,* plainly wishing to advertise his book through a famous scene. And secondly there is Greene's parody of a line from it. To have any effect a parody must take off something well known. Furthermore Greene is jealous, and he betrays his jealousy by parodying something that must have been not only well known but admired. The scene itself shows the very height of willful cruelty perpetrated by those who should have been the most civilized, the high aristocracy. It begins with Clifford, still ferocious from the loss of his father

at St. Albans, as described at the end of the previous
play, murdering York's son, Rutland, aged but twelve
and still under the charge of a tutor. Then York is captured by Queen Margaret, Clifford, and Northumberland.
Clifford is for killing him at once, but Margaret will not
let him off so lightly. She makes him stand upon a molehill, gives him a napkin stained in Rutland's blood to
wipe his tears, and crowns him with a paper crown,
accompanying her acts with words of such coarse contempt for himself and his sons as make her one of the
vituperators of genius:

> Brave warriors, Clifford and Northumberland,
> Come, make him stand upon this molehill here,
> That raught at mountains with outstretched arms,
> Yet parted but the shadow with his hand.
> What, was it you that would be England's king?
> Was't you that revell'd in our parliament
> And made a preachment of your high descent?
> Where are your mess of sons to back you now?
> The wanton Edward and the lusty George?
> And where's that valiant crook-back prodigy,
> Dicky your boy, that with his grumbling voice
> Was wont to cheer his dad in mutinies?
> Or, with the rest, where is your darling Rutland?
> Look, York: I stain'd this napkin with the blood
> That valiant Clifford with his rapier's point
> Made issue from the bosom of the boy;
> And if thine eyes can water for his death
> I'll give thee this to dry thy cheeks withal.

When she has done she again prevents Clifford from
killing York because she wishes to "hear the orisons he
makes." York rises to it in the speech from which Greene
got his quotation. It is far from mere bombast. York
thinks of all the things that are likely to make Margaret
most furious. He goes to his death undefeated, in bitter
contempt:

She-wolf of France, but worse than wolves of France,
Whose tongue more poisons than the adder's tooth,
How ill-beseeming is it in thy sex

To triumph, like an Amazonian trull,
Upon their woes whom fortune captivates!
But that thy face is visard-like, unchanging,
Made impudent with use of evil deeds,
I would assay, proud queen, to make thee blush.
To tell thee whence thou cam'st, of whom deriv'd,
Were shame enough to shame thee, wert thou not shameless.
Thy father bears the type of King of Naples,
Of both the Sicils and Jerusalem;
Yet not so wealthy as an English yeoman.
Hath that poor monarch taught thee to insult?
It needs not, nor it boots not thee, proud queen,
Unless the adage must be verified,
That beggars mounted run their horse to death.
'Tis beauty that doth oft make women proud;
But, God he knows, thy share thereof is small:
'Tis virtue that doth make them most admir'd;
The contrary doth make thee wonder'd at:
'Tis government that makes them seem divine;
The want thereof makes thee abominable.
Thou art as opposite to every good
As the Antipodes are unto us,
Or as the south to the septentrion.
O tiger's heart wrapt in a woman's hide,
How couldst thou drain the life-blood of the child,
To bid the father wipe his eyes withal,
And yet be seen to bear a woman's face?
Women are soft, mild, pitiful and flexible;
Thou stern, obdurate, flinty, rough, remorseless.

The episode gains much when set alongside the battle
of Towton, with which it is so carefully compared and
contrasted that the two make a beautiful pattern. While
at Wakefield we see the cruel authors of all this discord,
who ought to have known better, at Towton we see the
unhappy victims, who hate the part they are forced to
play. Henry has been led into the war by the fury of
his queen, the son who has killed his father records how

From London by the king I was press'd forth;
My father, being the Earl of Warwick's man,
Came on the part of York, press'd by his master.

And instead of glorying in their cruel deeds the surviving
father and son are broken with remorse. In both battles
the molehill figures, and with obvious intention. At Wakefield York *stands* on his molehill and instead of the real
crown he had hoped for is given one of paper. At Towton
Henry, the actual King, *sits* humbly on his molehill and
wishes he could abandon his authentic golden crown and
become a shepherd. Fate is impartial in denying to each
his different and contrasted aspiration. In style too the
episodes are contrasted. The first is written in a heightened version of the usual forthright powerful rhetorical
norm of Shakespeare's early blank verse. It is realistically
rhetorical rather than stylized: the language of law court,
marketplace, or house of parliament. The second, though
it contains touches of realism more genuine than the first,
is mainly ritual not rhetorical. It is slow-moving, full of
repetitions within the speeches, and antiphonic in the
way many of the speeches are arranged.

> So many hours must I tend my flock;
> So many hours must I take my rest;
> So many hours must I contemplate;
> So many hours must I sport myself.

That is Henry soliloquizing, but he bears his part later
in the antiphony of the surviving father and son.

> *Son.* How will my mother for a father's death
>   Take on with me and ne'er be satisfied!
> *Fath.* How will my wife for slaughter of my son
>   Shed seas of tears and ne'er be satisfied!
> *Hen.* How will the country for these woeful chances
>   Misthink the king and not be satisfied!

It is unfair to isolate this piece of stylized ritual writing
and to call it dull, primitive, and ingenuous. It forms part
of the great whole composed of the two battle scenes of
Wakefield and Towton. Coming after all the pomp and
rhetoric and forthright horror, it expresses worthily the
breakdown of violent human action into something hu-
miliated and devitalized. Life in these extremes falls back

on habit and routine; and the ritual repetitions together with the utter artlessness of the language express these straits into which life has come.

After the scene at Towton Shakespeare does not regain his full vitality till Richard's soliloquy in Act III Scene 2. But here he not only regains his vitality but shows us his genius suddenly enlarged. One has to compare this speech with York's two soliloquies in part two (at the end of I. 1 and III. 1) to see what has happened. York simply voices the motives Shakespeare has from outside put into his mouth; Richard appears to speak from within. And not only that, but to have grown then and there into the state of mind he expresses. He has just been witnessing Edward's courtship of Lady Grey, and it is the ecstasy of jealousy thereby aroused that both sharpens his malignity towards his brother and strengthens, in compensation for his own deficiencies in amorous scope, his already excessive ambitions. Such a change in presenting character implies of course a change in language; and here Shakespeare has indeed fully emerged from the κοινή of the period. He no longer adopts and embellishes the stereotyped phrases of the time, but, while strictly contemporary, fashions his speech anew. It is the old metal, the common stock of his time, but quite broken down and dissolved and then re-created after his own fashion, fresh with his own predominant interests, his own authentically experienced imagery, his own sense of how the lines ought to run and to be spoken. His very first image is both apt to himself and authentically Shakespeare's:

> Ay, Edward will use women honorably.
> Would he were wasted, marrow, bones, and all,
> That from his loins no hopeful branch may spring,
> To cross me from the golden time I look for.

Richard, as befits a diabolic character, is consistently well-informed on religious matters, sufficiently furnished with theological information to be efficiently profane. Near the end of part two, before the battle of St. Albans, he counters Young Clifford's defiance with

> Fie, charity, for shame! speak not in spite,
> For you shall sup with Jesu Christ tonight,

and this gratuitous religious reference is typical. Thus it is
likely that the hopeful branch springing from Edward's
loins should also suggest a religious reference: the tree of
Jesse. I have no doubt that Shakespeare was here drawing
on his memory of such pictures; and that the word *cross*
is a physical image suggested by the efficient massiveness
of the stem that springs in the works of art from the loins
of the recumbent Jesse. Similarly the image of the man lost
in a wilderness of thorn bushes (repeated at a culminating
point in *King John*) has its origin in something that
Shakespeare had experienced either himself or by report:

> And I, like one lost in a thorny wood,
> That rends the thorns and is rent with the thorns,
> Seeking the way and straying from the way,
> Not knowing how to find the open air
> But toiling desperately to find it out,
> Torment myself to catch the English crown.

A single line will suffice to illustrate the newly won sense
of just how the line should run dramatically:

> Flattering me with impossibilities.

Vague in rhythm at first reading, it soon falls into its
definitive shape:

> Flatt'ring me with—impossibilities.

The pause between preposition and noun both defines the
rhythm and adds a wealth of implication to the noun.

That the next scene (Queen Margaret and Warwick at
the court of the French King) should be a dull, routine
affair shows that Shakespeare's inclinations were at odds
with his will and duty. It is only in the last act, and as
Richard begins to emerge as the chief character, that
Shakespeare revives again. Clarence's shameless perjury
in forsaking Warwick and rejoining his brothers before
Coventry in the first scene is brought out strongly. Shake-

speare was preparing for his next play and Clarence's punishment there.

Few readers would deny that Richard's soliloquy both prepares for the next play and shows a treatment of character new in Shakespeare's History Plays. There remains yet another possible innovation, less likely to find universal acceptance. A. P. Rossiter has noticed that the elaborately patterned writing, used for the battle of Towton and illustrated above, occurs there for the first time, to be repeated several times through the rest of the play and becomes frequent and very important in *Richard III.* He thinks that this is a new departure, a reaction from a "documentary" to a "ritual" method of presenting historical material, creating a rift in the continuity of the tetralogy. Though I disagree about the importance of this rift and may interpret this ritual type of writing not quite as Rossiter does, I am greatly indebted to his observation and admire his detailed analysis of some of the main "ritual" passages. I fully agree with his associating the ritual technique with the Morality Play, but I think he is wrong in confining the Morality strain too closely to this single matter of style. There are other acts of ritual than verbal repetition and antiphony.

Generally, the Chronicle Play had substituted fact and direct statement for the rigidly contrasted and unrealistic presentation of good and evil used in the Morality Play. Shakespeare had accepted the substitution up to a point. But he impressed on his facts an interpretation of history that he derived neither from the Higden-Holinshed tradition followed by the Chronicle Plays nor from the now superannuated Morality but from Hall and the most intelligent creative writers current in his youth. Further, throughout the tetralogy he owed something to the Morality Play technique, the ritual method, though he used it in different degrees of frequency and obviousness. Rossiter admits some slight element of ritual in *1 Henry VI,* but he underestimates. Far from being mainly documentary, the three attempts made by Joan of Arc to ruin Talbot, worked out before Orleans, Rouen, and Bordeaux, are both violently untrue to history and make a regular pattern akin to ritual. The rhyme used in the culminating scene of the Talbots' death is not indeed as strongly patterned as some of the antiphonic writing in *3 Henry VI* and *Richard III* but it is the vehicle of a very unrealistic catastrophe. In *2 Henry VI*, where Rossiter finds no ritual element whatever, the characters are grouped at the opening in a severe balance that resembles the balancing of Virtues and Vices in a Morality. True, the groups are later broken and reformed, but this does not destroy the established formality. The scene where York unfolds his title to the throne to Salisbury and Warwick is incantatory in its enunciation of many great names: not unlike a ritual invocation of a god under many different titles or an enunciation of many divine attributes. And by standards of realism it is ridiculous. Thus though in the third part Shakespeare introduces (or borrows) a type of ritual he had not exploited before, he does not make the violent innovation of substituting a ritual style for something that had been almost entirely documentary; rather he develops in a different way a ritual method that had always been important.

Rossiter's observation confirms my opinion that Shakespeare was bored with the sheer documentation to which he was committed, and that, while unable to escape from it, he was impelled to develop independently of it, in other ways. One way was through Richard's character (which was already there in embryo), another was through developing the archaic Morality strain of historical presentation (already employed in the two earlier plays).

Finally, Rossiter points out how the most elaborate piece of stylistic ritual occurs in the scene immediately before Richard's first great soliloquy, Edward's courtship of Lady Grey with Clarence and Richard making ironic and indecent remarks in the background. Plainly Shakespeare wants it to carry much weight. Here is yet another indication that Shakespeare was growing restless and beginning to find new outlets for his powers. Tired by his grim and long fidelity to Hall's pattern of cause and effect in history, he temporarily departs from it by minimizing Edward IV's false oath before the walls of York (as described above) and erecting as the main cause of his downfall the less edifying but psychologically more interesting motive of his weakness for the female sex.

Temporarily, for in *Richard III* Hall's pattern of history is there in full seriousness.

Suggested References

The number of possible references is vast and grows alarmingly. (The *Shakespeare Quarterly* devotes one issue each year to a list of the previous year's work, and *Shakespeare Survey* —an annual publication—includes a substantial review of recent scholarship, as well as an occasional essay surveying a few decades of scholarship on a chosen topic.) Though no works are indispensable, those listed below have been found helpful.

1. Shakespeare's Times

Byrne, M. St. Clare. *Elizabethan Life in Town and Country*. Rev. ed. New York: Barnes & Noble, 1961. Chapters on manners, beliefs, education, etc., with illustrations.

Joseph, B. L. *Shakespeare's Eden: The Commonwealth of England 1558–1629*. New York: Barnes & Noble, 1971. An account of the social, political, economic, and cultural life of England.

Schoenbaum, S. *Shakespeare: The Globe and the World*. New York: Oxford University Press, 1979. A readable, handsomely illustrated book on the world of the Elizabethans.

Shakespeare's England. 2 vols. Oxford: Oxford University Press, 1916. A large collection of scholarly essays on a wide variety of topics (e.g., astrology, costume, gardening, horsemanship), with special attention to Shakespeare's references to these topics.

Stone, Laurence. *The Crisis of the Aristocracy, 1558–1641*, abridged edition. London: Oxford University Press, 1967.

2. Shakespeare

Barnet, Sylvan. *A Short Guide to Shakespeare*. New York: Harcourt Brace Jovanovich, 1974. An introduction to all of the works and to the dramatic traditions behind them.

Bentley, Gerald E. *Shakespeare: A Biographical Handbook.* New Haven, Conn.: Yale University Press, 1961. The facts about Shakespeare, with virtually no conjecture intermingled.

Bush, Geoffrey. *Shakespeare and the Natural Condition.* Cambridge, Mass.: Harvard University Press; London, 1956. A short, sensitive account of Shakespeare's view of "Nature," touching most of the works.

Chambers, E. K. *William Shakespeare: A Study of Facts and Problems.* 2 vols. London: Oxford University Press, 1930. An invaluable, detailed reference work; not for the casual reader.

Chute, Marchette. *Shakespeare of London.* New York: Dutton, Inc., 1949. A readable biography fused with portraits of Stratford and London life.

Clemen, Wolfgang H. *The Development of Shakespeare's Imagery.* Cambridge, Mass.: Harvard University Press, 1951. (Originally published in German, 1936.) A temperate account of a subject often abused.

Granville-Barker, Harley. *Prefaces to Shakespeare.* 2 vols. Princeton, N.J.: Princeton University Press, 1946–47. Essays on ten plays by a scholarly man of the theater.

Harbage, Alfred. *As They Liked It.* New York: Macmillan, 1947. A sensitive, long essay on Shakespeare, morality, and the audience's expectations.

Kernan, Alvin B., ed. *Modern Shakespearean Criticism: Essays on Style, Dramaturgy, and the Major Plays.* New York: Harcourt Brace Jovanovich, 1970. A collection of major formalist criticism.

————. "The Plays and the Playwrights." In *The Revels History of Drama in English,* general editors Clifford Leech and T. W. Craik. Vol. III. London: Methuen, 1975. A book-length essay surveying Elizabethan drama with substantial discussions of Shakespeare's plays.

Schoenbaum, S. *Shakespeare's Lives.* Oxford: Clarendon Press, 1970. A review of the evidence, and an examination of many biographies, including those by Baconians and other heretics.

Traversi, D. A. *An Approach to Shakespeare.* 3rd Rev. ed. New York: Doubleday, 1968–69. An analysis of the plays, beginning with words, images, and themes, rather than with characters.

Van Doren, Mark. *Shakespeare*. New York: Holt, 1939. Brief, perceptive readings of all of the plays.

3. Shakespeare's Theater

Beckerman, Bernard. *Shakespeare at the Globe, 1599–1609*. New York: Macmillan, 1962. On the playhouse and on Elizabethan dramaturgy, acting, and staging.

Chambers, E. K. *The Elizabethan Stage*. 4 vols. New York: Oxford University Press, 1945. A major reference work on theaters, theatrical companies, and staging at court.

Cook, Ann Jennalie. *The Privileged Playgoers of Shakespeare's London, 1576–1642*. Princeton, N.J.: Princeton University Press, 1981. Sees Shakespeare's audience as more middle-class and more intellectual than Harbage (below) does.

Gurr Andrew. *The Shakespearean Stage 1574–1642*. 2nd edition. Cambridge: Cambridge University Press, 1981. On the acting companies, the actors, the playhouses, the stages, and the audiences.

Harbage, Alfred. *Shakespeare's Audience*. New York: Columbia University Press, 1941. A study of the size and nature of the theatrical public, emphasizing its representativeness.

Hodges, C. Walter. *The Globe Restored*. London: Ernest Benn, 1953; New York: Coward-McCann, Inc., 1954. A well-illustrated and readable attempt to reconstruct the Globe Theatre.

Hosley, Richard. "The Playhouses." In *The Revels History of Drama in English*, general editors Clifford Leech and T. W. Craik. Vol. III. London: Methuen, 1975. An essay of one hundred pages on the physical aspects of the playhouses.

Kernodle, George R. *From Art to Theatre: Form and Convention in the Renaissance*. Chicago: University of Chicago Press, 1944. Pioneering and stimulating work on the symbolic and cultural meanings of theater construction.

Nagler, A. M. *Shakespeare's Stage*. Tr. by Ralph Manheim. New Haven, Conn.: Yale University Press, 1958. An ex-

cellent brief introduction to the physical aspect of the
playhouse.

Slater, Ann Pasternak. *Shakespeare the Director*. Totowa,
N.J.: Barnes and Noble, 1982. An analysis of theatrical
effects (e.g., kissing, kneeling) in stage directions and
dialogue.

Thomson, Peter. *Shakespeare's Theatre*. London: Routledge
and Kegan Paul, 1983. A discussion of how plays were
staged in Shakespeare's time.

4. Miscellaneous Reference Works

Abbott, E. A. *A Shakespearean Grammar*. New edition. New
York: Macmillan, 1877. An examination of differences between Elizabethan and modern grammar.

Bevington, David. *Shakespeare*. Arlington Heights, Ill.: A. H.
M. Publishing, 1978. A short guide to hundreds of important writings on the works.

Bullough, Geoffrey. *Narrative and Dramatic Sources of
Shakespeare*. 8 vols. New York: Columbia University
Press, 1957–1975. A collection of many of the books
Shakespeare drew upon with judicious comments.

Campbell, Oscar James, and Edward G. Quinn. *The Reader's
Encyclopedia of Shakespeare*. New York: Crowell, 1966.
More than 2,700 entries, from a few sentences to a few
pages on everything related to Shakespeare.

Gerg, W. W. *The Shakespeare First Folio*. New York: Oxford
University Press, 1955. A detailed yet readable history of
the first collection (1623) of Shakespeare's plays.

Kökeritz, Helge. *Shakespeare's Names*. New Haven, Conn.:
Yale University Press, 1959. A guide to the pronunciation
of some 1,800 names appearing in Shakespeare.

——. *Shakespeare's Pronunciation*. New Haven, Conn.:
Yale University Press, 1953. Contains much information
about puns and rhymes.

Muir, Kenneth. *The Sources of Shakespeare's Plays*. New
Haven, Conn.: Yale University Press, 1978. An account
of Shakespeare's use of his reading.

The Norton Facsimile: The First Folio of Shakespeare. Prepared by Charlton Hinman. New York: Norton, 1968. A

handsome and accurate facsimile of the first collection (1623) of Shakespeare's plays.

Onions, C. T. *A Shakespeare Glossary*. 2d ed., rev., with enlarged addenda. London: Oxford University Press, 1953. Definitions of words (or senses of words) now obsolete.

Partridge, Eric. *Shakespeare's Bawdy*. Rev. ed. New York: Dutton; London: Routledge & Kegan Paul, 1955. A glossary of bawdy words and phrases.

Shakespeare Quarterly. See headnote to Suggested References.

Shakespeare Survey. See headnote to Suggested References.

Shakespeare's Plays in Quarto. A Facsimile Edition. Ed. Michael J. B. Allen and Kenneth Muir. Berkeley, Calif.: University of California Press, 1981. A book of nine hundred pages, containing facsimiles of twenty-two of the quarto editions of Shakespeare's plays. An invaluable complement to *The Norton Facsimile. The First Folio of Shakespeare* (see above).

Smith, Gordon Ross. *A Classified Shakespeare Bibliography 1936–1958*. University Park, Pa.: Pennsylvania State University Press, 1963. A list of some 20,000 items on Shakespeare.

Spevack, Marvin. *The Harvard Concordance to Shakespeare*. Cambridge, Mass.: Harvard University Press, 1973. An index to Shakespeare's words.

Wells, Stanley, ed. *Shakespeare: Select Bibliographies*. London: Oxford University Press, 1973. Seventeen essays surveying scholarship and criticism of Shakespeare's life, work, and theater.

5. Henry VI

Alexander, Peter. *Shakespeare's Henry VI and Richard III*. Intro. Alfred W. Pollard. London: Cambridge University Press, 1929.

Berman, Ronald S. "Fathers and Sons in the Henry VI Plays," *Shakespeare Quarterly*, 13 (1962), 487–97.

Berry, Edward I. *Patterns of Decay: Shakespeare's Early Histories*. Charlottesville: University of Virginia Press, 1975.

Bevington, David. "The Domineering Female in *1 Henry VI*," *Shakespeare Studies* 2 (1966), 51–58.

Brockbank, J. P. "The Frame of Disorder—'Henry VI,'"
Shakespeare Institute Studies: Early Shakespeare, eds. John
Russell Brown and Bernard Harris. London: Edward
Arnold; New York: Schocken Books, 1966. Reprinted on
pages 205–15 (*1 Henry VI*), 206–17 (*2 Henry VI*), 194–
204 (*3 Henry VI*) of the Signet Classic edition.

Cairncross, Andrew S., ed. *The Arden Edition of the Works
of William Shakespeare: Henry VI.* London: Methuen;
Cambridge, Mass.: Harvard University Press. *The First
Part,* 1962; *The Second Part,* 1957; *The Third Part,* 1964.

Campbell, Lily B. *Shakespeare's "Histories": Mirrors of Elizabethan Policy.* San Marino, Calif.: The Huntington Library;
London: Cambridge University Press, 1947.

Clemen, Wolfgang H. "Anticipation and Foreboding in
Shakespeare's Early Histories," *Shakespeare Survey 6,* ed.
Allardyce Nicoll. Cambridge: The University Press, 1953.

Dash, Irene G. "The Paradox of Power: The Henry VI-
Richard III Tetralogy," Ch. 7 in *Wooing, Wedding, and
Power: Women in Shakespeare's Plays.* New York: Colum-
bia University Press, 1981.

Dollimore, Jonathan. *Political Shakespeare.* Ithaca, N.Y.:
Cornell University Press, 1985.

Doran, Madeleine. *Henry VI, Parts II and III, Their Relation to the Contention and the True Tragedy.* Iowa City:
University of Iowa Humanistic Studies, 4: 4 (1928).

Gaw, Allison. *The Origin and Development of 1 Henry VI in
Relation to Shakespeare, Marlowe, Peele, and Greene.* Los
Angeles: University of Southern California, 1926.

Greg, W. W., ed. *The True Tragedy of Richard Duke of York
(Henry the Sixth, Part III),* 1595. Shakespeare Quarto
Facsimiles, No. 11. London: Oxford University Press, 1958.

Hamilton, A. C. *The Early Shakespeare.* San Marino, Calif.:
The Huntington Library, 1967.

Hinchcliffe, Judith. *King Henry VI, Parts 1, 2, and 3 An
Annotated Bibliography.* New York & London: Garland,
1984.

Jackson, Sir Barry. "On Producing *Henry VI,*" *Shakespeare
Survey 6,* ed. Allardyce Nicoll. Cambridge: The Univer-
sity Press, 1963. Reprinted on pages 199–205 (*2 Henry
VI*) of the Signet Classic edition.

Jordan. John E. "The Reporter of *Henry VI, Part II*," *PMLA*, 64 (1949). 1089–1113.

Jorgensen. Paul A. *Shakespeare's Military World*. Berkeley: University of California Press, 1956.

Kirschbaum, Leo. "The Authorship of *1 Henry VI*," *PMLA*, 67 (1952), 809–22.

Leech, Clifford. *Shakespeare: The Chronicles*. Writers and Their Work. No. 146. London: Longmans, Green, 1962.

———. "The Two-Part Play: Marlowe and the Early Shakespeare." *Shakespeare Jahrbuch*, 92 (1958), 90–106.

Malone. Edmond. *A Dissertation on the Three Parts of "King Henry VI." Tending to Show that those Plays Were Not Originally Written by Shakespeare*. London, 1787.

Ornstein. Robert. *A Kingdom for a Stage: The Achievement of Shakespeare's History Plays*. Cambridge, Mass.: Harvard University Press. 1972.

Price. Hereward T. *Construction in Shakespeare*. Ann Arbor: University of Michigan Press, 1951.

Prior. Moody E. *The Drama of Power: Studies in Shakespeare's History Plays*. Evanston: Northwestern University Press. 1973.

Prouty. Charles T. *"The Contention" and Shakespeare's "2 Henry VI": A Comparative Study*. New Haven: Yale University Press. 1954.

Rackin. Phyllis R. "Anti-Historians: Women's Roles in Shakespeare's Histories." *Theatre Journal*. 37 (1985), 329–44. Reprinted in part on pages 216–29 of the Signet Classic edition of *1 Henry VI*.

Reese. Max Meredith. *The Cease of Majesty: A Study of Shakespeare's History Plays*. London: Edward Arnold, 1961: New York: St. Martin's Press, 1962.

Ribner. Irving. *The English History Play in the Age of Shakespeare*. Princeton: Princeton University Press; London: Oxford University Press. 1957. Revised edition: New York: Barnes & Noble; London: Methuen, 1965.

Riggs. David. *Shakespeare's Heroical Histories: "Henry VI" and Its Literary Tradition*. Cambridge, Mass.: Harvard University Press. 1971.

Sandoe. James. "King Henry the Sixth. Part II. Notes during Production," *Theatre Annual*, 13 (1955), 32–48.

Sprague, Arthur Colby. *Shakespeare's Histories: Plays for the Stage.* London: The Society for Theatre Research, 1964.

Swander, Homer D. "The Rediscovery of *Henry VI*," *Shakespeare Quarterly,* 29 (1978), 146–63.

Talbert, Ernest William. *Elizabethan Drama and Shakespeare's Early Plays: An Essay in Historical Criticism.* Chapel Hill: University of North Carolina Press, 1963.

Tillyard, E. M. W. *Shakespeare's History Plays.* London: Chatto and Windus, 1944; New York: Collier Books, 1962. Reprinted in part on pages 190–204 (*1 Henry VI*) and 205–17 (*3 Henry VI*) of the Signet Classic edition.

Turner, Robert Y. "Shakespeare and the Public Confrontation Scene in Early History Plays," *Modern Philology,* 72 (1964), 1–12.

Wilson, John Dover, ed. *The New Cambridge Shakespeare: Henry VI.* 3 volumes. London and New York: Cambridge University Press, 1952. Reissued in *The Cambridge Pocket Shakespeare,* 1961–62.

SIGNET CLASSICS   (0451)

THE SIGNET CLASSIC SHAKESPEARE SERIES

❑ MEASURE FOR MEASURE, S. Nagarajan, ed., University of Poona, India
(524098—$4.95)
❑ MACBETH, Sylvan Barnet, ed., Tufts University   (526775—$3.95)
❑THE MERCHANT OF VENICE, Kenneth Myrick, ed., Tufts University
(526805—$3.95)
❑ A MIDSUMMER NIGHT'S DREAM, Wolfgang Clemen, ed.,
University of Munich   (526961—$4.95)
❑ MUCH ADO ABOUT NOTHING, David Stevenson, ed., Hunter College
(526813—$4.95)
❑ OTHELLO, Alvan Kernan, ed., Yale University   (526856—$3.95)
❑ RICHARD II, Kenneth Muir, ed., University of Liverpool (522680—$4.95)
❑ RICHARD III, Mark Eccles, ed., University of Wisconsin (526953—$4.95)
❑ THE TAMING OF THE SHREW, Robert Heilman, ed., University of Washington
(526791—$3.95)
❑ THE TEMPEST, Robert Langbaum, ed., University of Virginia
(527127—$3.95)
❑ TROILUS AND CRESSIDA, Daniel Seltzer, ed., Harvard   (522974—$5.95)
❑ TWELFTH NIGHT, Herschel Clay Baker, ed., Harvard   (526767—$3.95)
❑ THE WINTER'S TALE, Frank Kermode, ed., University of Bristol
(527143—$4.95)
❑ THE SONNETS, William Burto, ed., Introduction by W.H. Auden
(522621—$4.95)
❑ JULIUS CAESAR, Barbara and William Rosen, ed., University of Connecticut
(526899—$3.95)
❑ KING LEAR, Russel Fraser, ed., Princeton University   (526937—$3.95)
❑ HAMLET, Sylvan Barnet, ed., Tufts University   (526929—$3.95)
❑ HENRY IV, Part I, Maynard Mack, ed., Yale University   (524055—$3.95)
❑ HENRY IV, Part II, Norman Holland, ed., Massachusetts Institute of Technology
(522532—$4.95)
❑ FOUR GREAT TRAGEDIES, Sylvan Barnet, ed., Tufts University
(527291—$6.95)

Prices slightly higher in Canada

Payable in U.S. funds only. No cash/COD accepted. Postage & handling: U.S./CAN. $2.75 for one book, $1.00 for each additional, not to exceed $6.75; Int'l $5.00 for one book, $1.00 each additional. We accept Visa, Amex, MC ($10.00 min.), checks ($15.00 fee for returned checks) and money orders. Call 800-788-6262 or 201-933-9292, fax 201-896-8569; refer to ad # SIGCL6 (10/99)

Penguin Putnam Inc.
P.O. Box 12289, Dept. B
Newark, NJ 07101-5289
Please allow 4-6 weeks for delivery.
Foreign and Canadian delivery 6-8 weeks.

Bill my: ❑ Visa ❑ MasterCard ❑ Amex _____(expires)
Card# _____
Signature _____

Bill to:
Name _____
Address _____City_____
State/ZIP _____Daytime Phone #_____

Ship to:
Name _____Book Total $ _____
Address _____Applicable Sales Tax $ _____
City _____Postage & Handling $ _____
State/ZIP _____Total Amount Due $ _____

This offer subject to change without notice.

PENGUIN CLASSICS

For over fifty years, Penguin has been the leading publisher of the classics of world literature in the English-reading world. Since the publication of the first Penguin Classic in 1946— E. V. Rieu's translation of *The Odyssey*—Penguin has been committed to making the greatest literary works available to everyone in authoritative editions with accurate yet accessible translations. The series now includes more than 1600 titles, the most significant works in all genres from every continent and every age, from the earliest creation myths to the masterpieces of the twentieth century.

Penguin is proud to announce that academics, teachers, students, and anyone who is passionate about the classics will be able to enjoy and participate in this world of excellence and innovation at

http://www.penguinclassics.com